Houghton Mifflin Harcourt

Teacher Edition

TEXAS SCIENCE FUSION

fusion [FYOO • zhuhn] a combination of two or more things that releases energy

Front Cover: *lion* ©Cesar Lucas Abreu/Stone/Getty Images; *grass* ©Nicholas Eveleigh/Stockbyte/Getty Images; *tulips* ©John McAnulty/Corbis; *soccer* ©Jon Feingersh Photography, Inc./Blend Images/Getty Images; *volcano* ©Westend61 GmbH/Alamy; *microscope* ©Thom Lang/Corbis.

Back Cover: *guitar* ©Brand Z/Alamy; *giraffe* ©Nicholas Eveleigh/Stockbyte/Getty Images; *observatory* ©Robert Llewellyn/Workbook Stock/Getty Images; *wind turbine* ©Comstock/Getty Images.

Printed in the U.S.A.

ISBN 978-0-544-02556-1

2 3 4 5 6 7 8 9 10 0877 21 20 19 18 17 16 15 14 13

4500428142 ABCDEFG

Teacher Edition Contents

About the Program

Units and Lessons

Resources, Professional Development, and Correlations

Consulting Authors

Michael A. DiSpezio

Global Educator
North Falmouth, Massachusetts

Michael DiSpezio is a renaissance educator who segued from the research laboratory of a Nobel Prize winner to the K–12 science classroom. He has authored or co-authored numerous textbooks and trade books. For nearly a decade he worked with the JASON Project, under the auspices of the National Geographic Society, where he designed curriculum, wrote lessons, and hosted dozens of studio and location broadcasts. Over the past two decades, DiSpezio has developed supplementary material for organizations and programs that include PBS Scientific American Frontiers, *Discover* Magazine, and the Discovery Channel. To all his projects, he brings his extensive background in science and his expertise in classroom teaching at the elementary, middle, and high school levels.

Marjorie Frank

Science Writer and Content-Area Reading Specialist
Brooklyn, New York

An educator and linguist by training, a writer and poet by nature, Marjorie Frank has authored and designed a generation of instructional materials in all subject areas, including past HMH Science programs. Her other credits include authoring science issues of an award-winning children's magazine, writing game-based digital assessments, developing blended learning materials for young children, and serving as instructional designer and co-author of pioneering school-to-work software for a nonprofit organization dedicated to improving reading and math skills for middle and high school learners. In addition, she has served on the adjunct faculty of Hunter, Manhattan, and Brooklyn Colleges, teaching courses in science methods, literacy, and writing.

Michael R. Heithaus

Executive Director, School of Environment, Arts, and Society
Associate Professor, Department of Biological Sciences
Florida International University
North Miami, Florida

Mike Heithaus joined the FIU Biology Department in 2003, has served as Director of the Marine Sciences Program, and is now the Executive Director of the School of Environment, Arts, and Society, which brings together the natural and social sciences and humanities to develop solutions to today's environmental challenges. His research focuses on predator-prey interactions and the ecological roles of large marine species. His long-term studies include the Shark Bay Ecosystem Project in Western Australia. He also served as a Research Fellow with National Geographic, using remote imaging in his research and hosting a *Crittercam* television series on the National Geographic Channel.

Donna M. Ogle

Professor of Reading and Language
National-Louis University
Chicago, Illinois

Creator of the well-known KWL strategy, Donna Ogle has directed many staff development projects translating theory and research into school practice in schools throughout the United States. She is a past president of the International Reading Association and has served as a consultant on literacy projects worldwide. Her extensive international experience includes coordinating the Reading and Writing for Critical Thinking Project in Eastern Europe and speaking and consulting on projects in several Latin American countries and in Asia. Her books include *Reading Comprehension: Strategies for Independent Learners; All Children Read;* and *Literacy for a Democratic Society.*

Classroom Management
Online teaching and planning

Texas ScienceFusion is a comprehensive, multimodal science program that provides all the digital tools teachers need to engage students in inquiry-based learning. *The Teacher Digital Management Center,* at thinkcentral.com, is designed to make it easier for teachers to access program resources to plan, teach, assess, and track.

- Program resources can be easily previewed in PDF format and downloaded for editing.
- Assign and schedule resources online, and they will appear in your students' inboxes.
- All quizzes and tests can be taken and automatically scored online.
- Easily monitor and track student progress toward mastery of the TEKS.

Teaching with Technology Made Easy

Texas ScienceFusion's 3,000+ animations, simulations, videos, & interactivities are organized to provide:

- flexible options for delivering exciting and engaging digital lessons;
- Digital Lessons Formative Assessment, for every lesson, ensures the important information is learned;
- multimodal learning options that connect online learning to concepts learned from reading, writing, and hands-on inquiry.

Digital Lessons Formative Assessment

Texas Essential Knowledge and Skills for Science

Grade 1 TEKS SCIENCE	**Units/Lessons**	**Teacher Edition Pages Flipchart (FC)**
1.1 Scientific investigation and reasoning. The student conducts classroom and outdoor investigations following home and school safety procedures and uses environmentally appropriate and responsible practices. The student is expected to:		
1.1A recognize and demonstrate safe practices as described in the Texas Safety Standards during classroom and outdoor investigations, including wearing safety goggles, washing hands, and using materials appropriately;	Safety in Science	T33–T34, FC 1–2
	Unit 1, Lesson 2	11A, FC 4
	Unit 2, Lessons 1, 3	53A, FC 11; 67A, FC 13
	Unit 4, Lesson 1, S.T.E.M.	123A, FC 19; 169–170B, FC 24
	Unit 5, Lessons 1, 2, 3, 4	177A, FC 25; 189A, FC 26; 199A, FC 27; 201A, FC 28
	Unit 8, Lesson 1	305A, FC 40
1.1B recognize the importance of safe practices to keep self and others safe and healthy; and	Safety in Science	T33–T34, FC 1–2
	Unit 1, Lesson 2	11A, FC 4
	Unit 2, Lessons 1, 2, 3	53A, FC 11; 65A, FC 12; 67A, FC 13
	Unit 3, S.T.E.M.	115–116B, FC 18
	Unit 4, Lessons 1, 4, S.T.E.M.	123A, FC 19; 155A, FC 22; FC 24
	Unit 5, Lessons 1, 2, 3, 4	177A, FC 25; 189A, FC 26; 199A, FC 27; 201A, FC 28
	Unit 6, Lesson 2	247A, FC 33
	Unit 7, Lessons 1, 2	273A, FC 36; 285A, FC 37
	Unit 8, Lessons 1, 2	305A, FC 40; 315A, FC 41
	Unit 9, Lesson 1	353A, FC 45
1.1C identify and learn how to use natural resources and materials, including conservation and reuse or recycling of paper, plastic, and metals.	Unit 2, Lessons 3, 4	67A–78A, FC 13; 79A, FC 14
	Unit 5, Lessons 1, 6	177–186A, FC 25; 217A–228A, FC 31
1.2 Scientific investigation and reasoning. The student develops abilities to ask questions and seek answers in classroom and outdoor investigations. The student is expected to:		

Grade 1 TEKS SCIENCE	Units/Lessons	Teacher Edition Pages Flipchart (FC)
1.2A ask questions about organisms, objects, and events observed in the natural world;	Unit 1, Lessons 2, 4, 6	11–12A; 23A–24A, FC 6; 35–44A
	Unit 2, Lessons 2, 3, 4	65–66A; 67A, FC 13; 79–80A
	Unit 3, Lesson 2	103–104A
	Unit 4, Lessons 1, 4	123A, FC 19; 155–156A
	Unit 5, Lessons 3, 4	199–200A; 201–202A
	Unit 6, Lesson 2	247–250A
	Unit 7, Lesson 3	295–296A
	Unit 8, Lessons 1, 3	305A, FC 40; 331–332A
	Unit 9, Lesson 2	353–356A
	Unit 10, Lesson 3	401–402A
1.2B plan and conduct simple descriptive investigations such as ways objects move;	Science Tools Activities	34B–34C, FC 8–9
	Unit 1, Lessons 1, 2, 3, 4, 5, 6	3A, FC 3; 11A–12A, FC 4; 13A, FC 5; 23A–24A, FC 6; 25A, FC 7; 35A–44A, FC 10
	Unit 2, Lessons 3, 4	67A, FC 13; 79A–80A, FC 14
	Unit 3, Lessons 1, 2, 3	89A, FC 15; 103A–104A, FC 16; 105A, FC 17
	Unit 4, Lessons 2, 3, 4, 5	135A, FC 20; 145A, FC 21; 155A–156A, FC 22; 157A, FC 23
	Unit 5, Lessons 1, 2, 3, 4, 5, 6	177A, FC 25; 189A, FC 26; 199A–200A, FC 27; 201A–202A, FC 28; 203A, FC 29; 217A, FC 31
	Unit 6, Lessons 1, 2, 3	235A, FC 32; 247A–250A, FC 33; 253A, FC 34
	Unit 7, Lessons 1, 2, 3	273A, FC 36; 285A, FC 37; 295A–296A, FC 38
	Unit 8, Lessons 1, 2, 3	305A, FC 40; 315A, FC 41; 331A–332A, FC 42
	Unit 9, Lessons 1, 2, 3	341A, FC 44; 353A–356A, FC 45; 359A, FC 47
	Unit 10, Lessons 1, 2, 3	379A, FC 48; 391A, FC 49; 401A–402A, FC 50

Texas Essential Knowledge and Skills for Scie...

Grade 1 TEKS SCIENCE	Units/Lessons	Teacher Edition Pages Flipchart (FC)
1.2C collect data and make observations using simple equipment such as hand lenses, primary balances, and non-standard measurement tools;	Science Tools Activities	34B–34C, FC 8–9
	Unit 1, Lessons 2, 3, 5, 6	11A, FC 4; 13A, FC 5; 25A–34A, FC 7; 35A, FC 10
	Unit 3, Lesson 2	103A, FC 16
	Unit 5, Lessons 3, 4	199A, FC 27; 201A, FC 28
	Unit 6, Lessons 1, 3	235A, FC 32; 253A, FC 34
	Unit 7, Lesson 3	295A, FC 38
	Unit 8, Lesson 2	315A, FC 41
	Unit 10, Lessons 1, 3	379A, FC 48; 401A, FC 50
1.2D record and organize data using pictures, numbers, and words; and	Unit 1, Lessons 1, 2, 3, 4, 5, 6	3A, FC 3; 11A–12A, FC 4; 13A–22A, FC 5; 23A–24A, FC 6; 25A, FC 7; 35A–44A, FC 10
	Unit 2, Lessons 1, 2, 3, 4	53A, FC 11; 65A–66A, FC 12; 67A, FC 13; 79A–80A, FC 14
	Unit 3, Lessons 1, 2, 3, S.T.E.M.	89A, FC 15; 103A–104A, FC 16; 105A, FC 17; 115–116B, FC 18
	Unit 4, Lessons 1, 2, 3, 4, 5, S.T.E.M.	123A, FC 19; 135A, FC 20; 145A, FC 21; 155A–156A, FC 22; 157A, FC 23; 169–170B, FC 24
	Unit 5, Lessons 1, 2, 3, 4, 5, S.T.E.M., Lesson 6	177A, FC 25; 189A, FC 26; 199A–200A, FC 27 201A–202A, FC 28; 203A, FC 29; 215–216B, FC 30; 217A, FC 31
	Unit 6, Lessons 1, 2, 3, S.T.E.M.	235A, FC 32; 247A–250A, FC 33; 253A, FC 34 265–266B, FC 35
	Unit 7, Lessons 1, 2, 3, S.T.E.M.	273A, FC 36; 285A, FC 37; 295A–296A, FC 38 297–298B, FC 39
	Unit 8, Lessons 1, 2, 3, S.T.E.M.	305A, FC 40; 315A, FC 41; 331A–332A, FC 42 333–334B, FC 43
	Unit 9, Lessons 1, 2, S.T.E.M., Lesson 3	341A, FC 44; 353A–356A, FC 45; 357–358B, FC 46; 359A, FC 47
	Unit 10, Lessons 1, 2, 3, S.T.E.M.	379A, FC 48; 391A, FC 49; 401A–402A, FC 50 403–404B, FC 51

Grade 1 TEKS SCIENCE	Units/Lessons	Teacher Edition Pages Flipchart (FC)
1.2E communicate observations and provide reasons for explanations using student-generated data from simple descriptive investigations.	Unit 1, Lessons 1, 2, 3, 4, 6	3A, FC 3; 11A, FC 4; 13A–22A, FC 5; 23A, FC 6; 35–44A
	Unit 2, Lessons 2, 4	65A, FC 12; 79A, FC 14
	Unit 4, Lessons 1, 2	123A, FC 19; 135A, FC 20
	Unit 5, Lessons 1, 2	177A, FC 25; 189A, FC 26
	Unit 7, Lessons 2, 3	285A, FC 37; 295A, FC 38
	Unit 9, Lessons 1, 2	341A, FC 44; 353A, FC 45
1.3 Scientific investigation and reasoning. The student knows that information and critical thinking are used in scientific problem solving. The student is expected to:		
1.3A identify and explain a problem such as finding a home for a classroom pet and propose a solution in his/her own words;	Unit 2, Lessons 1, 2	53A–64A, FC 11; 65A–66A, FC 12
	Unit 3, S.T.E.M.	115–116B, FC 18
	Unit 4, S.T.E.M.	169–170B, FC 24
	Unit 5, S.T.E.M.	215–216B, FC 30
	Unit 6, S.T.E.M.	265–266B, FC 35
	Unit 7, S.T.E.M.	297–298B, FC 39
	Unit 8, S.T.E.M.	329–330B, FC 43
	Unit 9, S.T.E.M.	357–358B, FC 46
	Unit 10, S.T.E.M.	403–404B, FC 51
1.3B make predictions based on observable patterns; and	Unit 6, Lessons 1, 2, 3	235A, FC 32; 247A–250A, FC 33; 253–264A
	Unit 7, Lesson 2	285–294A

Texas Essential Knowledge and Skills for Scie...

Grade 1 TEKS SCIENCE	Units/Lessons	Teacher Edition Pages Flipchart (FC)
1.3C describe what scientists do.	Unit 1, Lesson 6	35–44A
	Unit 1, People in Science	45–46
	Unit 2, People in Science	81–82
	Unit 3, Careers in Science	101–102
	Unit 4, People in Science	153–154
	Unit 5, People in Science	187–188
	Unit 6, People in Science	251–252
	Unit 7, People in Science	283–284
	Unit 8, People in Science	329–330
	Unit 9, Careers in Science	371–372
	Unit 10, People in Science	389–390
1.4 Scientific investigation and reasoning. The student uses age-appropriate tools and models to investigate the natural world. The student is expected to:		
1.4A collect, record, and compare information using tools, including computers, hand lenses, primary balances, cups, bowls, magnets, collecting nets, notebooks, and safety goggles; timing devices, including clocks and timers; non-standard measuring items such as paper clips and clothespins; weather instruments such as classroom demonstration thermometers and wind socks; and materials to support observations of habitats of organisms such as aquariums and terrariums; and	Science Tools Activities	34B–34C, FC 8–9
	Unit 1, Lessons 2, 5, 6	11A, FC 4; 25A–34A, FC 7; 35A, FC 10
	Unit 3, Lessons 2, 3	103A, FC 16; 105A, FC 17
	Unit 4, Lessons 2, 3	135A, FC 20; 145A, FC 21
	Unit 5, Lessons 1, 3, 4, 5	177A, FC 25; 199A, FC 27; 201A, FC 28; 203A, FC 29
	Unit 6, Lessons 1, 3, S.T.E.M.	235A, FC 32; 253A, FC 34; 251–252B
	Unit 7, Lessons 2, 3	285A, FC 37; 295A–296A, FC 38
	Unit 8, Lessons 1, 2, 3	305A, FC 40; 315A, FC 41; 331A–332A, FC 42
	Unit 9, Lesson 1	341A, FC 44
	Unit 10, Lessons 1, 3	379A, FC 48; 401A–402A, FC 50

Grade 1 TEKS SCIENCE	Units/Lessons	Teacher Edition Pages Flipchart (FC)
1.4B measure and compare organisms and objects using non-standard units.	Science Tools Activities	34B–34C, FC 9
	Unit 1, Lesson 5	25A–34A, FC 7
	Unit 7, Lesson 3	295A–296A, FC 38
	Unit 10, Lesson 3	401A–402A, FC 50
1.5 Matter and energy. The student knows that objects have properties and patterns. The student is expected to:		
1.5A classify objects by observable properties of the materials from which they are made such as larger and smaller, heavier and lighter, shape, color, and texture; and	Unit 2, Lessons 3, 4	67–78A; 79A–80A, FC 14
	Unit 3, Lesson 1	89A–100A, FC 15
1.5B predict and identify changes in materials caused by heating and cooling such as ice melting, water freezing, and water evaporating.	Unit 3, Lessons 2, 3	103A–104A, FC 16; 105A–114A, FC 17
1.6 Force, motion, and energy. The student knows that force, motion, and energy are related and are a part of everyday life. The student is expected to:		
1.6A identify and discuss how different forms of energy such as light, heat, and sound are important to everyday life;	Unit 4, Lesson 1	123A–134A, FC 19
1.6B predict and describe how a magnet can be used to push or pull an object;	Unit 4, Lesson 2	135A–144A, FC 20
1.6C describe the change in the location of an object such as closer to, nearer to, and farther from; and	Unit 4, Lesson 5	157A–168A, FC 23
1.6D demonstrate and record the ways that objects can move such as in a straight line, zig zag, up and down, back and forth, round and round, and fast and slow.	Unit 4, Lessons 3, 4	145A–152A, FC 21; 155A–156A, FC 22
1.7 Earth and space. The student knows that the natural world includes rocks, soil, and water that can be observed in cycles, patterns, and systems. The student is expected to:		
1.7A observe, compare, describe, and sort components of soil by size, texture, and color;	Unit 5, Lessons 2, 3, 4	189–198A; 199A–200A, FC 27; 201A–202A, FC 28
1.7B identify and describe a variety of natural sources of water, including streams, lakes, and oceans; and	Unit 5, Lesson 5	203A–214A, FC 29
1.7C gather evidence of how rocks, soil, and water help to make useful products.	Unit 5, Lesson 1	177A–186A, FC 25

Texas Essential Knowledge and Skills for Scie

Grade 1 TEKS SCIENCE	Units/Lessons	Teacher Edition Pages Flipchart (FC)
1.8 Earth and space. The student knows that the natural world includes the air around us and objects in the sky. The student is expected to:		
1.8A record weather information, including relative temperature, such as hot or cold, clear or cloudy, calm or windy, and rainy or icy;	Unit 6, Lessons 1, 2, S.T.E.M.	235A–246A, FC 32; 247A–250A, FC 33; 265A–266B, FC 35
1.8B observe and record changes in the appearance of objects in the sky such as clouds, the Moon, and stars, including the Sun;	Unit 7, Lessons 2, 3	285A–294A, FC 37; 295A–296A, FC 38
1.8C identify characteristics of the seasons of the year and day and night; and	Unit 6, Lesson 3	253A–264A, FC 34
	Unit 7, Lesson 1	273A–282A, FC 36
1.8D demonstrate that air is all around us and observe that wind is moving air.	Unit 6, Lesson 1	235A–246A, FC 32
1.9 Organisms and environments. The student knows that the living environment is composed of relationships between organisms and the life cycles that occur. The student is expected to:		
1.9A sort and classify living and nonliving things based upon whether or not they have basic needs and produce offspring;	Unit 8, Lesson 1	305A–314A, FC 40
1.9B analyze and record examples of interdependence found in various situations such as terrariums and aquariums or pet and caregiver; and	Unit 8, Lessons 2, 3	315A–328A, FC 41; 331A–332A, FC 42
1.9C gather evidence of interdependence among living organisms such as energy transfer through food chains and animals using plants for shelter.	Unit 8, Lesson 2	315A–328A, FC 41

Grade 1 TEKS SCIENCE	Units/Lessons	Teacher Edition Pages Flipchart (FC)
1.10 Organisms and environments. The student knows that organisms resemble their parents and have structures and processes that help them survive within their environments. The student is expected to:		
1.10A investigate how the external characteristics of an animal are related to where it lives, how it moves, and what it eats;	Unit 9, Lessons 1, 2	341A–352A, FC 44; 353A–356A, FC 45
1.10B identify and compare the parts of plants;	Unit 10, Lessons 1, 2, 3	379A–388A, FC 48; 391A–400B, FC 49; 401A–402A, FC 50
1.10C compare ways that young animals resemble their parents; and	Unit 9, Lesson 3	359A–370A, FC 47
1.10D observe and record life cycles of animals such as a chicken, frog, or fish.	Unit 9, Lesson 3	359A–370A, FC 47

Student Edition Contents

Levels of Inquiry Key ■ DIRECTED ■ GUIDED ■ INDEPENDENT

Track Your Progress

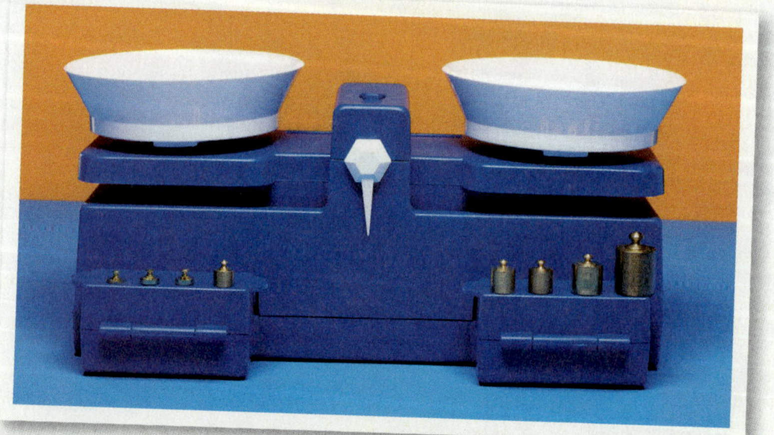

PHYSICAL SCIENCE

Safety in Science

Indoors Doing science is fun. But a science lab can be dangerous. Know the safety rules and listen to your teacher.

Follow these indoor science safety rules.

1. **Think ahead.** Study the steps. Follow them.
2. **Be neat.** Wipe up spills right away. Keep hair and clothing out of the way.
3. **Oops!** Tell your teacher if you spill or break something or if you get hurt.
4. **Watch your eyes.** Wear safety goggles when the teacher tells you.
5. **Ouch!** Do not touch sharp things.
6. **Yuck!** Do not eat or drink things.
7. **Don't get shocked.** Do not touch electric outlets.
8. **Keep it clean.** Clean up afterward. Wash your hands.

xxiii

Texas Safety Standards

Detailed science safety guidance is provided in the *Texas Safety Standards: Kindergarten Through Grade 12 Science* available from the Charles A. Dana Center at The University of Texas at Austin.

Contents

Ch. 1 Safe Working and Learning Environments
Ch. 2 Laboratory and Field Activities
Ch. 3 Safety Equipment and Supplies
Ch. 4 Laws, Rules, and Regulations
Ch. 5 Hazard Concerns
Ch. 6 Chemical Safety
Ch. 7 Safety Training and Professional Development

Safety in Science

Indoors

Use the following discussion points to emphasize key safety rules for indoor science activities.

What safety gear is the scientist in the picture using? She has on goggles, gloves, and a lab coat. **How does the gear keep her safer?** The goggles protect her eyes from harmful things; the gloves and lab coat protect her skin.

Why is it important to think ahead and study the steps before you begin an activity? You may get hurt because you don't know how to be safe during the activity.

Why do you need to keep long sleeves and hair out of the way during science activities? Hair and clothes can snag equipment and get stained. They can also catch fire.

Tell me what you would do if you spilled some water. Children should mention telling the teacher and helping clean up. **What could happen if the spill was not cleaned up?** Children should realize that water makes the floor slippery and increases the risk of falls.

Show children an ordinary pair of glasses (or sunglasses). Then show them safety goggles. **What is different about the safety goggles?** Children should recognize the sturdy material and protection all around the sides of the lenses. **How do you think these differences keep you safer during science activities?** The lenses are harder to break. The protection on the sides keeps liquids and objects from getting into your eyes.

Ask for a volunteer. Tell him or her to walk up to and point at a piece of safety equipment in the classroom, then tell the class when and how to use it.

Safety in Science (continued)

Outdoors

Use the following discussion points to emphasize key safety rules for outdoor science activities.

What outdoor safety gear is the scientist in the picture using? He is wearing a hard hat, goggles, boots, and coveralls. **How does the gear keep him safer?** The hard hat protects him from falling rocks; the clothing keeps him warm and protects him from scrapes and cuts.

How can clothing protect you outdoors? It protects you from scratches and from the sun.

Why are sturdy shoes important? You may need to walk a lot. Sturdy shoes protect your feet from sharp objects, plants, and biting insects.

Why is it not safe to taste anything outdoors? Many plants and animals are poisonous. Other things may have germs that will make you sick.

Why is it important to stay with your group? If you are with the group, someone will be there to help if you get hurt or have a problem. **Why should you stay on marked trails?** Marked trails are safer. Walking through wild areas may hurt the animals and plants.

Why do you think running and horseplay are more dangerous outdoors? You do not know the area. The ground may change quickly. You can fall and get hurt before you can stop.

Why is it especially important to wash your hands when you are done? Washing hands helps keep you from getting sick, and keeps you from rubbing grit into your eyes.

Assessment

Use the safety quiz on pages AG 1–AG 5 of the Assessment Guide to assess childrens' understanding of key safety rules and practices.

Outdoors Lots of science happens outdoors. Exploring the wilderness or your backyard is fun! But you need to be careful.

Follow these outdoor science safety rules.

1. **Think ahead.** Study the steps. Follow them.
2. **Dress right.** Wear clothes and shoes that are right for outdoors.
3. **Cover up.** Follow sun safety rules.
4. **Oops!** Tell your teacher if you break something or get hurt.
5. **Watch your eyes.** Tell your teacher right away if anything gets in your eyes. Wear goggles when your teacher tells you.
6. **Yuck!** Never taste anything outdoors.
7. **Stay together.** Stay on marked trails.
8. **Do not act wild.** No horseplay or pranks.
9. **Always walk.** No running!
10. **Clean up the area.** Throw away litter as your teacher tells you.
11. **Clean up.** Wash your hands with soap and water when you are done.

xxiv Safety in Science

Inquiry Flipchart

The numbered safety checklists on these two pages are reproduced on pages 1 and 2 of the *ScienceFusion* Inquiry Flipchart. Display the flipchart pages to help children recognize and demonstrate safe practices during science investigations.

ScienceFusion

Video-Based Projects

Available in Online Resources

This video series, hosted by program authors Michael Heithaus and Michael DiSpezio, develops science learning through real-world science and engineering challenges.

Ecology

Leave your lab coat at home! Not all science research takes place in a lab. Host Michael Heithaus takes you around the globe to see ecology field research, including tagging sharks and tracking sea turtles. Students research, graph, and analyze results to complete the project worksheets.

Grade	Video Title
3	Exploring the Galápagos Islands Tent-Making Bats
4	Alligators Up Close Rainforest Habitats
5	The Sea Turtles of Shark Bay

S.T.E.M. Science, Technology, Engineering, and Math

Host Michael DiSpezio poses a series of design problems that challenge students' ingenuity. Each video follows the engineering design process. Worksheets guide students through the process and help them document their results.

Grade	Video Title
3	Take It to Great Heights
4	It's a Bird! It's a Plane!
5	No Gas Needed Get Focused! A Cut Above **

** In Partnership with Children's Hospital Boston

Designed for Grades 3-5, the videos may also be viewed by primary-grade classes if appropriate.

Texas ScienceFusion

Program Scope and Sequence

The Texas Essential Knowledge and Skills for Science are organized into strands that fall into general science content areas. *Texas ScienceFusion* is made up of concise units of instruction that address all the TEKS for each grade level. Some units address TEKS from overlapping strands, and the Scientific Investigation and Reasoning TEKS are integrated within all the units. However, the following chart shows to which strands units are mostly aligned.

Texas ScienceFusion Grade Levels and Units

Content Area	TEKS STRANDS	GRADE K	GRADE 1	GRADE 2	GRADE 3
Nature of Science and STEM	**Scientific Investigation and Reasoning**	**Unit 1** Doing Science **Unit 2** Science and Technology	**Unit 1** How Scientists Work **Unit 2** Technology All Around Us	**Unit 1** Work Like a Scientist **Unit 2** Technology and Our World	**Unit 1** Investigating Questions **Unit 2** The Engineering Process
Physical Science	**Matter and Energy**	**Unit 3** Matter	**Unit 3** Matter	**Unit 3** Changes in Matter	**Unit 3** Properties of Matter
	Force, Motion, and Energy	**Unit 4** Energy **Unit 5** Motion	**Unit 4** Forces and Energy	**Unit 4** Energy, Motion, and Magnets	**Unit 4** Energy **Unit 5** Forces and Work

GRADE 4	GRADE 5	GRADE 6	GRADE 7	GRADE 8
Unit 1 Studying Science **Unit 2** The Engineering Process	**Unit 1** How Scientists Work **Unit 2** The Engineering Process	**Unit 1** The Nature of Science **Unit 2** Measurement and Data	**Unit 1** The Nature of Science **Unit 2** Measurement and Data	**Unit 1** The Nature of Science **Unit 2** Measurement and Data
Unit 3 Matter	**Unit 3** Matter	**Unit 3** Matter **Unit 4** Energy, Motion, and Forces	**Unit 6** Living Systems **Unit 7** Human Body Systems	**Unit 3** Introduction to Chemistry
Unit 4 Forms of Energy **Unit 5** Electricity and Circuits **Unit 6** Forces and Motion	**Unit 4** Forces and Motion **Unit 5** Forms of Energy **Unit 6** Light and Sound	**Unit 5** Energy Resources	**Unit 6** Living Systems	**Unit 4** Forces and Motion

Texas ScienceFusion Grade Levels and Units

Content Area	TEKS STRANDS	GRADE K	GRADE 1	GRADE 2	GRADE 3
Earth Science	Earth and Space	**Unit 6** Earth's Resources **Unit 7** Weather and the Seasons **Unit 8** Day and Night	**Unit 5** Earth's Resources **Unit 6** Weather and Seasons **Unit 7** Objects in the Sky	**Unit 5** Earth and Its Resources **Unit 6** All About Weather **Unit 7** The Solar System	**Unit 6** Earth's Surface **Unit 7** People and Resources **Unit 8** Water and Weather **Unit 9** Space
Life Science	Organisms and Environments	**Unit 9** Animals **Unit 10** Plants	**Unit 8** Living Things and Their Environments **Unit 9** Animals **Unit 10** Plants	**Unit 8** Animal and Plant Needs **Unit 9** Environments for Living Things **Unit 10** Animal and Plant Characteristics	**Unit 10** Ecosystems and Interactions **Unit 11** Living Things Grow and Change

GRADE 4	GRADE 5	GRADE 6	GRADE 7	GRADE 8
Unit 7 Earth's Surface **Unit 8** The Water Cycle and Weather **Unit 9** Patterns in the Sky	**Unit 7** Changes to Earth's Surface **Unit 8** Natural Resources **Unit 9** Weather and Climate **Unit 10** Earth, Sun, and Moon System	**Unit 6** Minerals and Rocks **Unit 7** The Dynamic Earth **Unit 8** The Solar System **Unit 9** Space Exploration	**Unit 8** Earth's Changing Surface **Unit 9** Living in Space	**Unit 5** The Earth-Moon-Sun System **Unit 6** The Universe **Unit 7** Processes That Shape Earth **Unit 8** Earth's Oceans and Atmosphere
Unit 10 Organisms and Their Environments **Unit 11** Plants and Animals	**Unit 11** Energy in Ecosystems **Unit 12** Heredity and Adaptation	**Unit 10** Organisms and Environments	**Unit 3** Cells **Unit 4** Reproduction and Heredity **Unit 5** The Diversity of Living Things **Unit 6** Living Systems **Unit 7** Human Body Systems	**Unit 9** Ecosystems

Program Pacing

The following pacing guide recommends days for the core print and digital instructional elements of each unit. Additional days can be added for optional inquiry, activities, and extensions.

DAYS	NATURE OF SCIENCE/ S.T.E.M.
Unit 1	**How Scientists Work**
9	Print or Digital Lesson Content
4	Inquiry Lesson or Virtual Lab
1	Unit Review and Assessment
Unit 2	**Technology All Around Us**
5	Print or Digital Lesson Content
2	Inquiry Lesson or Virtual Lab
1	Unit Review and Assessment
22 DAYS	

DAYS	PHYSICAL SCIENCE
Unit 3	**Matter**
5	Print or Digital Lesson Content
2	Inquiry Lesson or Virtual Lab
2	S.T.E.M. /Engineering and Technology
1	Unit Review and Assessment
Unit 4	**Forces and Energy**
9	Print or Digital Lesson Content
2	Inquiry Lesson or Virtual Lab
2	S.T.E.M. /Engineering and Technology
1	Unit Review and Assessment
24 DAYS	

DAYS	EARTH SCIENCE
Unit 5	**Earth's Resources**
9	Print or Digital Lesson Content
4	Inquiry Lesson or Virtual Lab
2	S.T.E.M. /Engineering and Technology
2	Unit Review and Assessment

DAYS	EARTH SCIENCE (continued)
Unit 6	**Weather and Seasons**
5	Print or Digital Lesson Content
2	Inquiry Lesson or Virtual Lab
2	S.T.E.M. /Engineering and Technology
1	Unit Review and Assessment
Unit 7	**Objects in the Sky**
5	Print or Digital Lesson Content
1	Inquiry Lesson or Virtual Lab
2	S.T.E.M. /Engineering and Technology
1	Unit Review and Assessment
36 DAYS	

DAYS	LIFE SCIENCE
Unit 8	**Living Things and Their Environments**
5	Print or Digital Lesson Content
2	Inquiry Lesson or Virtual Lab
2	S.T.E.M. /Engineering and Technology
1	Unit Review and Assessment
Unit 9	**Animals**
5	Print or Digital Lesson Content
2	Inquiry Lesson or Virtual Lab
2	S.T.E.M. /Engineering and Technology
1	Unit Review and Assessment
Unit 10	**Plants**
5	Print or Digital Lesson Content
2	Inquiry Lesson or Virtual Lab
2	S.T.E.M. /Engineering and Technology
1	Unit Review and Assessment
30 DAYS	

Unit 1

Unit 1

UNIT 1 How Scientists Work

Big Idea and Essential Questions

This Unit was designed to focus on this Big Idea and these Essential Questions.

Take It Home!
A School-Home Connection letter in English and Spanish is provided in Online Resources.

Big Idea

Scientists use inquiry skills and tools to help them find out information.

Essential Questions

L1 **What Are Senses?**

L2 **How Can We Use Our Senses?**

L3 **What Are Inquiry Skills?**

L4 **How Do We Use Inquiry Skills?**

L5 **What Are Science Tools?**

L6 **How Do Scientists Work?**

Professional Development

Houghton Mifflin Harcourt and **NSTA,** the **National Science Teachers Association,** have partnered to provide customized professional development resources for teachers using *ScienceFusion.*

The Professional Development Resources include:

- Do-it-yourself resources, where you can study at your own pace
- Live and archived online seminars
- Journal articles, many of which include lesson plans
- Fee-based eBooks, eBook chapters, online short courses, symposia, and conferences

Access to The NSTA Learning Center is provided in the *ScienceFusion* Online Resources.

NSTA National Science Teachers Association

The NSTA Learning Center

Unit Planning

Options for Instruction

Choose from **Interactive Worktext** and **Leveled Readers, Digital,** and **Inquiry** options to meet the Texas Essential Knowledge and Skills.

	LESSON 1	LESSON 2	LESSON 3
Essential Questions	**What Are Senses?**	✔ **Guided Inquiry** **How Can We Use Our Senses?**	**What Are Inquiry Skills?**
Texas Essential Knowledge and Skills		TEKS **1.2A, 1.2B, 1.2D**	TEKS **1.2D, 1.2E**
Interactive Worktext	☐ **Student Edition** pp. 3–10 • Your Senses • Learning With Your Senses	☐ **Student Edition** pp. 11–12 • Scaffolding for Inquiry	☐ **Student Edition** pp. 13–22 • Skills to Help You Learn
Leveled Readers	Parallel coverage of the lesson topics is provided in the **Extra Support, On-Level,** and **Enrichment** readers. See p. 1J for detailed reader information.		
Hands-On Inquiry	**Inquiry Flipchart** p. 3 **Shoebox Senses** ☐ Directed Inquiry **All Around Me** ☐ Independent Inquiry	**Inquiry Flipchart** p. 4 **How Can We Use Our Senses?** ☐ Guided Inquiry	**Inquiry Flipchart** p. 5 **Measure Up** ☐ Directed Inquiry **Animal Models** ☐ Independent Inquiry
Digital Curriculum	☐ **Digital Lesson** Online Resources Interactive presentation of lesson content 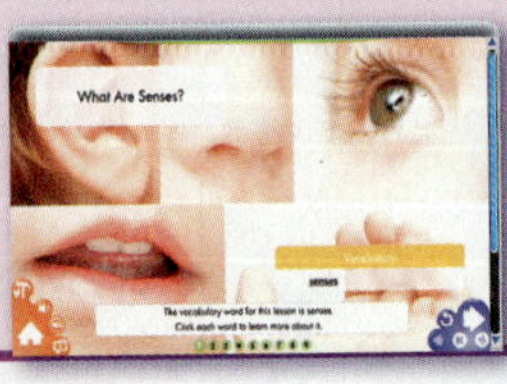	☐ **Virtual Lab** Online Resources Interactive scaffolded inquiry 	☐ **Digital Lesson** Online Resources Interactive presentation of lesson content 

LESSON 4

Guided Inquiry

How Do We Use Inquiry Skills?

TEKS 1.2A, 1.2B, 1.2D

☐ **Student Edition**
pp. 23–24
- Scaffolding for Inquiry

Inquiry Flipchart
p. 6

How Do We Use Inquiry Skills?
☐ Guided Inquiry

☐ **Virtual Lab**
Online Resources
Interactive scaffolded inquiry

LESSON 5

What Are Science Tools?

TEKS 1.2C, 1.4A, 1.4B

☐ **Student Edition**
pp. 25–34
- Tools to Explore
- Let's Measure!
- Measuring Up

Inquiry Flipchart
p. 7

It's Time to Measure
☐ Directed Inquiry

Balancing Act
☐ Independent Inquiry

☐ **Digital Lesson**
Online Resources
Interactive presentation of lesson content

LESSON 6

How Do Scientists Work?

TEKS 1.2A, 1.2B, 1.2D, 1.2E, 1.3C

☐ **Student Edition**
pp. 35–44
- Think Like a Scientist

Inquiry Flipchart
p. 10

Holding Water
☐ Directed Inquiry

My Fingerprints
☐ Independent Inquiry

☐ **Digital Lesson**
Online Resources
Interactive presentation of lesson content

OTHER UNIT FEATURES

People in Science, p. 45

Online Resources

Interactive Whiteboard Resources for Unit 1

Assessment

Formative Assessment
Sum It Up! and Brain Check
Student Edition, end of each lesson

Summative Assessment
Safety, Tools, Lesson Quizzes
Assessment Guide,
pp. AG 1–AG 15, pp. AG 18–AG 23

Unit 1 Review
Student Edition, pp. 47–50

Unit 1 Test
Assessment Guide,
pp. AG 26–AG 30

Performance Assessment
SHORT OPTION: Teacher Edition, p. 49
LONG OPTION: Assessment Guide, pp. AG 16–AG 17 and pp. AG 31–AG 32

RTI Response to Intervention
RTI Strategies, p. 1K

Online Assessment
Test-taking and automatic scoring
Banks of items from which to build tests

Planning for Inquiry

Use the following preview of Inquiry Activities and Lessons to gather and manage the materials needed for each lesson.

Activity	Inquiry and Design Process Skills Focus	Materials	Prep Tips, Troubleshooting, and Expected Results
Lesson 1 DIRECTED INQUIRY Flipchart p. 3 A **Shoebox Senses** **OBJECTIVE** Conduct simple descriptive investigations. 30 minutes pairs TEKS **1.2B**	• Plan and Conduct a Simple Investigation • Infer • Experiment	• small objects, such as toy cars, marbles, cotton balls, and blocks • shoeboxes (one for each pair of children)	**Prep Tips** Before the activity, cut a hole in the narrow end of each shoebox so children can reach in the box without having to take off the lid. Assemble a variety of small objects of different shapes, sizes, and textures from which children can choose. **Caution!** Warn children not to put anything sharp into the box. **Troubleshooting** If children repeatedly peek at the object being put in the box before conducting the investigation, you may wish to supervise them for one round of object identification. Alternatively, children may just need a reminder not to put the object in the box in view of their partners. **Expected Results** Children will find that even though they cannot see an object, they can often identify it using their sense of touch to feel its size, shape, and texture.
INDEPENDENT INQUIRY Flipchart p. 3 B **All Around Me** **OBJECTIVES** Plan and conduct simple investigations. Record and organize data. Communicate observations. 30 minutes individuals TEKS **1.2B, 1.2D, 1.2E**	• Observe • Communicate • Plan and Conduct a Simple Investigation	• Science Notebook	**Prep Tips** Suggest that children limit the scope of their investigation to one room in their home, such as a bedroom or the kitchen. Point out to children they may find it easier to use their senses of hearing and smelling to explore the room if they sit down and close their eyes. **Troubleshooting** Urge children to organize their investigation carefully. Suggest they write the name of each sense on a separate sheet of paper. Tell children to record their observations one sense at a time. **Expected Results** Children will make a plan to organize and record their observations of a room in their home. They will discover they can observe with senses other than their sense of sight. They will recognize that they can learn different information by using different senses.

Additional teaching support for all inquiry activities is available in **Online Resources.**

Science Notebook Strategies

- Lists of Kit-Supplied Materials
- Meeting Individual Needs
- Investigate More–Extensions and Variations
- and More!

Activity	Inquiry and Design Process Skills Focus	Materials	Prep Tips, Troubleshooting, and Expected Results
Lesson 2 INQUIRY GUIDED INQUIRY **Flipchart** p. 4 **Student Edition** pp. 11–12 **How Can We Use Our Senses?** **OBJECTIVES** • Recognize and demonstrate safe practices. • Conduct investigations. • Collect data and make observations using simple equipment. • Record and organize data. • Communicate observations. • Collect and compare informations using a hand lens. 15 minutes pairs TEKS **1.1A, 1.1B, 1.2B, 1.2C, 1.2D, 1.2E, 1.4A**	• Observe	• celery • hand lens	**Prep Tips** Gather enough celery so that each child can have a piece. Cut the celery into smaller pieces if necessary, making sure the pieces are still big enough for children to break in half. Also make sure that celery is fresh enough to audibly snap in half. Children may need to share hand lenses. **Caution!** Make sure that children do not put the celery in their mouths. **Troubleshooting** Remind children to think about how the celery tastes without actually putting it in their mouths. If children have not tasted celery before, they may make an educated guess based on how the celery smells or on their experiences with other green vegetables. **Expected Results** Children will discover that they can observe with senses beyond sight.

Go Digital! Virtual Lab

How Can We Use Our Senses?

Key inquiry skills: observe, predict, plan and conduct simple investigations

Children observe and use science tools as they explore how using the five senses can help us learn about the world around us.

Planning for Inquiry (continued)

Activity	Inquiry and Design Process Skills Focus	Materials	Prep Tips, Troubleshooting, and Expected Results
Lesson 3 DIRECTED INQUIRY **Flipchart** p. 5 **A Measure Up** **OBJECTIVES** Conduct investigations. Collect data using simple equipment. Record and organize data. Communicate observations. 30 minutes pairs TEKS **1.2B, 1.2C, 1.2D, 1.2E**	• Compare • Measure	• rulers or cloth tape measures • masking tape (optional)	**Prep Tips** Children should measure their own desks first, and use a teacher's desk as a longer object. If a teacher's desk is not available, children may use a table or the top of a bookshelf as an alternative. If the measuring tool is shorter than the desk or table, model how to mark where the tool ends with masking tape before repositioning it. **Caution!** Use only cloth tape measures. A retractable metal tape measure can cause injury. **Troubleshooting** Remind children that keeping good records will help them compare objects, so they should write down each measurement they take. Pairs may find it helpful to divide tasks–one partner can measure while the other records measurements. Children can then switch roles for the next object. **Expected Results** Children will practice using a tape measure or a ruler to measure length and compare objects by length. They will find that measuring–an inquiry skill–helps them find and compare the lengths of objects.
INDEPENDENT INQUIRY **Flipchart** p. 5 **B Animal Models** **OBJECTIVE** Plan and conduct simple descriptive investigations. 30 minutes individuals TEKS **1.2B**	• Compare • Formulate or Use Models	• construction paper • scissors • chenille sticks (optional) • nontoxic clay (optional) • toothpicks (optional: for drawing details on clay models) • newspaper (optional: for covering children's desks) • animal books (for reference)	**Prep Tips** Nontoxic clay and chenille sticks are available for purchase at craft and some toy stores. If children are using clay for their models, provide newspaper so they can cover their desks. **Troubleshooting** To ensure that children strive for scientific accuracy in their animal models, provide animal photo books to use as references. **Expected Results** Children will make models that approximate the appearance of various animals. They will recognize the differences between the models and the real animals, which may include size, dimensionality, and living versus nonliving qualities.

Additional teaching support for all inquiry activities is available in Online Resources.

Activity	Inquiry and Design Process Skills Focus	Materials	Prep Tips, Troubleshooting, and Expected Results
Lesson 4 INQUIRY GUIDED INQUIRY **Flipchart** p. 6 **Student Edition** pp. 23–24 **How Do We Use Inquiry Skills?** **OBJECTIVES** • Ask questions about organisms and objects observed in the natural world. • Conduct simple descriptive investigations. • Record and organize data. • Communicate observations and provide reasons for explanations using data. • Describe what scientists do. 15 minutes pairs TEKS **1.2A, 1.2B, 1.2D, 1.2E, 1.3A**	• Plan and Conduct a Simple Investigation • Draw Conclusions • Hypothesize • Experiment	• objects from nature, such as rocks, pinecones, leaves, shells, feathers, and fruits • science tools such as a balance, ruler, hand lens, and thermometer	**Prep Tips** If possible, plan time to take children outside to observe nature. Have them bring paper and pencils to record their ideas. When you return to the classroom, provide quiet time for children to think of questions and draw or write about their ideas. If an outdoor nature walk is not possible, assemble natural materials, such as rocks, pinecones, leaves, shells, feathers, and fruits or vegetables, in advance. **Caution!** Be aware of allergies to foods, nuts, and various plants. **Troubleshooting** Some of these objects will be more conducive to testing with certain science tools. For example, the mass of a leaf may not register on a balance, but the length of the leaf could be measured instead. As children formulate questions, you may wish to guide them toward methods that make sense for the objects they choose. **Expected Results** Children will choose two natural objects and investigate a scientific question about these objects. They will form a hypothesis, and then test it using science tools. They will draw conclusions based on the experiment.

Go Digital! Virtual Lab

How Do We Use Inquiry Skills?

Key Inquiry Skills: hypothesize, plan and conduct simple investigations, observe

Children experiment to determine the best conditions for a new visitor to the classroom—a pet lizard!

Planning for Inquiry (continued)

Activity	Inquiry and Design Process Skills Focus	Materials	Prep Tips, Troubleshooting, and Expected Results
Lesson 5 DIRECTED INQUIRY Flipchart p.7 **A It's Time to Measure** **OBJECTIVES** Conduct simple investigations. Record and organize data. Measure and compare objects using non-standard units. 20–25 minutes pairs TEKS **1.2B, 1.2C, 1.2D, 1.4A, 1.4B**	• Measure • Compare • Draw Conclusions	• ruler or tape measure • large object to measure	**Prep Tips** Model how to measure using hands. Place your hands side by side, fingers spread out and thumbs touching, along the bottom left edge of the bulletin board. Count, "One hand, two hands." Then, move your left hand over your right hand so your pinkie fingers touch, and count, "Three hands." Continue until you reach the bottom right edge of the bulletin board. Invite children to practice measuring with their hands. Explain that rulers and tape measures are tools that can be used to measure objects as well. These tools have units of measurement called inches and centimeters. Allow children to compare the size of an inch with the size of a centimeter on the ruler or the tape measure. If a classroom bulletin board is not available, children can measure a desk, a bookshelf, or a table. **Troubleshooting** If the ruler or tape measure is shorter than the bulletin board, model how to mark where the ruler or tape measure ends with masking tape before repositioning it. **Expected Results** Children will measure a large object using their hands. They will also use a ruler or a tape measure to measure in inches and in centimeters. Children will compare the results of their measurements with their classmates. As children compare their results, they will discover that measuring with standard units, such as inches and centimeters, is more reliable than measuring with nonstandard units, such as hands, that vary in size from person to person.
INDEPENDENT INQUIRY Flipchart p.7 **B Balancing Act** **OBJECTIVES** Plan and conduct simple investigations. Collect and compare information using a balance. 30 minutes individuals TEKS **1.2B, 1.2C, 1.2D, 1.4A, 1.4B**	• Compare • Order • Plan and Conduct a Simple Investigation	• balance • assortment of small classroom objects of varying weight	**Prep Tips** If children are unfamiliar with the way a balance works, model its use. To vary the difficulty of the investigation, challenge children to compare three objects after they compare two. Make sure you include objects that are heavy or light for their size, such as a small, solid ball and a larger, hollow ball. **Troubleshooting** Make sure children do not lean on the balance. Remind them to release each object onto the balance and let the balance settle before making their comparisons. **Expected Results** Children will be able to identify, using the balance, which objects are lighter and heavier and put them in order from lightest to heaviest. They will recognize that the mass of an object is not necessarily contingent upon its size.

Additional teaching support for all inquiry activities is available in Online Resources.

Activity	Inquiry and Design Process Skills Focus	Materials	Prep Tips, Troubleshooting, and Expected Results
Lesson 6 DIRECTED INQUIRY Flipchart p. 10 **A Holding Water** **OBJECTIVES** Conduct simple investigations. Record and organize data. Collect and compare information using cups and bowls. 40 minutes pairs TEKS **1.2B, 1.2C, 1.2D, 1.4A**	• Compare • Measure • Hypothesize • Experiment • Draw Conclusions	• bowls • cups • water • measuring cups	**Prep Tips** Provide a variety of clear, unbreakable cups and bowls. In advance, fill each with the same amount of water, making sure that some containers appear to be more full than others. To minimize mess, children can wear smocks to keep themselves dry and cover work surfaces with newspaper to catch drips and spills. **Caution!** Remind children to wipe up spills immediately. **Troubleshooting** If children have difficulty determining how to test their hypotheses, remind them that in previous investigations they used science tools to do their tests. If necessary, point out that the measuring cup is a science tool they can use to measure how much water is in each cup. **Expected Results** Children should find that although the containers are different shapes, and some appeared to hold more water than others, they all held the same amount of water at the start of the investigation.
INDEPENDENT INQUIRY Flipchart p. 10 **B My Fingerprints** **OBJECTIVES** Plan and conduct Investigations. Collect data and make observations using a hand lens. 30 minutes individuals TEKS **1.2B, 1.2C, 1.2D, 1.4A**	• Observe • Compare • Plan and Conduct a Simple Investigation • Draw Conclusions	• nontoxic inkpads • white paper • hand lenses	**Prep Tips** Model for children how to make a fingerprint stamp. Remind them not to touch their clothing after touching ink and to wash their hands right away. You may wish to provide children with smocks. **Caution!** Check for allergies to certain inks. **Troubleshooting** If you would like to simplify the experiment, have children make and compare only their thumbprints. You may also wish to have children stamp their fingerprints in small groups to avoid a crowd at the sink afterward. **Expected Results** Children will make fingerprints and examine them with a hand lens. They will recognize that each person has unique fingerprints.

Differentiated Instruction

Leveled Readers

The Leveled Readers provide parallel coverage of the unit topics and Texas Essential Knowledge and Skills. Each Reader is available in English and Spanish. Both versions are available online and on touchscreen mobile devices.

ON-LEVEL This Reader reinforces unit concepts and vocabulary and focuses on the Texas Essential Knowledge and Skills. It includes student response activities.

EXTRA SUPPORT This Reader shares title, illustrations, vocabulary, and concepts with the On-Level Reader. However, the text is linguistically accommodated to provide simplified sentence structures and comprehension aids for students who need a little extra support with content-area reading and vocabulary development. It also includes student response activities.

ENRICHMENT This high-interest nonfiction Reader enriches and extends unit concepts. It reinforces some of the unit vocabulary, but also includes stretch vocabulary. It also includes student response activities.

TEACHER GUIDE

The accompanying Teacher Guide provides teaching strategies and support for using all the Readers, as well as English and Spanish worksheets that focus on vocabulary development. A correlation to the Texas Essential Knowledge and Skills is included.

DIGITAL VERSIONS

All of these Leveled Readers are available online. They are also available in an innovative and engaging format for touchscreen mobile devices. For information about accessing these versions, see page T9.

RTI Response to Intervention

Response to Intervention is a process for identifying and supporting students who are not making expected progress toward essential learning goals.

The following ScienceFusion components have the flexibility to be used to provide Core Classroom Instruction (Tier 1), strategic intervention (Tier 2), and intensive intervention (Tier 3).

Component	Location	Strategies and Benefits
Student Edition, Active Reading prompts, Sum It Up, Brain Check	Active Reading throughout each lesson, Sum It Up and Brain Check at the end of each lesson	Student responses can be used as screening tools to assess whether intervention is needed.
Assessment Guide, Lesson Quizzes and TEKS DOK Skill Builder	pp. AG 18–AG 25	Student responses can be used as screening tools to assess whether intervention is needed.
Inquiry Flipcharts	Inquiry Flipchart pp. 4, 6	Directed Inquiry for students who learn best through directed or teacher-led hands-on activities.
Teacher Edition, Unit Review Answer Strategies	TE pp. 47–50	Suggestions for intervention, guidance, and remediation for each review question.
Leveled Readers	TE p. 1J	Content support for students not meeting the learning needs during core classroom instruction.
Leveled Readers, Teacher Guides and Vocabulary Worksheets	TE p. 1J	Direct instruction with small groups of students needing additional content at various readability levels.
Extra Support for Vocabulary and Concepts (online worksheets)	Online Resources	Support for individualized instruction with practice in essential content.
Online Student Edition with Audio	Online Resources	Provides learners with multiple-modality access to science concepts and information.
Interactive Digital Lessons and Virtual Labs	Online Resources	Provides individualized learning experiences. Lessons make content accessible through simulations, animations, videos, audio, and integrated assessment.
Interactive Whiteboard Resources	Online Resources	Reinforces key unit concepts through interactive vocabulary games and visuals and graphic organizers.
Leveled Readers, online and tablet versions	Online and Tablet Resources	Highlighted words and sentences synced with audio provide support for emerging or struggling readers.

Differentiated Instruction

English Language Learners

Choose from these instructional strategies to meet the needs of English language learners.

Vocabulary Cards are provided in Online Resources.

Unit Vocabulary

Lesson 1	Lesson 3	Lesson 5	Lesson 6
senses	inquiry skills	science tools thermometer	investigation

Preteach Vocabulary ELPS 3C

Say each word, and have children repeat after you. Point out that two of the Unit 1 words are compound words, and ask children to identify the ones that are. Use pantomime and display pictures or objects as you talk about each word. Then, have children use each word in a sentence.

Language Acquisition Strategies

Use Prior Experiences ELPS 1A, 4F, 5G

Point out the vocabulary word *senses* on TE page 4. Explain that *senses* means "the things your body uses to learn about the world around you." Have children use prior experiences to understand the meaning.

Beginning	Intermediate	Advanced/Advanced High
Ask children to act out and talk about how they use their senses when they eat a meal.	Have partners talk together about how they use their senses during a meal.	Have children write sentences that tell how they use each sense during a typical day.

Visual and Contextual Support **ELPS** 1E, 2E, 3D, 4F

Use the pictures on **TE pages 6–7** to help children understand how we use our senses to get information.

Beginning	Intermediate	Advanced/Advanced High
Point to each picture, and explain how you would use your senses to get information about that object. Ask children to point to the part of your body you use for each sense.	Point to the picture of the cat. Ask: *What does your sense of sight tell you about the cat? What other senses can you use? Which body parts would you use?*	Name each sense, and have children tell how they would use it to get information about the objects in the pictures.

Personal Dictionary **ELPS** 1C, 3D, 3H, 5B

Use information about the term *inquiry skills* on **TE page 14** to help children make personal dictionary entries. Throughout the unit, have children create entries, adding details, examples, and related words.

Beginning	Intermediate	Advanced/Advanced High
Start a word web by writing *inquiry skills* in a circle. Write a definition (*skills that help you find out information*). Elicit things children can do to get information (*look, measure, tell how things are alike*). Explain that these are inquiry skills. Have children add this information to their personal dictionary.	Have children define *inquiry skills* in their own words and draw a picture to represent its meaning in their personal dictionary. Ask them to explain how the children in the pictures are using inquiry skills to find information about things they see in nature.	Have children write a definition of *inquiry skills*, list examples, and write a context sentence in their entry. Ask children to explain how inquiry skills can help them find information.

Linguistic Support **ELPS** 1F, 2C, 2E

Provide linguistic support to help children understand the meaning of *classify* on **TE page 16.** Review that when we *classify*, we put objects into groups based on how they are alike.

Beginning	Intermediate	Advanced/Advanced High
Model classifying small manipulatives into groups by color, size, and shape.	Display assorted classroom objects. Ask children to tell or model and explain how they would sort them into groups.	Have children explain how they would classify these objects: pencil, desk, chair, crayon, table, marker.

Coordinating Conjunctions **ELPS** 4C, 5B, 5F

Display this sentence from **TE page 26:** *Science tools help you collect, record, and compare information.* Review the coordinating conjunctions *and, but, or,* and *nor*. Then, have children practice using them.

Beginning	Intermediate	Advanced/Advanced High
Display this sentence: *A ruler and a hand lens are science tools.* Circle the conjunction. Display this sentence: *I look at bugs and flowers with a hand lens.* Have children identify the conjunction.	Have children write a sentence that includes the names of two science tools and a conjunction. Then, have partners exchange papers and circle the conjunction.	Have children write two sentences about science tools. Ask them to use a conjunction in each sentence. Have Advanced High ELLs use a different conjunction in each sentence.

How Scientists Work

I Wonder Why

Use the photograph and question to build children's interest. Ask them to describe any experiences they have had with ocean animals. Encourage them to think about the work scientists might do with ocean animals to help them answer the "why" question.

Here's Why

Have children turn the page and read the response to the question. You may wish to share the following background with them.

More About...

Marine Scientists

A scientist who studies animals and other living things in the ocean is called a *marine biologist*. Marine biologists may focus on learning more about how ocean animals live or studying the plant life and health of ocean environments.

Scientists with the Texas State Aquarium educate visitors about gulf animals and conservation. The aquarium features a natural habitat for rehabilitated sea turtles.

Science Songs

See pp. TR40–TR43 for science songs you can use to reinforce content in this unit.

Professional Development **Science Background**

Use the keywords to access

- Professional Development from **The NSTA Learning Center**
- **SciLinks** for additional online content appropriate for children and teachers
- Teacher Science Background in the back of this Teacher Edition

Keywords

human body
scientific method
scientific tools

SCILINKS. THE WORLD'S A CLICK AWAY

Here's Why Scientists study ocean animals and other animals to learn about how they live.

In this unit, you will explore this Big Idea, the Essential Questions, and the Investigations on the Inquiry Flipchart.

Levels of Inquiry Key ■ DIRECTED ■ GUIDED ■ INDEPENDENT

Track Your Progress

Big Idea Scientists use inquiry skills and tools to help them find out information.

Essential Questions

Now I Get the Big Idea!

Science Notebook

Before you begin each lesson, be sure to write your thoughts about the Essential Question.

Go Digital

For a complete digital curriculum and resources that provide full coverage of the objectives for this unit, see the Online Resources for this program.

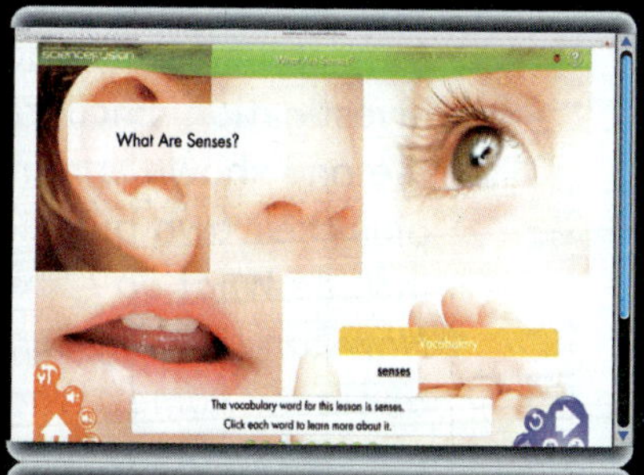

Big Idea and Essential Questions

Big Idea Scientists use inquiry skills and tools to help them find out information.

Post the Unit Big Idea on the board. Have children read the Essential Questions, which are also the titles of the lessons in this unit.

- Discuss how the Essential Questions can help them focus on the Big Idea.
- Have children read the Big Idea statement. The statement describes the main science concept they will be learning.
- Have children predict other ideas that will be taught in the lessons based on the titles, or have them give examples of pictures they expect to see.

Once they complete the unit, they should have a better understanding of the Big Idea.

Essential Questions You may use the following Science Notebook strategy for working with the Essential Questions before children begin the unit or before each lesson.

- Strategies for revisiting the Big Idea and Essential Questions are provided in Enduring Understandings on page 47A.

Notebook Science Notebook

- Have children copy the Essential Questions into their Science Notebooks. Suggest they leave writing lines between questions.
- Ask children to write responses to the Essential Questions. Urge children not to worry about whether their responses are correct. They should expect their ideas to change as they work in the unit. Comment that children will be able to review and revise their answers to the Essential Questions at the end of the unit.
- Tips and strategies for using Science Notebooks are provided throughout this unit, in the back of this Teacher Edition, and in Online Resources.

Options for Inquiry

FLIPCHART P. 3

Children can conduct these optional investigations at any time before, during, or in response to the lesson in the Student Edition.

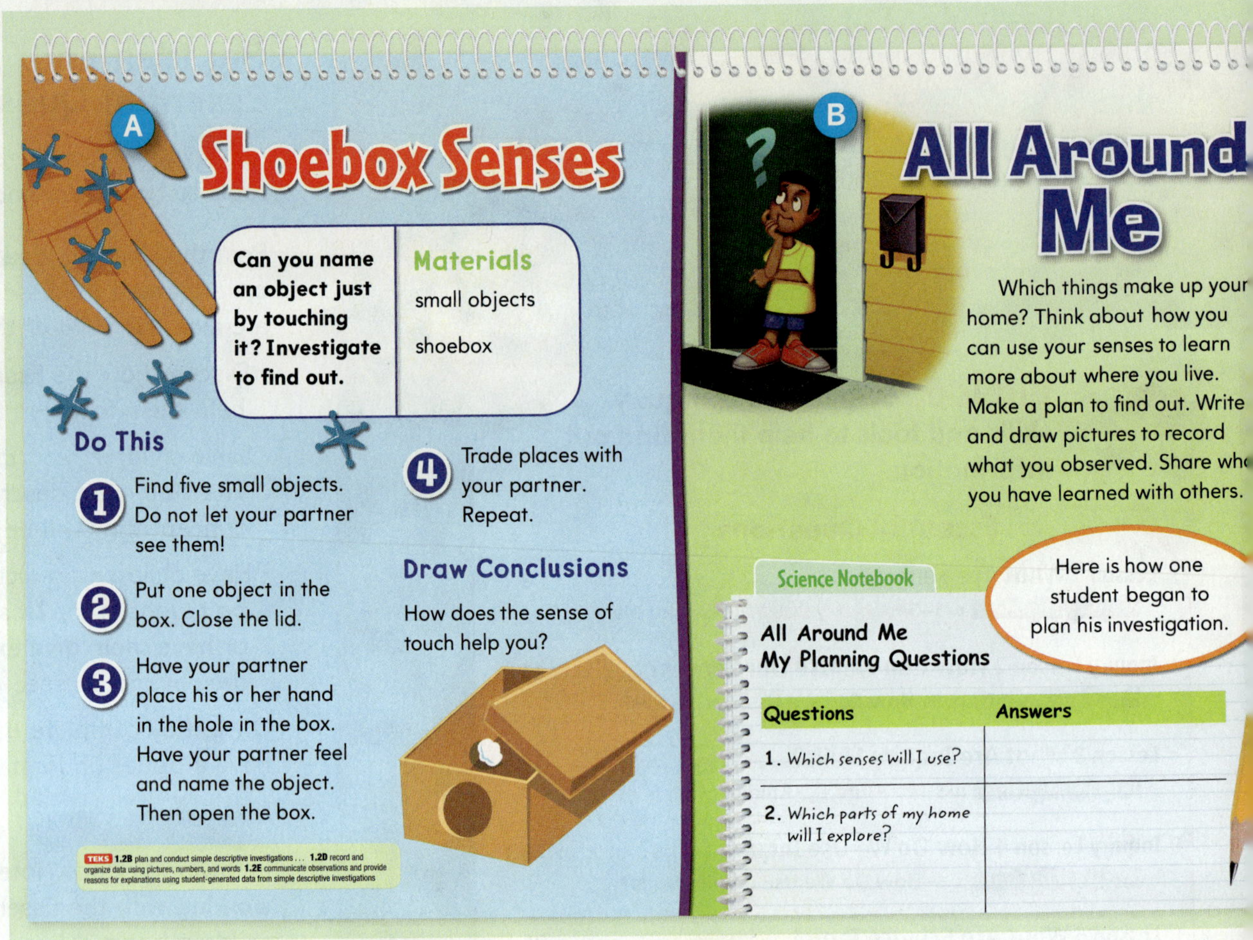
A
Shoebox Senses

Can you name an object just by touching it? Investigate to find out.

Materials
small objects
shoebox

Do This

1. Find five small objects. Do not let your partner see them!
2. Put one object in the box. Close the lid.
3. Have your partner place his or her hand in the hole in the box. Have your partner feel and name the object. Then open the box.
4. Trade places with your partner. Repeat.

Draw Conclusions

How does the sense of touch help you?

TEKS 1.2B plan and conduct simple descriptive investigations . . . 1.2D record and organize data using pictures, numbers, and words 1.2E communicate observations and provide reasons for explanations using student-generated data from simple descriptive investigations

B
All Around Me

Which things make up your home? Think about how you can use your senses to learn more about where you live. Make a plan to find out. Write and draw pictures to record what you observed. Share wh you have learned with others.

Directed Inquiry

A Shoebox Senses

30 minutes
pairs

Prep and Planning Tips

Before the activity, cut a hole in the narrow end of each shoebox so children can reach into the box without having to take off the lid.

Assemble a variety of small objects of different shapes, sizes, and textures from which children can choose.

Caution! Remind children to recognize the importance of safe practices to keep themselves and others safe and healthy. Warn children not to put anything sharp in the box.

Expected Results

Children will find that, even though they cannot see an object, they can often identify it using their sense of touch to feel its size, shape, and texture.

Independent Inquiry

B All Around Me

30 minutes
individuals

Prep and Planning Tips

See the Planning for Inquiry page for more information. Suggest that children limit the scope of their investigation to one room in their home, such as a bedroom or the kitchen. Point out that children may find it easier to use their senses of hearing and smelling to explore the room if they sit down and close their eyes.

Science Notebook

Children can use the Science Notebook as a model for planning and conducting their own investigation. Encourage them to make a chart like the one shown and include the sample questions plus their own questions. Additional questions may include *What do I observe using my sense of smell? How can I use my sense of touch to learn more about my home? What does my sense of hearing tell me about my home?*

Lesson 1

Essential Question

What Are Senses?

Engage Your Brain!

Find the answer to the question in the lesson.

Which sense is this child trying not to use?

the sense of

smell

Active Reading

Lesson Vocabulary

1. Preview the lesson.
2. Write the vocabulary term here.

senses

Inquiry Flipchart p. 3 — Shoebox Senses/All Around Me

3

Go Digital

An interactive digital lesson is available in the Online Resources. It is suitable for individuals, small groups, or may be projected or used on an interactive white board.

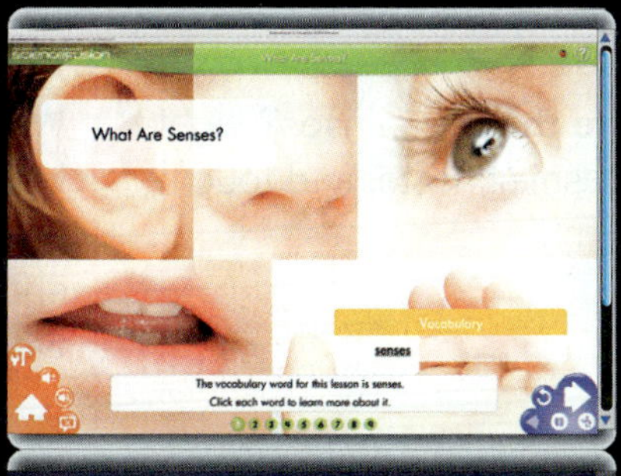

1 Engage/Explore

Objectives

- Plan and conduct simple investigations.
- Record and organize data.
- Communicate observations.
- Identify the five senses and the body part associated with each sense.
- Explain how the five senses help us learn.

Engage Your Brain!

Help children answer the question *Which sense is this child trying not to use?* Emphasize the word *not* in the question. Ask children whether they like the smell of cooking fish or sweaty sneakers. What would they do if those smells were nearby? How is that reaction like what the boy is doing to avoid the sock? Have children describe what the boy in the picture is doing.

Remind children to record their final answer to the question after reading the fifth page of this lesson.

Active Reading Annotations

Remind children that active readers "make texts their own" by marking them or writing notes to help them understand what they are reading. Encourage children to use pencil to make annotations and to feel free to change their marks and notes as they read. The goal of annotation is to help children remember what they have read.

Vocabulary and Interactive Glossary

Remind children to find and list the yellow highlighted terms from the lesson. As they proceed through the lesson and learn about the terms, they can add drawings or words in the extra spaces provided in some entries in the Interactive Glossary.

2 Explain

Generate Ideas

Read the heading aloud to children. Remind children that there are five senses, and challenge them to name all five. Ask volunteers to name them one by one, and write the words on the board. Ask children to find the matching word on the left page and point to it.

Active Reading Main Idea

Explain that the main, or most important, idea may be the first sentence in a paragraph. Or, it may be a different sentence. Active readers ask themselves, *What is this paragraph about?* The answer will be the main idea.

If children have difficulty locating the main idea on this page, read aloud the entire paragraph and have volunteers tell what it is about. Then have them find the sentence that states what the senses help you do.

Develop Science Vocabulary

senses Draw a word web on the board with *senses* in the middle and five bubbles around it. Have children copy the word web. Guide them as they suggest words for each bubble, and show them how to fill in *taste, touch, smell, sight,* and *hearing*.

Misconception Alert

Many children may think that sight is the only important sense to use when making observations. Point out that when scientists observe, they try to use many senses because each sense provides different information. Emphasize, however, how important it is not to smell or taste in science class, since many things are not safe to inhale, taste, or eat.

Your Senses

How do you learn about things? You use your five senses. Your **senses** are the way you learn about the world. The senses are sight, hearing, smell, taste, and touch. You use different body parts for different senses.

Active Reading

The main idea is the most important idea about something. Draw two lines under the main idea.

4

Differentiation—Leveled Questions

Extra Support

What are the five senses? sight, hearing, smell, taste, and touch

Challenge

Why do you think the senses are important to a scientist? Senses help scientists make observations and collect information about the world around them.

▶ Read the captions. Circle the name of the body parts you use for each sense.

5

Develop Science Concepts

How do you find out about things, such as what's happening in the world around you? through your senses

How many senses are there? Name them. five; sight, hearing, smell, taste, and touch

Interpret Visuals

Direct children's attention to the headphones on the left page. **Which sense would the girl be using if she was using the headphones?** hearing **Which body part does she use to hear?** her ears

Have children look at the flowers on the right page. **Which senses can you use to observe the flower?** smell, sight, touch **Which body part would you use to smell the flowers?** nose

Point to the scrapbook. Which sense is the girl using to look at the scrapbook? sight **Which body part do you use to see?** eyes

Have children point to the fruit. **Suppose you want to know if the fruit is sweet and juicy. What sense do you need?** taste **Which body part would you use to taste?** mouth

Have children find the cat. **Which sense tells you what the cat feels like?** touch **Which body part tells about touch?** your hands and skin

Review each part of the picture and have children point to the captions as you read each one aloud. Remind them to circle the body part word in the caption they use for each sense.

English Language Learners

ELPS 2E

Use Words for Body Parts Write these body parts on the board: *eyes, nose, ears, mouth,* and *hands.* Frame the word *eyes,* read it aloud, and point to your eyes. Have children say the word as they gesture the same way. Repeat with each body part. Next, say the words in random order and have children point to the correct body part. Finally, point to each body part and have children name it.

Notebook

Summarize Ideas

Remind children that the main idea tells what something is mostly about. Ask them to tell the main idea of these two pages orally or in writing by naming the five senses and summarizing what the senses do.

2 Explain (continued)

Notebook Generate Ideas

Read the heading aloud, and have children scan the two pages of the lesson to review the names of the five senses. Have them point to each word that indicates a sense as they find it on the page. Ask them to tell what they can learn from the senses.

Develop Science Concepts

Have children find the word *touching* and read what can be learned from that sense. Explain that *texture* means "how something feels." If possible, pass around a coarse wool sweater and a soft T-shirt or other objects with different textures.

How does this object feel? Encourage children to use texture words, like *soft, scratchy, rough, hard,* or *smooth* to describe what they feel. **Which sense did you use to figure out how these things feel?** the sense of touch

Write the words *loud, soft, noisy,* and *quiet* on the board. **What do these words describe?** kinds of noises or sounds **Which sense tells you a fire engine is coming down the street before you can see it?** the sense of hearing

Misconception Alert

Children may think that their hands are the only body part used to perceive touch. In fact, the sense of touch is distributed throughout the body with nerve endings in the skin and many other body parts. People can identify four different touch sensations: cold, heat, contact, and pain. These sensations are magnified by hairs on the skin, which act as an early warning system.

Learning with Your Senses

How can your senses help you learn? Look at the pictures. What would your senses tell you about each thing?

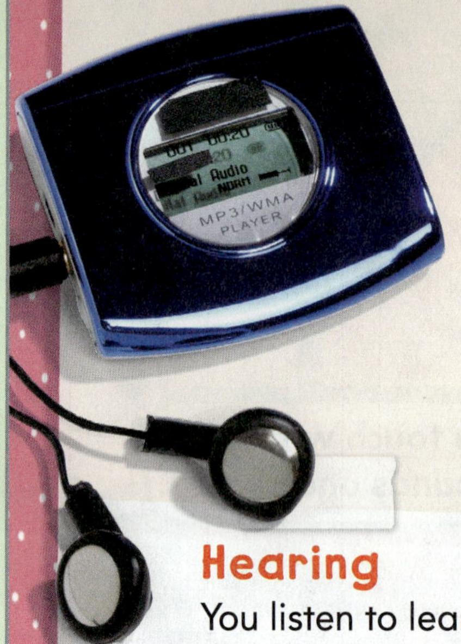

Hearing

You listen to learn how things sound.

Touching

You touch to learn about texture—how things feel.

▶ **Read the captions. Underline how you learn how things feel.**

6

Differentiation—Leveled Questions

Extra Support

Which sense do you use to learn about the color of a sweater? sight Which sense do you use to learn about its texture? touch

Challenge

Which sense do you think you use most? Explain. Sample answer: I use hearing most because I am always hearing things even when I am sleeping.

Seeing

You use sight to observe color, shape, and size.

Smelling

You use smell to learn how things smell.

Tasting

You taste to learn if foods are sweet, sour, or salty.

▶ **Read the captions. You use sight to observe three things. Circle the words.**

7

English Language Learners

ELPS 2E

Use Circles and Underlines
To ensure that children are able to mark their responses to the interactive text features on these two pages, model what it means to underline and circle. Write *circle* on the board, and demonstrate the action by circling it. Repeat for *underline.* Then have children write their first and last names and direct them to underline their first name and circle their last name.

Develop Science Concepts

Display a colored ball and have children describe it, including its size, shape, and color. **Which sense helped you observe this ball?** sight Help children find the caption "Seeing." Have them circle the three things they can observe with the sense of sight.

Direct children's attention to the picture above "Smelling." **What is something that smells good?** cookies baking, flowers **Name something that smells bad.** trash, dirty socks, gas fumes

Look at the food at the bottom of the right page. Would the food in this picture taste sweet, sour, or salty? Explain. They probably would taste sweet because fruits are usually sweet.

Taste and smell work together when you eat. Why is it hard to taste your food when you have a bad cold? If you have a stuffy nose, you cannot smell the food and that makes it hard to taste it.

Develop Inquiry Skills

DRAW CONCLUSIONS Point out that senses help us stay safe. **Which sense would help you avoid tripping over skates?** sight **Which sense would tell you an ambulance is coming?** hearing and sight

Notebook Summarize Ideas

Ask children to think about what they learned about how they can use the senses. Direct them to summarize the information orally or in a written two-column chart.

3 Extend/Evaluate

Sum It Up!

1. **Choose It!** Read the directions aloud to children, emphasizing the words *parts of the body* and *senses*. Ask them what they will do when they find a word that names a part of the body. Children should understand they will draw a circle around a word that names a body part. Then have them explain what they will do when they find a word that names one of the senses. Children should understand they will draw a line under a word that names a sense. Ask a volunteer to read the first word in the left-hand column. Have children tell whether the word should be circled or underlined and why. Children should circle the word. Call on volunteers to read the remaining words. Allow time for children to complete the activity on their own.
2. **Match It!** Read the directions aloud to children. Ask them to tell in their own words how they will complete this activity. They should understand that they will draw a line to match each object in the left-hand column with a sense described in the right-hand column. Ask a volunteer to identify each object in the left-hand column and to read the sentences in the right-hand column. Guide children through the first example by helping them match the pie with the sentence *You smell food baking*. Then ask children to complete the rest of the items on their own. They can look back at the pages with the heading "Learning with Your Senses" to review material about the senses.

Sum It Up!

1 Choose It!

Circle the words that name parts of the body. Underline the words that name senses.

nose	touch	smell
taste	eyes	mouth

2 Match It!

Look at each thing. Which sense helps you learn about it? Draw lines to match them.

You touch to feel how furry something is.

You see to read.

You smell food baking.

8

Brain Check

Lesson 1

Name ____________________

Word Play

You use different body parts for different senses. Label each body part with its sense.

hearing **sight** **smell** **taste** **touch**

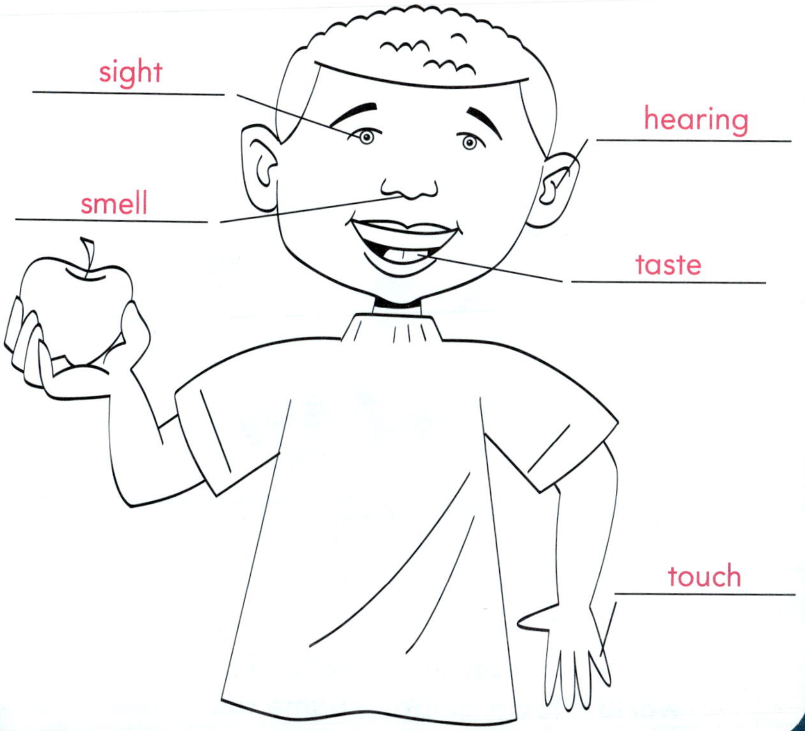

Answer Strategies

Word Play

- Begin the diagram by helping children read the words in the word bank. Ask what all of the words have in common, and guide children to understand that they name the five senses. Then have children follow along as you read the directions aloud.
- If children have difficulty completing the activity, explain that the boy shown in the diagram uses his senses to observe the apple. Have children point to the boy's eyes. **Which sense goes with your eyes?** sight Write the word *sight* on the line by the boy's eyes. Follow a similar process to help children label the other body parts.
- Once children label the diagram, have them check to make sure that they have written all five senses.
- To help improve recall of the five senses and their corresponding body parts, pair children and have them alternate naming a sense and the corresponding body part. Point out that they can use the Sum It Up! page to help them review and study for tests.

Assessment

Lesson Quiz

See Assessment Guide, p. AG 18.

3 Extend/Evaluate (continued)

Answer Strategies

Apply Concepts

- Before reading the directions, ask volunteers to read the words in each column on the page. Have children suggest ideas about what they think they will be doing on the page and then confirm or correct their ideas by reading aloud the directions.
- Then read the first word in the left-hand column. Encourage children to think of a sound they have heard. Ask them to name words that describe that sound. Suggest possible sound words, such as loud, soft, high, and low. Point out that the right-hand column has a word that describes sound. Have children find and point to the word.
- Before children draw a line to match the sense word with a word that goes with it, model your thinking for the first response: *I use my sense of hearing to hear sounds. Sounds may be high, low, loud, or soft. I'm going to look for one of those words in the list because those words go with hearing.*
- After children complete the rest of the page, ask them to summarize what they learned in the lesson. Encourage them to identify the five senses and how they help us learn.

Take It Home!

Suggest that children work with a family member to discuss ways we use our senses to learn about the world. You may want to play the "senses" game in class first to model it for children before they play it at home. Encourage children to share details of any versions they play at home.

Apply Concepts

Draw a line to the word that describes each sense.

hearing	hard
touching	loud
seeing	red
smelling	salty
tasting	fresh

Take It Home!

Family Members: Ask your child to tell how we use senses to learn about the world. Play a game to name the senses you use in different situations.

10

Make Connections

Easy

Art Connection

TEKS ART 1.2A

Draw With Your Eyes Open and Shut

- Distribute drawing paper and crayons, and show children how to fold the paper in half. On one half, have them draw an apple or other simple object.
- Tell children to close their eyes. Have them try to draw the same picture on the other half of the paper.
- Have children compare and contrast the pictures. Encourage discussion of how sight, touch, and other senses are important or unimportant in making art.

Average

Physical Education Connection

TEKS PE 1.3A, 1.7A

Analyze Senses Used in Sports and Games

- Let small groups of children work in an open area. Have them take turns acting out a sport or playground game for the group to guess.
- Ask the group to analyze how the senses are used to play this game or sport. For example, in kickball, you use sight to track the ball and touch to kick it.

Challenging

Writing Connection

TEKS ELA 1.24C

Write About Using Senses

- Write the following sentence frame on the board, and help children read it: "I use my sense of ________." Tell children that they will write the name of a sense and then draw a picture of something they observe with that sense.
- Challenge children to write at least two sentences and then share them with a partner.

Challenging

Health Connection

TEKS HEALTH 1.4A

Senses and Your Safety

- Write the following sentence on the board and help children read it aloud: *My senses can help keep me safe.* Have children brainstorm examples of how their senses can help keep them safe. For example, the sense of smell can detect smoke; the sense of hearing can detect sirens.
- List the five senses on the board. Allow time for pairs of children to write sentences about how each sense can help keep them safe.
- Have children make a class list on the board of ways their senses help keep them safe. Write their contributions next to the corresponding sense. You may wish to copy their class list onto chart paper and post it in the classroom.

Guided Inquiry

FLIPCHART P. 4

15 minutes
pairs

Children should follow the directions on the Flipchart. The accompanying pages in the Student Edition provide scaffolding for guided inquiry.

Inquiry Skills Focus Observe

Objectives

- Recognize and demonstrate safe practices.
- Plan and conduct simple descriptive investigations.
- Collect and compare information and make observations using simple equipment.
- Record and organize data. Communicate observations.

Prep and Planning Tips

See the Planning for Inquiry page for more information.

- Gather enough celery, or cut them into pieces, so that each child can have his or her own.
- Children may need to share hand lenses.

Caution! Be sure children recognize and demonstrate safe practices by using all materials appropriately. Make sure that children do not put the celery in their mouths to keep themselves safe and healthy.

Expected Results

Children will discover that they can observe with senses beyond sight.

1 Engage/Explore

Attention Grabber

Ask children to shut their eyes and provide them with a common, safe (i.e., not sharp or pointed) object on the desk in front of them. Have them observe and describe the object by using their senses other than sight (and taste) and try to identify it. After thirty seconds, have children open their eyes to check their guesses. Then allow time for children to discuss what it was like to observe without seeing.

Preview Activity

Before beginning the investigation, have children review the directions on the Inquiry Flipchart and the accompanying Student Edition response pages. Then have them complete the response pages as they follow the directions on the Flipchart.

Inquiry Flipchart p. 4

Lesson 2 INQUIRY

TEKS **1.2A** ask questions about organisms, objects, and events observed in the natural world **1.2B** plan and conduct simple descriptive investigations such as ways objects move **1.2D** record and organize data using pictures, numbers, and words

ame ____________________

Essential Question

How Can We Use Our Senses?

et a Purpose

ell what you want to find out.

want to use my senses to learn about celery.

hink About the Procedure

What will you observe?

will observe how celery looks, feels, smells, and sounds

hen it breaks. I will recall how it tastes.

How will you find out the sound of breaking celery?

vill break the celery.

11

Go Digital

A virtual lab experience is available with the Online Resources for this program.

1 Engage/Explore (continued)

Guide the Investigation

Develop Inquiry Skills

OBSERVE **Use your own words to tell what it means to observe.** Sample answer: It means to use your senses to notice things about the world around you.

What are the five senses you use to observe? sight, taste, touch, smell, and hearing

Which body part helps you observe by using sight? the eyes

Repeat for the other senses.

How will you observe in this investigation? I will use my senses to observe how celery looks, smells, sounds, and feels. I will think about how it tastes.

How will you observe what it feels like? I will touch it.

How will you observe what it sounds like? I will break it.

2 Explain

Develop Inquiry Skills

RECORD YOUR DATA Review the way the chart is organized. Direct attention to the left column, and have children read each sense.

Explain that children will write their observations for that sense in the right column under the heading *Observation*.

Children should understand that there are no right answers and that not everyone will have the same words or phrases to describe the celery. Explain that people may have different observations or use different words to describe what they observe. Also, the celery pieces are not exactly the same.

DRAW CONCLUSIONS Make sure that children understand that the conclusions they make should be based on their observations.

3 Extend/Evaluate

ASK MORE QUESTIONS Have pairs or small groups brainstorm questions they could ask about the celery. Ask volunteers to state a few of their questions to the class before children write their own answers. Questions could include ideas about how the celery changes after it is cooked or how observations of the celery compare to other vegetables.

Assessment

Lesson Quiz
See Assessment Guide, p. AG 19.

Record Your Data

In this chart, write to record what you observe.

Sample answers are provided

Sense	Observation
Sight	green, little ridges
Touch	a little hard, bumpy
Smell	smells a little like soil
Hear	snap when it breaks
Taste	tangy or bitter

Draw Conclusions

What did you find out about celery? How do you know?

I found out how celery looks, feels, smells, sounds when it breaks, and tastes. I know because I used my senses.

Ask More Questions

What other questions could you ask about celery and your senses?

Sample question: Does celery taste, smell, look, or feel different when it is cooked?

12

Differentiated Inquiry

Easy

Observe a Plant

Have children repeat the activity that they did on the Flipchart, but this time have them observe a different vegetable or fruit instead of a celery stalk. Remind them not to taste the object.

Average

Play I Spy

- Have partners use their senses to play a game of *I Spy* in the classroom.
- Have one child secretly choose an object in the room and describe how it looks, feels, sounds, and so on, one clue at a time, in the tradition of the game.
- Have the other child try to guess the identity of the object with as few clues as possible.

Average

Use Your Senses to Observe

- Have partners make "senses" cards on five separate index cards by writing the word or drawing a picture for each of the five senses.
- Have each child choose a classroom object to observe and then draw a card. The child must make an observation about the object using the sense on the card.
- Shuffle and reuse the cards. Partners can repeat the activity with a new object.

Challenging

Compare Observations

- Have children work in pairs to choose an object from the classroom that they can observe.
- Have them list their observations separately in a two-column chart and then compare their lists.

Options for Inquiry

FLIPCHART P. 5

Children can conduct these optional investigations at any time before, during, or in response to the lesson in the Student Edition.

Directed Inquiry

A Measure Up

30 minutes | pairs

Prep and Planning Tips

If a teacher's desk is not available, children can measure a table or top of a bookshelf. If the tape measure is shorter than the desk or table, model how to mark where it ends with masking tape before repositioning it.

Caution! Use only cloth tape measures. A retractable metal tape measure can cause injury.

Expected Results

Children will practice using a tape measure to measure length and comparing objects by length. They will find that the inquiry skill measure helps them find and compare the length of objects.

Independent Inquiry

B Animal Models

30 minutes | individuals

Prep and Planning Tips

See the Planning for Inquiry page for more information.

Caution! Remind children to recognize the importance of safe practices to keep themselves and others safe and healthy. Before children begin, review safety rules for using scissors in the classroom.

Science Notebook

Children can use the Science Notebook as a model for planning and conducting their own investigation. Encourage them to make a chart like the one shown and include the four sample questions plus their own questions. Additional questions may include *What parts of the animal should my model show? What reference materials do I need to learn about my animal?*

TEKS **1.2D** record and organize data using pictures, numbers, and words **1.2E** communicate observations and provide reasons for explanations using student-generated data from simple descriptive investigations

Lesson 3

Essential Question

What Are Inquiry Skills?

Engage Your Brain!

Find the answer to the question in the lesson.

What can you infer this boy is doing?

The boy is

playing outdoors .

Active Reading

Lesson Vocabulary

1. Preview the lesson.
2. Write the vocabulary term here.

inquiry skills

Inquiry Flipchart p. 5 — Measure Up/Animal Models

13

Go Digital

An interactive digital lesson is available in Online Resources. It is suitable for individuals, small groups, or may be projected or used on an interactive white board.

1 Engage/Explore

Objectives

- Plan and conduct simple investigations.
- Collect data using simple equipment.
- Record and organize data.
- Communicate observations.
- Identify inquiry skills and describe how to apply them during investigations.

Engage Your Brain!

Help children answer the question *What can you infer this boy is doing?* Ask volunteers to describe what the child in the picture is doing. Draw attention to the boy's surroundings. To help them infer, tell them to use what they observe in the picture and what they know from their experiences. *What do people do when they are dressed like the boy is and are located where he is?* Record children's ideas on the board.

Remind children to record their final answer when they find it on the next page.

Active Reading Annotations

Remind children that active readers "make texts their own" by marking them or writing notes to help them understand what they are reading. Encourage children to use pencil to make annotations and to feel free to change their marks and notes as they read. The goal of annotation is to help children remember what they have read.

Vocabulary and Interactive Glossary

Remind children to find and list the yellow highlighted terms from the lesson. As they proceed through the lesson and learn about the terms, they can add drawings or words in the extra spaces provided in some entries in the Interactive Glossary.

2 Explain

Notebook Generate Ideas

Read the heading aloud, and ask them to preview the subheadings on these pages to name four skills they will study. Have them read *observe, compare, predict,* and *measure*. Ask children to tell what they know about each of those skills or what they mean.

Develop Science Vocabulary

inquiry skills Explain that *inquiry* comes from the word *inquire,* which means "to ask" or "to want to know something." Point out that scientists use inquiry skills to help them find answers to questions they ask or to find out something they want to know.

Active Reading Compare

Explain that comparing things is finding ways they are alike. Active readers remember the way things are alike because they keep in mind the things being compared. Show children how to draw triangles so they can indicate which things are being compared.

Develop Science Concepts

What is an inquiry skill? a skill that helps you find out information **Name four of them.** observe, compare, predict, measure

Interpret Visuals

Tell children that this illustration can help them answer the Engage Your Brain! question. **What clues help you figure out, or infer, that these children are playing outdoors?** what they are wearing and where they are **What does it mean to infer?** You use clues to figure out something not told to you directly.

Skills to Help You Learn

Observe and Compare

How can you be like a scientist? You can use inquiry skills. **Inquiry skills** help you find out information. They help you learn about your world.

Active Reading

You can compare things. You find ways they are alike. A child on this page is comparing two things. Draw a triangle around the two things.

14

Differentiation—Leveled Questions

Extra Support

Two inquiry skills are observe and compare. What are two others? predict and measure

Challenge

What is something you could *observe* when you play outdoors? the colors of leaves **Compare?** the heights of buildings **Predict?** what the weather will do **Measure?** the height of a plant

Predict and Measure

▶ Read the labels. Circle the inquiry skill that helps you find the size of an object.

15

English Language Learners

ELPS 1E, 2C

Understand Words Used for Comparing Guide children in using the skill *compare* by focusing on the properties of size, shape, and color. As you ask *yes/no* questions, cue the property by gesturing. Display two identical books and ask *Are these books the same size (shape, color)?* Display two books that are the same shape and color, but are different sizes and repeat the questions. Repeat with books that are different colors and shapes.

TEKS 1.2D, 1.2E

Develop Science Concepts

What does it mean to observe? You use your senses to learn about the world around you.

What senses would you use to observe in a forest? sight, hearing, smell, touch

Explain that when we compare, we tell how things are the same. Show two classroom objects, such as a red crayon and a red marker. Ask children to compare them.

Is it possible to compare just one thing? Explain. No, you need at least two things so you can tell how one thing is the same as the other(s).

Explain that *predict* means "to make a good guess about will happen." **If you see dark clouds in the sky, what do you predict the weather will be? Explain.** I think it will rain. I know that dark clouds usually mean it will rain. **How is predicting different from simply guessing?** Predicting uses clues and things I already know to make a *good* guess. I just guess when I don't have enough information.

What science tools do you use to measure? What does each one measure? a ruler and tape measure measure length

Develop Inquiry Skills

COMPARE Have partners compare two or more leaves. Guide them to understand that they can compare by telling how features, like the size, shape, or color, are the same.

Notebook Summarize Ideas

Have children summarize the lesson concepts orally or in writing by identifying the four inquiry skills on this spread and explaining how they might use each one to think like a scientist.

2 Explain (continued)

Notebook Generate Ideas

Read the subheadings *Classify and Communicate,* and *Hypothesize and Plan an Investigation* aloud to children. Point out that these are four more inquiry skills that scientists use to find out information. Have children preview the illustrations, looking for clues that can help them figure out how to use these skills.

Develop Science Concepts

Explain that when you classify, you sort things into groups by how they are alike.

What is this child classifying? birds **You might classify the birds by their size. Another way to classify these birds is by color. Into what three color groups did the child classify these birds?** blue birds, red birds, and brown birds

Explain that after classifying, you can communicate the results by writing, speaking, drawing a picture, or making a chart.

To complete the chart at the bottom of the page, the child counted the number of blue birds. How many did she count? two Guide children to see that she showed the number of blue birds by coloring two spaces above the heading *blue.*

Why did the child color just one space above red? because there is one red bird

What is the first thing you need to do to communicate the number of brown birds? You need to count them. **How many brown birds are in the group?** three **How will you record and communicate this information on the chart?** I will color three spaces in above the heading *brown.*

Writing Connection

TEKS ELA 1.19

Write Complete Sentences
Remind children that they communicate the results of an investigation by writing, speaking, drawing, and/or making a chart. Have children look at the chart that communicates the number of birds by color. Have them copy and complete these sentence frames to communicate the resul shown in the chart.

They saw ___ blue birds. (two)

They saw ___ red bird. (one)

They saw ___ brown birds. (thre

Hypothesize and Plan an Investigation

▶ **Look at the picture. Which child made a hypothesis? Draw a line under the hypothesis.**

17

Differentiation—Leveled Questions

Extra Support

Why do you make a hypothesis before you plan an investigation? You make a hypothesis before you plan an investigation because the hypothesis tells what you will test and the investigation helps test the hypothesis.

Challenge

Think of a question about red and brown birds in a forest and state a hypothesis. Sample answer: There are more brown birds than red birds in the forest. **How could you investigate?** by doing a bird count

Interpret Visuals

Point out the speech bubbles on this page. Explain that these graphic features show what someone is saying. Have children describe what speech bubbles look like and identify what is being said inside each one.

Develop Science Concepts

Explain that when you hypothesize, or make a hypothesis, you tell what you think will happen before you actually test to find out. To test something, you plan an investigation by deciding what steps you will follow.

Have children point to the child who is hypothesizing, or making a hypothesis. **What is this child's hypothesis?** The big log will roll farther because it is heavier.

Have children underline this hypothesis and tell whether they agree with it. Point out that they do not have to agree and can make their own hypothesis.

Explain that *investigate* means "to explore or examine something to learn more about it." **What investigation do the children plan to test the hypothesis?** They plan to roll a big log and small log down the hill to see which rolls farther.

Develop Inquiry Skills

INVESTIGATE Explain that when you plan an investigation, you decide what steps to follow. **What steps could the children do to learn how logs of different sizes roll down a hill?** Sample answer: First, mark a start line. Then, put a big log at the start line and let it go. Next, measure how far the log rolls. Repeat for the small log. Last, compare the distances.

Notebook Summarize Ideas

Have children summarize these two pages orally or in writing by naming the four inquiry skills found on them and explaining each one.

2 Explain (continued)

Generate Ideas

Notebook

Read the headings. Explain that infer, draw conclusions, make a model, and sequence are also inquiry skills.

Develop Science Concepts

Explain that when people infer, they use clues to figure out something that is happening but is not said or explained directly.

Focus attention on the boy at the top of the left page, and have a volunteer read what he is saying. **What does this boy think about the containers?** The boy thinks that one container feels heavier than the other. **Using this information, what can the child infer about the containers?** The light container is empty or has less in it than the other.

Discuss *drawing conclusions.* Point out that an investigation starts with a question. Then information is collected to help answer it. Drawing a conclusion means using that information to try to answer the question. Look at the boy at the bottom of the left page, and read the speech bubble. **What information does the boy learn by tipping the containers over?** The boy observes that the heavy container had liquid in it. **What conclusion can the boy make by using this information?** Empty containers are lighter than full ones. Have children underline this conclusion.

Misconception Alert

Children often have difficulty distinguishing between inferring and drawing conclusions. The key difference is that inferring is "forward reasoning." You use what you know to make a supposition about something new. Drawing conclusions is "backward reasoning." You use prior knowledge and current observations to reach a conclusion. Be sure that children also understand that drawing conclusions does not involve actual "drawing."

Make a Model and Sequence

▶ Look at the picture. Things may happen in order.
Write 1 beside what happens first.
Write 2 beside what happens second.
Write 3 beside what happens third.
Write 4 beside what happens last.

Interpret Visuals

Focus attention on the model of the butterfly. **What did the child make?** a model of a butterfly **What does the model show?** what the butterfly looks like **How are the model and the real butterfly the same and different?** They have the same basic shape. The sizes and materials are different.

Explain that scientists make models to show how something works or to show its parts. **What could you learn about a butterfly by making this model?** Sample answer: You could learn about its body parts.

Active Reading Sequence

Explain that order is important in describing how something changes or how something is done. When order is important, active readers write numbers to help them remember the order in which things take place.

Direct children's attention to the drawings. **What do these drawings show?** how a butterfly changes during its life. **Explain that** *sequence* **means "to show the order in which events happen." What is the first event in this sequence?** A female butterfly lays eggs. **Write 1 by this drawing.** Guide children in numbering the remaining drawings in sequence.

Develop Inquiry Skills

SEQUENCE Have children use the numbered pictures to tell, in sequence, how a butterfly changes. Tell them to use the words *first, second, third,* and *last*. First, a butterfly egg is laid on a leaf. Second, a caterpillar grows. Third, it forms a hard shell. Last, it turns into a butterfly.

Notebook Summarize Ideas

Have children summarize these two pages orally or in writing by naming the four inquiry skills found on this spread and defining or explaining each one.

English Language Learners

ELPS 1E, 2C, 2E

Use Sequence Words Write *first, second, third,* and *last* on the board. Point to each word, pronounce it, and have children repeat it. Explain that these words help put things in order, or sequence. Act out a four-step process, such as brushing your teeth. Preface each step with the corresponding sequence word and have children hold up a finger to indicate the step number. Repeat the steps, and have children supply the words.

3 Extend/Evaluate

Sum It Up!

1. **Circle It!** Read the directions and the three choices aloud to children. If they have difficulty, call on volunteers to tell in their own words the meanings of the inquiry skills. To help them get started, model by saying *When you predict, you make a good guess about what you think will happen at a later time.*
2. **Choose It!** Have children study the picture and tell what the children in the picture are doing. Ask volunteers to read the answer choices while children listen for a match to what they see in the picture. If necessary, remind them that when they communicate, they share what they have learned; when they make a model, they make something to show what something is like or how it works; and when they sequence, they put things in order. After children respond, challenge them to tell how they would draw a picture to illustrate the two inquiry skills they did not circle.
3. **Draw It!** After children select, observe, and draw a classroom object, call on volunteers to talk about their drawings. Have children fill in the blanks of the sentence they write below the drawing.

Sum It Up!

1 Circle It!

You want to learn about something. Circle what you do to find out.

predict

classify

plan an investigation (circled)

2 Choose It!

What inquiry skill does this show?

communicate (circled)

make a model

sequence

3 Draw It!

Observe an object. Draw it. Tell about it.

Drawings and responses will vary.

This is a ______________. It is ______________.

20

Brain Check

Lesson 3

Name ____________________

Word Play

Circle the letters to spell the words. Then complete the sentence.

compare   classify   infer   measure
observe   predict   sequence

s	e	q	u	e	n	c	e	a
v	c	l	a	s	s	i	f	y
u	l	r	i	n	f	e	r	t
r	m	e	a	s	u	r	e	p
o	b	s	e	r	v	e	g	e
e	w	p	r	e	d	i	c	t
c	o	m	p	a	r	e	t	z

All the words in the puzzle are inquiry skills.

Answer Strategies

Word Play

- Have children point to each word in the word bank as you read it aloud. Explain that this is a word search puzzle, and that they will find each word in the word bank hidden in the puzzle. If children are unfamiliar with this puzzle format, replicate the first two lines on the board and show them how the words run across. Suggest to children that they cross out words in the word bank when they find them in the puzzle.
- When children complete the puzzle, read the incomplete sentence at the bottom of the page. Ask children to think about how all the words in the puzzle are alike. If children need help, suggest that they look at the first two pages of the lesson.
- To improve children's understanding, have pairs of children take turns reviewing the Brain Check answers and describing how they would use each inquiry skill. Point out that they can use the Sum It Up! page to help them review and study for tests.

Assessment

Lesson Quiz

See Assessment Guide, p. AG 20.

3 Extend/Evaluate (continued)

Answer Strategies

Apply Concepts

- Discuss the organization of the chart by showing how each row is like its own question. The first column gives a clue or definition; the second and third columns give two answer choices. Children will choose one of those words as the correct answer that matches the meaning in the left column. To help children keep their place in the chart, they can put a card or ruler under the row they are reading.
- Help children work through the first row before they continue on their own to complete the rest of the page.
- As a lesson follow-up, ask children to summarize what they learned about how inquiry skills can help them think like scientists. Have them name each skill and tell how they might use it to learn about the world.

Take It Home!

Have children work with a family member to discuss how they use inquiry skills around the house. Some ways these skills are used at home include classifying when unloading a dishwasher, predicting the weather when choosing clothes to wear, measuring laundry detergent, or communicating a phone message. Encourage children to use self-stick labels to mark these places around the house or draw and label pictures of the home activities to bring to class for discussion.

Apply Concepts

Circle the word that matches the meaning.

1 tell what you learn	communicate	observe
2 sort things into groups	sequence	classify
3 tell how things are alike and different	make a model	compare
4 put things in order	sequence	hypothesize
5 find out how much or how long	measure	infer
6 use your senses	make a model	observe
7 make a good guess about what will happen	predict	sequence
8 decide what steps to follow	draw conclusions	plan an investigation

Take It Home!

Family Members: Discuss with your child how inquiry skills are used around the home. For example, you measure when you cook and classify when you sort laundry.

22

Make Connections

Easy

Music Connection

TEKS MUSIC 1.2A

Sing About Observing

- Lead children in singing the traditional song "The Bear Went Over the Mountain."
- Call on volunteers to tell what the bear might observe going over the mountain.
- Repeat the activity by substituting other locations, such as a city, farm, beach, and forest.

Average

Social Studies Connection

TEKS SS 1.5A

Make a Model of Your Community

- Provide recycled cereal boxes and shoeboxes and clean milk cartons, as well as other art materials.
- Have small groups make models of buildings in your community, which you can put together to make a more complete model of the area.
- Discuss with children what they learned about their community by making these models.

Average

Math Connection

TEKS MATH 1.1C

Sequence Objects to Make Patterns

- Provide classroom materials, such as colored crayons, blocks, or counters.
- Have children sequence the materials to make a pattern. To help them get started, model patterns such as two chips and a crayon or alternating blue and red blocks.
- Have pairs of children take turns using the materials to make and extend patterns. One child makes a pattern and the other identifies the sequence of items and extends it.

Challenging

Art Connection

TEKS ART 1.2A

Make a Quilt to Show Inquiry Skills

- Assign pairs of children one of these inquiry skills: observe, compare, predict, measure, classify, communicate, hypothesize, plan an investigation, infer, draw conclusions, sequence, or make a model.
- Have them work together to draw and label a picture illustrating this skill. Tape the pictures together to make an "inquiry skills" quilt for display and discussion.

Guided Inquiry

FLIPCHART P. 6

15 minutes
pairs

Children should follow the directions on the Flipchart. The accompanying pages in the Student Edition provide scaffolding for guided inquiry.

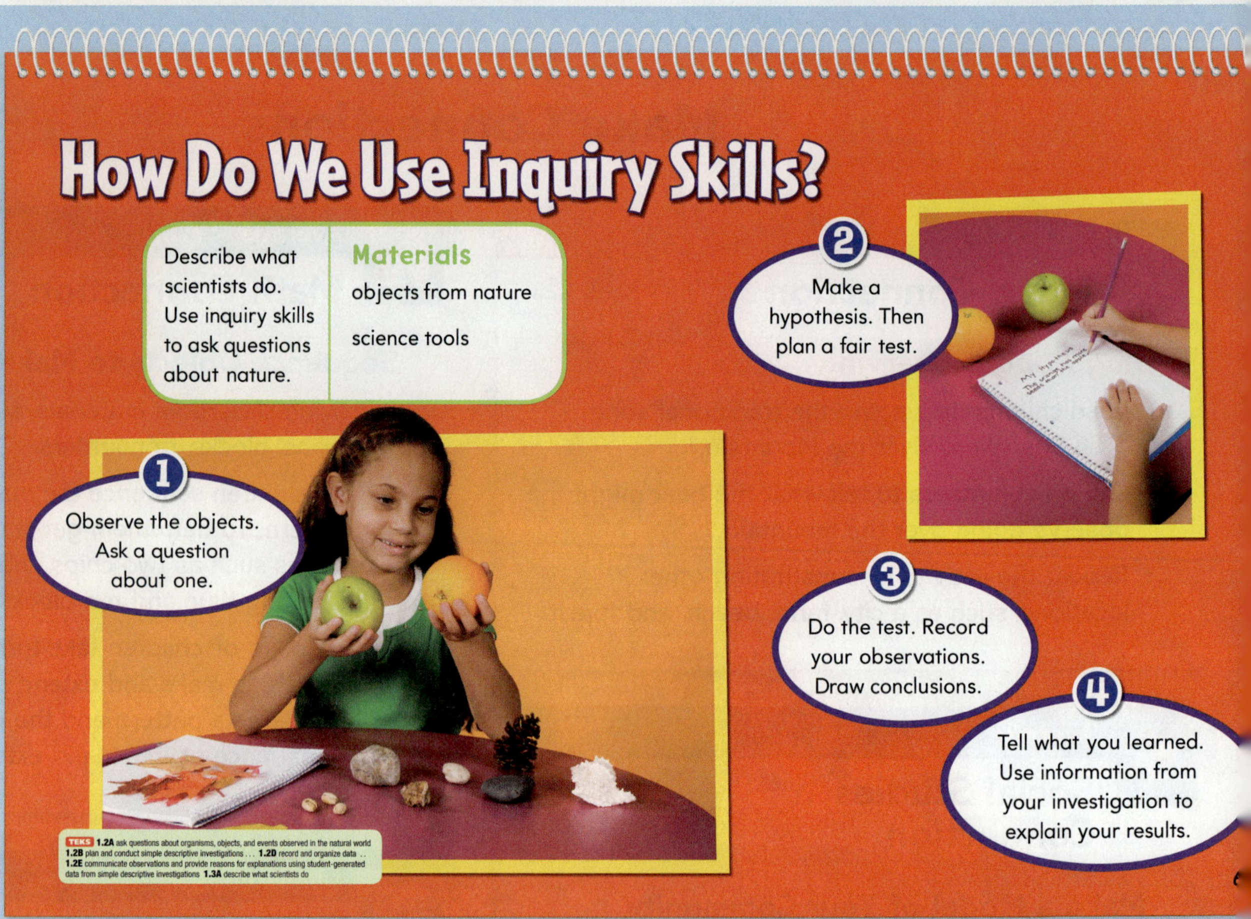

Inquiry Skills Focus Hypothesize, Plan an Investigation

Objectives

- Ask questions about organisms and objects observed in the natural world.
- Plan and conduct simple descriptive investigations.
- Record and organize data.
- Communicate observations and provide reasons for explanations using data from investigations.
- Describe what scientists do.

Prep and Planning Tips

See the Planning for Inquiry page for more information.

- If possible, bring children outside to observe nature.
- When you return to the classroom, provide time for children to think of questions and to draw or write about their ideas.

Expected Results

Children should be able to ask a question, write a hypothesis, plan an investigation, and draw conclusions from the question they wrote and the activity they planned.

1 Engage/Explore

Attention Grabber

Display a number of science tools such as a ruler, a hand lens, a scale, a balance, and a thermometer in a bin or on a large piece of poster board. Also display a number of interesting objects from nature, such as a geode, minerals, crystals, odd fruits or vegetables, or colorful leaves. Ask children to choose one object and talk about how they would use one of the science tools and inquiry skills to investigate it.

Preview Activity

Before beginning the investigation, have children review the directions on the Inquiry Flipchart and the accompanying Student Edition response pages. Then have them complete the response pages as they follow the directions on the Flipchart.

Inquiry Flipchart p. 6

Lesson 4
INQUIRY

TEKS **1.2A** ask questions about organisms, objects, and events observed in the natural world **1.2B** plan and conduct simple descriptive investigations such as ways objects move **1.2D** record and organize data using pictures, numbers, and words

Name ______________________

Essential Question

How Do We Use Inquiry Skills?

Set a Purpose

ell what you want to find out.

hildren should indicate the question they want to answer r learn more about. Sample question: Does an orange have ore seeds than an apple?

hink About the Procedure

What fair test did you plan? Write your plan here.

hildren should list the steps of the procedure for the st they have planned.

What science tools will you use for your test?

nswers will vary depending on the investigation.

23

Go Digital

A virtual lab experience is available with the Online Resources for this program.

1 Engage/Explore (continued)

Guide the Investigation

Develop Inquiry Skills

HYPOTHESIZE Remind children that an investigation starts with a question. A hypothesis is a best guess to the answer of that question *before* you do the investigation. In this inquiry, children will be describing what scientists do by completing an investigation of their own.

Suppose we were going to investigate the question "Does an orange have more seeds than an apple?" One hypothesis could be "An apple has more seeds than an orange." What could be a different hypothesis? An orange has more seeds than an apple.

What clues or knowledge did you use to make your hypothesis? Sample answer: I thought about what the inside of each fruit looks like.

PLAN AN INVESTIGATION **After you write a hypothesis, you are ready to plan the investigation. The investigation helps you collect information to answer the question. What would you do to figure out if the apple or orange has more seeds?** Sample answer: Cut open each fruit, count the seeds, and then compare the number of seeds in each one.

2 Explain

Develop Inquiry Skills

RECORD YOUR DATA Remind children that they should write and draw to record their observations. Point out that their observations should be based on the question that they chose, not the sample question you discussed with them, a hypothesis, or someone else's question. As a result, each person's answers will vary. Emphasize that what children record should be based on their observations and does not have to match the hypothesis.

DRAW CONCLUSIONS Explain that good conclusions try to answer the original question using the observations or information gathered in the investigation. Each child's conclusions, therefore, will vary depending on the question they studied and the observations made.

3 Extend/Evaluate

ASK MORE QUESTIONS Have children brainstorm other questions about the same topic that they could investigate. Have them think about how their conclusions lead them to other things they want to know.

As a follow-up, challenge children to write a hypothesis and plan an investigation to learn more about one of the questions.

Assessment

Lesson Quiz
See Assessment Guide, p. AG 21.

Record Your Data

Draw and write to record what you observe.

Children's responses will vary according to the questions they asked and the investigation they carried out.

Draw Conclusions

What conclusions can you draw?

Answers will depend on the investigation children carried out.

Ask More Questions

What other questions could you ask about the living things and objects observed around you?

Answers will depend on the investigation but should reflect the same topic.

24

Differentiated Inquiry

Easy

Tell What Science Tools Do

- Have children write the name or draw a picture of three science tools on one side of separate index cards.
- On the other side, have them write words or phrases to explain what the tool does.

Average

Write a Hypothesis

- Have children scan their science books for three science questions that interest them and challenge them to write a hypothesis for each one.
- Ask them to share their hypotheses with a partner and justify, or explain the reasoning behind, each one.

Average

Ask Testable Questions

- Have children practice asking "science" questions. Provide objects for children to observe and have them ask a "testable" question about two or three of them.
- Remind children to ask questions that they can investigate. Instead of asking *Is this rock pretty?* for example, they might ask *Will this rock scratch plastic?*
- Guide children to edit their questions or have partners work together to improve them.

Challenging

Plan Your Own Investigation

- Have partners think of an interesting question about something that fascinates them.
- Have them write or draw a step-by-step list showing the steps they would take to investigate that question.
- Have children present their ideas to the class or display a poster of the plan.

Options for Inquiry

FLIPCHART P. 7

Children can conduct these optional investigations at any time before, during, or in response to the lesson in the Student Edition.

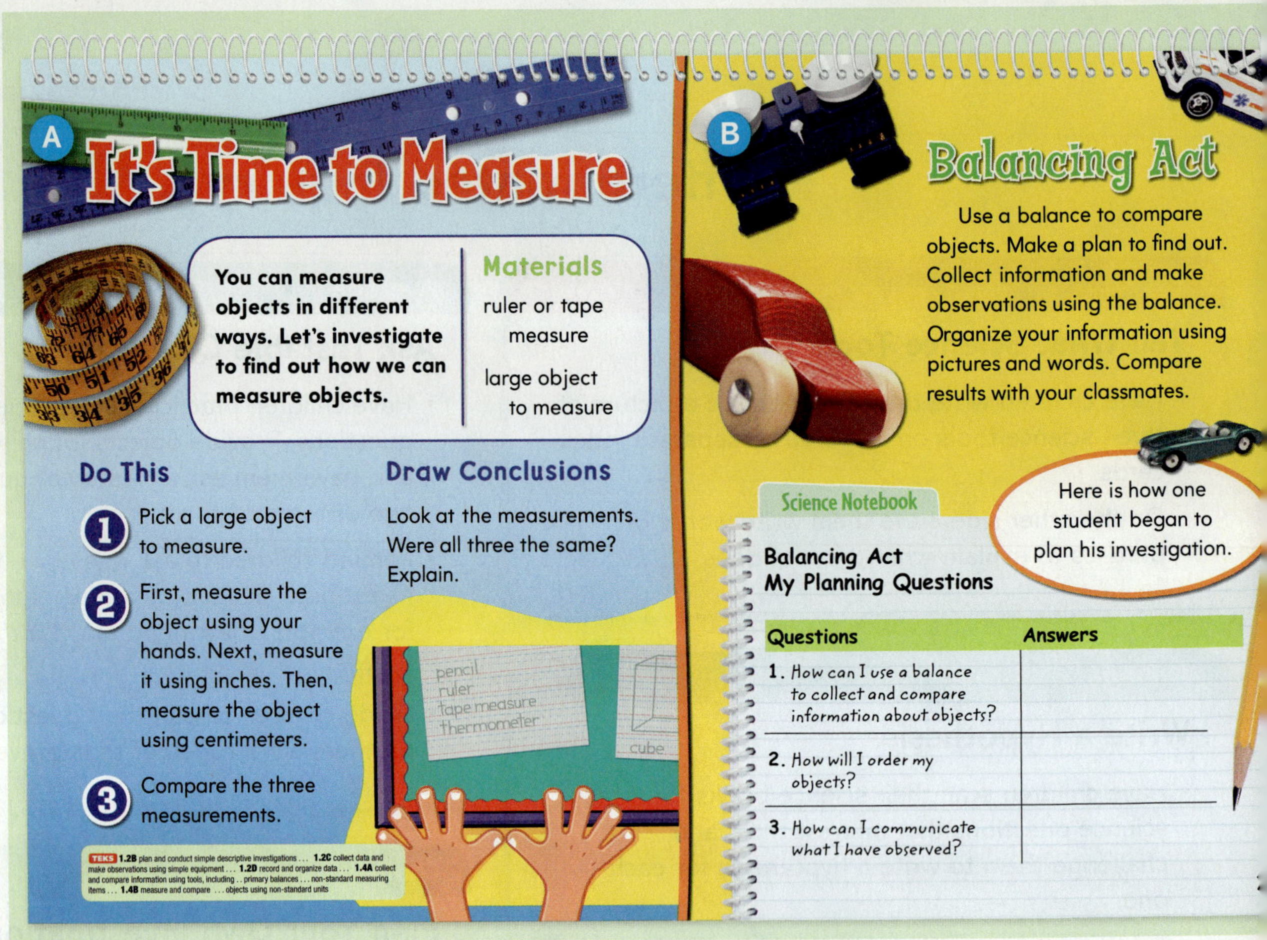

Directed Inquiry

A It's Time to Measure

20–25 minutes
pairs

Prep and Planning Tips

Model how to measure using hands. Continue until you reach the bottom right edge of the bulletin board. Invite children to practice measuring with their hands.

Explain that rulers and tape measures are tools that can be used to measure objects as well. These tools have units of measurement called inches and centimeters. Allow children to compare the size of an inch with the size of a centimeter.

Have children work in pairs and take turns measuring and checking their measurements.

Expected Results

Children will use their hands and a ruler or a tape measure to measure length and compare measurements. As children compare their results, they will discover that measuring with standard units is more reliable that measuring with nonstandard units.

Independent Inquiry

B Balancing Act

30 minutes
individuals

Prep and Planning Tips

See the Planning for Inquiry page for more information. If children are unfamiliar with the way a balance works, model its use. To vary the difficulty of the investigation, challenge children to compare two, three, or four objects. Make sure that you include objects that are heavy or light for their size.

Science Notebook

Children can use the Science Notebook as a model for planning and conducting their own investigation. Encourage them to make a chart like the one shown and include the four sample questions plus their own questions. Additional questions may include *Can I tell how heavy an object is by its size? What other ways can I order these objects? How will I record my results?*

TEKS **1.2C** collect data and make obervations using simple equipment ... **1.4A** collect, record, and compare information using tools ... **1.4B** measure and compare organisms and objects using non-standard units

Lesson 5

Essential Question

What Are Science Tools?

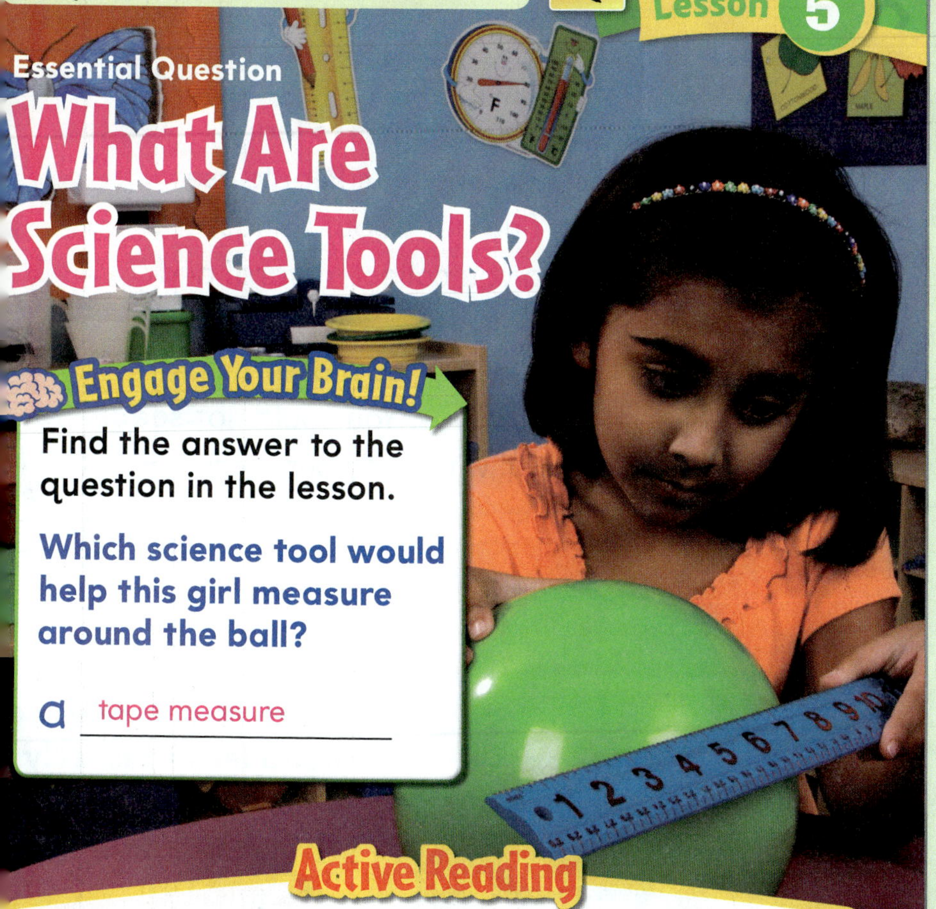

Engage Your Brain!

Find the answer to the question in the lesson.

Which science tool would help this girl measure around the ball?

a tape measure

Active Reading

Lesson Vocabulary

1. Preview the lesson.
2. Write the 2 vocabulary terms here.

science tools   thermometer

Inquiry Flipchart p. 7 — It's Time to Measure/Balancing Act
pp. 8–9 — Science Tools Activities

25

Go Digital

An interactive digital lesson is available in the Online Resources. It is suitable for individuals, small groups, or may be projected or used on an interactive white board.

1 Engage/Explore

Objectives

- Plan and conduct simple investgations.
- Collect data and make observations using simple equipment.
- Record and organize data.
- Collect and compare information using nonstandard measuring items.
- Measure and compare objects using nonstandard units.

Engage Your Brain!

Help children answer the question *Which science tool would help this girl measure around the ball?* Point out that the picture shows a ruler. Ask volunteers to share ideas about how they think a ruler is used. Have children describe tools they might use to measure around the ball. Record their ideas on the board or on a chart.

Remind children to record their final answer after reading the third page of this lesson.

Active Reading Annotations

Remind children that active readers "make texts their own" by marking them or writing notes to help them understand what they are reading. Encourage children to use pencil to make annotations and to feel free to change their marks and notes as they read. The goal of annotation is to help children remember what they have read.

Vocabulary and Interactive Glossary

Remind children to find and list the yellow highlighted terms from the lesson. As they proceed through the lesson and learn about the terms, they can add drawings or words in the extra spaces provided in some entries in the Interactive Glossary.

2 Explain

Notebook Generate Ideas

Lead a picture walk to preview the images. Ask children to identify any of the pictured science tools they already know and tell what they know about how the tools are used. Discuss how they think these tools might help them observe and learn more.

Active Reading Vocabulary

Explain that a vocabulary term may be highlighted in a color. Active readers pay attention to highlighted words because their meaning is given in the same sentence or in the next sentence.

Develop Science Vocabulary

science tools Explain that people in many jobs use tools. Have children brainstorm tools they have seen cooks, carpenters, doctors, or other people use. Explain that scientists also use tools. Reread the first paragraph and ask children to look and listen for the sentence that tells the meaning of *science tools*.

Develop Science Concepts

Explain to children that these two pages provide details about how science tools can help people collect and compare information as well as to help make observations.

What is a hand lens? a science tool that helps you see small things better

Would a scientist be more likely to use a hand lens to observe an ant or a cat? Explain. an ant; Ants are small, and a hand lens helps you observe things that are difficult to see with just your eyes.

What classroom objects might you observe with a hand lens? Accept all reasonable answers of small objects or objects with small parts or details.

Tools to Explore

You can use science tools to learn about the world around you. People use **science tools** to find out about things. Science tools help you collect, record, and compare information.

A hand lens is a science tool. It helps you observe small things. You could not see these things as well with just your eyes.

Active Reading

Find the sentence that tells about **science tools**. Draw a line under the sentence.

These children are using a hand lens to closely observe a flower.

26

English Language Learners

ELPS 1E, 2E

Make a Science Tools Dictionary To help children learn the names of science tools, have them make a physical dictionary. Provide a shelf or table where children can collect and display a hand lens, ruler, tape measure, measuring cup, balance, and thermometer. Then make index cards with a label for each tool. Read each word and have children repeat it after you. Have children match their labels to the tools.

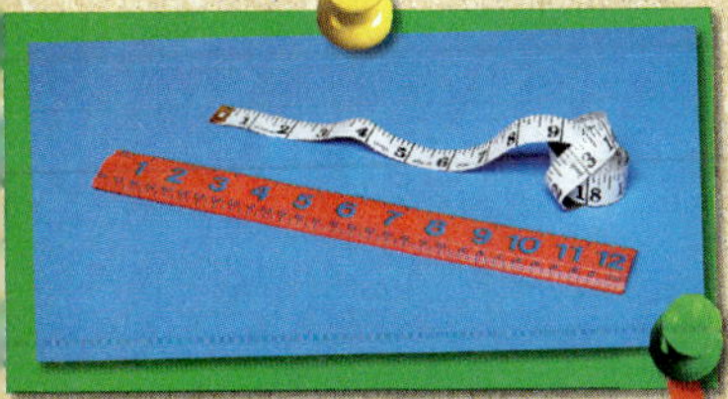

Ruler and Tape Measure

A ruler measures how long things are. A tape measure measures around things.

Measuring Cup

A measuring cup measures liquids.

Tools for Measuring

▶ **Read the labels. Circle the names of tools you use to measure.**

Balance

A balance compares how heavy things are.

Thermometer

A **thermometer** measures temperature. It tells how hot and cold things are.

TEKS 1.2C, 1.4A, 1.4B

Interpret Visuals

Help children learn about the science tools by focusing their attention on the pictures. Differentiate between a ruler and a tape measure. **What is the difference between a ruler and a tape measure?** A ruler cannot bend; a tape measure can. **Which tool can measure the length of a book?** a ruler or a tape measure **Which tool can measure around a tree?** a tape measure

Develop Science Vocabulary

thermometer Say that *thermometer* comes from the word *thermos*, meaning "hot" and the word *metron*, meaning "measure." Explain that this makes sense because a thermometer measures how hot or cold something is.

Develop Science Concepts

Suppose it snowed. Which science tools would you use to measure how deep the snow is and how cold the air is? a ruler to measure snow depth and a thermometer to measure temperature

Suppose you wanted to know which of your pet hamsters is heavier. Which tool would you use? a balance

Suppose you want to give a plant one cup of water. Which science tool would you need? Explain. I would need a measuring cup to figure out the amount of liquid.

Develop Inquiry Skills

COMPARE **How are a ruler, a balance, a measuring cup, and a thermometer the same?** They are all science tools used for measuring.

Notebook Summarize Ideas

Remind children that this section taught about science tools. Have them do an oral or written summary about science tools.

2 Explain (continued)

Notebook Generate Ideas

Read the heading aloud to children and direct their attention to the picture on this page. Have them identify the object being used for measuring. Ask children to name other objects that can be used for measuring, such as a book or clothespins. Display several paper clips. Ask a volunteer to show how to use paper clips to measure an index card.

Active Reading Main Idea

Explain that the main, or most important, idea may be the first sentence in a paragraph. Or it may be a different sentence. Active readers ask themselves, "What is this paragraph about?" The answer will be the main idea.

Develop Science Concepts

Which science tool would you use to measure how long an object is? a ruler or a tape measure

Display a ruler for children. Draw their attention to the units on the ruler. If the ruler has inches, explain the distance between the marks with numbers next to them is 1 inch. If the ruler has centimeters, explain the distance between the marks with numbers next to them is 1 centimeter. Point out that some rulers have inches on one side and centimeters on the other side. Ask for a volunteer to show how to use the ruler to measure an index card.

Why do you think a scientist is more likely to use a ruler for measuring than a paper clip? Guide children to understand that rulers show inches and centimeters. Both are standard units of measurement that are always the same size. Explain that paper clips come in different sizes, so something that is three small paper clips long would be a different length than something that is three large paper clips long.

Let's Measure!

You can measure objects in different ways. One way is to use another object such as a paper clip. Paper clips can help you collect and compare measurements.

You can also measure an object by using science tools. Many science tools have two kinds of units on them.

Active Reading

The main idea is the most important idea about something. Draw two lines under the main idea.

28

Differentiation—Leveled Questions

Extra Support

What are some things you could measure with a ruler or a tape measure? Sample answers: the length, the width, or the height of objects such as books, chairs, tables, or sheets of paper

Challenge

Suppose you measure a book in inches and in centimeters. Would there be more inches or more centimeters? more centimeters because centimeters are smaller than inches

Tools and Measurements

Tool	Unit of Measurement	
measuring cup	ounce	milliliter
ruler	inch	centimeter
tape measure	inch	centimeter
thermometer	degree Fahrenheit	degree Celsius

▶ **Look at the three pictures. Record the measurement on the line paired with each picture.**

12 inches

29 centimeters

English Language Learners

ELPS 1E, 2C, 2E

Understanding Measurement Terms Children may have difficulty with the terms *inch* and *centimeter* as units of measurement. For *inch*, say the word and clap once as you say it. Have children repeat several times. Follow the same process with *centimeter*. Clap once for each syllable. Write the words on the board. Point to the syllables as you read the words aloud with children. Have children point to an inch and a centimeter on a ruler.

Develop Inquiry Skills

COMMUNICATE Draw children's attention to the chart. Explain that a chart is a way to communicate information so it is easy to read and understand. Have children point to the *Tools* heading, and have them read it aloud with you. Explain that a heading names a group of items, which are listed under it. Have children point to the words under the *Tools* heading—one at a time—as you read them aloud. Follow a similar process for the *Units of Measurement* heading.

Then have children point to the words *measuring cup* and move their finger to the right until they reach the word *ounce*. Read the word aloud. Explain that some measuring cups use ounces as a unit of measurement. Have children continue moving their finger across the row and stop at the word *milliliter*. Point out that some measuring cups use milliliters as a unit of measurement. Follow the same procedure to discuss the other tools and corresponding units of measurement listed in the chart.

If children have difficulty following with their fingers, suggest they use an index card to help focus their attention on each row as it is discussed.

Interpret Visuals

Direct children's attention to the two small pictures at the bottom of this page. Point to the image of the ruler on the left. Explain that this side of the ruler measures in inches. Point to the image of the ruler on the right. Explain that this side of the ruler measures in centimeters.

Which is longer—1 inch or 1 centimeter?
1 inch

Ask children to place their finger on the inches side of the ruler where the folder ends. Have children identify the number they see on the ruler. Explain that this number shows inches. Follow a similar procedure with the centimeter ruler. Then have children complete the activity on their own.

2 Explain (continued)

Notebook Generate Ideas

Read the heading aloud to children, and focus their attention on the photograph. Discuss what the girl is doing and the tool she is using. (finding the length of the rug with her shoes)

Explain that when something "measures up," it does a good job or meets a purpose. Discuss whether using shoes "measures up" or is a good way to do the job of finding the length of the rug.

Develop Science Concepts

Display a crayon and a long marker. **If you measure your desk with the crayon and the marker, would you find the same measurements? Explain.** No, they would be different because the crayon and marker are different lengths.

Which science tools could you use to get an accurate measurement of the length of your desk? You could use either the ruler or tape measure to get an accurate measure of length.

Develop Inquiry Skills

INFER Which tool is the girl using to measure the rug? her shoes **Will the measurement be the same if both children measure the rug with the girl's shoes? Why?** Yes, because they would both be using the same tool. **What would happen if the children used different shoes? Why?** The measurements would be different because the shoes would be different lengths. **Why is this a bad way to measure?** People do not know about the tool you used. The measurements would be different. **How is the boy measuring the rug?** with a ruler **Is it better to measure the rug with a ruler or shoes? Why?** A ruler, because that way the measurement will be more accurate and the same each time you measure.

Why It Matters

Measuring Up

Why should we use science tools to measure? What would happen if we used different things to measure the same object? We might get different measurements.

This girl is using her shoes to measure the rug.

30

Writing Connection

TEKS ELA 1.24C

Write a Descriptive Caption
Lead a brainstorming session in which children discuss how they could use science tools to measure length, volume, or temperature in the classroom or at home. Then have them draw a picture showing themselves using a science tool in a real-life situation. Have children write or dictate a caption that describes their picture. Remind them to include the name of the science tool in their caption.

Do the Math!
Measure Length

Measure how long a bookcase is. Use a small shoe, a large shoe, and a ruler or a tape measure. The ruler or tape measure should have units in centimeters and inches on it.

How long is the bookcase when you measure

1. with a small shoe?
   about _____ small shoes long
2. with a big shoe?
   about _____ big shoes long
3. with a ruler or a tape measure?
   about _____ centimeters long
   about _____ inches long

Compare all four measurements. Why should you use a ruler or a tape measure to measure the bookcase?

Sample answer: If you use a ruler or a tape measure, you will always know how long the object is. If you use shoes, you will not know how long it is. Shoes are all different sizes.

31

Do the Math!

TEKS MATH 1.7C

Measure Length

Children can complete this activity individually, in pairs, or in small groups. You will need to collect enough shoes in advance for children to use or share.

Read and discuss the directions aloud. Make sure that children understand that they will measure the *same* bookcase (or other object) four times. If a bookcase is not available, you can substitute something else. If you have a large object available in multiples, such as a window, this might make it easier to coordinate several groups working at the same time.

After completing the measurements, read the final question aloud and encourage discussion. Poll the class and record all the different measurements for the big shoes and the small shoes. Then record the measurements obtained by using a tape measure or ruler. Help children understand that all of the measurements made with the tape measure or ruler are the same because the measuring tool used the same units and gave a standard answer. Have children write or dictate their answer to the question.

Notebook Summarize Ideas

Have children discuss what they learned about why science tools "measure up" and why nonstandard tools like shoes do not. Ask them to summarize orally or in writing what they learned from the lesson and by completing the Do the Math! activity.

23 Math Connection

TEKS MATH 1.3A, 1.5D, 1.7D

Solve Problems Have children use manipulatives, a number line, or other strategy to solve these problems:

A yellow piece of chalk is 3 inches long. A white piece of chalk is 2 inches long. How long are the pieces together? (5 inches)

How much longer is the yellow chalk than the white chalk? (1 inch)

Challenge children to measure two pieces of chalk to the nearest inch, then write and solve their own similar problems.

3 Extend/Evaluate

Sum It Up!

1. **Choose It!** Read the directions aloud to children, emphasizing the word *not,* and explain to children that they will draw an *X* on one of the tools pictured. If children have difficulty, suggest that they revisit the "Tools to Explore" pages that describe science tools and how they are used. Point out that all of the tools, except one, are used to measure.
2. **Circle It!** Read the directions with children. Then have them suppose they wanted to read the letters or words on a coin. As they look at the picture of each tool, they should think about whether that tool would help them observe the details of the coin. If it would, they should circle that tool.
3. **Match It!** Read the directions aloud to children. Ask them to tell in their own words how they will complete this activity. They should understand that they will draw a line to match a tool in the left-hand column with a unit of measurement in the right-hand column. Ask a volunteer to read aloud the words in the left-hand column. Guide children to understand that these words name science tools. Follow the same process with the words in the right-hand column. Point out that these words name units of measurement. Guide children through the first example by helping them match *thermometer* with *degree Celsius.* Then ask children to complete the rest of the items on their own. They can look back at the pages with the heading "Let's Measure!" to review the material about science tools and their units of measurement.

Sum It Up!

1 Choose It!

Which tool is not used to measure? Mark an X on it.

2 Circle It!

Which tool helps you observe small things? Circle it.

3 Match It!

Draw a line to match the tool with the kind of unit found on it.

thermometer	centimeter
ruler	degree Celsius
measuring cup	milliliter

32

Brain Check

Lesson 5

Name ____________

Word Play

Draw a line to the science tool whose name completes the sentence.

1. Measure temperature with a ________.
2. Measure water with a ________.
3. Observe an ant with a ________.
4. Compare how heavy with a ________.
5. Measure length with a ________.

33

Answer Strategies

Word Play

- Before reading the directions, ask volunteers to name the objects pictured in the right-hand column. Guide children to understand that these objects are all science tools. Ask a volunteer to describe each tool. Then have children suggest ideas about what they think they will be doing on the page. Confirm or correct their ideas by reading aloud the directions.
- Read the first entry in the left-hand column and discuss which science tool children would use to measure the temperature of something. Encourage them to look back at the pictures in the section titled "Tools to Explore" if they need help remembering how each tool is used.
- Before children draw a line to match, model your thinking for the first response: *I want to measure temperature, or how hot or cold something is. So I need a thermometer to help me.*
- After children complete the rest of the page, ask them to name the tools and suggest a question each tool could help answer, such as "How long is a sheet of paper?" To help children remember how science tools are used, have pairs of children take turns naming one tool and describing one way it is used. Point out that they can use the Sum It Up! page to help them review and study for tests.

Assessment

Lesson Quiz
See Assessment Guide, p. AG 22.

Safety in Science Quiz
See Assessment Guide, pp. AG 1–AG 5.

Science Tools Quiz
See Assessment Guide, pp. AG 6–AG 15.

3 Extend/Evaluate (continued)

Answer Strategies

Apply Concepts

- Have children compare the length of the crayon and the marker to identify which is longer.
- Give pairs of children five paper clips. Have children describe and demonstrate how to use the paper clips to measure length. Children should place the paper clips end to end across a distance.
- Have pairs take turns measuring the crayon and the marker. Make sure children record their measurements. Have them compare the number of paper clips needed to measure each object.
- Invite children to select a science tool appropriate for measuring length. Write the names of the tools on the board. Have them refer to the board as they write the name of the tool they selected.
- Invite children to compare the methods they used to measure the objects. Remind them that paper clips can be different sizes, and the measurement changes based on the size of the paper clip used. Point out that scientists use tools to measure in inches and centimeters, which are always the same size.
- Ask children to name the science tools they learned about in this lesson, to explain why they are important, and to summarize what they learned about them.

Take It Home!

Suggest that children discuss different science tools with a family member. Point out that science tools are used in homes on a daily basis. For example, measuring cups are used in cooking. Children may want to pick one room, such as the kitchen, to hunt for science tools. Have children report back to the class on the different science tools they found.

Apply Concepts

Measure each object using paper clips. Then use a science tool to measure each object in centimeters and inches. Record your answers. Compare your measurements.

_____ paper clips _____ centimeters _____ inches

_____ paper clips _____ centimeters _____ inches

Check children's work.

Which science tool did you use to measure the objects the second time?

Sample answer: a ruler

Take It Home!

Family Members: Discuss with your child kinds of science tools. Go on a hunt together to find out how science tools are used in your home.

34

Make Connections

Easy

Art Connection

TEKS ART 1.2A

With and Without a Hand Lens

- Give pairs of children drawing paper, crayons, a hand lens to share, and two small objects, such as a leaf and a small stone, one for each child.
- Have children draw the object they have been given twice—once using their eyes alone and once using the hand lens. Suggest that children divide their paper into two sides to make their drawings.
- Have children compare their finished drawings and describe details the hand lens helped them to observe and include.

Average

Physical Education Connection

TEKS PE 1.3D

Standing Long Jump

- Explain that the standing long jump is an athletic contest. The long jump is done by standing with feet together and toes at a starting line. From there, the athlete tries to jump as far as possible. The length of a jump is the distance between the starting line and the place where the jumper's heels land.
- Use masking tape to fix a tape measure on the floor in an open area of the classroom. Draw a chalk line at the beginning of the tape as the starting point.
- Tell children to take turns making and measuring long jumps. Suggest children record their own measurements and compare the distance of their first jump with the distance of their later jumps.

Challenging

Music Connection

TEKS MUSIC 1.4A, 1.4B

Measured Music

- Provide each child with a measuring cup and two or three plastic 1-liter bottles.
- Ask children to measure and pour one cup of water into one bottle and two cups of water into the other bottle. If a third bottle is available, children can pour three cups of water into that bottle.
- Demonstrate how to blow across the top of a bottle to hear a sound. Tell children not to share bottles or put their mouths on the bottles, but to blow over the tops. Invite them to experiment with the different sounds their bottles make. Challenge them to make a rhythm or melody.

Challenging

Math Connection

TEKS MATH 1.1C

Compare Weight

- Provide pairs of children with a balance, classroom objects, drawing paper, and crayons.
- Ask children to select two objects and draw them. Have them estimate which is heavier and circle it in blue. Then have them use the balance to compare the objects and mark the heavier object in red.
- Have children repeat the activity by using other pairs of objects. When they finish, they can describe how a science tool helped them in this investigation.

Collecting

FLIPCHART p. 8

25–30 minutes

small groups

Science Tool Tips

Cups and Bowls

Children can use cups and bowls to collect, sort, and store materials or small objects. For longer activities, cups or bowls can be covered with lids or plastic wrap and stored for later use.

Caution! Glass or ceramic cups and bowls can break and cause injury. Use paper or plastic whenever possible. Reusable cups and bowls should be thoroughly cleaned.

Computer

Help children understand how to distinguish reliable from unreliable websites. If used with great care, children can use mobile computing devices such as laptops, tablets, and smartphones "in the field" to collect and record data.

Collecting Net

Model how to gently collect and remove animals from a collecting net to prevent harm. Allow time for children to practice this skill with an inanimate object before trying it with real insects and other animals.

Try It!

CUPS AND BOWLS Provide children with four soil samples such as sandy soil, clay soil, potting soil, and soil with mulch—all readily available at a garden store.

COMPUTER Challenge children to identify at least one fact from a reliable .gov or .edu website.

COLLECTING NET Group children into teams if the number of insects is limited.

Tool Time

Review children's questions and plans for safety and reasonableness. Any outdoor investigations should be completed with a partner and under adult supervision. Here are some investigation ideas to share with children:

- Which kind of soil holds the most water?
- How many different kinds of insects are found on school grounds?

Science Tools for Measuring

Timer and Clock

- Use a timer or clock to compare the times it takes to do things.
- Always record the time shown on the timer or clock.

Try It! Use tape to mark a starting and a finish line. Time a partner running from start to finish. Record the time using a timer. Then time your partner hopping. Record the time using a clock. Compare the two times.

Paper Clips and Clothespins

- Use paper clips and clothespins to compare the lengths of objects.
- Line them up from end to end of an object. Observe how many it takes.

Try It! Use paper clips to measure your desk and a book. Record each length. Then compare. Repeat using clothespins.

Balance

- Use a balance to compare how heavy objects are.
- Use objects like blocks to see how many it takes to make the sides even.

Try It! Place a book on one side of the balance. Place blocks on the other side. When the sides are even, compare.

Tool Time Think about how you could use one of these tools to measure and compare. Plan how to do it. Then conduct an investigation.

1.2B plan and conduct simple descriptive investigations . . . **1.2C** collect data … using simple equipment … primary balances, and non-standard measurement tools **1.4A** collect and compare information using tools, g … primary balances, … ; timing devices, including clocks and timers; non-standard measuring items such as ips and clothespins; ... **1.4B** measure and compare … objects using non-standard units

9

Measuring

FLIPCHART p. 9

25–30 minutes

small groups

Science Tool Tips

Timer and Clock

Timers and clocks can both measure elapsed time, or the amount of time between events. A timer can be reset to "0" so the elapsed time can be read off from this starting point. When using a clock, though, children must always record both the start and stop times and find the difference to know the elapsed time.

Balance

A balance can be used to compare how heavy objects are. An object that sits lower on one pan is heavier than the other.

Tools for Non-standard Units

Be sure children understand that any *uniform* object can be used as a non-standard unit. Challenge them to identify other classroom objects, such as identical, unused crayons or pencils, which could be used as non-standard units of length.

Try It!

TIMER AND CLOCK Allow time for children to discuss the differences they found between using a timer and clock.

Tool Time

Here are some investigation ideas to share with children:

- Does it take longer to walk 30 feet forward or 15 feet backward?
- Which is heavier—a box of crayons or a box of chalk?
- How could you measure the length of a classroom rug without a meter stick or yardstick?

Assessment

Science Tools Quiz

Assess students' understanding of science tools with the Science Tools Quiz, AG pp. 6–15.

Options for Inquiry

FLIPCHART P. 10

Children can conduct these optional investigations at any time before, during, or in response to the lesson in the Student Edition.

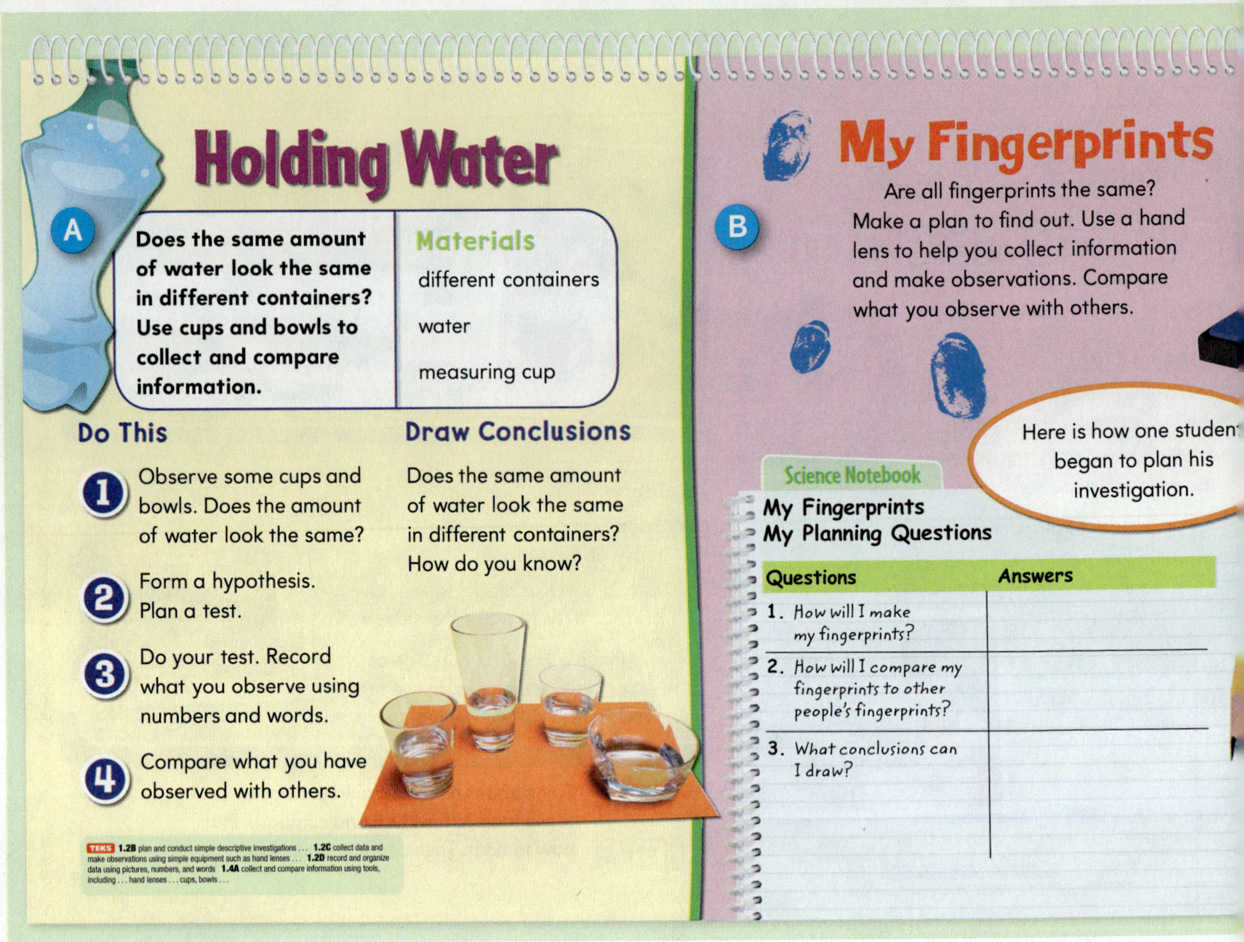

Holding Water

A **Does the same amount of water look the same in different containers? Use cups and bowls to collect and compare information.**

Materials
different containers
water
measuring cup

Do This

1. Observe some cups and bowls. Does the amount of water look the same?
2. Form a hypothesis. Plan a test.
3. Do your test. Record what you observe using numbers and words.
4. Compare what you have observed with others.

Draw Conclusions

Does the same amount of water look the same in different containers? How do you know?

TEKS **1.2B** plan and conduct simple descriptive investigations . . . **1.2C** collect data and make observations using simple equipment such as hand lenses . . . **1.2D** record and organize data using pictures, numbers, and words **1.4A** collect and compare information using tools, including . . . hand lenses . . . cups, bowls . . .

My Fingerprints

B Are all fingerprints the same? Make a plan to find out. Use a hand lens to help you collect information and make observations. Compare what you observe with others.

Here is how one studen[t] began to plan his investigation.

Science Notebook

My Fingerprints
My Planning Questions

Questions	Answers
1. How will I make my fingerprints?	
2. How will I compare my fingerprints to other people's fingerprints?	
3. What conclusions can I draw?	

Directed Inquiry

A Holding Water

40 minutes
pairs

Prep and Planning Tips

Children can wear smocks to keep them dry and cover work surfaces with newspaper to catch drips and spills. Whenever possible, provide clear, unbreakable cups and bowls for children to use to collect and compare information.

Children will be making a hypothesis before they plan and conduct a test. They can write or say that hypothesis.

Caution! Remind children to wipe up spills immediately.

Expected Results

Children should find that though the cups and bowls are different shapes, they hold the same amount of liquid. Depending on the shape of the container, it may appear that some containers hold more.

Independent Inquiry

B My Fingerprints

30 minutes
individuals

Prep and Planning Tips

See the Planning for Inquiry page for more information. Children can use washable ink or paint for this investigation. Review how to use a hand lens to help collect data and make observations.

Caution! Check for allergies to certain inks. Be sure children recognize and demonstrate safe practices by washing their hands after the investigation and using all materials appropriately.

Science Notebook

Children can use the Science Notebook as a model for planning and conducting their own investigation. Encourage them to make a chart like the one shown and include the sample questions plus their own questions.

TEKS 1.2A ask questions about . . . events observed in the natural world 1.2B plan and conduct simple descriptive investigations . . . 1.2D record and organize data . . . 1.2E communicate observations and provide reasons for explanations . . . 1.3C describe what scientists do

Lesson 6

Essential Question

How Do Scientists Work?

Engage Your Brain!

Find the answer to the question in the lesson.

How do you paint a rainbow using only three colors of paint?

You can mix

the colors to make new ones.

Active Reading

Lesson Vocabulary

1. Preview the lesson.
2. Write the vocabulary term here.

investigation

Inquiry Flipchart p. 10 — Holding Water/My Fingerprints

35

Go Digital

An interactive digital lesson is available in Online Resources. It is suitable for individuals, small groups, or may be projected or used on an interactive white board.

1 Engage/Explore

Objectives

- Ask questions about organisms, objects, and events observed in the natural world.
- Plan and conduct simple investigations.
- Collect and compare data and make observations using simple equipment and tools.
- Record and organize data. Share observations.
- Describe what scientists do.

Engage Your Brain!

Help children answer the question *How do you paint a rainbow using only three colors of paint?* Emphasize that a rainbow has seven colors. Ask children whether they have ever mixed paints. Encourage them to tell about colors they have made by mixing. Record these experiments on the board.

Remind children to record their final answer to the question when they find it on the seventh page of the lesson.

Active Reading Annotations

Remind children that active readers "make texts their own" by marking them or writing notes to help them understand what they are reading. Encourage children to use pencil to make annotations and to feel free to change their marks and notes as they read. The goal of annotation is to help children remember what they have read.

Vocabulary and Interactive Glossary

Remind children to find and list the yellow highlighted terms from the lesson. As they proceed through the lesson and learn about the terms, they can add drawings or words in the extra spaces provided in some entries in the Interactive Glossary.

2 Explain

Notebook Generate Ideas

Remind children they have learned about the tools and inquiry skills that scientists use. Explain that in this lesson they will learn how scientists think and work.

Read the heading and subheadings on these pages aloud. Ask children to share what they know about observing, hypothesizing, and making a plan.

Develop Science Vocabulary

investigation Write *investigation* on the board and ask children if it reminds them of another word they already know. Lead children to identify *investigate* as the word *investigation* reminds them of. Explain that *investigation* is a noun formed from the verb *investigate*.

Explain that investigate comes from a Latin word meaning "to track down." Point out that when scientists plan an investigation they follow steps that help them track down the answer to a question.

Active Reading Clue Words

Explain that some words are clues to ways ideas are connected. The word *first* hints that information about order is coming. Active readers look for clue words to help them remember how ideas are connected. Direct attention to the text under *Observe*. Have children locate the clue word and draw a box around it.

Interpret Visuals

Direct children's attention to the picture on the left page. **What are the children observing?** yellow paint and blue paint **What question do they ask about the paints?** They ask what would happen if they mixed yellow paint and blue paint.

Think Like a Scientist

Scientists plan an investigation when they want to learn more. An **investigation** is a test scientists do. There are different plans for investigations. Here is one plan.

Observe

First observe something. Ask a question about it.

Active Reading

Clue words can help you find the order of things. **First** is a clue word. Draw a box around this clue word.

36

Differentiation—Leveled Questions

Extra Support

Why do scientists plan an investigation? They want to learn more about something.

Challenge

First, you observe. What steps come next? ask a question, hypothesize, plan a fair test

Hypothesize and Make a Plan

Next, make a hypothesis. State something you can test. Plan a fair test to see whether you are correct.

My Hypothesis

Blue paint and yellow paint mix to make green.

My Plan

1. Put yellow paint on a plate.
2. Put blue paint on a plate.
3. Mix the paints.

▶ **Do you think yellow paint and blue paint mix to make green? Circle your answer.**

Yes (circled) **No**

37

English Language Learners

ELPS 1C, 2C, 3B

Use Color Words Write the color words yellow, blue, and green on a chart. Then display crayons of the same color and name them for children to repeat. Expand the list to include other color words such as red, orange, purple, black, brown, and white. Then have children draw a swatch of each color and label it.

Develop Science Concepts

Point out that scientists investigate to learn more about something they want to know. Emphasize that there are many ways to investigate, but one way is to start with the steps shown on these two pages. Review those steps by having children follow the headings across the pages and looking for clue words like *first* and *next*.

What is the first step? You observe and ask a question. **What comes next?** You make a hypothesis. **What do you do after you make a hypothesis?** plan a fair test **What is the difference between a question and a hypothesis?** A question asks something you want to find out. A hypothesis is a statement you can test. Ask a volunteer to read the hypothesis about blue paint and yellow paint as an example, and then read the question at the bottom aloud. Have children circle whether they agree.

Turn this question into a hypothesis: What happens if you mix red and white paints? Sample answer: Red paint and white paint mix to make pink.

Walk children through the steps in the plan. Mention that sometimes people investigate by observing rather than experimenting; for example, watching birds eat or fish swim.

Develop Inquiry Skills

IDENTIFY AND CONTROL VARIABLES

Explain that a fair test tests only the things you want to know about. **You mix red paint, blue paint, and yellow paint to see if blue and yellow make green. Why isn't this test fair?** It's not fair to mix in red because you can't tell what blue and yellow do.

Notebook Summarize Ideas

Have children summarize the lesson orally or in writing by identifying the first three steps, in order, in planning an investigation.

2 Explain (continued)

Notebook Generate Ideas

Read the subheadings *Conduct the Test and Draw Conclusions* aloud to children. Point out that these subheadings name the next two steps in an investigation. Have children preview the photographs, looking for clues that can help them figure out what happens in each step.

Active Reading Main Idea

Explain that the main, or most important, idea may be the first sentence in a paragraph. Or, it may be a different sentence. Active readers ask themselves, "What is this paragraph mostly about?" The answer will be the main idea.

Read the sentences on this page aloud and ask children to tell what they are mostly about. Then reread each sentence with them and have them find and draw two lines under the sentence that tells this main idea.

Develop Science Concepts

What happens after you plan the test? You do the test. You follow the steps in the plan and observe what happens.

Then what do you do? You draw conclusions. **What does that mean?** You look at the results and compare them with others. You use the results to figure out what you learned and try to answer the original question.

Conduct the Test

Do the test. Follow the steps of your plan. Observe what happens.

Active Reading

The main idea is the most important idea about something. Draw two lines under the main idea.

We can mix the paints to see what happens.

38

Differentiation—Leveled Questions

Extra Support

What are two things you can do to make sure that the results of a test are correct? You can compare your results with others. You can repeat the test to see if you get the same results.

Challenge

What might scientists do if a test fails to prove a hypothesis? Sample answer: They might repea the test again just to be sure. Or they might state a new hypothesi and come up with a plan to test i

Draw Conclusions

Draw conclusions from your test. What did you learn? Compare your results with your classmates' results. Use information you have collected to explain your results.

What would happen if you did the test again? How do you know?

▶ **Circle the color that yellow and blue make when you mix them.**

39

English Language Learners

ELPS 1A

Recognize Cognates Point out the Spanish equivalents of the words in the steps so children can see how closely the words parallel their English counterparts. These parallels might help English language learners remember the meanings of these new words: *observar/to observe; hipótesis/hypothesis; el plan/the plan; la investigación/the investigation; la conclusión/the conclusion.*

Interpret Visuals

Direct children to the photograph on the left page. **How did the children do their test?** They mixed blue paint and yellow paint. **What happened?** They made green paint.

Have children look at the *Draw Conclusions* section on the right page. **What conclusion could you make from the test?** You can conclude that yellow paint and blue paint mix to make green paint. You know because one of the children shows a finger with green paint.

How does this conclusion compare to the hypothesis? It supports the hypothesis. **Must a conclusion support a hypothesis? Explain.** No, the conclusion is based on results and can show that a hypothesis is not supported.

Do you think the children are surprised by the conclusion? Explain. They probably are not surprised because their hypothesis said that this would happen.

What do you think would happen if the children compared their results with their classmates' results? Explain. They might find that their classmates had the same results because they did the same thing. **What do you think would happen if the children did the test again? Why?** They would get the same results because they did a fair test.

Develop Inquiry Skills

EXPERIMENT Have children state a hypothesis about mixing red paint and yellow paint and then follow a plan to investigate. What conclusion can they draw?

Notebook Summarize Ideas

Have children continue to summarize the steps in an investigation by adding the steps they learned on these two pages to the ones from the previous two pages.

2 Explain (continued)

Notebook Generate Ideas

Read the heading aloud to children. Point out that *record* has different pronunciations and different meanings. Say that the use of *record* on this page means "to make a note of something." Then have children preview the photograph and look for ways to record the results of an investigation.

Active Reading Details

Explain that a detail sentence may give an example. Or, it may describe something. Active readers ask themselves, "What topic does this detail sentence tell about?" The answer will help readers keep the main idea in mind.

Read the text under the heading on this page aloud. Remind children that a detail can give an example. Discuss the two examples of ways to record results mentioned in the text. Have children choose one, underline it, and then draw an arrow connecting it to the main idea.

Develop Science Concepts

What does it mean to record information? You make a note of it.

What are some ways to record? You can write or draw.

Interpret Visuals

How does the girl on the left page record what they learned in the investigation? She draws a picture. She draws two patches, one yellow and one blue. Where they overlap, she shows that they make green.

Record What You Observe

Scientists record what they learn from an investigation. You can keep a record in a science notebook. You can draw pictures. You can write. You can also use numbers.

Active Reading

A detail is a fact about a main idea. Draw one line under a detail. Draw an arrow to the main idea it tells about.

40

Writing Connection

TEKS ELA 1.24C

Add Labels to Drawings Explain that scientists sometimes record what they observe by drawing and writing, rather than using just one way or the other. Labels, for example, can be added to a drawing. Have children reproduce the girl's drawing of the results of the color mixing investigation and label the colors.

Communciate

You can share what you have observed and learned with others. Writing, drawing, and speaking are ways to communicate.

▶ **Describe what scientists do.**

They observe, hypothesize, plan and do investigations, draw conclusions, record, and communicate.

41

Develop Science Concepts

Why is it important to record what you observe in an investigation? Recording is a way of helping you remember the results. Recording also lets you share your results with others.

Choose an investigation that children completed in Lessons 1 through 4 and discuss it briefly to refresh their memories. Ask them to describe how they recorded the results. Encourage children to come up with other ways they could have recorded their results. While discussing an investigation children conducted, go over all of the steps they took to complete it. This will help them answer the interactive on this page.

Develop Inquiry Skills

COMMUNICATE Remind children that it is important to communicate the results of an investigation to others. **Suppose you did this color-mixing investigation. How could you communicate your results to others?** I could read it aloud. I could show a drawing or a chart of what happened. **Why is it important to communicate your results with others?** You can compare results. Others can see what you did and see if they get the same results.

Notebook Summarize Ideas

Share this main idea statement: *Scientists record and communicate what they learn from an investigation.* Ask children to expand this summary statement by giving two examples of ways they can record and communicate the results of their investigations.

3 Extend/Evaluate

Sum It Up!

1. **Write It!** Ask volunteers to read the statements in the directions. Remind children that only one thing changes at a time in a fair test. **You must drop the block and feather from the same height. What else must you do to make the test fair?** You must drop the objects at the same time. Children can write or dictate their answers. As an additional challenge, ask them to identify what kind of statement this is: *The block will fall faster than the feather.* (hypothesis)
2. **Circle It!** After you read the directions aloud, have volunteers read the answer choices and talk about what each one means. Encourage them to draw a picture or make notes below each answer choice if they need help remembering the meaning. Then they can go back to the clues to figure out the answer. Children can look back at the lesson photographs that show what happens during each part of an investigation to help them work out the solution. After children circle the correct answer, review that recording results can mean drawing or writing.

Sum It Up!

1 Write It!

You have a  **and a**  **.**
You will drop them.
You think the block will fall faster.
How can you test your idea?

drop them both at the same time

2 Circle It!

You do the steps in an investigation.
Now you draw what happens.
Which step are you doing?
Circle it.

Observe. Plan a fair test.
Record what you observe.

42

Brain Check

Lesson 6

Name ______________________

Word Play

Unscramble the word to complete each sentence. Use these words if you need help.

observe	hypothesize	investigation	record

ntiovetigansi

1. To learn more about something, you do an ___investigation___.

eyhtpoheszi

2. When you make a statement you can test, you ___hypothesize___.

dreorc

3. After you do a test, you should ___record___ your results.

beosver

4. When you look at something closely, you ___observe___ it.

43

Answer Strategies

Word Play

- Focus children's attention on the word bank, and have children point to each word as you read it aloud. Then point out the scrambled word in front of each sentence. Explain that to solve this puzzle, children can unscramble the letters to make one of the words found in the word bank; they can use this word to complete the sentence. Point out that the page is organized in rows–the letters in the left-hand column unscramble to make the word that completes the sentence to the right.
- Read the first sentence frame aloud. Then ask which word from the word bank would best complete it. As a hint, point out that they can count the letters in a scrambled word and find a word in the word bank with the same number of letters.
- As children complete the sentences, have them read their completed sentences aloud to check that they make sense.
- Remind children that they can use the Sum It Up! page to help them review and study for tests.

Assessment

Lesson Quiz

See Assessment Guide, p. AG 23.

3 Extend/Evaluate (continued)

Answer Strategies

Apply Concepts

- Review the idea of "sequence" and that it shows the order of things that happen. Write the numbers 1 to 5 on the board and say that these numbers can show order with 1 being first and 5 being last.
- Have individuals or pairs copy the five steps on the page on separate index cards. They can move the cards around until they find the correct order, number the cards, and then use the cards to go back and number the steps on the page.
- Remind children that the headings in the lesson show the order of the steps in an investigation and they could use those headings to help them order the steps.

Take It Home!

Have children work with a family member to plan and carry out a simple investigation, such as finding out whether water or orange juice freezes faster. Children should think about something that interests them or a question they want to answer as a place to start. Remind them that the last step in an investigation is to communicate results, so they should bring the results to class to share with others.

Apply Concepts

Can air move a penny and a feather? Describe what a scientist does. Tell how a scientist might investigate. Write a number from 1 to 5 to show the order.

2 Write a plan.

1 Ask a question–
Can air move a penny and a feather?

4 Record what you observe.

5 Share your results.

3 Follow your plan.

Take It Home!

Family Members: Ask your child to tell you about the steps of an investigation. Then plan and conduct an investigation you and your child can try at home.

44

Make Connections

Easy

Art Connection

TEKS ART 1.2A

Mix Colors to Make a Rainbow

- Remind children of the Engage Your Brain! question.
- Give them red, blue, and yellow crayons or paint, and have them mix these colors to draw a rainbow: red, orange, yellow, green, blue, and purple.

Average

Health Connection

TEKS HEALTH 1.7C

Write a Hypothesis About Hand Washing

- Discuss with children the health benefits of washing their hands after science activities, before eating, and when their hands are dirty.
- Have children use that information to state a hypothesis about hand washing. They might, for example, state that washing hands gets rid of germs.

Average

Math Connection

TEKS MATH 1.6D

Investigate Shapes

- Remind children that sometimes they can investigate by carefully observing.
- Show children three labeled shapes: a triangle, a rectangle, and a circle.
- Ask *Which shape has the most sides?* Have children write or dictate a plan to investigate this question.

Challenging

Physical Education Connection

TEKS 1.3A

Explore Footedness

- Ask the question *Can I kick a ball farther with one foot than the other?*
- Have children write a hypothesis and a plan to conduct a fair test.
- If space and time allow, take children to an open area and have them follow their plan, record what they observe, and share their results.

People in Science

Objectives

- Describe what scientists do.
- Realize that the work of scientists in the past is helpful now.
- Understand that scientific inventions help make our lives better.

Notebook Generate Ideas

Have children remember a time when they were in a car and it was raining. Ask them how the driver kept the rain off the front window. Focus children's attention on the title on this page, and explain that Mary Anderson had a lot to do with the windshield wipers that drivers depend on today. Share background information with children. Ask questions to ascertain prior knowledge.

What do windshield wipers do? They move water and snow off the windshield.

Why are they important? They help drivers see better through the glass.

Background

- In 1902, while visiting New York on a snowy day, Mary Anderson saw that trolley drivers had to lean out the window to wipe the windshield clean. That observation sparked her design for the first windshield wiper. Patented in 1903, the first wiper had a manually operated lever. When pulled, it activated a swinging arm with a rubber blade that wiped the windshield clean.
- When Anderson tried to sell the rights in 1905, car companies rejected it. They said they did not consider it useful enough to justify its cost. By 1916, however, wipers had become standard equipment.
- Robert Kearns invented the intermittent wiper with an electric motor in the 1960s. This advance allowed the blades to start and stop without running all the time.

TEKS 1.3C describe what scientists do

People in Scien

Learn About . . . Mary Anderson

In 1902, Mary Anderson observed something. In bad weather, drivers had trouble seeing. They had to drive with the window open. Or they had to get out to clean off the windshield. Anderson got an idea. She invented the windshield wiper.

Fun Fac
By the 1
all cars
windshi
wipers.

Writing Connection

TEKS ELA 1.24

Write About Windshield Wipers Ask children to suppose that they were looking through the windshield while driving on a rainy day. Tell them to draw two scenes showing what they would see with and without windshield wipers. Have them write or dictate a sentence under each drawing telling why Mary Anderson's invention helps people stay safe today.

UNIT 2 Technology All Around Us

Big Idea and Essential Questions

This Unit was designed to focus on this Big Idea and these Essential Questions.

Big Idea

Engineers use a process to design and build something new. They use many different kinds of materials.

Essential Questions

L1 **How Do Engineers Work?**

L2 **How Can We Solve a Problem?**

L3 **What Materials Make Up Objects?**

L4 **How Can Materials Be Sorted?**

Take It Home!
A School-Home Connection letter in English and Spanish is provided in Online Resources.

Professional Development

Houghton Mifflin Harcourt and **NSTA,** the **National Science Teachers Association,** have partnered to provide customized professional development resources for teachers using *ScienceFusion*.

The Professional Development Resources include:

- Do-it-yourself resources, where you can study at your own pace
- Live and archived online seminars
- Journal articles, many of which include lesson plans
- Fee-based eBooks, eBook chapters, online short courses, symposia, and conferences

Access to The NSTA Learning Center is provided in the *ScienceFusion* Online Resources.

NSTA National Science Teachers Association

The NSTA Learning Center

Unit Planning

Options for Instruction

Choose from **Interactive Worktext** and **Leveled Readers, Digital,** and **Inquiry** options to meet the Texas Essential Knowledge and Skills.

	LESSON 1	LESSON 2	LESSON 3
Essential Questions	**How Do Engineers Work?**	✔ Guided Inquiry **How Can We Solve a Problem?**	**What Materials Make Up Objects?**
Texas Essential Knowledge and Skills	TEKS 1.3A	TEKS 1.2A, 1.2D, 1.3A	TEKS 1.1C, 1.5A
Interactive Worktext	☐ **Student Edition** pp. 53–64 • Problem Solvers • The Design Process	☐ **Student Edition** pp. 65–66 • Scaffolding for Inquiry	☐ **Student Edition** pp. 67–78 • Play Your Part • A Material World • Made to Order • Everyday Materials
Leveled Readers	Parallel coverage of the lesson topics is provided in the **Extra Support, On-Level,** and **Enrichment** readers. See p. 51H for detailed reader information.		
Hands-On Inquiry	**Inquiry Flipchart** p. 11 **Don't Crack Up!** ☐ Directed Inquiry **Make It Fly!** ☐ Independent Inquiry	**Inquiry Flipchart** p. 12 **How Can We Solve a Problem?** ☐ Guided Inquiry	**Inquiry Flipchart** p. 13 **Build It!** ☐ Directed Inquiry **Materials Mission** ☐ Independent Inquiry
Digital Curriculum	☐ **Digital Lesson** **Online Resources** Interactive presentation of lesson content 	☐ **Virtual Lab** **Online Resources** Interactive scaffolded inquiry 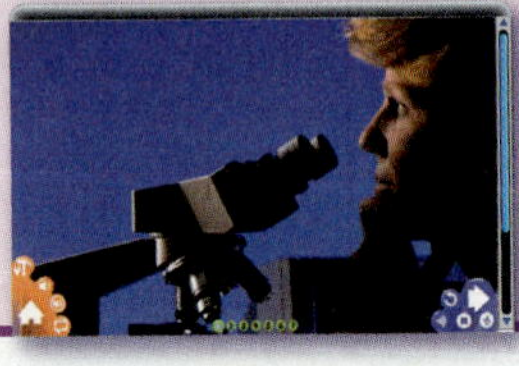	☐ **Digital Lesson** **Online Resources** Interactive presentation of lesson content 

Enduring Understandings

Revisit the Big Idea and Essential Questions

Big Idea **Scientists use inquiry skills and tools to help them find out information.**

To explore the Big Idea, post the inquiry skills discussed in this unit on the board. Have children work in groups of three or four to name tools that support each inquiry skill. Then, have them tell how the inquiry skills and tools help scientists find out information. Have children add their ideas to their Science Notebooks.

- hypothesize
- draw conclusions
- plan an investigation
- observe

Essential Questions

Post the Essential Questions, and use the following prompts to guide a discussion.

Lessons/Essential Questions	Prompts
L1 **What Are Senses?**	• Name the five senses.
L2 **How Can We Use Our Senses?**	• Demonstrate three ways you can use your senses.
L3 **What Are Inquiry Skills?**	• Name three inquiry skills.
L4 **How Do We Use Inquiry Skills?**	• Explain one way you can use inquiry skills.
L5 **What Are Science Tools?**	• Name three tools that a scientist might use.
L6 **How Do Scientists Work?**	• Describe how a scientist might work to solve a problem.

Notebook Science Notebook

You may use the following strategies after children complete the unit or after each lesson.

- Have children review and edit the responses to the Essential Questions they drafted at the beginning of the unit. Suggest they cross out sentences or ideas that are unnecessary or inappropriate.
- Have children draw a picture depicting each of the five senses in their Science Notebooks. Ask them to write or draw one way a scientist can use that sense to find information.

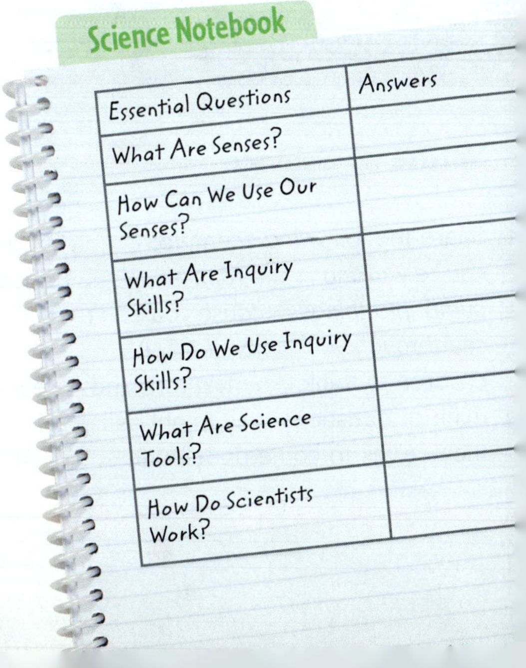

This Leads to That

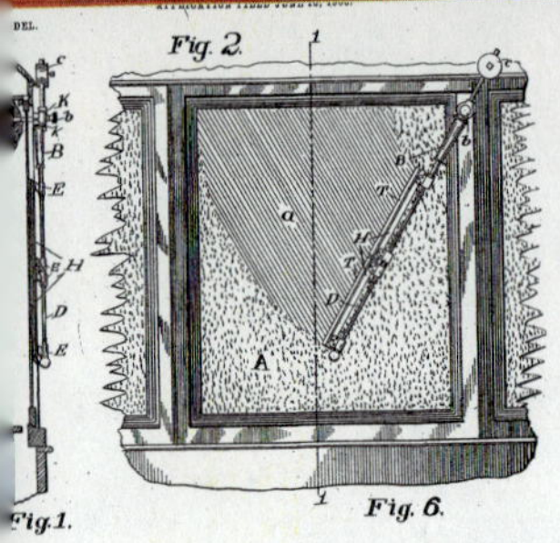

Mary Anderson invented the first windshield wiper. This shows an early drawing.

Robert Kearns invented a windshield wiper that went on and off as needed.

How does Mary Anderson's invention help people today?

People use windshield wipers to clear their windshield so they can see better when driving in rain or snow.

Nature of Science

Share the following scenario: *You're walking in the rain. You bump into things because you can't see through your umbrella.* Tell children to think like inventors and think of questions they might ask themselves to come up with an invention to solve this problem. Encourage them to use inquiry skills when coming up with their questions. Sample answers: What real-world problem do I observe? How could I solve it? How could I test it?

TEKS 1.3C

Develop Science Concepts

What real-world problem did Mary Anderson want to solve? She wanted to find a better way to keep a windshield clean in bad weather. **How did she discover this problem?** She saw people driving with an open window or having to get out of their vehicle to clean the windshield.

How did she solve this problem? She invented the windshield wiper to clean a windshield. **How did the windshield wiper work?** A blade moved back and forth across the windshield.

Develop Inquiry Skills

OBSERVE **Mary Anderson saw people leaning out of windows to wipe windshields. What inquiry skill did she use when she saw that problem? Explain how she used the skill.** She observed. She saw that people could not see through the windshield and was inspired to find a solution. **How does the skill "observe" help scientists solve problems?** Sample answer: It can help them decide what problems they want to solve or to see what happens in the world around them.

COMMUNICATE Focus attention on the drawing of the first windshield wiper. **What inquiry skill did Anderson use when she made this drawing?** communicate **What information does this drawing communicate?** It shows wiper parts and how they work.

Notebook Summarize Ideas

Ask children to think about their own experiences seeing how a windshield wiper works before they answer the question at the bottom of the right page. Encourage them to answer in a complete sentence, completing this sentence frame as needed: People use windshield wipers to _____.

Unit 1 Review

Name ______________________

Vocabulary Review

Use the terms in the box to complete the sentences.

inquiry skills
investigation
senses

1. You learn about the world by using your senses ______________________.

TEKS 1.3C

2. To find out information, scientists use inquiry skills ______________________.

TEKS 1.2B, 1.3C

3. To learn more, scientists plan an investigation ______________________.

Science Concepts

Fill in the letter of the choice that best answers the question.

4. What can you learn from listening to music?
   - Ⓐ how it feels
   - Ⓑ how it looks
   - Ⓒ how it sounds

TEKS 1.4A

5. Which science tool can Sandra use to collect and compare air temperatures?
   - Ⓐ balance
   - Ⓑ measuring cup
   - Ⓒ thermometer

Item Analysis

Items	TEKS	Depth of Knowledge	Cognitive Complexity
1		1	Low
2	**1.3C**	1	Low
3	**1.2B, 1.3C**	1	Low
4		1	Low
5	**1.4A**	2	Moderate

Unit Review

Answer Key

Vocabulary Review (5 points each)

1. **senses**
   Elicit from children the names of the five senses. Have volunteers tell how each sense can be used to learn about the world.
2. **inquiry skills**
   Review what all inquiry skills have in common.
3. **investigation**
   To learn more, you do an investigation. Ask volunteers to give an example of how they can learn more by doing an investigation.

Science Concepts (7 points each)

4. **C**
   Direct children's attention to the word *listening*. Have them tell which sense is used to listen. Guide them to associate the sense of hearing with sound.
5. **C**
   If possible, display each tool in the answer choices as children name it. Ask them to tell how each one is used.

Assessment

Unit 1 Test and Performance Assessments

See Assessment Guide, pp. AG 26–AG 30 for Unit 1 Test. See pp. AG 16–AG 17 and pp. AG 31–AG 32 for Performance Tasks with Long Option rubric.

Unit Review *continued*

Answer Key

Science Concepts (7 points each)

6. B
Have children act out what the boy is doing in the picture. Ask them to point to the body part they are using to observe. Then, have them tell what they use their nose for.

7. B
Review the meaning of each answer choice with children. Then, emphasize that writing results is one way to communicate.

8. A
Have children name each pictured tool and explain how it is used.

TEKS 1.2A

6. What question is the boy trying to answer about the flower?

Ⓐ Are the flower petals soft or hard?

Ⓑ How does the flower smell?

Ⓒ Does the flower stem make a sound if it breaks?

TEKS 1.3C

7. A scientist does a fair test and writes about the results. What is the scientist doing?

Ⓐ classifying

Ⓑ communicating

Ⓒ measuring

TEKS 1.4A, 1.4B

8. You have two toy cars. You want to compare which is heavier. Which science tool will you use?

Ⓐ 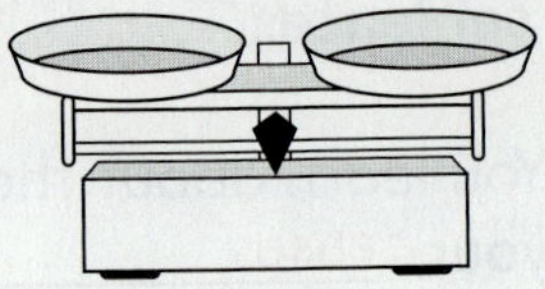

Ⓑ 

Ⓒ 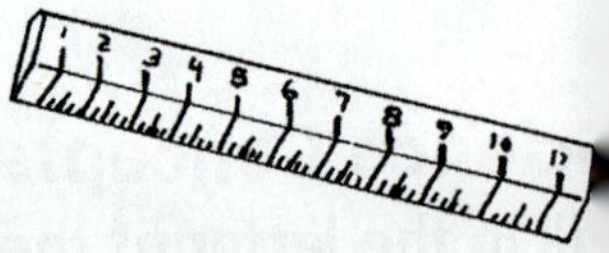

Item Analysis *(continued)*

Items	TEKS	Depth of Knowledge	Cognitive Complexity
6	**1.2A**	2	Moderate
7	**1.3C**	2	Low
8	**1.4A, 1.4B**	1	Low

TEKS 1.2C

9. Pablo uses a hand lens to collect information about a plant. What does he observe?
   - Ⓐ the weight of the plant
   - Ⓑ the height of the plant
   - Ⓒ how the plant looks up close

10. Which step in an investigation is shown?

   - Ⓐ doing a test
   - Ⓑ drawing a conclusion
   - Ⓒ recording results

TEKS 1.2D, 1.2E

11. Alma does an investigation to find out how a bean plant grows. What can she do to communicate her results?
   - Ⓐ She can draw a picture of the bean plant each day.
   - Ⓑ She can ask a question about whether the plant needs water to grow.
   - Ⓒ She can repeat the investigation.

TEKS 1.2A

12. You are doing an investigation about different soils. What question could you use your sense of sight to answer?
   - Ⓐ How are the textures of the soils different?
   - Ⓑ How are the colors of the soils different?
   - Ⓒ How are the smells of the soils different?

Item Analysis *(continued)*

Items	TEKS	Depth of Knowledge	Cognitive Complexity
9	**1.2C**	2	Moderate
10		2	Moderate
11	**1.2D, 1.2E**	2	Moderate
12	**1.2A**	2	Moderate

Unit Review *continued*

Answer Key

Science Concepts (7 points each)

9. C

Have children look at a hand lens or a picture of one to review what it can do. If necessary, review the meanings of *weight* and *height*.

10. A

Have children describe what they see in the picture. Then, have children review the steps in an investigation.

11. A

Remind children that writing and drawing are both ways to communicate.

12. B

Have children look at pictures of different soils and name which property they can observe using just their eyes.

Short Option Performance Assessment

Task

Make Observations in the Classroom
Have children observe different eye colors of their classmates. Tell them to count the number of children with each eye color and record this information in a chart. Then, have them make a bar graph using the data from the chart. Have children write a conclusion about the most common eye color among the general population, based on the data from their classmates.

Rubric

Preparation Show children how to make a chart to record the data.

Scoring Rubric—Performance Indicators

___ Correctly collects, records, and graphs data about eye color among classmates.

___ Correctly identifies a pattern in the data.

___ Makes a valid conclusion about eye color that can be supported by the data.

Observations and Rubric Scores

3 2 1 0

Unit Review *continued*

Answer Key

Inquiry and the Big Idea (11 points each)

13.

- **a.** touch
- **b.** how the dog feels

Have children act out what they see in the picture. Ask them to describe what they are doing and try to suppose what senses they would use and what they would detect.

14. First, I would do a test by rolling both cars using the same amount of force. Next, I would record my observations. Then I would communicate my results.

Review the steps in an investigation. Have volunteers conduct the investigation outlined and ask them to describe the steps they take to test the hypothesis.

UNIT 1

Inquiry and the Big Idea

Write the answers to these questions.

13. Look at this picture.

a. What sense is the girl using?

touch

b. What can she learn by petting the dog?

how the dog feels

TEKS 1.2B

14. You want to plan and conduct an investigation about how fast two toy cars roll. Your hypothesis is that a metal car rolls faster than a wooden car. What steps would you follow to test your hypothesis?

First, I would do a test by rolling both cars using the same amount of force. Next, I would record my observations. Then I would communicate my results.

50 **Unit 1** Unit Review

Item Analysis

Items	TEKS	Depth of Knowledge	Cognitive Complexity
13		3	High
14	**1.2B**	3	High

LESSON 4

Guided Inquiry

How Can Materials Be Sorted?

TEKS 1.2A, 1.2B, 1.2D, 1.5A

- [ ] **Student Edition**
pp. 79–80
- Scaffolding for Inquiry

Inquiry Flipchart
p. 14

How Can Materials Be Sorted?
- [ ] Guided Inquiry

- [ ] **Virtual Lab**
Online Resources
Interactive scaffolded inquiry

OTHER UNIT FEATURES

People in Science, p. 81

Online Resources

Interactive Whiteboard Resources for Unit 2

Assessment

Formative Assessment
Sum It Up! and Brain Check
Student Edition, end of each lesson

Summative Assessment
Lesson Quizzes
Assessment Guide, pp. AG 33–AG 36

Unit 2 Review
Student Edition, pp. 83–86

Unit 2 Test
Assessment Guide, pp. AG 39–AG 43

Performance Assessment
SHORT OPTION: Teacher Edition, p. 85
LONG OPTION: Assessment Guide, pp. AG 44–AG 45

RTI Response to Intervention
RTI Strategies, p. 51I

Online Assessment
Test-taking and automatic scoring
Banks of items from which to build tests

Teacher Notes

Planning for Inquiry

Use the following preview of Inquiry Activities and Lessons to gather and manage the materials needed for each lesson.

Activity	Inquiry and Design Process Skills Focus	Materials	Prep Tips, Troubleshooting, and Expected Results
Lesson 1 DIRECTED INQUIRY Flipchart p. 11 A **Don't Crack Up!** **OBJECTIVES** Record and organize data. Identify and explain a problem and propose a solution. 20–30 minutes small groups TEKS **1.2D, 1.3A**	• Plan and Conduct a Simple Investigation • Predict • Formulate or Use Models • Experiment	• foam • tape • fabric scraps • cardboard tubes • hard-boiled eggs	**Prep Tips** Prior to the activity, hard boil eggs. Brainstorm additional materials, such as packing peanuts, bubble wrap, corrugated cardboard, cotton batting, shredded paper, or popped popcorn. Explain that while children are limited to the materials provided, they may choose the materials and the design for the landing pad. If you substitute fresh eggs, cover the area with newspapers and trash bags. To ensure that children drop their eggs from the same height, place a 4-foot high marker at the drop site. **Caution!** Be aware of possible allergies. Have children wash their hands after this activity. **Troubleshooting** If children have difficulty deciding how to use the materials, suggest they model their landing pads on pillows or fragile mail packages. You may wish to bring extra eggs in case children accidentally drop them before the experiment begins. **Expected Results** Children will draw conclusions about the effectiveness of their landing pad designs. As they analyze the effectiveness of the design process, they should think about and name each step.
INDEPENDENT INQUIRY Flipchart p. 11 B **Make It Fly!** **OBJECTIVES** Recognize and demonstrate safe practices. Identify and explain a problem and propose a solution. 20–25 minutes pairs TEKS **1.1A, 1.1B, 1.3A**	• Plan and Conduct a Simple Investigation • Formulate or Use Models • Experiment	• heavyweight paper (two sheets for each pair of children)	**Prep Tips** Heavyweight paper will work best. Have children test their airplanes outside on a day that is not windy. Use masking tape to mark where the thrower will stand and to mark each landing spot. Have children write their names on the masking tape to avoid confusion. **Caution!** Be aware of chances for injury. Have children wear goggles when testing their airplanes. **Troubleshooting** Instead of having children measure the total distance their plane flies, have the class observe as you measure out 25 feet and put a masking tape line down at the 25-foot mark. **Expected Results** Children will design and construct a paper airplane and test it to see how far it flies. If the airplane flies less than 25 feet, they will repeat the steps of the design process to design a paper airplane that will travel farther.

RTI Response to Intervention

Response to Intervention is a process for identifying and supporting students who are not making expected progress toward essential learning goals.

The following *ScienceFusion* components have the flexibility to be used to provide Core Classroom Instruction (Tier 1), strategic intervention (Tier 2), and intensive intervention (Tier 3).

Component	Location	Strategies and Benefits
Student Edition, Active Reading prompts, Sum It Up, Brain Check	Active Reading throughout each lesson, Sum It Up and Brain Check at the end of each lesson	Student responses can be used as screening tools to assess whether intervention is needed.
Assessment Guide, Lesson Quizzes and TEKS DOK Skill Builder	pp. AG 33–AG 38	Student responses can be used as screening tools to assess whether intervention is needed.
Inquiry Flipcharts	Inquiry Flipchart pp. 12, 14	Directed Inquiry for students who learn best through directed or teacher-led hands-on activities.
Teacher Edition, Unit Review Answer Strategies	TE pp. 83–86	Suggestions for intervention, guidance, and remediation for each review question.
Leveled Readers	TE p. 51H	Content support for students not meeting the learning needs during core classroom instruction.
Leveled Readers, Teacher Guides and Vocabulary Worksheets	TE p. 51H	Direct instruction with small groups of students needing additional content at various readability levels.
Extra Support for Vocabulary and Concepts (online worksheets)	Online Resources	Support for individualized instruction with practice in essential content.
Online Student Edition with Audio	Online Resources	Provides learners with multiple-modality access to science concepts and information.
Interactive Digital Lessons and Virtual Labs	Online Resources	Provides individualized learning experiences. Lessons make content accessible through simulations, animations, videos, audio, and integrated assessment.
Interactive Whiteboard Resources	Online Resources	Reinforces key unit concepts through interactive vocabulary games and visuals and graphic organizers.
Leveled Readers, online and tablet versions	Online and Tablet Resources	Highlighted words and sentences synced with audio provide support for emerging or struggling readers.

Differentiated Instruction

English Language Learners

Choose from these instructional strategies to meet the needs of English language learners.

Vocabulary Cards are provided in Online Resources.

Unit Vocabulary

Lesson 1	Lesson 3
engineer	materials
design process	natural
	human-made

Preteach Vocabulary ELPS 2B

As you preteach vocabulary, model pronunciation and have children repeat. For Unit 2 vocabulary, draw attention to the long *e* sound in *design*, the short *e* sound in *engineer*, and the silent *e* in *human-made*.

Language Acquisition Strategies

Concept Cards ELPS 1C, 1E, 3D, 5B

Have children make concept cards for the terms *engineer* and *design process* on TE pages 54–55. Throughout the unit, have children make cards, adding details, examples, and related words.

Beginning	Intermediate	Advanced/Advanced High
Start a word web by writing *engineer* in a circle. Elicit examples of things an engineer does (*solves problems, designs robots, plans roads*). Then, have children orally complete the sentence frame: *An engineer* ___.	Have children refer to the pictures as they tell a partner what an engineer does. Have children add the sentences to their concept card.	Have children tell a partner in their own words what the terms mean. Children can add the definitions to their concept cards.

Visual Support ELPS 1F, 3H, 4F

Use the illustration on **TE pages 68–69** to support children's understanding of the relationship between parts and a whole.

Beginning	Intermediate	Advanced/Advanced High
Point to and name each part of the bicycle. Explain that each part is needed to make a whole bicycle. Have children name the parts of a familiar object, such as a car.	Review the information in the picture. Use simple language and the illustration to help children understand that a bicycle is made up of different parts. Have children tell a partner about something that is made of many parts.	Review the information in the picture. Then, have partners collaborate to explain how the parts work together to make the bicycle work.

Respond to Questions ELPS 1A, 2I, 3C, 3E

After children read **TE pages 70–71,** lead a discussion of the materials they have in and around their homes.

Beginning	Intermediate	Advanced/Advanced High
Ask *yes/no* questions about the kinds of materials children have in and around their homes.	Ask simple questions about the kinds of materials children have in and around their homes. Have children respond in words or phrases.	Have partners interview each other about the kinds of materials in and around their homes.

Peer Support ELPS 2D, 2I, 4F

Have children use **TE pages 72–73** to practice using teacher and peer support.

Beginning	Intermediate	Advanced/Advanced High
Have children ask questions about anything they did not understand or found confusing. Use specific information on the page to answer each question.	Ask children to list two facts they learned about natural and human-made materials. Then, have partners compare lists and check each other's facts.	Have partners summarize what they learned about natural and human-made materials. Have children verify that their partner mentioned all the most important information.

Monitor Understanding ELPS 2D, 2I, 3F

Read aloud the information about Dr. Eugene Tsui on **TE page 81.** Have children practice monitoring their understanding.

Beginning	Intermediate	Advanced/Advanced High
Ask questions to help children monitor their understanding: *What is Dr. Tsui's job? What does an architect do? What can you say about Dr. Tsui's clothes?*	Have children summarize the information for a partner. Then, ask partners to retell what their partner said in their own words.	Have partners take turns asking and answering questions about what they heard.

Technology All Around Us

I Wonder How

If time allows, visit the school playground so children can examine the different structures there. Talk about how the parts might have been planned and built. Then use the discussion, the photograph, and any other information children have about designs and building to interest them in the unit topic and help them answer the "how" question.

Here's How

Have children turn the page and read the response to the question. You may wish to share the following background with them.

More About...

Architects and Playgrounds

Today's playgrounds are usually a lot more than just some swings and a slide. Architects are designing exciting playgrounds all over the country. Every playground begins with a problem to solve: how can the architect design a place with challenging and fun activities for children that are also safe and age-appropriate? The solution can take many forms. The playground in this photograph has slides, towers, and bridges decorated with butterflies. It also has interactive areas for childen and their families.

Science Songs

See pp. TR40–TR43 for science songs you can use to reinforce content in this unit.

Professional Development Science Background

Use the keywords to access

- Professional Development from **The NSTA Learning Center**
- **SciLinks** for additional online content appropriate for children and teachers
- Teacher Science Background in the back of this Teacher Edition

Keywords

engineering and technology
engineering design process
natural resources

SCILINKS. THE WORLD'S A CLICK AWAY

Here's How An engineer drew ideas on a plan. The plan had many fun things for kids.

In this unit, you will explore this Big Idea, the Essential Questions, and the Investigations on the Inquiry Flipchart.

Levels of Inquiry Key ■ DIRECTED ■ GUIDED ■ INDEPENDENT

Track Your Progress

Big Idea Engineers use a process to design and build something new. They use many different kinds of materials.

Essential Questions

Now I Get the Big Idea!

Science Notebook

Before you begin each lesson, be sure to write your thoughts about the Essential Question.

Go Digital

For a complete digital curriculum and resources that provide full coverage of the objectives for this unit, see the Online Resources for this program.

Big Idea and Essential Questions

Big Idea Engineers use a process to design and build something new. They use many different kinds of materials.

Post the Unit Big Idea on the board. Have students read the Essential Questions, which are also the titles of the lessons in this unit.

- Discuss how the Essential Questions can help keep them focused on the Big Idea.
- Have children read the Big Idea statement. The statement describes the main science concepts that they will be learning.
- Have children predict other ideas that will be taught in the lessons based on the titles, or have them give examples of pictures they expect to see.

Once they complete the unit, they should have a better understanding of the Big Idea.

Essential Questions You may use the following Science Notebook strategy for working with the Essential Questions before children begin the unit or before each lesson.

- Strategies for revisiting the Big Idea and Essential Questions are provided in Enduring Understandings on p. 83A.

Notebook Science Notebook

- Have children copy the Essential Questions into their Science Notebooks. Suggest they leave several writing lines between questions.
- Ask children to write responses to the Essential Questions. Urge them not to worry about whether their responses are correct. They should expect their ideas to change as they work in the unit. Comment that children will be able to review and revise their answers to the Essential Questions at the end of the unit.
- Tips and strategies for using Science Notebooks are provided throughout this unit, in the back of this Teacher Edition, and in Online Resources.

Options for Inquiry

FLIPCHART P. 11

Children can conduct these optional investigations at any time before, during, or in response to the lesson in the Student Edition.

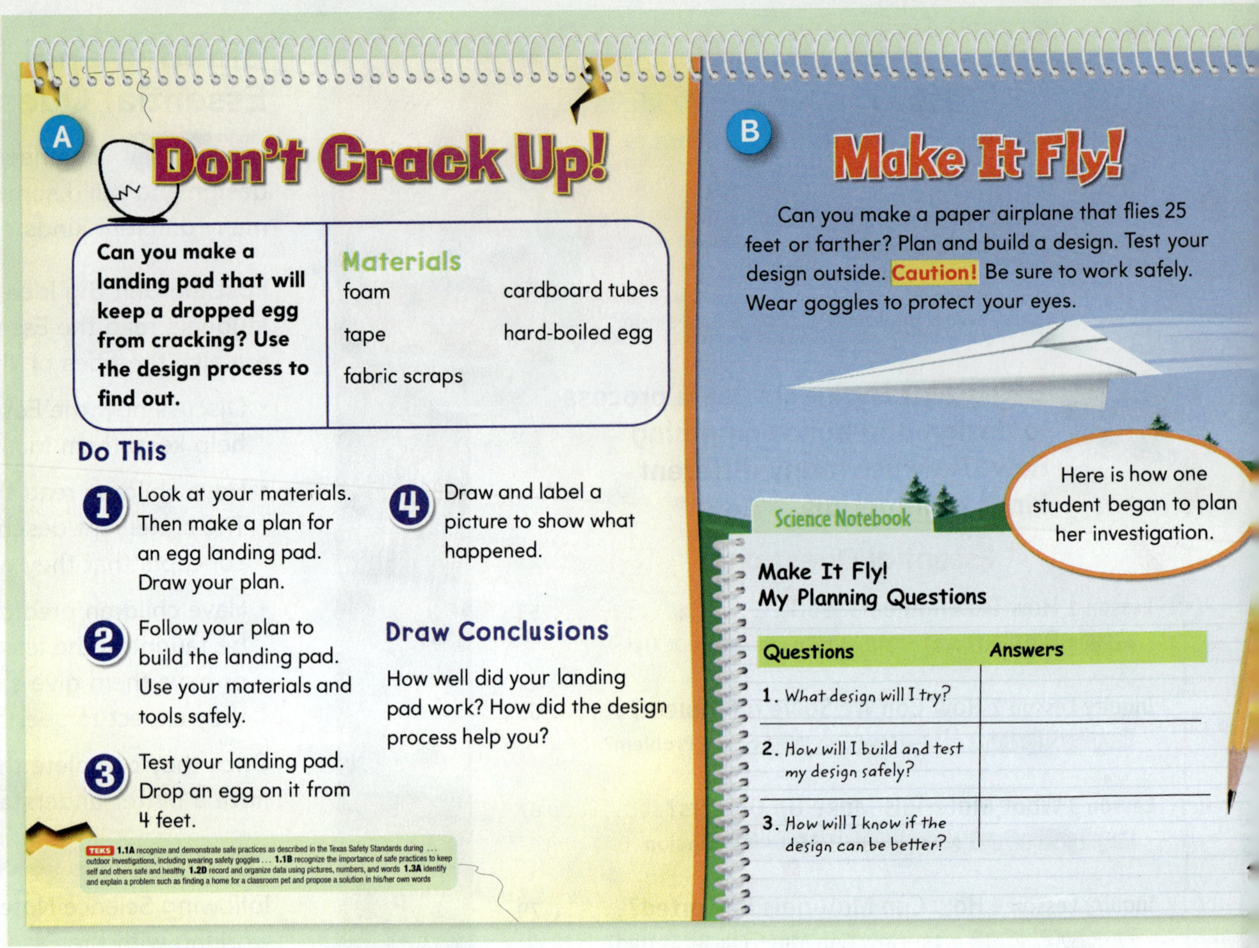

A **Don't Crack Up!**

Can you make a landing pad that will keep a dropped egg from cracking? Use the design process to find out.

Materials	
foam	cardboard tubes
tape	hard-boiled egg
fabric scraps	

Do This

1. Look at your materials. Then make a plan for an egg landing pad. Draw your plan.
2. Follow your plan to build the landing pad. Use your materials and tools safely.
3. Test your landing pad. Drop an egg on it from 4 feet.
4. Draw and label a picture to show what happened.

Draw Conclusions

How well did your landing pad work? How did the design process help you?

TEKS **1.1A** recognize and demonstrate safe practices as described in the Texas Safety Standards during . . . outdoor investigations, including wearing safety goggles . . . **1.1B** recognize the importance of safe practices to keep self and others safe and healthy **1.2D** record and organize data using pictures, numbers, and words **1.3A** identify and explain a problem such as finding a home for a classroom pet and propose a solution in his/her own words

B **Make It Fly!**

Can you make a paper airplane that flies 25 feet or farther? Plan and build a design. Test your design outside. **Caution!** Be sure to work safely. Wear goggles to protect your eyes.

Here is how one student began to plan her investigation.

Science Notebook

Make It Fly!
My Planning Questions

Questions	Answers
1. What design will I try?	
2. How will I build and test my design safely?	
3. How will I know if the design can be better?	

Directed Inquiry

A Don't Crack Up!

20–30 minutes
small groups

Prep and Planning Tips

In addition to the materials listed, brainstorm others, such as packing peanuts, bubble wrap, corrugated cardboard, cotton batting, shredded paper, popped popcorn, or tissue paper. Explain that while children are limited to the materials provided, they may choose which materials to use and come up with their own design of the landing pad. If you decide to substitute fresh eggs for hard-boiled ones, cover the area with newspapers and large plastic trash bags. To ensure all children drop their eggs from the same height, place a 4-foot-high marker at the drop site. Have children write and draw to record their observations.

Expected Results

Based on the egg's condition after it is dropped, children can draw conclusions about the effectiveness of the design of their landing pad. As they analyze the effectiveness of the design process, remind them to think about and name each step.

Independent Inquiry

B Make It Fly!

20–25 minutes
pairs

Prep and Planning Tips

See the Planning for Inquiry page for more information. Have children test their airplanes outside. Be sure that children recognize and demonstrate safe practices to keep themselves safe by wearing safety goggles. Use masking tape to mark each plane's landing spot.

Science Notebook

Children can use the Science Notebook as a model for planning and conducting their own investigation. Encourage them to include the sample questions plus questions of their own. Remind children to follow the design process as they plan and carry out their investigations.

TEKS 1.3A identify and explain a problem such as finding a home for a classroom pet and propose a solution in his/her own words

Lesson 1

Essential Question

How Do Engineers Work?

Engage Your Brain!

Find the answer to the question in the lesson.

How do you scratch an itch you can not reach?

You can

design a tool to reach it

______________________.

Active Reading

Lesson Vocabulary

1. Preview the lesson.
2. Write the 2 vocabulary terms here.

engineer ______ design process ______

Inquiry Flipchart p. 11 — Don't Crack Up!/Make It Fly!

53

Go Digital

An interactive digital lesson is available in Online Resources. It is suitable for individuals, small groups, or may be projected or used on an interactive white board.

1 Engage/Explore

Objectives

- Recognize and demonstrate the importance of safe practices.
- Record and organize data.
- Identify and explain a problem and propose a solution in his/her own words.

Engage Your Brain!

Help children answer the question *How do you scratch an itch you can not reach?* Focus children's attention on the picture, and ask what the bear is doing to scratch its itch. Have children share what they might do to scratch an itch in the middle of their back, and record their responses on the board.

Remind children to record their final answer to the question when they find it on the fourth page of the lesson.

Active Reading **Annotations**

Remind children that active readers "make texts their own" by marking them or writing notes to help them understand what they are reading. Encourage children to use pencil to make annotations and to feel free to change their marks and notes as they read. The goal of annotation is to help children remember what they read.

Vocabulary and Interactive Glossary

Remind children to find and list the yellow highlighted terms from the lesson. As they proceed through the lesson and learn about the terms, they should add drawings or words in the extra spaces provided in some of the entries in the Interactive Glossary.

2 Explain

Notebook Generate Ideas

Call on a volunteer to read aloud the heading. Then have children preview the images shown on these two pages by asking them to describe what each person is doing. Guide the discussion by asking: **What problems do you think these people are trying to solve? What materials are they using?**

Develop Science Vocabulary

engineer Write the word on the board and have children clap out the syllables as they read it after you. Explain that different kinds of engineers are trained to solve different kinds of problems. Have children point to the engineers pictured on these pages as you read aloud their job titles. Have children circle the names of these engineers.

design process Explain that a process is a set of steps or procedures that people follow in order to do something. Remind children that they use a process when they write a story or when they solve a story problem. A design process is a plan with steps that engineers follow to find good solutions.

Active Reading Details

Explain that a detail sentence may give an example, or it may describe something. Active readers ask themselves, "What topic does this detail sentence tell about?" The answer will help readers keep the main idea in mind.

Problem Solvers

An **engineer** is a person who uses math and science to solve everyday problems. Engineers work on many kinds of problems. Some engineers design robots. Others plan roads. Some design cars.

Active Reading

A detail is a fact about a main idea. Draw one line under a detail. Draw an arrow to the main idea it tells about.

Children can also underline any of the last 3 sentences of the paragraph with an arrow pointing to the first sentence.

▶ **Circle the names of three kinds of engineers.**

robotics engineer

54

Differentiation—Leveled Questions

Extra Support

How do engineers go about solving a problem? They use the steps in a design process.

Challenge

Suppose you wanted to be an engineer. What could you do right now to begin working toward that goal? Sample answer: I could work hard in math and science classes because those are skills engineers use.

Engineers use a design process to solve problems. A **design process** is a plan with steps that help engineers find good solutions.

The Design Process

1. Find a Problem
2. Plan and Build
3. Test and Improve
4. Redesign
5. Communicate

mechanical engineer

civil engineer

55

English Language Learners

ELPS 1E, 2C, 2E

Explore Word Meanings
Children may have difficulty understanding the meaning of the abstract term *design process*. Give a concrete example of a familiar process by leading children through a pantomime of the steps in brushing their teeth. Then ask them to suppose they had a problem getting the toothpaste out of the tube. Explain that they could make, or design, something that would help them do this. The steps they would use to solve the problem are the *design process*.

TEKS 1.3A

Develop Science Concepts

What two skills do engineers use to solve everyday problems? math and science

What details support the main idea that engineers solve everyday problems? Some engineers make robots, while others build roads or design better cars. Remind children to underline one detail and draw an arrow to the main idea it supports.

Interpret Visuals

Focus attention on the photographs of the engineers. Tell children to use clues in these pictures as well as the text to answer these questions. **What kinds of things might a civil engineer design?** Sample answers: buildings, a wind farm

What kinds of things might a mechanical engineer design? Sample answer: machines

Develop Inquiry Skills

SEQUENCE Point out that the steps in the design process are numbered and appear in a certain order. **What is the first step in the design process?** Find a Problem

What do engineers do after they plan and build the solution to a problem? They test and improve it.

Why might it be important to follow the steps of the design process in order? If an engineer did the steps out of order, he or she might not find good solutions.

Notebook Summarize Ideas

Remind children that details often provide examples. Have children summarize the details in the text that provide examples of types of engineers and the steps they follow to solve everyday problems.

2 Explain (continued)

Notebook Generate Ideas

Have children reach around and try to scratch the middle of their backs. Have them describe why this is so difficult. Ask children what they might do to try to solve this problem, and list their ideas on the board.

Develop Science Concepts

Identify and explain Jack's problem in your own words. Sample answer: Jack wants to find a way to scratch an itch in the middle of his back. **Guide children to record this answer in the interactive.**

What are some other everyday problems that you might want to design a solution for? Sample answer: I would like to design a tool to help me reach objects in high places or find a way to clean my room more quickly.

What does it mean to brainstorm? It means to think of many different ideas to solve a problem.

The Design Process

1 Find a Problem

Jack has an itch he can not reach. How can he scratch it? The steps of this design process show Jack what to do.

Jack identifies his problem. He needs to find a way to scratch his back. He brainstorms ways to solve his problem.

Jack tries to scratch his back.

▶ **Identify and explain Jack's problem.**

Jack has an itch. He wants to

find a way to scratch his back.

56

Differentiation—Leveled Questions

Extra Support

What is the first step in the design process? The first step is to find and identify a problem.

Challenge

Why is it important to state the problem clearly before you begin to solve it? Sample answer: If I don't have a clear idea of the problem I want to solve, I might waste time finding the wrong solution.

Brain Check

Lesson 1

Name ______________________

Word Play

Write a label for each picture.

choose materials | build | engineer | test

choose materials

test

build

engineer

Answer Strategies

Word Play

- After helping children read the directions, call on volunteers to read the words in the word box. Then have children study each picture and describe what they see. Remind them that one of the words in the word box can be used to describe each picture.
- Have children work individually or with a partner to complete the labeling task. Once they finish, have them take turns sharing an oral sentence using the word they have written to describe each picture.

Assessment

Lesson Quiz

See Assessment Guide, p. AG 33.

3 Extend/Evaluate (continued)

Answer Strategies

Apply Concepts

- Remind children that this lesson was about the step-by-step approach that engineers use to solve everyday problems. Have children recall the name of this process. Then ask them to follow along as you read aloud the directions at the top of the list.
- Explain to children that the steps shown are out of order. Have children work independently to order the steps. If they need help recalling the correct sequence, have them look back at the pages of the lesson.
- Once children complete the sequence, check it as a group. Then call on volunteers to describe how Jack applied each of these steps to solve an everyday problem.

Take It Home!

Suggest that children work with a family member to identify and explain a household problem that they can solve by applying the steps in the design process. Encourage them to bring in their test results and describe whether their solution solved the problem they identified.

Apply Concepts

Write numbers to put the steps of the design process in order. The first one is done for you.

The Design Process

3 Test and Improve

1 Find a Problem

5 Communicate

4 Redesign

2 Plan and Build

Take It Home!

Family Members: Help your child identify and explain a problem at home, such as a messy "junk drawer." Have your child come up with a solution using the design process.

64

Make Connections

Easy

Language Arts Connection

TEKS ELA 1.23A, 1.24A, 1.27A

Interview a Problem Solver

- Invite an engineer or other problem solver, such as the school custodian, to visit the class to discuss how he or she solves problems.
- Have children brainstorm questions they can ask following the presentation. Remind them to practice good listening and speaking skills. Review that these include being active and attentive listeners, looking at the speaker, waiting to ask questions until the end of the presentation, and thanking the speaker.

Average

Writing Connection

TEKS ELA 1.19A, 1.19C

Write a Plan to Solve a Problem

- Have children look at the lesson and study Jack's diagram for the back scratcher. Have them write a description of his plan for the back scratcher.
- Encourage children to think of a problem and a solution to the problem. Have them write a description of their solution. Ask children to share their plans in small groups, and encourage comments.

Challenging

Social Studies Connection

TEKS SS 1.6A

Solve Weather Problems

- Remind children that the weather and climate are different around the world. Working with partners, have children identify problems that engineers might try to solve in a place that is very hot, very wet, or very cold.
- Have them choose one problem, such as how to keep a dog's feet warm in a very cold climate, and use the design process to come up with a solution to this problem.

Challenging

Health Connection

TEKS HEALTH 1.3B

Explore Everyday Problems in Health

- Explain that physical challenges may make it difficult for some people to lift things off the floor, hear a phone ring, or walk up stairs.
- Have children choose one of these or another everyday problem caused by a physical challenge. Have children work in small groups to brainstorm possible solutions to this problem.
- Then have them do research to find out if engineers have invented solutions for the problem.

Guided Inquiry

FLIPCHART P. 12

30–40 minutes
small groups

Children should follow the directions on the Flipchart. The accompanying pages in the Student Edition provide scaffolding for guided inquiry.

Inquiry Skills Focus Plan an Investigation

Objectives

- Recognize and demonstrate the importance of safe practices.
- Ask questions about objects observed in the natural world.
- Record and organize data. Communicate observations and provide reasons for explanations using data.
- Identify and explain a problem such as finding a home for a classroom pet and propose a solution in his/her own words.

Prep and Planning Tips

See the Planning for Inquiry page for more information.

- Do not provide special materials for this activity; working within the limitations of classroom objects and craft materials is the challenge of the investigation.

Caution! Be sure children recognize the importance of safe practices to keep themselves and others safe and healthy. Tell children to be careful when handling scissors.

Expected Results

Groups will make a variety of structures.

1 Engage/Explore

Attention Grabber

Display several pictures showing animals in various kinds of shelters. Discuss with children the importance that each shelter provides for each animal. Also provide reference materials for children to peruse that will help them decide what kind of shelter their classroom pet needs. Explain to children that in this activity they will be designing and building a shelter for their classroom pet. If your classroom does not have a pet, then brainstorm what kind of pet you would like to have and what kind of shelter it needs.

Preview Activity

Before beginning the investigation, have children review the directions on the Inquiry Flipchart and the accompanying Student Edition response pages. Then have them complete the response pages as they follow the directions on the Flipchart.

TEKS 1.1C, 1.5A

Brain Check

Lesson 3

Name ____________

Word Play

Color the letters to spell the vocabulary words. Write the words to complete the sentences.

human-made materials natural

n	a	t	u	r	a	l	t	w	k
c	t	o	w	r	e	g	y	p	s
h	u	m	a	n	m	a	d	e	y
g	m	a	t	e	r	i	a	l	s
k	n	y	u	o	s	d	x	p	m

1. Objects are made of materials.
2. Materials made in a lab are human-made.
3. Materials found in nature are natural.

77

Answer Strategies

Word Play

- Begin this puzzle by helping children read the words in the word box. Then, have them locate and color the letters to spell out each word in the word-search puzzle. Point out that the words in this puzzle can begin at any place in each row of letters.
- Guide children in reading each open sentence, and explain that one of the words in the word box will complete it. Have children check that each completed sentence makes sense by reading it aloud.
- To help improve recall of basic concepts of the lesson, have children take turns using each word in a sentence. Then, ask children to provide examples of objects made from natural or human-made materials or both.

Assessment

Lesson Quiz

See Assessment Guide, p. AG 35.

3 Extend/Evaluate (continued)

Answer Strategies

Apply Concepts

- Help children read the three headings in the top row of the chart. Then, direct attention to the first column and call on volunteers to identify and describe each object.
- Ask children what materials are used to make each object. Explain that they will fill in the second column of the chart with this information.
- Discuss with children what they know about natural materials, human-made materials, or objects that are a combination of both. Encourage children to look back at the lesson pages to review this information and give examples of objects made from each type of material. Then, have them fill in the third column of the chart.

Take It Home!

Suggest children work with family members to identify the parts and materials that make up a household object and then report back to class with a visual presentation. Children can draw the whole object, show its separate parts, and list the materials it is made from. Then, they can describe whether these materials are natural, human-made, or both by classifying them.

Apply Concepts

Complete the chart. Identify and classify the materials each object is made from.

Materials Chart

Object	Material	Natural, human-made, or both
1 	plastic	human-made
2 	metal plastic	both
3 	cotton	natural

Take It Home!

Family Members: Play a game with your child to identify the parts and materials of objects around the home. Classify the materials as natural, human-made, or both.

78

Make Connections

Easy

Art Connection

TEKS ART 1.1A

Sort Classroom Toys

- Provide small groups with bags labeled *Natural Materials, Human-Made Materials,* and *Both.*
- Then, have groups find a small object for each bag.
- When children finish, have them share what they found with another group.

Average

Social Studies Connection

TEKS SS 1.6B

Identify Building Materials from Around the World

- Remind children that glass, brick, wood, and metal were used to build the house shown in the lesson. Point out that temperature, rainfall, and materials available can determine how a house is built.
- Ask children to find pictures of homes in different parts of the world and identify the materials used. Have them identify whether each material is natural or human-made.

Challenging

Physical Education Connection

TEKS PE 1.5B

Identify Materials Used in Safety Gear

- Have children brainstorm a list of safety gear used in different sports. For example they might list helmets, knee pads, wrist guards, and proper clothing and shoes.
- Help them research to find out the material(s) each object is made of and whether the materials are natural, human-made, or a combination of both. Discuss the importance of wearing safety gear to protect oneself.

Challenging

Writing Connection

TEKS ELA 1.6D, 1.24C

Write Labels

- Provide children with three sticky notes or index cards. Help them write the word "natural" on each of the notes or cards to make three labels.
- Have children search the classroom for objects made entirely or partly from natural materials, such as rock or wood, and place those labels on the appropriate object or its part.
- Challenge children to repeat the activity for "human-made," writing the labels on their own or working with a partner.

Guided Inquiry

FLIPCHART P. 14

30 minutes
individuals

Children should follow the directions on the Flipchart. The accompanying pages in the Student Edition provide scaffolding for guided inquiry.

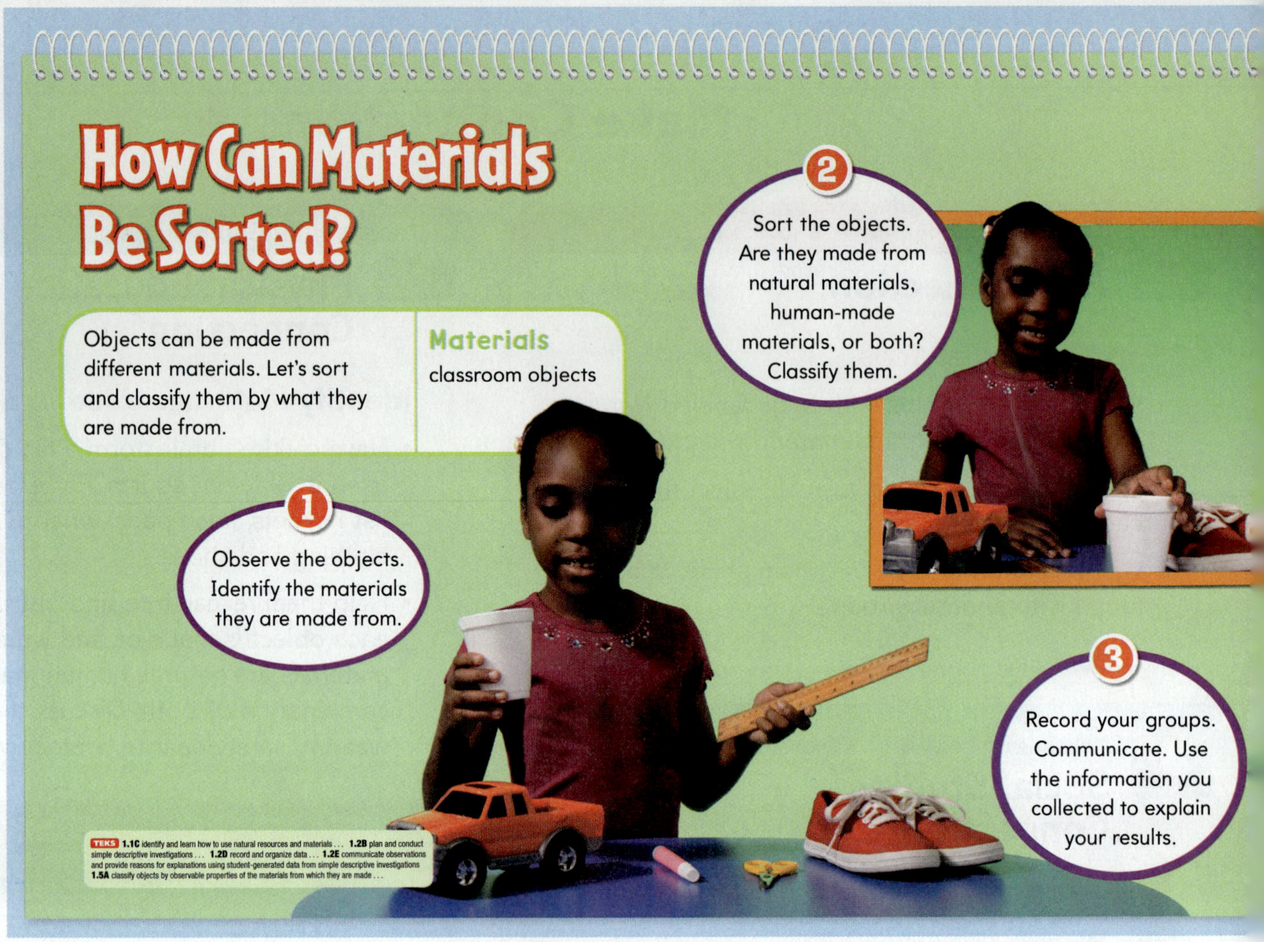

Inquiry Skills Focus Sort, Classify

Objectives

- Identify materials. Ask questions about objects observed in the natural world.
- Plan and conduct investigations. Record and organize data.
- Communicate observations and provide reasons for explanations using data.
- Classify objects by observable properties of the materials from which they are made.

Prep and Planning Tips

See the Planning for Inquiry page for more information.

- Make a set of four to six small objects constructed from various natural and human-made materials. Include at least one object that is a combination of both.

Expected Results

Children should identify, sort, and classify materials by the following criteria: natural, human-made, or a combination of both. They should communicate their observations and provide reasons for explanations about the information they collected.

1 Engage/Explore

Attention Grabber

Have each child examine a pencil and ask *What is this pencil made of?* Prompt them with follow-up questions such as *What is the soft material at the tip? What hard brownish material is the object mostly made of? What material wraps around the eraser and holds it in place?* List responses on the board and read the finished list aloud. Then, explain that children will learn to identify, compare, and classify the materials that objects are made of.

Preview Activity

Before beginning the investigation, have children review the directions on the Inquiry Flipchart and the accompanying Student Edition response pages. Then, have them complete the response pages as they follow the directions on the Flipchart.

Inquiry Flipchart p. 14

Lesson 4
INQUIRY

TEKS **1.2A** ask questions about organisms, objects, and events observed in the natural world **1.2B** plan and conduct simple descriptive investigations such as ways objects move **1.2D** record and organize data using pictures, numbers, and words **1.5A** classify objects by observable properties of the materials from which they are made . . .

ame ____________

Essential Question

How Can Materials Be Sorted?

et a Purpose

ell what you want to do.

want to sort and classify objects by the materials they are

ade from.

hink About the Procedure

What will you observe about the objects?

vill observe the materials that make up

e objects.

How will you sort the objects?

vill sort the objects by the materials they are made from—

tural materials, human-made materials, and both.

79

Go Digital

A virtual lab experience is available with the Online Resources for this program.

1 Engage/Explore (continued)

Guide the Investigation

Develop Inquiry Skills

SORT/CLASSIFY Remind children that when they sort and classify, they form groups of things that are alike in some way. Then, work with them to briefly brainstorm a list of situations from their everyday lives that require sorting and classifying, such as putting away clean clothes or organizing art or sports supplies.

Why are some objects made out of more than one material? Sample answer: The parts of an object do different jobs, and so the parts may be made out of different materials.

What are some natural materials you can identify? Sample answers: wood, rocks, clay, objects made from plants such as some kinds of cloth, and some foods.

What are some human-made materials you can identify? Sample answer: plastic, nylon

Which senses helped you identify the different parts of your object? Sample answer: I was able to figure out what the parts were by touching and looking at the object.

Share this tip with children. If they are unsure of whether a material is natural or human-made, they can ask themselves: "Did this material come from a plant, an animal, or from Earth? Could I find something made out of this material if I took a nature walk?" If their answers are no, then the material is probably not natural.

2 Explain

Develop Inquiry Skills

RECORD YOUR DATA Read the chart headings aloud. Discuss with children how they will use the table to record the groups they made. Point out to children that they may use pictures or words as they fill in the chart.

If children have difficulty naming the materials their objects are made of, provide simple descriptors (such as *metal, plastic,* etc.) but do not let children get distracted by these terms. Tell children that they can get the information they need about materials by observing them with their senses, even if they do not know the name for each thing.

DRAW CONCLUSIONS Help children note that they used their senses to observe, sort, and classify the different objects. If time allows, ask them to compare charts with one another and draw some additional conclusions about which category of object might be most common in the world around them.

3 Extend/Evaluate

ASK MORE QUESTIONS Discuss children's responses to the items. Some children may raise questions about other objects and what they could be made of. As an extension activity, encourage children to plan investigations or research the answers to their questions.

Assessment

Lesson Quiz
See Assessment Guide, p. AG 36.

Record Your Data

Classify the objects using the chart below. Draw or write to record how you grouped the objects.

Natural	Human-made	Both
Check that children write		
or draw the objects in the		
correct column.		

Draw Conclusions

How could you tell what objects were made of?

Sample answer: I used my senses and what I know about materials and where they come from.

Ask More Questions

What other questions could you ask about objects and materials?

Sample answer: What materials are an object's parts made of?

80

Differentiated Inquiry

Easy

Use Senses to Observe Objects

- Have children choose objects they observed in the main inquiry activity, tell about the materials they were made from, and explain how they used their senses to learn about the materials.
- If necessary, provide prompts they may use as they respond orally, such as
  I saw this material was _____.
  I felt this material was _______.

Average

Sort Similar Materials

- Arrange sets of objects made from similar materials, such as objects that are all made from different types of paper or different types of cloth.
- Provide small groups with the sets and have each small group sort and classify their objects into categories they choose themselves. Ask them to make a chart to show how they classified.

Easy

Sort Another Way

- Have children brainstorm another way they might sort and classify materials, such as by whether they are hard or soft, heavy or light, or bend or do not bend.
- Provide small groups with the same sets of objects as used in the main inquiry activity, and have them sort and classify again according to the new criteria.

Challenging

Play "Wood, Cloth, Plastic"

- Tell children they will play a game called "Wood, Cloth, Plastic." You will name an object that you would like to build, and they will discuss which of these three materials would be best for the job. For example: *I want to build a tall fence next to my house to keep animals out* or *I want to make a light object I can use to carry things from one place to another.*
- Have children explain their reasoning as they choose an appropriate material for each scenario.

People in Science

Objectives

- Describe what scientists do.
- Describe the contributions made by Dr. Eugene Tsui.
- Explain that engineers use a process to solve problems.

Notebook Generate Ideas

Share the following background information with children before you assign the feature. Ask questions to ascertain children's prior knowledge.

Look at the building in the photograph. What is interesting about it? Sample answer: It is an unusual shape for a building.

Do you think Dr. Tsui's job sounds easy or hard? Why? Sample answer: I think it sounds hard because there are a lot of steps to making a building. Also, he went to school for many years to be an architect, which means he probably had to learn a lot of things.

Background

- Dr. Eugene Tsui was born in Cleveland, Ohio. Both of his parents came from China, and Dr. Tsui speaks both English and Chinese. Today, Dr. Tsui lives outside of San Francisco, California.
- Dr. Tsui is an architect, or a person who designs buildings. In order to become an architect, Dr. Tsui went to school for many years. He also worked for and studied with another famous architect named Bruce Goff.
- Today, Dr. Tsui is famous for using shapes and patterns found in nature in his buildings.

TEKS 1.3C describe what scientists do

People in Science

Get to Know Dr. Eugene Tsui

Dr. Eugene Tsui is an architect. This is a kind of engineer. An architect designs homes and other buildings.

Dr. Tsui studies forms in nature, such as sea shells. He bases his designs on what he learns. Dr. Tsui says that nature is our greatest teacher.

Fun Fact

Dr. Tsui also designs his own clothes.

Writing Connection

TEKS ELA 1.19A

Write to Express Write the following sentence frame on the board or chart paper, read it aloud, and have children copy it: *I want to live in a house shaped like* _______. Help children complete the sentence in their own words. If time allows, provide other frames, such as *It would be made of* _______ or *The color would be* _______. Ask volunteers to read aloud what they wrote.

Dr. Tsui's Designs

▶ Draw a line from each building to the natural form it is based on.

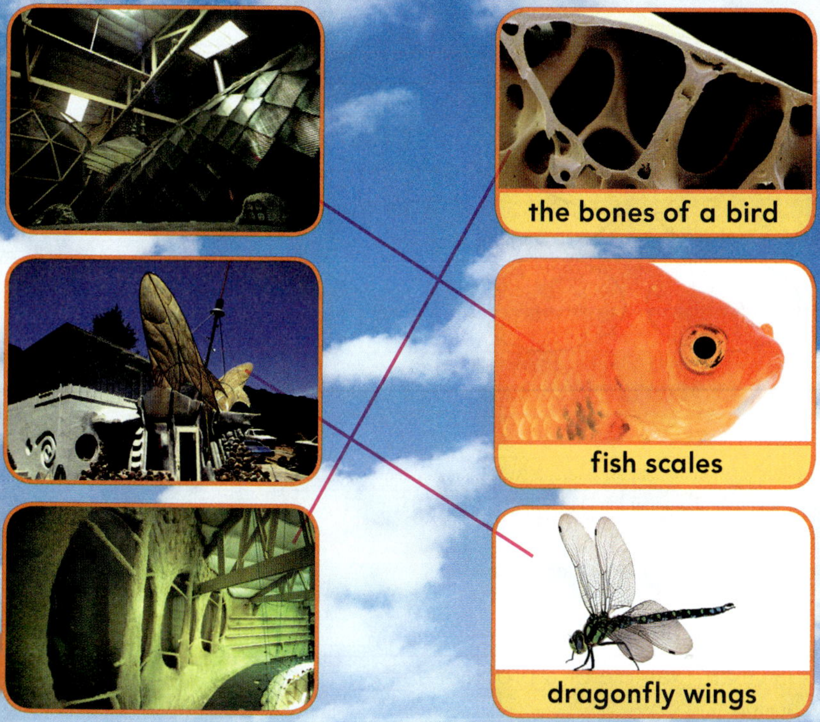

▶ Think about a form from nature. Use it to design your own building.

Design Process

Tell children that Dr. Tsui has steps he follows when he designs a building. In that way, he is like a scientist conducting an experiment. Ask children to think about what some of Dr. Tsui's steps might be. Encourage them to use what they know about the steps of the design process for help. Guide them to understand that both an architect and a scientist must decide on materials to use, draw plans in preparation, and use skills such as observing and drawing conclusions.

TEKS 1.3C

Develop Science Concepts

What are buildings usually made of? They are made of materials like wood, metal, and bricks.

Many buildings are cube- or box-shaped. Why do you think people usually make buildings in those shapes? Sample answer: The design is simple and easy to build.

How is Dr. Tsui like a scientist? Sample answer: He is like a scientist because he studies nature.

Develop Inquiry Skills

COMPARE/CONTRAST Remind children that when they compare and contrast, they tell how things are the same and different.

Choose one of the buildings shown in your book. How is it like a thing from nature? Sample answer: The fish building is like a real fish because it is covered with scales that look like fish scales.

How is the building different from the natural object? Sample answer: It is different because it is made of a different material, it is much bigger, and it was made by people.

Notebook Summarize Ideas

Have each child summarize the main idea of these pages by discussing this question with a partner: How is Dr. Eugene Tsui like a scientist?

Enduring Understandings

Revisit the Big Idea and Essential Questions

Big Idea **Engineers use a process to design and build something new. They use many different kinds of materials.**

To explore the Big Idea, challenge children to generate word webs that contain vocabulary words from the unit. Have them work in groups of three or four. Help them write the vocabulary word in the center circle, then ask them to write, draw, or dictate related words to fill in the surrounding circles. Have children add their webs to their Science Notebooks.

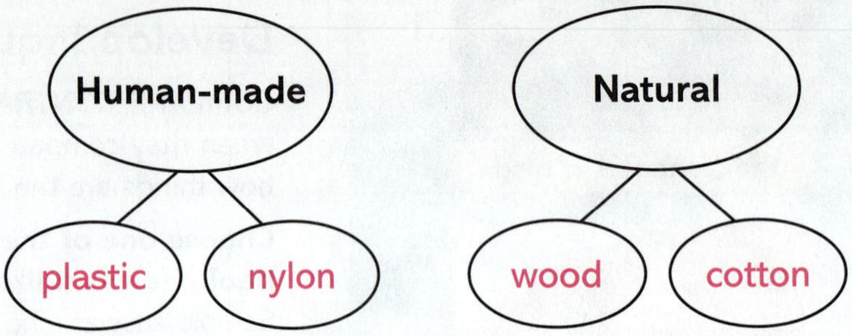

Essential Questions

Post the Essential Questions, and use the following prompts to guide a discussion.

Lessons/Essential Questions	Prompts
L1 **How Do Engineers Work?**	• Describe how engineers work.
L2 **How Can We Solve a Problem?**	• Give an example of a problem and how we can work to solve it.
L3 **What Materials Make Up Objects?**	• Name three types of materials that make up objects.
L4 **How Can Materials Be Sorted?**	• Demonstrate how to sort a group of materials.

Notebook Science Notebook

You may use the following strategies after children complete the unit or after each lesson.

- Have children review and edit the responses to the Essential Questions they drafted at the beginning of the unit. Suggest they cross out sentences or ideas that are unnecessary or inappropriate.
- Have children draw tic-tac-toe boards in their Science Notebooks. Have partners play together, with one partner being "human-made" and the other partner being "natural." Ask them to write or draw an example of their kind of material in a box on each turn. The first player to get three in a row wins.

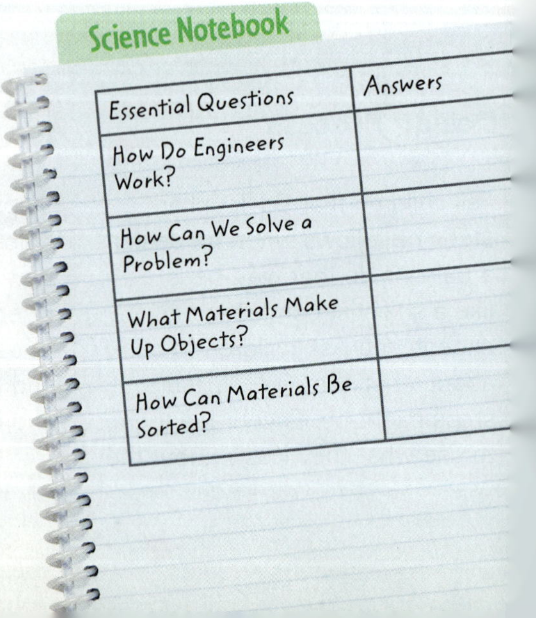

Unit 2 Review

Name ____________________

/ocabulary Review

Jse the terms in the box to complete he sentences.

engineer
materials
natural

. An engineer ________ might try to solve a problem such as how to build a better car.

EKS 1.1C

. Brick, metal, and wood are all different materials ________.

KS 1.1C

. Cotton and wood are natural ________ things found in nature.

cience Concepts

ll in the letter of the choice that best nswers the question.

KS 1.1C, 1.5A

A cotton shirt has a metal zipper. How can you classify the materials that make up the shirt?

Ⓐ natural
Ⓑ human-made
Ⓒ both natural and human-made

TEKS 1.3A

5. Yazan observes that the food in a bird feeder is hard for birds to get. What step of the design process has he just completed?

Ⓐ Communicate
Ⓑ Find a Problem
Ⓒ Test and Improve

Item Analysis

Items	TEKS	Depth of Knowledge	Cognitive Complexity
1		1	Low
2	**1.1C**	1	Low
3	**1.1C**	1	Low
4	**1.1C, 1.5A**	2	Moderate
5	**1.3A**	2	Moderate

Unit Review

Answer Key

Vocabulary Review (5 points each)

1. engineer

   Elicit from children examples of what an engineer does.

2. materials

   Reinforce that materials can make up an object by displaying a recent art or craft project, such as a collage. Have children name the materials used to make it.

3. natural

   Point out that the word *nature* is in the same word family as *natural.* Ask children to name some natural materials. Elicit from children that the opposite of *natural* is *human-made.*

Science Concepts (7 points each)

4. A

   Direct children's attention to the words *cotton* and *metal.* Have them tell whether each material is natural or human-made. Make sure children understand that cotton comes from a plant. Explain that some metals, such as copper and iron, exist naturally. Other metals are made by combining natural metals.

5. B

   Review the steps in the design process. As needed, review the meanings of words like *communicate, problem,* and *improve.*

Assessment

Unit 2 Test and Performance Assessment

See Assessment Guide, pp. AG 39–AG 45, for Unit Test and Performance Task with Long Option rubric.

Unit Review *continued*

Answer Key

Science Concepts (7 points each)

6. B

If available, display a wooden object and a plastic object so children can see these materials in real life. Make sure children understand that plastic is made in a lab, and is therefore made from a human-made material.

7. A

Fold a piece of paper in half to demonstrate what will happen to the bike described in the problem. Have children describe what happens to the size and shape of the paper.

8. C

Make sure children understand that wood comes from trees, which are found in nature.

9. B

Emphasize that regardless of the problem an engineer or other person is trying to solve, the steps of the design process are the same. Therefore, Raj will want to plan and build a better solution.

UNIT 2

TEKS 1.1C

6. Cara is looking at two objects.

Which object is made from a human-made material?

Ⓐ the wooden chair

Ⓑ the plastic bucket

Ⓒ both are made from human-made materials

TEKS 1.3A

7. An engineer designs a bike that folds in half. What problem might she be trying to solve?

Ⓐ Bikes cannot fit in small spaces.

Ⓑ Bikes are hard to ride.

Ⓒ Bikes are too slow.

TEKS 1.1C

8. Which object is made from natural materials?

Ⓐ a nylon shirt

Ⓑ a plastic bottle

Ⓒ a wood table

TEKS 1.3A

9. Raj's pencil stand falls over when it is full. How can he try to solve this problem?

Ⓐ He can throw the pencil stand away.

Ⓑ He can plan and build a better pencil stand.

Ⓒ He can find a different problem to solve.

Item Analysis *(continued)*

Items	TEKS	Depth of Knowledge	Cognitive Complexity
6	**1.1C**	2	Low
7	**1.3A**	2	Moderate
8	**1.1C**	2	Low
9	**1.3A**	2	Moderate

TEKS 1.3A

10. A river is between two towns. People want to drive from one town to the other. Two engineers talk about the problem.

How do they plan to solve it?

Ⓐ build a tunnel under the river

Ⓑ build a bridge over the river

Ⓒ give boats to the people in the towns

TEKS 1.2E

11. You use the design process to design a sun hat. How can you communicate what you did?

Ⓐ Test that the hat blocks the sun.

Ⓑ Tell others how your design works.

Ⓒ Redesign the hat and make changes.

TEKS 1.1C

12. Which object is made of both natural materials and human-made materials?

Ⓐ a metal bucket with a wooden handle

Ⓑ a wooden door with a metal handle

Ⓒ a cotton bag with a plastic handle

Item Analysis *(continued)*

Items	TEKS	Depth of Knowledge	Cognitive Complexity
10	**1.3A**	2	High
11	**1.2E**	3	Moderate
12	**1.1C**	2	Moderate

Unit Review *continued*

Answer Key

Science Concepts (7 points each)

10. B

Point out to children they must use the art to correctly answer the question. The other answer choices offer valid solutions, but they do not reflect what is shown in the illustration.

11. B

Children need to define *communicate* to solve this problem. Ask, "What does it mean to *communicate*?"

12. C

Children can refer to the highlighted lesson vocabulary terms to distinguish between natural and human-made materials.

Short Option Performance Assessment

Task

Build a Book Holder

Have children use the design process to build a book holder to make more room on their desks. This could be a bookshelf on top of their desks, a sturdy set of bookends, or a way for them to hang books from the sides of their desks.

Rubric

Preparation Provide materials, such as scrap wood, cardboard, paper-towel tubes, glue, tape, scissors, and string.

Scoring Rubric—Performance Indicators

___ Identifies and explains the problem: children need more room on their desks.

___ Thinks of a solution and brainstorms a list of characteristics the book holder should have.

___ Plans and builds the book holder.

___ Tests and improves the book holder.

Observations and Rubric Scores

3 2 1 0

Unit Review *continued*

Answer Key

Inquiry and the Big Idea (11 points each)

13.

a. Group 1 has objects made from natural materials. Group 2 has objects made from human-made materials.

b. Sample answer: a metal key for Group 1 and a plastic bottle for Group 2

Have children recall how they sorted materials in some of the lessons in this unit. Help them draw comparisons between how they sorted materials and how Geeta sorted materials.

14.

a. He needs to plan and build a solution.

b. He can put the tool in front of the door to see if it blocks the cold air.

c. He should redesign the tool and test it again.

Review with children the steps in the design process. Have children execute the design process to solve the same problem that Michael has.

UNIT 2

Inquiry and the Big Idea

Write the answers to these questions.

TEKS 1.1C, 1.5A

13. Geeta sorted objects into these two groups.

Group 1	Group 2
wooden pencil	plastic toy
metal fork	nylon jacket

a. How did she classify the objects?

Group 1 has objects made from natural materials.

Group 2 has objects made from human-made materials.

b. Name one thing that could be added to each group.

Sample answer: a metal key for Group 1 and a plastic bottle for Group 2

TEKS 1.3A

14. Cold air is coming in under Michael's door. He wants to use the design process to find a solution.

a. What should Michael do first?

He needs to plan and build a solution.

b. Michael builds a tool. How can he test it?

He can put the tool in front of the door to see if it blocks the cold air.

c. What should he do if the tool does not work?

He should redesign the tool and test it again.

86 **Unit 2** Unit Review

Item Analysis

Items	TEKS	Depth of Knowledge	Cognitive Complexity
13	**1.1C, 1.5A**	3	High
14	**1.3A**	3	High

UNIT 3 Matter

Big Idea and Essential Questions

This Unit was designed to focus on this Big Idea and these Essential Questions.

Take It Home!
A School-Home Connection letter in English and Spanish is provided in Online Resources.

Big Idea

All objects are matter. Matter can change in different ways.

Essential Questions

L1 **What Can We Observe About Objects?**

L2 **How Can We Measure Temperature?**

L3 **How Does Heating and Cooling Change Matter?**

Professional Development

Houghton Mifflin Harcourt and **NSTA,** the **National Science Teachers Association,** have partnered to provide customized professional development resources for teachers using *ScienceFusion*.

The Professional Development Resources include:

- Do-it-yourself resources, where you can study at your own pace
- Live and archived online seminars
- Journal articles, many of which include lesson plans
- Fee-based eBooks, eBook chapters, online short courses, symposia, and conferences

Access to The NSTA Learning Center is provided in the *ScienceFusion* Online Resources.

NSTA National Science Teachers Association

The NSTA Learning Center

Unit Planning

Options for Instruction

Choose from **Interactive Worktext** and **Leveled Readers**, **Digital**, and **Inquiry** options to meet the Texas Essential Knowledge and Skills.

	LESSON 1	LESSON 2	LESSON 3
Essential Questions	**What Can We Observe About Objects?**	✔ Guided Inquiry **How Can We Measure Temperature?**	**How Does Heating and Cooling Change Matter?**
Texas Essential Knowledge and Skills	TEKS 1.5A	TEKS 1.2A, 1.2B, 1.2D, 1.5B	TEKS 1.5B
Interactive Worktext	☐ **Student Edition** pp. 89–100 • Why Matter Matters • What's It Like? • Heavy or Light? • Hot or Cold? • Will It Sink or Will It Float?	☐ **Student Edition** pp. 103–104 • Scaffolding for Inquiry	☐ **Student Edition** pp. 105–114 • Freeze in Place • Melt Away • Up in the Air • Cool It!
Leveled Readers	Parallel coverage of the lesson topics is provided in the **Extra Support**, **On-Level**, and **Enrichment** readers. See p. 87H for detailed reader information.		
Hands-On Inquiry	**Inquiry Flipchart** p. 15 **Sort It Out!** ☐ Directed Inquiry **What's the Weight?** ☐ Independent Inquiry	**Inquiry Flipchart** p. 16 **How Can We Measure Temperature?** ☐ Guided Inquiry	**Inquiry Flipchart** p. 17 **Water to Gas** ☐ Directed Inquiry **Water Changes** ☐ Independent Inquiry
Digital Curriculum	☐ **Digital Lesson** Online Resources Interactive presentation of lesson content 	☐ **Virtual Lab** Online Resources Interactive scaffolded inquiry 	☐ **Digital Lesson** Online Resources Interactive presentation of lesson content 

OTHER UNIT FEATURES

Careers in Science, p. 101

S.T.E.M. Engineering and Technology, pp. 115–116B

Online Resources

Interactive Whiteboard Resources for Unit 3

Assessment

Formative Assessment

Sum It Up! and Brain Check

Student Edition, end of each lesson

Summative Assessment

Lesson Quizzes

Assessment Guide, pp. AG 46–AG 48

Unit 3 Review

Student Edition, pp. 117–120

Unit 3 Test

Assessment Guide, pp. AG 51–AG 55

Performance Assessment

SHORT OPTION: Teacher Edition, p. 119

LONG OPTION: Assessment Guide, pp. AG 56–AG 57

RTI Response to Intervention

RTI Strategies, p. 87I

Online Assessment

Test-taking and automatic scoring

Banks of items from which to build tests

Teacher Notes

Planning for Inquiry

Use the following preview of Inquiry Activities and Lessons to gather and manage the materials needed for each lesson.

Activity	Inquiry and Design Process Skills Focus	Materials	Prep Tips, Troubleshooting, and Expected Results
Lesson 1 DIRECTED INQUIRY Flipchart p.15 A **Sort It Out!** **OBJECTIVES** Conduct simple descriptive investigations. Record and organize data. Classify objects by observable properties of the materials from which they are made. 15 minutes small groups TEKS **1.2B, 1.2D, 1.5A**	• Observe • Compare • Classify	• classroom objects	**Prep Tips** To prepare, gather an assortment of classroom objects that children can sort based on their properties. Objects should be small enough for children to handle easily. For example, small balls, writing tools, paper clips, and blocks are appropriate. If possible, include a few less familiar objects. You may wish to provide groups with shoeboxes they can use to sort their objects. **Troubleshooting** Make sure your assortment of items includes at least a few items of the same color, a few of roughly the same size, and a few with the same texture or shape. Alert children that it's fine if the amount of objects in each group varies, as long as they are able to group at least two objects together and justify their groupings. **Expected Results** Children will be able to observe and classify the objects according to different properties. They will also be able to describe and explain their groupings. Children should focus on observed properties, such as size, weight, texture, color, and shape.
INDEPENDENT INQUIRY Flipchart p.15 B **What's the Weight?** **OBJECTIVES** Plan and conduct simple investigations. Record and organize data. Classify objects by observable properties. 15 minutes individuals TEKS **1.2B, 1.2D, 1.5A**	• Compare • Measure	• classroom objects of varying weights • scale	**Prep Tips** Gather a variety of objects that children can weigh. Avoid objects that are breakable, sharp-edged, or overly heavy. If possible, include objects that are heavy or light for their size, such as a small bag of flour and a large beach ball. A bathroom scale or a kitchen scale will work for this activity, although a kitchen scale will only be able to handle small objects. Demonstrate use of the scale before children begin. **Troubleshooting** Remind children not to weigh down the scale with their hands or feet while weighing objects. **Expected Results** Children will use a scale to weigh classroom objects and identify which is heavier based on the amount registered on the scale.

Additional teaching support for all inquiry activities is available in **Online Resources.**

Science Notebook Strategies

- Lists of Kit-Supplied Materials
- Meeting Individual Needs
- Investigate More—Extensions and Variations
- and More!

Activity	Inquiry and Design Process Skills Focus	Materials	Prep Tips, Troubleshooting, and Expected Results
Lesson 2 INQUIRY GUIDED INQUIRY **Flipchart** p. 16 **Student Edition** pp. 103–104 **How Can We Measure Temperature?** **OBJECTIVES** • Conduct simple descriptive investigations. • Collect and compare data and make observations using thermometers. • Record and organize data. • Identify changes in materials caused by heating. 45 minutes pairs TEKS **1.2B, 1.2C, 1.2D, 1.4A, 1.5B**	• Measure • Experiment • Identify and Control Variables	• two thermometers • black paper • white paper	**Prep Tips** Cut sheets of black and white construction paper in half. Then, fold each piece in half lengthwise and staple it on three sides to form a pocket. Each pair should have a black paper pocket and a white paper pocket. Review with children how to read the temperature. After they record the beginning temperature, have them wait 30 minutes before recording new data. **Caution!** Make sure children do not put thermometers in their mouths. **Troubleshooting** Paper color should be the only difference between the two thermometers. Make sure the thermometers are adjacent in position, and both are in direct sunlight. **Expected Results** Children should find that the thermometer in the dark paper pocket gets warmer than the one in the light paper pocket.

Go Digital! Virtual Lab

How Can We Measure Temperature?

Key Inquiry Skills: observe, measure, plan and conduct simple investigations, record data, predict

Children measure and record temperatures and use the temperatures to compare different types of matter.

Planning for Inquiry (continued)

Activity	Inquiry and Design Process Skills Focus	Materials	Prep Tips, Troubleshooting, and Expected Results
Lesson 3 DIRECTED INQUIRY Flipchart p.17 A **Water to Gas** **OBJECTIVES** Conduct simple descriptive investigations. Record and organize data. Collect and compare information using timers. Predict and identify changes in materials caused by heating. 25–30 minutes pairs TEKS **1.2B, 1.2D, 1.4A, 1.5B**	• Predict • Compare • Draw Conclusions	• small cups • water • colored construction paper • water droppers • timers • markers	**Prep Tips** Water droppers are available for purchase from teacher-supply stores, drugstores, and online suppliers. Dark-colored construction paper will work best for this activity. Show children how to use the water droppers by squeezing the bulb, dipping the dropper in the water, and then releasing the bulb to fill the dropper with water. Then, demonstrate how to release the water droplets on the paper. **Troubleshooting** Show children how to place all ten water drops in one place to make one spot, rather than making dots of water all over the paper. Also make sure children do not soak one tiny spot of the paper to the point that it wears through. **Expected Results** Children will find that the wet spot gets smaller. They should conclude that heat from the sun or lamp warmed the water and dried the paper. They should recognize that the water changed from a liquid to a gas.
INDEPENDENT INQUIRY Flipchart p.17 B **Water Changes** **OBJECTIVES** Conduct simple descriptive investigations. Record and organize data. Collect and compare information using clocks. Predict and identify changes in materials caused by heating and cooling. 30 minutes small groups TEKS **1.2B, 1.2D, 1.4A, 1.5B**	• Predict • Compare • Plan and Conduct a Simple Investigation	• small cups of water • ice cubes	**Prep Tips** In advance, make enough ice cubes to give one to each group. Before the activity, talk to school personnel about setting aside room in the freezer. Fill a small cup with water for each group about one-third full so the water will fully freeze during the activity. **Troubleshooting** If children have difficulty using a clock to tell time, identify the starting and stopping times as a class and have children record the times in their Science Notebooks. **Expected Results** Children should observe that the cooled water changed from a liquid to a solid and the heated water changed from a solid to a liquid.

Additional teaching support for all inquiry activities is available in Online Resources.

Activity	Inquiry and Design Process Skills Focus	Materials	Prep Tips, Troubleshooting, and Expected Results
S.T.E.M. Engineering and Technology Flipchart p.18 **Think About Process: Write a Recipe** **OBJECTIVES** • Recognize and demonstrate safe practices. • Record and organize data. • Identify and explain a problem and propose a solution. 25 minutes individuals TEKS **1.1B, 1.2D, 1.3A**	 1 Find a Problem 2 Plan and Build 3 Test and Improve 4 Redesign 5 Communicate	• children's cookbooks and a variety of simple recipes	**Prep Tips** Have on hand several children's cookbooks and simple recipes. Tell children that they will be writing their own recipes for a favorite sandwich. You may wish to prepare children for the activity by suggesting they make their favorite sandwiches at home and take notes on the process. **Expected Results** Children will write a recipe for a favorite sandwich, listing the ingredients and amounts needed and the steps in the process.

Differentiated Instruction

Leveled Readers

The Leveled Readers provide parallel coverage of the unit topics and Texas Essential Knowledge and Skills. Each Reader is available in English and Spanish. Both versions are available online and on touchscreen mobile devices.

ON-LEVEL This Reader reinforces unit concepts and vocabulary and focuses on the Texas Essential Knowledge and Skills. It includes student response activities.

EXTRA SUPPORT This Reader shares title, illustrations, vocabulary, and concepts with the On-Level Reader. However, the text is linguistically accommodated to provide simplified sentence structures and comprehension aids for students who need a little extra support with content-area reading and vocabulary development. It also includes student response activities.

ENRICHMENT This high-interest nonfiction Reader enriches and extends unit concepts. It reinforces some of the unit vocabulary, but also includes stretch vocabulary. It also includes student response activities.

TEACHER GUIDE
The accompanying Teacher Guide provides teaching strategies and support for using all the Readers, as well as English and Spanish worksheets that focus on vocabulary development. A correlation to the Texas Essential Knowledge and Skills is included.

DIGITAL VERSIONS

All of these Leveled Readers are available online. They are also available in an innovative and engaging format for touchscreen mobile devices. For information about accessing these versions, see page T9.

RTI Response to Intervention

Response to Intervention is a process for identifying and supporting students who are not making expected progress toward essential learning goals.

The following *ScienceFusion* components have the flexibility to be used to provide Core Classroom Instruction (Tier 1), strategic intervention (Tier 2), and intensive intervention (Tier 3).

Component	Location	Strategies and Benefits
Student Edition, Active Reading prompts, Sum It Up, Brain Check	Active Reading throughout each lesson, Sum It Up and Brain Check at the end of each lesson	Student responses can be used as screening tools to assess whether intervention is needed.
Assessment Guide, Lesson Quizzes and TEKS DOK Skill Builder	pp. AG 46–AG 50	Student responses can be used as screening tools to assess whether intervention is needed.
Inquiry Flipcharts	Inquiry Flipchart p. 16	Directed Inquiry for students who learn best through directed or teacher-led hands-on activities.
Teacher Edition, Unit Review Answer Strategies	TE pp. 117–120	Suggestions for intervention, guidance, and remediation for each review question.
Leveled Readers	TE p. 87H	Content support for students not meeting the learning needs during core classroom instruction.
Leveled Readers, Teacher Guides and Vocabulary Worksheets	TE p. 87H	Direct instruction with small groups of students needing additional content at various readability levels.
Extra Support for Vocabulary and Concepts (online worksheets)	Online Resources	Support for individualized instruction with practice in essential content.
Online Student Edition with Audio	Online Resources	Provides learners with multiple-modality access to science concepts and information.
Interactive Digital Lessons and Virtual Labs	Online Resources	Provides individualized learning experiences. Lessons make content accessible through simulations, animations, videos, audio, and integrated assessment.
Interactive Whiteboard Resources	Online Resources	Reinforces key unit concepts through interactive vocabulary games and visuals and graphic organizers.
Leveled Readers, online and tablet versions	Online and Tablet Resources	Highlighted words and sentences synced with audio provide support for emerging or struggling readers.

Differentiated Instruction

English Language Learners

Choose from these instructional strategies to meet the needs of English language learners.

Vocabulary Cards are provided in Online Resources.

Unit Vocabulary

Lesson 1	Lesson 3
matter	freeze
property	melt
texture	evaporate
weight	condense
temperature	

Preteach Vocabulary ELPS 3C

Use accessible language to define *matter, property, texture, weight,* and *temperature*. Then, display and discuss classroom objects to develop children's understanding of the Lesson 1 terms. Model using each word in a sentence, and have children repeat it.

Language Acquisition Strategies

Describe Objects ELPS 3C

Have children use complete sentences to describe the objects shown on **TE pages 90–91.**

Beginning	Intermediate	Advanced/Advanced High
Point to the ball on page 90. Model describing it in complete sentences: *The ball is round. The ball has many colors.* Have children use sentences to describe other objects: *The table is ___. The bed is ___.*	Have children describe each object by completing a sentence frame: *The [name of object] is ___ and ___.*	Have partners take turns describing objects in complete sentences. Challenge Advanced High ELLs to say two sentences about each object.

Visual and Contextual Support ELPS 1C, 4F

Before children read **TE page 92,** write the properties listed at the top of the page (*size, shape, color, texture*) in a chart.

Beginning	Intermediate	Advanced/Advanced High
Use objects to develop understanding of each property. For size, for example, display a small and large ball. For texture, invite children to touch a smooth ruler and a rough brush.	Read aloud each word as you point to it, and have children repeat after you. Then, have children copy the chart and work together to list words and/or draw pictures related to each property.	Read aloud each word as you point to it, and have children repeat after you. Then, have children work in pairs to write sentences about each property and list examples that illustrate it.

Vocabulary Development ELPS 2C, 4C

Before children complete the math problem on **TE page 94,** develop their understanding of the verb *order*. Use number or picture cards that are appropriate for each proficiency level.

Beginning	Intermediate	Advanced/Advanced High
Define the word *order*. Model placing a series of number cards in order. Use the word *order* as you describe what you are doing. Display the first card. Pass out the remaining cards, and have children put them in the correct order.	Display a set of picture cards that show a simple series of events. Have children place the cards in the correct order.	Give partners a set of picture cards that show a simple series of events. Have children put the cards in order and then use complete sentences to tell about the events.

Taking Notes ELPS 2G, 2I, 4I

Use **TE pages 106–107** to have children practice note-taking skills.

Beginning	Intermediate	Advanced/Advanced High
Read aloud the first paragraph. Work together to identify the most important information. Model writing notes for the paragraph. Have children copy your notes.	Read aloud the first paragraph. Ask children to identify the most important information. Have them record this information as notes.	Have children take notes about the information on these pages. Then, have partners review their notes and determine if they recorded all the key ideas.

Vocabulary Support ELPS 1A, 1F, 4F

Provide support to enhance children's understanding of the terms *evaporate* and *condense* on **TE pages 110–111.**

Beginning	Intermediate	Advanced/Advanced High
Point out details in the pictures as you discuss what happens to water when it evaporates and condenses. Guide children to understand that these terms tell what happens when water changes form.	Have children work in pairs to explain what happens to water when it evaporates and when it condenses. Ask them to refer to details in the pictures to support their explanations.	Have partners explain how water changes when it evaporates and when it condenses. Challenge Advanced High ELLs to explain why *evaporate* and *condense* are antonyms.

Matter

I Wonder Why

Play a simple game of Twenty Questions. Tell children that you are thinking of an object. They have to figure out what it is by asking yes or no questions about the object. For example, Is it red? Is it smooth? Is it sweet? After children identify the object, point out that they have identified it according to its properties. Relate this concept to the sandcastle in the photograph. Point out that *brown* and *rough* are properties of the sandcastle. Guide children to understand that all matter has properties.

Here's Why

Have children turn the page and read the response to the question. You may wish to share the following background with them.

More About...

Properties of Sand

Sand is made from broken pieces of rocks. Sand found at the beach may also contain pieces of shells and corals. The properties of these rocks, shells, and corals affect the properties of the sand. The make-up of sand varies depending on the rocks and sea creatures in the area. For example, Bermuda's pink sand comes from the red shell of a tiny sea animal that lives nearby. Hawaii's black sand is broken bits of volcanic rock from the islands' volcanoes.

Science Songs

See pp. TR40-TR43 for science songs you can use to reinforce content in this unit.

Professional Development **Science Background**

Use the keywords to access

- Professional Development from **The NSTA Learning Center**
- **SciLinks** for additional online content appropriate for children and teachers
- Teacher Science Background in the back of this Teacher Edition

Keywords

changes in matter
measuring matter
properties of matter

SCiLINKS THE WORLD'S A CLICK AWAY

Here's Why Brown and rough are properties of the sandcastle. A property is one part of what something is like.

In this unit, you will explore this Big Idea, the Essential Questions, and the Investigations on the Inquiry Flipchart.

Levels of Inquiry Key ■ DIRECTED ■ GUIDED ■ INDEPENDENT

Track Your Progress

Big Idea All objects are matter. Matter can change in different ways.

Essential Questions

Science Notebook

Before you begin each lesson, be sure to write your thoughts about the Essential Question.

Go Digital

For a complete digital curriculum and resources that provide full coverage of the objectives for this unit, see the Online Resources for this program.

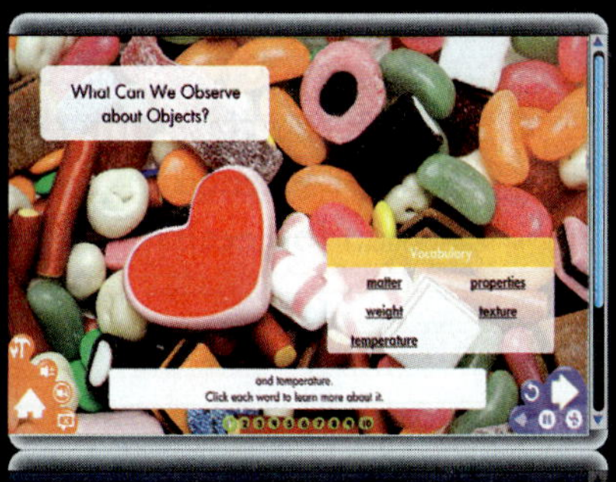

Big Idea and Essential Questions

Big Idea All objects are matter. Matter can change in different ways.

Post the Unit Big Idea on the board. Have children read the Essential Questions, which are also the titles of the lessons in this unit.

- Discuss how the Essential Questions can help keep them focused on the Big Idea.
- Have children read the Big Idea statement. The statement describes the main science concept that they will be learning.
- Have children predict other ideas that will be taught in the lessons based on the titles, or have them give examples of pictures they expect to see.

Once they complete the unit, they should have a better understanding of the Big Idea.

Essential Questions You may use the following Science Notebook strategy for working with the Essential Questions before children begin the unit or before each lesson.

- Strategies for revisiting the Big Idea and Essential Questions are provided in Enduring Understandings on p. 117A.

Notebook Science Notebook

- Have children copy the Essential Questions into their Science Notebooks. Suggest they leave several writing lines between questions.
- Ask children to write responses to the Essential Questions. Urge them not to worry about whether their responses are correct. They should expect their ideas to change as they work in the unit. Comment that children will be able to review and revise their answers to the Essential Questions at the end of the unit.
- Tips and strategies for using Science Notebooks are provided throughout this unit, in the back of this Teacher Edition, and in the Online Resources.

Options for Inquiry

FLIPCHART P. 15

Children can conduct these optional investigations at any time before, during, or in response to the lesson in the Student Edition.

Directed Inquiry

A Sort It Out!

15 minutes
small groups

Prep and Planning Tips

To prepare, gather an assortment of classroom objects that children can sort based on their properties. Objects should be small enough for children to handle easily. For example, small balls, writing tools, paper clips, and blocks are appropriate. If possible, also include a few less-familiar objects.

You may wish to provide groups with shoeboxes that they can use as they sort their objects.

Expected Outcomes

Children will be able to observe and classify the objects according to different properties. Children will be able to describe and explain their groupings. Children should focus on observed properties such as size, weight, texture, color and shape.

Independent Inquiry

B What's the Weight?

15 minutes
individuals

Prep and Planning Tips

See the Planning for Inquiry page for more information. Gather a variety of objects that children can weigh. Avoid objects that are breakable or have sharp edges.

Science Notebook

Children can use the Science Notebook as a model for planning and conducting their investigations. Encourage them to make a chart like the one shown. Ask volunteers to share their comparisons with the class or a small group. Suggest they use this sentence frame: [Object] is [heavier/lighter] than [object].

TEKS **1.5A** classify objects by observable properties of the materials from which they are made such as larger and smaller, heavier and lighter, shape, color, and texture

Lesson 1

Essential Question

What Can We Observe About Objects?

Engage Your Brain!

Find the answer to the question in the lesson.

How are the blocks in this rabbit the same?

They are all

matter .

Active Reading

Lesson Vocabulary

1. Preview the lesson.
2. Write the 5 vocabulary terms here.

matter
weight
property
temperature
texture

Inquiry Flipchart p. 15—Sort It Out!/What's the Weight?

89

Go Digital

An interactive digital lesson is available in the Online Resources. It is suitable for individuals, small groups, or may be projected or used on an interactive white board.

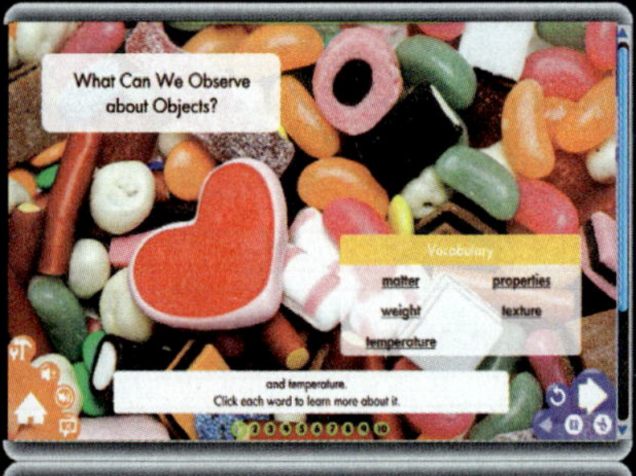

1 Engage/Explore

Objectives

- Plan and conduct simple investigations.
- Record and organize data.
- Classify objects by observable properties of the materials from which they are made such as larger and smaller, heavier and lighter, shape, color, and texture.

Engage Your Brain!

Have children brainstorm answers to the question *How are the blocks in this rabbit the same?* Tell them that desks, crayons, and other objects are also the same as the blocks in one way. Give them a hint by pointing out that the answer to the question has to do with everything around them. Record children's responses on the board.

Remind children to record their final answer to the question when they find it on the second page of the lesson.

Active Reading Annotations

Remind children that active readers "make texts their own" by marking them or writing notes to help them understand what they are reading. Encourage children to use a pencil to make annotations and to feel free to change their marks and notes as they read. The goal of annotation is to help children remember what they have read.

Vocabulary and Interactive Glossary

Remind children to find and list the yellow highlighted terms from the lesson. As they proceed through the lesson and learn about the terms, they can add drawings or words in the extra spaces provided in some entries in the Interactive Glossary.

2 Explain

Notebook Generate Ideas

Read the heading aloud with children. Explain that *matter* has many meanings. *Matter* can mean "something that is important." In science, it refers to anything that takes up space. With children, make a list of things that are matter. Have volunteers explain why things from the list "matter" to them.

Active Reading Main Idea

Explain that the main, or most important, idea may be the first sentence or another sentence in a paragraph. To find the main idea, active readers ask themselves, "What is this paragraph mostly about?" The answer will be the main idea. Children should draw two lines under the sentence that answers the question *What is this paragraph mostly about?*

Develop Science Vocabulary

matter Point to any matter in the classroom. Explain that matter is anything that takes up space. Explain that when the word *matter* is used in everyday language, it has many meanings. Ask volunteers to share any meanings for *matter* that are different from the scientific meaning. Then explain several meanings using sentences such as these: *What's the matter (trouble) with the car? That is a matter (situation) for the police. My grades matter (are important) to me.*

Why Matter Matters

Look around. What do you see? Are there trees, toys, or books? These things are matter. **Matter** is anything that takes up space. Even the air you breathe is matter!

Active Reading

The main idea is the most important idea about something. Draw two lines under the main idea.

90

Develop Science Concepts

What do you know is true about the ball, the clock, and the boy? They are all matter.

What other things do you see in the boy's room that are matter? Sample answers: water in fishbowl, bed, truck, and blocks.

Develop Inquiry Skills

COMPARE/CONTRAST **What do you do when you compare things?** You tell how they are alike. **What do you do when you contrast things?** You tell how they are different.

You know the ball, the clock, and the boy are alike because they are all matter. What are some ways that the ball, the clock, and the boy are different? Sample answers: They are different shapes and sizes. The ball and the clock are round. They are nonliving, and the boy is living.

Notebook Summarize Ideas

Have children look at the objects again and think about the main idea on these pages. Ask if their ideas about matter have changed since they read these pages. Have them summarize the main idea orally or in writing.

Differentiation—Leveled Questions

Extra Support

What are examples of matter in your classroom? Have children draw to respond. Check their drawings. Sample drawings might show desks, a chalkboard, a teacher, children, books, toys, a window, and so on.

Challenge

How do you use matter? Why does it matter to you? Sample answer: Because everything around me is matter, I use it in everything I do. I eat and drink matter. It matters to me because I am matter.

2 Explain (continued)

Notebook Generate Ideas

Read the heading aloud to children. Point out that all matter is not alike. Provide an example of a familiar object, such as a crayon. Ask children to brainstorm a list of types of matter that are different from the crayon in some way. Have volunteers describe the differences.

Active Reading Vocabulary

Explain that a vocabulary word may be highlighted in a color. Point out to children the two highlighted words. Active readers pay attention to highlighted words because their meaning is given in the same sentence or the next sentence.

Develop Science Concepts

What are some of the properties of matter? size, shape, color, texture

What are some words that describe an object's size? big and small

Look at the pictures of the cars. How do you know which car does not belong? Children should explain that the car that is a different size than the others does not belong.

What are some ways to describe an object's shape? round, square, star-shaped, and heart-shaped

What are some other objects that are red? Accept all reasonable answers. Sample answers: an apple, a stop sign.

Name some objects that are soft. Accept all reasonable answers. Sample answers: pillow, cotton ball, and a puppy's fur.

What's It Like?

A **property** of matter is one part of what something is like. Some properties are size, shape, color, and texture. **Texture** is what an object feels like.

Active Reading

Find the sentence that tells the meaning of **property**. Draw a line under the sentence.

Size

Big and **small** are words that tell about size.

Shape

Star and **heart** are words that tell about shape.

92

English Language Learners

ELPS 1E, 2C, 2E

Use Words for Properties Children may have difficulty understanding the meaning of *properties*. Write on the board: *properties, size, shape, color,* and *texture*. Have pairs of children draw pictures of a big bear and a small mouse, a round plate and a square book, a red apple and a yellow banana, a soft pillow and a hard rock. Ask them to describe each picture; for example: *A property of the bear is that it is big. Red is a property of the apple*

You can classify objects by the properties of the materials they are made from. When you classify, you put things that are alike in the same group.

▶ **In each box, draw an X on the object that does not belong.**

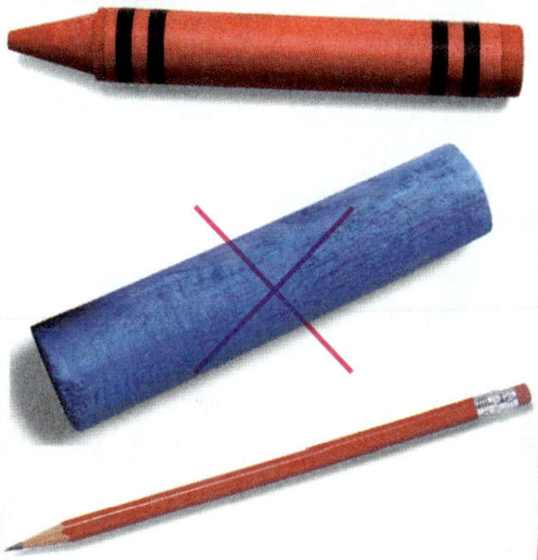

Color

Red and **blue** are words that tell about color.

Texture

Soft and **hard** are words that tell about texture.

93

Math Connection

TEKS MATH 1.8A, 1.8B

Make a Graph Write these color names on the board: *red, blue, yellow*. Ask children to identify and record in a tally chart the number of objects in the classroom that are each color. Then have them make a bar graph to show the results. Invite volunteers to summarize the information in the bar graph.

Develop Science Vocabulary

property Children may think of the word *property* as meaning something that belongs to them. Explain that in science, a *property* is a characteristic that describes things. A property of matter is one part of what something is like. For example, *round* is a property of a ball.

texture Gather materials that have different textures such as cotton balls, rocks, a scarf, and a penny. Have children touch each material and tell about its texture. Explain to children that texture is what an object feels like.

Develop Inquiry Skills

CLASSIFY Point out to children that when they group objects by how they are alike, they are classifying. Have children look at the pictures on these two pages. Lead the class in a discussion about how properties can be used to classify objects. Then gather a few objects from around the classroom. Provide children the opportunity to classify the objects by size, shape, color, and texture.

Interpret Visuals

Focus children's attention to the pictures of the cars grouped together.

Why are these pictures shown in a group? They show the same kind of object. **How are the cars alike?** They have the same shape. **How are they different?** One of them is a different size. **What is this picture trying to show?** The picture shows how objects can vary in size. Objects can be big or small.

Notebook Summarize Ideas

Ask children to think about the main idea and details on these pages. Have them summarize orally or in writing some properties that are used to describe and classify matter.

2 Explain (continued)

Notebook Generate Ideas

Write *heavy, light, hot,* and *cold* on the board. Then read the words aloud with children. Point to a heavy item such as a desk, and ask children whether it is heavy or light. Repeat with a light item such as a pencil. Have children take turns naming an item for other children to observe and then identify them as heavy or light. Do the same for *hot* and *cold*. Have volunteers describe the difference between *heavy* and *light* and *hot* and *cold*.

Do the Math!

TEKS MATH 1.1C

Order by Weight

Ask children what it means to order. They can practice ordering by putting groups of three pencils in order from shortest to tallest. Discuss with children how they can estimate weight by holding objects in their hands to see how heavy or light they feel. Once they have ordered the objects, have children compare their responses. Ask volunteers to discuss how they knew the order.

Develop Science Concepts

Which would be heavier—a jar filled with pennies or a jar filled with one-dollar bills? Sample answer: A jar filled with pennies would be heavier.

Tell about a time you measured the temperature. Sample answers: checking temperature for the weather, during an illness, for a science class.

How do you know if a food is hot? Explain. Sample answers: It may feel warm to touch. It might have steam coming off of it.

Heavy or Light?

Some things you pick up feel light. Others feel heavy. **Weight** is the measure of how heavy an object feels. You can classify objects by their weight.

Do the Math!

Order by Weight

Order from light to heavy. Write 1 for lightest. Write 3 for heaviest.

paint
3

paper clip
1

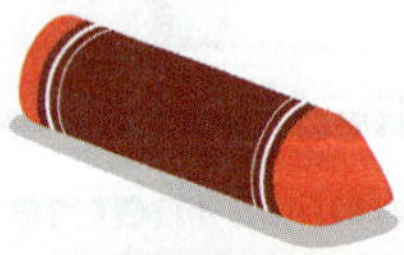

marker
2

94

English Language Learners

ELPS 1E, 2C, 2E

Understand Multiple-Meaning Words Children may have difficulty understanding the meaning of *light*. Have them act out lifting objects that are light. Discuss other meanings such as "not dark" and "energy that lets us see." Then say sentences such as *That paper is light. The sun's light makes the room bright. It is light outside during the day.* Have children identify the meanings of *light*. Then have them write and share their own sentences using the meanings of *light*.

Hot or Cold?

How hot is a pizza? How cold is an ice pop? You can find out by using temperature. **Temperature** is the measure of how hot or cold something is.

pizza

ice pop

hot cocoa

lemonade

▶ **Draw something hot.**

Check that children draw something hot.

▶ **Draw something cold.**

Check that children draw something cold.

95

Differentiation—Leveled Questions

Extra Support

What are your favorite cold foods and hot foods? Have children make a list of each. Sample answers: cold foods: ice cream, potato salad, juice; hot foods: soup, cocoa, mashed potatoes, steamed broccoli, pizza.

Challenge

How do you make a hot drink cold? Sample answers: put an ice cube in it; put the drink in the freezer.

Develop Science Vocabulary

weight Tell children that weight is the measure of how heavy an object feels. Point out to children that the weight of a heavy object can make it difficult to pick up. Demonstrate by trying to pick up a desk. Explain that the weight of a light object makes it easy to pick up. Demonstrate by holding up a crayon. Explain to children that they cannot determine weight based on the size of an object. Some large objects such as a balloon are light. Some small objects such as a rock may be heavy.

temperature Write the word on the board and help children break it into syllables so they can read it more easily. Explain to children that temperature is the measure of how hot or cold something is.

Develop Inquiry Skills

INFER **You have a basketball and a small rubber bouncy ball. You throw both of them. Which do you think will travel farther? Explain.** The small ball will travel farther, because it weighs less and is easier to throw.

When is the temperature usually colder, in the early afternoon or late at night? Explain. It's colder late at night; at night the sun does not warm the air. The temperature goes down, and the air feels cooler.

Notebook Summarize Ideas

Have children look at the photographs again. Ask them to think about the information presented in these visuals and then summarize the main idea about weight and the main idea about temperature orally or in writing.

2 Explain (continued)

Notebook Generate Ideas

Read the title of the page aloud with children and ask them to look at the photographs. Ask children to share experiences they have had in a bathtub or swimming pool with objects that sink or float. Discuss with children the properties of the objects that were able to float and compare them to the properties of the objects that sank.

Develop Science Concepts

How is the shape of the clay boat different from the shape of the clay ball? The boat has a long flat bottom and is spread out. The ball is round and solid.

How might knowing an object's shape help you predict if an object will sink or float? The shape of an object affects whether it will float or sink. An object that is flat might float better.

Suppose the clay boat had a heavy rock attached to it by a rope. What do you think might happen to the boat? The rock would sink and might pull the boat under the water too.

Misconception Alert

Children may assume that heavy objects sink and light objects float. Point out that some very heavy objects, such as big ships, float while light things, such as grains of sand, can be found at the bottom of the ocean. Remind them that an object's shape is one property that helps it sink or float whatever its weight.

Why It Matters

Will It Sink or Will It Float?

Think about things in a tub or a pool. A sponge may stay on top of the water. A bar of soap may go to the bottom.

An object that floats stays on top of a liquid. An object that sinks falls to the bottom.

▶ **Circle what floats. Draw an X on what sinks.**

96

Writing Connection

TEKS ELA 1.24C

Write Fact Cards Direct children to make properties of matter cards for four of the properties discussed in the lesson. Each card should include the name of the property, such as texture, on one side of the card and phrases or pictures that help them understand its meaning. On the other side, children should write words that can be used to tell about that property, such as *rough, bumpy,* and *smooth*.

How Does That Boat Float?

Look at the clay boat and the clay ball. The ball sinks. The boat floats. Why? The ball and the boat have different shapes. The shape of the boat helps it float. Sometimes changing the shape of something makes it sink or float.

97

TEKS 1.5A

Interpret Visuals

Ask children to compare the clay boat to the real boat.

How are the clay boat and the real boat alike? They both have a similar shape.

How are the clay boat and the real boat different? The clay boat has paper people in it and the real boat is filled with people. They are made of different materials.

Why do you think both boats float? Sample answer: The boats float because of their shape. They have curved bottoms and a shape like a bowl. This shape helps them float on the water.

Do you think changing the shape of the clay boat to a clay ball will make it sink? Yes, because when the clay is in the shape of a boat it has a long flat bottom and is spread out so it floats. When you change the shape of the clay boat into a ball then it is round and solid so it sinks.

Develop Inquiry Skills

INFER **How might an object that floats help a person who is swimming?** Sample answer: A swimmer can use a floating object to stay on top of the water.

How might an object that sinks help someone explore the bottom of the ocean? Someone exploring the bottom of the ocean could hold onto an object that sinks so it would be easier to stay under the water.

Notebook Summarize Ideas

Have children look again at the photographs on these pages. Have them think about the information presented in these visuals to understand why boats float. Ask them to summarize the main idea orally, in a drawing, or in writing.

3 Extend/Evaluate

Sum It Up!

1. **Choose It!** Before children complete the activity, draw a square, a circle, and a triangle on the board. Ask children to name the shapes and label the drawings as you review. As you read the directions with children, refer to the drawings when they say a shape name.
2. **Mark It!** Tell children to look closely at the visuals to compare their sizes. Ask children to underline the size word in the directions.
3. **Write It!** Suggest that children go back to the second spread in the lesson to review the information about texture if needed.

Sum It Up!

1 Choose It!

Classify the objects. Circle each blue shape. Draw an X on each square. Underline each big circle.

2 Mark It!

Draw an X on the small dog.

3 Write It!

Is this toy soft or hard? Write the word.

soft

98

Brain Check

Lesson 1

Name ______________________

Word Play

Write the word from the box for each clue.

property	weight	texture	temperature

the measure of how hot or cold something is

t e (m 1) p e r (a 2) t u r e

the way something feels

(t 3) e x (t 4) u r e

the measure of how heavy something feels

w (e 5) i g h t

a part of what something is like

p r o p e (r 6) t y

Solve the riddle. Write the circled letters in order on the lines below.

I am anything that takes up space.

What am I? m a t t e r (1 2 3 4 5 6)

99

Answer Strategies

Word Play

- If children have difficulty matching the correct word to its definition, provide examples to help them. For example, to give a hint for *property*, say "You can tell what something is like from its size, shape, color, or texture." Encourage children to refer to the pages where the words are defined.
- Before children look at the circled letters, ask them whether they know the answer to the riddle. Have them write the answer below the numbers and then check their answer by writing the circled letters in order. Then ask children to provide examples of matter.

Assessment

Lesson Quiz

See Assessment Guide, p. AG 46.

3 Extend/Evaluate (continued)

Answer Strategies

Apply Concepts

- Make sure that children know how to fill in a Venn diagram. Review that the center section shows where two objects are the same.
- Discuss with children what they know about objects that sink and float. Encourage them to look back at the lesson pages to review sinking and floating.
- Ask children to share what they know about temperature. Then ask volunteers to explain how they know whether something is hot or cold.

Take It Home!

Suggest that children work with family members to describe the properties of matter for several objects in their homes. Children should then classify the objects according to their properties and then report back to the class with a visual presentation. Have children discuss the properties they used to classify the objects, such as size, shape, color, texture, and weight.

Apply Concepts

1. Classify these shapes by their properties. Draw each one in the diagram.

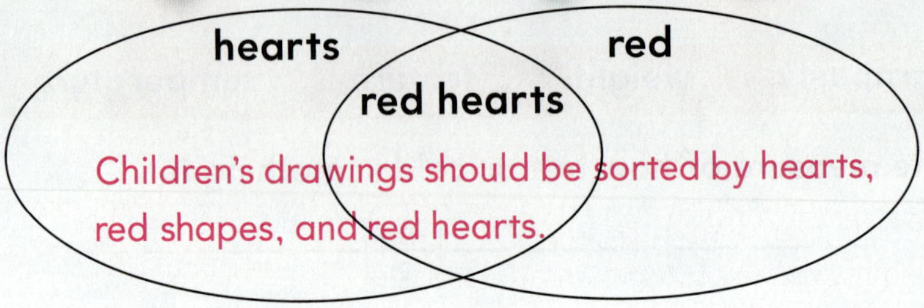

2. Circle each thing that floats.

Draw an X on each thing that sinks.

3. Name or draw something hot. Sample answer: hot dog

Name or draw something cold. Sample answer: ice

Take It Home! **Family Members:** Ask your child to tell you about the properties of matter. Point out objects at home. Have your child classify the objects by their properties.

Make Connections

Easy

Physical Education Connection

TEKS PE 1.7A

Weightlifting

- Explain that some people lift weights as a form of exercise. To demonstrate why, provide two hand weights (1 pound per weight) or small objects that can be used in place of weights, such as a water-filled milk container or a heavy book.
- Have children take turns lifting each "weight" off the ground a few times, being careful to lift with both hands and keep back straight while bending at the waist. Have them tell which body parts they exercised as they did this.

Easy

Art Connection

TEKS ART 1.2C

Make Soft Collages

- Discuss why clothing is made with matter that has a soft texture. Provide soft fabric scraps for children to use to make collages.
- Tell them to use different-colored fabrics and to cut the pieces into different shapes and sizes. Then ask children to describe their collages.

Average

Writing Connection

TEKS ELA 1.24C

Illustrate Sentences

- Have children name two objects that float and two that sink. Ask them to draw the objects on or under water. Have them write a sentence about each object; for example: *The boat floats on the water. The shell sinks to the bottom.*
- Ask children to share their work with the class.

Challenging

Math Connection

TEKS MATH 1.1C

Sort and Order

- Provide groups with buttons of different colors, sizes, textures, and number of buttonholes. Have each group choose a way to sort the buttons by a physical property.
- After the groups finish sorting, they should count the number of buttons in each category and order their totals from least to greatest.
- Members of each group should present their sorting criterion and their ordered results to the class.

Careers in Science

Objectives

- Describe what scientists do.
- Realize that scientists come from all backgrounds.
- Identify the role of technology in the work of scientists.

Notebook Generate Ideas

Hold up a plastic bottle and ask children to describe its properties. Prompt them to tell what the bottle is made of—plastic. Then read the title "Ask a Polymer [PAHL•uh•mer] Scientist" aloud with children. Ask children what they think a polymer is and what the plastic container might have to do with this scientist. Discuss the following information with the class and then read these pages aloud to them.

Background

- One of the first people to experiment with polymers was Charles Goodyear. As early as 1839, he experimented with natural rubber from latex, which he found in sap from tropical trees. His discovery has made it possible for vehicles to travel on vulcanized rubber tires.
- In the early 1900s, Leo Baekeland experimented with polymers and invented plastics. He developed a plastic that he called Bakelite. It was used first on telephones, radios, furniture, and cars. Today, plastics are used almost everywhere.
- Protein in foods such as milk and cheese and starch in foods such as potatoes and pasta are polymers.
- Other examples of things made from polymers are tires, plastic bottles, glue, foam cups, and gum.
- Some polymers can be recycled easily. Milk jugs, for example, can be recycled into objects such as fences, pens, and benches.

TEKS 1.3C describe what scientists do

Careers in Science

Ask a Polymer Scientist

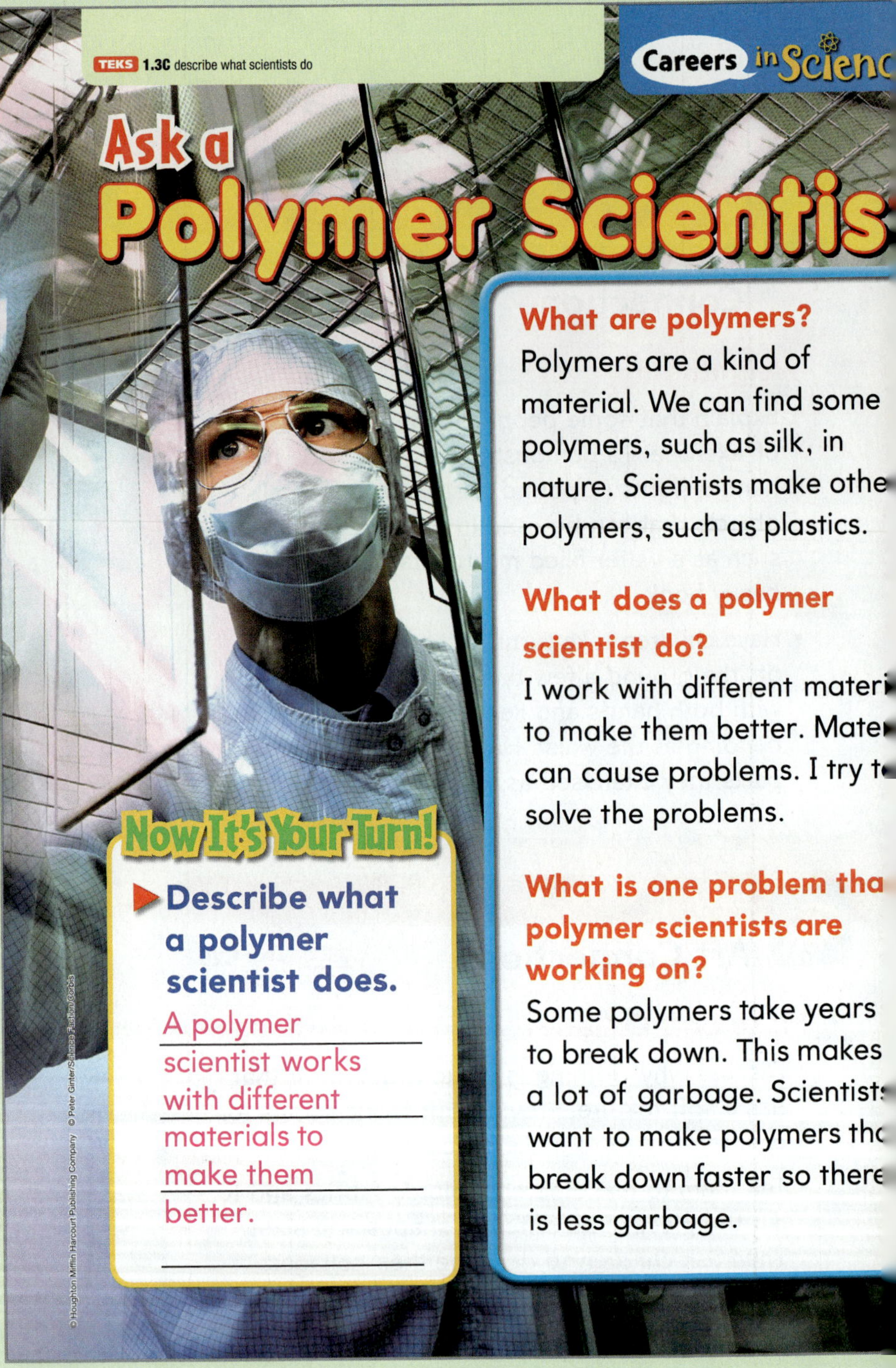

What are polymers?
Polymers are a kind of material. We can find some polymers, such as silk, in nature. Scientists make other polymers, such as plastics.

What does a polymer scientist do?
I work with different materials to make them better. Materials can cause problems. I try to solve the problems.

What is one problem that polymer scientists are working on?
Some polymers take years to break down. This makes a lot of garbage. Scientists want to make polymers that break down faster so there is less garbage.

Now It's Your Turn!

▶ **Describe what a polymer scientist does.**

A polymer scientist works with different materials to make them better.

Writing Connection

TEKS ELA 1.19C

Write to Persuade Explain to children that sometimes they write to persuade other people to share their ideas or opinions. Then discuss what a polymer scientist does, and ask children if they think it is an important job. Have them draw pictures and use simple text to explain their ideas about the importance of a polymer scientist. Have children share their drawings and sentences in small groups.

Polymer Play

Think about what a polymer scientist studies. Make a list of polymers on the lines below.

1. rubber
2. plastic
3. foam
4. Accept all reasonable answers.

rubber ball

foam peanuts

plastic toy

plastic bags

Fun Fact

A lobster's shell is a polymer.

Nature of Science

Provide the following scenario: You want to make a better polymer, but first you have to find out what polymers are like. Ask children to choose a polymer they want to improve. Tell them to think about its properties such as size, texture, and so on. Then have them tell three questions to which they would need to find answers to improve the polymer. Sample questions: How strong is it? How much will it stretch before it breaks? How hard is it to scratch? What happens if it gets hot or cold? Can I see through it?

Develop Science Concepts

What are two properties of polymers? Sample answer: They are strong. They may take years to break down.

Describe what a polymer scientist does. Sample answer: A polymer scientist works with different materials to make them better.

What do you find most interesting about polymers? Sample answer: that they appear in nature and are human-made

Write a question to ask a polymer scientist. Sample answer: How do you become a polymer scientist?

Develop Inquiry Skills

INFER **What inquiry skills do you think polymer scientists use to identify a problem?** Sample answer: observe, infer, and communicate

What steps do you think they most likely take to solve a problem? Sample answer: hypothesize, use models, experiment, and draw conclusions

How do you think making polymers that break down faster will help people now and in the future? Sample answer: There will be less garbage in landfills. People will be able to recycle more. It will help the environment.

Notebook Summarize Ideas

Children can use photographs and what they have learned about a polymer scientist to list polymers. Direct children to think about the information presented on these pages and then summarize the main idea orally or in writing.

Guided Inquiry

FLIPCHART P. 16

45 minutes

pairs

Children should follow the directions on the Flipchart. The accompanying Lesson Inquiry pages in the Student Edition provide scaffolding for guided inquiry.

Inquiry Skills Focus Measure

Objectives

- Ask questions about objects and events observed in the world.
- Plan and conduct simple descriptive investigations.
- Collect and compare information and make observations using thermometers. Record and organize data.
- Identify changes in materials caused by heating.

Prep and Planning Tips

See the Planning for Inquiry page for more information.

- Cut sheets of black and white construction paper in half. Then fold each piece in half lengthwise and staple it on three sides to form a pocket for each pair of children.
- Review with children how to read the temperature. After children record the beginning temperature, have them wait 30 minutes before they record new data.

Caution! Tell children not to put thermometers in their mouths.

Expected Outcomes

Children should find that the thermometer in or under dark paper gets warmer than the one in or under light paper.

1 Engage/Explore

Attention Grabber

Collect 10 or 12 pictures of hot and cold foods and other items, such as cookies out of the oven, an ice cream cone, a snowman, and a campfire. Gather children around a table and present the pictures. Have children sort and classify the pictures by temperature. Children should understand that the groups show objects that are hot or cold. Large yarn circles or pieces of poster board can be used to collect the pictures in each group.

Preview Activity

Before beginning the investigation, have children review the directions on the Inquiry Flipchart and the accompanying Student Edition response pages. Then have them complete the response pages as they follow directions on the Flipchart.

Inquiry Flipchart p. 16

Lesson 2
INQUIRY

TEKS 1.2A Ask questions about organisms, objects, and events observed in the natural world **1.2B** plan and conduct simple descriptive investigations such as ways objects move **1.2D** record and organize data using pictures, numbers, and words **1.5B** predict and identify changes in materials caused by heating and cooling such as ice melting, water freezing, and water evaporating

Name ______________________

Essential Question

How Can We Measure Temperature?

Set a Purpose

Tell what you will find out.

I will find out whether light colors or dark colors warm up faster.

Think About the Procedure

1. How will you test whether light colors or dark colors warm up faster?

I will put thermometers under light paper and dark paper and see which warms up faster.

2. How do you know which color warms up faster?

I will read the temperatures on the thermometers. I know that the higher the liquid in the thermometer, the warmer it is.

103

Go Digital

A virtual lab experience is available with the Online Resources for this program.

1 Engage/Explore (continued)

Guide the Investigation

Develop Inquiry Skills

MEASURE Remind children that when they measure, they find the size, weight, or amount of something. They will often use a tool to measure. The measurement will often be a number with a unit of measure, like inches or pounds.

What tool do you use to measure temperature? a thermometer

Why is it a good idea to get an exact number when measuring temperature? Sample answer: Getting an exact number helps us to be accurate and to compare.

When the liquid in a thermometer moves higher, what does that mean? It means that the temperature is getting hotter.

When the liquid in a thermometer moves lower, what does that mean? It means that the temperature is getting cooler.

What do you think might happen if you did not read the measurement on the thermometer correctly? The results of my investigation would not be correct.

2 Explain

Develop Inquiry Skills

RECORD YOUR DATA Discuss with children how they will use the table to record the temperature at the beginning and 30 minutes later for both colors of paper. Children may choose to write the temperature in degrees, or they may want to draw a picture of the thermometers with the accurate temperature at both times.

DRAW CONCLUSIONS Ask children to communicate which thermometer had a higher ending temperature—the one used to measure the temperature of the black paper or the white paper. Ask children how much higher the temperature of the black paper was than the white paper.

Continue the discussion by asking children why people usually wear light-colored clothing in summer and dark-colored clothing in winter. Help them understand that dark colors absorb light so they are warmer and light colors reflect light so they are cooler.

3 Extend/Evaluate

ASK MORE QUESTIONS

Discuss children's responses to the items. Some children may raise questions about whether the temperature is cooler in the shade than in the sun and how other materials might affect temperature. As an extension activity, encourage children to plan investigations or research the answers to their questions.

Assessment

Lesson Quiz

See Assessment Guide, p. AG 47.

Record Your Data

In this chart, record the temperature at the beginning and the temperature after 30 minutes. Compare them.

Color	Beginning Temperature	Temperature After 30 Minutes
White		
Black		

Draw Conclusions

Do light colors or dark colors warm up faster?

Dark colors warm up faster.

Ask More Questions

What other questions about temperature could you ask?

Sample answers: Is the temperature in the sun warmer than the temperature in the shade? Would foil warm up faster than dark colors?

104

Differentiated Inquiry

Easy

Measure Temperature

- Provide groups with a thermometer and two plastic cups. Have them fill one cup with ice water and one with warm water.
- Ask them to put the thermometer in the warm water and observe until the liquid stops moving. Have them record the temperature and how it changed. Children can draw a thermometer with an arrow showing the direction the liquid moved.
- Make sure that children reset the thermometer to room temperature. Then have groups repeat for the ice water. Children should draw conclusions, such as the higher numbers mean higher temperatures or more heat and lower numbers mean lower temperatures or less heat.

Average

Find Changes in Temperature

- Have children measure the temperature of a cup of water, then add ice to it and measure the temperature again. Ask them to find the difference in temperature.
- Challenge children to find the difference in temperature between two locations or other liquids. Allow them to choose the temperatures to compare, and then present their findings.

Challenging

Compare Indoor and Outdoor Temperatures

- Tell partners they are going to measure temperature in two places inside the school, such as the media center and cafeteria, and two places outside the school, such as the playground and front entrance. Each pair will measure the same places. Have children predict the warmer areas.
- Partners can then measure the temperature in each place and record it.
- Partners should graph their results and compare them with those of another pair.

Challenging

Compare Materials

- Provide groups with metal, plastic, and wooden long-handled spoons and a container of very warm water. Caution children not to touch the water.
- Have children put the spoons in the water for 5 minutes. After that time, they should touch the handles, compare how warm they are, and record their results in writing.
- Ask children to draw conclusions; for example, the metal spoon allows heat to travel so its handle feels hot. Wood and plastic do not get as warm as metal. Ask groups to compare results and recognize that if different people do the same experiment they should get similar results.

Options for Inquiry

FLIPCHART P. 17

Children can conduct these optional investigations at any time before, during, or in response to the lesson in the Student Edition.

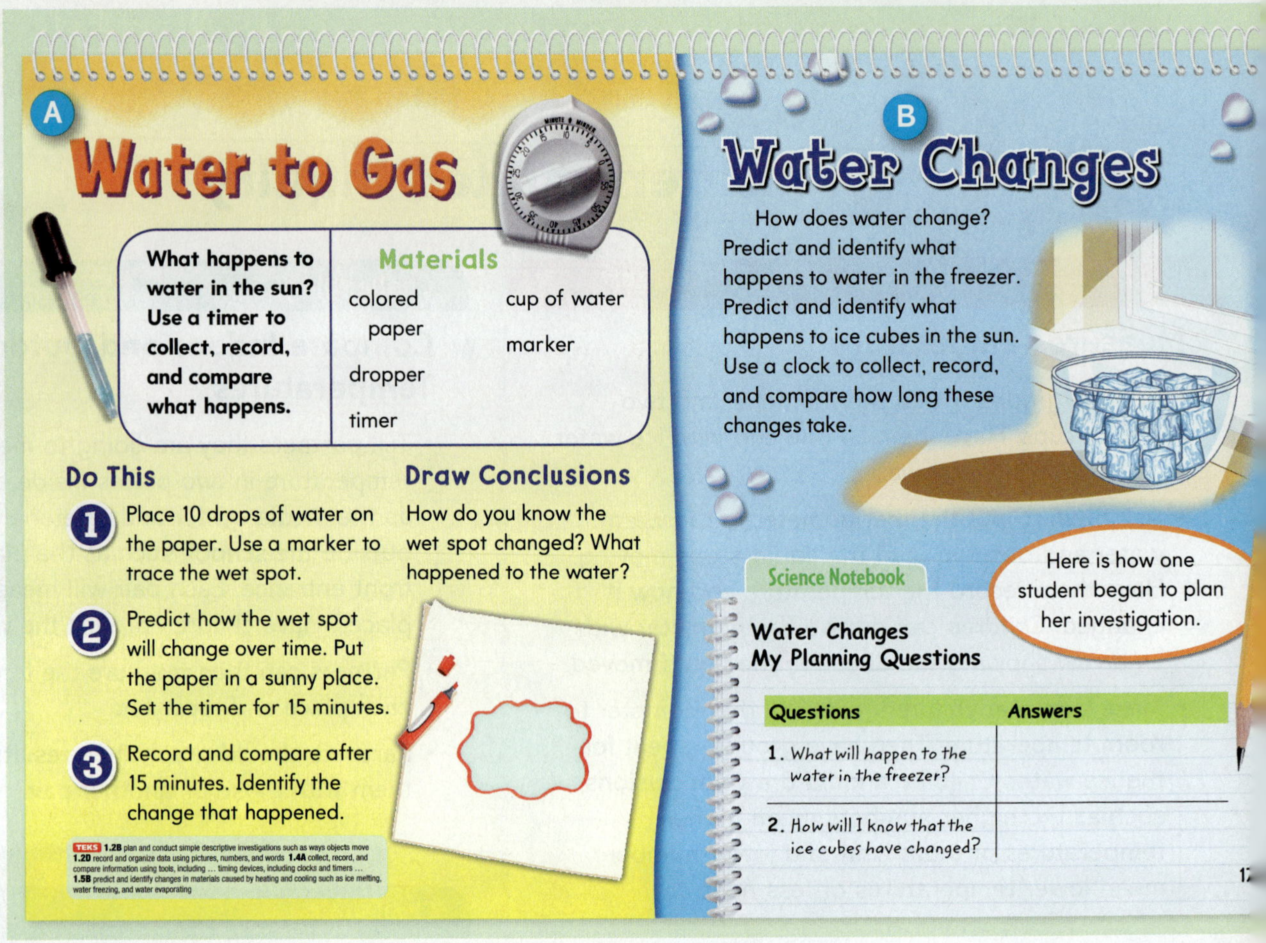

Directed Inquiry

A Water to Gas

25–30 minutes
pairs

Prep and Planning Tips

Locate a sunny location to place children's papers. Provide a small cup of water for each pair. Model how to fill the dropper with water. Demonstrate how to drop the water in one spot, in the middle of the paper, to make one large water spot that children can trace.

Show children how to set the timer by turning the dial so that the point lines up with 15.

Children can use their Science Notebooks to record and organize their information.

Expected Results

Children will predict and identify the changed that happened. They should notice that the wet spot got smaller. Guide them to conclude that heat from the sun caused the water to evaporate.

Independent Inquiry

B Water Changes

30 minutes
small groups

Prep and Planning Tips

See the Planning for Inquiry page for more information. Have ice cubes available ahead of time for children to use. Use small cups of water for the first part of the investigation. This will ensure that the water will fully freeze during the course of the activity.

Science Notebook

Children can use the Science Notebook page shown on the Flipchart as a model for planning and conducting their own investigation. Children should include questions for both parts of the investigation. Encourage them to think about tools, such as clocks or timers, that help them collect, record, and compare information. Have them record two sets of answers for any predictions: what they think will happen and what actually happened.

TEKS 1.5B predict and identify changes in materials caused by heating and cooling such as ice melting, water freezing, and water evaporating

Lesson 3

Essential Question

How Does Heating and Cooling Change Matter?

Engage Your Brain!

Find the answer to the question in the lesson.

How does water turn to ice?

It ___freezes___.

Active Reading

Lesson Vocabulary

1. Preview the lesson.
2. Write the 4 vocabulary terms here.

freeze	evaporate
melt	condense

Inquiry Flipchart p. 17—Water to Gas/Water Changes

105

Go Digital

An interactive digital lesson is available in Online Resources. It is suitable for individuals, small groups, or may be projected or used on an interactive white board.

1 Engage/Explore

Objectives

- Plan and conduct simple investigations.
- Collect, record, and compare information using timing devices, such as clocks and timers.
- Record and organize data using pictures and words.
- Predict and identify changes in materials caused by heating and cooling.

Engage Your Brain!

Explain that the photograph shows a figure carved out of ice. Point out that the ice sculpture is like a giant ice cube. Help children answer the question *How does water turn to ice?* by asking them to share experiences they may have had making ice cubes. Ask them how they think the water turned into ice. Record their ideas.

Remind children to record their final answer to the question when they find it on the second and third pages of the lesson.

Active Reading Annotations

Remind children that active readers "make texts their own" by marking them or writing notes to help them understand what they are reading. Encourage children to use pencil to make annotations and to feel free to change their marks and notes as they read. The goal of annotation is to help children remember what they have read.

Vocabulary and Interactive Glossary

Remind children to find and list the yellow highlighted terms from the lesson. As they proceed through the lesson and learn about the terms, they can add drawings or words in the extra spaces provided in some entries in the Interactive Glossary.

2 Explain

Notebook Generate Ideas

Have children look at the two photographs on this page. Explain that they show the same lake during summer and winter. Ask children to describe the lake in each photograph, noting the changes they see.

Active Reading Vocabulary

Explain that a vocabulary word may be highlighted in a color. Active readers pay attention to highlighted words because their meaning is given in the same sentence or the next sentence.

Develop Science Vocabulary

freeze Tell children that in science *freeze* means to change from a liquid to a solid. Explain that when the word *freeze* is used in everyday language, it has other meanings, such as "to stop moving suddenly" or "get very cold." You may wish to explain all three meanings using sentences such as: "Let's freeze (stand completely still) in place." "In winter the water in this lake will freeze (change from a liquid to a solid)." "In winter I wear warm boots so my feet will not freeze (get very cold)."

Develop Inquiry Skills

INFER Remind children that when they infer, they use what they already know to draw a conclusion about a new image or concept.

How can you tell that it is very cold in the second picture? There is snow and ice. The lake is frozen.

Identify how the lake changed. It changed from a liquid to a solid. **What caused the lake to become a solid?** The lake lost heat, which caused it to freeze.

Freeze in Place

Cooling changes water. Taking away heat makes water freeze. **Freeze** means to change from a liquid to a solid. Water freezes into ice. Other liquids, such as juice, can freeze, too.

Active Reading

Find the sentence that tells the meaning of **freeze**. Draw a line under the sentence.

1

2

A lake can freeze into ice.

106

English Language Learners

ELPS 1E, 1F, 2E

Children may have trouble distinguishing between the meaning of the verb *freeze* and the adjective *freezing*. Pantomime shaking and hugging your body to indicate that you are cold.

Explain that when you say, "I am freezing," it means you feel very cold. Point to the photograph of the frozen lake, and explain that *freeze* also describes what happens when a liquid (water) turns into a solid (ice).

The water turns to ice.
Ice is solid and cold.

Water is a liquid.
Water loses heat when it goes into a cold place.

▶ **Identify what happens to water when it is cooled.**

It freezes.

107

Differentiation—Leveled Questions

Extra Support

What happens when you cool water? It loses heat and can freeze and become a solid.

Challenge

Look at the pictures. Why did the water that turned to ice come out in a shape? Children should infer that when water freezes, it takes the shape of the mold into which it was poured.

TEKS 1.5B

Interpret Visuals

Draw attention to how the girl handles the water in each photograph. Use the following questions to move children toward identifying how cooling causes the water to lose heat, and completing the interactivity.

How does the girl get the water into the molds? She pours it. **How does the water move?** It flows. **Time passes between the first picture and the second picture. During this time, the water goes into a freezer. What happens to the water in the freezer?** It loses heat and freezes. **Now look at the water that has frozen into ice. Why can't it pour like it did before?** It is a solid. **What words could you use to describe the ice in the second picture?** Sample answers: solid, cold

Develop Inquiry Skills

COMPARE Remind children that when they compare, they tell how things are alike. **What does it feel like inside a freezer?** very cold

How is winter weather like the air inside a freezer? They are both cold.

What is the same about how water cools in the freezer and in the winter weather? Water loses heat in the freezer and in winter weather. Losing heat makes water freeze and turn into ice in both places.

Develop Science Concepts

Predict what would happen to water left outside on a cold winter day. I think it would lose heat and freeze into ice.

Notebook Summarize Ideas

Have children summarize orally or in writing the main ideas of these two pages. They should be able to predict and identify changes in materials caused by cooling.

2 Explain (continued)

Notebook Generate Ideas

Ask children if they have ever eaten an ice pop outside on a hot day. Ask them to describe how the heat changed their cold treat and discuss why it changed.

Develop Science Vocabulary

melt Explain that *melt* and *freeze* are antonyms, or opposites. When an object freezes, it changes from a liquid to a solid. When it melts, it changes from a solid to a liquid. Write the words *liquid* and *solid* on the board. Draw an arrow from the word *liquid* to the word *solid* and label the diagram *freeze*. Then have children repeat for the word *melt*.

Develop Science Concepts

Identify what happens to ice when heat is added to it. The ice melts and turns from a solid to a liquid.

How might the ice look while it is still melting? The cubes will get smaller. There will be more and more liquid water.

Besides ice cubes, what other solid things might melt in the sun? ice pops, snow

Interpret Visuals

Make clear to children that the two pictures show the same glass of water, before and after it spends some time in the sun.

What will happen to the ice in the first glass when heat is added? It will change from a solid to a liquid. **Why can't you see ice cubes in the second glass?** They melted.

What shape did the water have when it was frozen? It was shaped like cubes. **How is the water in the second glass different from the ice in the first glass?** The ice was solid. The water is liquid and you can pour it.

Melt Away

Heat from the sun warms ice. Then what? The ice melts! **Melt** means to change from a solid to a liquid. Ice melts and changes into water. Other solids melt when heated, too.

1 The ice is still frozen.

2 Heat melts the ice.

108

Differentiation—Leveled Questions

Extra Support

What makes ice cubes melt? adding heat

Challenge

How are melting and freezing water alike? Sample answer: In both melting and freezing, water changes form.

1

What happens when crayons are left out in the sun?

2

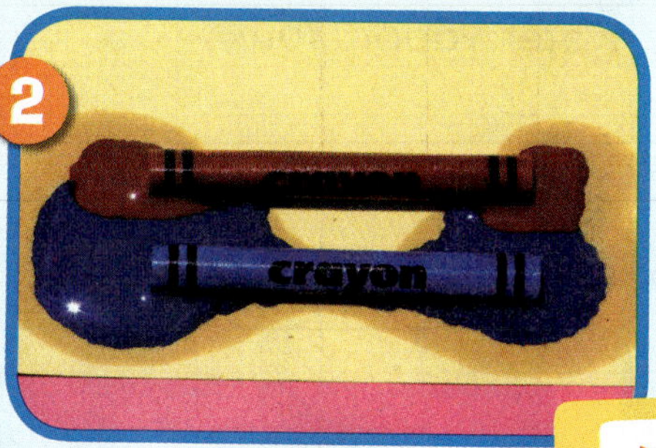

Heat from the sun melts them. They become a liquid.

1

2

▶ What will happen to ice cream left in the sun? Draw to predict it!

Childen's drawings should show melted ice cream.

109

3 **Math Connection** TEKS MATH 1.1A

Compare Times On a chart or the board, draw an ice cream cone, an ice cube, and a large block of ice. Label the ice cream *5 minutes*, the ice cube *15 minutes*, and the block of ice *30 minutes*. Explain that the labels show how long it might take each object to melt. Ask children questions such as: *Which object took the longest to melt?* (block of ice) *Which object melted the fastest?* (ice cream) *How much longer did it take the ice cube to melt than the ice cream?* (10 minutes)

TEKS 1.5B

Develop Science Concepts

Use the following questions to help children identify how heat causes materials, such as frozen ice cream, to change and then use this information to complete the interactivity.

Look at the ice cream. Is it a solid or a liquid? It is a solid. **How do you know?** Sample answers: It has its own shape. It is standing up in the cone. Nothing is dripping down the sides of the cone.

Think about what the sun did to the ice and the crayons. What do you predict will happen to the ice cream in the sun? Sample answer: I predicted that the ice cream would melt like the crayons and the ice did.

How will the ice cream look after it melts? It will be a liquid. It will lose its shape. It will look like a puddle.

Develop Inquiry Skills

Have children look closely at the two pictures on this page. Point out that in the first picture, the crayons are solid and have a shape, and that in the second picture, the crayons changed but the paper wrappers did not.

INFER **Why did the crayons change from solid to liquid?** They were left in the sun. The heat from the sun melted them.

Why didn't the paper wrappers change? Heat from the sun wasn't strong enough to cause the paper wrappers to melt.

Notebook Summarize Ideas

Ask children to summarize orally or in writing the main ideas of these two pages. They should be able to predict and identify changes in materials caused by heating, such as objects that melt, or change from a solid to a liquid.

2 Explain (continued)

Generate Ideas

Notebook

Have children tell what happens when they hang a wet towel to dry. Draw their attention to the page heading. Explain that when the towel dries, the water goes "up in the air."

Develop Science Vocabulary

evaporate Help children pronounce the word *evaporate* and allow time for them to practice saying and writing it. Explain that *evaporate* means to change from a liquid to a gas.

condense Point out that *evaporate* and *condense* are antonyms, or opposites. Guide them to understand that the terms are antonyms because *evaporate* means to change from a liquid to a gas and *condense* means to change from a gas to a liquid.

Develop Science Concepts

What happened to the puddle? The water evaporated. It changed from a liquid to a gas.

Why can't we see the water anymore? The water turned into a gas, which we cannot see.

Develop Inquiry Skills

PREDICT Remind children that to predict is to tell what they think will happen. **What do you think will happen to the water in the footprints?** The water will evaporate. **Why?** Heat from the sun will turn the water into a gas.

Misconception Alert

Children might think that when puddles disappear, they soak into the ground. That can happen to some extent, but most of the water evaporates. Remind them that when they hang a towel to dry, it is not on the ground. The water must evaporate.

Up in the Air

Water dries. Where does it go? It evaporates. **Evaporate** means to change from a liquid to a gas. The more heat you add, the faster the water will evaporate. Water in the air is called water vapor. You can not see it.

1 **The puddle is liquid.**

2 **Heat turns the puddle into a gas.**

▶ Predict what will happen to the water in these footprints in the sun.

The water in the footprints will evaporate.

110

English Language Learners

ELPS **1E, 1F, 2E**

Children may have trouble understanding the scientific meaning of the word *gas*. Explain that in everyday use, the word *gas* refers to a liquid that people use as fuel for their cars. Explain that *gas* also names a state of matter that we cannot see.

Use *gas* in two sentences to show the two meanings. Then have children use *gas* in their own sentences to demonstrate their understanding of its meanings.

Cool It!

What happens when water vapor cools? Cooling makes water vapor condense into water. **Condense** means to change from a gas to a liquid.

Active Reading

An effect tells what happens. Draw two lines under an effect.

Water vapor condenses into water on the mirror.

111

Writing Connection

TEKS ELA 1.6A, 1.20A

Write Using Key Terms

Display a word bank with the words *freeze, melt, evaporate*, and *condense*. Have children use each word to complete one of these sentence frames: *Ice cubes ___ in the sun. Heat makes water ___. Some lakes ___ in winter. Cool air makes water ___.* After children complete each sentence, have them choose a word and use it to write their own sentence.

Active Reading **Effect**

Point out that sometimes one thing happens *because* something else happens. What happens is the effect. To find an effect, active readers ask themselves, What happened? The answer will be the effect.

Develop Science Concepts

Have children look at the bathroom mirror. **What is covering the mirror?** drops of water **Where did the drops come from?** Water vapor in the air cooled into liquid drops of water on the mirror. **What is water vapor?** water in the form of a gas **Identify the change that happened.** The water condensed, or changed from a gas to a liquid.

Misconception Alert

Children might have difficulty understanding that water in the form of a gas is part of the air around them, since they cannot see it. Point out that children can feel it as humidity or see it indirectly after it cools on a mirror or forms dew on morning grass.

Develop Inquiry Skills

COMPARE **How is melting like evaporating?** Both changes happen when heat is added. **How is freezing like condensing?** Both changes happen when heat is lost or taken away. **How is freezing like evaporating?** Both change water or other kinds of matter to a different state.

Notebook Summarize Ideas

Ask children to summarize orally or in writing what causes water to evaporate and condense and what happens when it does. They should be able to predict and identify changes in materials caused by heating and cooling.

3 Extend/Evaluate

Sum It Up!

1. **Mark It!** Before children complete the activity, ask them to think about how heat from the sun affects a puddle of water. After you read the directions with children, emphasize that they are using an X to mark their answer choice, not to cross out the wrong answer.
2. **Circle It!** Suggest that children go back to the lesson and look at the pictures of the frozen lake and the ice cubes. As necessary, review the meaning of *frozen*.
3. **Draw It!** Encourage partners to brainstorm a list of things that can melt before children choose something to draw for this activity.

Sum It Up!

1 Mark It!

Predict which one will evaporate faster. Mark it with an X.

2 Circle It!

Identify which one is frozen. Circle it.

3 Draw It!

Draw an object before and after it melts.

Before	After

Check that children have drawn an object before and after it melts.

112

Brain Check

Lesson 3

Name ______________________

Word Play

Write the word that describes the underlined words in each sentence.

melt   freeze   evaporate   condense

1. Heating makes a solid turn into a liquid. melt
2. Heating makes a liquid turn into a gas. evaporate
3. Cooling makes a liquid turn into a solid. freeze
4. Cooling makes a gas turn into a liquid. condense

113

TEKS 1.5B

Answer Strategies

Word Play

- If children have difficulty matching the correct word to its definition, provide questions or sentence frames to help them. For example, for *melt*, say "When ice cubes are left in the sun, they do this."
- Encourage children to refer back to the pages where the words are defined for additional ways to figure out the meanings.

Assessment

Lesson Quiz

See Assessment Guide, p. AG 48.

3 Extend/Evaluate (continued)

Answer Strategies

Apply Concepts

- Be sure children understand the meaning of the word *effect*. Explain that sometimes one thing happens *because* something else happens. What happens is the effect.
- Model how to read the sentence in the first box and then ask, *What happened?* Tell children that the answer will be the effect.
- Work together to identify the answer in the first row of the chart. Then have children complete the chart in pairs or individually. If children have difficulty, you can make a word box with the answers to aid them.

Take It Home!

Draw on the board a three-column chart with the headings *Freeze, Melt,* and *Evaporate* for children to copy and share at home with family members. Encourage them to bring their completed charts to class to share with partners or small groups. Suggest that children start their home search in the kitchen and work from there to other parts of the home.

Apply Concepts

Identify the change that happened. Write the missing word for each effect.

Cause	Effect
Gas is cooled.	It condenses into a liquid.
Water is heated.	It evaporates into a gas.
Water is cooled.	It freezes into a solid.
Ice is heated.	It melts into water.

Take It Home!

Family Members: Work with your child to identify foods, liquids, and other materials in your home that can freeze, melt, and evaporate.

114

Guide the Activity

Develop Inquiry Skills

USE NUMBERS Poll children to find out their favorite kinds of sandwiches. Have children help you tally the votes for each kind.

SEQUENCE Have children list the ingredients for making their sandwiches. Have them visualize each step of the process as they write their directions. Ask: **Do you need an adult helper for any of your steps?**

COMMUNICATE Encourage children to use visuals, such as drawings or photographs, and written steps to tell about their recipes.

Strategies for Success

Before beginning the investigation, have children review the directions on the *Inquiry Flipchart*. If a child is having difficulty, pair him or her with another child who is writing a recipe for the same sandwich. Suggest children list the ingredients first and then pantomime making the sandwich to identify each step. Ask: **Did you forget an ingredient or a tool? Are your steps in order?**

Science Notebook

During the Activity Have children write rough drafts of their recipes and then check that all ingredients are listed and that the steps are in order.

2 Explain

Develop the Engineering Design Process

Use the following steps of the engineering design process to provide context and support for the analyses that children are doing in the flipchart activity.

1. FIND A PROBLEM **Use your own words to identify and explain the problem.** I need to write a recipe for my favorite sandwich. I need to include all the ingredients and tools and write the steps in order.

3. TEST AND IMPROVE **What did you change about your recipe after you tested it?** Sample answers: I decided to use less grape jelly in the recipe; I added a can opener as one of the tools needed.

3 Extend/Evaluate

Quick Check

What is your recipe about? Sample answer: My recipe is a set of steps about how to make a cheese sandwich.

What did you learn about recipes when you tried to write your own? Sample answer: I learned to include every detail. It is easy to forget a small step, tool, or ingredient. You have to say exactly what you mean.

4. REDESIGN Have partners trade recipes and provide feedback that identifies any unclear steps. **How could you rewrite this part to make it easier to understand?** Accept reasonable answers.

5. COMMUNICATE Have children who wrote recipes for the same kind of sandwich compare their recipes. Talk about how the ingredients or steps vary.

Science Notebook

After the Activity Check to see that children have listed all the ingredients, tools, and steps needed to make the sandwich. If they have included any steps that require adult assistance, be sure that a special note is included.

Michael DiSpezio's Tips & Tricks

Guiding the Activity Establish a home connection by having children bring in and share their favorite family recipes. With recipes in hand, review the concepts of ingredients, tools, and steps. To introduce the higher-order skill of sequencing, display the steps to a simple recipe out of order. Challenge children to put the steps in order. Don't overlook the visual nature of food recipes. If appropriate, have children make pictures that illustrate the steps of sandwich building.

Enduring Understandings

Revisit the Big Idea and Essential Questions

Big Idea **All objects are matter. Matter can change in different ways.**

To explore the Big Idea, post the vocabulary words on the board. Then, challenge children to explain how each word relates to the Big Idea. As an additional challenge, ask children to identify ways that the vocabulary words relate to each other.

- matter
- property
- weight
- texture
- temperature
- melt
- freeze
- condense
- evaporate

Essential Questions

Post the Essential Questions, and use the following prompts to guide a discussion.

Lessons/Essential Questions	Prompts
L1 **What Can We Observe About Objects?**	• Pick an object. Name three things you observe about it.
L2 **How Can We Measure Temperature?**	• Show with your hand what happens to the liquid inside a thermometer as the temperature gets warmer.
L3 **How Does Heating and Cooling Change Matter?**	• Describe what happens when you freeze water.

Science Notebook

You may use the following strategies after children complete the unit or after each lesson.

- Have children review and edit the responses to the Essential Questions they drafted at the beginning of the unit. Suggest they cross out sentences or ideas that are unnecessary or inappropriate.
- Have children draw tic-tac-toe boards in their Science Notebooks. Have partners play together, with one partner being "properties of matter" and the other partner being "changes to matter." Ask them to write or draw an example of either a property or a change to matter in a box on each turn. The first player to get three in a row wins.

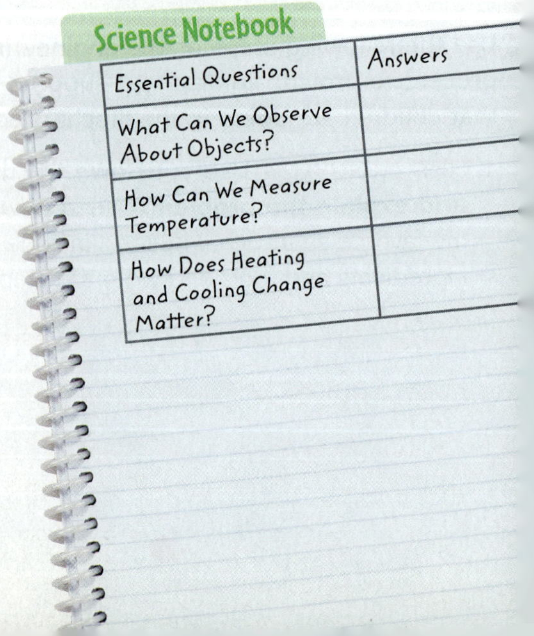

Unit 3 Review

Name ______________________

Vocabulary Review

Use the terms in the box to complete the sentences.

condense
property
texture

TEKS 1.5A

1. One part of what something is like is a property ______________.

TEKS 1.5A

2. You can classify an object by its texture ______________, or how hard or soft it is.

TEKS 1.5B

3. To condense ______________ is to cool and change from a gas to a liquid.

Science Concepts

Fill in the letter of the choice that best answers the question.

TEKS 1.5A

4. How is all matter the **same**?
   - Ⓐ All matter has the same shape.
   - Ⓑ All matter takes up space.
   - Ⓒ All matter is made from natural materials.

TEKS 1.2B, 1.5A

5. John is conducting an investigation. He picks up two objects. One is heavier than the other. How can he classify the objects?
   - Ⓐ by color
   - Ⓑ by shape
   - Ⓒ by weight

Item Analysis

Items	TEKS	Depth of Knowledge	Cognitive Complexity
1	**1.5A**	1	Low
2	**1.5A**	1	Low
3	**1.5B**	1	Low
4	**1.5A**	1	Low
5	**1.2B, 1.5A**	1	Low

Unit Review

Answer Key

Vocabulary Review (5 points each)

1. property

   Have children name properties, such as size, shape, color, and texture.

2. texture

   Display some classroom objects that have different textures. Ask volunteers to touch them and describe how they feel. Make a list of the descriptive words. Reinforce that these words describe texture.

3. condense

   Point out the key phrase *gas to a liquid,* and have children identify the word in the word box that matches that definition.

Science Concepts (7 points each)

4. B

   Set out examples of different kinds of matter for children to observe and compare as they consider the answer choices.

5. C

   Review the answer choices. Then ask, "Does how heavy something feels relate to its color?" Repeat the question, substituting the other answer choices. When children can answer *yes,* they have found the correct answer.

Assessment

Unit 3 Test and Performance Assessment

See Assessment Guide, pp. AG 51–AG 57, for Unit Test and Performance Task with Long Option rubric.

Unit Review *continued*

Answer Key

Science Concepts (7 points each)

6. B

Be sure children read the question carefully and look at the picture to identify that the boy is putting the tray of water in a freezer (a cold place).

7. A

If necessary, rephrase the question: "How are the two groups of rocks sorted?" Or, "What property is different about the two groups of rocks?"

8. B

Review how to read a thermometer and remind children that the cup with the highest temperature is the hottest.

UNIT 3

TEKS 1.2B, 1.5B

6. The boy puts the tray in a cold place. What does he predict will happen to the water in the tray?

Ⓐ It will evaporate.
Ⓑ It will freeze.
Ⓒ It will melt.

TEKS 1.5A

7. How are these rocks classified?

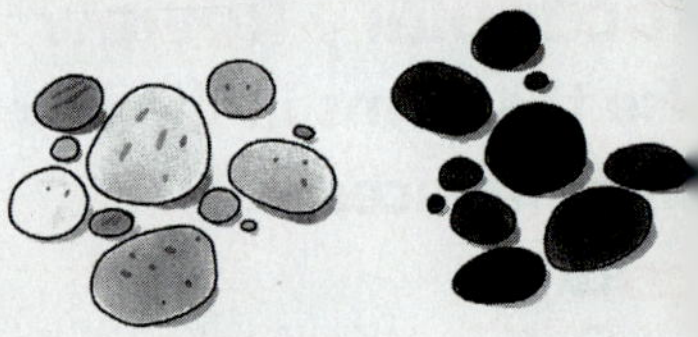

Ⓐ by color
Ⓑ by shape
Ⓒ by size

TEKS 1.4A

8. Use the cups of water and the thermometers to compare temperatures. Which cup has the hottest water?

Ⓐ cup 1
Ⓑ cup 2
Ⓒ cup 3

118 **Unit 3** Unit Review

Item Analysis *(continued)*

Items	TEKS	Depth of Knowledge	Cognitive Complexity
6	**1.2B, 1.5B**	2	Moderate
7	**1.5A**	2	Moderate
8	**1.4A**	2	Moderate

TEKS 1.5B

9. How is the ice cube changing? Identify it.

Ⓐ It is freezing.
Ⓑ It is melting.
Ⓒ It is condensing.

TEKS 1.5A

10. You observe a group of square blocks and a group of round blocks. How are they classified?

Ⓐ by color
Ⓑ by size
Ⓒ by shape

TEKS 1.2B, 1.4A

11. Jin measures the temperature at different times. Compare them. At which time is it coldest?

Time of Day	Temperature
morning	32 °F
afternoon	42 °F
night	25 °F

Ⓐ morning
Ⓑ afternoon
Ⓒ night

TEKS 1.5B

12. A lake freezes into ice. What can you tell about the temperature where the lake is?

Ⓐ It is cold.
Ⓑ It is hot.
Ⓒ It is warm.

Item Analysis *(continued)*

Items	TEKS	Depth of Knowledge	Cognitive Complexity
9	**1.5B**	1	Low
10	**1.5A**	2	Moderate
11	**1.2B, 1.4A**	2	Moderate
12	**1.5B**	2	Moderate

Unit Review *continued*

Answer Key

Science Concepts (7 points each)

9. B

Have children describe the picture. Be sure they identify the ice cube and notice the liquid water at the bottom of the cube.

10. C

Have children name synonyms for *classified,* such as *grouped* or *sorted,* to help them understand this question.

11. C

It might help children to remove the "° F" labels from the temperatures and just compare the numbers.

12. A

Remind children that freezing is when a liquid changes to a solid.

Short Option Performance Assessment

Task

Properties of Matter
Ask each child to choose an item from a paper bag, name the object, and describe its properties. Then, have children classify all of the objects into groups and tell what property they used to classify the objects.

Rubric

Preparation Fill a large brown bag with an assortment of small classroom objects, such as a pencil, paper clip, eraser, and block.

Scoring Rubric—Performance Indicators

___ Accurately identifies the object.
___ Describes the object using its properties.
___ Classifies the objects and identifies the property used to classify.

Observations and Rubric Scores

3 2 1 0

Review *continued*

r Key

and the Big Idea (11 points each)

B; Its thermometer shows a higher temperature.

b. B is on a dark piece of paper. Darker colors absorb more heat and warm up faster than lighter colors.

Have children review how to measure temperature. Draw their attention to the differences in the color of the paper, and reinforce that darker colors absorb more heat than lighter colors.

14. Sample answer: I think the puddle will evaporate, or change from a liquid to a gas. The sun provides heat and heat makes liquids like water change to gas.

Review that there are three forms of matter—solid, liquid, and gas. Remind children that the sun will heat the liquid water in the puddle, and have them discuss what happens to liquid water when it is heated.

UNIT 3

Inquiry and the Big Idea

Write the answers to these questions.

TEKS 1.2B, 1.4A, 1.5B

13. These two cups started with water at 25 °C.

They both stayed in the sun for 30 minutes.

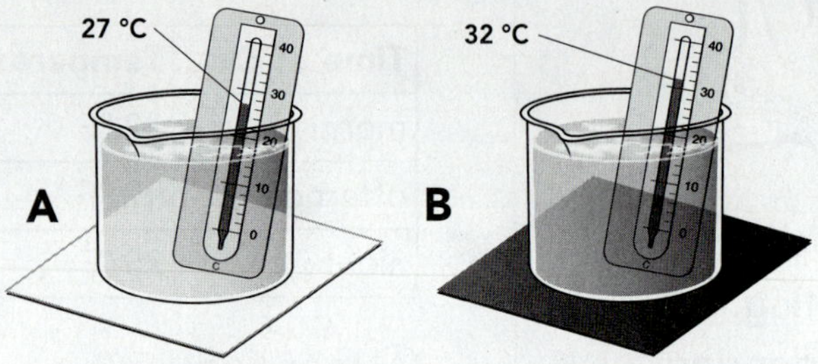

a. Identify the cup of water that heated up more. How can you tell?

B; Its thermometer shows a higher temperature.

b. Why did this happen?

B is on a dark piece of paper. Darker colors absorb more heat and warm up faster than lighter colors.

TEKS 1.5B

14. The sun shines on a puddle. Predict how the puddle will change. Explain.

Sample answer: I think the puddle will evaporate, or change from a liquid to a gas. The sun provides heat and heat makes liquids like water change to gas.

Item Analysis

Items	TEKS	Depth of Knowledge	Cognitive Complexity
13	**1.2B, 1.4A, 1.5B**	3	High
14	**1.5B**	3	High

TEKS 1.6D

10. Which do you move round and round on?

Ⓐ a merry-go-round

Ⓑ a slide

Ⓒ a swing

TEKS 1.6C

11. You can describe how the location of an object changes. How does the ball's location change when the boy throws it?

Ⓐ The ball moves closer to the boy.

Ⓑ The ball moves farther from the boy.

Ⓒ The ball stays in the same place.

TEKS 1.2A, 1.6D

12. What question does the picture answer?

Ⓐ How can a ball move?

Ⓑ Who wins the game?

Ⓒ Is the ball filled with air?

UNIT 4

Item Analysis *(continued)*

Items	TEKS	Depth of Knowledge	Cognitive Complexity
10	**1.6D**	2	Low
11	**1.6C**	2	Low
12	**1.2A, 1.6D**	2	Moderate

Unit Review *continued*

Answer Key

Science Concepts (7 points each)

10. A

Have children demonstrate with their finger what the motion named in the question looks like.

11. B

Children can think about a time when they threw a ball or act out the action using a paper ball or other similar prop.

12. A

Have children first describe what they see in the picture, and then talk about the question in each answer choice to determine if the picture provides enough information to answer it.

Short Option Performance Assessment

Task

Maze Race

Have children construct a maze with straight lines and another maze with zigzag sections. Then, have them predict whether it would be faster to push a marble through the straight or the zigzag maze. Have children test their predictions by timing how long it takes to push the marble through each of the mazes.

Rubric

Preparation Provide children with marbles, masking tape, cardboard tubes, tagboard, rulers, blocks, scissors, and a timer.

Scoring Rubric—Performance Indicators

___ Makes and tests predictions.

___ Identifies straight and zigzag paths.

___ Explains how a push can be used to move an object and to change its location.

Observations and Rubric Scores

3 2 1 0

Unit Review *continued*

Answer Key

Inquiry and the Big Idea (11 points each)

13. **The two N poles are lined up. The magnets are repelling. I know because like poles repel.**

Have children look carefully at the picture to recognize that there are two separate magnets set close to each other. Point out the N and the S on each magnet identify the magnet's poles. Once children notice that the two N poles are close to each other, ask, "What happens when two like poles are near each other?"

14.

a. **a push; The force will push the ball farther away from the bat and the girl.**

b. **Sample answers: speed, location**

Have children pantomime or act out the motion of hitting a ball using a paper ball or similar object. Make sure they understand that the motion is a push.

UNIT 4

Inquiry and the Big Idea

Write the answers to these questions.

TEKS 1.4A, 1.6B

13. Compare the magnets. Describe what they are doing. How do you know?

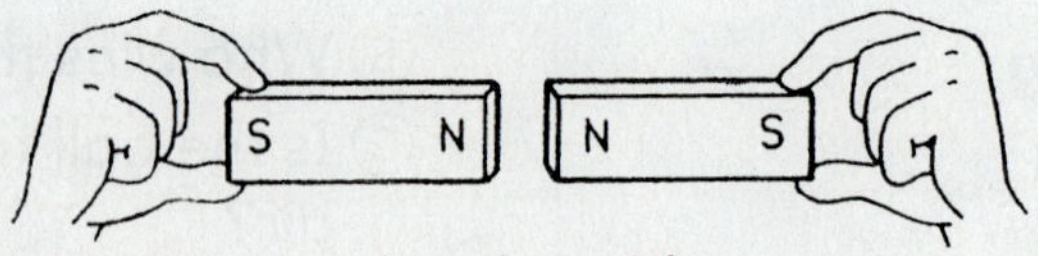

The two N poles are lined up. The magnets are repelling. I know because like poles repel.

TEKS 1.6C, 1.6D

14. Look at the picture.

a. What kind of force is being put on the ball? Describe how the location of the ball will change.

a push; The force will push the ball farther away from the bat and the girl.

b. Name two things that the force can change about the ball.

Sample answers: speed, location

Item Analysis

Items	TEKS	Depth of Knowledge	Cognitive Complexity
13	**1.4A, 1.6B**	2	High
14	**1.6C, 1.6D**	3	High

UNIT 4 Forces and Energy

Big Idea and Essential Questions

This Unit was designed to focus on this Big Idea and these Essential Questions.

Take It Home!
A School-Home Connection letter in English and Spanish is provided in Online Resources.

Big Idea

Forces change the way objects move. Magnets attract some objects and repel others. Energy can cause matter to move or change.

Essential Questions

- L1 **How Do We Use Energy?**
- L2 **How Do Magnets Move Objects?**
- L3 **How Do Objects Move?**
- L4 **How Can We Move a Ball?**
- L5 **How Can We Change the Way Objects Move?**

Professional Development

Houghton Mifflin Harcourt and **NSTA,** the **National Science Teachers Association,** have partnered to provide customized professional development resources for teachers using *ScienceFusion.*

The Professional Development Resources include:

- Do-it-yourself resources, where you can study at your own pace
- Live and archived online seminars
- Journal articles, many of which include lesson plans
- Fee-based eBooks, eBook chapters, online short courses, symposia, and conferences

Access to The NSTA Learning Center is provided in the *ScienceFusion* Online Resources.

NSTA National Science Teachers Association

The NSTA Learning Center

Unit Planning

Options for Instruction

Choose from **Interactive Worktext** and **Leveled Readers, Digital,** and **Inquiry** options to meet the Texas Essential Knowledge and Skills.

	LESSON 1	LESSON 2	LESSON 3
Essential Questions	**How Do We Use Energy?**	**How Do Magnets Move Objects?**	**How Do Objects Move?**
Texas Essential Knowledge and Skills	TEKS 1.6A	TEKS 1.6B	TEKS 1.6D
Interactive Worktext	☐ Student Edition pp. 123–134 • Full of Energy • Energy All Around • Electricity at Home • Kinds of Energy	☐ Student Edition pp. 135–144 • It's Magnetic • Get Together • Go Away!	☐ Student Edition pp. 145–152 • Set Things in Motion • It's Your Move!
Leveled Readers	Parallel coverage of the lesson topics is provided in the Extra Support, On-Level, and Enrichment readers. See p. 121J for detailed reader information.		
Hands-On Inquiry	Inquiry Flipchart p. 19 **Making Toast** ☐ Directed Inquiry **My Energy Survey** ☐ Independent Inquiry	Inquiry Flipchart p. 20 **Push and Pull** ☐ Directed Inquiry **Which Magnet Will Win?** ☐ Independent Inquiry	Inquiry Flipchart p. 21 **Marble Race** ☐ Directed Inquiry **Testing Toys** ☐ Independent Inquiry
Digital Curriculum	☐ Digital Lesson Online Resources Interactive presentation of lesson content 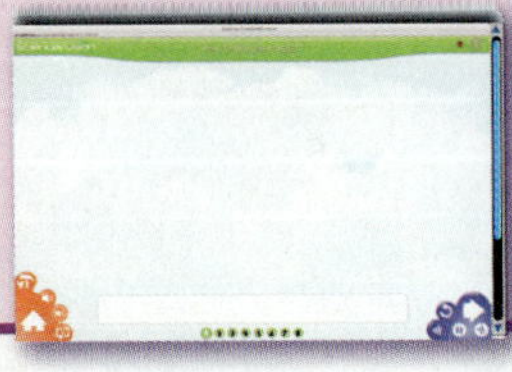	☐ Digital Lesson Online Resources Interactive presentation of lesson content 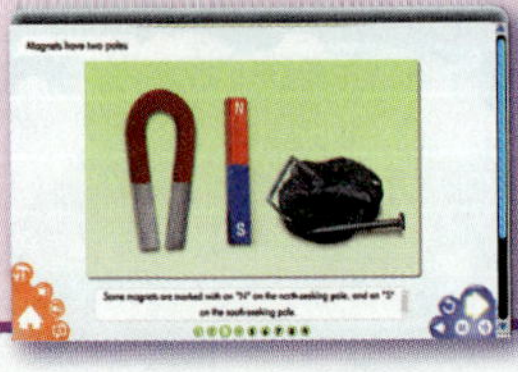	☐ Digital Lesson Online Resources Interactive presentation of lesson content 

LESSON 4

Guided Inquiry

How Can We Move a Ball?

TEKS 1.2A, 1.2B, 1.2D, 1.6D

☐ **Student Edition**
pp. 155–156

- Scaffolding for Inquiry

Inquiry Flipchart
p. 22

How Can We Move a Ball?

☐ Guided Inquiry

☐ **Virtual Lab**
Online Resources

Interactive scaffolded inquiry

LESSON 5

How Can We Change the Way Objects Move?

TEKS 1.6C

☐ **Student Edition**
pp. 157–168

- In Full Force
- Using Force
- What Makes That Coaster Move?

Inquiry Flipchart
p. 23

Changing Motion

☐ Directed Inquiry

Changing Location

☐ Independent Inquiry

☐ **Digital Lesson**
Online Resources

Interactive presentation of lesson content

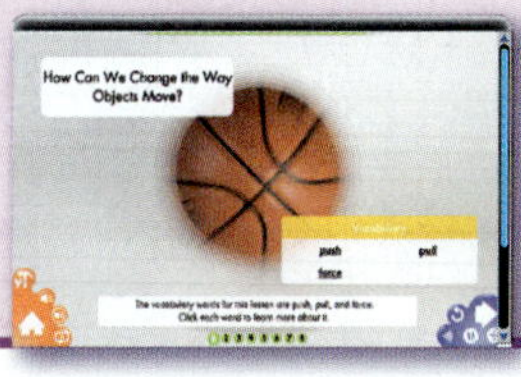

OTHER UNIT FEATURES

People in Science, p. 153

S.T.E.M. Engineering and Technology, pp. 169–170B

Online Resources

Interactive Whiteboard Resources for Unit 4

Assessment

Formative Assessment
Sum It Up! and Brain Check
Student Edition, end of each lesson

Summative Assessment
Lesson Quizzes
Assessment Guide, pp. AG 58–AG 62

Unit 4 Review
Student Edition, pp. 171–174

Unit 4 Test
Assessment Guide, pp. AG 65–AG 69

Performance Assessment
SHORT OPTION: Teacher Edition, p. 173
LONG OPTION: Assessment Guide, pp. AG 70–AG 71

RTI Response to Intervention

RTI Strategies, p. 121K

Online Assessment
Test-taking and automatic scoring
Banks of items from which to build tests

Planning for Inquiry

Use the following preview of Inquiry Activities and Lessons to gather and manage the materials needed for each lesson.

Activity	Inquiry and Design Process Skills Focus	Materials	Prep Tips, Troubleshooting, and Expected Results
Lesson 1 DIRECTED INQUIRY Flipchart p.19 **A Making Toast** **OBJECTIVES** Recognize and demonstrate safe practices. Record and organize data. Identify and discuss how different forms of energy are important to everyday life. 15 minutes small groups TEKS **1.1A, 1.1B, 1.2D, 1.6A**	• Plan and Conduct a Simple Investigation • Observe • Draw Conclusions	• slices of bread • toaster • paper plates (optional)	**Prep Tips** Before the activity, set up a toaster near an electric outlet. Have a package of sliced bread ready. **Caution!** Remind children that they should never put their fingers or any other objects inside the toaster or the electric outlet at any time. Make sure that children are aware of the cord. Explain that they should stay away from it and should not pull on it. **Troubleshooting** Set the dial on the toaster to a medium setting. This will ensure that the bread shows changes but does not burn. **Expected Results** Children should observe that the bread has now been cooked. Electricity from the outlet moved through the cord. When the toaster was turned on, the electricity changed to heat, causing the bread to cook. Children should note that heat is important to everyday life because it helps cook our food.
INDEPENDENT INQUIRY Flipchart p.19 **B My Energy Survey** **OBJECTIVES** Ask questions about objects and events observed in the natural world. Record and organize data. Communicate observations. Identify and discuss how different forms of energy are important to everyday life. 15 minutes pairs TEKS **1.2A, 1.2D, 1.2E, 1.6A**	• Gather, Record, Display, or Interpret Data • Communicate • Plan and Conduct a Simple Investigation	• a variety of energy examples found at school	**Prep Tips** Before the activity, request permission for children to survey people in the school's front office or custodial office. The activity can be performed only in the classroom, but children might wish to visit other parts of the school in order to see how energy is used elsewhere. **Troubleshooting** School personnel may not have time to be interviewed by each pair of children. Schedule a time for a staff member to meet with the class, and invite pairs to take turns asking one of the questions from their list. **Expected Results** Children should recognize that their school uses many different kinds of energy, including electricity, heat, light, and sound.

Additional teaching support for all inquiry activities is available in **Online Resources.**

Science Notebook Strategies

- Lists of Kit-Supplied Materials
- Meeting Individual Needs
- Investigate More—Extensions and Variations
- and More!

Activity	Inquiry and Design Process Skills Focus	Materials	Prep Tips, Troubleshooting, and Expected Results
Lesson 2 DIRECTED INQUIRY Flipchart p.20 A **Push and Pull** **OBJECTIVES** Plan and conduct simple investigations. Record and organize data. Communicate observations and provide reasons for explanations using data. Predict and describe how a magnet can be used to push or pull an object. 20 minutes individuals TEKS **1.2B, 1.2D, 1.2E, 1.6B**	• Gather, Record, Display, or Interpret Data • Predict • Compare • Communicate	• magnets (two for each child) • small objects made of iron or steel	**Prep Tips** Before the activity, gather enough small objects made of iron or steel so that each child will have several objects to experiment with. Some possible objects are paper clips, washers, bolts, and screws with flat ends. Small magnets are available for purchase from craft stores, teacher-supply stores, and online suppliers. **Caution!** Make sure metal hardware items are clean and do not have any sharp edges. **Troubleshooting** If children attract several objects at once with their magnet, suggest that they set aside all but one object for testing at a time. **Expected Results** Children will find that the magnets attract items made of iron and steel. They should notice that magnets attract when unlike poles are aligned and repel when like poles are aligned.
INDEPENDENT INQUIRY Flipchart p.20 B **Which Magnet Will Win?** **OBJECTIVES** Plan and conduct simple investigations. Record and organize data. Collect and compare information using magnets. 25–30 minutes pairs TEKS **1.2B, 1.2D, 1.4A**	• Compare • Gather, Record, Display, or Interpret Data • Plan and Conduct a Simple Investigation	• two magnets about the same size and shape (for each pair) • small cup of paper clips (one for each pair) • ruler (optional)	**Prep Tips** Magnets are available for purchase from craft stores, teacher-supply stores, and online suppliers. Before the activity, experiment with the magnets to ensure that one magnet is stronger than the other. Place a handful of paper clips in a small cup for each pair, and have children empty the paper clips into a small pile before beginning the investigation. Before children begin the activity, suggest that they make a two-column chart to organize their questions and answers. **Troubleshooting** Make sure that children hold both magnets at approximately the same distance above the pile of paper clips. If they have difficulty with this part, suggest that one partner hold a ruler to keep track of the distance. **Expected Results** Children should find that even though the magnets are about the same size and shape, that one is stronger than the other.

Planning for Inquiry (continued)

Activity	Inquiry and Design Process Skills Focus	Materials	Prep Tips, Troubleshooting, and Expected Results
Lesson 3 DIRECTED INQUIRY **Flipchart** p.21 **A Marble Race** **OBJECTIVES** Plan and conduct simple investigations. Record and organize data. Collect and compare information using timers. Demonstrate and record the ways that objects can move. 25 minutes pairs TEKS **1.2B, 1.2D, 1.4A, 1.6D**	• Observe • Identify and Control Variables • Experiment	• 3 clear cups (for each pair) • water • shampoo • clear cooking oil • 3 equal-sized marbles (for each pair) • timer	**Prep Tips** Gather marbles that are all the same size. As children fill the cups with liquid, direct them to leave about an inch between the top of each liquid and the rim of the cup. You may wish to complete this step yourself to avoid spills or place cups on a cookie sheet to catch spills. If desired, label the cups with masking tape to indicate which liquid is in each. For best results, use clear or translucently colored shampoo and nearly clear cooking oil, such as peanut or canola oil. Review how to use a timer with children. **Caution!** Tell children not to put the marbles in their mouths. Have them wash their hands immediately after the activity. **Troubleshooting** Remind children to drop each marble in its cup gently, to avoid splashing, and to make sure all marbles enter the liquid with the same amount of force. **Expected Results** Children will observe that the thicker the liquid, the more slowly the marble moves through it. They will note that the marble moves most quickly through the water and most slowly through the shampoo.
INDEPENDENT INQUIRY **Flipchart** p.21 **B Testing Toys** **OBJECTIVES** Plan and conduct simple investigations. Record and organize data. Demonstrate and record the ways that objects can move. 15 minutes individuals TEKS **1.2B, 1.2D, 1.6D**	• Observe • Compare • Plan and Conduct a Simple Investigation	• 3 or more toys that move in different ways	**Prep Tips** Gather toys that children can use for observation. The toys should be able to move in a variety of ways. Possible toys include pinwheels, toy vehicles, tops, marbles, abaci, and wind-up objects. You may wish to review or demonstrate the terms *straight line, zigzag, back and forth, round and round, up and down,* and *fast and slow* before children begin. **Troubleshooting** If you can't gather enough objects for the investigation, you may wish to supplement your available supply with online videos showing movement. For example, you might find videos of a pendulum, a moving train, and a sled being pulled. **Expected Results** Children will observe that toys may move in a variety of ways, such as in straight lines, back and forth, in a zigzag pattern, up and down, fast and slow, or around in a circle.

Additional teaching support for all inquiry activities is available in Online Resources.

Activity	Inquiry and Design Process Skills Focus	Materials	Prep Tips, Troubleshooting, and Expected Results
Lesson 4 INQUIRY GUIDED INQUIRY Flipchart p.22 **Student Edition** pp.155–156 **How Can We Move a Ball?** **OBJECTIVES** • Recognize the importance of safe practices. • Plan and conduct simple investigations. • Record and organize data. • Demonstrate and record the ways that objects can move. 25 minutes pairs TEKS **1.1B, 1.2B, 1.2D, 1.6D**	• Compare	• thick string • safety scissors • small ball (one for each pair) • ramp • tape (optional)	**Prep Tips** In advance, find thick string or rope that is thick enough to keep a small ball from rolling over the top of it. Each pair of children will need a small, firm ball, such as a tennis ball. Encourage children to help you collect balls in order to have enough for the entire class to perform the activity together. You might need to clear some classroom space so each pair has enough room for the investigation or find some extra space in a hallway. Be sure to have enough ramps ahead of time or have children build their own. **Caution!** Review scissors safety rules with children. **Troubleshooting** If children have difficulty cutting the thick string, precut 3-foot pieces for them. If they have trouble keeping their string in place, help them use tape to attach the string to the floor. Also be sure children space the string so the ball can roll freely inside the track. **Expected Results** Children should recognize that there is a connection between the track's and ramp's shapes and how the ball moves.

Go Digital! Virtual Lab

How Can We Move a Ball?

Key Inquiry Skills: compare, record, plan and conduct an investigation, communicate

Children will experiment to see the different ways that objects can move.

Planning for Inquiry (continued)

Activity	Inquiry and Design Process Skills Focus	Materials	Prep Tips, Troubleshooting, and Expected Results
Lesson 5 DIRECTED INQUIRY Flipchart p.23 A **Changing Motion** **OBJECTIVES** Plan and conduct simple investigations. Describe the change in location of an object. 15 minutes · individuals TEKS **1.2B, 1.6C**	• Observe • Plan and Conduct a Simple Investigation	• golf balls • paper cups • rulers • classroom objects (to block the golf ball and make it change direction)	**Prep Tips** To prepare, place the golf ball and the ruler in the paper cup. Provide one set of materials for each child. Set children up in a large space, if possible, so their golf balls do not knock into each other, or have children take turns. Provide children with pencils and paper so they can record what they do each time. Have them refer to their notes when they review the activity at the end. Children can put an object in place to change the ball's direction or change its direction by blocking it with a foot. **Troubleshooting** Encourage children to tap the ball gently to set it in motion rather than apply a continuous force. This will help avoid the misconception that an object must have a continuously applied force to keep it moving. **Expected Results** Children should determine which forces must be applied to put the ball into motion, stop its motion, and change its direction.
INDEPENDENT INQUIRY Flipchart p.23 B **Changing Location** **OBJECTIVES** Plan and conduct simple investigations. Record and organize data. Describe the change in location of an object. 30 minutes · small groups TEKS **1.2B, 1.2D, 1.6C**	• Plan and Conduct a Simple Investigation • Record	• assortment of classroom objects	**Prep Tips** Gather several classroom objects ahead of time. Review forces with children, such as pushes and pulls, and what it means to move one object closer to, nearer to, and farther from another object. Be sure children have their Science Notebooks on hand to record all their observations. **Troubleshooting** Guide children to think of a way to organize their information ahead of time, such as in a chart. **Expected Results** Children should determine that forces, such as pushes and pulls, can change the location of an object by moving it closer to, nearer to, and farther from another object.

Additional teaching support for all inquiry activities is available in Online Resources.

<table>
<tr><th>Activity</th><th>Inquiry and Design Process Skills Focus</th><th>Materials</th><th>Prep Tips, Troubleshooting, and Expected Results</th></tr>
<tr>
<td>

S.T.E.M.

Engineering and Technology

Flipchart p.24

Build It: Paper Airplanes

OBJECTIVES

- Recognize and demonstrate safe practices.
- Record and organize data.
- Identify and explain a problem and propose a solution in his/her own words.

30 minutes

individuals or pairs

TEKS **1.1A, 1.1B, 1.2D, 1.3A**

</td>
<td>

1 Find a Problem
2 Plan and Build
3 Test and Improve
4 Redesign
5 Communicate

</td>
<td>

- construction paper
- printer paper
- safety goggles

</td>
<td>

Prep Tips Have available for each child or pair $8\frac{1}{2}$ x 11 sheets of paper in at least two different weights, such as construction paper and printer paper. Ahead of time, clear an area outside for children to test their airplanes. Have a small group help you mark off a starting line and 6-inch increments from the starting line to 20 or 30 feet.

Expected Results Children will build and fly paper airplanes that are made of different kinds of paper to see which flies farthest.

</td>
</tr>
</table>

Differentiated Instruction

Leveled Readers

The Leveled Readers provide parallel coverage of the unit topics and Texas Essential Knowledge and Skills. Each Reader is available in English and Spanish. Both versions are available online and on touchscreen mobile devices.

ON-LEVEL This Reader reinforces unit concepts and vocabulary and focuses on the Texas Essential Knowledge and Skills. It includes student response activities.

EXTRA SUPPORT This Reader shares title, illustrations, vocabulary, and concepts with the On-Level Reader. However, the text is linguistically accommodated to provide simplified sentence structures and comprehension aids for students who need a little extra support with content-area reading and vocabulary development. It also includes student response activities.

ENRICHMENT This high-interest nonfiction Reader enriches and extends unit concepts. It reinforces some of the unit vocabulary, but also includes stretch vocabulary. It also includes student response activities.

TEACHER GUIDE
The accompanying Teacher Guide provides teaching strategies and support for using all the Readers, as well as English and Spanish worksheets that focus on vocabulary development. A correlation to the Texas Essential Knowledge and Skills is included.

DIGITAL VERSIONS

All of these Leveled Readers are available online. They are also available in an innovative and engaging format for touchscreen mobile devices. For information about accessing these versions, see page T9.

RTI Response to Intervention

Response to Intervention is a process for identifying and supporting students who are not making expected progress toward essential learning goals.

The following *ScienceFusion* components have the flexibility to be used to provide Core Classroom Instruction (Tier 1), strategic intervention (Tier 2), and intensive intervention (Tier 3).

Component	Location	Strategies and Benefits
Student Edition, Active Reading prompts, Sum It Up, Brain Check	Active Reading throughout each lesson, Sum It Up and Brain Check at the end of each lesson	Student responses can be used as screening tools to assess whether intervention is needed.
Assessment Guide, Lesson Quizzes and TEKS DOK Skill Builder	pp. AG 58–AG 64	Student responses can be used as screening tools to assess whether intervention is needed.
Inquiry Flipcharts	Inquiry Flipchart p. 22	Directed Inquiry for students who learn best through directed or teacher-led hands-on activities.
Teacher Edition, Unit Review Answer Strategies	TE pp. 171–174	Suggestions for intervention, guidance, and remediation for each review question.
Leveled Readers	TE p. 121J	Content support for students not meeting the learning needs during core classroom instruction.
Leveled Readers, Teacher Guides and Vocabulary Worksheets	TE p. 121J	Direct instruction with small groups of students needing additional content at various readability levels.
Extra Support for Vocabulary and Concepts (online worksheets)	Online Resources	Support for individualized instruction with practice in essential content.
Online Student Edition with Audio	Online Resources	Provides learners with multiple-modality access to science concepts and information.
Interactive Digital Lessons and Virtual Labs	Online Resources	Provides individualized learning experiences. Lessons make content accessible through simulations, animations, videos, audio, and integrated assessment.
Interactive Whiteboard Resources	Online Resources	Reinforces key unit concepts through interactive vocabulary games and visuals and graphic organizers.
Leveled Readers, online and tablet versions	Online and Tablet Resources	Highlighted words and sentences synced with audio provide support for emerging or struggling readers.

Differentiated Instruction

English Language Learners

Choose from these instructional strategies to meet the needs of English language learners.

Vocabulary Cards are provided in Online Resources.

Unit Vocabulary

Lesson 1	Lesson 2	Lesson 3	Lesson 5
energy	magnet	motion	push
heat	pole	speed	pull
light	attract		force
sound	repel		
electricity			

Preteach Vocabulary ELPS 3C

Use pantomime, visuals, and simplified language to preteach the words *attract, repel, push,* and *pull.* Use each word in a sentence, and have children repeat after you.

Language Acquisition Strategies

Ask for Information ELPS 2C, 3D, 3F

Provide a word bank that includes *sound, light,* and *heat.* Have children use these words to ask questions about the kinds of energy featured on TE pages 124–125.

Beginning	Intermediate	Advanced/Advanced High
Display this question frame: *What kind of energy is ___?* Use a word from the word bank to complete the question, and work with children to answer it. Repeat with the other words.	Have partners take turns completing this question frame with a word from the word bank: *What kind of energy is ___?* Have partners work together to answer it.	Have partners complete these question frames with pairs of words from the word bank: *How are ___ and ___ alike? How are ___ and ___ different?* Have partners work together to answer each question.

Share Information ELPS 1A, 3E, 3F

Before children read TE pages 126–127, have them share information about their own experiences with energy.

Beginning	Intermediate	Advanced/Advanced High
Use forced-choice questions to help children share information: *Does the sun provide sound or light energy? Would you use heat energy to cook food or listen to music? Does light energy warm your body or help you see things?*	Have children complete sentence frames such as these: *We use ___ energy to cook our food. ___ energy helps me see. ___ energy keeps me warm. ___ energy helps me hear music.*	Have partners take turns explaining how they use different kinds of energy throughout the day. Challenge Advanced High ELLs to identify the source of each kind of energy.

Use Accessible Language ELPS 1A, 1C, 1F, 2E

Use accessible language to develop children's understanding of the word *pole* before they read TE page 137.

Beginning	Intermediate	Advanced/Advanced High
Display a globe. Point to the North Pole and the South Pole as you explain that Earth has two poles. Display a magnet. Explain that a magnet is like Earth because it also has two poles at opposite ends.	Draw a picture of a flagpole and a fishing pole. Have children define *pole* in their own words. Then, explain that *pole* also means a place on a magnet with the strongest pull. Have children point to the poles on the magnet in the picture.	Children may know *pole* in reference to a flagpole or a fishing pole. Explain that *pole* also means a place on a magnet with the strongest pull. Have children write one sentence for each meaning of *pole*.

Vocabulary Practice ELPS 1A, 2C, 3D, 3F

After children read TE page 162, have them practice using the words *nearer to, closer to,* and *farther from.* Display assorted objects on a table. Model using the words in simple sentences to describe where the objects are in relation to one another.

Beginning	Intermediate	Advanced/Advanced High
Then, have children use one of the words to tell about two of the objects.	Ask partners to use the words to tell about objects in the classroom: *The __ is nearer to the ___. The ___ is farther from the ___.*	Have partners choose two classroom objects and use the words to describe where these objects are in relation to one another.

Use Learning Strategies ELPS 1D, 3G, 3H

Have children refer to TE pages 164–165 as they tell what makes a roller coaster move. Guide them to use learning strategies.

Beginning	Intermediate	Advanced/Advanced High
Model ways children can request help: *Can you help me ___? I don't understand ___. Would you please repeat that? Would you please explain ___?* Have children repeat after you.	Provide sentence frames to help children use synonyms: *It is the same as ___. It is like ___. It is similar to ___.*	Have children use sentence frames to convey ideas by defining or describing them: *It has ___. It includes ___. Let me rephrase that.*

Forces and Energy

I Wonder Why

Direct children's attention to the main picture and ask them to tell what they think is happening, using any experiences they may have had playing miniature golf. Call on volunteers to describe what happens to a ball when you hit it with another object, such as a golf putter or a baseball bat. Encourage children to brainstorm reasons for why the ball moves, in order to begin answering the question.

Here's Why

Have children turn the page and read the response to the question. You may wish to share the following background with them.

More About...

Miniature Golf

In miniature golf, or minigolf, each player uses a putter to hit a golf ball through a series of obstacles into a series of holes. The ball may have to travel through hollow logs and tunnels, over hills, or even between the moving blades of a windmill! A player uses force to move the putter in order to hit the ball. The force from the putter pushes the ball forward to a different location. A player may do this several times until the ball finally reaches the hole.

Science Songs

See pp. TR40–TR43 for science songs you can use to reinforce content in this unit.

UNIT 4

Forces and Energy

Big Idea

Forces change the way objects move Magnets attract some objects and repel others. Ener can cause matter move or change.

TEKS 1.2A, 1.2B, 1.2D, 1.2E, 1.3C, 1. 1.6B, 1.6C, 1.6D

miniature golf course

I Wonder Why

The ball moves when you hit it. Why?

Turn the page to find out.

Professional Development Science Background

Use the keywords to access
- Professional Development from **The NSTA Learning Center**
- **SciLinks** for additional online content appropriate for children and teachers
- Teacher Science Background in the back of this Teacher Edition

Keywords

energy, forces, gravity, magnetism, motion

SCILINKS THE WORLD'S A CLICK AWAY

Here's Why A force pushes the ball and makes it move to a new location.

In this unit, you will explore this Big Idea, the Essential Questions, and the Investigations on the Inquiry Flipchart.

Levels of Inquiry Key ■ DIRECTED ■ GUIDED ■ INDEPENDENT

Track Your Progress

Big Idea Forces change the way objects move. Magnets attract some objects and repel others. Energy can cause matter to move or change.

Essential Questions

Science Notebook

Before you begin each lesson, be sure to write your thoughts about the Essential Question.

Go Digital

For a complete digital curriculum and resources that provide full coverage of the objectives for this unit, see the Online Resources for this program.

Big Idea and Essential Questions

Big Idea Forces change the way objects move. Magnets attract some objects and repel others. Energy can cause matter to move or change.

Post the Unit Big Idea on the board. Have children read the Essential Questions, which are also the titles of the lessons in this unit.

- Discuss how the Essential Questions can help them focus on the Big Idea.
- Have children read the Big Idea statements. The statements describe the main science concepts they will be learning.
- Have children predict other ideas that will be taught in the lessons based on the titles, or have them give examples of pictures they expect to see.

Once they complete the unit, they should have a better understanding of the Big Idea.

Essential Questions You may use the following Science Notebook strategy for working with the Essential Questions before children begin the unit or before each lesson.

- Strategies for revisiting the Big Idea and Essential Questions are provided in Enduring Understandings on page 171A.

Notebook Science Notebook

- Have children copy the Essential Questions into their Science Notebooks. Suggest they leave writing lines between questions.
- Ask children to write responses to the Essential Questions. Urge children not to worry about whether their responses are correct. They should expect their ideas to change as they work in the unit. Comment that children will be able to review and revise their answers to the Essential Questions at the end of the unit.
- Tips and strategies for using Science Notebooks are provided throughout this unit, in the back of this Teacher Edition, and in Online Resources.

Options for Inquiry

FLIPCHART P. 19

Children can conduct these optional investigations at any time before, during, or in response to the lesson in the Student Edition.

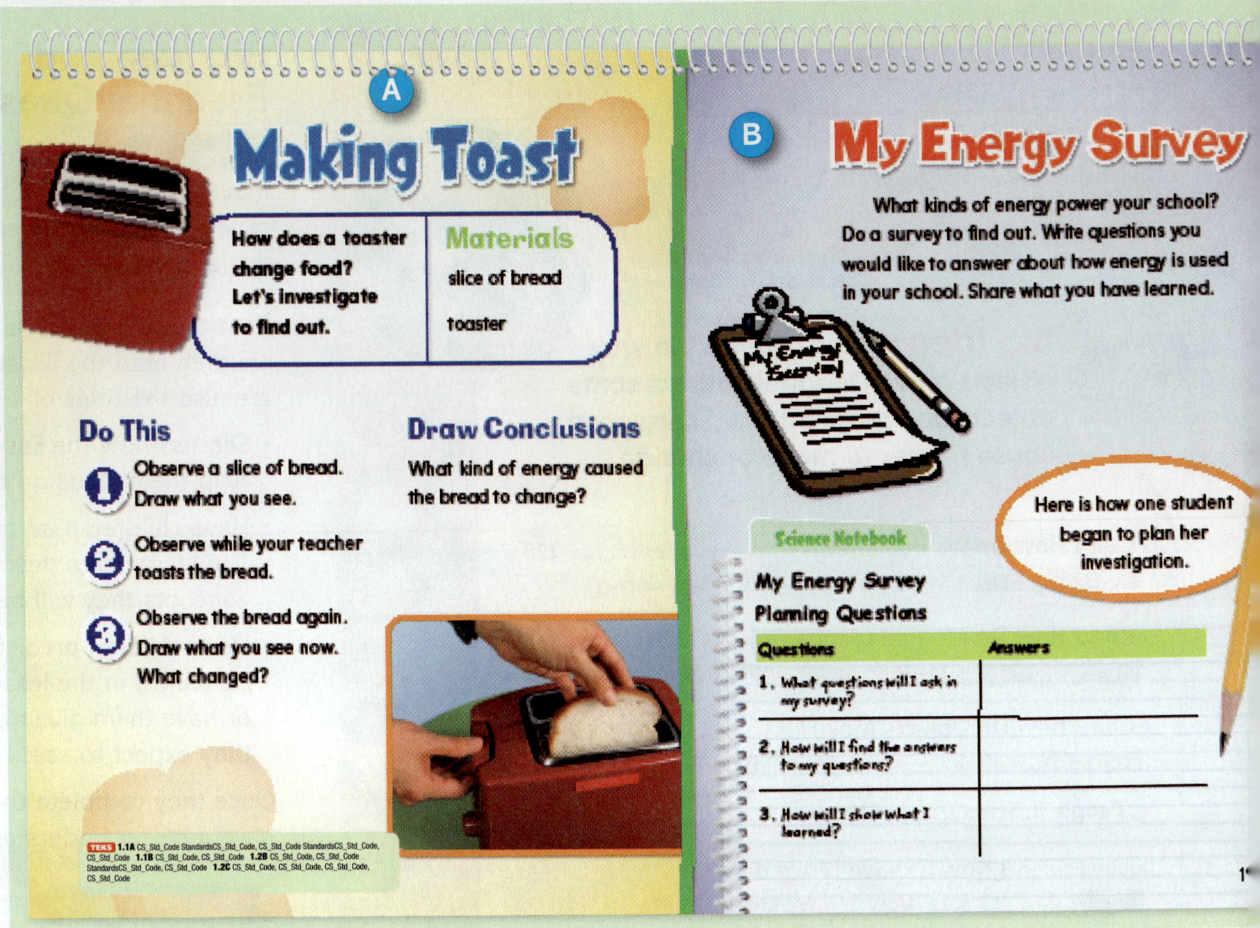

Directed Inquiry

A Making Toast

15 minutes
small groups

Prep and Planning Tips

Set up the toaster on a table near an electric outlet. Have sliced bread ready ahead of time.

Make sure children observe the bread before and after it has been toasted. Have them record their observations using pictures and words.

Caution! Be sure children recognize and demonstrate safe practices to keep themselves and others safe and healthy by reminding them never to put their fingers or any other objects inside the toaster at any time and to use all materials appropriately. Make sure that children are alert to the cord and keep them away from it.

Expected Results

Children should observe that the bread has now been cooked. Electricity from the outlet moved through the cord. When the toaster was turned on, the electricity changed to heat, causing the bread to cook. Children should note that heat is important to everyday life because it helps to cook our food.

Independent Inquiry

B My Energy Survey

15 minutes
pairs

Prep and Planning Tips

See the Planning for Inquiry page for more information. Get permission in advance for children to survey people in the school's front office or custodial office.

Science Notebook

Children can use the Science Notebook as a model for planning and conducting their own investigation. Encourage them to make a chart like the one shown and include any of the sample questions plus their own questions. Additional questions may include *Which kind of energy keeps our school warm in winter? Which kind of energy helps us to see at school?* Ask volunteers to share with the class.

TEKS 1.6A identify and discuss how different forms of energy such as light, heat, and sound are important to everyday life

Lesson 1

Essential Question

How Do We Use Energy?

Engage Your Brain!

Find the answer to the question in the lesson.

What kind of energy lets us see the truck at night?

light energy

Active Reading

Lesson Vocabulary

1. Preview the lesson.
2. Write the 5 vocabulary terms here.

energy, light, electricity, heat, sound

Inquiry Flipchart p. 19—Making Toast/My Energy Survey

123

Go Digital

An interactive digital lesson is available in Online Resources. It is suitable for individuals, small groups, or may be projected or used on an interactive white board.

1 Engage/Explore

Objectives

- Recognize and demonstrate the importance of safe practices.
- Ask questions about events observed in the natural world.
- Plan and conduct simple investigations.
- Record and organize data.
- Communicate observations.
- Identify and discuss how different forms of energy such as light, heat, and sound are important to everyday life.

Engage Your Brain!

Help children answer the question *What kind of energy lets us see the truck at night?* by describing this scenario: *A fire truck leaves a firehouse at night. Firefighters turn on the siren so people can hear it. What can they do to make sure people see it?* Have children describe fire trucks they have seen. Remind children to record their final answers to the question when they find it on the third page of the lesson.

Active Reading Annotations

Remind children that active readers "make texts their own" by marking them or writing notes to help them understand what they are reading. Encourage children to use pencil to make annotations and to feel free to change their marks and notes as they read. The goal of annotation is to help children remember what they have read.

Vocabulary and Interactive Glossary

Remind children to find and list the yellow highlighted terms from the lesson. As they proceed through the lesson and learn about the terms, they can add drawings or words in the extra spaces provided in some entries in the Interactive Glossary.

2 Explain

Notebook Generate Ideas

Read the heading aloud to children. Explain that energy makes matter change or move. Have children preview the images and tell where they see energy at work. Record their responses on the board.

Active Reading Vocabulary

Explain to children that a vocabulary word may be highlighted in a color. Active readers pay attention to highlighted words because their meaning is given in the same sentence or in the next sentence.

Develop Science Concepts

What effects can energy have on matter? Energy causes matter to move or change.

Look through the window in the picture. Which image is an example of heat energy? the boiling pot on the stove

Which kind of energy helps us see inside the classroom? light energy

Which kind of energy would you hear on the playground? sound energy

What kinds of energy does the sun give off? How do you know? heat and light; I know it gives off heat because it makes things on Earth warm. I know it gives off light because it helps us see.

Heat energy is important to everyday life. Point to the part of the picture showing the greenhouse and the sun. How does heat energy help plants? Heat from the sun helps plants grow.

Have children use this information to answer the interactive.

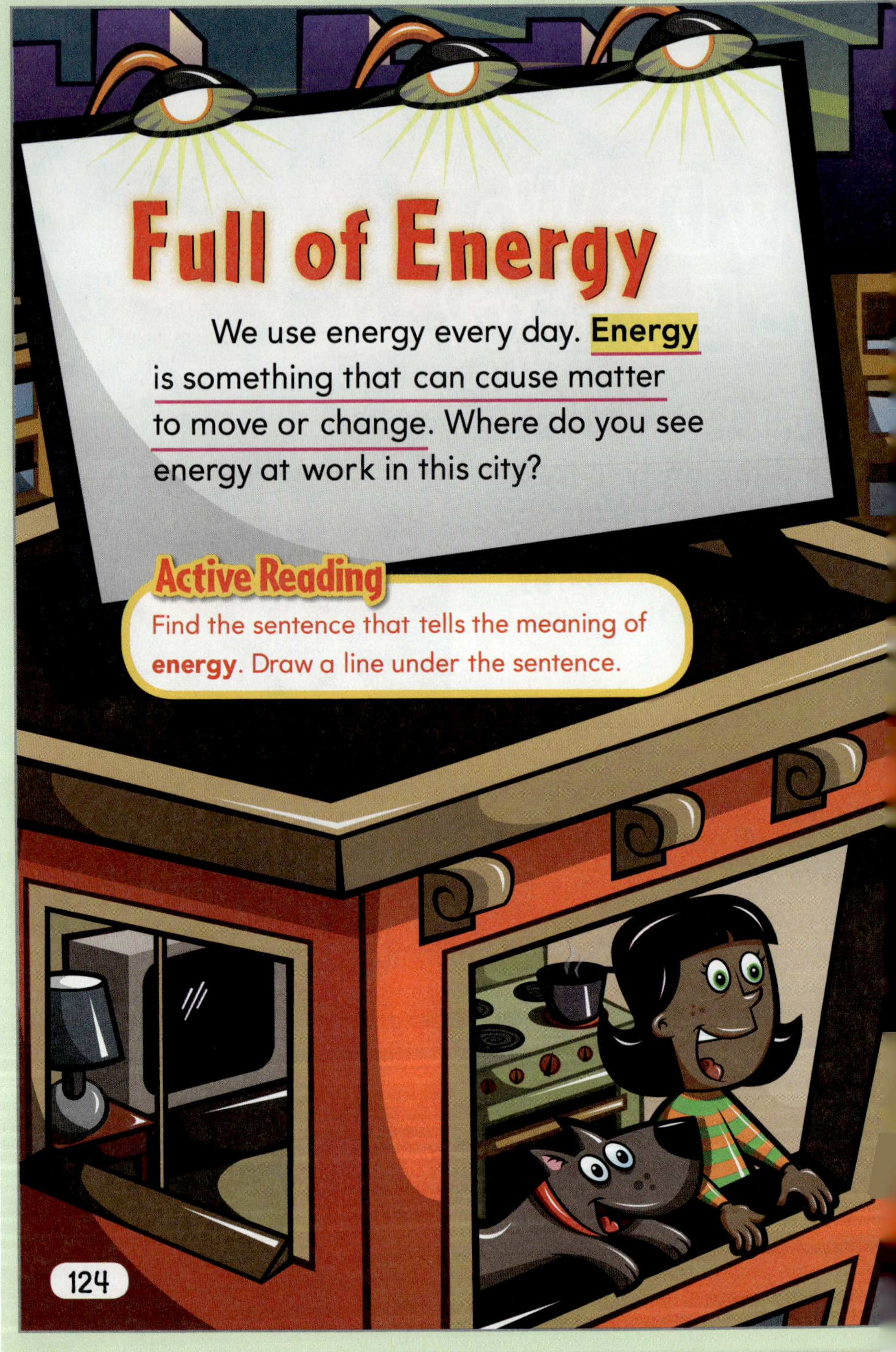

Full of Energy

We use energy every day. **Energy** is something that can cause matter to move or change. Where do you see energy at work in this city?

Active Reading

Find the sentence that tells the meaning of **energy**. Draw a line under the sentence.

124

Differentiation—Leveled Questions

Extra Support

What is energy? Energy is something that makes matter move or change.

Challenge

What observations can you make to tell that you see the effects of energy? You can observe that matter moves or changes; for example, a windmill turns or water boils.

Heat is energy that makes things warmer. The sun gives off heat. **Light** is energy that lets you see. Lamps give off light. The sun gives off light, too. **Sound** is energy that you can hear. People talking and busy city streets are sounds we can hear.

▶ **Discuss how heat energy helps plants.**

Heat from the sun

helps plants grow.

125

English Language Learners

ELPS 1E, 1F, 2E

Understand Multiple-Meaning Words Children may be confused by the multiple meanings of the word *light*. Explain that meanings include "energy that lets us see;" "not heavy;" or "not dark in color." Use the word in sentences to help children differentiate the meanings, for example: *The sun gives off light. The chair is light and easy to carry. The color of Ann's hair is light brown.* Ask volunteers to identify the meaning of *light* in each sentence. Then have them make and share their own sentences.

Develop Science Vocabulary

energy Tell children that *energy* comes from the Greek word *energos,* which means "active." Point out that energy is needed for things to move around and be active.

heat Explain that *heat* comes from words meaning "hot" or "fever." Remind children that heat makes things warm or hot.

light Point to the movie marquee in the picture. Discuss why it is so easy to see the sign. Then ask how the picture would be different if there were no light.

sound Have children sound out and pronounce the word *sound*, paying attention to the vowel sound. Say other words that rhyme with *sound*, such as pound, round, and found.

Interpret Visuals

Have children look at the city scene on these two pages. Discuss the different forms of energy that can be seen.

Which kind of energy helps us see the sign? light energy **Which kind of energy helps us hear the taxi?** sound energy **How does heat energy help us?** It keeps us warm, cooks food, and helps plants grow. **Which kinds of energy can be seen around your town?** Sample answer: Light and sound energy; I see streetlights turned on at night and hear people talking as they are walking on the streets.

Notebook Summarize Ideas

Have children review the main idea they learned about energy and summarize orally or in writing what they learned about it on these two pages.

2 Explain (continued)

Notebook Generate Ideas

Read the heading aloud to children. Guide them to understand that if something is "all around," it is seen or used a lot of the time. Have them start a list of ways they use energy each day.

Develop Science Concepts

Use the following questions to help children identify and discuss how they use energy in their everyday lives. They can use ideas from this discussion to complete the interactivity on this spread.

It is daytime in the park, and the sun is out. What two kinds of energy does the sun provide? light energy and heat energy

How is energy being used in the park? Light energy from the sun is helping people see the park. Light energy from the streetlight is helping people see the park when it is nighttime. It also helps people see the food stand. Sound energy is helping people hear the music and the animals in the park. Heat energy is cooking food for the people. Heat energy from the sun is warming the park.

Identify and discuss why energy is important to our everyday lives. There are many things we could not do without energy, such as see at night or cook food.

Suppose you want to order something from the food stand. Discuss, or talk about, how you might use sound energy to give your order. I could talk to the person working at the food stand. Sound energy would let the person hear my voice.

Energy All Around

Think about a day in the park. The sun provides light and heat. Birds make sounds. Light, heat, and sound energy are a big part of everyday life. How do you use them in your life?

Sound energy lets you hear music.

126

Differentiation—Leveled Questions

Extra Support

What are three kinds of energy? heat, light, and sound Which kind helps you cook food? heat energy

Challenge

How are the sun and a streetligh alike? Both give off light. How ar they different? Sample answer: The sun gives off light during the day. A streetlight can give off ligh during the day and at night.

▶ **Name three kinds of energy. Identify and discuss how they are important to everyday life.**

Sample answers: Light energy helps us see things. Heat energy cooks our food. Sound energy helps us hear.

Interpret Visuals

Point out the guitar as well as the radio next to the girl playing the guitar.

Which kind of energy do these two things show? How do you know? They show sound energy. I know because they both provide energy you can hear.

What else do you see in the pictures that might make sound energy? Sample answers: birds, plane, people, dog

How do you use sound energy every day? Sample answer: I use sound energy when I talk to my friends and listen to my teacher.

Develop Inquiry Skills

COMPARE/CONTRAST Review that *compare* means to tell how things are alike. *Contrast* means to tell how they are different. **How are light, heat, and sound all alike?** They are kinds of energy.

How are heat, light, and sound different? They let you do different things. Heat is energy that keeps you warm. Light is energy that lets you see. Sound is energy you can hear.

Notebook Summarize Ideas

Direct children to return to their lists of ways they use energy each day and to use the picture on these two pages to add items based on what they learned. Have them summarize orally or in writing the key ideas about energy and how it can be used in everyday life.

Writing Connection

TEKS ELA 1.19A

Energy Diary Have children write a diary entry describing how they used energy one day this week. In their entries, they should include mentions of sound, light, and heat energy, and tell why each form of energy was useful. For extra support, you may wish to prompt them with questions such as: *What did you see yesterday? What did you hear yesterday? How did you stay warm yesterday?*

2 Explain (continued)

Generate Ideas

Read the heading aloud to children. Then ask them to look at the images and compare what they see to objects in their homes. Have them name objects they use every day that work because of electricity.

Active Reading Vocabulary

Explain to children that a vocabulary word may be highlighted in a color. Active readers pay attention to highlighted words because their meaning is given in the same sentence or in the next sentence.

Develop Science Vocabulary

electricity Write the word on the board and help children break it into syllables. Read it aloud, and have children clap once for each syllable, *e-lec-tric-i-ty,* as they repeat it.

Develop Science Concepts

Look at the picture. Do you see something that you turn on when it is dark in a room? Draw an X on it. Children should draw an X on any of the lamps on these two pages.

How does electricity get to the electric stove, the lamp, and other electrical things? It moves from an outlet to the object through a cord.

What happens after the electricity reaches the appliance? The electricity is changed into heat, light, or sound.

What are two examples of electricity being changed into heat? an electric stove, a toaster, a microwave, an iron, a hair dryer

What are some things that you use electricity for? lights, to run computers, to cook, to clean clothes

Electricity at Home

Things like toasters, lamps, and radios change electricity into heat, light, and sound. **Electricity** is energy that provides power for many things we use each day.

Sample answer:

Active Reading

Find the sentence that tells the meaning of **electricity**. Draw a line under the sentence.

128

Differentiation—Leveled Questions

Extra Support

Name two objects you use at home that run on electricity. Sample answers: computer, television, radio, stove

Challenge

Tell children that electricity can change into other kinds of energy. **Name three of those kinds and give an example of a way each is found at home.** light from a lamp; heat in a toaster; sound from a radio

Writing Connection

TEKS ELA 1.24C

Write a List Ask children to make a list of three things they do every day or week during which they use electricity. For example, do they brush their teeth with an electric toothbrush? Does an adult cook them toast or eggs? Do they listen to the radio? Children can illustrate their lists and then share them with a partner.

TEKS 1.6A

Interpret Visuals

Point to the image of the light in the hall outside the door.

What kind of energy does this picture show? How do you know? It shows light energy. I know this because light is energy that lets us see.

Look at the picture of the ceiling fan. How is it helping? The fan is helping cool the girl and the dog in the room.

Misconception Alert

Explain that a ceiling fan does not actually lower the air temperature in a room. It makes people in the room feel cooler because of the evaporation of perspiration. However, an air-conditioning (AC) unit can lower the air temperature. AC units run on electricity. Air conditioning keeps many homes much cooler when the outside temperature is high.

Develop Inquiry Skills

INFER **Look at the images. How is heat changing the objects on the stove and in the oven?** The stove is boiling the liquid in the pot. The oven is cooking food.

Clarify for children that heat is energy that moves from something warmer to something cooler, which is why the water boils and the food gets cooked.

Why do you think electricity is useful? It is useful because it provides power for things people use every day. Electricity helps cool our homes, light our homes, and cook our food.

Notebook Summarize Ideas

Direct children to think about the lesson vocabulary they have learned so far and ask them to use those terms to summarize what they learned on these two pages.

2 Explain (continued)

Notebook Generate Ideas

Ask children to look at the photographs and share what they already know about dams, wind farms, and solar panels. Record their ideas on the board. Tell children that you will look back at these ideas after reading the pages that follow.

Develop Science Concepts

Why is energy important? It powers the things people use each day.

How are wind, water, and energy from the sun alike? They can all make electricity.

Explain to children that the dam blocks water and uses water energy to make electricity.

Interpret Visuals

Ask children to observe the photograph of the wind turbines on the right-hand page.

Look at the wind turbines. What makes the blades turn? wind

What kind of energy powers the wind turbines? wind energy

Direct children to the photograph of the solar panels on the right-hand page.

Look at the solar panels. What is their source of energy? the sun

What is a solar panel? A solar panel collects energy from the sun and changes it to electricity.

Why It Matters

Kinds of Energy

Many kinds of energy provide power for the things we use each day. You can see some of these kinds of energy on these pages. People use most of them to produce electricity.

This dam uses water to produce electricity.

▶ Identify two kinds of energy you see on these pages.

Sample answers: wind and water energy

130

Math Connection

TEKS MATH 1.5D

Solve an Energy Sentence
Explain that for every 100 parts of solar energy reaching Earth, 30 parts are reflected, or bounced back, into space. Ask children to figure out how many parts actually reach Earth's surface. Guide them to write and solve the subtraction sentence: 100 – 30 = 70 to find the answer.

Wind farms collect energy from the wind.

Solar panels collect energy from the sun.

Do the Math!

Solve a Problem

Read the word problem. Answer the question.

There are two solar panels on each house. How many solar panels are there on four houses?

eight solar panels

131

TEKS 1.6A

Do the Math!

TEKS MATH 1.3A, 1.3E, 1.5D

Solve a Problem

Encourage children to draw a picture, use a number line, or make a model to solve the problem. Explain that children can group the solar panels by twos and skip-count to find the total number. If children are having difficulty, you may want to draw a number line on the board and model how to skip-count.

Develop Inquiry Skills

DRAW CONCLUSIONS **What are some of the advantages of using solar panels to make electricity?** Solar panels use energy from the sun, so there is a lot of energy available. They do not make waste. **What do you think some of the problems are?** They do not work in the dark or on cloudy days. Maybe they are expensive to set up.

Notebook Summarize Ideas

Have children look at the list of their original ideas about dams, wind farms, and solar panels. Ask whether their ideas about them have changed since they read this section and to summarize those ideas orally or in writing.

English Language Learners

ELPS 1E, 1F, 2A, 2E

Understand Homographs Read these sentences aloud, and stress the difference in pronunciation:
The *wind* is blowing the leaves.
You should *wind up* that yarn.

Explain that homographs are words that are spelled the same but have different meanings and may have different pronunciations. In the first sentence, *wind* is a noun that means "moving air." In the second one, *wind* is a verb that means "to wrap something around." Ask children to say their own sentences using the homographs.

3 Extend/Evaluate

Sum It Up!

1. **Label It!** After children read the directions, have them look closely at the visuals, name each item, and tell what it does. If children need help, ask questions about each item, such as: *What does a ringing phone tell you? What does a stove do to your food? How does a lamp help you at night?*
2. **Choose It!** Guide children to identify the type of energy each sentence describes. If they need help, list the words *heat*, *light*, and *sound* on the board. Then have children match each type of energy with a sentence and identify which sentence tells about light energy.
3. **Draw It!** Before children draw an answer, they may want to make a list of three ways they use electricity and then choose one way from their list to draw.

Sum It Up!

1 Label It!

Look at the pictures. Identify the kind of energy you see. Label it.

sound

heat

light

2 Choose It!

Circle the sentence that tells about light energy.

We use it to cook food.
It lets us see. (circled)
It is energy we can hear.

3 Draw It!

Draw a way that you use electricity.

Check children's drawings. Sample answers: a child using a lamp, a TV, an electric toy

132

Brain Check

Lesson 1

Name ____________________

Word Play

Write a word for each clue. Find each word in the word search. Then answer the question.

1. something that can make matter move or change e n e r g y
2. energy that lets us see l i g h t
3. energy we can hear s o u n d
4. energy that makes things warmer h e a t

t	e	q	o	r	s	g	u	a
e	y	b	p	a	w	c	o	c
n	u	s	o	u	n	d	h	e
e	s	a	v	d	b	w	g	l
r	o	b	c	h	s	x	u	i
g	n	a	e	e	t	u	q	g
y	r	b	k	a	f	d	b	h
d	e	h	p	t	n	h	o	t
k	g	u	b	s	t	z	f	a

Which kind of energy provides power for many things we use? electricity

133

Answer Strategies

Word Play

- With children, read the directions and then each clue aloud. If they have difficulty identifying the correct word for the clues, encourage them to make a list of the highlighted vocabulary terms from the lesson to refer to as they go through the clues. This list will also help children spell the words correctly. Remind them that each blank will have one letter so the number of blanks shows the number of letters in the answer.
- To help children find the words in the word search, suggest that they look for distinct and interesting letter combinations in each word such as *gy, ght,* and *ea*. Point out that words go from left to right or from top to bottom but never backward or diagonally.

Assessment

Lesson Quiz

See Assessment Guide, p. AG 58.

3 Extend/Evaluate (continued)

Answer Strategies

Apply Concepts

- Explain that the left column of the chart gives a problem that people can use energy to solve, and the words in the box list types of energy they can use to solve it. Review the meaning of each column head, reminding children that *discuss* means *talk about*, and *identify* means *find* or *show*.
- Ask children to share what they know about the scenarios described in the left column. For example, some children may have seen a nighttime sports game on television.
- If necessary, ask questions such as the following to help them think about each problem differently: *Which kind of energy helps the players see the ball? Which kind of energy helps you stay warm? Which kind of energy helps you hear someone knocking?*

Take It Home!

Suggest that children work with a family member to list and classify four ways energy is used at home (to cook, to cool, to light, to power objects) and then report back to the class.

Apply Concepts

Read each problem. Write the kind of energy you can use to solve it.

heat light sound

Discuss the Problem	Identify an Energy Solution
A soccer team wants to play a game at night.	light
It is cold in the classroom.	heat
You want to know when someone is at the door.	sound

Take It Home!

Family Members: Ask your child to tell you about energy. Ask him or her to point out ways that energy is used around your home.

134

Make Connections

Easy

Writing Connection TEKS ELA 1.19A

Tell About Wind or Water Energy

- Ask children to write two or three sentences about a personal experience involving wind or water energy and how it can move or change things.
- Provide ideas that children can use for inspiration, such as wind blowing leaves, a kite, or a sailboat; water moving a raft or a boat; or a visit to a wind farm or a dam.
- Ask children to read their sentences to the class.

Easy

Art Connection TEKS ART 1.2C

Conserve Energy

- Remind children of the importance of saving, or conserving, energy so that it is not wasted.
- Have children work in small groups to name a way they can conserve energy in the classroom, such as turning off lights when they leave, keeping the room cooler in winter and bundling up, or carpooling to school.
- Have groups make posters, mobiles, or other art reminders, such as light plates, to hang in the classroom to show classmates how to help.

Average

Math Connection TEKS MATH 1.5D

Solve the Problem

- Read children the following word problem:

  The solar farm in Smithville has 8 solar panels. The solar farm in Brownsboro has 12 solar panels. How many more panels does the farm in Brownsboro have?
- Guide children in setting up a number sentence to solve the problem.

Challenging

Social Studies Connection TEKS SS 1.17C, 1.18A, 1.18B

Research the History of Windmills

- Work with children to locate online or print reference materials about windmills and their uses.
- Then have them work with partners to research the history of windmills and how they have been used over time. Ask them to discuss how windmills were used for energy.
- Have children organize the facts you find together as a time line or poster.

Options for Inquiry

FLIPCHART P. 20

Children can conduct these optional investigations at any time before, during, or in response to the lesson in the Student Edition.

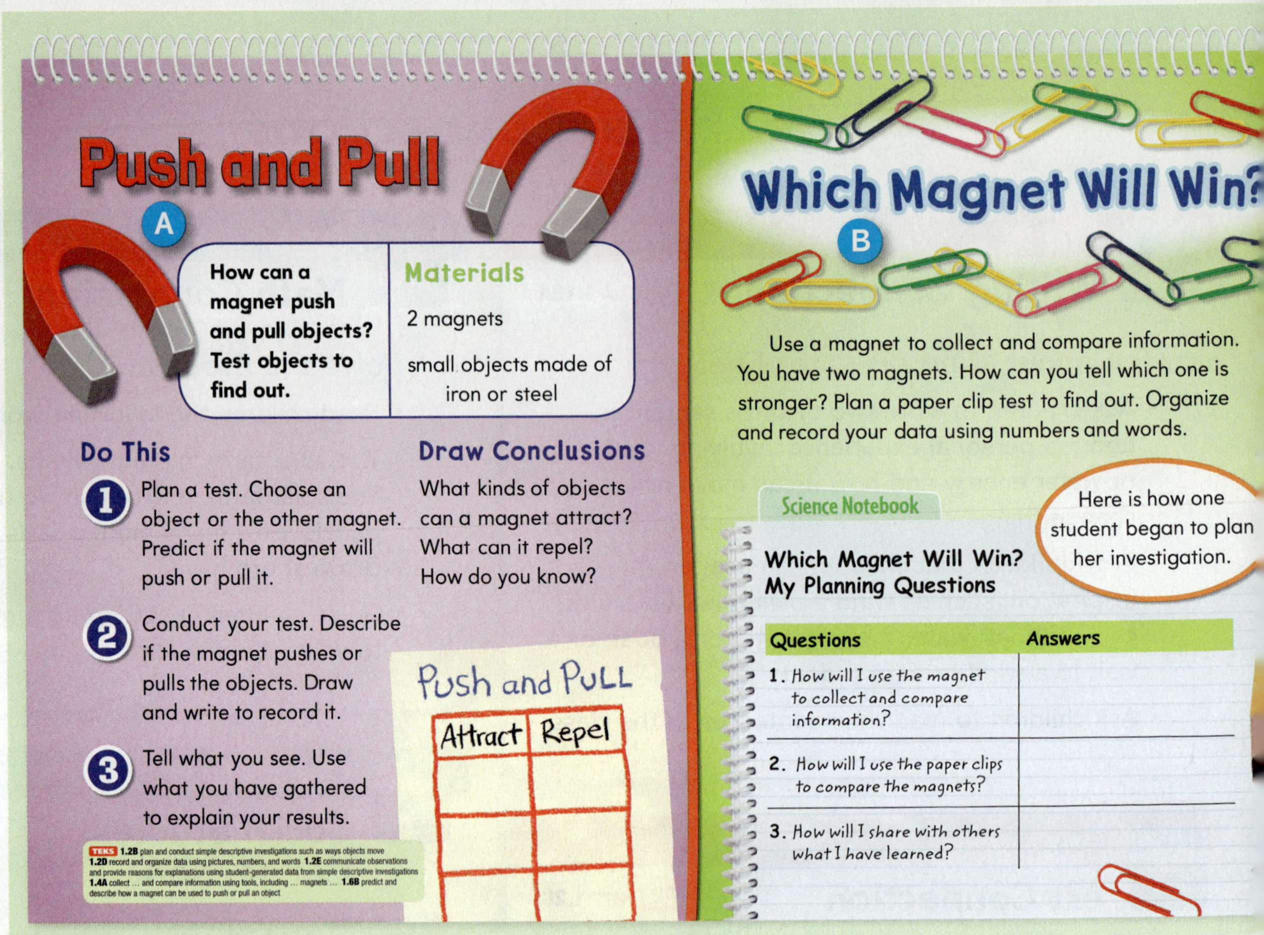

Directed Inquiry

A Push and Pull

20 minutes
individuals

Prep and Planning Tips

Provide iron and steel items such as paper clips, washers, and screws with flat, not pointy, ends. Have children record and organize their information in a chart.

Guide children in testing each item. Bar magnets are preferable for this activity. Have them use the magnet to attract and repel a second magnet.

After children test each item, they should draw and label a picture in the appropriate column.

Have children communicate their observations and provide reasons for explanations using data from the investigation.

Expected Results

Children will predict and describe how a magnet can be used to push or pull various objects. They should notice that magnets attract items made of iron and steel, and also attract other magnets when opposite poles line up. They should understand that magnets repel when like poles line up.

Independent Inquiry

B Which Magnet Will Win?

25–30 minutes
pairs

Prep and Planning Tips

See the Planning for Inquiry page for more information. Provide each pair with two magnets of varying strength. The magnets should be about the same size and shape.

Science Notebook

Children can use the Science Notebook page shown on the Flipchart as a model for planning and conducting their own investigation. Children should think about what they already know about magnets and how they attract some objects and have varying strengths. Remind them that they can make a two-column chart to organize their questions and answers.

TEKS 1.6B predict and describe how a magnet can be used to push or pull an object

Lesson 2

Essential Question

How Do Magnets Move Objects?

Engage Your Brain!

Find the answer to the question in the lesson.

What does a magnet do to iron and steel objects?

It ___attracts___ them.

Active Reading

Lesson Vocabulary

1. Preview the lesson.
2. Write the 4 vocabulary terms here.

magnet ______ attract ______

pole ______ repel ______

Inquiry Flipchart p. 20—Push and Pull/Which Magnet Will Win?

135

Go Digital

An interactive digital lesson is available in Online Resources. It is suitable for individuals, small groups, or it may be projected or used on an interactive white board.

TEKS 1.2B, 1.2D, 1.2E, 1.4A, 1.6B

1 Engage/Explore

Objectives

- Plan and conduct simple investigations.
- Collect and compare information using tools, including magnets.
- Record and organize data.
- Communicate observations and provide reasons for explanations from investigations.
- Predict and describe how a magnet can be used to push or pull an object.

Engage Your Brain!

Help children brainstorm answers to the question *What does a magnet do to iron and steel objects?* Explain that the photograph shows someone fishing using toys. Ask children why they think the toy fish sticks to the pole. Record their ideas on a chart or on the board. Remind children to record their final answer to the question when they find it on the fourth page of the lesson.

Active Reading Annotations

Remind children that active readers "make texts their own" by marking them or writing notes to help them understand what they are reading. Encourage children to use pencil to make annotations and to feel free to change their marks and notes as they read. The goal of annotation is to help children remember what they have read.

Vocabulary and Interactive Glossary

Remind children to find and list the yellow highlighted terms from the lesson. As they proceed through the lesson and learn about the terms, they can add drawings or words in the extra spaces provided in some entries in the Interactive Glossary.

2 Explain

Notebook Generate Ideas

Ask children if they have ever stuck an object to a refrigerator or board without using tape or glue. Encourage them to talk about how they use magnets.

Develop Science Vocabulary

magnet Explain that the word *magnet* comes from the old names for rocks that had the ability to attract iron or steel. In different languages, the rocks were called "magnete," "magnetum," or "Magnes lithos." All of those names derived from a region called Magnesia, where the rocks were dug up.

Active Reading **Details**

Explain that a detail sentence may give an example. Or, it may describe something. Active readers ask themselves, What topic does this detail sentence tell about? The answer will help readers keep the main idea in mind.

Develop Science Concepts

Why are the paper clips sticking to the magnets? The magnets pulled the paper clips toward them.

Which magnet has more paper clips? the one on the right

Why do you think the magnet on the right has more paper clips? It is stronger than the magnet on the left.

It's Magnetic

What is pulling the paper clips? It is a magnet. A **magnet** pulls iron or steel objects. It can push or pull other magnets, too. Magnets can have different strengths.

Active Reading

A detail is a fact about a main idea. Draw one line under a detail. Draw an arrow to the main idea it tells about.

The magnet on the right is stronger. It pulls more than the other magnet.

136

English Language Learners

ELPS 1E, 1F, 2E

Reinforce Vocabulary Children may have trouble understanding the scientific meaning of the word *pole*. Display a bar magnet, point to each end, and say *This place on the magnet is called a pole.* Demonstrate using each end of the magnet to attract paper clips as you say *The pole is on the end of the magnet. It is the place where the magnet's pull is the strongest.* Then have children use the word *pole* in their own sentences to demonstrate that they understand its scientific meaning.

Magnets have two poles. **Poles** are where the pull is the strongest. A magnet has an **N** pole and an **S** pole.

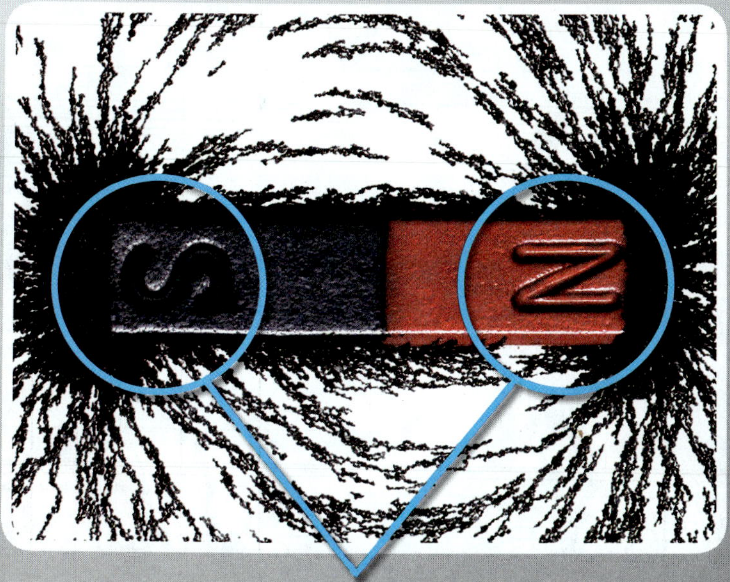

▶ **Look at the magnet. Where is the pull the strongest?**

Sample answer: at the N pole and the S pole

137

Differentiation—Leveled Questions

Extra Support

What is a magnet? An object that can push or pull iron or steel objects.

Challenge

Would a magnet pick up an iron nail? Tell why or why not. Yes, because a magnet can pick up objects made of iron and steel.

Develop Science Vocabulary

pole Use the visual on the right page to point out each pole on the magnet. Explain that the word *pole* can have different meanings in everyday language and in science. Then illustrate those meanings using sentences such as the following: "I caught a fish with my fishing pole." (a long piece of wood or plastic) "Each magnet has two poles." (places where the pull is the strongest)

Interpret Visuals

Read the paragraph of text with children. Then have them examine the picture of the bar magnet, and describe the poles. **What do we call the places on a magnet where the pull is the strongest?** the poles

Point out the circled poles on the magnet. **What are the names of the poles on the magnet in this picture?** N pole and S pole

Guide children to write these names as the answer on the line for the interactivity.

Develop Inquiry Skills

COMPARE Explain that Earth has two poles at opposite ends called the North and South poles. **How are Earth and a magnet the same?** They both have poles at opposite ends.

Notebook Summarize Ideas

Have children summarize orally or in writing the main ideas of these two pages. They should be able to describe how a magnet pulls iron or steel objects. Children should also be able to identify the poles of a magnet and what they do.

2 Explain (continued)

Notebook Generate Ideas

Discuss with children what they do when they pull an object closer. Ask for a volunteer to pantomime this action. Have children predict how using a magnet to pull an object might be similar and different.

Develop Science Vocabulary

attract Explain that *attract* means to pull something closer. To reinforce the meaning, lead children in making a word web with words or phrases that describe what a magnet does when it attracts, such as *together, toward, closer,* and *pull*.

Develop Science Concepts

Guide children to predict and describe how magnets would be used in different situations. **Suppose you are watching a magnet attract a pair of scissors. Describe what the magnet is doing to the scissors and tell why it can do this.** The magnet is pulling the scissors toward itself. It can do this because the scissors are made of iron or steel.

Now suppose you are trying to attract a wooden block with a magnet. Predict if the magnet will attract the block. I think the magnet will not attract the block. **Why?** The block is not made of iron or steel.

Interpret Visuals

Have children look at the objects in the picture on this page. **How are the objects on the left different from the objects on the right?** The objects on the left are not made of iron or steel. The objects on the right are made of iron or steel. **How do you know?** I know because the wood truck on the left is not attracted to the magnet and the button on the right is.

Get Together

A magnet can attract things. **Attract** means to pull something. A magnet pulls things made of iron or steel. It can pull things without touching them.

Differentiation—Leveled Questions

Extra Support
What does *attract* mean? to pull something closer

Challenge
How can magnets attract each other? line up the opposite poles of two magnets

Opposite poles attract each other. The N and S poles attract.

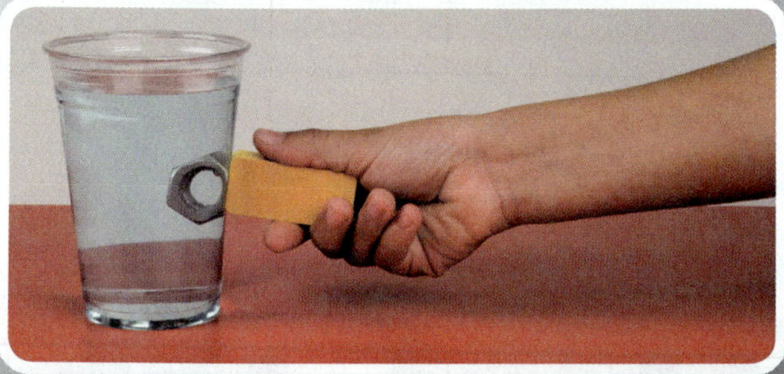

The magnet pulls the object through the cup and the water without touching it.

▶ **Describe how a magnet can be used to pull an object.**

Sample answer: A magnet will pull an

object made of iron or steel.

139

Math Connection

TEKS MATH 1.3A, 1.5D

Magnetic Numbers Place a set of magnetic numbers from 1 through 10 on the board. Invite volunteers to come up to the board. Have them make one digit addition and subtraction number sentences for their classmates to solve.

TEKS 1.6B

Interpret Visuals

Have children look at the top picture. Point out the two arrows. **What do the arrows show?** the direction the magnets are pulling **Why are the arrows pointing toward each other?** to show the magnets are attracting

Develop Science Concepts

Does a magnet have to touch an object to attract it? Explain. No, a magnet does not have to touch an object to attract it. A magnet can attract an object through another object.

Develop Inquiry Skills

INFER Direct children's attention to the picture of the cup. **Describe how the magnet is being used to pull the washer.** The magnet is attracting the washer inside the cup because it is made of iron or steel. **How do you know the magnet is not attracting the cup?** The cup is made of plastic. A magnet does not attract objects made of plastic.

PREDICT **Predict what would happen if you replaced the washer in the cup with a small leaf. Explain.** The magnet would not attract the leaf because it is not made of iron or steel.

Misconception Alert

Children may assume that any kind of metal is "magnetic." Explain that aluminum cans are made of metal, but they do not contain iron or steel. This means that they are not magnetic. Demonstrate this fact by placing a magnet near an empty aluminum can. Point out that the magnet does not attract the can.

Notebook Summarize Ideas

Have children summarize orally or in writing the main idea and a few important details of these two pages.

2 Explain (continued)

Notebook Generate Ideas

Review with children what magnets do when they attract. Have them use their hands to mimic two magnets attracting. Then ask them to use their hands to show what two magnets might look like if they were doing the opposite of attracting, repelling.

Active Reading Main Idea

Explain that the main, or most important, idea may be the first sentence in a paragraph. Or, it may be a different sentence. Active readers ask themselves, What is this paragraph mostly about? The answer will be the main idea.

Develop Science Vocabulary

repel Explain that when two objects repel, they push away from each other. Point out that *attract* and *repel* are opposites. To reinforce this idea, draw two arrows pointing towards each other and two arrows pointing away from each other. Call on volunteers to help you label the pairs of arrows *attract* and *repel*.

Develop Science Concepts

Have children look at the first picture on this page and point out the two arrows. **Why are the arrows pointing away from each other?** They are pointing away to show that the magnets are repelling each other. **What else shows that the magnets are repelling instead of attracting?** There is a space between the magnets. **Predict how a magnet can be used to push another magnet.** You can put two like poles together to make the magnets repel. **What do you think would happen if you put two N poles together?** The magnets would repel. **What do you think would happen if you put two S poles together?** The magnets would repel.

Go Away!

A magnet does not always pull. Two magnets may repel. **Repel** means to push away. Like poles repel.

Active Reading

The main idea is the most important idea about something. Draw two lines under the main idea.

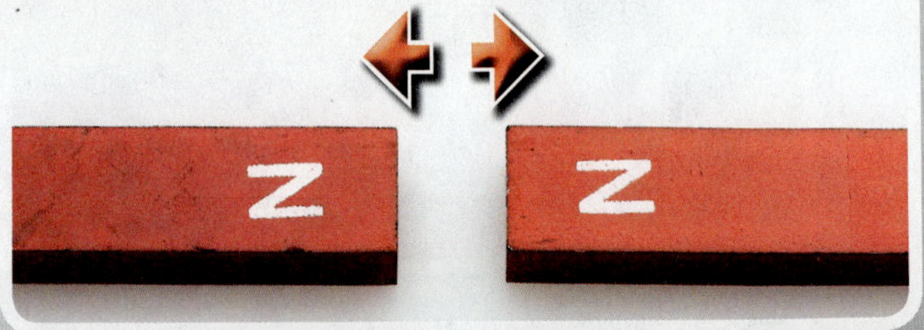

The two N poles and the two S poles repel each other.

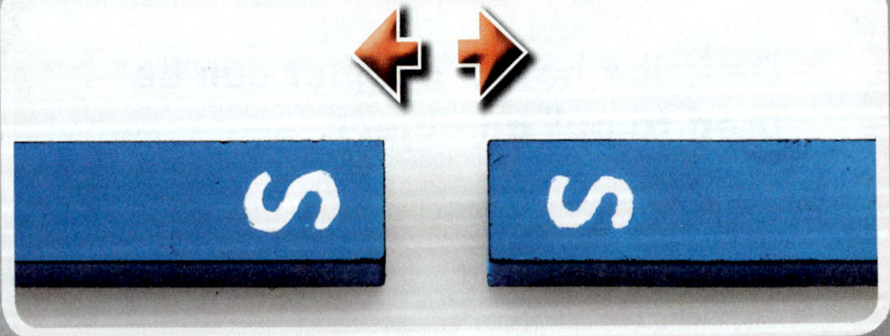

140

English Language Learners

ELPS 1E, 1F, 2E

Multiple Meanings Children may be confused by the use of the word *like* on this page. Say: *We use the word like to show that we enjoy something.* For example, *I like math* or *I like to ride my bike.* Explain that on this page, *like* has a different meaning. Say: *Here the word like means "similar" or "alike."* Use pairs of objects to reinforce the meaning. For example, say *A pen and a pencil are like objects.* Have children identify two like objects and use them in a sentence: *A ___ and a ___ are like objects.*

▶ **Predict how this magnet could repel, or push, another magnet. Draw to show it.**

Check children's drawings to make sure that like poles are lined up on the two magnets.

Writing Connection

TEKS ELA 1.6A, 1.20A, 1.24C

Vocabulary Riddles Display a word bank with the words *magnet, attract, repel*, and *pole*. Model writing a clue for the word *repel*: *I say "go away!"* Have children write each word on an index card and a clue about its meaning on the back. Collect the completed cards, and read aloud the clues. Challenge children to name each vocabulary word.

TEKS 1.6B

Develop Science Concepts

When you want to push something away from you, what can you do? Sample answer: I can push it with my hand. **How is this different from the way a magnet pushes away another magnet?** Sample answer: A magnet does not have to touch the other magnet to push it away.

What is an example of two "like" poles? Sample answers: two N poles; two S poles. **Why do we call them "like" poles?** Sample answer: They are the same kind of pole.

Describe how a magnet can be used to push another magnet. You can use two magnets to repel each other by lining up like poles.

Why is *repel* the opposite of *attract*? *Repel* means to push something away and *attract* means to bring it closer.

Use the following questions to help children plan out what they will draw for the interactivity. **Describe what happens when two magnets repel each other.** They push away from each other.

What makes the magnets repel? What position are the poles in? The N poles of both magnets are lined up, or the S poles of both magnets are lined up.

Check that children draw a second magnet so that like poles of the two magnets are lined up.

Notebook Summarize Ideas

Have children summarize orally or in writing what causes magnets to repel. Guide them to describe the effect of like poles aligning.

3 Extend/Evaluate

Sum It Up!

1. **Circle It!** Before children complete the activity, remind them that a magnet attracts objects made of iron or steel. Before they circle an object, ask them to look at all three objects and identify each one. Discuss the materials each object is made from to help them identify the one a magnet would be attracted to.
2. **Draw It!** If children have difficulty with the activity, direct them back to the pictures of magnets attracting and repelling in the lesson, and have them note the position of the poles in each one. Encourage children to include arrows in their own pictures to show how the magnets are attracting and repelling.

Sum It Up!

1 Circle It!

Predict which object a magnet will attract. Circle it.

2 Draw It!

In the first box, draw magnets attracting. In the second box, draw magnets repelling.

Attract	Repel

Check children's work to be sure they draw one image of magnets attracting and one image of magnets repelling.

TEKS 1.6B

Brain Check

Lesson 2

Name ____________________

Word Play

Read each statement. Write your answer on the line below.

1. Describe what a magnet does when it attracts.

Sample answer: It pulls an object toward it.

2. Describe what a magnet does when it repels.

Sample answer: It pushes another magnet away.

3. Describe the poles of a magnet.

Sample answer: The poles have the strongest pull.

143

Answer Strategies

Word Play

- Before children complete the activity, review the meanings of the words *attract, repel,* and *pole*. Invite volunteers to describe each picture and use the words to tell what the magnets are doing.
- Children can complete the activity independently or you can complete it as a group. Read aloud each statement. Work together to make a sample answer sentence. Then write the sentence on the board and have children copy it on their papers.

Assessment

Lesson Quiz

See Assessment Guide, p. AG 59.

3 Extend/Evaluate (continued)

Answer Strategies

Apply Concepts

- Model how children will complete the activity by reading aloud the first set of clues.
- Explain that the answer names something that magnets do and encourage children to look back at the yellow highlighted terms in the lesson to see which one applies. Once they know the answer, have them write the word on the line.
- After children understand how to complete the process, have them work in pairs or independently to complete the rest of the page.

Take It Home!

If possible, send home with children a magnet that they can use to test objects. If not, have them make their lists based on what they know about what household objects are made of—that is, whether the household objects they identify are made of iron or steel, or not. Children should bring their completed charts to class for additional discussion and to compare with other children. Consider making one large chart that compiles all of the children's objects for the entire class.

Apply Concepts

Write the word that goes with each set of clues.

Answer	Clues
attract	opposite poles do this; pull toward
repel	push away; like poles do this

Take It Home!

Family Members: Work with your child to identify household objects that a magnet will attract, as well as items it will not attract.

144

Make Connections

Easy

Art Connection

TEKS ART 1.2A, 1.2C
THEATRE 1.1D

Magnet Puppets

- Ask children to draw a few characters on cardboard and cut them out. Then have them attach a steel paper clip to the back and figure out a way that they can hold up the "puppets" using magnets. For example, children could attach a magnet to the end of a dowel or a pencil and swap out the puppets to change characters.
- Partners or small groups should write and perform a short puppet skit for the class, changing out the characters as needed.

Average

Math Connection

TEKS MATH 1.3A

Solve Addition Problems

- Give each pair of children a magnet and a supply of paper clips. Have partners take turns using the magnet to pick up paper clips. Ask, *How many paper clips in all did you pick up?*
- Ask children to count how many paper clips they picked up each time and write an addition sentence to solve the problem. Children can repeat the activity.

Average

Writing Connection

TEKS ELA 1.6A, 1.20A, 1.24C

Make a Picture Dictionary

Display the following words: *magnet, attract, repel*, and *pole*. Have children make a picture dictionary for these words. On each page, children should write the word and draw a picture to show the word's meaning.

Challenging

Social Studies Connection

TEKS SS 1.16A, 1.18B

Design a Magnetic Tool

- Point out that many of the tools we use at home, such as some can openers, use magnets.
- Have children design a new invention that uses magnets. Children can draw their tool and write labels, captions, or sentences to tell about it.

Options for Inquiry

FLIPCHART P. 21

Children can conduct these optional investigations at any time before, during, or in response to the lesson in the Student Edition.

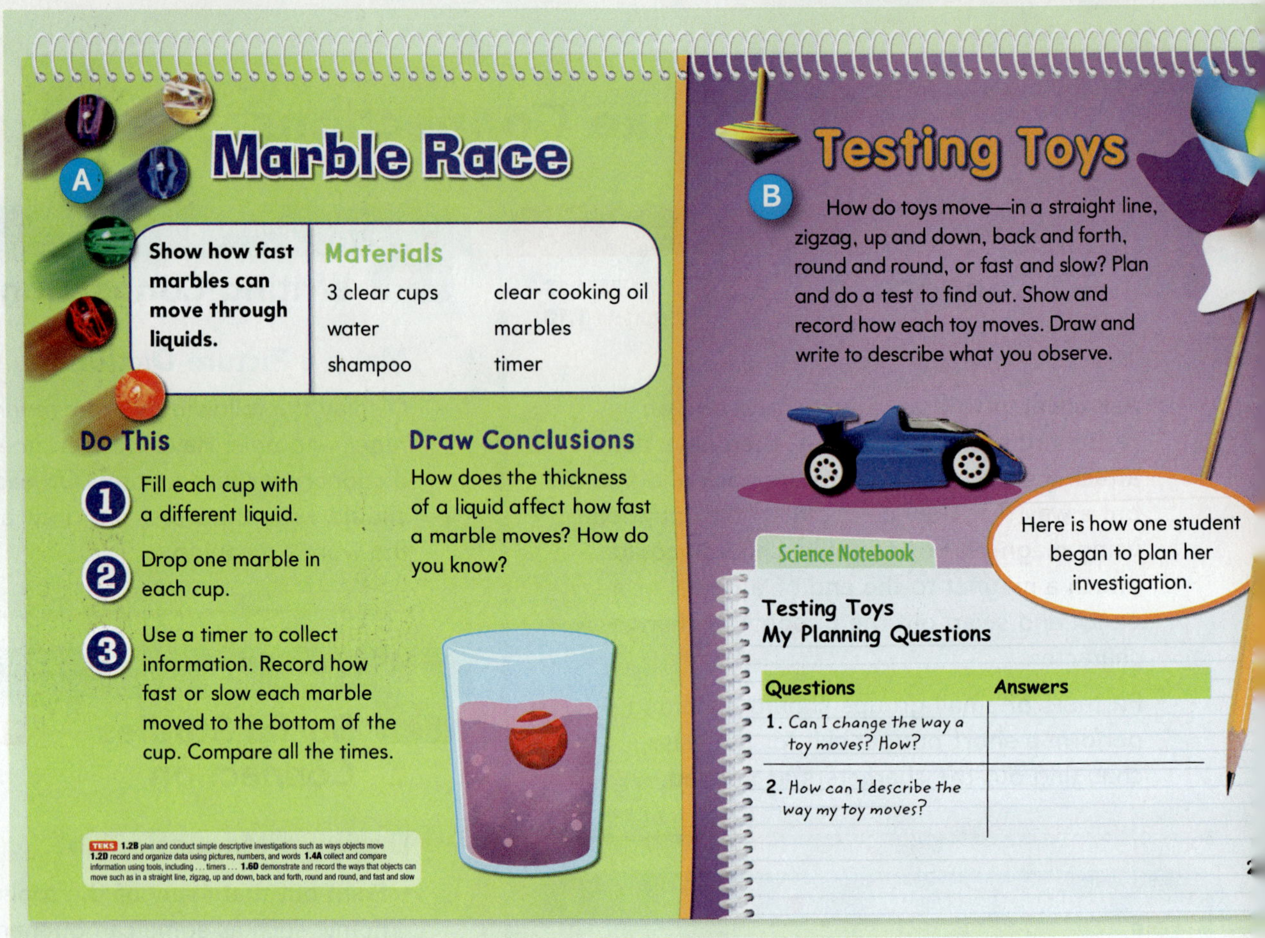

Directed Inquiry

A Marble Race

25 minutes | pairs

Prep and Planning Tips

- Gather marbles that are all the same size.
- Review with children how to use a timer to help them collect and compare information.
- As children fill the cups with liquid, direct them to leave about an inch between the top of each liquid and the rim of the cup. You may wish to label the cups to indicate which liquid is in each.
- Consider placing the cups on a cookie sheet to catch spills.

Caution! Tell children not to put the marbles in their mouths. Have them wash their hands immediately after the activity.

Expected Results

Children will be able to observe that the thicker the liquid, the more slowly the marble moves through it. For example, children should observe that the marble moves fastest through the water and the most slowly through the shampoo.

Independent Inquiry

B Testing Toys

15 minutes | individuals

Prep and Planning Tips

See the Planning for Inquiry page for more information. Gather three or more toys that children can use for observation. The toys should be able to move in a variety of ways. You may wish to review or demonstrate the terms *straight line, zigzag, back and forth,* and *round and round* before children begin the activity.

Science Notebook

Children can use the Science Notebook as a model for planning and conducting their investigation. Encourage them to make a chart like the one shown and include the two sample questions plus any questions of their own. Additional questions may include *How do I predict the toy will move if I push it and let go? How many ways can I make the toy move?*

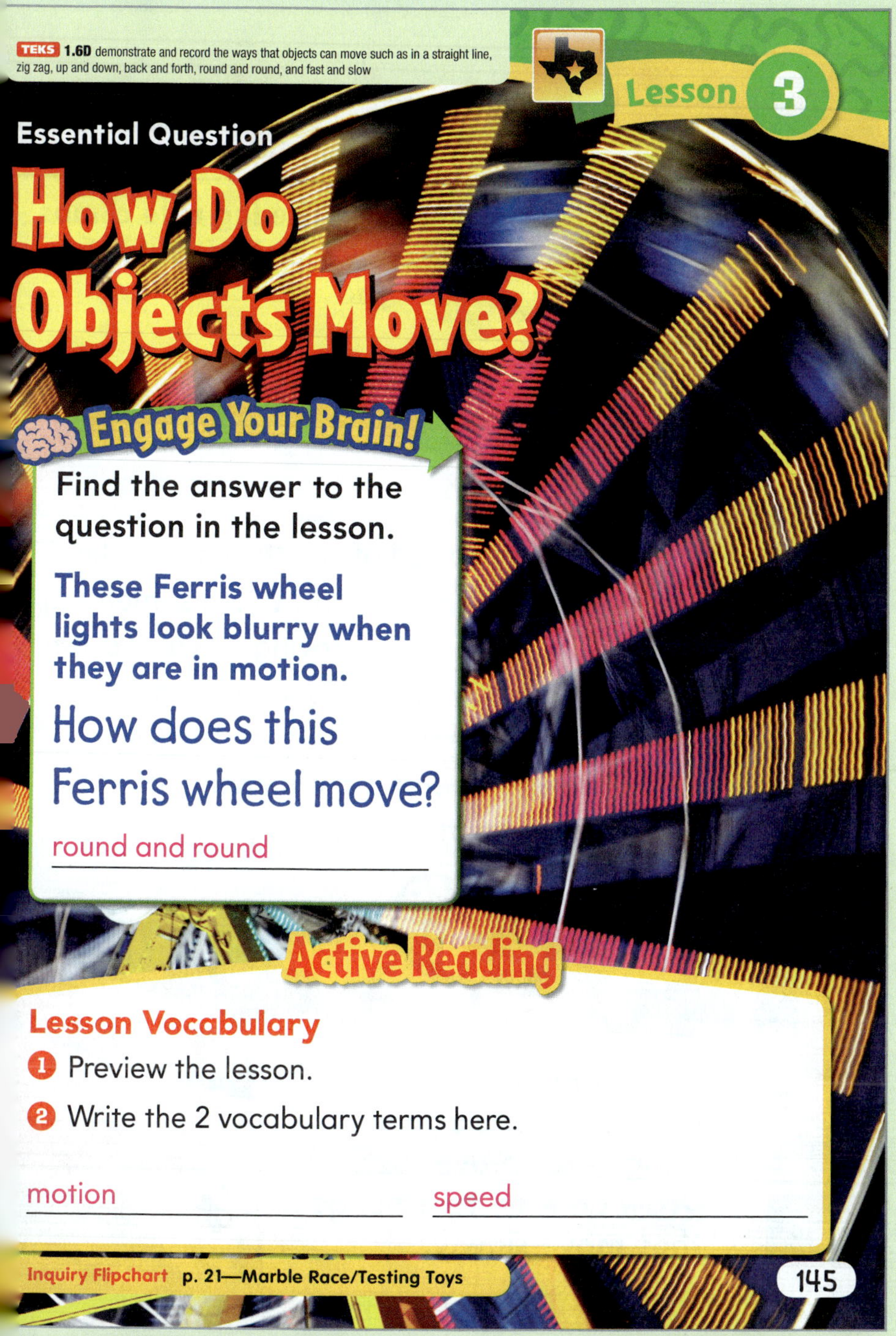

TEKS 1.6D demonstrate and record the ways that objects can move such as in a straight line, zig zag, up and down, back and forth, round and round, and fast and slow

Lesson 3

Essential Question

How Do Objects Move?

Engage Your Brain!

Find the answer to the question in the lesson.

These Ferris wheel lights look blurry when they are in motion.

How does this Ferris wheel move?

round and round

Active Reading

Lesson Vocabulary

1. Preview the lesson.
2. Write the 2 vocabulary terms here.

motion ______ speed ______

Inquiry Flipchart p. 21—Marble Race/Testing Toys

145

Go Digital

An interactive digital lesson is available in Online Resources. It is suitable for individuals, small groups, or may be projected or used on an interactive white board.

1 Engage/Explore

Objectives

- Plan and conduct simple investigations.
- Record and organize data.
- Collect and compare information using tools including timers.
- Demonstrate and record the ways that objects can move such as in a straight line, zig zag, up and down, back and forth, round and round, and fast and slow.

Engage Your Brain!

Ask children to identify the object shown in the photo and tell how it works. Ask why this object might have lights on it. Then have them brainstorm answers to the question *How does this Ferris wheel move?*

Remind children to record their final answer to the question when they find it on the fourth and fifth pages of this lesson.

Active Reading Annotations

Remind children that active readers "make texts their own" by marking them or writing notes to help them understand what they are reading. Encourage children to use their pencil to make annotations and to feel free to change their marks and notes as they read. The goal of annotation is to help children remember what they have read.

Vocabulary and Interactive Glossary

Remind children to find and list the yellow highlighted terms from the lesson. As they proceed through the lesson and learn about the terms, they can add drawings or words in the extra spaces provided in some of the entries in the Interactive Glossary.

2 Explain

Notebook Generate Ideas

Read the heading of the page aloud with children. Explain that things all around us are in motion because they are moving. Call on volunteers to point out things in the picture that are in motion. Ask children to brainstorm a list of ways that things move, such as floating, flying, walking, pushing, pulling, and so forth.

Direct children to the captions and read them aloud. Ask children how the captions help them understand what *speed* means.

Develop Science Concepts

Why do you think the log ride climbs slowly? Why do you think it zooms down fast? It climbs slowly because it is going uphill. It zooms down fast because it is going downhill.

Do you think the water in the picture is in motion? What makes you think so? Yes, the water is moving. It is rippling and splashing.

Do you think the rabbit can move both slowly and quickly? Explain. Yes, a rabbit can run very fast. It can also move so slowly you can hardly see it moving, such as when it is sitting and breathing.

What are some ways you move? I can walk, run, and jump. I can move my arms, legs, head, and hands. I can move slow or fast.

Set Things in Motion

The log ride climbs up the hill slowly.

log ride

Look at all of the things in motion! **Motion** is movement. When something is in motion, it is moving. Up and down is one way that objects can move.

Planes fly fast. A turtle walks slowly. **Speed** is the measure of how fast something moves.

▶ Record the ways objects can move. Circle two things that move fast. Draw an X on two things that move slowly.

146

Differentiation—Leveled Questions

Extra Support

How can you make a wagon move? You can push or pull a wagon to make it move.

Challenge

How can you change the speed of a wagon? Explain. Sample answer: You can pull the wagon less to make it go more slowly. You can pull it harder to make it go faster.

Do the Math!
Make a Bar Graph

Pam went on three rides. This graph shows how long she waited for each ride.

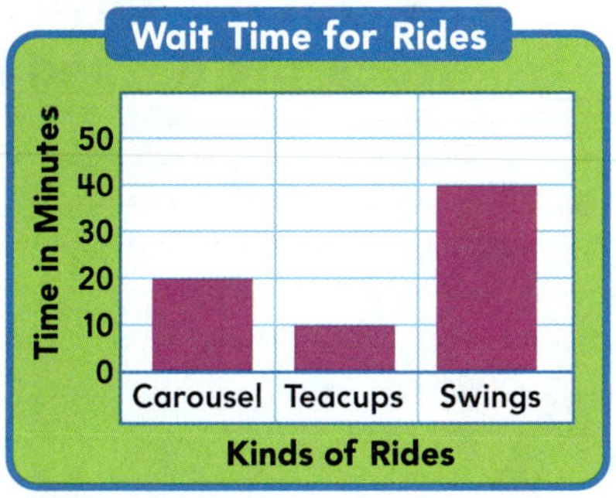

Use the graph to answer the questions.

1. Which ride had the shortest wait?

   teacups

2. How does the graph tell you?

   The bar for the teacups is the shortest.

he log ride zooms
lown the hill fast.

147

English Language Learners

ELPS 1A, 1E, 2C

Reinforce Object Words and Content Vocabulary Help children become familiar with the names of the different objects on these pages. Point to each object, say its name, ask children to repeat after you, and make a circle around the object as they say its name.

Also point out to Spanish-speaking children the cognate of motion *(movimiento)* and the Spanish equivalent for speed *(velocidad).*

TEKS 1.6D

Develop Science Vocabulary

motion Explain that *motion* and *movement* are synonyms, or words with the same or almost the same meanings. Give a sentence that uses *movement* such as *The ball's movement really surprised us* and then say it again with *motion* in place of *movement.* Have children notice that the meaning of the sentence does not change because the two words mean the same thing.

speed Point out that *speed* is the measure of how fast something moves. However, children may hear other words that have *speed* in them. List examples, with context sentences, and have children use what they know about *speed* to guess the meaning of *speedy* and *speeding.*

Interpret Visuals

Ask children to describe what the children in the picture are doing. They are riding in a log on a water ride. **Which children are going slowly?** the children going up the ride **Which children are going fast?** the children going down the ride

Do the Math!

TEKS MATH 1.8C

Make a Bar Graph

Review the graph with children. Ask them to identify where the rides are listed and where the wait times are located on the graph. Review with children what the bars show. Help them conclude that the shortest bar represents the shortest time and the longest bar represents the longest time.

Notebook Summarize Ideas

Ask children whether their ideas about motion and speed have changed since they read this section. Have them summarize the main idea orally or in writing.

2 Explain (continued)

Generate Ideas

Notebook

Read the heading aloud to children. Direct them to the pictures of the amusement park rides across the bottom of the pages. Call on volunteers to describe amusement park rides they have been on. Encourage them to explain how each ride moved and how it felt to be on the ride.

Point out to children that like amusement park rides, objects can move in many different ways. Then ask them to demonstrate or name ways in which things can move. Explain that they will be learning more about how things move as they read these pages.

Active Reading Details

Explain that a detail sentence may give an example. Or, it may describe something. Active readers ask themselves, "What topic does this detail sentence tell about?" The answer will help readers keep the main idea in mind.

Develop Science Concepts

How is moving back and forth different from moving in a straight line? When you move in a straight line, you go in only one direction. When you move back and forth, you move in opposite directions over and over again.

Look at the picture of the bumper cars. Why aren't the bumper cars going in a straight line? The cars bump into one another and push each other in different directions. People steer the cars in different directions.

How is the way a Ferris wheel moves like the way a merry-go-round moves? They both go round and round.

It's Your Move!

Objects can move in other ways, too. They can move in a straight line, zigzag, back and forth, or round and round.

▶ **Record the ways objects can move. Trace the dashed lines below.**

straight line

zigzag

148

Differentiation—Leveled Questions

Extra Support

What are four ways things can move? in a straight line, back and forth, round and round, zigzag

Challenge

What is a way something might move that is not shown on these pages? Sample answer: Objects can move up and down.

TEKS 1.6D

Interpret Visuals

Ask children to describe and compare how the roller coaster and the bumper cars in the pictures move. Point out the arrows in the pictures and the arrows at the ends of the dashed lines. Have children explain how these help them understand the objects' movements.

Repeat with the pictures of the boat ride and the Ferris wheel. Point out to children that pictures often include information that helps the reader understand what the picture is trying to show or demonstrate.

Develop Inquiry Skills

CONTRAST **How do the bumper cars and the Ferris wheel move differently?** The bumper cars zigzag and the Ferris wheel goes round and round.

How do the roller coaster and the boat ride move differently? The roller coaster moves in a straight line. The boat ride moves back and forth.

Misconception Alert

Children may get the impression that every object can move in only one way. Explain that many objects can move in many different ways. Demonstrate how a ball can be used to move in all four of the directions described on these pages. Point out that people can also move in many ways, such as in a straight line, round and round, and zigzag.

Notebook Summarize Ideas

Have children look again at the pictures and captions on these two pages. Have them work with partners to summarize the details presented on these pages about how amusement park rides can move. Then have children explain how these details relate to the main idea of the lesson.

English Language Learners

ELPS 1H, 2C, 2E

Clarify Expressions Clarify the heading *It's Your Move!* Have children draw a line under the word *Move* in the heading. Explain that in a game, a *turn* may be called a *move* because with each turn, a player moves a piece. Therefore, the expression *It's your move* is another way to say *It's your turn to move (or do) something.* Reinforce this concept by having children act out *moves* they might make when playing their favorite games or sports.

3 Extend/Evaluate

Sum It Up!

1. **Draw It!** Have children read the direction line either silently or aloud. Call on a volunteer to tell in his or her own words what children are supposed to do. If necessary, help children read the labels. Suggest that they picture in their minds what each type of motion looks like. Suggest that children go back to the previous two pages to find pictures that illustrate each kind of motion.
2. **Circle It!** Have children read the direction line. Then ask *Which object should you circle?* Help children understand that they are to circle the object that goes fast. You may wish to review each pair of pictures with children so there is no confusion about what the pictures show. Suggest that children refer to *Set Things in Motion* to review objects that move fast and slowly. Point out to children that they should correct wrong responses so they can use the Sum It Up! page to study for tests.

Sum It Up!

1 Draw It!

Read the labels. Record how objects move. Draw an arrow to show the kind of motion.

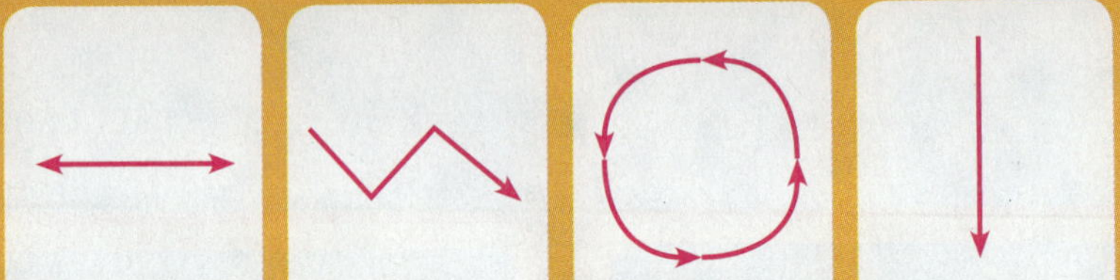

back and forth	zigzag	round and round	straight line

2 Circle It!

Look at each pair of objects. Circle the one that goes fast.

150

Brain Check

Lesson 3

Name ____________________

Word Play

Work your way through the maze to match the word with its meaning.

Answer Strategies

Word Play

- Check to make sure that children understand what a maze is and how it is used. If necessary, demonstrate using this maze but in a way that does not give the answer away.
- You can have children refer to the page on which each term is defined or discussed. As a challenge activity, ask children to construct their own mazes using the same terms and definitions.
- To help children better communicate the main ideas of the lesson, ask them to use each term in a sentence. If they have trouble, pair children and ask them to think of the sentence together.

Assessment

Lesson Quiz

See Assessment Guide, p. AG 60.

3 Extend/Evaluate (continued)

Answer Strategies

Apply Concepts

- If children are not familiar with a word web, explain that the most important word, phrase, or idea goes in the middle of the web. Details about this important idea go in the surrounding circles.
- Encourage children to look back at the lesson pages as needed. Tell them to pay particular attention to the descriptions of the way things move.
- As a lesson follow-up, ask children to summarize what they learned in the lesson. Encourage them to name new facts and ideas that they never knew about before they read the lesson.

Take It Home!

Suggest that children work with family members to identify objects in motion around their homes. Have them demonstrate and describe the motion with words like *fast, slow, straight, zigzag, up and down, round and round,* and *back and forth.* You may wish to provide suggestions of objects they may want to look at, such as toys, doors and drawers, fixtures such as knobs and light switches, and appliances such as vacuum cleaners. Children should record the different ways objects can move. They can present their findings to the class.

Apply Concepts

Complete the word web. Record how objects can move.

The Way Things Move

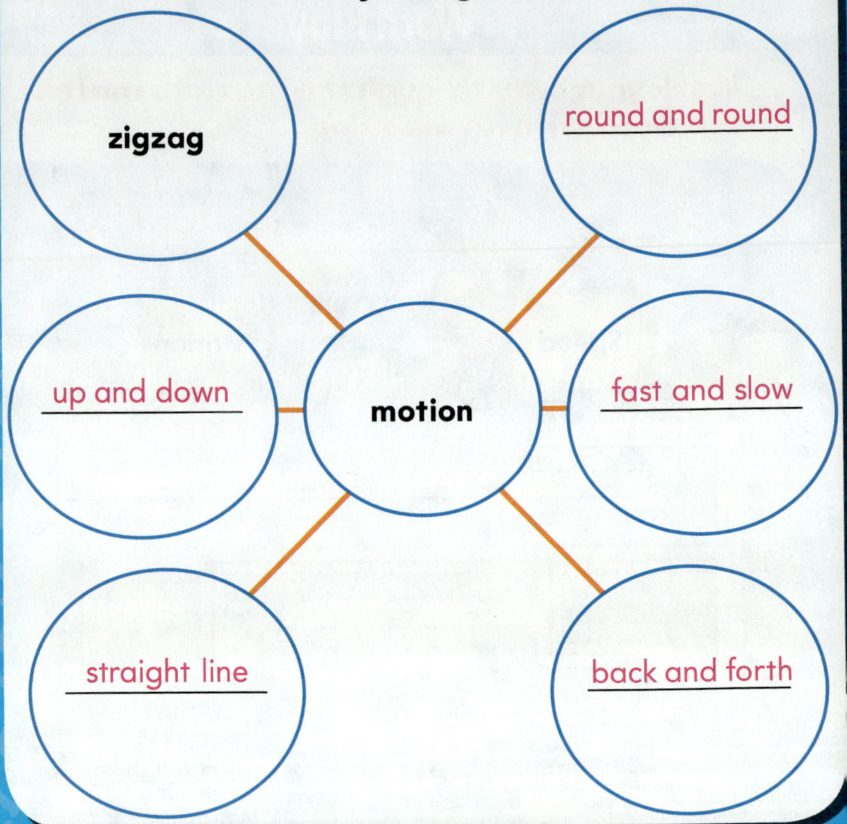

Take It Home! **Family Members:** Discuss with your child the motion and speed of different objects. Ask them to show and record the different ways objects can move.

Make Connections

Easy

Art Connection

TEKS ART 1.2A

Draw Motion

- Give each child a sheet of art paper and some finger paints.
- Have children make finger paintings using these motions: straight line, zigzag, up and down, back and forth, and round and round.
- Encourage them to try to show *movement* in their paintings and to make them as colorful as possible.
- Have children share their work and identify the paths they made.

Easy

Physical Education Connection

TEKS PE 1.7A

Play a Motion Game

- Have children play a variation of the "Hokey Pokey" game, adding words for specific types of motion. For example, "Put your left foot in, take your left foot out, put your left foot in, and shake it *back and forth*!"
- Make up as many verses as possible using different motion words.

Average

Language Arts Connection

TEKS ELA 1.4B

Find Motion in Books

- Provide small groups of children with a favorite book from the classroom reading center.
- Have children look through the book to find examples of things in motion. Invite children to share what they found with the class.

Challenging

Writing Connection

TEKS ELA 1.19A

Write About Motion

- Have children think of a sport or active game that they like to play. Ask them to think about how their body moves when they play the game.
- Have them write a description that tells about the motion. Before children begin to write, you may wish to suggest they act out the motions from the game they have chosen and to draw their movement.
- Have children use their drawings to write descriptions of how their bodies moved.

People in Science

Objectives

- Describe what scientists do.
- Recognize that scientists come from all backgrounds.
- Identify the role of technology in the work of scientists.

Notebook Generate Ideas

Share the following background information with children before you assign the feature. Ask questions to ascertain children's prior knowledge.

Look at the picture of Isaac Newton. How can you tell that he lived long ago? Sample answer: You can tell by his clothes.

Why do you think a scientist like Isaac Newton would want to study how objects move? Sample answer: If we understand how things move, it might help us understand more about motion and to predict how things will move in the future.

Background

- Isaac Newton was born in England in 1642, more than 370 years ago. He lived to be 85 years old.
- As a boy, Newton liked to invent things. He invented a windmill that could grind wheat, a water clock, and a sundial.
- Newton left school when he was 14, but he spent so much time reading, he was sent back to school.
- Newton was a professor at Cambridge University, where he taught mathematics.

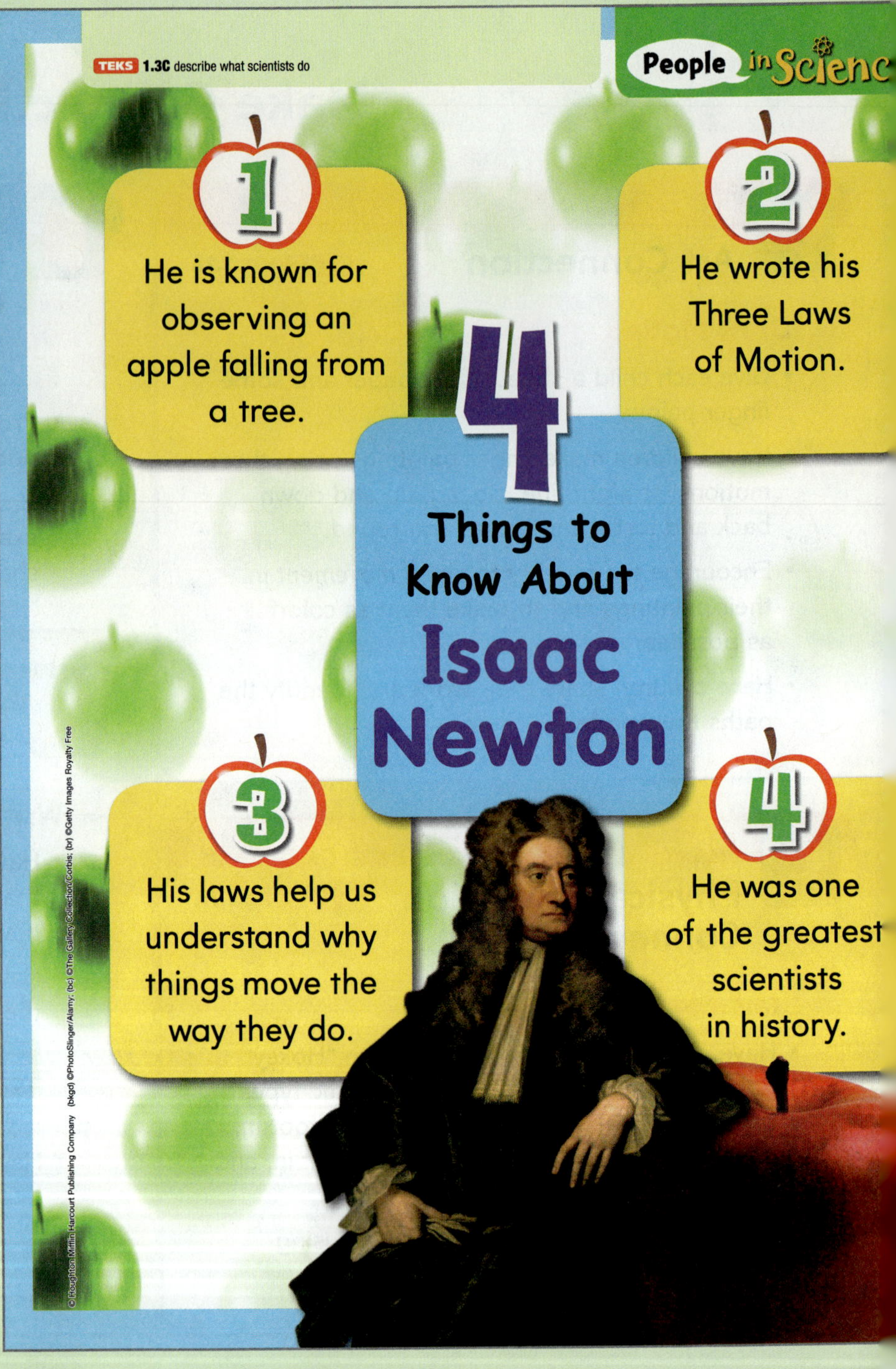

Writing Connection

TEKS ELA 1.2

Write to Inform Have children prepare four fact cards based on the information about Isaac Newton in this feature. Each card should include a word, phrase, or drawing that tells about Isaac Newton. Remind children that a fact is something that can be proved to be true. As a challenge, some children could verify their facts by finding a second source of information either in an online or print encyclopedia or in other nonfiction books.

ple in Science continued

bjects in Motion

hink about what you know bout Isaac Newton. Then write ne answer to each question.

Nature of Science

Provide the following scenario: You are standing in the schoolyard when all of a sudden a ball rolls past you. *Where did the ball come from? What started the ball moving? How fast was it going? In what direction was it moving?* These are questions a scientist might ask. Scientists try to find the answers to questions and problems. Ask children to list three ways they could begin to investigate, or find out, the answer to their questions about the moving ball.

Develop Science Concepts

What is the difference between motion and speed? Motion is movement. Speed is the measure of how fast something moves.

What are some ways things can move? They can move in a straight line, zigzag, back and forth, round and round, up and down, or fast and slow.

What is the difference between a push and a pull? A push moves an object away from you. A pull moves an object closer to you.

Develop Inquiry Skills

OBSERVE Remind children that carefully seeing or observing what happens is an important skill scientists use to arrive at new ideas and to help them draw conclusions.

Describe what Isaac Newton did. He wrote his Three Laws of Motion.

What did Isaac Newton observe that helped him form his Three Laws of Motion? He observed an apple falling from a tree.

What are some things you can observe when you see an object move? Sample answer: how fast the object is moving, what causes it to move

Notebook Summarize Ideas

Have children look again at the pictures and captions on these pages. Invite them to think about the information presented and then summarize the main idea for partners.

Guided Inquiry

FLIPCHART P. 22

25 minutes
pairs

Children should follow the directions on the Flipchart. The accompanying pages in the Student Edition provide scaffolding for guided inquiry.

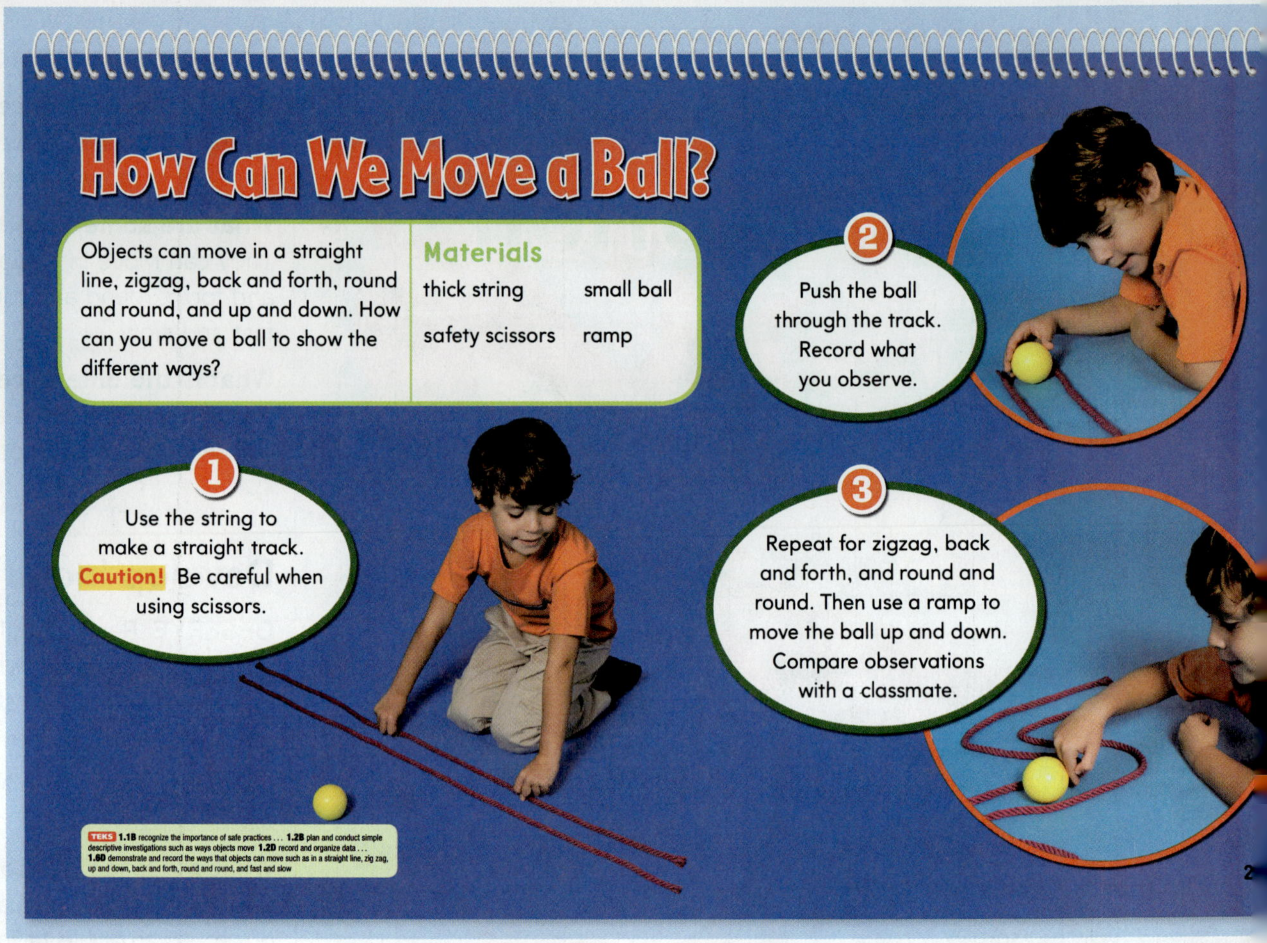

Inquiry Skills Focus Compare

Objectives

- Recognize the importance of safe practices.
- Ask questions about objects observed in the natural world.
- Plan and conduct simple investigations.
- Record and organize data.
- Demonstrate and record the ways that objects can move.

Prep and Planning Tips

See the Planning for Inquiry page for more information.

- If children are having trouble keeping strings in place, help them use tape to attach the string to the floor.

Caution! Be sure children recognize the importance of safe practices to keep themselves and others safe and healthy. Review with children that they should never run with scissors and should always point scissors away from their body.

Expected Results

Children should determine what happens when they change the shape of the track and add a ramp to the activity.

1 Engage/Explore

Attention Grabber

Demonstrate juggling two small, soft balls. Ask children to describe how the balls move using words from the previous lesson, such as *fast, slowly, round and round,* and so forth. If you drop a ball, have them use describing words to tell how that ball moved, too!

Preview Activity

Before beginning the investigation, have children review the directions on the Inquiry Flipchart and the accompanying Student Edition response pages. Then, have them complete the response pages as they follow directions on the Flipchart.

Inquiry Flipchart p. 22

Lesson 4
INQUIRY

TEKS **1.2A** ask questions about organisms, objects, and events observed in the natural world **1.2B** plan and conduct simple descriptive investigations such as ways objects move **1.2D** record and organize data using pictures, numbers, and words **1.6D** demonstrate and record the ways that objects can move such as in a straight line, zig zag, up and down, back and forth, round and round, and fast and slow

ame ______________________

Essential Question

How Can We Move a Ball?

Set a Purpose

ell what you will do in this investigation.

will show the different ways objects can move.

hink About the Procedure

What kinds of motion will you show?

will show straight-line, zigzag, back-and-forth,

ound-and-round, and up and down motions.

How will you show the motion?

will use string to make tracks and push a ball through the

acks to show motion. I will also use a ramp to show motion.

155

Go Digital

A virtual lab experience is available with the Online Resources for this program.

1 Engage/Explore (continued)

Guide the Investigation

Develop Inquiry Skills

COMPARE As children complete each part of the activity, ask them to compare how the ball moved along the tracks they made. You may wish to ask how the ball moves differently on this track than the one before. Also ask how the ball moved when they used the ramp. Ask questions such as the ones below as they plan and complete the activity.

How many different tracks will you need to make? Why? I will need to make four different tracks, one to show each kind of motion.

What do you think might happen if you do not make your tracks carefully? The ball may go outside of the track or go in a different direction than I planned.

How might your tracks look different from your classmates' tracks? Sample answer: My track might be longer or shorter than my classmates' track. We might be making tracks that show different kinds of motion.

What do you think might happen if you push the ball too hard or make it go too fast? It might not follow the track. It might even roll outside of the track.

What do you think you will use the ramp for? Sample answer: to show how a ball can move up and down

2 Explain

Develop Inquiry Skills

RECORD YOUR DATA Discuss with children how they will use the table to record their observations of the ball's movement. Children should be able to draw lines and arrows to illustrate the different ways the ball moved along the tracks they made as well as the ramp. You may wish to read aloud and review the phrases in the *Motion* column before children begin.

DRAW CONCLUSIONS Ask children to demonstrate moving their hands or bodies in a straight line in one direction only, then moving back and forth. Have them refer to their charts if needed to review how the two motions are alike and different.

Continue the discussion by asking children to demonstrate moving round and round, up and down, and moving in a zigzag. Invite them to compare the types of movement and tell how they are different. Help children conclude that objects move in different ways.

3 Extend/Evaluate

ASK MORE QUESTIONS Discuss children's responses. Some children may raise questions about whether an object can move in just one way or more than one way. Some may ask how to make an object move fast or slowly. Focus their questions about how a ball can move on things that can be tested. As an extension activity, have children plan an investigation.

Assessment

Lesson Quiz

See Assessment Guide, p. AG 61.

Record Your Data

Draw to record what you did. Check children's answers.

Motion	Drawing
Straight line	
Zigzag	
Back and forth	
Round and round	
Up and down	

Draw Conclusions

How can a ball move? How do you know?

A ball can move in a straight line, in a zigzag, back and forth, round and round, and up and down. I know because I demonstrated it by moving the ball through the track and up and down the ramp.

Ask More Questions

What questions can you ask about how objects move?

Sample answer: How can you use classroom objects to show how a ball moves fast and slowly?

156

Differentiated Inquiry

Easy

Move and Stop an Object

- Suspend a block or some other small object from a string tied to the middle of a meter stick. Rest each end of the meter stick on a desk so the block hangs down between two desks.
- Ask children how they could make the block swing back and forth. Record their ideas. Then have children test their ideas to see if they work.
- Set the block in motion. Ask children to name different ways that they might stop the block from moving. Have them name as many ways as possible and record their answers. Then have them test which ideas work.

Easy

Act Out Motion

- Tell children that they are going to act out different kinds of motion. After they pantomime each kind of motion, ask them to name the kind of motion they performed.
- Have children act out pushing a ball forward (straight line), bouncing a ball up and down (up and down), swinging on a swing (back and forth), skiing down a hill (zigzag), and riding on a merry-go-round (round and round).
- To extend the activity, have children suggest activities of their own and tell the kind of motion they illustrate.

Average

Make a Table

- Have each child draw a two-column chart. At the top of the chart, they should label the columns *Motion* and *Object*. Under *Motion,* they should list these words: *straight line, zigzag, back and forth, round and round, and up and down.*
- Have children fill in the *Object* column with the names of objects that illustrate the kinds of motion listed in the *Motion* column.
- When children finish, have them share their charts with one another.

Challenging

Make a Motion Graph

- Have children choose four or five different moving toys. Provide them with drawing paper, colorful paper squares, and glue.
- Have the group test how each toy can move (straight, zigzag, back and forth, round and round, fast and slow, and up and down) and note their results.
- Children should then work together to make a bar graph showing how many ways each toy can move. Help them by drawing the chart outline, writing the title *How Many Ways?,* and labeling each row with the name of one of the toys. Children can use glue to add the squares to the chart.
- Children should observe that a single object can move in several ways.

Options for Inquiry

FLIPCHART P. 23

Children can conduct these optional investigations at any time before, during, or in response to the lesson in the Student Edition.

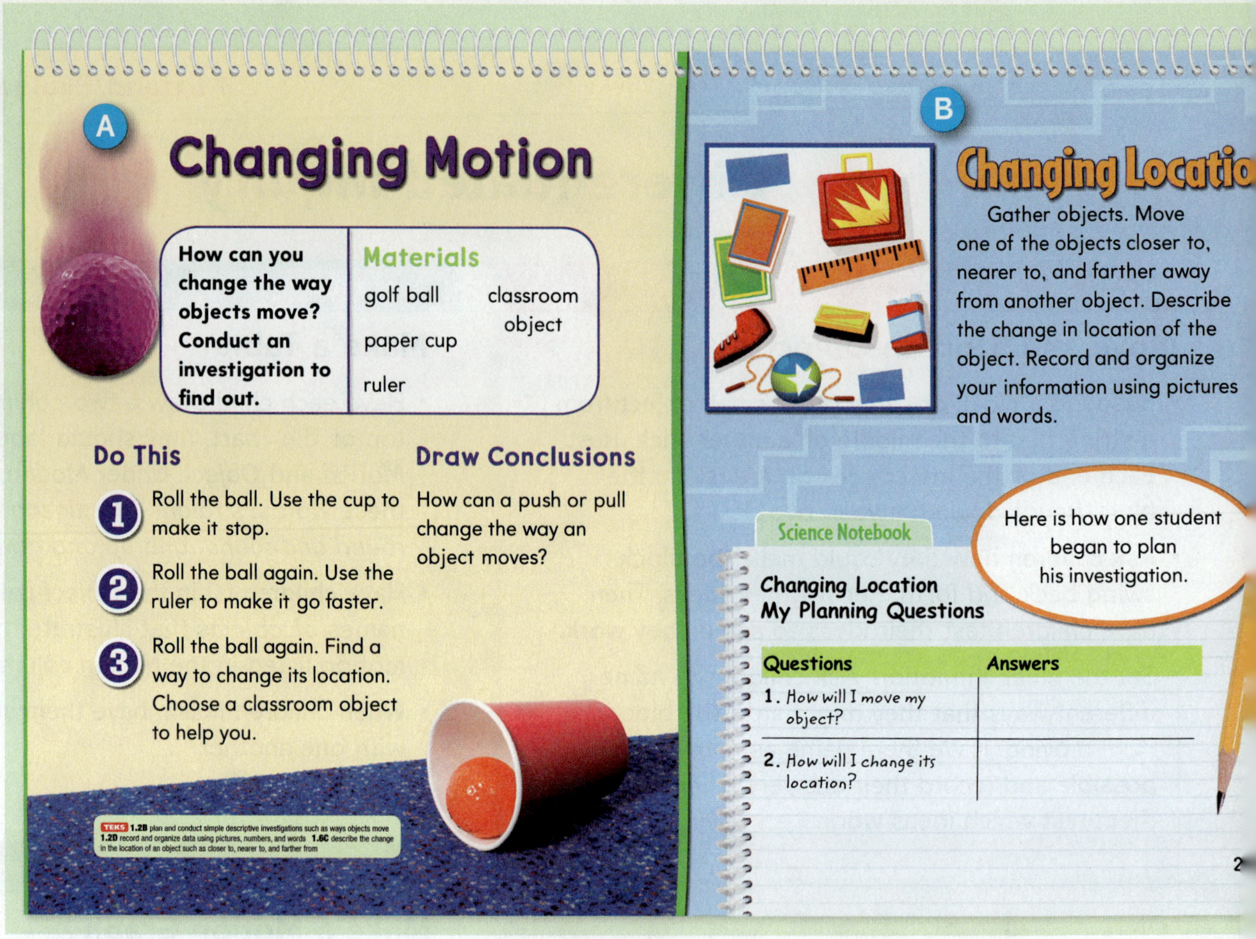

A

Changing Motion

How can you change the way objects move? Conduct an investigation to find out.

Materials
golf ball
paper cup
ruler
classroom object

Do This

1. Roll the ball. Use the cup to make it stop.
2. Roll the ball again. Use the ruler to make it go faster.
3. Roll the ball again. Find a way to change its location. Choose a classroom object to help you.

Draw Conclusions

How can a push or pull change the way an object moves?

TEKS **1.2B** plan and conduct simple descriptive investigations such as ways objects move **1.2D** record and organize data using pictures, numbers, and words **1.6C** describe the change in the location of an object such as closer to, nearer to, and farther from

B

Changing Locatio

Gather objects. Move one of the objects closer to, nearer to, and farther away from another object. Describe the change in location of the object. Record and organize your information using pictures and words.

Science Notebook

Changing Location
My Planning Questions

Questions	Answers
1. How will I move my object?	
2. How will I change its location?	

Here is how one student began to plan his investigation.

Directed Inquiry

A Changing Motion

15 minutes
individuals

Prep and Planning Tips

To prepare, place the golf ball and the ruler in the paper cup. Provide one set of materials for each child.

Encourage children to tap the ball rather than apply a continuous force to make it go faster and change direction. This will help avoid the misconception that an object must have a continuously applied force to keep it moving.

Provide children with pencil and paper so they can record what they do each time. Have them refer to their notes when they review the activity at the end.

Expected Results

Children should determine what force needs to be applied to stop or change the motion of the ball.

Independent Inquiry

B Changing Location

30 minutes
small groups

Prep and Planning Tips

See the Planning for Inquiry page for more information. Gather classroom objects that children can use. Review with them how they can use forces, such as pushes and pulls, to change the location of an object. Remind children to use words, such as *closer to, nearer to,* and *farther from* to describe the change in location.

Notebook

Science Notebook

Children can use the Science Notebook as a model for planning and conducting their own investigation. Encourage them to make a chart like the one shown and include the sample questions plus any questions of their own. Have children record and organize their information using pictures and words.

TEKS 1.6C describe the change in location of an object such as closer to, nearer to, and farther from

Lesson 5

Essential Question

How Can We Change the Way Objects Move?

Engage Your Brain!

Find the answer to the question in the lesson.

How is pushing a swing like pulling a wagon?

A push and a pull are both

forces ______.

Active Reading

Lesson Vocabulary

1. Preview the lesson.
2. Write the 3 vocabulary terms here.

push ______ force ______

pull ______

Inquiry Flipchart p. 23—Changing Motion/Changing Location

157

Go Digital

An interactive digital lesson is available in the Online Resources. It is suitable for individuals, small groups, or may be projected or used on an interactive white board.

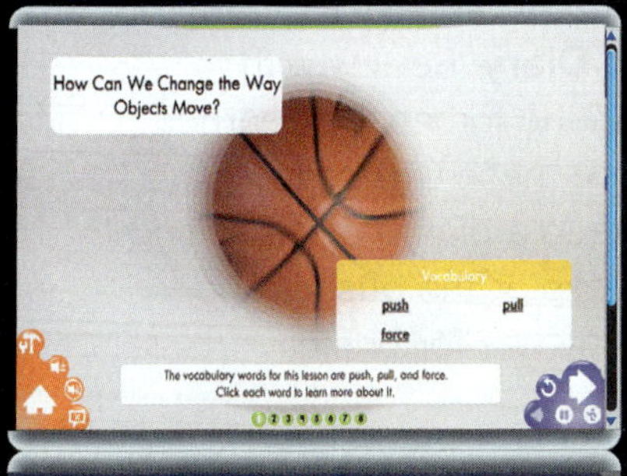

1 Engage/Explore

Objectives

- Plan and conduct simple investigations such as ways objects move.
- Record and organize data using pictures and words.
- Describe the change in the location of an object such as closer to, nearer to, and farther from.

Engage Your Brain!

Have children brainstorm an answer to the question *How is pushing a swing like pulling a wagon?* Give them a hint by explaining that the answer to the question has to do with how we make objects move and how pushing and pulling are alike. Record children's responses on the board.

Remind them to record their final answer to the question when they find it on the second and third pages of the lesson.

Active Reading Annotations

Remind children that active readers "make texts their own" by marking them or writing notes to help them understand what they are reading. Encourage children to use a pencil to make annotations and to feel free to change their marks and notes as they read. The goal of annotation is to help children remember what they have read.

Vocabulary and Interactive Glossary

Remind children to find and list the yellow highlighted terms from the lesson. As they proceed through the lesson and learn about the terms, they can add drawings or words in the extra spaces provided in some of the entries in the Interactive Glossary.

2 Explain

Notebook Generate Ideas

Read the heading of the page aloud with children, and point out that they use a force whenever they make an object move. Ask children to brainstorm a list of ways they make things move, such as pushing, pulling, throwing, lifting, and putting down.

Active Reading Vocabulary

Explain to children that a vocabulary word may be highlighted in a color. Active readers pay attention to highlighted words because their meaning is given in the same sentence or the next sentence. In this lesson, the meaning of the word *force* is given in the sentence after it is first used.

Develop Science Vocabulary

push and **pull** Explain to children that the words *push* and *pull* are antonyms, or words with opposite meanings. Reinforce this concept by pointing out other word pairs from this unit that are opposites such as *fast* and *slow*, *up* and *down*, and *straight* and *round*.

force Read aloud the sentence that gives the meaning of the word *force* as it is used in this lesson. Explain that here, the word *force* means something that can make an object start or stop moving. A force can also make an object change its speed and direction. Explain that *force* can also mean "strength" or power."

Develop Science Concepts

Do you think both the girl and the boy are helping the wagon move? Why or why not?
Yes; the girl is pushing and the boy is pulling. Both forces help the wagon move.

In Full Force

What makes the wagon move? The girl gives it a push. A **push** moves an object away from you. The boy gives the wagon a pull. A **pull** moves an object closer to you.

Pushes and pulls are forces. A **force** makes an object move or stop moving. When the girl and boy push and pull the wagon, it starts to move.

Draw yourself pushing something.

Check to see that children draw themselves pushing something, such as a shopping cart or swing.

158

Writing Connection

TEKS ELA 1.19

Forces Diary Review with children the forces they learned about on these two pages. Have them keep a diary in their science notebooks of the pushes and pulls they use for one day. Guide children to use one page for recording their pushes and one page for recording their pulls. Have children share their diary entries in small groups.

▶ **Draw yourself pulling something.**

Check to see that children draw themselves pulling something, such as a wagon or chair.

Active Reading

Find the sentence that tells the meaning of **force**. Draw a line under the sentence.

159

Differentiation—Leveled Questions

Extra Support

How do you know that a push or a pull is a force? A force is something that makes an object move, and a push and a pull both make objects move.

Challenge

Tell if throwing a ball to another person is a push or a pull. Why? Throwing a ball to another person is a push, because you are moving the ball away from yourself.

Develop Science Concepts

Do you think it is easier or harder for two people to move the wagon than if one person worked alone? Why? It is easier for two people to move the wagon because two people together are stronger than one.

How is pushing the wagon different from pulling the wagon? Pushing moves the wagon away. Pulling moves the wagon closer.

What happens when you pull an object? It moves closer to me. **What happens when you push an object?** It moves away from me.

Interpret Visuals

Have children read the interactive instructions on each page. Encourage them to brainstorm objects they have pushed and objects they have pulled.

Like the girl and boy in the picture, what are some things you have pushed and what are some things you have pulled? Sample answers: specific toys, sporting equipment, wagon, sled

Develop Inquiry Skills

COMPARE/CONTRAST **How is what the girl and the boy are doing different?** The girl is pushing the wagon away from herself. The boy is pulling the wagon toward himself.

How is what they are doing alike? They are both using force to move the wagon. Pushes and pulls are both forces.

Notebook Summarize Ideas

Have children look at the photographs again and think about the main idea. Ask if their ideas about pushes and pulls have changed since they read this section. Have them draw and label pictures to summarize the main idea about pushing and pulling.

2 Explain (continued)

Notebook Generate Ideas

Read the heading aloud to children. Point out that not only can they use a force like a push or a pull to make objects move, but they can also use a force to change the way an object is moving.

Point out that they will be learning about ways a force can be used to change motion as they read the next few pages. Ask children to brainstorm some ways that a force can change the way an object moves. Encourage them to review the images for ideas. List their suggestions on the board.

Develop Science Concepts

How is kicking a ball different from catching a ball? Kicking sets the ball in motion. Catching the ball stops it from moving.

How can you make a ball go faster or more slowly by kicking it? The ball goes fast or slow depending on how hard you kick it.

How can you make a wagon go faster by pushing it? The harder you push the wagon, the faster it will go.

What happens when you give something a push? It will move away from you.

How can you move something closer to you? You could pull it.

Using Force

Look at the pictures. How does a force move a ball? A force can change the way an object moves. It can change a ball's speed or location.

Changing Speed

Force can change an object's speed. It can make something start moving or stop moving. It can make something go faster or more slowly.

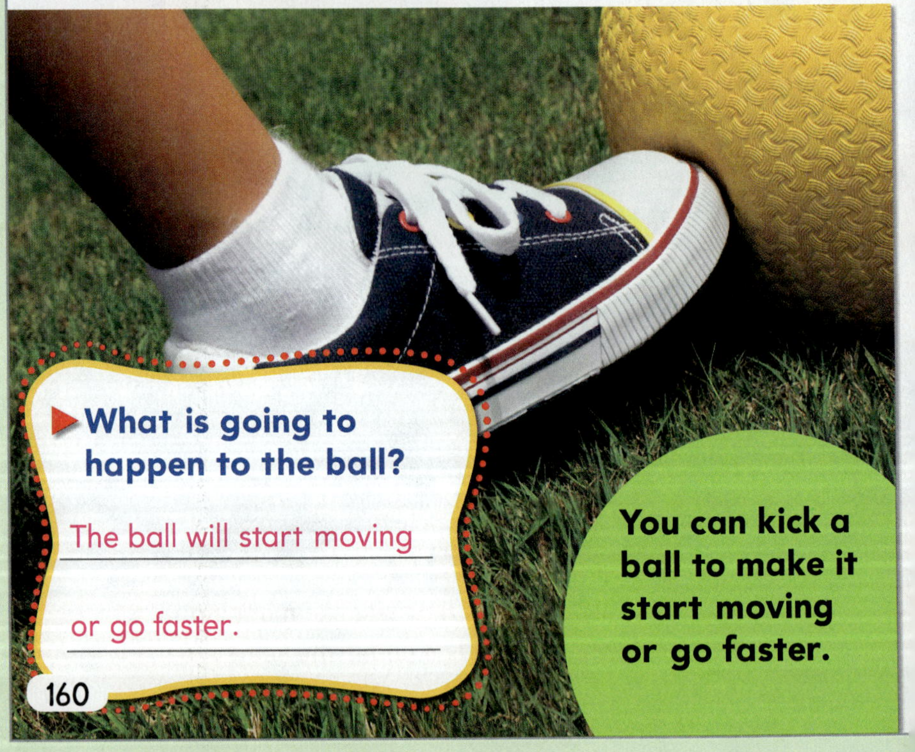

English Language Learners

ELPS 1E, 1F, 2E

Reinforce Content Words Point to the word *Speed* in the heading *Changing Speed,* and have children underline the word. Say the word aloud, and have children repeat it after you. Explain that speed is how fast an object moves. Work with children to make a web of words that can describe the speed of things, such as *fast, speedy, quick,* or *slow*. Help children read the list with you. Have them draw or find pictures to illustrate something going at a fast speed and something going at a slow speed

Describe how the motion of the cars change.

1 The cars start moving.

2 The cars move faster down the hill.

3 The cars stop at the end.

161

Math Connection

TEKS MATH 1.5D

Solve a Word Problem Share the following word problem with children:

Jake and Alexa race their toy cars down a hill. Jake's car speeds down the hill in 10 seconds. Alexa's car speeds down the hill in 7 seconds. How much faster is Alexa's car?

Help children write a subtraction sentence to solve the problem:

10 – 7 = 3. So Alexa's car was 3 seconds faster than Jake's.

Misconception Alert

Children may have the impression that objects must have a continuously applied force to keep moving. Direct their attention to the ball being kicked. Point out that once the ball is set in motion, it continues to move with nothing pushing it. Ask children to offer other examples of objects being set in motion and staying in motion, such as giving a toy car a push to set it in motion or throwing a ball.

Interpret Visuals

Direct children to the three pictures of the cars going down the hill. Point out that the pictures show three events in order from first to last. First, two friends push the other friends' cars from the top of a hill. Next, the cars go faster and faster down the hill.

What happens last? The cars stop at the bottom of the hill.

Develop Inquiry Skills

SEQUENCE **Why do you think the pictures are arranged from first to last?** The pictures show the order in which things happen. If the pictures were not shown in order, it would be hard to figure out what happened to the cars.

If you could add another picture to the end of this sequence, what might it show? Sample answer: The picture could show the two friends pushing the cars back up the hill.

Notebook Summarize Ideas

Have children brainstorm ideas about ways objects can be made to go faster or more slowly and how they can be made to start and stop moving. Ask them to summarize these pages by describing what happens to the ball from the time it is placed in front of the kicker until the catcher stops it.

2 Explain (continued)

Notebook Generate Ideas

Have children look at the pictures, headings, and labels to preview what these pages are about. Ask them about past experiences they have had that look like what they are seeing or reading, such as playing with toys or swinging on swings.

Active Reading Details

Explain to children that a detail sentence may give an example. Or, it may describe something. Active readers ask themselves "What topic does this detail sentence tell about?" The answer will help readers keep the main idea in mind. In this case, the detail sentence tells more about location words.

Develop Science Concepts

Find the two small pictures at the bottom of the page. Look at the picture on the left. Now look at the picture on the right. What changed from one picture to the next? The trucks are in different locations.

Describe how the location of the green truck changed. Did it move closer to or farther from the yellow truck? It moved farther from the yellow truck.

How do you know? Sample answer: In the picture on the left, the green truck is next to the yellow truck. In the picture on the right, there is more space between them.

What made the green truck move? A force made it move.

Changing Location

The toys are in different places. Some are nearer, or closer, to the yellow truck. Others are farther from it.

Nearer, closer, and **farther** are location words. Location tells where something is. A force can move something to a new location.

Active Reading

A detail is a fact about a main idea. Draw one line under a detail. Draw an arrow to the main idea it tells about.

The green truck is closer to the yellow truck.

A force moved it farther from the yellow truck.

162

English Language Learners

ELPS 1D, 2E, 4F

Location Words Have children circle the location words *nearer* and *farther* on the page. Point out that these words have opposite meanings. Use two objects to demonstrate those meanings, saying each word as you demonstrate. Repeat for *nearer* and *closer*, having children underline the words and explaining that the words mean nearly the same thing. Finally, have partners take turns saying each word and moving classroom objects to demonstrate their understanding.

What's Your Location?

Think about pushing a friend on a swing. Your friend moves farther from you and then comes nearer, or closer. Forces can move things closer to and farther from you.

▶ **Describe how this swing changes location as it moves.**

Sample answer: The swing moves farther from the dad when he pushes it. It moves closer to him when it swings back.

Differentiation—Leveled Questions

Extra Support

A force can change the speed of an object. What else can it change about an object? its location

Challenge

Describe how you can change the location of a toy car. Use the word force in your answer. Sample answer: I can use a force to push the car farther away from me. I can use a force to pull it closer to me.

Interpret Visuals

Direct children to the picture of the swing. Have them point to both the person moving the swing and the person swinging. Ask children to use the picture to describe how the location of the swing changes when the person pushes it. Encourage them to use location words such as *nearer to* and *farther from* to describe the motion.

Then ask: **How does the father make the swing change location?** He uses a force to push the swing farther away from him. If necessary, suggest that children think about a time when they were in a swing and describe how and why the location of the swing changed.

Develop Inquiry Skills

OBSERVE **How does the location of the green truck change?** It moves farther away from the yellow truck. **How does the location of the swing change?** The swing moves farther away from the father.

COMPARE **How are those two changes the same?** The green truck and the swing both moved farther away from another object.

Notebook Summarize Ideas

Have children look again at the pictures, headings, and captions. Ask them to think about the information they learned on these two pages and then summarize the important ideas orally to a partner or in a few written phrases.

2 Explain (continued)

Notebook Generate Ideas

Ask children to share experiences they have had on amusement park rides. Have them describe the motion of the rides they have been on. Then have children predict what they will learn on this page about what makes the coaster in the picture move. Have them read to find out if their predictions are correct.

Develop Science Concepts

What do you think causes the coaster to start moving? the force from a motor

How is the coaster moving when it goes up a hill? It moves slowly.

How does the coaster's motion change when it goes down a hill? It goes faster and faster.

How does the coaster's location change? It goes up and down.

What do you think causes the location of the coaster to change? Forces cause the location of the coaster to change.

How are the movement of a coaster and a swing alike and different? Sample answers: They both can change speed and location. The coaster goes much faster than the swing.

Think about how gravity pulls the coaster down to Earth. What else might gravity pull to Earth? Sample answers: rain, a ball after you throw it, a ball if you drop it, paper airplanes

Explain to children that gravity pulls things to Earth even if nothing is touching them.

Why It Matters

What Makes That Coaster Move?

Roller coasters are fun! They go up and down, fast and slow, round and round. People on the ride might yell as they change speed and location. What makes the coaster move?

A motor pulls a chain. The chain pulls the car up the first hill.

164

Writing Connection

TEKS ELA 1.6D, 1.24C

Make Flash Cards Have children use location words to make four flash cards. On one side, have children write a pair of location words that are opposites. On the other side, have them draw a picture that shows what the words mean. Word pairs might include *up/down, in/out, above/below, nearer to/farther from, under/over.* Have children share their cards with one another. They can take turns showing each other the picture side of the card and guessing the words that are written on the back of the card.

Gravity is the force that pulls the car down. Gravity pulls all things toward Earth.

▶ **What pulls the car down the hill?**

gravity

165

Interpret Visuals

Ask children to use a finger to trace the coaster's track. Have them identify how the coaster's motion changes as the track changes.

How does the coaster's motion change as it goes along the track? It goes up and down. It curves. It goes fast and slow.

Direct children to the captions on each page. Point out that captions are often used to give information about pictures. Ask children to read the captions silently.

What did you learn from the captions? I learned what makes the coaster move.

Develop Inquiry Skills

INFER **What effect does the coaster's motion have on the people riding it?** It causes them to move quickly. It makes them go fast and slowly.

Notebook Summarize Ideas

Have children think about the main idea of these two pages. Ask if the predictions they made about what makes the coaster move were correct. Then have them summarize the main idea orally.

Differentiation—Leveled Questions

Extra Support

What makes the coaster move up and down? The force from a motor and a chain pull the car up. Gravity pulls the car down.

Challenge

What can you infer about other rides after learning about the coaster? Other rides probably use motors and gravity to help them move, too.

3 Extend/Evaluate

Sum It Up!

1. **Solve It!** Tell children to draw a line under the most important clue of the riddle: *I can be a push or a pull.* If necessary, have them review the vocabulary words at the beginning of the lesson.
2. **Circle It!** Remind children that we can use a force to change the way an object moves. Have them reread the section *Using Force* to review what these changes are.
3. **Label It!** Instruct children to look at both pictures before labeling. If they have difficulty identifying the spatial relationships between the two balls, remind them that objects that are closer to each other have less space between them, while objects that are farther away from each other have more space between them.

Sum It Up!

1 Solve It!

Write the word that solves the riddle.

I move a box
when it is full.
I can be a push
or a pull.
What am I?

force

2 Circle It!

Forces can change objects. Circle the words that tell the kinds of changes.

speed (circled) | color
size | location (circled)
shape

3 Label It!

Describe the ball's change in location. Write <u>nearer to</u> or <u>farther from</u> below each picture.

nearer to

farther from

166

Brain Check

Lesson 5

Name ____________________

Word Play

Complete the letter by using these words.

speed	push	pull
force	closer	farther

Dear Jen,

Yesterday my brother and I played trains. The front car can ___pull___ other cars. I gave my train a ___push___. It moved ___farther___ from me. It moved ___closer___ to my brother. My brother sent the train down a hill. The ___force___ made it go so fast! It picked up ___speed___ as it went down. It was fun to make the trains move!

Your friend,

Amy

167

TEKS 1.6C

Answer Strategies

Word Play

- Read the directions with children and make sure that they understand what to do. Review each word in the box at the top of the page. You may wish to have children refer to the pages in the lesson on which these words occur and are discussed.
- If children are unfamiliar with cloze passages, tell them that they should use clues in the sentences as well as what they learned from the lesson to fill in the missing words.
- If children find parts of the cloze passage to be particularly difficult, make certain to review the relevant concept.
- To help children better communicate the main ideas of the lesson, ask them to use each word in a sentence of their own. If they have trouble, pair children and ask them to think of a sentence together.

Assessment

Lesson Quiz

See Assessment Guide, p. AG 62.

3 Extend/Evaluate (continued)

Answer Strategies

Apply Concepts

- If children have difficulty filling in the chart, work through the activity orally and elicit responses by putting the chart information in question form. For example, ask: *What is something a force can change about an object?* and *How does a swing move when you use a force to push it?*
- Encourage children to look back at the lesson pages as needed. Tell them to pay particular attention to how the words are used and the examples given.
- As a lesson follow-up, ask children to summarize what they learned in the lesson. Encourage them to name facts and ideas that they never knew before.

Take It Home!

Suggest that children work with family members to gather information about things that move in their homes and then report back to the class. Have them look for examples of pushes and pulls and explain how these forces change motion.

Apply Concepts

Complete the chart. Write a word on each blank line.

nearer to | farther from | location

Cause	Effect
Force	changes the location of an object.
Force	pushes a swing farther from you.
Force	moves a ball nearer to a bat.

Take It Home!

Family Members: Ask your child to tell you about forces and motion. Have your child point out examples of pushes and pulls and explain how those forces change motion.

168

Make Connections

Easy

Art Connection

TEKS ART 1.2C

Make a Poster

- Provide children with poster board and markers. Have them write the headings *Pushes* and *Pulls*.
- Supply them with old magazines and safety scissors.
- Have them look for pictures that show objects being pushed or pulled, cut out their favorite ones, and tape or paste them to the poster board under the appropriate headings.

Caution! Remind children to be careful when they are using scissors. If in doubt, provide pictures already cut from magazines.

Easy

Writing Connection

TEKS ELA 1.19A

Write a Description

- Have children brainstorm playground games that involve pushes and pulls. (Possibilities include tug-of-war, hopscotch, capture the flag, and soccer.)
- Have individuals or pairs choose a favorite game, name an action, and write whether the action involves a push or a pull. For example, in soccer you kick the ball; you push it away from you.
- Ask children to share their writing.

Average

Social Studies Connection

TEKS SS 1.16C

Draw a Tool

- Have children think about a tool they have used and how they changed its speed and location. For example, when you use a broom or a shovel, you push it to change its speed and location.
- Have children draw their tool and write a label or a caption that summarizes how it changes speed and location. Have them write a sentence at the bottom that tells why the tool is useful.

Challenging

Health Connection

TEKS HEALTH 1.4B

Make a Diagram

- Point out to children that in some kinds of exercise, you push against gravity. Have children draw pictures that show how they exercise.
- Have them label the body parts that they use to push against gravity.
- Before children draw, you may wish to have them pantomime the exercise to help identify the body parts that push against gravity.
- Have children share their drawings and talk about them in small groups.

S.T.E.M.

Engineering and Technology

Objectives

- Identify and explain a problem and propose a solution in his/her own words.
- Identify the contributions the Wright brothers made to aviation.
- Describe how the design of airplanes has changed over the years.

Notebook Generate Ideas

Share the background information before you assign the feature. Ask questions to ascertain children's prior knowledge.

Have you ever flown on an airplane? What was it like, or what do you think it would be like? Accept all reasonable answers.

Why might people need airplanes? People may need to get from place to place more quickly than they could if they drove a car or took a train or a boat.

Background

- One of the keys to the Wright brothers' success was their observation of birds. They noticed that air moving over certain parts of the wings helped lift a bird into the air. They also noticed that a bird would change or move its wings if it wanted to turn during a flight.
- The Wright brothers thought that they could use what they learned about birds to control their aircraft. For some years before the first motorized flight, the men tested different ideas. They designed gliders—airplanes without engines—and flew them as kites and as manned, piloted vehicles.
- During the glider tests, the Wright brothers discovered their gliders needed a tail to help them balance. After more tests, the brothers began work on a motorized airplane. A year later, they made their first successful flight.

TEKS 1.3A identify and explain a problem such as finding a home for a classroom pet and propse a solution in his/her own words

S.T.E.M.

Engineering and Technolog

Fly to the Sky

The First Flight

Wilbur and Orville Wright were brothers and inventors. They had a problem. The brothers wanted to fly an airplane. Together they came up with a solution. First, they made designs of their plane. Next, they built it. Then, they tested it. After a few tries, their plane flew.

This is one of the Wright Brothers' planes.

Today's planes look different and have more parts.

College & Career Readiness

CCRS III.A.1, III.B.1, III.B.3 III.C.1, III.D.1, III.D.

Aeronautical Engineers This feature provides an opportunity to develop children's awareness of STEM careers related to airplanes and flying, such as aeronautical engineers. Suggest children go online to find out more about aeronautical engineers.

Help children find relevant artic and have them talk about if the articles are current and accurat Children should write three sentences about what they learned about aeronautical engineers using scientific vocabulary.

S.T.E.M. continued

ane Parts

:h part of a plane has a job to do. The gs help lift it. The tail keeps it flying straight. propeller moves the plane forward.

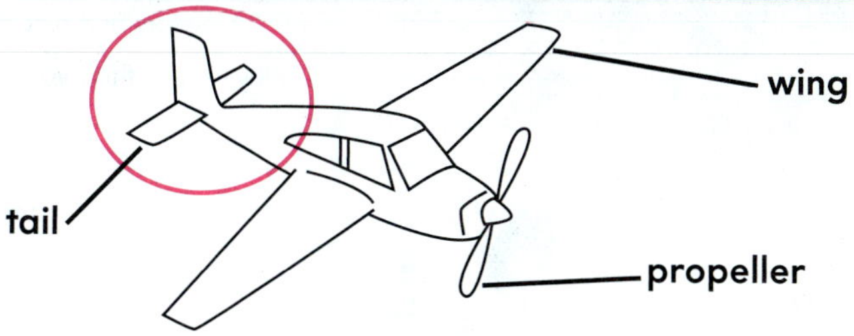

the picture of the plane to answer the questions.

Which part keeps the plane flying straight? Circle it.

What would happen if the wings on the plane were missing? Explain.

wings help lift the plane. If they were missing, the plane

ld not be able to fly.

ld On It!

Build your own paper airplanes. Complete **Build It: Paper Airplanes** on the Inquiry Flipchart.

Build On It!

In **Build It: Paper Airplanes,** the design challenge associated with this lesson, children use the steps of the engineering design process to design and build paper airplanes that fly far. For more details, see the pages that follow.

Other opportunities to apply the design process appear throughout the *Inquiry Flipchart.*

TEKS 1.3A

Develop S.T.E.M. Concepts

When children have completed reading the feature, ask questions to help them reflect on the design process and how it is used to make new technology and help solve problems.

What problem do airplanes solve? They provide a way for people to travel quickly from place to place.

How did the Wright brothers use the design process to invent their plane? They made designs and built them. Then they tested their designs until they found one that worked.

What are some parts that make up an airplane? The wings, tail, and propeller are some parts of a plane. **What does each one do?** The wings help lift the plane, the tail keeps it flying straight, and the propeller moves it forward.

Develop Inquiry Skills

OBSERVE Ask children to carefully observe the diagram of the airplane. **What are the labeled parts in the diagram?** wing, tail, and propeller **How does the drawing help you understand more about an airplane's parts?** The drawing shows where the parts are and how they fit together.

PREDICT **What would happen if any one of these parts were missing?** The airplane would not fly.

Why do you think so? Each part of the plane has a job to do to help the plane fly. If one part were missing, the whole plane would not work.

Notebook Summarize Ideas

Ask children to summarize what they learned about the Wright brothers and how they used the design process to invent the first airplane. Then have children explain how the parts of a plane have different jobs and that the parts are all needed for the technology to work.

S.T.E.M.

Engineering and Technology

FLIPCHART P. 24

30 minutes

individual or pairs

Objectives

- Recognize and demonstrate safe practices.
- Record and organize data.
- Identify and explain a problem and propose a solution in his/her own words.

Prep and Planning Tips

- Have available for each child or pair 8½ x 11 sheets of paper in at least two different weights, such as construction paper and printer paper.
- Ahead of time, clear an area outside for plane flying. Have a small group help you mark off a starting line and 6-inch increments from the starting line to 20 or 30 feet.
- **Caution!** Be sure children recognize and demonstrate safe practices to keep themselves and others safe and healthy. Children should wear goggles to protect their eyes. Instruct them to use all materials appropriately.

Expected Results

Children will build and fly paper airplanes that are made of different kinds of paper to see which flies farthest.

1 Engage/Explore

Attention Grabber

Make a simple paper airplane, and show it to children. Ask them to predict how far it will fly if you toss it from the front of the classroom. Then toss it so children can see whether their predictions were correct.

Preview Activity

Before beginning the activity, have children review the directions on the Engineering and Technology Flipchart page.

Enduring Understandings

Revisit the Big Idea and Essential Questions

Big Idea **Forces change the way objects move. Magnets attract some objects and repel others. Energy can cause matter to move or change.**

To explore the Big Idea, post key terms from the unit on the board and challenge children to explain different ways word pairs are connected. For example, a child might explain that they are using *force* when they *pull* open a door. Prompt children with the following pairings.

- motion, speed
- force, motion
- force, pull
- force, push
- push, pull
- electricity, light
- light, heat
- attract, repel
- magnet, pole

Essential Questions

Post the Essential Questions, and use the following prompts to guide a discussion.

Lessons/Essential Questions	Prompts
L1 **How Do We Use Energy?**	• Give two examples of how energy is used in the classroom.
L2 **How Do Magnets Move Objects?**	• Demonstrate how to pick up a paper clip with a magnet.
L3 **How Do Objects Move?**	• Using things from the classroom, demonstrate different ways objects move.
L4 **How Can We Move a Ball?**	• Explain what happens when you kick a soccer ball.
L5 **How Can We Change the Way Objects Move?**	• Name at least two ways that you could change the way a ball moves.

Notebook Science Notebook

You may use the following strategies after children complete the unit or after each lesson.

- Have children review and edit the responses to the Essential Questions they drafted at the beginning of the unit. Suggest they cross out sentences or ideas that are unnecessary or inappropriate.
- Have children draft flash card facts in their Science Notebooks to prepare for a game. After generating the facts, children can make a game by writing a question on one side of an index card and the answer on the back. The cards can be drawn and collected as questions are answered correctly.

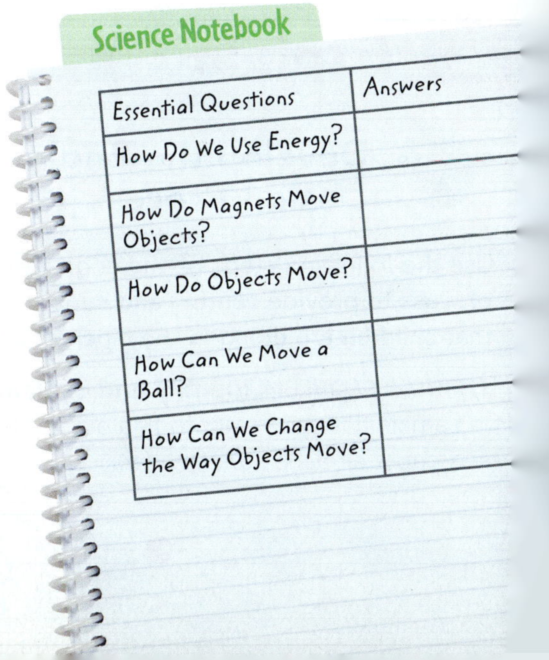

Guide the Activity

Develop Inquiry Skills

OBSERVE Allow children time to handle the available paper. You may also wish to provide books and other reference materials with paper airplane designs if children want to try different designs.

MEASURE Help children measure how far their planes fly. You may wish to use standard measurements, such as inches and feet, or nonstandard measurements, such as the number of "kid feet" that each plane flies.

GATHER AND RECORD DATA Have each child or each pair observe and record how far each plane flies. Help them display the data in chart form.

Strategies for Success

Before beginning the investigation, have children review the directions on the *Inquiry Flipchart*. Then find directions for a simple paper airplane from a book or online resource. Write the directions on the board. Then demonstrate how to make an airplane. When children fly their planes, have them begin at the same starting point and toss their planes with the same amount of force each time.

Science Notebook

During the Activity Have children write their names on their planes and "A" or "B" to tell which plane is which. Children may need guidance in measuring and recording distances in their Science Notebooks. You may want to demonstrate this step or have children do it in teams.

2 Explain

Develop the Engineering Design Process

Use the following steps of the engineering design process to provide context and support for the analyses that children are doing in the flipchart activity.

1. **FIND A PROBLEM** **Identify and explain the problem.** Sample answer: I want to find out the best way to make a paper airplane so it flies far.
2.
3. **TEST AND IMPROVE** **How can you test your airplanes?** I can fly each one, measure how far they fly, and compare the measurements. **How can you improve your airplanes so they fly farther?** I can try different kinds of paper and designs.

3 Extend/Evaluate

Quick Check

What was the same about your two airplanes? Sample answer: The airplanes had the same design and were tossed with the same amount of force. **What was different?** Sample answer: The kind and weight of the paper I used was different. **How do you know which plane flew farther?** I measured how far each plane flew and then compared the two measurements.

4. **REDESIGN** Have children try out other designs, using their own ideas or ideas from research.
5. **COMMUNICATE** Have children share their results. Ask them to tell how far each airplane flew and whether the weight of the paper had any effect on how far the plane flew.

Science Notebook

After the Activity Check children's notebooks to see that they recorded the flight distances accurately.

Michael DiSpezio's Tips & Tricks

Expecting Variation Be aware that paper plane performance is often inconsistent and may not demonstrate differences only because of designs or differences in paper weight. How the plane is launched, how its wings have sagged, or how local breezes have changed can all affect the range in performance. That variability, however, is okay as long as children understand the possible factors involved. It's all part of the learning process.

Unit 4 Review

Name ______________________

Vocabulary Review

Use the terms in the box to complete the sentences.

heat
magnet
motion

1. If something is moving, it is in motion.

TEKS 1.6A

2. Heat is a kind of energy people use to keep warm.

TEKS 1.6B

3. A magnet can pull objects made of iron or steel.

Science Concepts

Fill in the letter of the choice that best answers the question.

TEKS 1.6D

4. A ball is hanging from a string. You pull the ball back and let it go. What kind of motion does the ball make?
   - Ⓐ back and forth
   - Ⓑ round and round
   - Ⓒ straight line

TEKS 1.6A

5. Which sentence identifies a way that sound energy is important?
   - Ⓐ It lets people cook food.
   - Ⓑ It can warn people of danger.
   - Ⓒ It gives people light to see at night.

Item Analysis

Items	TEKS	Depth of Knowledge	Cognitive Complexity
1		1	Low
2	**1.6A**	1	Low
3	**1.6B**	1	Low
4	**1.6D**	2	Moderate
5	**1.6A**	2	Moderate

Unit Review

Answer Key

Vocabulary Review (5 points each)

1. motion

   Point out the word *moving* in the sentence. If necessary, review the section on motion.

2. heat

   Remind children that some kinds of energy are sound and light. Ask them to think of another kind of energy that keeps them warm.

3. magnet

   Children can look back through the unit for pictures of objects that are pulling steel and iron objects, such as paper clips. Ask them to identify the objects doing the pulling.

Science Concepts (7 points each)

4. A

   Ask children to demonstrate each answer choice by acting out the motion or drawing it with an arrow.

5. B

   Remind children that sound is energy you can hear.

Assessment

Unit 4 Test and Performance Assessment

See Assessment Guide, pp. AG 65–AG 71, for Unit Test and Performance Task with Long Option rubric.

Unit Review *continued*

Answer Key

Science Concepts (7 points each)

6. B

Point out that if the fire is not giving off a kind of energy in an answer choice then the entire answer choice must be incorrect. Both parts of the answer choice must be true for the answer choice to be the correct one.

7. B

Point out that something that needs electricity to run is usually plugged into an outlet. Ask, "Which of these objects must be plugged in to run?"

8. C

Be sure children read all of the answer choices before making their final selection. Explain that they should choose the most complete answer choice, not one that is only partially true.

9. A

Ask, "What kinds of objects can a magnet attract?" Guide children to understand that they must choose an object made of iron or steel. Discuss why answer choices B and C are incorrect.

UNIT 4

TEKS 1.6A

6. Which kinds of energy is the fire giving off? Identify them.

Ⓐ heat and sound
Ⓑ light and heat (circled)
Ⓒ light and sound

TEKS 1.6A

7. Which of these objects needs electricity to work?

Ⓐ a baseball bat
Ⓑ a lamp (circled)
Ⓒ a marker

TEKS 1.6C

8. What can a force do?

Ⓐ stop an object
Ⓑ move an object
Ⓒ move or stop an object (circled)

TEKS 1.4A, 1.6B

9. Which of these objects will a magnet attract? Predict it.

Ⓐ (circled)

Ⓑ

Ⓒ

172 **Unit 4** Unit Review

Item Analysis *(continued)*

Items	TEKS	Depth of Knowledge	Cognitive Complexity
6	**1.6A**	2	Moderate
7	**1.6A**	2	Low
8	**1.6C**	1	Low
9	**1.4A, 1.6B**	2	Moderate

UNIT 5 Earth's Resources

Big Idea and Essential Questions

This Unit was designed to focus on this Big Idea and these Essential Questions.

Big Idea

There are many kinds of resources on Earth.

Essential Questions

L1 **What Can We Find on Earth?**

L2 **What Is Soil?**

L3 **What Do We Find in Soil?**

L4 **How Do Soils Differ?**

L5 **Where Can We Find Water?**

L6 **How Can We Save Resources?**

Take It Home! A School-Home Connection letter in English and Spanish is provided in Online Resources.

Professional Development

Houghton Mifflin Harcourt and **NSTA,** the **National Science Teachers Association,** have partnered to provide customized professional development resources for teachers using *ScienceFusion*.

The Professional Development Resources include:

- Do-it-yourself resources, where you can study at your own pace
- Live and archived online seminars
- Journal articles, many of which include lesson plans
- Fee-based eBooks, eBook chapters, online short courses, symposia, and conferences

Access to The NSTA Learning Center is provided in the *ScienceFusion* Online Resources.

NSTA National Science Teachers Association

The NSTA Learning Center

Unit Planning

Options for Instruction

Choose from **Interactive Worktext** and **Leveled Readers**, **Digital**, and **Inquiry** options to meet the Texas Essential Knowledge and Skills.

	LESSON 1	LESSON 2	LESSON 3
Essential Questions	**What Can We Find on Earth?**	**What Is Soil?**	✔ Guided Inquiry **What Do We Find in Soil?**
Texas Essential Knowledge and Skills	TEKS 1.1C, 1.7C	TEKS 1.7A	TEKS 1.2A, 1.2B, 1.2D, 1.7A
Interactive Worktext	☐ Student Edition pp. 177–186 • All Natural • Air • Water • Plants and Animals • Rocks • Soil	☐ Student Edition pp. 189–198 • Super Soil • The Scoop on Soil • In the Mix	☐ Student Edition pp. 199–200 • Scaffolding for Inquiry
Leveled Readers	Parallel coverage of the lesson topics is provided in the Extra Support, On-Level, and Enrichment readers. See p. 175J for detailed reader information.		
Hands-On Inquiry	Inquiry Flipchart p. 25 **Just Add Water** ☐ Directed Inquiry **Resources All Around** ☐ Independent Inquiry	Inquiry Flipchart p. 26 **Cleaning Crew** ☐ Directed Inquiry **How Much Water?** ☐ Independent Inquiry	Inquiry Flipchart p. 27 **What Do We Find in Soil?** ☐ Guided Inquiry
Digital Curriculum	☐ Digital Lesson **Online Resources** Interactive presentation of lesson content 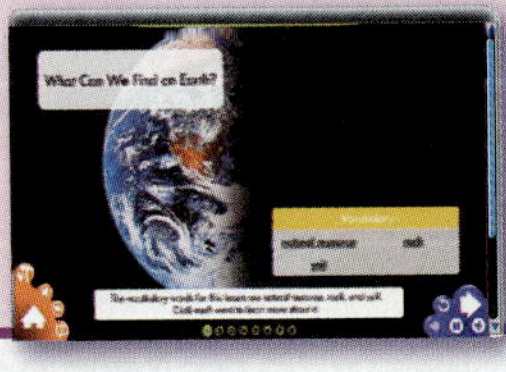	☐ Digital Lesson **Online Resources** Interactive presentation of lesson content 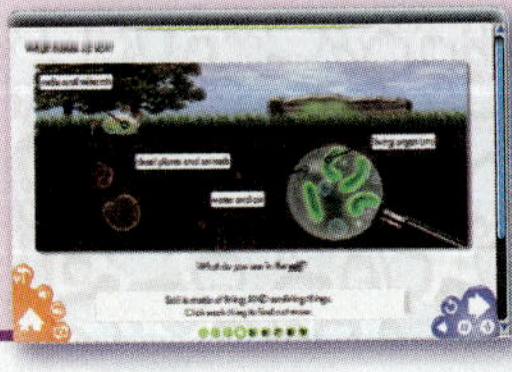	☐ Virtual Lab **Online Resources** Interactive scaffolded inquiry 

LESSON 4

✔ Guided Inquiry

How Do Soils Differ?

TEKS 1.2A, 1.2B, 1.2D, 1.7A

☐ **Student Edition**
pp. 201–202
- Scaffolding for Inquiry

Inquiry Flipchart
p. 28

How Do Soils Differ?
☐ Guided Inquiry

☐ **Virtual Lab**
Online Resources
Interactive scaffolded inquiry

LESSON 5

Where Can We Find Water?

TEKS 1.7B

☐ **Student Edition**
pp. 203–214
- So Fresh
- So Salty
- Wonderful Water
- Jump Into Safety!

Inquiry Flipchart
p. 29

Pass the Salt?
☐ Directed Inquiry

Water Watch
☐ Independent Inquiry

☐ **Digital Lesson**
Online Resources
Interactive presentation of lesson content

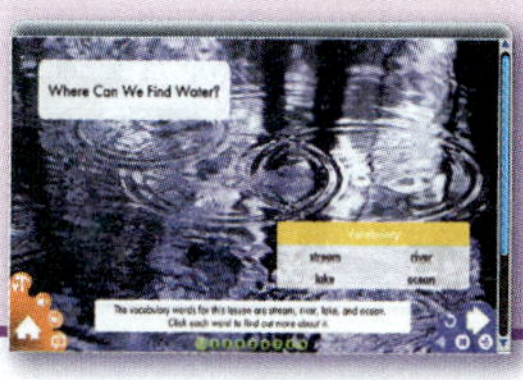

LESSON 6

How Can We Save Resources?

TEKS 1.1C

☐ **Student Edition**
pp. 217–228
- What a Waste!
- Pollution Solutions
- Care for Earth!
- Good As New

Inquiry Flipchart
p. 31

Trash on the Grass
☐ Directed Inquiry

Ready, Set, Recycle!
☐ Independent Inquiry

☐ **Digital Lesson**
Online Resources
Interactive presentation of lesson content

OTHER UNIT FEATURES

People in Science, p. 187

S.T.E.M. Engineering and Technology, pp. 215–216B

Online Resources

Interactive Whiteboard Resources for Unit 5

Assessment

Formative Assessment
Sum It Up! and Brain Check
Student Edition, end of each lesson

Summative Assessment
Lesson Quizzes
Assessment Guide, pp. AG 72–AG 77

Unit 5 Review
Student Edition, pp. 229–232

Unit 5 Test
Assessment Guide, pp. AG 80–AG 84

Performance Assessment
SHORT OPTION: Teacher Edition, p. 231
LONG OPTION: Assessment Guide, pp. AG 85–AG 86

RTI Response to Intervention
RTI Strategies, p. 175K

Online Assessment
Test-taking and automatic scoring
Banks of items from which to build tests

Planning for Inquiry

Use the following preview of Inquiry Activities and Lessons to gather and manage the materials needed for each lesson.

Activity	Inquiry and Design Process Skills Focus	Materials	Prep Tips, Troubleshooting, and Expected Results
Lesson 1 DIRECTED INQUIRY **Flipchart** p.25 **A Just Add Water** **OBJECTIVES** Recognize and demonstrate safe practices. Plan and conduct simple investigations. Record and organize data. Communicate observations. Record and compare information using notebooks. Gather evidence of how water helps to make useful products. 15–20 minutes pairs TEKS **1.1A, 1.1B, 1.2B, 1.2D, 1.2E, 1.4A, 1.7C**	• Observe • Compare • Gather, Record, Display, or Interpret Data	• plastic spoons (one for each pair) • large container of powdered drink mix • clear plastic cups of water (one for each pair)	**Prep Tips** Consider having children cover their workspace with butcher paper in case of spills and to make it easier to clean up after the activity. Give each pair of children a clear plastic cup of water and a spoon. Tell children that when they are ready for Step 2 of the activity, they should raise their hands and you will hold the container of powdered drink mix while they scoop out one spoonful. **Caution!** Due to possible allergies, make sure children do not actually drink the mixture during the activity. **Troubleshooting** If children do not notice a difference once they have poured the powdered drink mix into the water, suggest that they use their spoon to gently stir the mixture. **Expected Results** Children will observe that the powdered drink mix dissolved in the water and became a useful product (a drinkable beverage).
INDEPENDENT INQUIRY **Flipchart** p.25 **B Resources All Around** **OBJECTIVES** Recognize and demonstrate safe practices. Identify natural resources. Plan and conduct simple investigations. Gather evidence of how rocks and soil help to make useful products. 20 minutes pairs TEKS **1.1A, 1.1B, 1.1C, 1.2B, 1.7C**	• Observe • Gather, Record, Display, or Interpret Data • Plan and Conduct a Simple Investigation	• pictures of products that use rocks and soil (optional)	**Prep Tips** If possible, plan time to take children outside to gather evidence by drawing or writing their ideas. If outdoor exploration is not possible, gather pictures of products made from rocks and soil in advance. **Caution!** Have children wash their hands after they touch any rocks or soil. Be sure all materials are handled with care. **Troubleshooting** Before children gather their evidence, work as a group to brainstorm examples of rock- and soil-based products, such as bricks, asphalt, and clay flowerpots. **Expected Results** Children will recognize that a variety of products they see and use every day are made from rocks and soil.

Additional teaching support for all inquiry activities is available in **Online Resources.**

Science Notebook Strategies

- Lists of Kit-Supplied Materials
- Meeting Individual Needs
- Investigate More—Extensions and Variations
- and More!

Activity	Inquiry and Design Process Skills Focus	Materials	Prep Tips, Troubleshooting, and Expected Results
Lesson 2 DIRECTED INQUIRY Flipchart p.26 **A Cleaning Crew** **OBJECTIVES** Recognize and demonstrate safe practices. Plan and conduct simple investigations. 30–40 minutes small groups TEKS **1.1A, 1.1B, 1.2B**	• Plan and Conduct a Simple Investigation • Experiment • Draw Conclusions	• bowl • small cup of grape drink • paper cup • pencil • small cup of soil • coffee filter and tea bag (optional)	**Prep Tips** In advance, purchase a bag of potting soil. Use noncarbonated grape drink. Before the investigation, measure out a small amount of grape drink for each group. You may want to display a coffee filter and tea bag for children. Identify these items as filters, and explain what filters do. Explain that the grape drink represents dirty water. **Caution!** Warn children to keep their fingers away from the bottom of the cup when they poke holes in it. Remind children not to drink the liquid. Ensure that children wash their hands when the activity is over. **Troubleshooting** If you anticipate that children will have trouble poking the holes in the cup, prepare the cups ahead of time. Remind children that they should not pour the grape drink into the cup unless they are holding the cup over the bowl. **Expected Results** Children will observe that the liquid that flows out of the bottom of the cup is lighter in color. Children should conclude that soil can clean dirty water. The soil acts as a filter because it removes some of the "dirt" from the "water."
INDEPENDENT INQUIRY Flipchart p.26 **B How Much Water?** **OBJECTIVES** Recognize and demonstrate safe practices. Plan and conduct simple investigations. Record and organize data. Communicate observations. 25 minutes small groups TEKS **1.1A, 1.1B, 1.2B, 1.2D, 1.2E**	• Observe • Compare • Plan and Conduct a Simple Investigation • Experiment	• 2 to 3 different soils per group • 2 to 3 coffee filters per group • plastic cups • water • dry and wet measuring cups • rubber bands or tape • plastic gloves	**Prep Tips** If possible, include samples of potting, sandy, and clay soils. Beforehand, measure out soil samples for each group. Show children how to make a filtering device by attaching a coffee filter to a plastic cup. Make sure the filter forms a concave surface in the cup, which children can fill with about 1 cup of soil. Demonstrate how to slowly pour 1 cup of water from a measuring cup into the filter. Wait about 30 seconds. Then, discard the filter and the soil. Pour the water back into the measuring cup to see how much of it the soil absorbed. **Troubleshooting** Have children fill the measuring cup to the 1-cup mark each time and pour it slowly. **Expected Results** Children will observe that different soils hold different amounts of water. They may recognize that water moves most slowly through clay soil and most quickly through sandy soil.

Planning for Inquiry (continued)

Activity	Inquiry and Design Process Skills Focus	Materials	Prep Tips, Troubleshooting, and Expected Results
Lesson 3 INQUIRY GUIDED INQUIRY **Flipchart** p.27 **Student Edition** pp. 199–200 **What Do We Find in Soil?** **OBJECTIVE** • Observe and compare components of soil. 30 minutes · individuals TEKS **1.1A, 1.1B, 1.2B, 1.2C, 1.2D, 1.4A, 1.7A**	• Plan an Investigation • Observe • Compare	• soil samples (one for each child) • paper plates (two for each child) • tools, such as forceps and sieves • hand lenses • gloves • safety goggles	**Prep Tips** Avoid using commercial potting soil. Forceps are available for purchase from online suppliers. If possible, request that each child bring a sieve from home. **Caution!** Children should not put their hands or any materials near or in their mouths. They should wear goggles and gloves. Even if children wear gloves, have them wash their hands once they have completed their investigation. **Expected Results** Children will recognize that soil has different parts, but their actual results will vary depending on the samples they use.

Go Digital! Virtual Lab

What Do We Find in Soil?

Key Inquiry Skills: plan and conduct an investigation, observe, compare, record

Children observe the different components that make up soil.

Activity	Inquiry and Design Process Skills Focus	Materials	Prep Tips, Troubleshooting, and Expected Results
Lesson 4 INQUIRY GUIDED INQUIRY **Flipchart** p.28 **Student Edition** pp. 201–202 **How Do Soils Differ?** **OBJECTIVE** • Observe, compare, describe, and sort components of soil. 30 minutes · individuals or pairs TEKS **1.1A, 1.1B, 1.2B, 1.2C, 1.2D, 1.4A, 1.7A**	• Compare • Observe	• soil samples • hand lenses • plastic gloves • goggles	**Prep Tips** Supply two very different soil samples for each child or pair. You can purchase sand and natural clay at many craft stores. Different potting soils are available at nurseries. **Caution!** Remind children to wear goggles and gloves and to wash their hands after the activity. **Expected Results** Children should observe, compare, describe, and sort components of two soil samples.

Go Digital! Virtual Lab

How Do Soils Differ?

Key Inquiry Skills: observe, compare, infer, experiment

Children compare different kinds of soil and how well they support the growth of tomato plants.

Additional teaching support for all inquiry activities is available in Online Resources.

Activity	Inquiry and Design Process Skills Focus	Materials	Prep Tips, Troubleshooting, and Expected Results
Lesson 5 DIRECTED INQUIRY Flipchart p.29 **A Pass the Salt?** **OBJECTIVES** Plan and conduct simple investigations. Record and organize data. Identify and describe a variety of natural sources of water. 15 minutes to set up; 5 minutes a day for the next few days pairs TEKS **1.2B, 1.2D, 1.7B**	• Observe • Compare • Experiment	• 2 romaine lettuce leaves • cup of salt water • cup of fresh water • labels • markers (for labels)	**Prep Tips** Prepare the salt water in advance. Mix 4 teaspoons of salt into 1 liter of water. This will make enough salt water for two 16-oz cups. If children do not see you do the preparations, be sure to explain how the cups differ. Divide the class into pairs or small groups, depending on the number of cups and lettuce leaves you have. Before children immerse the leaves, remind them to note the appearance of each, for the sake of comparison later on. You may wish to have children note, such factors as color and springiness, or instruct them to break off a piece of the lettuce stalk to hear the sound it makes. **Caution!** Have children immediately notify you of any spills. Water can make surfaces slippery and cause falls. Remind children not to put any of the investigation materials in their mouths. **Troubleshooting** Make sure all lettuce leaves are fresh and healthy before the investigation starts. Keep them refrigerated or in a cooler until you need them. Once the leaves are in the cups, keep them out of direct sunlight to make sure the water stays cool. **Expected Results** After a few days, children should notice that the romaine leaf in the salt water is wilting. The one in the fresh water is looking healthy.
INDEPENDENT INQUIRY Flipchart p.29 **B Water Watch** **OBJECTIVES** Plan and conduct simple investigations. Record and organize data. Record and compare information using notebooks. Identify and describe a variety of natural sources of water. 30 minutes individuals TEKS **1.2B, 1.2D, 1.4A, 1.7B**	• Observe • Gather, Record, Display, or Interpret Data • Plan and Conduct a Simple Investigation	• clipboards (optional)	**Prep Tips** Before the activity, have children brainstorm different ways they use water at home and at school, such as to shower, wash hands, do dishes, or water plants. Work with the class or small groups to devise an effective chart for recording information about water use. Make sure children have their charts in place before they complete the at-home portion of the activity. **Troubleshooting** To aid children's memories throughout the day, you may wish to have them carry around clipboards so they can record water use wherever they are, or set aside time at different intervals during the day for them to recall and record information. **Expected Results** Children will keep a record of how they use water each day, both at home and at school. They will note that people use water in many different ways, such as to drink, bathe, water plants, and clean.

Planning for Inquiry (continued)

Activity	Inquiry and Design Process Skills Focus	Materials	Prep Tips, Troubleshooting, and Expected Results
S.T.E.M. Engineering and Technology Flipchart p.30 **Design It: Water Filter** **OBJECTIVES** • Record and organize data. • Identify and explain a problem and propose a solution in his/her own words. 40 minutes · small groups TEKS 1.2D, 1.3A	 1 Find a Problem 2 Plan and Build 3 Test and Improve 4 Redesign 5 Communicate	• sand • soil • cotton balls • paper cups • plastic cups of water • bits of paper, plastic, leaf parts, and twigs	**Prep Tips** Assemble the materials needed. Coffee filters and folded paper towels can substitute for the cotton balls. For each group, prepare a mixture of dirty water that can include bits of paper, plastic, leaf parts, twigs, and soil. **Expected Results** Children will use the materials to filter the dirty water. They will determine that fine materials, such as cotton balls, remove more debris from the water than coarser materials, such as sand.

Additional teaching support for all inquiry activities is available in Online Resources.

Activity	Inquiry and Design Process Skills Focus	Materials	Prep Tips, Troubleshooting, and Expected Results
Lesson 6 DIRECTED INQUIRY Flipchart p.31 A **Trash on the Grass** **OBJECTIVES** Plan and conduct simple investigations. Record and organize data. 5–10 minutes each day for a week small groups TEKS **1.2B, 1.2D**	• Observe • Compare • Formulate or Use Models • Experiment	• small pieces of paper • grass in a planter • water • spray bottle (optional: to mist grass)	**Prep Tips** The activity will take 5–10 minutes each day for about a week. If lawn grass is not available near your school, you can often purchase a patch of wheatgrass at a health food or pet store. **Troubleshooting** In Step 3, check daily for changes. You may wish to weigh down the pieces of paper with rocks to make sure they don't move. **Caution!** Be aware of possible allergies to grass. **Expected Results** Children will see that littered grass begins to yellow and get brittle. They will recognize that land pollution negatively affects grass.
INDEPENDENT INQUIRY Flipchart p.31 B **Ready, Set, Recycle!** **OBJECTIVES** Identify and learn how to use natural resources and materials, including conservation and reuse or recycling of paper, plastic, and metals. Plan and conduct simple investigations. 25 minutes small groups TEKS **1.1C, 1.2B**	• Classify • Plan and Conduct a Simple Investigation	• recyclable objects • reusable objects	**Prep Tips** You may wish to place recyclable objects around the room and treat this investigation like a scavenger hunt. Possible materials include paper goods, metal, and plastic. Brainstorm with children ways they can reuse some of the objects they found. Discuss ways children can help save resources by conserving. **Troubleshooting** Make sure children identify a good sample size of materials—including representative metal, plastic, and paper objects—before deciding on a sorting method. If necessary, lead them toward sorting by type of material, rather than irrelevant recycling criteria, such as size or color. **Expected Results** Children should come up with a plan for how to reuse and recycle materials as well as ways to conserve natural resources.

Differentiated Instruction

Leveled Readers

The Leveled Readers provide parallel coverage of the unit topics and Texas Essential Knowledge and Skills. Each Reader is available in English and Spanish. Both versions are available online and on touchscreen mobile devices.

ON-LEVEL This Reader reinforces unit concepts and vocabulary and focuses on the Texas Essential Knowledge and Skills. It includes student response activities.

EXTRA SUPPORT This Reader shares title, illustrations, vocabulary, and concepts with the On-Level Reader. However, the text is linguistically accommodated to provide simplified sentence structures and comprehension aids for students who need a little extra support with content-area reading and vocabulary development. It also includes student response activities.

ENRICHMENT This high-interest nonfiction Reader enriches and extends unit concepts. It reinforces some of the unit vocabulary, but also includes stretch vocabulary. It also includes student response activities.

TEACHER GUIDE

The accompanying Teacher Guide provides teaching strategies and support for using all the Readers, as well as English and Spanish worksheets that focus on vocabulary development. A correlation to the Texas Essential Knowledge and Skills is included.

DIGITAL VERSIONS

All of these Leveled Readers are available online. They are also available in an innovative and engaging format for touchscreen mobile devices. For information about accessing these versions, see page T9.

RTI Response to Intervention

Response to Intervention is a process for identifying and supporting students who are not making expected progress toward essential learning goals.

The following *ScienceFusion* components have the flexibility to be used to provide Core Classroom Instruction (Tier 1), strategic intervention (Tier 2), and intensive intervention (Tier 3).

Component	Location	Strategies and Benefits
Student Edition, Active Reading prompts, Sum It Up, Brain Check	Active Reading throughout each lesson, Sum It Up and Brain Check at the end of each lesson	Student responses can be used as screening tools to assess whether intervention is needed.
Assessment Guide, Lesson Quizzes and TEKS DOK Skill Builder	pp. AG 72–AG 79	Student responses can be used as screening tools to assess whether intervention is needed.
Inquiry Flipcharts	Inquiry Flipchart pp. 27, 28	Directed Inquiry for students who learn best through directed or teacher-led hands-on activities.
Teacher Edition, Unit Review Answer Strategies	TE pp. 229–232	Suggestions for intervention, guidance, and remediation for each review question.
Leveled Readers	TE p. 175J	Content support for students not meeting the learning needs during core classroom instruction.
Leveled Readers, Teacher Guides and Vocabulary Worksheets	TE p. 175J	Direct instruction with small groups of students needing additional content at various readability levels.
Extra Support for Vocabulary and Concepts (online worksheets)	Online Resources	Support for individualized instruction with practice in essential content.
Online Student Edition with Audio	Online Resources	Provides learners with multiple-modality access to science concepts and information.
Interactive Digital Lessons and Virtual Labs	Online Resources	Provides individualized learning experiences. Lessons make content accessible through simulations, animations, videos, audio, and integrated assessment.
Interactive Whiteboard Resources	Online Resources	Reinforces key unit concepts through interactive vocabulary games and visuals and graphic organizers.
Leveled Readers, online and tablet versions	Online and Tablet Resources	Highlighted words and sentences synced with audio provide support for emerging or struggling readers.

Differentiated Instruction

English Language Learners

Choose from these instructional strategies to meet the needs of English language learners.

Vocabulary Cards are provided in Online Resources.

Unit Vocabulary

Lesson 1	Lesson 2	Lesson 5	Lesson 6
natural resource	soil	stream	pollution
product	sand	river	conservation
rock	silt	lake	reduce
soil	clay	ocean	reuse
	property		recycle

Preteach Vocabulary ELPS 3C

Point out the prefix *re-* in the words *reduce, reuse,* and *recycle*. Explain that *re-* means "again." Define each word, and use it in a sentence. Then, have children use each word in their own sentence.

Language Acquisition Strategies

Reading Support ELPS 1C, 2E, 4E

Provide support to help children read the content on TE pages 178–179.

Beginning	Intermediate	Advanced/Advanced High
Use a bilingual dictionary to preteach the meaning of key content words, including *natural, resource, air, water,* and *product*. Have children make vocabulary flash cards that include the word and a picture.	Have children skim the text and identify any words that are unfamiliar or difficult to pronounce. Say and define each word.	Children may have difficulty with the words *natural, resource,* and *breathe*. Pronounce each word and have them repeat after you. Have children ask questions to clarify the meaning or pronunciation of words they do not know.

Visual and Contextual Support **ELPS** 1F, 3B, 3H, 4F

Use the pictures on **TE pages 180–181** to explain why plants and animals are natural resources.

Beginning	Intermediate	Advanced/Advanced High
Use accessible language to define natural resources. Ask *yes/no* questions about the resources and products pictured. Help children see that many things they use and eat come from plants and animals.	Use simple language and the pictures to explain that many of the things we use and eat come from plants and animals. Have children explain what they have learned to a partner.	Review the examples of products that come from plants and animals. Then, have small groups collaborate to make a visual that shows three things they use or eat and the plants and animals that provide these products.

Language Support **ELPS** 1F, 2C, 4F

Help children understand the meaning of the heading "The Scoop on Soil" on **TE page 192.** Explain that when we get "the scoop" on something, we get information about it.

Beginning	Intermediate	Advanced/Advanced High
Act out a scene in which you get the scoop about a friend's new puppy. Explain that you were getting information about your friend's new pet.	Ask a volunteer to tell you about something he or she did over the weekend. Explain that you were getting the scoop about what happened.	Have children take turns getting the scoop about a partner's favorite activity or hobby.

Academic Language **ELPS** 2C, 2E

Point out the word *compare* on **TE page 195.** Develop children's understanding of this word.

Beginning	Intermediate	Advanced/Advanced High
Explain that when we compare, we tell how things are the same. Display two classroom objects and use simplified language to model comparing them.	Have children use sentence frames to practice comparing two classroom objects: *A ___ is like a ___. These objects are the same because ___. These objects are both ___.*	Have partners take turns explaining how two classroom objects are the same. Ask children to identify at least two ways they are alike.

Follow Commands **ELPS** 2C, 3B

Review the list of water safety tips on **TE page 210.** Review imperative sentences.

Beginning	Intermediate	Advanced/Advanced High
Explain that a command tells you to do something. Give children simple commands, such as: *Raise your hand. Point to your pencil.* Then, have partners take turns giving simple commands about water safety.	Point out that a command begins with a verb, or an action word. State simple commands related to water safety. Have children identify the verb in each sentence.	Have partners take turns giving and following simple commands about water safety. Challenge Advanced High ELLs to say compound sentences, such as *Learn to swim, but don't swim alone!*

UNIT 5

Earth's Resources

I Wonder Why

Have children look at the trash in the picture and ask them to name any rules they know about throwing away trash. Talk about reasons why trash on the beach should be cleaned up and have children share ideas that will help them answer the "why" question.

Here's Why

Have children turn the page and read the response to the question. You may wish to share the following background with them.

More About...

Coastal Cleanup

For one day each year, thousands of volunteers around the world unite for an International Coastal Cleanup. In one day alone, they remove millions of pounds of garbage from coastal environments. Much of the garbage removed by the cleanup is plastic bags, bottles, and food wrappers.

A central mission of the International Coastal Cleanup is to educate people about the impact of garbage on the environment. People can easily help lessen the amount of such garbage by remembering to reduce, reuse, and recycle.

Science Songs

See pp. TR40–TR45 for science songs you can use to reinforce content in this unit.

Professional Development — Science Background

Use the keywords to access

- Professional Development from **The NSTA Learning Center**
- **SciLinks** for additional online content appropriate for children and teachers
- Teacher Science Background in the back of this Teacher Edition

Keywords

conservation, rocks, minerals, soil, oceans

SCI LINKS THE WORLD'S A CLICK AWAY

Here's Why Trash can be harmful to land, water, and living things at the beach.

In this unit, you will explore this Big Idea, the Essential Questions, and the Investigations on the Inquiry Flipchart.

Levels of Inquiry Key ■ DIRECTED ■ GUIDED ■ INDEPENDENT

Track Your Progress

Big Idea There are many kinds of resources on Earth.

Essential Questions

Science Notebook

Before you begin each lesson, be sure to write your thoughts about the Essential Question.

Go Digital

For a complete digital curriculum and resources that provide full coverage of the objectives for this unit, see the Online Resources for this program.

Big Idea and Essential Questions

Big Idea There are many kinds of resources on Earth.

Post the Unit Big Idea on the board. Have children read the Essential Questions, which are also the titles of the lessons in this unit.

- Discuss how the Essential Questions can help keep them focused on the Big Idea.
- Have children read the Big Idea statement. The statement describes the main science concept that they will be learning.
- Have children predict other ideas that will be taught in the lessons based on the titles, or have them give examples of pictures they expect to see.

Once they complete the unit, they should have a better understanding of the Big Idea.

Essential Questions You may use the following Science Notebook strategy for working with the Essential Questions before children begin the unit or before each lesson.

- Strategies for revisiting the Big Idea and Essential Questions are provided in Enduring Understandings on p. 229A.

Notebook Science Notebook

- Have children copy the Essential Questions into their Science Notebooks. Suggest they leave writing lines between questions.
- Ask children to write responses to the Essential Questions. Urge them not to worry about whether their responses are correct. They should expect their ideas to change as they work in the unit. Comment that children will be able to review and revise their answers to the Essential Questions at the end of the unit.
- Tips and strategies for using Science Notebooks are provided throughout this unit, in the back of this Teacher Edition, and in the Online Resources.

Options for Inquiry

FLIPCHART P. 25

Children can conduct these optional investigations at any time before, during, or in response to the lesson in the Student Edition.

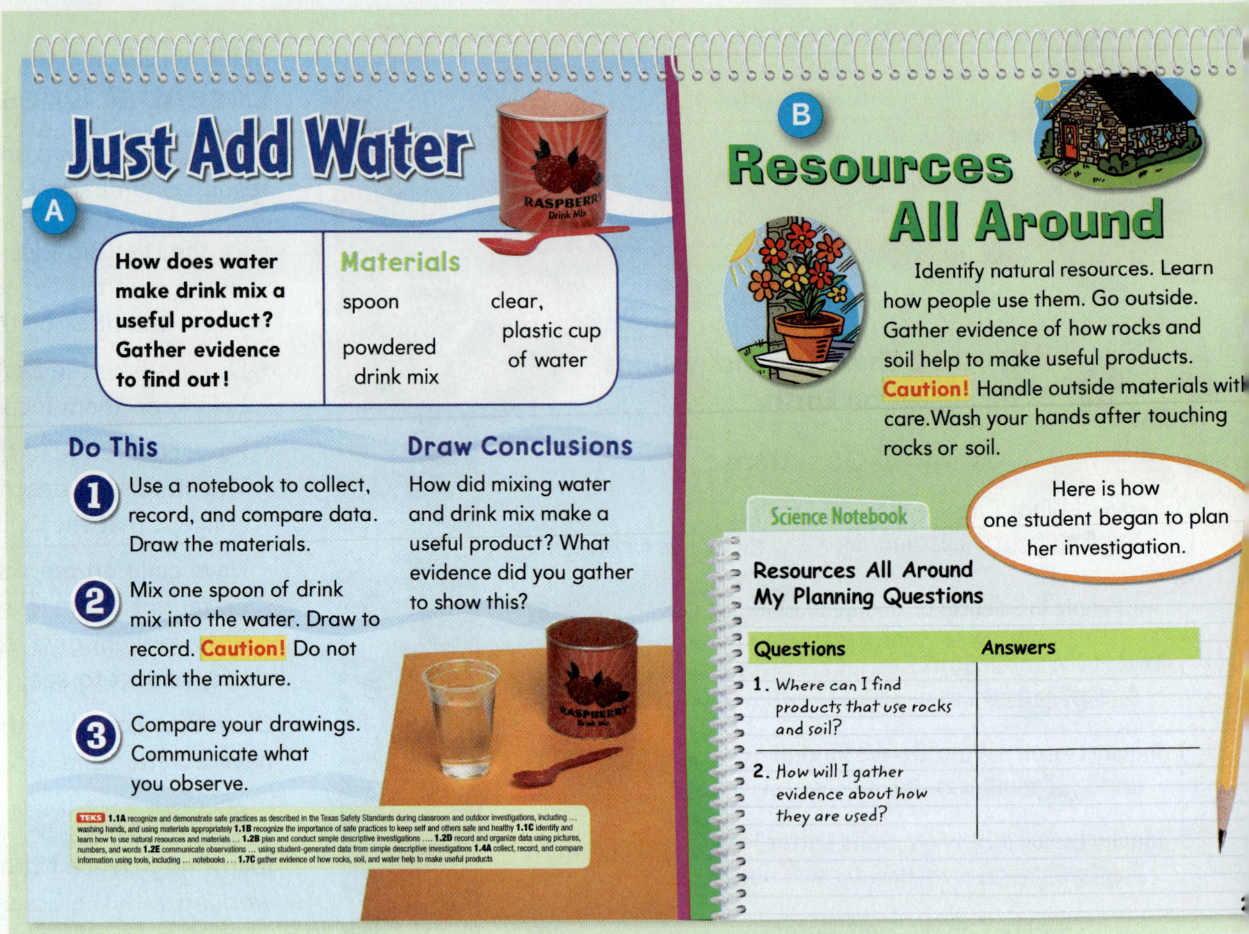

A Just Add Water

How does water make drink mix a useful product? Gather evidence to find out!

Materials
spoon
powdered drink mix
clear, plastic cup of water

Do This

1. Use a notebook to collect, record, and compare data. Draw the materials.
2. Mix one spoon of drink mix into the water. Draw to record. **Caution!** Do not drink the mixture.
3. Compare your drawings. Communicate what you observe.

Draw Conclusions
How did mixing water and drink mix make a useful product? What evidence did you gather to show this?

TEKS **1.1A** recognize and demonstrate safe practices as described in the Texas Safety Standards during classroom and outdoor investigations, including ... washing hands, and using materials appropriately **1.1B** recognize the importance of safe practices to keep self and others safe and healthy **1.1C** identify and learn how to use natural resources and materials ... **1.2B** plan and conduct simple descriptive investigations .... **1.2D** record and organize data using pictures, numbers, and words **1.2E** communicate observations ... using student-generated data from simple descriptive investigations **1.4A** collect, record, and compare information using tools, including ... notebooks . . . **1.7C** gather evidence of how rocks, soil, and water help to make useful products

B Resources All Around

Identify natural resources. Learn how people use them. Go outside. Gather evidence of how rocks and soil help to make useful products. **Caution!** Handle outside materials with care. Wash your hands after touching rocks or soil.

Here is how one student began to plan her investigation.

Science Notebook

Resources All Around
My Planning Questions

Questions	Answers
1. Where can I find products that use rocks and soil?	
2. How will I gather evidence about how they are used?	

Directed Inquiry

A Just Add Water

15–20 minutes
pairs

Prep and Planning Tips

Review with children what makes something a useful product. Distribute enough clear plastic cups, spoons, and drink mix for each pair, or, if necessary, complete the activity as a group.

Make sure children use their notebooks to compare their drawings of before and after the materials are mixed. Have them communicate what they have learned with others and explain their results using data from the inquiry.

Caution! Remind children of the importance to use safe pratices to keep themselves safe and healthy. Due to possible allergies, make sure children do not actually drink the mix. Be sure children recognize and demonstrate how to use all materials appropriately.

Expected Results

Children should observe that water is needed to dissolve powdered drink mix to make it into a useful product.

Independent Inquiry

B Resources All Around

15–20 minutes
pairs

Prep and Planning Tips

See the Planning for Inquiry page for more information. You may wish to have children brainstorm rock- and soil-based products before beginning the activity. Be sure children recognize and demonstrate safe practices by using any materials they find outside appropriately and to wash their hands.

Science Notebook

Children can use the Science Notebook page shown on the Flipchart as a model for planning and conducting their own investigation. Remind them that to gather evidence means to find out. Children will try to find out more about how people use products made out of rocks and soil, and record what they find in their notebooks.

TEKS **1.1C** identify and learn how to use natural resources and materials, including nservation and reuse or recycling of paper, plastic, and metals **1.7C** gather evidence of how cks, soil, and water help to make useful products

Lesson 1

Essential Question

What Can We Find on Earth?

Engage Your Brain!

Find the answer in the lesson.

The Great Sphinx was built long ago.

It was built from rock.

Active Reading

Lesson Vocabulary

1. Preview the lesson.
2. Write the 4 vocabulary terms here.

natural resource — rock

product — soil

Inquiry Flipchart p. 25 — Just Add Water/Resources All Around

177

Go Digital

An interactive digital lesson is available in Online Resources. It is suitable for individuals, small groups, or may be projected or used on an interactive white board.

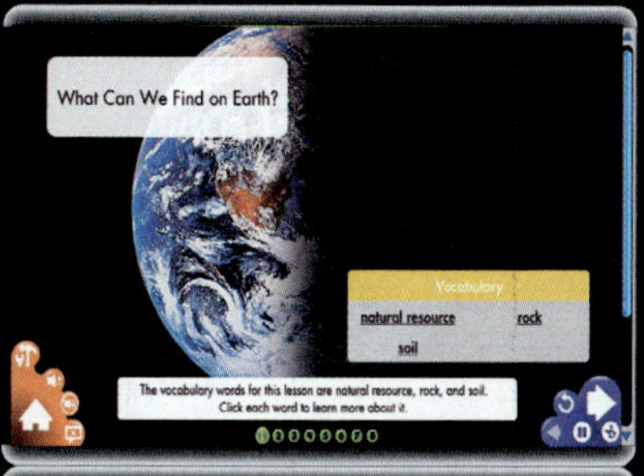

1 Engage/Explore

Objectives

- Recognize and demonstrate safe practices.
- Identify natural resources.
- Plan and conduct simple investigations.
- Record and organize data.
- Collect, record, and compare information using notebooks.
- Communicate observations and provide reasons for explanations.
- Gather evidence of how rocks, soil, and water help to make useful products.

Engage Your Brain!

Ask children to look at the photograph of the Great Sphinx and think about sculptures, skyscrapers, and other buildings to identify common building materials. They should look closely at the picture to help figure out the answer.

Remind them to record their final answer to the question when they find it on the sixth page of this lesson.

Active Reading Annotations

Remind children that active readers "make texts their own" by marking them or writing notes to help them understand what they are reading. Encourage children to use pencil to make annotations and to feel free to change their marks and notes as they read. The goal of annotation is to help children remember what they have read.

Vocabulary and Interactive Glossary

Remind children to find and list the yellow highlighted terms from the lesson. As they proceed through the lesson and learn about the terms, they should add drawings or words in the extra spaces provided in some of the entries in the Interactive Glossary.

2 Explain

Notebook Generate Ideas

Talk with children about the air around them. Ask how they can tell it is there.

Have you ever seen leaves on a tree move? What makes that happen? Have children share experiences they have had on windy days.

Active Reading Main Idea

Explain to children that drawing a line under the main idea can help them to remember what they read. If they go back to a page later, the underlined words will help them easily review the main idea.

Develop Science Vocabulary

natural resource Write *natural resource* on the board or a chart. Explain to children that *natural means* "from nature" and *resource* means "something you can use." Therefore, a natural resource is something from nature that people can use.

Develop Science Concepts

What is a natural resource? something from nature that people can use

Identify two natural resources. air and water

Display wood from a tree, soil, a rock, and an apple. Ask children to think about the definition of *natural resource* to identify which objects they think are natural resources and explain why. Guide them to understand that all the items are natural resources because they come from nature and people use them.

All Natural

What do you use from Earth? You use natural resources. A **natural resource** is anything from nature that people can use.

Air

Air is a natural resource. We breathe air. Wind is moving air. This hang glider uses wind to move. A wind farm changes wind into useful energy. Energy gives light and heat to our homes.

Active Reading

Draw two lines under the main idea.

178

English Language Learners

ELPS 1E, 2E

Recognize Earth Words Tell children that they will be learning about air, water, plants, animals, rocks, and soil in this lesson. Point to a visual of each term from the lesson pages. Say the word aloud, and have children repeat after yo Then point to the visuals again and have children write the word that goes with each visual in thei Student Edition.

Water

We use water every day. We drink it and bathe with it. Water also helps to make useful products, such as shampoo. A **product** is something made by people or machines for people to use.

There is water in this iced tea.

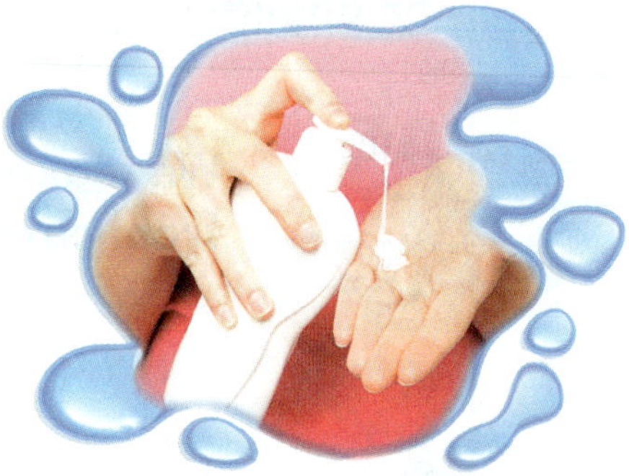

There is water in this lotion.

We use water to care for plants.

▶ **Identify a product made with water. Tell why it is useful.**

Sample answer: My shampoo has water in it. It is useful because it cleans my hair.

Differentiation—Leveled Questions

Extra Support

What natural resource do you use when you breathe? air

What natural resource do you use to wash your hands? water

Challenge

What questions would you ask to find out if something is a natural resource? Does it come from nature? Do people use it?

Develop Science Vocabulary

product Write *produce* → *product* on the board. Explain that the word *product* comes from *produce*. Point out that *produce* means "to make by hand or by machine." Therefore, a product is something made by hand or by machine.

Develop Science Concepts

Use these questions to help children identify natural resources and also identify how water makes useful products.

Why is wind a natural resource? It is something from nature that people can use.

What are two ways that people can use air? They can use air to breathe and they can use wind to make useful energy.

How have you used water today? Sample answer: I drank water and used it for brushing my teeth and washing my hands.

Why is water useful when you are caring for a plant? Water helps keep plants alive.

Water is also in products like lotion and shampoo. Why are these products useful? Lotion helps to keep your skin from getting dry. Shampoo cleans your hair.

Interpret Visuals

Direct children to the pictures on the right. Ask them to describe what they see. Tell them that they are gathering evidence, or finding out, about how water helps to make useful products. They can use their answers to complete the interactivity.

Notebook Summarize Ideas

Have children look back at the main idea they underlined and use that information to summarize the main idea and key supporting details orally or in writing.

2 Explain (continued)

Notebook Generate Ideas

Read the heading aloud to children. Have them observe the size and style of the letters of the heading and then compare them to the headings on the previous two pages. Guide children to see that the lesson is all about natural resources and that the subheadings give examples of natural resources.

People use natural resources. Plants and animals are natural resources. What are some ways that people use plants and animals? Allow time for children to brainstorm ideas and make a list on the board.

Develop Science Concepts

How do people use plants? Name three different ways. Sample answer: as food, for clothes, to make things we need

Look at the pictures of the cotton, tree, and tomato plant. Which one is being used as food? the tomato

How can a tomato be used as food? It can be used in tomato sauce, ketchup, salsa, or sliced on sandwiches.

What are some of your favorite plants to eat? Accept all reasonable responses.

Explain to children that when we use natural resources for food, clothing, or other things we need that we may refer to them as "products."

Plants and Animals

Plants and animals are natural resources, too. We use them for food. We also use them to make clothes and other things we need.

▶ **Look at the pictures. Circle the useful product that comes from each plant or animal.**

Differentiation—Leveled Questions

Extra Support
Why are plants and animals natural resources? They come from nature and people use them for food, clothes, and other things such as buildings.

Challenge
Think about peanut butter on an apple as a snack. Does this snack come from plants? **Explain.** Yes, the peanuts come from a plant. Apples are the fruit of an apple tree.

We make a sweater from a sheep's wool.

We make cheese from a cow's milk.

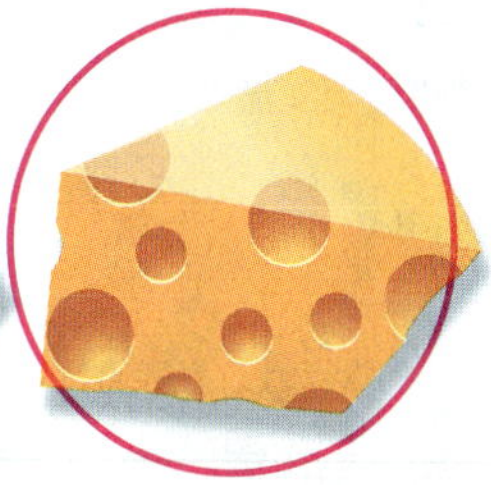

We get eggs from a hen.

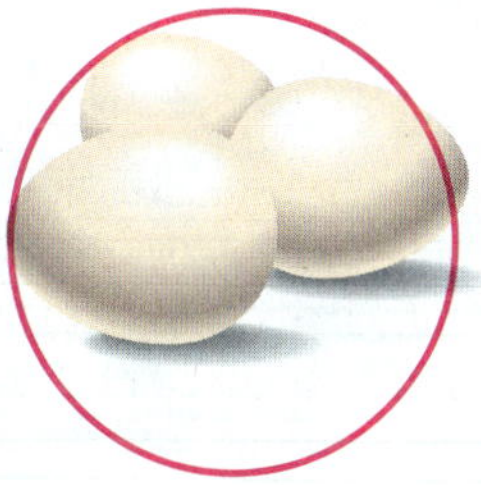

181

Writing Connection

TEKS ELA 1.24C

Make a Chart List the following clothing materials on the board: *wool, cotton, silk, polyester,* and *nylon.* Have children copy the names in the left column of a two-column chart. They should then research each one to write in the right column whether the material comes from a plant, an animal, or neither.

TEKS 1.1C, 1.7C

Interpret Visuals

Have children look at the picture of the sheep at the top of the page. **How does the picture show people using the sheep as a natural resource?** The wool from the sheep is used to make clothes.

Develop Inquiry Skills

CLASSIFY/USE NUMBERS **Look at the six pictures of the things we get from plants and animals. How many are foods? How many are clothes? How many are other things?** Three are foods, two are clothes, and one is a toy.

Have children make a bar graph to show the results.

Notebook Summarize Ideas

Ask children to review the visuals on the two pages and use them to tell orally or in writing what they learned about plants and animals as natural resources. Ask them to explain what the item in the picture shows and what natural resource was used to make it.

2 Explain (continued)

Notebook Generate Ideas

Ask children to preview these two pages by finding and pointing to the two headings that are about the same size and style as the headings *Air, Water,* and *Plants and Animals* on the previous pages.

What do the headings say? *Rocks and Soil* **If these headings look about the same as the others, what do they tell you about rocks and soil?** Like air, water, and plants and animals, rocks and soil are natural resources.

Active Reading Vocabulary

Explain that a vocabulary word may be highlighted in a color. Active readers pay attention to highlighted words because their meaning is given in the same sentence or the next sentence.

Develop Science Vocabulary

rock Tell children about the expression *hard as a rock.* Explain that the expression is used because rocks are hard.

Develop Science Concepts

What useful products are made from rocks? Sample answers: buildings, jewelry, salt

Why do you think rocks make a good building material? They are hard, strong, and will not break easily.

Misconception Alert

Children may think that rock is the only material used for building. Point out that many materials are used. Encourage them to think of others, such as wood, metal, and plastic.

Rocks

Rocks are a natural resource. A **rock** is a hard, nonliving object from the ground. We use rocks to build things. Rocks can also be used to make useful products like jewelry or salt.

Active Reading

Find the sentence that tells the meaning of **rock.** Draw a line under the sentence.

house made from rocks

182

123 Math Connection

TEKS MATH 1.8A, 1.8B

Make a Tally Chart Have children make a tally chart to classify ten objects from the classroom or around the school. Have them tally whether they come from plants, animals, rocks, or none of these sources. As an extension activity, challenge children to show the results as a bar graph.

Make Connections

Easy

Art Connection

TEKS ART 1.1B, 1.2C

Make Art from Natural Resources

- Provide art supplies and natural resources, such as plant parts and rocks, for children to make artwork. Children may make a painting with leaves glued to it or a sculpture made of rocks. You might want to provide time for children to collect their own natural resources to include in their art.
- Talk about the art supplies they used. Explain that paper comes from trees, paints can come from plants, and brushes are often made of wood and animal hair.

Average

Social Studies Connection

TEKS SS 1.6B

Research Resources Around the World

- Remind children that fruits are a natural resource. Explain that some other cultures and countries eat fruits that are less familiar than apples or bananas. Ask children whether they have heard of, seen, or eaten kumquats, lychees, durians, cherimoyas, or melanos.
- Help small groups research an exotic fruit and make a report. They should include the name of the fruit, a description or picture if possible, information about where and how it grows, how it is used, and any other interesting facts.

Average

Math Connection

TEKS MATH 1.3B, 1.3E

Solve a Math Problem

- Give pairs of children 12 rocks and a small box.
- Have one partner put some of the rocks under (or in) the box. The other partner will count the visible rocks to figure out how many rocks are in the box, and then explain how they solved the problem.
- Have partners change roles and repeat the activity several times.

Challenging

Writing Connection

TEKS ELA 1.18B

Write a Natural Resource Poem

- Have children choose a natural resource they read about in the lesson and write a 4- to 8-line poem about it. The poem should include at least two facts or important details about the natural resource.
- Remind children that their poem does not have to rhyme, but should have the same, or nearly the same, number of syllables in each line.

People in Science

Objectives

- Describe what scientists do.
- Know that scientists come from all backgrounds.
- Recognize that the work of scientists helps people.

Notebook Generate Ideas

Share the following background information with children before you assign the feature. Ask questions to ascertain children's prior knowledge.

Based on the pictures, what plants do you think Dr. George Washington Carver studied? Explain. Sample answer: I think he studied peanut plants. I think so because the first page shows him thinking about peanuts, with a peanut plant behind him.

How do you think Dr. Carver might have felt about being the first African American student at his school? Explain. Sample answer: He might have felt proud because he did something important. He might have felt nervous because he was the first.

Background

- George Washington Carver was born in 1864. He was born on a farm in Missouri.
- Carver was the first African American student at the school now known as Iowa State University. He studied agricultural science, or the science of farms and farming.
- Dr. Carver became a scientist, inventor, and teacher. He dedicated his life to helping farmers by studying and inventing ways to keep farm soils healthy. He won many awards and medals for his work. He died in 1943.

TEKS 1.3C describe what scientists do

People in Science

Learn About . . .

Dr. George Washington Carver

Dr. George Washington Carver was a scientist. He worked with farmers. Dr. Carver showed them how to plant peanuts to keep their soil good for growing crops.

Fun Fact

Dr. Carver invented peanut shampoo!

Writing Connection

TEKS ELA 1.24C

Write Captions Have children draw a picture of Dr. George Washington Carver at work. Remind them to base their drawings on what they have learned about him as a scientist, inventor, and teacher. Then have children write or dictate captions for their drawings. Tell them to use complete sentences.

ople in Science continued

This Leads to That

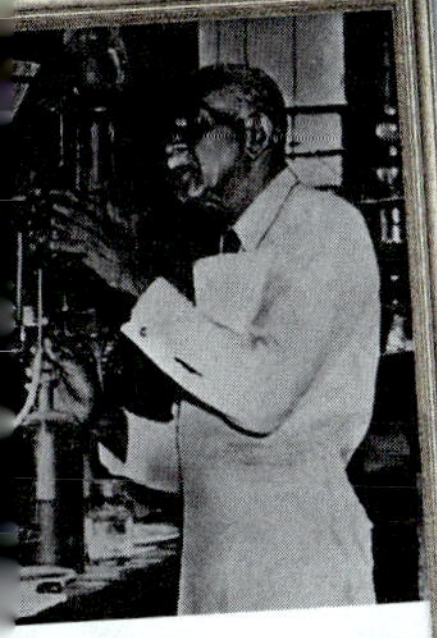

. George
ashington Carver
udied farming.

He taught farmers how to make their soil rich.

Today, farmers around the world use his ideas.

Describe what Dr. Carver did to help farmers.

He taught farmers how to keep their soil good for growing crops by planting peanuts.

Science, Technology, and Society

Tell children that people have been farming for thousands of years and that as long as people have been farming, they have tried to invent ways to make their work easier. Then help children list tools or other inventions that help with the work of growing plants.

You may prompt children by displaying pictures or actual objects for tools they would already be familiar with such as shovels, watering cans, and so on. Help children name these tools and discuss how each one makes growing plants easier.

Develop Science Concepts

How can soils be different? Soils can have different things in them, like bits of rock or once-living things. They can also look different because of their color or texture.

Crops are plants that farmers grow for food or to sell to people. Why might a farmer growing crops want to keep the soil rich? If the soil is rich, the crops might grow better. Then the farmer might have more crops to eat or sell.

What might a soil that is good for growing crops be like? It might hold water well, so the crops could get water they need. It might have lots of bits of once-living things, which would make it rich.

Develop Inquiry Skills

EXPERIMENT Remind children that when they experiment, they investigate a question they have about science and draw conclusions based on what they observe.

Suppose you wanted to know whether certain soils were good for growing peanut plants. How would you experiment to find out? Sample answer: I would try to grow peanut plants in those soils. I would compare how the plants grew in the soils.

If possible, have children grow the same type of plants in different kinds of soil, such as potting soil, clay soil, and sandy soil, to see which soil is best for growing those plants.

Notebook Summarize Ideas

Have children look again at the pictures and captions on these pages. Ask them to think about the information presented and then summarize the main idea for partners.

Options for Inquiry

FLIPCHART P. 26

Children can conduct these optional investigations at any time before, during, or in response to the lesson in the Student Edition.

A Cleaning Crew

Can soil clean dirty water? Investigate to find out.	Materials
	pencil, bowl, paper cup, grape drink, soil

Do This

1. Carefully, use a pencil to poke three holes in the bottom of the cup.
2. Fill the cup halfway with soil.
3. Hold the cup over a bowl. Pour some grape drink into the cup.
4. Observe the liquid that comes out of the bottom of the cup. Compare it to the grape drink.

Draw Conclusions

Can soil clean dirty water? How do you know?

TEKS **1.1A** recognize and demonstrate safe practices as described in the Texas Safety Standards . . . **1.1B** recognize the importance of safe practices . . . **1.2B** plan and conduct simple descriptive investigations . . . **1.2D** record and organize data . . . **1.2E** communicate observations and provide reasons for explanations using student-generated data from simple descriptive investigations

B How Much Water?

Gather soil samples. Which soil holds the most water? Make a plan to find out.

Use coffee filters and water to test the samples. Record and share your observations. Use the information you gathered to explain your results. **Caution!** Be sure to wash your hands and to use all materials the right way.

Science Notebook

Here is how one student began to plan his investigation.

How Much Water?
My Planning Questions

Questions	Answers
1. Which kinds of soil will I test? How much water will I use?	
2. How do I know which holds the most water?	

Directed Inquiry

A Cleaning Crew

30–40 minutes
small groups

Prep and Planning Tips

Use non-carbonated grape drink. Before the investigation, you may want to measure the grape drink. You may also wish to display a coffee filter and tea bag for children and identify them as filters. Make sure children understand what filters do.

Caution! Be sure children recognize the importance of safe practices to keep themselves safe and healthy by keeping their fingers away from the bottom of the cup when poking holes. Remind them not to drink the liquid, and caution them against touching their faces. Have them demonstrate safe practices by washing their hands at the end of the investigation.

Expected Results

Children will observe that the liquid flowing out of the bottom of the cup is lighter in color. They should conclude that soil can clean dirty water because when water passes through soil it acts as a filter.

Independent Inquiry

B How Much Water?

25 minutes
small groups

Prep and Planning Tips

See the Planning for Inquiry page for more information. Before the investigation, measure out different soil samples on paper plates. If possible, include samples of potting soil, sandy soil, and clay soil, and provide children with plastic measuring cups.

Caution! Be sure children recognize and demonstrate safe practices to keep themselves safe and healthy by washing their hands and using all materials appropriately.

Science Notebook

Children can use the Science Notebook as a model for planning and conducting their own investigation. Encourage them to make a chart like the one shown and include the sample questions plus their own questions.

TEKS **1.7A** observe, compare, describe, and sort components of soil by size, texture, and color

Lesson 2

Essential Question

What Is Soil?

Engage Your Brain!

Find the answer to the question in the lesson.

How can people use soil?

to grow plants

Active Reading

Lesson Vocabulary

1. Preview the lesson.
2. Write the 5 vocabulary terms here.

soil | clay
sand | property
silt

Inquiry Flipchart p. 26—Cleaning Crew/How Much Water?

189

Go Digital

An interactive digital lesson is available in Online Resources. It is suitable for individuals, small groups, or may be projected or used on an interactive white board.

1 Engage/Explore

Objectives

- Recognize and demonstrate safe practices.
- Plan and conduct simple investigations.
- Record and organize data.
- Communicate observations and provide reasons for explanations using data from investigations.
- Observe, compare, describe, and sort components of soil by size, texture, and color.

Engage Your Brain!

Help children answer the question *How can people use soil?* Focus their attention on the photograph of the radishes. Ask children to recall other things they have seen growing in soil.

Remind children to record their final answer to the question when they find it on the second page of the lesson.

Active Reading Annotations

Remind children that active readers "make texts their own" by marking them or writing notes to help them understand what they are reading. Encourage children to use pencil to make annotations and to feel free to change their marks and notes as they read. The goal of annotation is to help children remember what they have read.

Vocabulary and Interactive Glossary

Remind children to find and list the yellow highlighted terms from the lesson. As they proceed through the lesson and learn about the terms, they can add drawings or words in the extra spaces provided in some of the entries in the Interactive Glossary.

2 Explain

Notebook Generate Ideas

Read the heading aloud to children, and explain that if we say that something is *super*, we mean that it is very good. **Why do you think soil is super?** Encourage speculation and record ideas. Guide children to the idea that soil is super because plants grow in it.

Active Reading Vocabulary

Explain that a vocabulary word may be highlighted in a color. Active readers pay attention to highlighted words because their meaning is given in the same or the next sentence.

Develop Science Vocabulary

soil Write *soil* on the board. Explain that soil comes from a word meaning "ground." Discuss the connection between soil and the ground.

Develop Science Concepts

What is soil made of? small pieces of rock and once-living things **What are these once-living things made up of?** bits of dead plants and animals

How do wind and water help in making soil? Wind and water break down rock into tiny bits.

What are some ways that soil is important? Sample answer: Plants grow in soil. Without soil for plants, people might not get the food they need.

Revisit the Engage Your Brain! question, and have children finalize their response.

Super Soil

Soil is made up of small pieces of rock and once-living things. We use soil to grow plants.

Active Reading

Find the sentence that tells the meaning of **soil**. Draw a line under the sentence.

Soil forms a layer on parts of Earth's surface.

190

Differentiation—Leveled Questions

Extra Support

What three things make up soil? bits of dead plants, bits of dead animals, bits of rock

Challenge

Why is soil important to animals? Plants grow in soil and many animals eat plants for food.

Soil forms when wind and water break down rock. The bits of rock form the base of soil.

At the same time, dead plants and animals fall to the ground. These once-living things break down into bits. The bits become part of soil, too.

Soil is a mix of many tiny pieces.

▶ **Look at the picture. Describe the color and texture of the soil.**

Sample answer: The color is dark brown. The texture is rough because there are rocks mixed in it.

191

English Language Learners

ELPS 1C, 1E

Explore Related Words
Help children explore words related to *soil*. Write the words *dirt* and *mud* on the board. Point to each word as you pronounce it. Explain that the word *dirt* is sometimes used when talking about soil. Mud is very wet soil. Help children make a word web or other organizer to show how the words relate.

TEKS 1.7A

Interpret Visuals

Look at the picture of the field that spreads across both pages. Where is the soil in this picture? It is on the ground. Plants are growing in it.

Direct children's attention to the photograph of the soil sample in the trowel. **Describe the color and texture of the soil.** Sample answer: The color of the soil is dark brown. The texture is rough because there are bits of rock and plant matter mixed in.

Remind children to record their observations about this soil sample on the lines at the bottom of the page.

Develop Inquiry Skills

SEQUENCE **Suppose you wanted to tell a friend how soil is formed. Use the words *first*, *next*, and *last* to describe these steps in order.** Sample answer: First, wind and water break rock into tiny bits. Plants and animals die and fall to the ground. Next, small pieces of rock become part of soil. Once-living things break down into bits. Last, all the bits mix together to form soil.

Notebook Summarize Ideas

To summarize the important ideas in this section orally or in writing, have children complete these sentences:

Soil is made up of _____.

Soil is important because ______.

2 Explain (continued)

Notebook Generate Ideas

Explain that getting "the scoop" on something means learning all about it. Have children recall the two things that make up soil. Explain that on these two pages, they will learn more about the four parts that make up soil.

Active Reading Vocabulary

Explain that a vocabulary word may be highlighted in a color. Active readers pay attention to highlighted words because their meaning is given in the same sentence or the next sentence. Remind children to find and underline the meaning of *sand*.

Develop Science Vocabulary

sand Pass around a damp sample of sand, or have children observe the sand picture closely. Ask children to tell what it feels like or what they think it would feel like. Children should note its large grains and rough texture.

silt Have children observe the silt picture or a silt sample. They should note its fine texture, almost like flour.

clay Have children observe the clay picture or a damp clay sample. They should notice its fine texture, which sticks together.

Develop Science Concepts

What four parts make up soil? sand, silt, clay, and once-living things

How can soil from one place be different from soil in another place? Different amounts of sand, clay, silt, or once-living things in the soil can cause soils to be different.

How might soil from a garden be different from soil from an empty, dried-out lot without many plants or animals in it? The garden soil would probably have more once-living things.

The Scoop on Soil

Sand, silt, clay, and once-living things make up soil. Different amounts of these parts make soils different.

Active Reading

Find the sentence that tells what **sand** is made of. Draw a line under the sentence.

Farm soil has many once-living things.

192

Differentiation—Leveled Questions

Extra Support

Suppose you were a gardener and you found plants were not growing well in the soil in your garden. What might you do? add more once-living things to the soil

Challenge

Cactus plants have roots that rot if they stay wet for a long time. What kind of soil would you use to grow a cactus plant? Why? I would use sandy soil, because it does not hold water well.

TEKS 1.7A

Soil is a mix of these four parts.

Sand is made of large bits of rock. It does not hold water well.

Silt is made of medium bits of rock. It holds water fairly well.

Clay is made of small bits of rock. Clay holds water so well that clay sticks together.

Once-living things are bits of dead plants and animals. They make soil rich, or good for plants.

▶ **Circle the part of soil that makes soil good for growing plants.**

193

Writing Connection

TEKS ELA 1.24C

Write a Description Give partners a soil sample. After they observe it, have them write several sentences on a large index card telling how it feels and how it looks. Randomly display the samples and cards from four or five pairs. Have the group work together to match the samples with the cards. After each match is made, ask children to identify which clues in the description were most helpful in making the match.

Interpret Visuals

Focus children's attention on the chart. **What four parts of soil are shown in the chart?** sand, silt, clay, and once-living things

Point out the captions beside the soil photographs, and help children read them. **What information do the captions provide?** They identify and describe the parts of soil.

What does the caption tell you about sand? It has large bits of rock; it does not hold water well.

What do you know about silt? It has medium bits of rock; it holds water fairly well.

How would you describe clay? It is made of tiny bits of rock; it is sticky and holds water well.

Discuss which part of soil is most important in helping plants grow. Remind children to circle this picture.

Misconception Alert

Children may think that color determines soil type. In fact, soil type is mostly determined by the size of particles in the soil.

Develop Inquiry Skills

COMPARE Explain that scientists also use the color of parts of soil to determine the rocks the parts of soil came from. **How would you compare the color of the four parts of soil shown on this page?** The sand is tan; the silt is grayish-brown; the clay is reddish-brown; the once-living things look dark brown.

Notebook Summarize Ideas

Have children look at the pictures and recall the new vocabulary they learned. Then have them think about information found in the pictures and captions. Have them summarize orally or in writing what they learned.

2 Explain (continued)

Notebook Generate Ideas

Read the heading aloud, and have children preview the pictures. Ask children what they already know about soils. **How do we know if a soil has more sand or more clay? How do we know if a soil has a lot of once-living things?** Compile a list of ideas on the board.

Develop Science Vocabulary

property Display a book and have children describe its shape, color, size, and texture. Explain that a book's shape, color, size, and texture are all properties of the book because they tell what the book is like. Then discuss with children some properties of soil.

Active Reading Clue Words

Explain that some words are clues to ways ideas are connected. *Different* and *but* hint that information about how things differ is coming. Active readers look for clue words to help them remember how ideas connect. As children read, remind them to find and draw boxes around these clue words.

Develop Science Concepts

Remind children that a mixture contains different kinds of objects that are mixed together. **How do we know that soil is a mixture?** Soil is made up of different amounts of sand, clay, silt, and once-living things that are all mixed together.

How can soils have different properties? Soils can have different properties depending on how much sand, silt, clay, or once-living things make up the soil.

In the Mix

There are many soils. But each soil is a mix of things. The mix gives each soil different properties. A **property** is one part of what something is like. The chart on the right shows some properties of soil.

Active Reading

Clue words can help you find ways things are different. **But** and **different** are clue words. Draw boxes around these words.

This rich garden soil is dark brown.

194

English Language Learners

ELPS 1C, 1E

Explore Word Meanings
Children may have difficulty understanding the scientific meaning of *property*. Write the word on the board, and have children say it. Explain that when scientists use this word, they are talking about things that make an object like it is, such as its color, its shape, its size, and its texture. Make a word web to summarize these examples of properties.

▶ **Compare and describe the parts of soil. Write labels to complete the chart.**

Color The rock in soil helps give soil its color. Soil can be orange, gray, tan, and yellow, too.

red — brown — black

Size of Rock Bits The rock bits may be different sizes. Clay has small bits. Sand has large ones.

small — medium — large

Texture The size and shape of the rock bits make soils feel different.

smooth — gritty — lumpy

Amount of Once-Living Things Once-living things make soil rich. Rich soil is good for plants.

few — some — many

195

Interpret Visuals

Direct children to the chart, and read the directions. Children will be describing and comparing the different properties and parts of soil. Explain that the words in colored type are four properties of soil. Call on a volunteer to read these properties aloud. Point out the soil samples pictured under the description of each property. Make sure that children understand that they will label one soil sample in each row.

What gives soil its color? rock in soil **What three colors are shown in these soil samples?** red, brown, black
Have children write *brown* under the soil sample with a missing label in the top row.

What is the second property of soil identified in this chart? size of rock bits
What size rock bits does sand have? large
Pause so children can label the soil sample.

What is texture? how something feels **Why do soils have different textures?** Soils have different textures because of the different sizes and shapes of the rock bits found in them.
What are three textures of soil? smooth, gritty, lumpy

What is the fourth property of soil? amount of once-living things **Which soil sample would be best for gardening?** the one with the most once-living things

Have children supply the missing labels in the third and fourth rows.

Notebook

Summarize Ideas

Direct children to think about four properties they could use to compare soil samples. Have them summarize these properties by making an oral or written list.

Math Connection

TEKS MATH 1.1C

Compare the Weights of Soils
Explain to children that the weight of a soil sample is one property of that sample. Then provide a balance and three labeled 2-cup soil samples in plastic bags. Explain to children that each bag contains the same amount of soil, and ask them to predict whether some of the samples are heavier than others. Have pairs or small groups compare the samples. Finally, have them arrange the samples in order from lightest to heaviest using their observations.

3 Extend/Evaluate

Sum It Up!

1. **Write It!** Remind children that soil is a mixture of four things. Challenge them to recall the three sizes of rock bits plus one other thing that make up soil. Have them reread the fifth page of the lesson if they need help.
2. **Order It!** Remind children that they should think about the order of the stages in which a plant becomes part of the soil. Help children read all the steps, and tell them to think about what happens first, next, and last. Point out that they should mark the thing that happens first with a 1 and the thing that happens last with a 3. If children need help, remind them that this information can be found in the lesson.
3. **Draw It!** Tell children they can refer to the chart about soil properties to find pictures showing various properties of soil. Explain that they can use this information to draw a soil sample that is tan, has large rock bits, has a gritty texture, and has only a few once-living things.

Sum It Up!

1 Write It!

List the four parts that make up soil.

sand

silt

clay

once-living things

2 Order It!

Write 1, 2, 3 to order how a plant becomes part of soil.

2 The plant begins to break into pieces.

1 A plant dies and falls to the ground.

3 The pieces get smaller and become part of soil.

3 Draw It!

Draw soil that has these properties.

tan | large rock bits | gritty | few once-living things

Children's drawings should show soil that is tan, gritty, with large rock bits and few once-living things.

196

TEKS 1.7A

Brain Check

Lesson 2

Name ______________________

Word Play

Observe and compare the parts of soil. Match each part of soil to its description. Then add a detail about the size of rock bits.

sand

silt

clay

It holds water so well that it sticks together.

It is made of small bits of rock.

It does not hold water well.

It is made of large bits of rock.

It holds water fairly well.

It is made of medium bits of rock.

197

Answer Strategies

Word Play

- Begin this exercise by having children study the photographs of the soils and read the incomplete descriptions. Children should observe and compare each soil sample. You can help lead them through the activity. **Which description on the right-hand side best describes the properties of sand?** After children match the photograph to its description, tell them to add one more property of sand regarding the size of the rock bits. Repeat this procedure to match and complete the remaining descriptions of silt and clay.
- If children need to review the parts of soil and their properties, direct them to look back at the lesson and study the descriptions of sand, silt, and clay.
- Have pairs of children take turns asking each other questions about sand, silt, and clay.

Assessment

Lesson Quiz

See Assessment Guide, p. AG 73.

3 Extend/Evaluate (continued)

Answer Strategies

Apply Concepts

- Explain that this diagram is a sequence chart. Each box has space for a description of a step in the process of soil formation.
- Encourage children to look back at the lesson pages to find information about soil. Tell them to look for the steps of the process under the heading *Super Soil*.
- After children write the two missing steps, have them reread the chart to make sure that the sequence makes sense.
- As a lesson follow-up, ask children to summarize what they learned in the lesson. Encourage them to share information that they did not know about before reading the lesson.

Take It Home!

Have children work with a family member to observe, describe, and compare parts of soil in their area. Encourage them to talk about the properties of each type of soil and how the soil is being used. Have them share the results of their observations with the class.

Apply Concepts

Fill in the chart. Describe how soil forms.

How Soil Forms

Sample answer: Water and wind break down rock into smaller pieces. Plants and animals die and fall to the ground.

↓

Sample answer: Small pieces of rock become part of soil. Once-living things break down into bits.

↓

All the bits mix together to make soil.

Take It Home! **Family Members:** Walk with your child near your home to observe soil. Have your child describe and compare the parts of soil.

198

Make Connections

Easy

Art Connection

TEKS ART 1.2A, 1.2C

Paint with Soil

- Provide children with sand, clay, and silt soil, white finger paint, and paper. Have children mix a small quantity of each soil with paint and use it to finger-paint landscape scenes. As children work, encourage them to notice differences in the way the paints feel.
- After their paintings dry, have children comment on the way soil changed the appearance of the paint. Remind children to wash their hands.

Average

Social Studies Connection

TEKS SS 1.6B

Learn About Clay Homes

- Tell children that in some parts of the world, people have long used clay to build their homes. Provide resources with pictures of clay homes (such as those made from adobe), and have small groups of children model them by using real clay or modeling clay.
- Have children discuss what makes clay a good building material.

Average

Math Connection

TEKS MATH 1.7D

Measure Soil Settlement

- Fill a clear jar with potting soil or sand, and have children use rulers to measure the soil's depth. Then screw the lid onto the jar and shake it up and down, allowing children to take turns carefully shaking it, too.
- Have them measure the depth of soil again. Then have them compare the measurements. Children should observe that the soil was less deep in the jar after it was shaken.
- Lead them in discussing why the soil settled.

Challenging

Writing Connection

TEKS ELA 1.19C

Write About Soil Properties

- Share this verse about soil sung to the tune "Row Your Boat": *Sand, sand, sand I see/Sand is all around/Sand is rough/and often dry/Sand is tan or brown.*
- Have children work in small groups to write their own lyrics describing soils. After they rehearse, have them share their lyrics with the class.

Guided Inquiry

FLIPCHART P. 27

30 minutes

individuals

Children shoud follow the directions on the Flipchart. The accompanying pages in the Student Edition provide scaffolding for guided inquiry.

Inquiry Skills Focus Plan an Investigation

Objectives

- Recognize and demonstrate safe practices.
- Ask questions about objects observed in the natural world.
- Plan and conduct investigations. Record and organize data.
- Collect and compare information and make observations using hand lenses and safety goggles.
- Observe and compare components of soil.

Prep and Planning Tips

- See the Planning for Inquiry page for more information. Place a scoop of fresh soil on a plate for each child. Do not use commercial potting soil, which may contain synthetic ingredients.

Caution! Be sure children recognize and demonstrate safe practices to keep themselves and others safe and healthy by washing hands and using all materials appropriately. Children should wear goggles to protect their eyes.

Expected Results

Children use tools to find and separate out components of soil. They should find that soil has different parts.

1 Engage/Explore

Attention Grabber

Display a small potted plant for children, making sure that the soil is visible to children at the bottom of the pot. Ask *What is in this pot?* As children mention soil, prompt them to be more specific based on what they have learned about the different parts of soil. Help them recall that soil is not uniform but is made up of many smaller parts. Encourage them to be specific as they describe the soil parts they might find in the pot.

Preview Activity

Before beginning the investigation, have children review the directions on the Inquiry Flipchart and the accompanying Student Edition response pages. Then, have them complete the response pages as they follow the directions on the Flipchart.

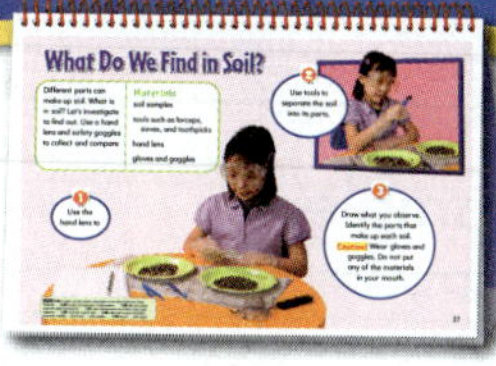

Inquiry Flipchart p. 27

Lesson 3
INQUIRY

TEKS 1.2A ask questions about organisms, objects, and events observed in the natural world 1.2B plan and conduct simple descriptive investigations such as ways objects move 1.2D record and organize data using pictures, numbers, and words 1.7A observe, compare, describe, and sort components of soil by size, texture, and color

Name ___________________

Essential Question

What Do We Find in Soil?

Set a Purpose

Tell what you want to find out.

I want to separate soil into its parts so I can identify the parts that make it up.

Think About the Procedure

1. What tools do you have?

sieve, forceps, toothpicks, hand lens

2. Tell about one way you will use a tool to separate the soil into parts.

Sample answer: I will put the soil through a sieve. A sieve will help me separate out large objects in soil from small ones.

199

Go Digital

A virtual lab experience is available with the Online Resources for this program.

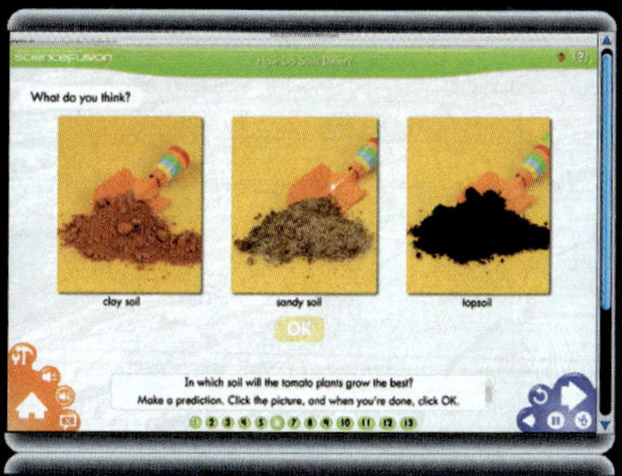

1 Engage/Explore (continued)

Guide the Investigation

Develop Inquiry Skills

PLAN AN INVESTIGATION Display the investigation materials. Have children discuss how they might use these materials to learn about soil. Work with them to decide on concrete steps they will take using these materials. Explain that when they decide on steps they will take to learn about something, they are planning an investigation.

Why is it helpful to plan the steps you will take for an investigation before you start? Sample answer: If I plan the steps, then I will know exactly what to do. Otherwise, I might make mistakes or do things out of order.

What do you predict you will find in the soil? Sample answer: I predict I will find bits of once-living things, like old plants, as well as small bits of rock. I might even find little pieces of trash or things made by humans.

2 Explain

Develop Inquiry Skills

RECORD YOUR DATA Point out the area on children's recording sheets where they can draw and label what they saw. If possible, provide your own labeled soil drawing on the board or chart paper, or have a volunteer share one as an example to children who are less practiced at making labels. Point out that each label is placed near the thing it tells about and that labels only need to include one or two words.

DRAW CONCLUSIONS Have children use their labeled pictures to draw conclusions about what their soil samples included. Allow time for all children to share what they learned. Have children tell what surprised or interested them most. You may wish to make a list of unusual things children found to emphasize the variety of materials that end up in soil.

If possible, also take a minute to have children tell how planning their investigations beforehand helped them. Ask them to draw a conclusion about why scientists plan their investigations.

3 Extend/Evaluate

ASK MORE QUESTIONS Discuss children's responses to the items. Some children may raise questions about other parts of soil. As an extension activity, encourage children to plan investigations or research the answers to their questions.

Assessment

Lesson Quiz
See Assessment Guide, p. AG 74.

Record Your Data

Draw and label the parts in your soil sample.

Check children's work. Children should draw and label the parts they find in the soil sample.

Draw Conclusions

What parts make up your soil?

Sample answer: The soil has bits of rock, dead plant parts, and silt.

Ask More Questions

What other questions can you ask about soil?

Sample answer: Are soils made up of different parts in other places? How are other soil samples the same and different?

200

Differentiated Inquiry

Easy

Choose Tools

- Display the tools used in the investigation. Ask *If you could only use one of these tools to learn about soil, which one would you choose?*
- Have children who chose the same tools work in groups to observe new soil samples.
- Have each group share what they discovered and reflect on the usefulness of the tool they chose. Work with them to draw conclusions about why scientists often use more than one tool to observe things.

Average

Determine Whether a Sample Is Soil

- Provide a sample of wood chips or small pebbles, such as one might use to line a path or garden. Ask *Is it soil?* Have children explain their reasoning.
- Have children use toothpicks and a hand lens to observe the sample closely. Ask again: *Is it soil?* Help children understand that although the sample may contain some parts found in soil, it is different in that it does not contain a mixture of many different parts and the pieces are bigger.

Average

Draw Conclusions About Soil

- Tell children where the soil used for their investigation came from, such as your backyard or a garden supply store. Then, have children look back at their labeled drawings showing the different things they found. Say *How do you think each thing got into the soil? Draw conclusions.*
- Have children write and draw an explanation for where each part of their soil sample came from. Allow them to look at science or other reference materials for help.

Challenging

Investigate How Well Soil Holds Water

- Remind children that some soils hold water well, while others do not. Have children predict whether the soil they observed in this activity will hold water well and explain their reasoning.
- Have children plan an investigation in which they test their predictions. You may provide a sieve or filter paper to aid children in their investigation.

Guided Inquiry

FLIPCHART P. 28

30 minutes

individuals or pairs

Children should follow the directions on the Flipchart. The accompanying pages in the Student Edition provide scaffolding for guided inquiry.

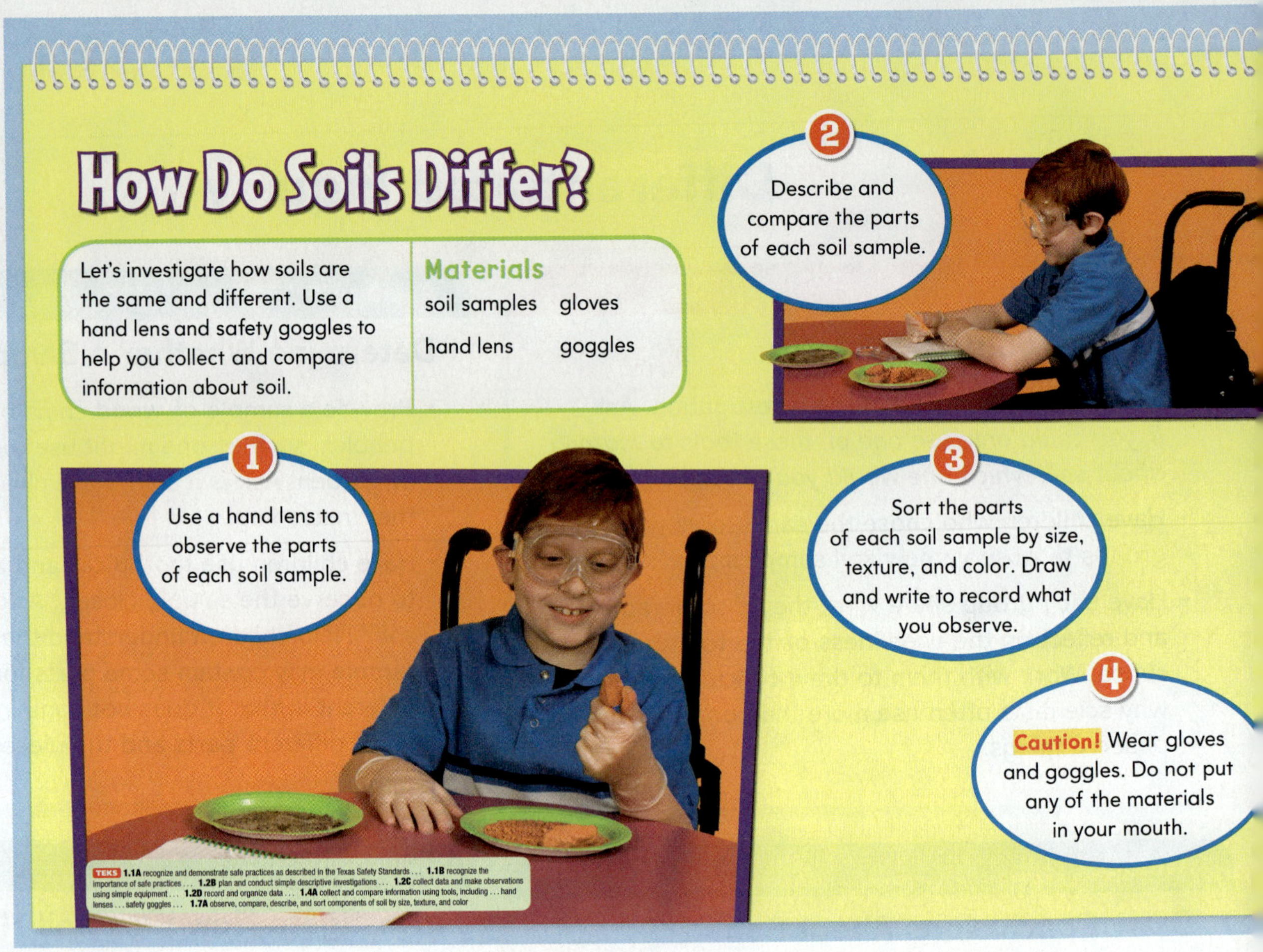

Inquiry Skills Focus Compare

Objectives

- Recognize and demonstrate safe practices.
- Ask questions about objects observed in the natural world.
- Plan and conduct investigations. Record and organize data.
- Collect, compare, and make observations using hand lenses and safety goggles.
- Observe, compare, describe, and sort components of soil.

Prep and Planning Tips

- See the Planning for Inquiry page for more information. Supply two very different soil samples for each child or pair.

Caution! Be sure children recognize and demonstrate the importance of safe practices to keep themselves and others safe and healthy by using all materials appropriately, wearing gloves, wearing safety goggles, and washing their hands.

Expected Results

By comparing the two samples, children should observe that soils can vary widely in their contents and appearance.

1 Engage/Explore

Attention Grabber

Hold up a chunk of clay for children, using natural clay if it is available in your area. Let children feel and shape it with their hands. Tell children that clay is a part of soil. Ask *How is soil that has a lot of clay different from other soils?* Point out that when children tell how things are alike and different, they are comparing and contrasting them. Then, explain that they will be comparing and contrasting other kinds of soil today, too.

Preview Activity

Before beginning the investigation, have children review the directions on the Inquiry Flipchart and the accompanying Student Edition response pages. Then, have them complete the response pages as they follow the directions on the Flipchart.

TEKS 1.1A, 1.1B, 1.2A, 1.2B, 1.2C, 1.2D, 1.4A, 1.7A

Inquiry Flipchart p. 28

Lesson 4
INQUIRY

TEKS **1.2A** ask questions about organisms, objects, and events observed in the natural world **1.2B** plan and conduct simple descriptive investigations such as ways objects move **1.2D** record and organize data using pictures, numbers, and words **1.7A** observe, compare, describe, and sort components of soil by size, texture, and color

Name ____________________

Essential Question

How Do Soils Differ?

Set a Purpose

Tell what you want to find out.

I want to observe, compare, describe, and sort the different parts of each soil sample by size, color, and texture.

Think About the Procedure

1. How many soil samples will you compare?

Sample answer: I will compare two soil samples.

2. Name some properties of soil that you will observe.

Sample answer: Some properties I will observe are color, texture, and size of the rock bits.

201

Go Digital

A virtual lab experience is available with the Online Resources for this program.

1 Engage/Explore (continued)

Guide the Investigation

Develop Inquiry Skills

COMPARE/CONTRAST Remind children that when they compare and contrast, they tell how things are alike and different. Ask the following questions as children plan and complete the activity.

What senses are you using to compare the soil samples? sight and touch **How would you describe the soil samples?** Sample answer: One soil sample is red in color and smooth while the other soil sample is dark brown with bits of plants and rocks.

Why don't we use our sense of taste to observe things from nature, like soil? Sample answer: There might be germs on the soil. Tasting the soil might make us sick.

Do you think the samples you are looking at came from the same place in nature? Explain. Sample answer: No, I think they came from different places. I don't think a dry, sandy soil would be right next to a damp, rich soil on the ground.

What can you observe with the hand lens that you could not observe without it? Sample answer: I can see tiny grains of rock, insects, and other very small things.

2 Explain

Develop Inquiry Skills

RECORD YOUR DATA Point out the chart on children's recording sheets, and read the headings aloud. Remind children that a *property* is one part of what something is like, such as its size or shape. The properties listed on this chart are color, texture, and the size of bits in the soil. Have children draw and write their observations on their charts.

DRAW CONCLUSIONS Have children use their charts to describe, compare, and contrast how their soil samples were the same and different. Encourage them to use words such as *alike*, *both*, and *different* as they talk about the samples. Also encourage them to be specific as they talk about how and why they sorted their soil samples as they did.

3 Extend/Evaluate

ASK MORE QUESTIONS Discuss children's responses to the items. Some children may raise questions about other ways soils can be alike and different. As an extension activity, encourage children to plan investigations or research the answers to their questions.

Assessment

Lesson Quiz

See Assessment Guide, p. AG 75.

Record Your Data

Check children's observations.

Describe and sort the parts of soil. Draw and write to record what you observe.

Property	Soil Sample 1	Soil Sample 2
Color		
Texture		
Size of Bits		

Draw Conclusions

Compare. How are the soils the same and different?

Sample answer: Both soils had small rock bits. Soil 1 was dark and had twigs in it. Soil 2 was light and had no twigs in it.

Ask More Questions

What other questions could you ask about the different parts of soil?

Sample answer: Why are soils different colors?

202

Differentiated Inquiry

Easy

Compare Soil by Touch

- Have partners add the same amount of water to their two soil samples from the main activity.
- Have them try to shape damp soil into a ball; each partner works with their own sample of soil. Also, have them try to roll the soil ball between their thumb and forefinger and observe the grain size and whether the soil holds water well.

Caution! For all of these activities, have children follow the usual safety tips for handling soil, such as wearing gloves and goggles. Remind them not to put soil in or near their mouths. Ask them to wash their hands after the activity.

Average

Observe Changes in Organic Matter

- Talk with children about how once-living things become soil. *Does this take a long time? What does it look like?* Then, fill a shallow container with rich soil. Add to it a few citrus peels and green leaves. Have children observe as you mix these items with the soil. Cover the container.
- Revisit the container every day as the items break down. Have children observe how they brown and break down into smaller pieces. Make a final note when the items have become indistinguishable from the rest of the soil.

Easy

Observe Soil Colors

- Take children on a nature walk. Have them observe you collect two soil samples: one from near the surface and one from about a foot under the surface in the same spot.
- Take children back to the classroom and have them compare the soils. In particular, direct attention to the colors of the soils; explain that darker soils have more once-living things, while red or white soils have more rock bits in them.
- Have children observe the soil samples with a hand lens to find other ways they are different.

Challenging

Compare How Soils Help Plants Grow

- Ask *Which of the soils you observed would be better for growing plants? Why?* Have children explain their predictions and their reasoning.
- Have children test their predictions by putting each type of soil into a small pot, spraying it with a little water, and putting a bean plant in the pot.
- Have children observe and compare the two pots over a few weeks to determine whether their predictions were correct. Remind them to spray the pots periodically with water if needed.

Options for Inquiry

FLIPCHART P. 29

Children can conduct these optional investigations at any time before, during, or in response to the lesson in the Student Edition.

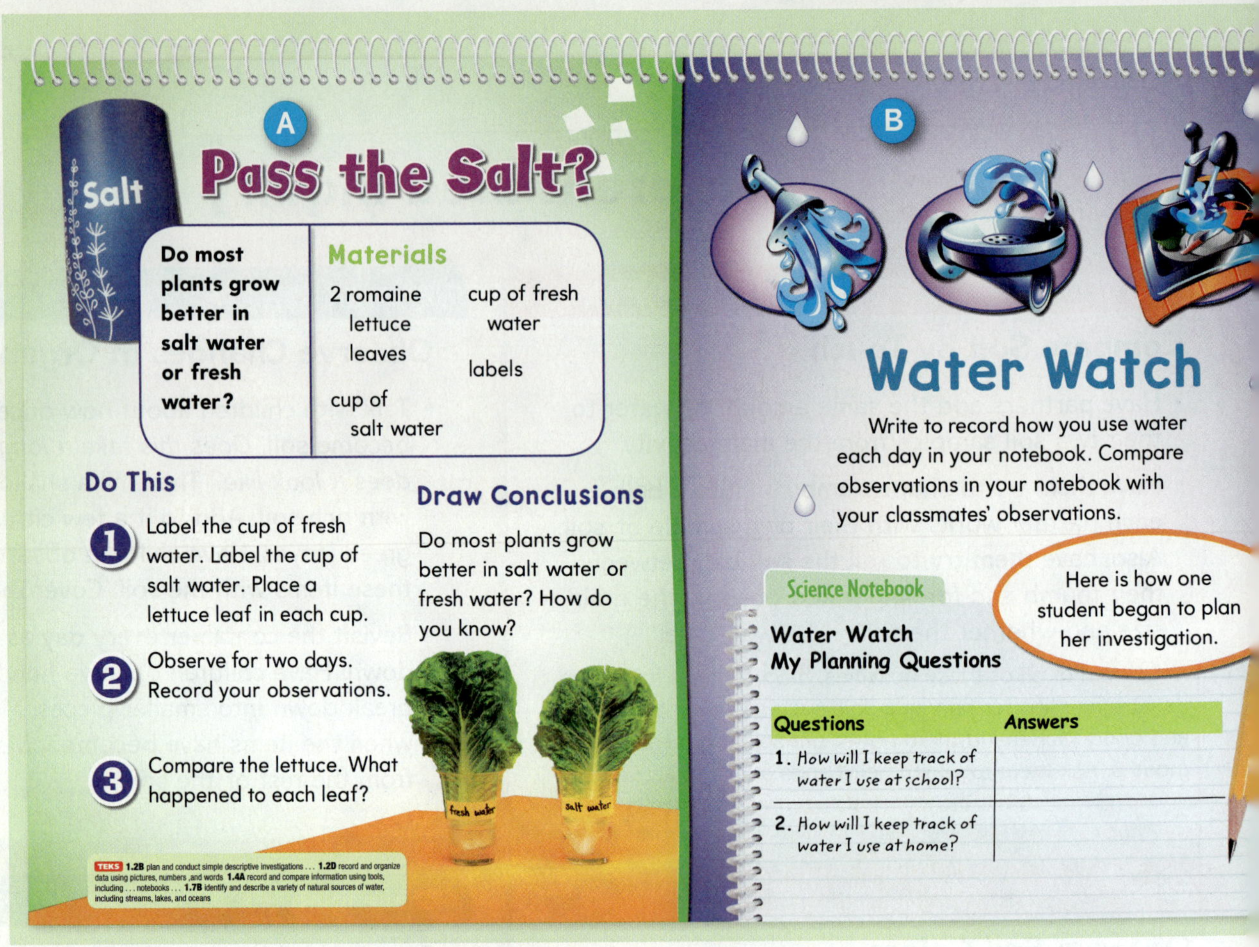

Directed Inquiry

A Pass the Salt?

15 minutes
pairs

Prep and Planning Tips

Prepare the salt water in advance. Mix 4 teaspoons of salt into 1 liter of water. This will make enough salt water for two 16-oz cups.

Divide the class into pairs or small groups, depending on the number of romaine leaves you have. It will take about 15 minutes for children to set up the activity and make their initial observations. Then they will need 5 minutes a day for the next few days to water and observe their plants.

Expected Results

After a few days, children should notice that the romaine leaf in the salt water is wilting. The one in fresh water is doing well and looking healthy.

Independent Inquiry

B Water Watch

30 minutes
individuals

Prep and Planning Tips

See the Planning for Inquiry page for more information. This activity can be completed all at once in school, with children remembering how they used water during one day. It can also be done throughout the day. Children would discuss the activity and set up their recording charts in class and then complete them throughout the course of a day.

Notebook

Science Notebook

Children can use the Science Notebook as a model for planning and conducting their own investigation. Children will need to figure out how to record the information, so allow time for pairs to discuss or sketch ideas for how to organize a chart. They might want to head one column *Home* and a second column *School*.

TEKS 1.7B identify and describe a variety of natural sources of water, including streams, lakes, and oceans

Lesson 5

Essential Question

Where Can We Find Water?

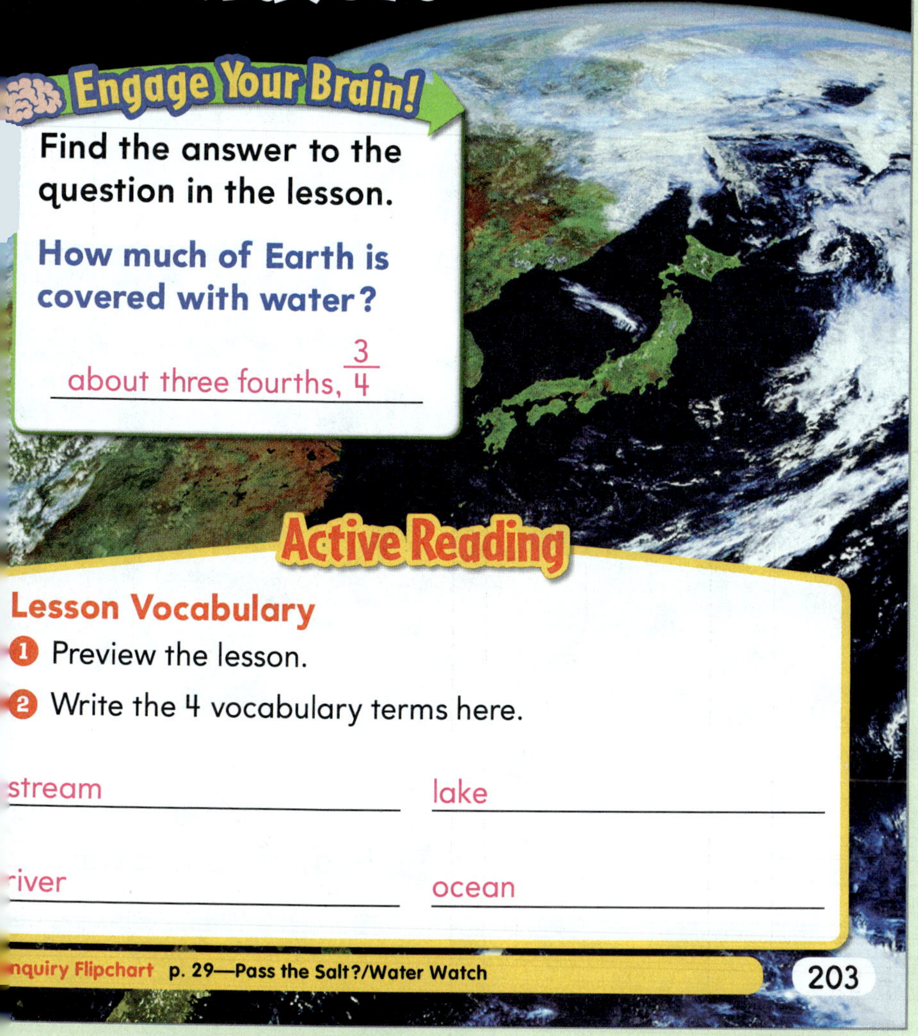

Engage Your Brain!

Find the answer to the question in the lesson.

How much of Earth is covered with water?

about three fourths, $\frac{3}{4}$

Active Reading

Lesson Vocabulary

1. Preview the lesson.
2. Write the 4 vocabulary terms here.

stream, lake, river, ocean

Inquiry Flipchart p. 29—Pass the Salt?/Water Watch

203

Go Digital

An interactive digital lesson is available in Online Resources. It is suitable for individuals, small groups, or may be projected or used on an interactive white board.

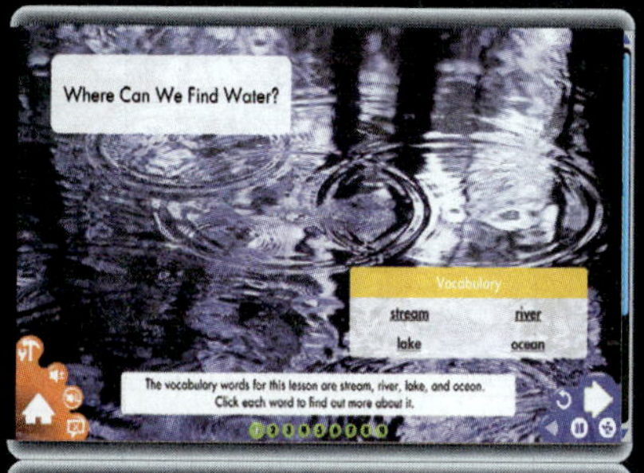

1 Engage/Explore

Objectives

- Plan and conduct simple investigations.
- Record and organize data.
- Record and compare information using notebooks.
- Identify and describe a variety of natural sources of water, including streams, lakes, and oceans.

Engage Your Brain!

Have children brainstorm answers to this question: *How much of Earth is covered with water?* Show them a globe or a world map. Point out that the blue areas are water and ask for predictions about how much of the map or globe is blue.

Remind them to record their final answer to the question when they find it on the fifth page of this lesson.

Active Reading Annotations

Remind children that active readers "make texts their own" by marking them or writing notes to help them understand what they are reading. Encourage children to use pencil to make annotations and to feel free to change their marks and notes as they read. The goal of annotation is to help children remember what they have read.

Vocabulary and Interactive Glossary

Remind children to find and list the yellow highlighted terms from the lesson. As they proceed through the lesson and learn about the terms, they should add drawings or words in the extra spaces provided in some of the entries in the Interactive Glossary.

2 Explain

Notebook Generate Ideas

Read the heading aloud to children. Tell them that it refers to fresh water, or water that is not salty. Explain that the water we drink is fresh water. Ask children where they think we find fresh water in nature, and then have them scan the subheadings on the spread to name three places where fresh water can be found. (streams, rivers, lakes)

Develop Science Vocabulary

stream Review that a stream is a small body of flowing water.

river Review that a river is a large body of flowing water. To clarify the difference between *stream* and *river,* turn on the tap of a sink gently and say *stream.* Then turn the faucet on hard and say *river.* If a sink is not available, pour water instead.

Develop Science Concepts

What is the difference between fresh water and salt water? Fresh water does not contain large amounts of salt. Salt water contains large amounts of salt.

Identify two sources of fresh water that flow. streams and rivers

How can you describe streams and rivers? A stream is a small body of flowing water. A river is a large body of flowing water.

Review that streams can flow into a river. Have children draw a picture to show this relationship.

So Fresh

Most plants and animals need fresh water. People need fresh water, too. Fresh water is not salty. You can find sources of fresh water in many places.

streams

A **stream** is a small body of flowing water.

rivers

Some streams flow into rivers. A **river** is a large body of flowing water.

204

English Language Learners

ELPS 2C, 2E

Learn Multiple-Meaning Words Write *fresh* on the board. Explain that it is a multiple-meaning word that can mean "not salty" or "new or recent" as in *fresh food.* Say sentences that use the various meanings, such as *This food is fresh or The stream has fresh water.* Ask children to raise their hands when they hear the use that means "new or recent."

Look at the pictures. Identify the three bodies of water. Circle their names. Describe each one by drawing a line under a sentence that tells about it.

lakes

A lake is a body of water with land all around it. Water in a lake does not flow.

205

Develop Science Vocabulary

lake Explain that a lake is a body of water with land all around it. Make an indentation with modeling clay and fill it with water to model a lake.

Develop Science Concepts

Look at the picture of the lakes on the right page. How do they look different from the stream and the river? Lakes do not flow.

Why do you think the water in a lake does not flow? Land is all around a lake, so the water does not have anywhere to flow.

Develop Inquiry Skills

COMPARE/CONTRAST **How are a lake, a stream, and a river all the same?** They are sources of fresh water.

How are a stream and a river different from a lake? A stream and a river flow. A lake does not.

Guide children to use this information to help them answer the interactive.

Notebook Summarize Ideas

Have children think about what they learned about water that they did not already know. Have them summarize those ideas, and the main ideas about streams, rivers, and lakes, orally or in writing.

Differentiation—Leveled Questions

Extra Support

Which kind of fresh water sources flow? streams and rivers Which do not? lakes

Challenge

Do you think it is possible for a river to become a stream? Why or why not? Sample answer: Yes, because a river can flow into areas where it becomes narrower and smaller, until it is just a small stream.

2 Explain (continued)

Notebook Generate Ideas

Ask children to talk about experiences they might have had at the ocean or beach, or have seen in movies or on television. Talk about how visiting the ocean is different from visiting a lake, stream, or river.

Active Reading Details

Review that a detail is a fact about a main idea. Explain that a detail sentence may give an example or describe something. Active readers ask, "What topic does this detail sentence tell about?" The answer helps them keep the main idea in mind and better understand it.

Develop Science Vocabulary

ocean The ancient Greeks imagined Oceanus (also known as Okeanos) as the great god of the waters. It was said that he was the source of all water on Earth, controlling rivers, lakes, streams, oceans, wells, and rain through underground caverns. The word *ocean* that we use today relates to Oceanus. Explain this relationship to children. Encourage children to imagine Oceanus and draw pictures of what they imagine.

Develop Science Concepts

Identify and describe the body of water seen on these two pages. The body of water is an ocean. It has salty water.

Why don't we drink ocean water? It is salty. We live by drinking fresh water, not salt water.

Why do you think that animals that live in the ocean cannot live in lakes? The animals need to live in salt water to stay alive. They could not live in fresh water.

So Salty

You can find water in oceans too. An **ocean** is a large body of salty water. Most of Earth's water is in oceans.

Active Reading

A detail is a fact about a main idea. Draw one line under a detail. Draw an arrow to the main idea it tells about.

▶ Identify the body of water you see on the page. Circle the name of it. Describe the body of water by writing a sentence about it.

An ocean is a large body of salty water.

206

Differentiation—Leveled Questions

Extra Support

Where is most of the water on Earth found? in the oceans

Challenge

What is the closest ocean to where you live? Use a map to fi[nd] out. Guide children to use a map to find the closest ocean.

surfer in ocean

Do the Math!

Model Fractions

About $\frac{3}{4}$, or three fourths, of Earth is covered with water. The rest is covered with land.

This circle models Earth's water and land. It has 4 parts. Color the parts to show how much water is on Earth.

Now look at the circle. How much of Earth is covered with land?

Answer: $\frac{1}{4}$

207

3 Math Connection

TEKS MATH 1.1A, 1.5G

Solve a Problem About 97 gallons of every 100 gallons of water on Earth are salt water. Challenge children to figure out how many gallons per hundred are fresh water. After children solve the problem, put these numbers in perspective. Explain that if all of the world's water fit in a very large glass, only one small spoonful would be drinkable fresh water.

TEKS 1.7B

Do the Math!

TEKS MATH 1.6H

Model Fractions

Point out that the circle looks like a pizza or pie cut into four slices. Have children point to each piece as you count the pieces together.

Explain that the fraction ¾ means the same as 3 out of 4, or 3 of the 4 slices. **How many slices will you color to show ¾ or 3 out of 4?** 3 slices Guide children to color three of the slices.

To answer the question at the bottom, children need to look at the part of the circle that is not colored. **How many pieces are not colored?** 1 **How many pieces are there in all?** 4 **Which number belongs on the top of the fraction?** 1 **Which number belongs on the bottom?** 4 **How do we write the fraction?** ¼

Notebook

Summarize Ideas

Ask children to find one sentence that tells the most important thing they read on these two pages. Say that this sentence is the main idea. Have them use the main idea to summarize orally or in writing what they learned about the oceans.

2 Explain (continued)

Notebook Generate Ideas

Read the heading aloud to children. Discuss what *wonderful* means, and have children identify words that mean about the same thing. Use the heading as a clue to talk about what these two pages might be about.

Why is water wonderful? Brainstorm ideas with children and list them on the board.

Active Reading Main Idea

Review that the main idea is the most important idea about something. Explain that the main idea may be the first sentence in a paragraph. The heading might also give an idea about the main idea of a page.

Develop Science Concepts

Name three kinds of living things that need fresh water to live. people, animals, and plants

According to the pictures and captions on the left page, how do people and animals use water? Sample answer: They drink it.

What kind of water would you give your plants or animals, fresh water or salt water? fresh water

Misconception Alert

Children might think that plants, animals, and people can use salt water to stay healthy. Explain that most living things can use only fresh water to meet their basic needs. Fresh water is much more uncommon on Earth than salt water. If salt water can be *desalinated* (that is, have the salt removed and turned into fresh water), then it can be used. This process, though, is uncommon and expensive. Only plants and animals that live in salt water can use salt water.

Wonderful Water

All living things need water. Plants, animals, and people need it to stay healthy.

Active Reading

The main idea is the most important idea about something. Draw two lines under the main idea.

People drink water.

Animals drink water.

208

Writing Connection

TEKS ELA 1.18A

Write a Water Story Ask children to write a fictional paragraph about a child who helps to save or clean water. The story should include one specific thing the child does to benefit water. Children who have trouble writing complete sentences can be paired with a more writing proficient partner.

Water flows through this dam.

Save Earth's water!

We must protect water and keep it clean.

Follow these tips to help.

1. Use less water for baths and showers.
2. Fix leaky pipes or faucets.
3. Put trash in trash cans! Do not put trash in water.

Plants need water too.

▶ Add your own tip for protecting Earth's water.

Sample answer: Turn off running water while you brush your teeth.

209

English Language Learners

ELPS 2C, 2E

Understand Language Use a toy animal or doll to gesture or pantomime the meaning of *protect* as you explain that it means "to keep safe." Have children use their own examples to gesture the same meaning. Help children understand that they cannot protect water in exactly the same way, but they can keep it safe by saving it and keeping it clean.

Develop Science Concepts

Review the tips for protecting water and keeping it clean. Choose one you think you could do every day and tell how you will do it. Sample answer: I will take shorter showers to save water.

How does using less water when we bathe help to protect it? It makes the water last longer so that it is not wasted.

Why do you think it is important to keep trash out of the water? Trash in the water pollutes it, or makes it dirty. Then we have to clean it before we use it.

What other ways can we protect water? Write your own idea. Accept all reasonable answers.

Develop Inquiry Skills

INFER **What do you think would happen if we did not protect water?** We would not have clean water to drink and for other important uses. The water in lakes, rivers, and oceans may become dirty and make animals sick.

Notebook Summarize Ideas

Ask children to work in a group to review the details they read about protecting water. Ask each child in the group to name one thing that they can do to save and protect water.

2 Explain (continued)

Notebook Generate Ideas

Read the heading aloud to children and explain that these two pages are about being safe in and around the water. Ask children to name activities people do in the water when they need to be safe, such as swimming or boating. Allow time for them to talk about experiences they have had with those activities and the things they did to stay safe, such as wearing a life jacket or swimming while a lifeguard is on duty.

Develop Science Concepts

Why do we follow safety rules? They keep people safe in the water.

What kind of weather would be unsafe for swimming or boating? thunderstorms

What does a life jacket do? It helps you float in the water.

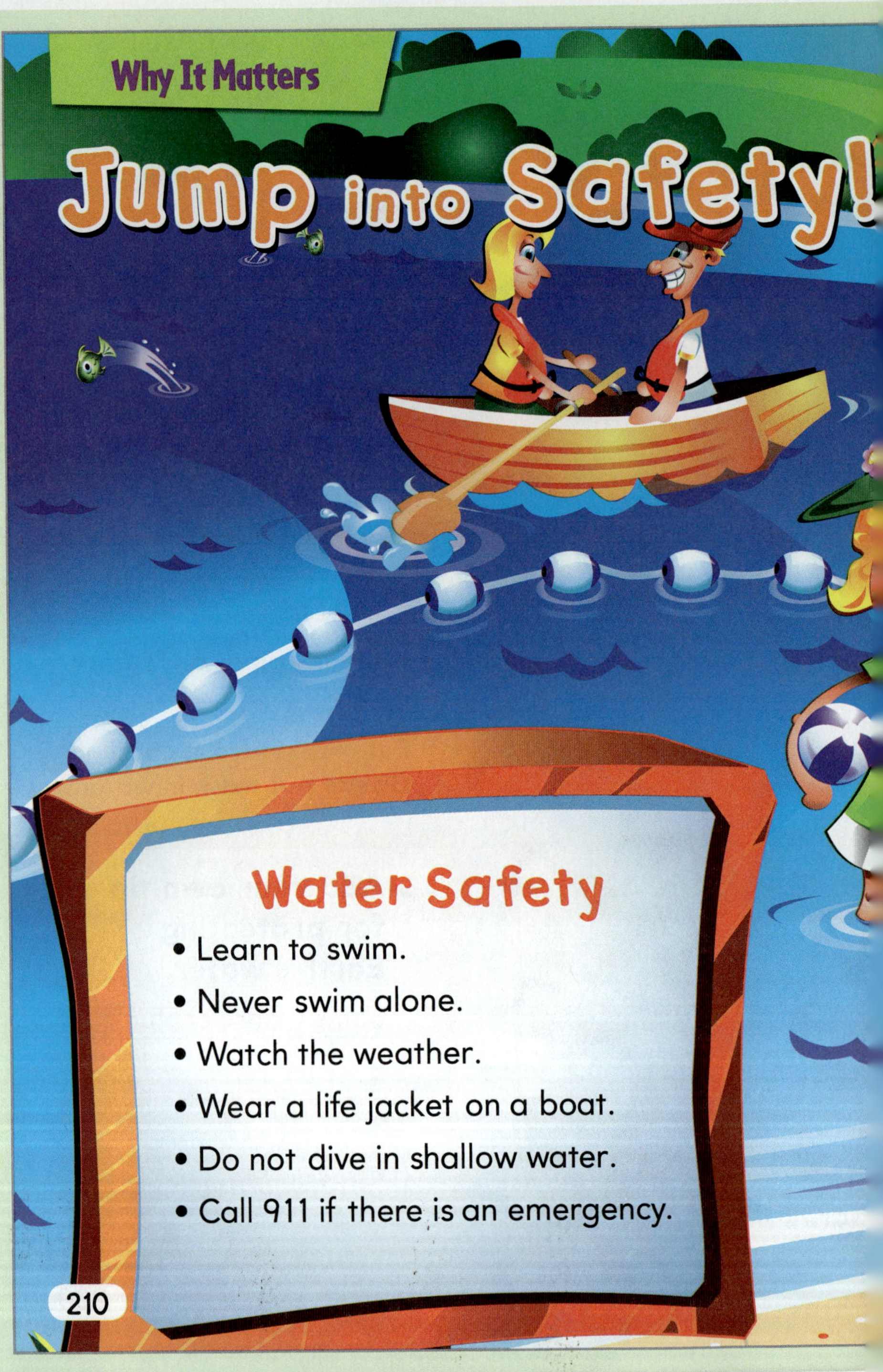

123 Math Connection

TEKS MATH 1.1

Work Backward to Solve a Problem Have pairs work together to solve this problem and show or explain the solution: Some number of people were in a boat. The lifeguard said, "That boat is not safe with so many people in it! Three of you must get out!" So three people left the boat. Now there are five people in the boat. How many were ther to start?

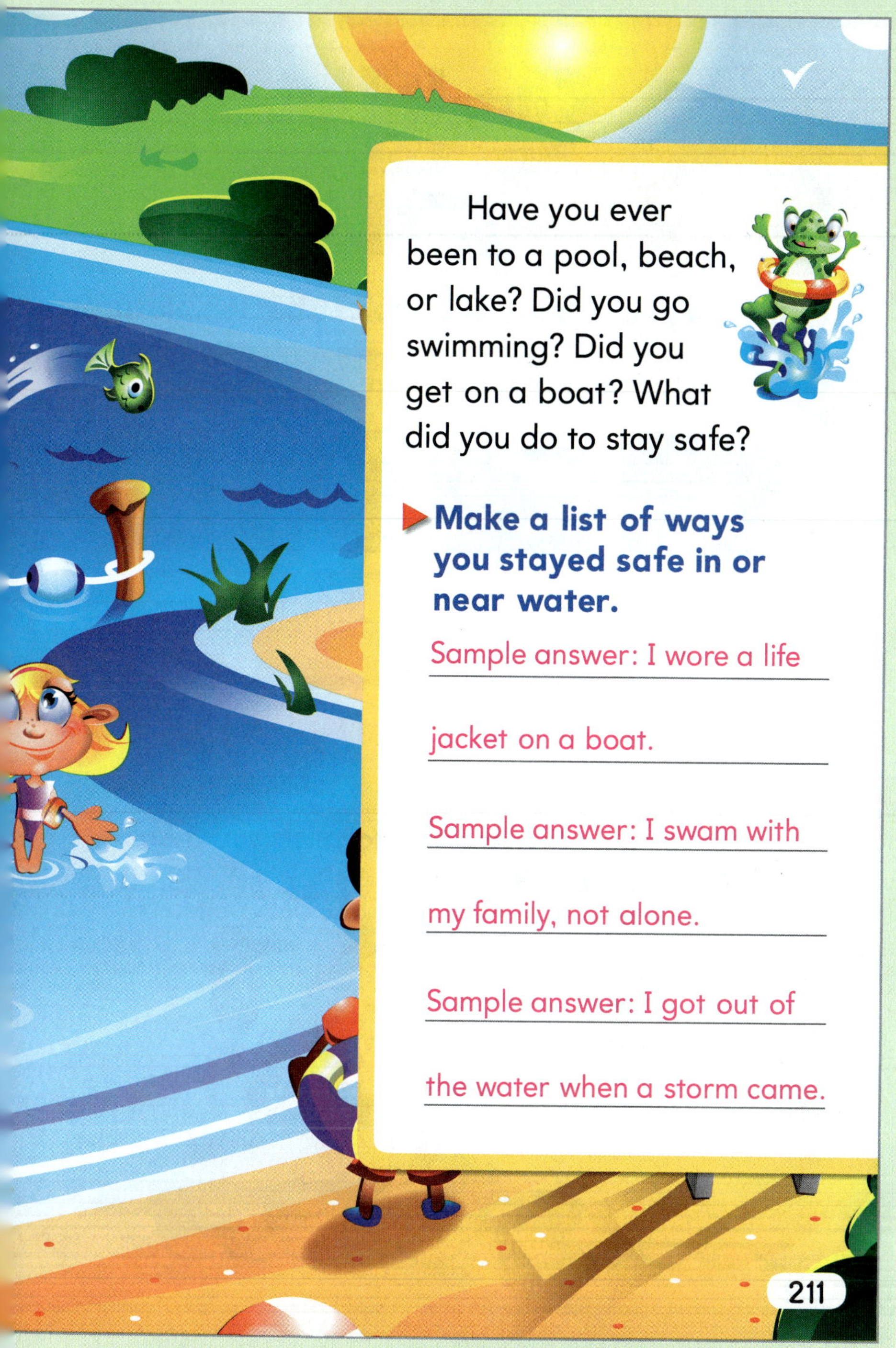

Have you ever been to a pool, beach, or lake? Did you go swimming? Did you get on a boat? What did you do to stay safe?

▶ **Make a list of ways you stayed safe in or near water.**

Sample answer: I wore a life jacket on a boat.

Sample answer: I swam with my family, not alone.

Sample answer: I got out of the water when a storm came.

211

Interpret Visuals

Guide children though the picture of water activities. Ask volunteers to take turns pointing out an activity they see that they would enjoy doing and name something they would do to make that activity safe. Keep the safety ideas as a list on the board or a chart and use that list as a reference when children write their lists of water safety rules.

Notebook Summarize Ideas

Direct children to look again at the picture and review the rules listed on these two pages. Then have them summarize orally or in writing the key ideas that they learned.

3 Extend/Evaluate

Sum It Up!

1. **Label It!** To help identify and label each body of water, suggest that children ask themselves questions such as *Is this fresh water or salt water? Is this water flowing or still?* They can look back in the lesson for help with the answers.
2. **Draw It!** Explain to children that they should look closely at the picture and think about the safety rules they just talked about to decide what they should draw on the picture.

Sum It Up!

1 Label It!

Identify each body of water. Label the pictures.

stream lake river ocean

river

lake

ocean

stream

2 Draw It!

What can the people do to be safe on the water? Draw on the picture.

Children should draw life vests on the boaters.

212

TEKS 1.7B

Brain Check

Lesson 5

Name ____________________

Word Play

Fill in the blanks. Use these words to describe the different bodies of water.

ocean	lake	stream	river	fresh water

Most lakes have f r e s h (w) a t e r.

An o c e (a) n has salty water.

A s (t) r e a m is a small body of water.

A l a k (e) has water that does not flow.

Streams can flow together to make a (r) i v e r.

Then use the circled letters to fill in the blanks below.

We use w a t e r in many ways!

Answer Strategies

Word Play

- Explain that there are two parts to this activity. The first is to answer each question with a word from the word bank by filling in the blanks with one letter on each blank. Guide children to spell the words correctly by using the words in the word bank as a reference. The answer to the second part depends on spelling each word correctly.
- Then explain that the circled letters should be placed in order into the blanks at the bottom of the page to complete the sentence. Challenge children to figure out the answer to the sentence at the bottom before they fill in the letters. They might be able to use the context of the lesson and the number of blanks to find the answer.

Assessment

Lesson Quiz

See Assessment Guide, p. AG 76.

3 Extend/Evaluate (continued)

Answer Strategies

Apply Concepts

- Point out that the four bullets under question 2 indicate that children should list four different answers for that question. Tell them that they need not write those answers as complete sentences.

Take It Home!

Suggest that children talk with a family member to help them identify and describe different sources of water. Then have children make a list of ways they can save water at home and then show it to a family member to discuss. Encourage the family member to add to the list and talk about water use in the family. Children can bring their family lists to class to compile them into a large poster. That poster can be displayed in class as a reminder of things children can do at home or in school.

Apply Concepts

Write your answer to each question.

1. Why do we need water?

Responses will vary but should indicate uses for water such as drinking, bathing, watering plants, and traveling.

2. How can we stay safe around water?

- Children should list four ways to stay
- safe around water such as wearing life
- vests, learning to swim, and calling 911
- in an emergency.

Take It Home!

Family Members: Help your child to identify and describe different bodies of water. Then work with your child to identify ways to save water at home.

214

Make Connections

Easy

Music Connection TEKS MUSIC 1.2A

Sing "Row Your Boat"

- Teach children the song "Row Your Boat." Ask them to identify the body of water named in the song. *(stream)*
- Have them rewrite the lyrics to replace *stream* with *lake* and fix the rhyme for *stream* and *dream*. Repeat for *river*.

Average

Math Connection TEKS MATH 1.2F

Compare River Lengths

- Tell children that the three longest rivers in the world are the Amazon (South America, 3,890 miles), the Nile (Africa, 4,135 miles) and the Yangtze (China, 3,917 miles).
- Have children order the three rivers from longest to shortest.

Easy

Writing Connection TEKS ELA 1.24C

Write About Water Fun

- At the bottom of a large sheet of paper, ask children to write a phrase or sentence about a time that they enjoyed playing in or around the water. Have them draw a picture on the rest of the paper to accompany the writing.
- Ask children to show their work and tell about it to the class. Then display the drawings and writing.

Challenging

Social Studies Connection TEKS SS 1.5A

Identify Oceans of the World

- Have groups use a world map or online resources to identify the names of the world's oceans.
- When they finish, ask groups to compare their lists, adding any names that they did not include.

S.T.E.M.

Engineering and Technology

Objective

- Identify and explain a problem and propose a solution in his/her own words.

Generate Ideas

Notebook

Share the background information before you assign the feature. Ask questions to ascertain children's prior knowledge.

What is a dam? A dam is a wall across a river.

Why have people developed dams? Sample answer: to collect water

Background

- A dam is a wall, or barrier, built across a river. It can stop or slow the flow of water in a river. Water collects behind the dam to form a lake.
- People first built dams to collect water for drinking and farming. The water collected by a dam is sent through pipes to farms and cities.
- Dams also help people in other ways. They help control flooding by holding back the river when heavy rains fall. In times when there is little or no rain, the dam releases water slowly so that the river flows evenly. Other dams use waterpower to make electricity.
- As helpful as dams are, they can also harm the environment. The lake that forms behind a dam covers land that was once home to animals and, sometimes, people. The dam collects water, but it also traps silt and sand that contain nutrients. Animals and plants below the dam cannot get these nutrients.
- Dams also affect the fish that live in the river. A dam can stop fish from migrating.

TEKS 1.3A identify and explain a problem such as finding a home for a classroom pet and propose a solution in his/her own words

S.T.E.M.

Engineering and Technology

Technology and the Environment

Dams

A dam is a wall built across a river. It slows the flow of the river. A dam can be helpful. It is built to help solve problems. It can provide water for drinking and for crops. It can also control floods.

A dam can also harm the environment. Fish, like salmon, can not move across some dams. Some animals lose their homes.

College & Career Readiness CCRS III.B.1, III.B.3, III.C.1, III.D.1

Civil Engineers This feature provides an opportunity to develop children's awareness of STEM careers related to civil engineering. Suggest children go online to find out more about civil engineers. Civil engineers plan, design, construct, and maintain structures. These structures include dams, roads, and bridge Have children make a poster to share what they learned about civil engineers. Share technical articles with children. Encourag children to use technical vocabulary in their posters.

S.T.E.M. continued

Helpful and Harmful

How are dams helpful? How are dams harmful? Use your ideas to complete the chart.

Effects of Dams	
Helpful	**Harmful**
Sample answers:	Sample answers:
Dams provide drinking water and water for crops.	Some animals lose homes.
Dams can control flooding.	Dams can affect how animals move around.

Build On It!

Learn more about water and technology. Complete **Design It: Water Filter** on the Inquiry Flipchart.

Build On It!

In **Design It: Water Filter**, the design challenge associated with this lesson, children use the steps of the engineering design process to make a water filter from everyday materials. For more details, see the pages that follow.

Other opportunities to apply the design process appear throughout the *Inquiry Flipchart*.

Develop S.T.E.M. Concepts

When children have completed reading the feature, ask questions to help them reflect on dams.

How can dams harm the environment? Animals may lose their homes. Some fish cannot move around.

What other kinds of technology do you know that can harm the environment? Sample answer: A car is a kind of technology that can cause air pollution.

Develop Inquiry Skills

INFER **In what ways do dams improve life for people?** They store and provide water for farming and drinking. They can control flooding.

A dam is a kind of system. What might happen if part of the dam breaks or is missing? Sample answer: The dam might break and release all the water it is holding. It would cause the river to flood.

COMPARE Ask questions to help children identify both the helpful and harmful effects of dams. **How do dams help store water?** Water collects behind the dam.

How do people use the water a dam collects? for farming and drinking

How does a dam change the environment? Animals behind the dam may lose their homes. Fish may not be able to move around.

IDENTIFY VARIABLES **If you were an engineer building a dam, what question could you ask about the environment?** Sample answer: How can I improve my dam so that fish can still swim upstream?

Notebook Summarize Ideas

Ask children to summarize what they learned about dams. Have them share the helpful and harmful aspects of dams and tell how dams can change the environment.

S.T.E.M.

Engineering and Technology

FLIPCHART P. 30

40 minutes

small groups

Objectives

- Record and organize data.
- Identify and explain a problem and propose a solution in his/her own words.

Prep and Planning Tips

- Assemble the materials needed for the lesson. Coffee filters and folded paper towels can substitute for the cotton balls.
- Prepare for each group a mixture of dirty water. It can include bits of paper, plastic, leaf parts, twigs, and soil. Clear, plastic, two-liter soft drink bottles make good receptacles for the mixture.

Expected Results

Children will use the materials to filter the dirty water. They will determine that finer materials, such as cotton balls, will remove more debris from the water than coarser materials, such as sand.

1 Engage/Explore

Attention Grabber

Show children a jar filled with a sand and pebble mixture. Call on volunteers to suggest ways in which they might be able to separate the sand from the pebbles. Suggest a strainer or a sieve if children do not. Then display a sieve and slowly pour the mixture over it. Note with children how the sieve filters the mixture—the sand falls through the holes of the sieve, leaving the pebbles behind. Tell children that the water we drink goes through a water treatment plant that filters the water many times before it comes into our homes.

Preview Activity

Before beginning the activity, have children review the directions on the Engineering and Technology Flipchart page.

Guide the Activity

Develop Inquiry Skills

HYPOTHESIZE **Which material would you use to filter out large bits in the water?** I would use the sand or soil to filter out the large bits.

Which material would you use to filter out small bits in the water? I would use the cotton balls because holes in the cotton are small and can trap small bits of debris.

EXPERIMENT Have children test their hypotheses by pouring the dirty water through each of the materials.

Caution! Tell children not to taste or drink the water even if it looks clean. Bacteria and germs too small to be seen may still be in the filtered water.

Strategies for Success

Before beginning the *investigation,* have children review the directions on the *Inquiry Flipchart*. Help them understand that their goal is to find a way to filter the debris out of the water. As children begin to plan and build their filters, have them articulate to you the function of each material and how it will help them filter objects out of the water.

Science Notebook

During the Activity As children experiment, remind them to take notes on what they observe. Children can record their notes in a chart with the headings: Soil, Sand, and Cotton Balls. Tell them to refer to their notes to help them plan and design their water filter.

2 Explain

Develop the Engineering Design Process

Use the following steps of the engineering design process to provide context and support for the analyses that children are doing in the flipchart activity.

1. FIND A PROBLEM **Use your own words to identify and explain the problem.** I need to design a filter to clean dirty water.
2. PLAN AND BUILD **How did experimenting help you plan your water filter?** Sample answer: I learned that the large bits should be filtered out of the water first so that they do not clog the cotton balls.
3. TEST AND IMPROVE If children can build and test their filters, have them do so. Prompt discussion: *How well did your filter work? What could you do to improve it?*

3 Extend/Evaluate

Quick Check

How did you know if your filter was working well? Sample answer: The water that came out through the filter did not have bits in it. It was clear and clean.

What problems did you have with the filter? Sample answer: I could not find materials to filter the small bits.

4. REDESIGN Explain that water treatment plants filter water through different layers of filters. **What layers would you include to redesign your water filter?**
5. COMMUNICATE Have groups share their findings with the class by demonstrating how their filters work.

Science Notebook

After the Activity Check that children have drawn and labeled their designs. Have them read what they wrote about their designs. Suggest that children also add their ideas for improving or redesigning the water filters.

Michael DiSpezio's Tips & Tricks

Guiding the Activity Demonstrate how a screen or colander can act like a filter, separating a water/pasta mixture. Then have children apply this observation to the microscopic filtering performed by coffee filters, tea bags, or cotton balls. Obtain and use clean sand or soil from a pet or garden supply store. Use clear plastic cups so that the improved water quality can be readily observed. This activity can get messy, so have clean-up materials ready. Also, distribute protective eyewear if appropriate.

Options for Inquiry

FLIPCHART P. 31

Children can conduct these optional investigations at any time before, during, or in response to the lesson in the Student Edition.

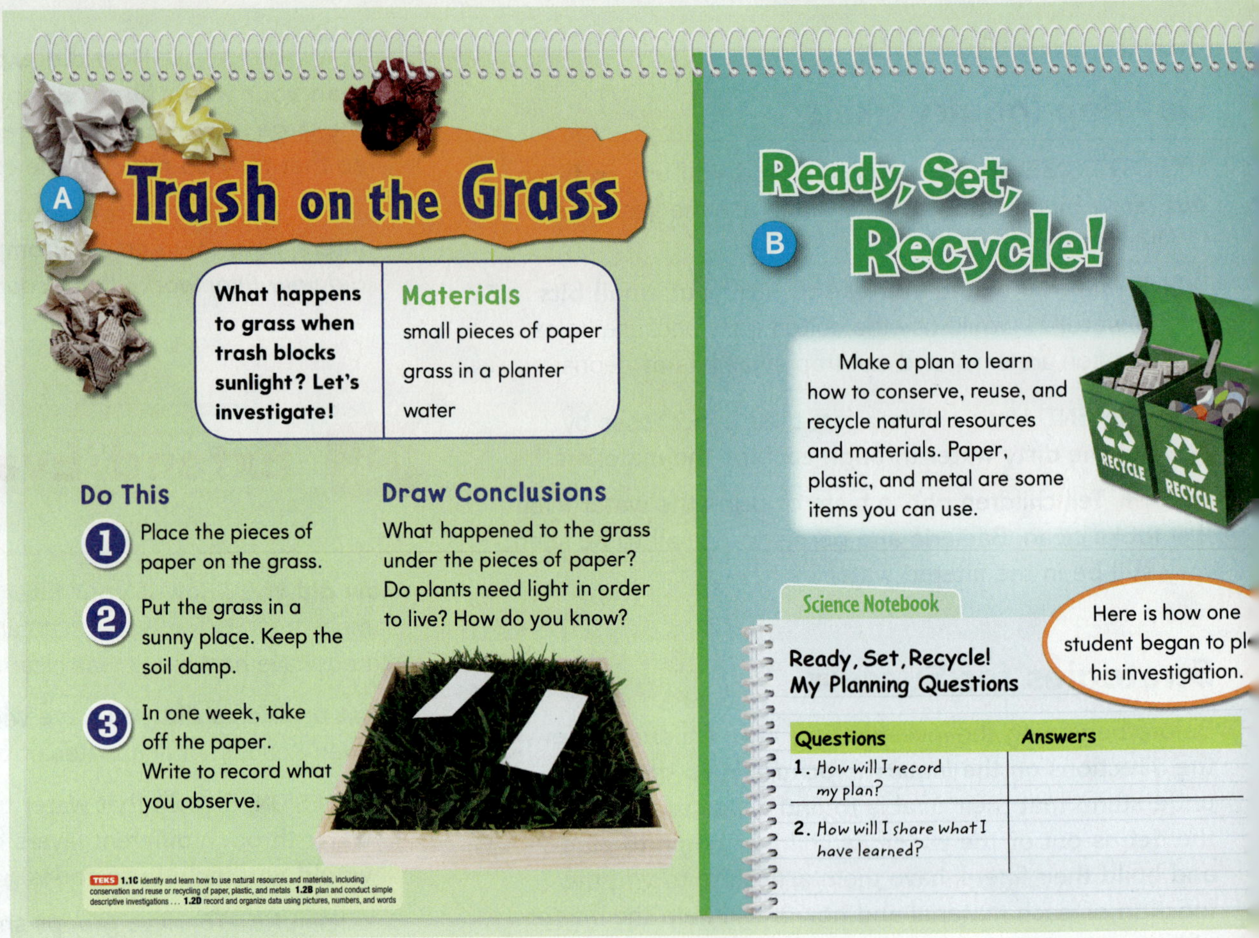

Directed Inquiry

A Trash on the Grass

5–10 minutes
small groups

Prep and Planning Tips

The activity will take about 5–10 minutes each day for about a week.

If lawn grass is not available, you can often purchase a patch of wheatgrass at a health food or pet store. Trim the grass in advance of the activity.

Depending on how many patches of grass you can make available, children can do the activity as individuals, pairs, or small groups. They can share spray bottles used for watering the patches of grass.

Expected Results

After a week, children will observe that the grass loses its green color and turns pale and brittle where trash has prevented light from reaching it. Guide them to conclude that grass cannot grow or live if trash blocks the light.

Independent Inquiry

B Ready, Set, Recycle!

25 minutes
small groups

Prep and Planning Tips

See the Planning for Inquiry page for more information. Discuss ways that children already recycle, reuse, or conserve resources and materials at home or at school.

Caution! If children execute a recycling plan in your classroom, remind them to recognize and demonstrate safe practices to keep themselves and others safe and healthy by not putting food waste, breakables, or sharp objects in the recycling containers.

Science Notebook

Children can use the Science Notebook page as a model for planning and conducting their own investigation. Have them include the sample questions plus their own questions. Encourage them to walk around the classroom for ideas.

TEKS 1.1C identify and learn how to use natural resources and materials, including conservation and reuse or recycling of paper, plastic, and metals

Lesson 6

Essential Question

How Can We Save Resources?

Engage Your Brain!

Find the answer to the question in the lesson.

This art uses old things to make something new. How does this help Earth?

It makes less

trash.

Active Reading

Lesson Vocabulary

1. Preview the lesson.
2. Write the 5 vocabulary terms here.

pollution	reuse
conservation	recycle
reduce	

Inquiry Flipchart p. 31—Trash on the Grass/Ready, Set, Recycle!

217

Go Digital

An interactive digital lesson is available in Online Resources. It is suitable for individuals, small groups, or may be projected or used on an interactive white board.

1 Engage/Explore

Objectives

- Identify and learn how to use natural resources and materials, including conservation and reuse or recycling of paper, plastic, and metals.
- Plan and conduct simple investigations.
- Record and organize data.

Engage Your Brain!

Ask children to identify some of the different kinds of trash they see in the artwork. Help them answer the question *How does this help Earth?* by discussing what would have happened to the trash if the artist did not reuse it. Record children's responses on the board.

Remind children to record their final answer to the question when they find it on the sixth and seventh pages of the lesson.

Active Reading Annotations

Remind children that active readers "make texts their own" by marking them or writing notes to help them understand what they are reading. Encourage them to use pencil to make annotations and to feel free to change their marks and notes as they read. The goal of annotation is to help children remember what they have read.

Vocabulary and Interactive Glossary

Remind children to find and list the yellow highlighted terms from the lesson. As they proceed through the lesson and learn about the terms, they can add drawings or words in the extra spaces provided in some entries in the Interactive Glossary.

2 Explain

Notebook Generate Ideas

Point out the title and explain that "What a Waste!" means that it is a shame to let something go bad or to not use it in the right way. Model an example: *What a waste to not eat that good food!* Then ask children to give their own examples. Have them preview the "waste" they might be learning about on these pages.

Active Reading Vocabulary

Explain that a vocabulary word may be highlighted in a color. Active readers pay attention to highlighted words because their meaning is given in the same sentence or the next sentence.

Develop Science Vocabulary

pollution Explain that *pollute* is a verb, or action word, that means "to spoil something by making it dirty." The word *pollution* is the noun that comes from *pollute*. Therefore, *pollution* is waste that makes something dirty.

Develop Science Concepts

Have children look at the parts of nature seen in the picture. **What three natural things can be harmed by pollution?** air, land, water

How can pollution hurt people? Pollution can make people sick. It can make the air and water dirty.

What a Waste!

Pollution is waste that harms land, water, and air. It can make people and animals sick. Plants can be harmed, too. Pollution makes water unsafe to drink. It also makes the air dirty. Dirty air is unsafe to breathe. We all need clean resources.

Active Reading

Find the sentence that tells the meaning of **pollution**. Draw a line under the sentence.

218

Differentiation—Leveled Questions

Extra Support

What is pollution? waste that harms air, land, and water

Challenge

Name things in nature that can sometimes cause pollution. How might fires or floods harm natural resources? Smoke from fires can make the air dirty. Floods can wash waste into clean water.

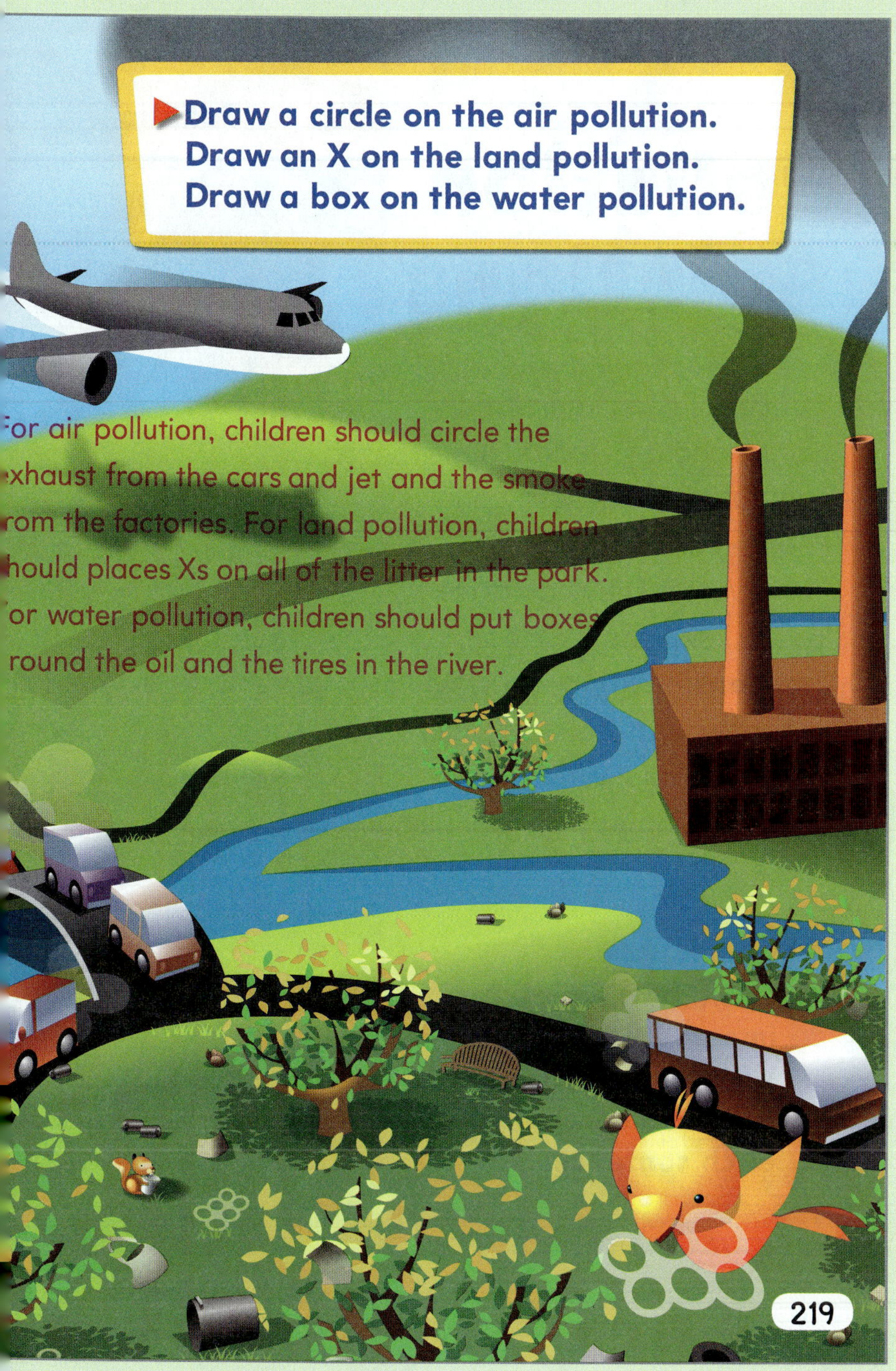

English Language Learners

ELPS 1E, 2C, 2E

Explore Word Meanings
Children may be unfamiliar with the term *natural resource*. Write it on the board, and have them pronounce it after you. Explain that *natural* means "something found in nature" and that a *resource* is anything that people can use. Have children put the two parts of the definition together to explain the meaning of *natural resource*.

TEKS 1.1C

Interpret Visuals

Focus attention on the illustration. **Would this park be a good place to play? Why?** No, the park is dirty and full of trash. **Would you want to swim in the water? Explain.** No, waste from the factory has made the water dirty. **How do you think the air would smell? Why?** The air would not smell good because of the smoke from the factory, plane, and cars.

Which part of this picture shows land pollution? How do you know? The lot filled with cars and the park show land pollution. I know because of the trash and tires on the ground. **What should you draw on these parts of the picture?** an X

Repeat this procedure or have children work independently to identify and mark water pollution with a box and air pollution with a circle.

Develop Inquiry Skills

COMMUNICATE **What would you say to the mayor of the town in the picture to explain why it is important to clean up the pollution?** Sample answer: The pollution is bad for people's health.

Notebook Summarize Ideas

Direct children to review the meaning of the term *pollution*. Have them summarize orally or in writing how pollution affects air, water, and land.

2 Explain (continued)

Notebook Generate Ideas

Ask a volunteer to read the rhyming heading: "Pollution Solutions." Guide children to understand that solutions are ways to solve problems. Challenge them to brainstorm ways that pollution problems might be solved. Record these ideas on the board and add to this list as you work through the pages.

Develop Science Concepts

How can people reduce air pollution? by driving less and riding bicycles more

Suppose you pick up candy wrappers on the playground. What pollution problem are you trying to solve? land pollution

Why might towns have laws that stop people and businesses from dumping waste into rivers or lakes? These laws help keep water clean.

Why do you think it is important for people to solve pollution problems? It is not safe for people to live with pollution on the land and in the air and water.

What do you do to solve pollution problems? I put trash in trash cans.

What is conservation? It is a way to protect natural resources and materials.

How can you help conserve natural resources and materials at home or in school? Accept all reasonable answers.

Develop Science Vocabulary

conservation Help children pronounce the word *conservation.* Say each syllable slowly and clearly and have children repeat each one after you. You can also have children practice spelling the word by writing each syllable on separate index cards and then putting the pieces together.

Pollution Solutions

People can keep land, water, and air clean. They can put trash in trash cans. People can keep waste away from water. They can drive less to keep the air clean.

Conservation is a way to protect natural resources and materials. When you conserve something, you use less of it.

▶ **Look at the pictures in each row. Write land, water, or air to complete each sentence.**

220

Pollution

English Language Learners

ELPS 4A, 5B

Explore Word Endings Help children understand how the word ending *-ion* turns action words (verbs) like *pollute* into nouns. Write *pollute* on the board and discuss its meaning. Then show children how to drop the letter "e" and add the word ending *-ion* to make *pollution*. Discuss how the two words are alike and different. Repeat for other words, such as *act/action*.

TEKS 1.1C

How to Help

People ride bikes. This keeps the air **clean.**

People keep waste out of the river. This keeps the water **clean.**

People put trash in cans. This keeps the land **clean.**

Interpret Visuals

Direct children's attention to the three pairs of circles. Ask them to point to each one in turn as a volunteer describes what is happening. **What does each pair of circles show?** It shows a pollution problem in the first circle and a way to help solve the problem in the second circle.

Which kind of pollution do you see in the top row of circles? air pollution **What are people doing to help solve this problem?** They are riding bikes instead of driving cars.

Ask a volunteer to read aloud the caption that goes with the top two circles and have children identify a word to complete the sentence. Once the word *air* is identified, have them write it in the blank. If children need help with spelling, remind them to check the underlined words in the interactive box.

Follow a similar procedure or have children work independently to complete the other two captions.

Notebook Summarize Ideas

Direct children to think about the pollution solutions described in this section of the lesson. Have them return to the list they compiled before reading and add to the pollution solutions. Then have them summarize these solutions orally or in writing.

Writing Connection

TEKS ELA 1.24C

Make a Pollution Solution Poster Have small groups brainstorm and write slogans to convince classmates to be part of a pollution solution. To help them get started, share examples such as: *Stash your trash* and *Litter makes people bitter!* After children select a slogan, have them illustrate it on the poster.

2 Explain (continued)

Notebook Generate Ideas

Have children scan for the highlighted words on this page to identify the three ways they will learn to care for Earth. Ask them to explain what they know about the meanings of these three words.

Active Reading Effect

Point out that sometimes one thing happens because something else happens. What happens is the effect. To find an effect, active readers ask themselves, "What happened?" The answer will be the effect.

Develop Science Vocabulary

reduce, reuse, recycle Write the words *reuse* and *recycle* on the board. Have children repeat them with you, emphasizing the first syllable. Explain that in each word, the letters *re-* form a word part that means "to do again." Have children use this information to arrive at their own meanings of *reuse* and *recycle*. Explain that to *reduce* means "to make something less in amount."

Develop Science Concepts

How are reduce and reuse the same? Both are ways to care for Earth. **How are they different?** Reduce is to use less of something; reuse is to use something again.

How are you caring for Earth when you decorate a plastic bottle to use as a vase? You are reusing the bottle rather than throwing it away. Reusing the bottle makes less trash.

In what ways do you reduce, reuse, or recycle? Explain. Sample answers: I put bottles and cans in a recycle bin. I reuse shopping bags. I use less water when I turn off the faucet.

Care for Earth!

You can learn how to reduce, reuse, and recycle natural resources and materials. This makes less trash.

To **reduce** is to use less of something. You use less water when you turn the faucet off. To **reuse** is to use something again. You can reuse a can to make a pencil holder. To **recycle** is to use old things to make new things. You can recycle the plastic in bottles to make something new.

reduce

Active Reading

An effect tells what happens. Draw two lines under an effect of **reducing**, **reusing**, and **recycling**.

222

Differentiation—Leveled Questions

Extra Support

What does it mean to reuse? How is that different from recycling? *Reuse* means to use something again. *Recycle* means to make old things into new things.

Challenge

Of reduce, reuse, and recycle, which one do you think is most important in caring for Earth? Explain. Sample answer: Reduce, because if you make less trash then you do not have to reuse or recycle it.

3 Math Connection

TEKS MATH 1.3A

Solve a Problem Explain that it takes about 5 gallons of water to brush your teeth if you leave the water running while you brush. You can show a gallon milk container to help children visualize the amount of water that action wastes. Have children use manipulatives or pictures to calculate about how many gallons of water it would take if you brush your teeth two times a day. (10 gallons of water)

TEKS 1.1C

Interpret Visuals

Focus attention on the illustrations of the children caring for resources. **What is the boy doing at the sink?** turning off the faucet **Is he trying to recycle, reuse, or reduce water?** reduce **What word should you write on the line?** reduce

Point out the symbol on the bin held by the girl. **What does this symbol stand for?** recycle **Why is the girl putting the bottle in this bin?** She is recycling it. **What word should you write to show what the girl is doing?** recycle

Have children label the third picture to tell what the two children are doing with the can. Then have them use the word *reuse* to explain what is happening in the picture.

Develop Inquiry Skills

INFER Remind children that when they *infer,* they use clues to figure out something that is happening but that is not said or explained directly. **How can you reduce your water use at home? What effects might this have?** Sample answers: Take quick showers. Turn off the water while brushing your teeth or washing dishes. Use certain kinds of faucets and toilets. All of these things save water.

Notebook Summarize Ideas

Have children hold up three fingers as they recall the three actions that help care for Earth: reduce, reuse, recycle. Have them use those three words to summarize orally or in writing how to care for Earth.

2 Explain (continued)

Notebook Generate Ideas

Help children scan the classroom for items that might have been made from recycled materials, such as fleece clothing, plastic bottles, paper, or cans. Ask them to share what they know about how products are recycled and why.

Develop Science Concepts

How does a plastic bottle change when it is recycled into a shirt? A plastic bottle is hard and stiff. A shirt is soft.

What do you get when you buy a greeting card made from recycled paper? You are getting old paper that has been recycled into the new paper used to make the card.

Misconception Alert

Children may find it difficult to understand the difference between reusing and recycling. Explain that when a product is recycled, it goes to a factory where it is turned into something new. When something is reused, it is used again without changing what it is made of. Crushing and melting down glass bottles to make glass tiles is recycling. Using a glass bottle as a vase is reusing the bottle.

Develop Inquiry Skills

SEQUENCE Remind children that when they *sequence*, they put things in order. Clue words such as *first*, *next*, and *last* can help tell the sequence of events.

Think about how old cans are recycled to make new baseball bats. What happens first? The cans are collected. **Then what happens?** The cans are taken to a factory and melted down. **What is the last step?** The melted metal is used to make the new bats.

Why It Matters

Good As New

Have you ever worn a shirt made from plastic bottles? Have you ever reused a plastic milk jug as a bird feeder? We can recycle and reuse many old things. Metal from cans may be recycled to make a new baseball bat. A metal can may also be reused as a planter. Paper can be reused and recycled, too.

▶ **Match each object on the left to what it became on the right.**

224

English Language Learners

ELPS 2C

Explore Idioms Children may have difficulty understanding the meaning of the expression "good as new." Write it on the board, and help children read it aloud. Explain that when something is as good as new, we mean that something old has been fixed so that it looks or works as well as something new.

Do the Math!

Solve a Word Problem

Solve the problem.

5 plastic bottles make 1 shirt.

How many shirts do 10 plastic bottles make?

2 shirts

225

Interpret Visuals

Have children point to the objects on the left and explain that they were made into the new objects on the right through recycling or reusing. **Point to the milk jug. What is it made of?** plastic **Which of the new objects is made of recycled milk jugs?** the playground equipment **How do you know?** Slides and other playground parts may be made of plastic. Have children write the number one next to the picture of the playground equipment.

Repeat this procedure to help children match the other two picture pairs. Ask them which object they think changes the most during the recycling process.

Do the Math! TEKS MATH 1.3A

Solve a Word Problem

Have a volunteer read aloud the word problem. Then discuss what information children know and what they need to find out. Ask them to study the picture. Encourage them to draw 10 bottles and circle sets of bottles to help solve the problem. Pairs of children can work together to strategize and find a solution.

Notebook Summarize Ideas

Have children look back at the pictures they matched. Ask them to think about the information presented in these visuals and then summarize orally or in writing what they learned about reusing objects and recycling old objects into new ones.

3 Extend/Evaluate

Sum It Up!

1. **Draw It!** If children need support, suggest that they scan back through the lesson for examples of land and water pollution. They can also think about pollution they have seen in their own community.
2. **Match It!** Call on volunteers to read the three words. If children have difficulty recalling the meanings of the terms, have them look for the highlighted versions in the lesson to find the definitions. They may want to make their own picture dictionaries for the terms before they draw lines to complete the activity.

Sum It Up!

1 Draw It!

Draw a picture of land pollution. Draw a picture of water pollution.

land	water
Check children's drawings.	Check children's drawings.

2 Match It!

Draw a line to match each word to the picture it tells about.

recycle reduce reuse

Brain Check

Lesson 6

Name ____________________

Word Play

Use the words to complete the letter.

pollution **reduce** **reuse** **recycle** **conservation**

Dear Ben,

I just joined a club. We ___recycle___ paper so it can be made into new things. We ___reuse___ cans to make pencil holders. It is a good idea to shut off lights when we leave rooms. This helps ___reduce___ our use of resources. ___Conservation___ is another way to protect our resources.

Soon we will clean up trash in the park. ___Pollution___ could harm the living things there. Let's go to the park together!

Your Friend,
Ming

TEKS 1.1C

Answer Strategies

Word Play

- Ask volunteers to read aloud and define the terms in the word box. If they need help, have them scan through the lesson looking for the yellow highlighted words.
- Explain that this activity is a letter written to a boy named Ben. Have children follow along as you read aloud the letter, pausing briefly at each blank. Tell them to point to each blank line so they know where to write the words.
- Point out that children will use words from the word box to write the missing words in the letter. Remind them to look for word clues in the sentence that will help them figure out which word to use. Once children fill in a blank, have them reread the sentence to be sure it makes sense.

Assessment

Lesson Quiz

See Assessment Guide, p. AG 77.

3 Extend/Evaluate (continued)

Answer Strategies

Apply Concepts

- Explain to children that this page is a cause-and-effect chart. Remind children that an effect is what happens and a cause is why something happens.
- In this chart, the causes are on the left and the effects are on the right. Sometimes, the cause is missing from the chart, and sometimes the effect is missing. Children will need to look over the text in each row to locate which piece of information they need to write.
- If children need to review examples of causes and effects that come from recycling, reusing, and reducing the use of natural resources, suggest that they look back at the section of the lesson titled "Care for Earth!"

Take It Home!

Family members can go on a household scavenger hunt to locate items that can be recycled and reused. Ask children to keep a record of what they find and then share those results with the class. They can also keep a list of ways they reduce the use of resources in their homes and share that with the class as well.

Apply Concepts

Write a word from the box to fill in the blanks.

reduce | reuse | recycle

Cause		Effect
I reuse a bottle as a flower vase.	→	I make less trash.
I recycle cans.	→	The old cans are used to make new pots.
I turn off the water when I brush my teeth.	→	I reduce the amount of water I use.

Take It Home!

Family Members: Work with your child to identify household items that can be recycled or reused. Find ways to reduce the use of resources in your home.

228

Make Connections

Easy

Music Connection

TEKS MUSIC 1.2A

Compose and Sing Song Lyrics

- Sing "The Mulberry Bush" with children.
- Have partners compose their own lyrics about recycling, reusing, or reducing. For example: "This is the way we recycle our trash, recycle our trash, recycle our trash. This is the way we recycle our trash, so early Saturday morning."
- Have partners share their lyrics with the class.

Average

Art Connection

TEKS ART 1.2C

Reuse Resources to Make a Sculpture

- Remind children that the artist in the Lesson Opener reused trash to make art.
- Ask children to collect materials such as clean cartons, boxes, buttons, and fabric scraps. Have them use the materials to make a sculpture.
- Display the sculptures in a class exhibit. Ask children to list the materials along with the sculptures.

Average

Social Studies Connection

TEKS SS 1.16A, 1.17B

Pollution Solution Report

Ask pairs to use books or online sources to research a way that other children have developed a real-world pollution solution. Have them present their findings orally to the class.

Challenging

Writing Connection

TEKS ELA 1.24C

Design a Board Game About Pollution

- Divide children into small groups. Then display board games as models and discuss how children could make their own game about pollution. Children could copy games they know, modifying the content to be about pollution, or they could make their own game with new rules and goals.
- Children can reuse materials, such as buttons as markers and a number cube to indicate moves. They can share their game with another group and play it as time allows.

Enduring Understandings

Revisit the Big Idea and Essential Questions

Big Idea **There are many kinds of resources on Earth.**

To explore the Big Idea, challenge children to generate word webs. Have them work in groups of three or four. Help each group write a word or a category in the center circle. Then, ask the children to write or dictate words to fill in the surrounding circles. Have them add their webs to their Science Notebooks.

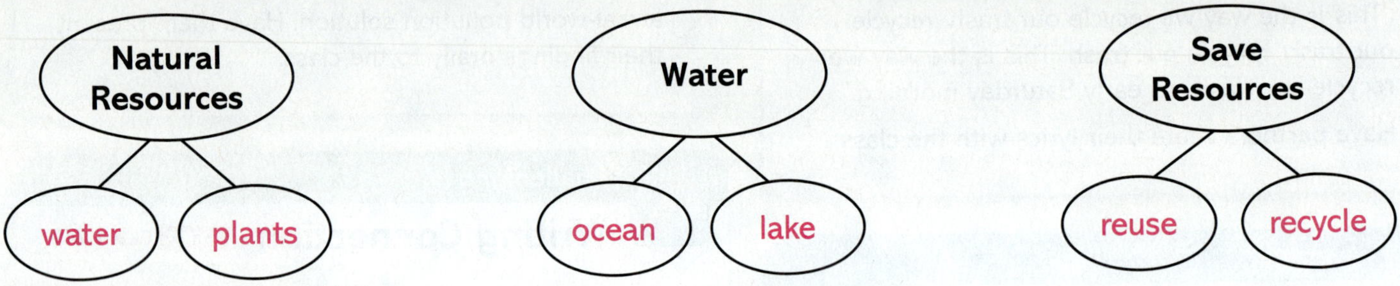

Essential Questions

Post the Essential Questions, and use the following prompts to guide a discussion.

Lessons/Essential Questions	Prompts
L1 **What Can We Find on Earth?**	• Name at least three natural resources found on Earth.
L2 **What Is Soil?**	• Explain what soil is.
L3 **What Do We Find in Soil?**	• Describe the different components found in soil.
L4 **How Do Soils Differ?**	• Describe how two types of soil are different.
L5 **Where Can We Find Water?**	• Name places we can find water.
L6 **How Can We Save Resources?**	• Demonstrate at least one way you can save resources.

Notebook Science Notebook

You may use the following strategies after children complete the unit or after each lesson.

- Have children review and edit the responses to the Essential Questions they drafted at the beginning of the unit. Suggest they cross out sentences or ideas that are unnecessary or inappropriate.
- Have children draft flash card facts in their Science Notebooks to prepare for a game. After generating the facts, children can make a game by writing a question on one side of an index card and the answer on the back. The cards can be drawn and collected as questions are answered correctly.

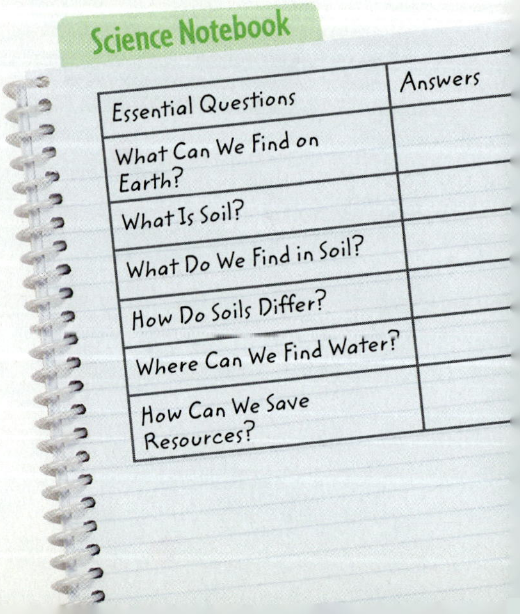
Science Notebook

Essential Questions	Answers
What Can We Find on Earth?	
What Is Soil?	
What Do We Find in Soil?	
How Do Soils Differ?	
Where Can We Find Water?	
How Can We Save Resources?	

Unit 5 Review

Name ______________________

ocabulary Review

se the terms in the box to complete he sentences.

ocean
product
recycle

TEKS 1.1C

. When you recycle ______________ paper, you use old paper to make new paper.

EKS 1.7B

. An ocean ______________ is a large body of salty water.

EKS 1.7C

. A brick is a product ______________ that is made from soil.

cience Concepts

ill in the letter of the choice that best nswers the question.

KS 1.2B, 1.7A

. Nick investigates. He observes that one soil is smooth and one is lumpy. What property of the soil did Nick observe?

- Ⓐ color
- Ⓑ texture
- Ⓒ size of rock bits

TEKS 1.7B

5. Which body of water has land all around it? Identify it.

- Ⓐ lake
- Ⓑ river
- Ⓒ stream

Item Analysis

Items	TEKS	Depth of Knowledge	Cognitive Complexity
1	**1.1C**	1	Low
2	**1.7B**	1	Low
3	**1.7C**	1	Low
4	**1.2B, 1.7A**	2	Moderate
5	**1.7B**	1	Low

Unit Review

Answer Key

Vocabulary Review (5 points each)

1. **recycle**
   Remind children that the prefix *re-* means "again."
2. **ocean**
   Children can look back at the lesson pages to identify the water source that is large and salty.
3. **product**
   Remind children that products are things that people use and are often made from natural resources like rocks or soil.

Science Concepts (7 points each)

4. **B**
   Have children underline the key words *smooth* and *lumpy* in the second sentence. Ask what property these words can describe.
5. **A**
   Have children describe each answer choice. They can refer to the lesson pages in order to reread definitions or look at pictures of each one.

Assessment

Unit 5 Test and Performance Assessment

See Assessment Guide, pp. AG 80–AG 86, for Unit Test and Performance Task with Long Option rubric.

Unit Review *continued*

Answer Key

Science Concepts (7 points each)

6. C
Ask children to identify what is shown in the picture. After children choose their answer, have them explain why the other answer choices are incorrect.

7. B
Explain that children will need to know the definition of silt to answer this question.

8. B
Remind children that scientists can tell a great deal about soil from its color. For example, a dark black soil may have a lot of nutrients or a light brown soil may be sandy.

9. A
Be sure children can identify each picture and understand that answer choice A refers to the shampoo in the bottle, not the bottle itself.

UNIT 5

TEKS 1.7C

6. How does the soil in this garden help to make useful products?

Ⓐ It helps to make statues.

Ⓑ It helps to make jewelry.

Ⓒ It helps grow food for people to eat.

TEKS 1.7A

7. What is silt made of?

Ⓐ large bits of rock

Ⓑ medium bits of rock

Ⓒ small bits of rock

TEKS 1.7A

8. Why are soils different colors?

Ⓐ They get different amounts of rain.

Ⓑ They have different materials in them.

Ⓒ They hold different amounts of water.

TEKS 1.7C

9. Water can help make useful products. Which of these products includes water?

Ⓐ 

Ⓑ 

Ⓒ 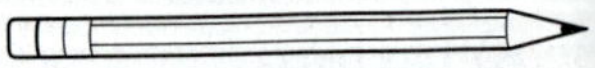

Item Analysis *(continued)*

Items	TEKS	Depth of Knowledge	Cognitive Complexity
6	**1.7C**	3	High
7	**1.7A**	1	Low
8	**1.7A**	2	Moderate
9	**1.7C**	2	Low

TEKS 1.2C, 1.7A

10. Tim is using tools to separate soil into parts. Which tool could he use?

Ⓐ a balance
Ⓑ a sieve
Ⓒ a thermometer

TEKS 1.2C, 1.4A, 1.7A

11. Jill wants to observe the size of the bits in this soil. Which tool should she use?

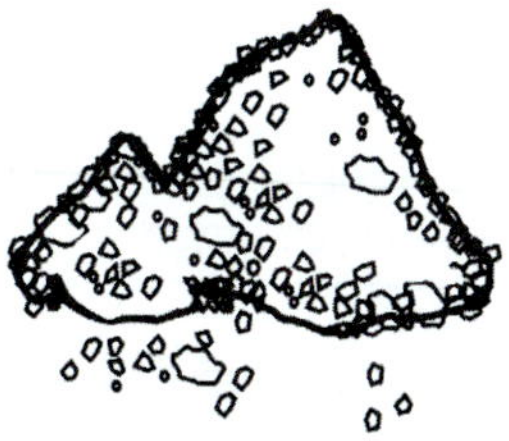

Ⓐ a balance
Ⓑ a hand lens
Ⓒ a thermometer

TEKS 1.1C

12. This bird feeder is made from a plastic milk jug.

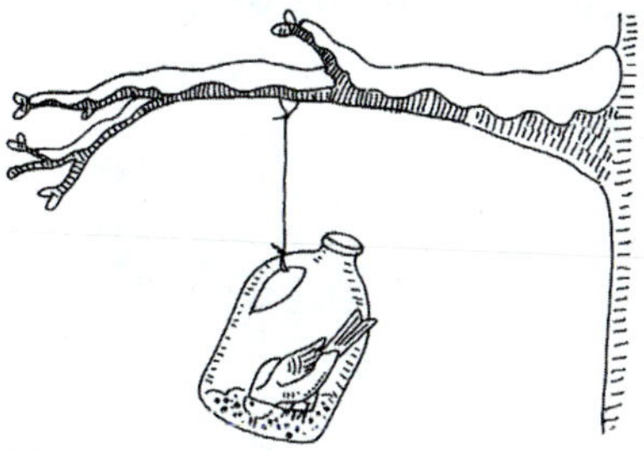

Which word describes how the milk jug is being used?

Ⓐ recycle
Ⓑ reduce
Ⓒ reuse

UNIT 5

Item Analysis *(continued)*

Items	TEKS	Depth of Knowledge	Cognitive Complexity
10	**1.2C, 1.7A**	2	Moderate
11	**1.2C, 1.4A, 1.7A**	2	Moderate
12	**1.1C**	2	Moderate

Unit Review *continued*

Answer Key

Science Concepts (7 points each)

10. B

If possible, have examples of each tool to remind children what each one looks like and what it does. Children can also look back at pictures in the lesson pages as a reference.

11. B

Ask, "Will a ____ help us better observe the size of bits in soil?" and substitute each answer choice one at a time. When the answer is *yes,* children have found the correct answer.

12. C

Have children explain why the milk jug was reused, not recycled or reduced.

Short Option Performance Assessment

Task

Compare Soils
Have children observe, describe, and compare different kinds of soil. Ask children to identify each sample. Then, have children feel the texture of each sample and describe it, using words such as *smooth, sticky, grainy, powdery,* and *lumpy.*

Rubric

Preparation Collect soil samples for children to observe. Provide tools they might need, such as hand lenses or sieves, as well as gloves.

Scoring Rubric—Performance Indicators

___ Accurately identifies each soil sample.
___ Describes and compares each soil sample.

Observations and Rubric Scores

3 2 1 0

Unit Review *continued*

Answer Key

Inquiry and the Big Idea (11 points each)

13.

a. People can use rocks to build houses, walls, or roads.

b. People can use water to help make products like shampoo and lotion.

Have children give examples of how classroom, school, or playground objects make use of natural resources. Prompt discussion with questions, such as, "What is the wall in front of our school made from?"

14. I can reuse shopping bags to hold or carry other things. This helps the environment because it makes less trash.

Remind children that when something is reused, it is not thrown away.

UNIT 5

Inquiry and the Big Idea

Write the answers to these questions.

TEKS 1.7C

13. Describe a way each of these natural resources helps to make useful products.

a.

People can use rocks to build houses, walls, or roads.

b.

People can use water to help make products like shampoo and lotion.

TEKS 1.1C

14. Describe how you can reuse something at home or at school. How does learning to reuse things help the environment?

I can reuse shopping bags to hold or carry other things.

This helps the environment because it makes less trash.

Item Analysis

Items	TEKS	Depth of Knowledge	Cognitive Complexity
13	**1.7C**	3	Moderate
14	**1.1C**	3	High

Unit Planning

Options for Instruction

Choose from **Interactive Worktext** and **Leveled Readers, Digital,** and **Inquiry** options to meet the Texas Essential Knowledge and Skills.

	LESSON 1	LESSON 2	LESSON 3
Essential Questions	**What Is Weather?**	✔ Guided Inquiry **What Can We Observe About Weather?**	**What Are Seasons?**
Texas Essential Knowledge and Skills	TEKS 1.8A, 1.8D	TEKS 1.2A, 1.2B, 1.2D, 1.3B, 1.8A	TEKS 1.3B, 1.8C
Interactive Worktext	☐ Student Edition pp. 235–246 • Weather Watch • Measure It! • Catch the Wind • Predict It!	☐ Student Edition pp. 247–250 • Scaffolding for Inquiry	☐ Student Edition pp. 253–264 • Spring Into Spring • Sunny Summer • Fall Into Fall • Winter Weather
Leveled Readers	Parallel coverage of the lesson topics is provided in the **Extra Support, On-Level,** and **Enrichment** readers. See p. 233H for detailed reader information.		
Hands-On Inquiry	Inquiry Flipchart p. 32 **Hot or Cold?** ☐ Directed Inquiry **Windsock Workshop** ☐ Independent Inquiry	Inquiry Flipchart p. 33 **What Can We Observe About Weather?** ☐ Guided Inquiry	Inquiry Flipchart p. 34 **Keeping Warm** ☐ Directed Inquiry **Turn Over a New Leaf** ☐ Independent Inquiry
D	☐ Digital Lesson Online Resources Interactive presentation of lesson content 	☐ Virtual Lab Online Resources Interactive scaffolded inquiry 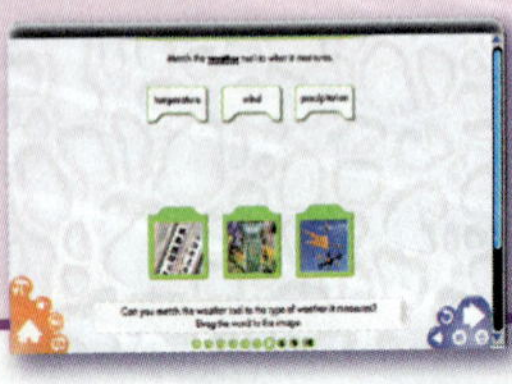	☐ Digital Lesson Online Resources Interactive presentation of lesson content 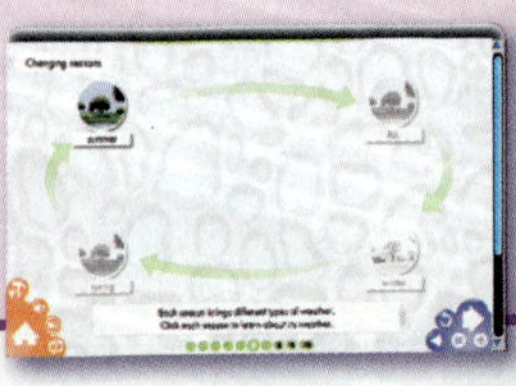

OTHER UNIT FEATURES

People in Science, p. 251

S.T.E.M. Engineering and Technology, pp. 265–266B

Online Resources

Interactive Whiteboard Resources for Unit 6

Assessment

Formative Assessment
Sum It Up! and Brain Check
Student Edition, end of each lesson

Summative Assessment
Lesson Quizzes
Assessment Guide, pp. AG 87–AG 89

Unit 6 Review
Student Edition, pp. 267–270

Unit 6 Test
Assessment Guide, pp. AG 92–AG 96

Performance Assessment
SHORT OPTION: Teacher Edition, p. 269
LONG OPTION: Assessment Guide, pp. AG 97–AG 98

RTI Response to Intervention

RTI Strategies, p. 233I

Online Assessment
Test-taking and automatic scoring
Banks of items from which to build tests

Teacher Notes

Planning for Inquiry

Use the following preview of Inquiry Activities and Lessons to gather and manage the materials needed for each lesson.

Activity	Inquiry and Design Process Skills Focus	Materials	Prep Tips, Troubleshooting, and Expected Results
Lesson 1 DIRECTED INQUIRY Flipchart p.32 A **Hot or Cold?** **OBJECTIVES** Plan and conduct simple investigations. Record and organize data. Make predictions based on observable patterns. Collect and compare information using thermometers. Record weather information. 5–10 minutes twice per day for 5 days small groups TEKS **1.2B, 1.2C, 1.2D, 1.3B, 1.4A, 1.8A**	• Compare • Gather, Record, Display, or Interpret Data • Measure	• thermometers • clipboards (optional)	**Prep Tips** Review how to read a thermometer. If possible, provide one for each small group. Place small markers, such as dowels or sticks, in the ground labeled with each group's name so children can conduct their measurements in the same spot. You may wish to set an alarm as a reminder of when to read the temperature. **Troubleshooting** It may be necessary to shake down the columns in some thermometers. Be sure that all thermometers are at room temperature before starting. If you are unable to use thermometers outside, you may wish to have children track the outside temperature using an online weather report. **Expected Results** Children will observe that the temperature typically rises from morning to afternoon, and that this pattern repeats each day. Variations may occur, however, depending on weather conditions.
INDEPENDENT INQUIRY Flipchart p.32 B **Windsock Workshop** **OBJECTIVES** Plan and conduct simple investigations. Record and organize data. Collect and compare information using windsocks. Record weather information. Demonstrate that air is all around us and observe that wind is moving air. 20 minutes individuals TEKS **1.2B, 1.2D, 1.4A, 1.8A, 1.8D**	• Observe • Compare • Gather, Record, Display or Interpret Data • Plan and Conduct a Simple Investigation	• construction paper • tape • scissors • ribbons or crepe paper • handheld hole puncher • string • clothesline (optional)	**Prep Tips** Use a handheld hole puncher to punch two holes in the top of each child's windsock. Thread a long piece of string through the holes, and tie a knot at the ends to secure it. You might conduct the investigation over several days so children can collect data on both windy and calm days. Consider hanging a clothesline outside the classroom to attach children's windsocks. **Caution!** Review scissors safety rules before children begin the activity. **Troubleshooting** If children have difficulty assembling the windsocks on their own, complete this part of the activity as a group. **Expected Results** Children should observe that the windsock moves on windy days and hangs still on calm days. They should recognize that the windsock shows the direction of the wind.

Additional teaching support for all inquiry activities is available in **Online Resources.**

Science Notebook Strategies

- Lists of Kit-Supplied Materials
- Meeting Individual Needs
- Investigate More—Extensions and Variations
- and More!

Activity	Inquiry and Design Process Skills Focus	Materials	Prep Tips, Troubleshooting, and Expected Results
Lesson 2 INQUIRY GUIDED INQUIRY **Flipchart** p.33 **Student Edition** pp. 247–250 **What Can We Observe About Weather?** OBJECTIVES • Recognize the importance of safe practices. • Plan and conduct simple investigations. • Record and organize data. • Make predictions based on observable patterns. • Record weather information, including relative temperature. 15–20 minutes for setup; 15 minutes each day for 5 days to record weather individuals TEKS **1.1B, 1.2B, 1.2D, 1.3B, 1.8A**	• Observe • Compare • Gather, Record, Display, or Interpret Data • Predict	• picture cards on Student Edition p. 249 • safety scissors • glue sticks	**Prep Tips** Have children cut apart the picture cards. Set aside 15 minutes per day for them to observe the weather and paste the appropriate picture cards into their charts. Explain to children that they may use more than one picture card per day (for example, it may be both sunny and cold). If children independently notice a change in the weather during a different time during the day, encourage them to record that as well. **Caution!** Instruct children to be careful with scissors. **Troubleshooting** Remind children that, although they cannot see wind, they can hear it and notice its effects on objects like trees or flags. Check children's work periodically to make sure they are recording the weather accurately. This will ensure that they have the right information to make a reasonable weather prediction for the sixth day. **Expected Results** Children will record the weather using weather symbols for a period of five days, and describe different types of weather using words like *sunny*, *cloudy*, *clear*, *rainy*, *icy*, *hot*, *cold*, *calm*, and *windy*. They should note patterns and differences in the weather, and use their observations to make predictions about upcoming weather.

Go Digital! Virtual Lab

What Can We Observe About Weather?

Key Inquiry Skills: observe, infer, predict

Children make observations about weather conditions and then match an activity to the weather conditions.

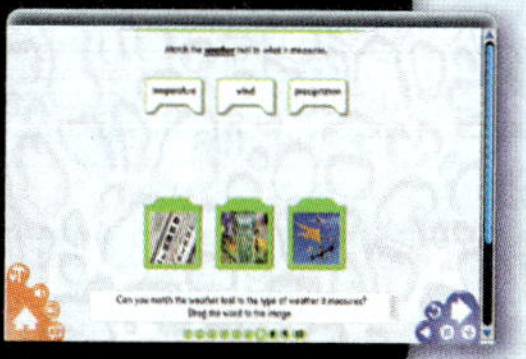

Planning for Inquiry (continued)

Activity	Inquiry and Design Process Skills Focus	Materials	Prep Tips, Troubleshooting, and Expected Results
Lesson 3 DIRECTED INQUIRY Flipchart p.34 **A Keeping Warm** **OBJECTIVES** Plan and conduct simple investigations. Collect data using simple equipment. Record and organize data. Collect and compare information using thermometers. Identify characteristics of the seasons. 25 minutes pairs TEKS **1.2B, 1.2C, 1.2D, 1.4A, 1.8C**	• Compare • Gather, Record, Display, or Interpret Data • Measure • Experiment	• thermometers (3 for each pair) • ball of yarn (1 for each pair) • socks (1 for each pair)	**Prep Tips** Children can do this investigation in small groups if materials are scarce. Make sure the thermometers register the same room temperature at the beginning of the investigation. Check that the yarn balls are loose enough for children to insert a thermometer. Use thick athletic or wool socks rather than thin dress socks. **Troubleshooting** Make sure children hold the thermometers by their edges while reading them, so the warmth of their hands does not affect the temperature reading. If it is not possible to give a ball of yarn to each pair, give pairs a few feet of yarn each and have them wrap the thermometers tightly, securing the end of the yarn with tape. If you don't have a refrigerator to use, a cooler or a container full of ice will also work. **Expected Results** Children will observe that the thermometers in the sock and yarn register higher temperatures than the bare thermometer. They should conclude that the sock and the yarn insulate, or protect, the thermometer from the cold.
INDEPENDENT INQUIRY Flipchart p.34 **B Turn Over a New Leaf** **OBJECTIVES** Plan and conduct simple investigations. Record and organize data. Identify characteristics of the seasons. 20 minutes individuals TEKS **1.2B, 1.2D, 1.8C**	• Compare • Predict • Formulate or Use Models	• drawing paper • crayons or markers	**Prep Tips** Have children use previous experiences and knowledge of the seasons to help them complete this activity. If they have difficulty, show pictures or online videos depicting the weather in all four seasons along with activities people do and clothes they wear. **Expected Results** Children should identify characteristics of the seasons by writing and drawing in their charts.

Additional teaching support for all inquiry activities is available in Online Resources.

Activity	Inquiry and Design Process Skills Focus	Materials	Prep Tips, Troubleshooting, and Expected Results
S.T.E.M. Engineering and Technology Flipchart p.35 **Build It: Rain Gauge** OBJECTIVES • Record and organize data. • Identify and explain a problem and propose a solution in his/her own words. • Record weather information. 20–25 minutes, plus 10 minutes each day for 2 weeks (optional) small groups TEKS **1.2D, 1.3A, 1.8A**	 **1 Find a Problem** **2 Plan and Build** **3 Test and Improve** **4 Redesign** **5 Communicate**	• half-liter plastic bottles • ruler • masking tape • marking pen	**Prep Tips** Ask children to help you collect clean half-liter plastic bottles. Divide the class into as many groups as you have bottles. Cut the tops off the bottles in advance. Also have available a ruler, masking tape, and a permanent marking pen for each group. **Expected Results** Children will build a rain gauge. As an optional extension, they will use it to observe and measure precipitation that collects in it.

Differentiated Instruction

Leveled Readers

The Leveled Readers provide parallel coverage of the unit topics and Texas Essential Knowledge and Skills. Each Reader is available in English and Spanish. Both versions are available online and on touchscreen mobile devices.

ON-LEVEL This Reader reinforces unit concepts and vocabulary and focuses on the Texas Essential Knowledge and Skills. It includes student response activities.

EXTRA SUPPORT This Reader shares title, illustrations, vocabulary, and concepts with the On-Level Reader. However, the text is linguistically accommodated to provide simplified sentence structures and comprehension aids for students who need a little extra support with content-area reading and vocabulary development. It also includes student response activities.

ENRICHMENT This high-interest nonfiction Reader enriches and extends unit concepts. It reinforces some of the unit vocabulary, but also includes stretch vocabulary. It also includes student response activities.

TEACHER GUIDE

The accompanying Teacher Guide provides teaching strategies and support for using all the Readers, as well as English and Spanish worksheets that focus on vocabulary development. A correlation to the Texas Essential Knowledge and Skills is included.

DIGITAL VERSIONS

All of these Leveled Readers are available online. They are also available in an innovative and engaging format for touchscreen mobile devices. For information about accessing these versions, see page T9.

RTI Response to Intervention

Response to Intervention is a process for identifying and supporting students who are not making expected progress toward essential learning goals.

The following *ScienceFusion* components have the flexibility to be used to provide Core Classroom Instruction (Tier 1), strategic intervention (Tier 2), and intensive intervention (Tier 3).

Component	Location	Strategies and Benefits
Student Edition, Active Reading prompts, Sum It Up, Brain Check	Active Reading throughout each lesson, Sum It Up and Brain Check at the end of each lesson	Student responses can be used as screening tools to assess whether intervention is needed.
Assessment Guide, Lesson Quizzes and TEKS DOK Skill Builder	pp. AG 87–AG 91	Student responses can be used as screening tools to assess whether intervention is needed.
Inquiry Flipcharts	Inquiry Flipchart p. 33	Directed Inquiry for students who learn best through directed or teacher-led hands-on activities.
Teacher Edition, Unit Review Answer Strategies	TE pp. 267–270	Suggestions for intervention, guidance, and remediation for each review question.
Leveled Readers	TE p. 233H	Content support for students not meeting the learning needs during core classroom instruction.
Leveled Readers, Teacher Guides and Vocabulary Worksheets	TE p. 233H	Direct instruction with small groups of students needing additional content at various readability levels.
Extra Support for Vocabulary and Concepts (online worksheets)	Online Resources	Support for individualized instruction with practice in essential content.
Online Student Edition with Audio	Online Resources	Provides learners with multiple-modality access to science concepts and information.
Interactive Digital Lessons and Virtual Labs	Online Resources	Provides individualized learning experiences. Lessons make content accessible through simulations, animations, videos, audio, and integrated assessment.
Interactive Whiteboard Resources	Online Resources	Reinforces key unit concepts through interactive vocabulary games and visuals and graphic organizers.
Leveled Readers, online and tablet versions	Online and Tablet Resources	Highlighted words and sentences synced with audio provide support for emerging or struggling readers.

Differentiated Instruction

English Language Learners

Choose from these instructional strategies to meet the needs of English language learners.

Vocabulary Cards are provided in Online Resources.

Unit Vocabulary

Lesson 1	**Lesson 3**
wind	season
weather	weather pattern
temperature	
windsock	

Preteach Vocabulary ELPS 2B

As you preteach vocabulary, model pronunciation and have children repeat. For Unit 6 vocabulary, draw attention to the short *e* sound in *weather* and *temperature* and the long *e* sound in *season*.

Language Acquisition Strategies

Reading Environmental Print ELPS 2I, 4C, 4F

Display a weather forecast that includes visuals of the types of weather listed on **TE pages 236–237.**

Beginning	Intermediate	Advanced/Advanced High
Explain that a weather forecast uses pictures to show what the weather will be like each day. Ask *yes/no* questions about the information in the visual.	Have children use the information in the weather forecast to answer simple questions: *On which day will it be windy? On Friday, will you wear sandals or rain boots?*	Have partners take turns telling what they will wear each day based on the weather forecast.

TEKS 1.8A record weather information, including relative temperature, such as hot or cold, clear or cloudy, calm or windy, and rainy or icy 1.8D demonstrate that air is all around us and observe that wind is moving air

Lesson 1

Essential Question

What Is Weather?

Engage Your Brain!

Find the answer to the question in the lesson.

Rainbows usually follow rainy weather. Which tool could you use to measure rainfall?

a rain gauge

Active Reading

Lesson Vocabulary

1. Preview the lesson.
2. Write the 4 vocabulary terms here.

wind	temperature
weather	windsock

Inquiry Flipchart p. 32—Hot or Cold?/Windsock Workshop

235

Go Digital

An interactive digital lesson is available in Online Resources. It is suitable for individuals, small groups, or may be projected or used on an interactive white board.

1 Engage/Explore

Objectives

- Plan and conduct simple investigations.
- Record and organize data.
- Make predictions based on observable patterns.
- Collect and compare information using tools, such as classroom demonstration thermometers and windsocks.
- Record weather information.
- Demonstrate that air is all around us and observe that wind is moving air.

Engage Your Brain!

Ask children to look at the photograph and describe the sky and weather they see. Guide them to understand that it has been raining. Have them use what they know about weather tools to help answer the question *Which tool could you use to measure rainfall?* Record children's responses on the board.

Remind them to record their final answer to the question when they find it on the fifth page of the lesson.

Active Reading Annotations

Remind children that active readers "make texts their own" by marking them or writing notes to help them understand what they are reading. Encourage them to use pencil to make annotations and to feel free to change their marks and notes as they read. The goal of annotation is to help children remember what they have read.

Vocabulary and Interactive Glossary

Remind children to find and list the yellow highlighted terms from the lesson. As they proceed through the lesson and learn about the terms, they can add drawings or words in the extra spaces provided in some of the entries in the Interactive Glossary.

2 Explain

Notebook Generate Ideas

Read aloud the heading, and discuss its meaning. Then direct children to look outside, "watch" today's weather, and describe what they see. List their phrases and weather words on the board. Add to this list as you work through the spread.

Develop Science Vocabulary

wind Have children blow on a small piece of paper to make it move. Review that wind is moving air. Explain that this activity shows that although air cannot be seen, its effects can.

weather Write the homophones *weather* and *whether* and have children pronounce them with you. Explain that while the words sound the same, they have different meanings. *Weather* is what the air is like outside, and *whether* means "if" or "in case of." Use each word in a sentence, and have children identify which word is being used.

Active Reading Details

Explain that a detail sentence may give an example or describe something. Active readers ask themselves, What topic does this detail sentence tell about? The answer will help readers keep the main idea in mind.

Develop Science Concepts

What is weather? what the air outside is like

What are some words that can describe the weather? sunny, rainy, cloudy, clear, icy, snowy, hot, cold, windy, calm

Will the weather tomorrow be the same as today? Explain. Sample answer: Maybe; weather can stay the same, or it can change from day to day.

Weather Watch

Look outside. Is it sunny? Is the air warm or cool? Are there any clouds? Do you feel any wind? **Wind** is air that moves.

Weather is what the air outside is like. Weather may change during the day. It may also change from day to day and from month to month.

Active Reading

A detail is a fact about a main idea. Draw one line under a detail. Draw an arrow to the main idea the detail tells about.

Is it cloudy or sunny?

Is it windy or calm?

236

English Language Learners

ELPS 1E, 1F, 5B

Reinforce Weather Adjectives
Write the base words *cloud*, *snow*, and *rain* on the board. Have children read the words with you, copy them, and draw a picture for each word. Then point out that some describing words end in the letter *y*. For each base word, show how to add the ending *-y*. Have children copy the adjectives next to the base words. Then help them use weather words to complete the following sentence frame: *You can see _____ on a _____ day.* (clouds, cloudy; snow, snowy; rain, rainy)

s it rainy or icy?

Is it hot or cold?

Is it cloudy or clear?

▶ Record weather information. Read the captions. Circle the word that tells about the weather in each picture.

237

Differentiation—Leveled Questions

Extra Support

What are some kinds of weather? Weather can be sunny, windy, calm, rainy, icy, hot, cold, cloudy, or clear.

Challenge

How might wind affect the weather? Sample answer: Wind can bring cold or warm air, or clouds.

Interpret Visuals

Focus children's attention on the caption under the first photograph on the left page. **What does this caption ask?** Is it cloudy or sunny? **Which word would you circle? Why?** You would circle the word *sunny* because the photograph shows the sun in the sky. **Guide children to understand that they are going to be recording weather information.**

Follow a similar procedure or have children work independently to circle the adjective for each remaining image. Ask children to explain what clues helped them select each answer.

Misconception Alert

Children may confuse weather with the concept of climate. Explain that *weather* is what the air is like today or for a few days. *Climate* is the weather over a long period of time. Use sentences to help clarify: *Today the weather is cloudy. Our climate has hot summers and cool, rainy winters.*

Develop Inquiry Skills

PREDICT Remind children that when they predict, they use their knowledge to make a best guess about what will happen in the future. **Suppose that the weather today is warm and sunny. What weather would you predict for tomorrow? Explain.** Sample answer: It might be a warm, sunny day because the weather tomorrow is often like the weather today.

What kind of weather would you predict if the air was very cold and you saw low gray clouds? Sample answer: a snowy or icy day

Notebook Summarize Ideas

Ask children to use the photographs and captions on these two pages to summarize orally or in writing the details they learned about weather.

2 Explain (continued)

Generate Ideas

Display a ruler, a balance, and other tools, such as a hammer or screwdriver. Discuss how these objects are alike. Help children identify them as tools. Ask them to speculate about the kinds of tools that can be used to measure weather.

Develop Science Vocabulary

temperature Review that *temperature* is the measure of how hot or cold something is and a *thermometer* is the tool used to make that measurement. Name other things that are measured, such as length, and have children name a tool used to measure it.

Active Reading Vocabulary

Explain that a vocabulary word may be highlighted in yellow. Active readers pay attention to a highlighted word because its meaning is given in the same sentence or the next sentence.

Develop Science Concepts

Name some weather tools. rain gauge, thermometer

Which tool measures temperature? thermometer **Which tool measures the amount of rain that falls?** rain gauge

What units does each tool use to measure? thermometer: degrees; rain gauge: inches or centimeters

What are some forms of water that fall from the sky that you can measure with a rain gauge? rain, snow, sleet, hail

Measure It!

You can use tools to measure weather. A thermometer is a tool that measures temperature. **Temperature** is the measure of how hot or cold something is. Temperature is measured in degrees.

Active Reading

Find the sentence that tells the meaning of **temperature.** Draw a line under the sentence.

thermometer

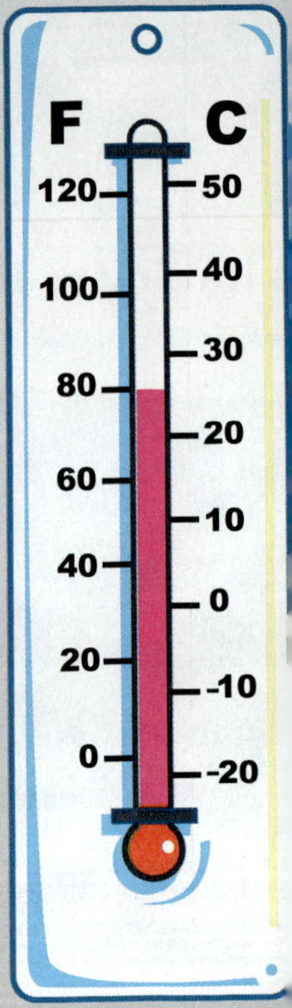

▶ **Color the thermometer to show 80 °F.**

238

Differentiation—Leveled Questions

Extra Support

Name two tools that measure weather. What does each one do? A thermometer measures temperature. A rain gauge measures how much rain (or other form of water) falls from the sky.

Challenge

How could you measure how much snow falls? Sample answer: I would use a ruler to measure how deep the snow is or use a rain gauge to collect snowfall.

Rain, snow, sleet, and hail are forms of water that fall from the sky. A rain gauge is a tool that measures how much water falls.

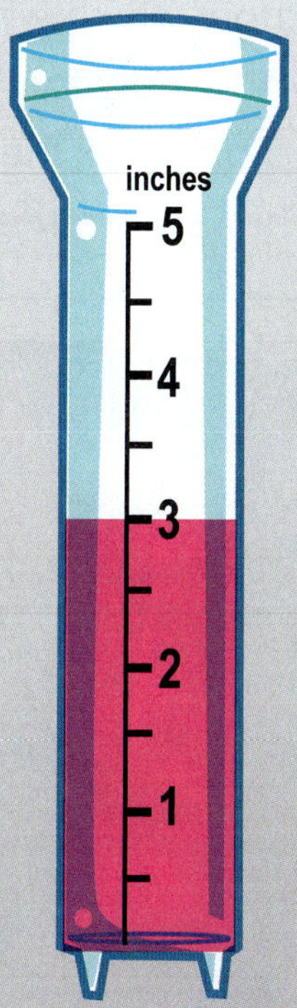

▶ **Color the rain gauge to show that three inches of rain fell.**

239

English Language Learners

ELPS 1E, 1F, 2E

Reinforce Weather Tool Names
Write *thermometer* and *rain gauge* on the board and read the words with children. Ask questions such as the following and have children name the tool they would use: *How hot is it? Do you need an umbrella?* Then have children follow your models to ask and answer oral questions about weather tools.

Interpret Visuals

Direct attention to the large thermometer, and have children identify the two letters at the top and the degrees underneath. Explain to children that the letter *F* stands for Fahrenheit and the letter *C* stands for Celsius. **Why do you think the numbers under them are different?** The numbers on the left show the temperature using the Fahrenheit scale. The numbers on the right show the temperature using the Celsius scale.

If you wanted to show a temperature in degrees Fahrenheit, which set of numbers would you use? the one on the left

Have children locate 80° on the Fahrenheit scale and use a red crayon to color the column up to this point.

Have children point to the rain gauge. **What is the unit of measurement used on this weather tool?** inches **How many inches on this rain gauge will you color?** 3 inches

Have children locate 3 inches on the rain gauge and use a blue crayon to color the column up to this point.

Develop Inquiry Skills

COMPARE/CONTRAST **How are a rain gauge and a thermometer alike? How are they different?** Both are tools that measure weather. A thermometer measures temperature. A rain gauge measures rainfall.

Notebook Summarize Ideas

Ask children what they learned about weather measurement tools. Have them identify two different tools, tell what each one measures, and briefly summarize how to use each one. They can present the information orally or in writing.

2 Explain (continued)

Generate Ideas

Notebook

Read the heading aloud to children. Explain that no one can really "catch the wind," but there are ways for people to observe it. Have children brainstorm different things people might want to observe about the wind.

Develop Science Vocabulary

windsock Explain that a *windsock* is a tool that shows the direction of the wind. Direct children's attention to the picture of the windsock. Have volunteers tell why they think a windsock got its name.

Develop Science Concepts

What kind of air is wind? Wind is air that moves. **What does it do when it blows?** It moves.

How can you tell that the wind is blowing? Sample answer: It moves things.

Windsocks help us observe that wind is moving air. How does a windsock demonstrate, or show, which way the wind is blowing? It blows the same way the wind blows.

Interpret Visuals

Draw attention to the windsock. Explain that a windsock is made out of fabric in a tube or sock shape. Then use these questions to guide children through the Interactivity.

The windsock in the picture is full of air. How did the air get into the windsock? It blew into the tube of fabric. **How do you think the wind changed the way the windsock looked?** It made the windsock puff up. **Why do you think the windsock is blowing in the direction you see here?** That is the way the wind is blowing. **What does a windsock show about the wind?** the direction of the wind

Catch the Wind

Air moves all around us. How do you know which way it moves? How do you know how fast it moves? You can use tools to observe the wind. A **windsock** is a tool that shows the direction of the wind.

It is a windy day. The windsock is filled with air.

240

Writing Connection

TEKS ELA 1.18B, 1.20A

Put the Wind in Words Have children write a poem about a windy day. Remind them to use sensory details to describe how the wind feels and the sounds it makes, and to also tell how it moves other objects, such as trees, boats, flags, and hair. When children finish, have partners switch papers and illustrate each other's poems.

This tool measures wind speed.

he wind vane shows e direction the ind is coming from.

▶ **Observe that wind is moving air. What makes the windsock move?**

The windsock is moving because it is full of air.

Differentiation—Leveled Questions

Extra Support

How could you demonstrate that the wind is blowing? Sample answer: Use a windsock to show that the wind is blowing.

Challenge

How is a person's long hair similar to a windsock? Sample answer: The direction his or her hair blows tells which way the wind is blowing from.

Interpret Visuals

Draw attention to the two images on the right page. Discuss with children that both tools measure different things about the wind. Explain that the top image is called an anemometer, which measures wind speed. The bottom image is a wind vane that shows the direction the wind is coming from. **What are two things that people use wind tools to measure?** wind speed and wind direction

Develop Science Concepts

How does a wind vane show the wind's direction? The arrow on a wind vane points in the direction the wind is coming from.

What does the wind vane do when the wind blows? It spins, or turns, to show the direction.

If it were very windy outside, how might the wine vane look? It would be spinning very quickly.

Why might people want to know how fast the wind is blowing? It would help them know whether the wind was strong enough to cause damage.

Develop Inquiry Skills

COMPARE/CONTRAST Remind children that when they compare, they tell how things are alike. When they contrast, they tell how things are different.

How is a windsock like a wind vane? They both show the direction of the wind.

How are a windsock and a wind vane different? A windsock fills with air when the wind blows and a wind vane spins.

Notebook Summarize Ideas

Have children summarize key details about how people measure the wind. Remind children to look back at the photographs and captions to help them summarize these ideas orally or in writing.

2 Explain (continued)

Notebook Generate Ideas

Share a weather report like the following, modifying it for your area: *Tomorrow the weather will be sunny and warm with rain moving into the area in the evening.* Point out that a weather report is what scientists think will probably happen with the weather. Ask children to share weather reports they have heard. Have them tell how these reports help them plan what to do or wear.

Develop Science Concepts

Review the meaning of *predict*. Talk about what it means for weather scientists or other people to predict the weather. Guide children to understand that people use information to make a best guess about what the weather will be like in the future.

Why are changes in temperature and rainfall important to weather scientists? These changes help scientists predict what the weather might be.

What other weather tools do scientists use to predict weather? weather satellites, weather stations, and weather balloons

Interpret Visuals

Focus children's attention on the weather chart at the bottom of the page. **What information is given in the chart?** days of the week and temperature for each day **What would come next in the chart if you added to it?** the temperature for Thursday

Why It Matters

Predict It!

Scientists observe and track weather over time. They look for changes in weather. They use tools to learn what the weather may be. Scientists use what they learn to make a weather report. A weather report helps people. They can get ready for the coming weather.

weather satellit

Do the Math!

Compare Numbers

Monday	Tuesday	Wednesday

50 °F	40 °F	45 °F

242

Writing Connection

TEKS ELA 1.19C

Write a Description Ask children to each choose one weather tool presented in this lesson and write a brief description of how it looks and works. Then divide children into small groups. Have them tak turns presenting their written descriptions of tools for other group members to guess the toc described.

We use these tools to observe and track weather.

weather station

weather balloon

Look at the temperatures on the left.
Write one of them in the empty box below.
Write >, <, or = to compare the two numbers.

Check children's work.

45 °F	◯	______ °F

243

3 Math Connection

TEKS MATH 1.2G

Compare Temperatures Have children use thermometers to measure temperatures in two locations. Then have them use <, >, or = to write a number sentence that compares the two temperatures.

TEKS 1.8A, 1.8D

Interpret Visuals

Have children point to each weather tool and ask a volunteer to read the caption. **Which weather tool records weather on land?** the weather station **Which weather tool records weather in the sky?** the weather balloon **Which weather tool records weather from space?** the weather satellite **What kind of information could a weather satellite show?** clouds or storms from high above Earth; weather from all over the world

Do the Math!

TEKS MATH 1.2G

Compare Numbers

Remind children that they can compare numbers by using the symbols <, >, or =. Review the meaning of each symbol and how to compare numbers using place value.

Develop Inquiry Skills

INFER **How might a weather report predicting a windstorm help people?** Sample answer: People could tie down things that might blow away, make sure animals are safe, put up storm shutters, or find a safe place to be out of the storm.

Notebook Summarize Ideas

Have children review the photographs of the weather tools on these pages. Then ask them to summarize orally or in writing what they learned by completing this sentence: *Scientists use weather tools to ________.*

3 Extend/Evaluate

Sum It Up!

1. **Draw It!** Have children follow along as you read the directions aloud. Suggest that they look outside the classroom windows or take note during an outside activity of what the weather is like today. If children need help, suggest that they look back at the weather pictures on the first spread of the lesson.
2. **Circle It!** After reading the directions, encourage children to close their eyes and imagine what a windsock looks like when it is filled with moving air, or wind. They can reference the third spread of the lesson as a reminder if necessary.
3. **Match It!** Before children make the matches, have them identify each weather tool. If they have difficulty identifying the objects, suggest that they go back to the section "Measure It!" to review these tools and their functions.

Sum It Up!

1 Draw It!

Look outside. Draw to record the weather you observe.

Check to see that children have drawn a picture of today's weather.

2 Circle It!

Circle the picture that shows wind is moving air.

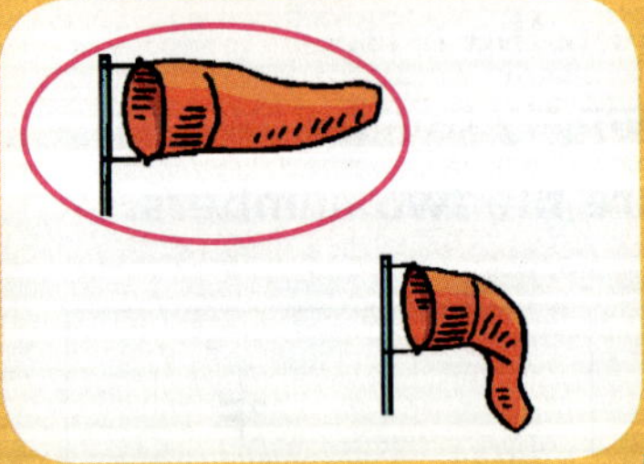

3 Match It!

Match the words to the pictures.

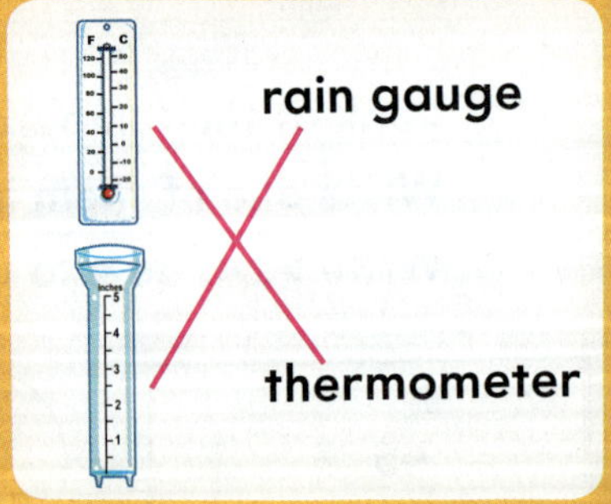

244

Brain Check

Lesson 1

Name ____________

Word Play

Unscramble the word to complete each sentence.

wind   weather   temperature   windsock

1. trwahee   W e a t h e r is what the air outside is like.
2. ueeratpmret   T e m p e r a t u r e is how hot or cold something is.
3. ndiw   Air that moves is called w i n d.
4. diwnoskc   A w i n d s o c k is a tool that shows the direction of the wind.

245

TEKS 1.8A, 1.8D

Answer Strategies

Word Play

- Ask volunteers to read the words in the word box and explain that each word is shown in scrambled form next to the clue it answers. Encourage children to try to solve the problems by using the clues first without unscrambling the words, and then unscramble the words if necessary.
- Children can look back through the lesson to find definitions of the words in the word box if they need to review the meanings. You may wish to have children read all clues with a partner or small groups and discuss possible answers before filling in the answers.

Assessment

Lesson Quiz

See Assessment Guide, p. AG 87.

3 Extend/Evaluate (continued)

Answer Strategies

Apply Concepts

- Remind children that when they infer, they use what they observe and what they already know to figure out what is not stated. To clarify, share this example: if a child came into the classroom wearing wet boots, you could infer that it was raining outside.
- Read the directions aloud. Then ask volunteers to read the weather words in the word box. Discuss the organization of the chart. Point out that an observation is stated in the left column and an inference that can be made is in the right column.
- Explain that children will complete the inference with one of the weather adjectives found in the word box at the top of the page.
- Complete the first inference with children. Discuss how they knew that the word *hot* should be used to complete the sentence.
- After children complete the page, have them share their completed inferences and explain what clues and prior knowledge they used to complete each one.

Take It Home!

Ask children to work with family members to read or listen to a weather forecast. Have children make and present a report to the class showing their predictions and the actual weather that happened during the week.

Apply Concepts

Write a word from the box to fill in the blanks.

cold windy sunny hot

Observation	Inference
Children are swimming in the lake.	The day is hot.
Air is moving the trees back and forth.	The day is windy.
People are wearing warm coats.	The day is cold.
People are wearing sunglasses.	The day is sunny.

Take It Home!

Family Members: Look up the weather forecast with your child. Together, predict the weather for the coming week. Have your child record the weather for the week.

246

Make Connections

Easy

Writing Connection

TEKS ELA 1.24A, 1.28

Present a Weather Report

- Have partners write and present a weather report for the day's weather to the class. They can gather evidence by observing the weather outside, or by looking at a local weather report online.
- Ask them to also use available weather tools, such as windsocks and thermometers, and to include at least two weather words from the lesson.

Average

Social Studies Connection

TEKS SS 1.6A

Observe Weather in Different Parts of the Country

Provide access to an online weather site that gives information about weather in different parts of the United States. Give a brief overview of how to interpret this information. Have children identify parts of the country that are hot, cold, clear, rainy, snowy, and so on.

Average

Writing Connection

TEKS ELA 1.19A

Write Journal Entries

- Ask children to write journal entries for one week describing the weather each day and what they did during free time on those days.
- After a week, have children look back through the journal for patterns that relate the weather to their behavior.

Challenging

Math Connection

TEKS MATH 1.2G

Collect and Compare Temperature Data

- Pair children and provide them with thermometers.
- Have them record the outside temperature in a shady spot at two-hour intervals from the beginning to the end of the school day.
- Have them compare pairs of temperatures recorded at two-hour intervals using the symbols $>$, $=$, and $<$.

Guided Inquiry

FLIPCHART P. 33

15–20 minutes plus 15 minutes each day for five days

individuals

Children should follow the directions on the Flipchart. The accompanying pages in the Student Edition provide scaffolding for guided inquiry.

Inquiry Skills Focus Observe

Objectives

- Recognize the importance of safe practices.
- Ask questions about events observed in the natural world.
- Plan and conduct investigations. Record and organize data.
- Make predictions based on observable patterns.
- Record weather information, including relative temperature.

Prep and Planning Tips

See the Planning for Inquiry page for more information.

- **Caution!** Be sure children recognize the importance of safe practices to keep themselves and others safe and healthy by using scissors appropriately. Review scissors safety.
- Give children envelopes to store the picture cards.
- Allow 15 minutes each day at the same time for five days so children can observe and record the weather. If weather permits, allow them to go outside.

Expected Results

Children will observe and record weather changes from day to day. They should note patterns and differences in the weather.

1 Engage/Explore

Attention Grabber

Make large picture cards that show a variety of common things, including the sun, clouds, and rain. Use the cards to play an identification game. Hold up the card and ask children to say the word that the picture stands for. Explain to children that they will use picture cards to stand for words or ideas in the Inquiry.

Preview Activity

Before beginning the investigation, have children review the directions on the Inquiry Flipchart and the accompanying Student Edition response pages. Then have them complete the response pages as they follow the directions on the Flipchart.

Inquiry Flipchart p. 33

Lesson 2

INQUIRY

TEKS 1.2A ask questions about … events observed in the natural world **1.2B** plan and conduct simple descriptive investigations … **1.2D** record and organize data using pictures, numbers, and words **1.3B** make predictions based on observable patterns **1.8A** record weather information, including relative temperature, such as hot or cold, clear or cloudy, calm or windy, and rainy or icy

Name ______________________

Essential Question

What Can We Observe About Weather?

Set a Purpose

Tell what you want to find out.

want to find out how the weather changes for five days.

will predict the weather on the sixth day.

Think About the Procedure

When will you observe the weather?

will observe the weather at the same time each day.

What will you observe?

will observe if the day is hot or cold. I will see if the sky is

oudy or clear and sunny. I will see if it is raining outside.

247

Go Digital

virtual lab experience is vailable with the Online esources for this program.

1 Engage/Explore (continued)

Guide the Investigation

Develop Inquiry Skills

OBSERVE Explain that *observe* means to look closely at something. It is a way to gather information. Remind children that they use their senses to observe.

How can you use your senses to observe the weather? Sample answer: You can look to see if it is sunny or rainy. You can feel if it is hot or cold. You can use your ears to hear if it is windy.

Why should you observe the weather at the same time every day? You don't want the time of day to change your results. You want to see how things change from day to day, not at different times of the day.

Do you think you should observe the weather in the same place every day? Why? Yes, the weather might be different in different places. For example, there might be more wind in an open area than near trees.

Why do people observe the weather? Sample answers: to know what to wear, to know when to travel, or to know how to be safe

PREDICT **What does it mean to "predict" something?** It means to make a best guess about what will happen in the future.

How will you predict the weather on the sixth day? Sample answer: I will look at the weather from the few days before. I will use those patterns and information to make a best guess about what will happen on the sixth day. If the weather has been sunny for a few days, for example, I would predict that it will be sunny on the sixth day.

2 Explain

Develop Inquiry Skills

RECORD YOUR DATA Discuss with children how they will use the chart to record the weather for each day. Read the headings across the top with children, and point out that the chart includes five school days.

Tell children that they will glue the appropriate weather card or cards in the chart to match each day's weather. Review the words on the picture cards: *clear, cloudy, rainy, icy, hot, cold, windy,* and *calm*. Discuss what they tell about weather.

DRAW CONCLUSIONS Be sure that children can justify their answers by using the weather cards in the chart. Ask them to refer to the chart to explain their conclusions.

As children compare their observations with partners or in small groups, encourage them to first note the similarities in weather from day to day and then the differences. Have children compare their predictions about the weather for the sixth day with the actual weather for that day.

3 Extend/Evaluate

ASK MORE QUESTIONS Some children may raise questions about the specific temperature each day. They may ask about weather that involves other observations or weather tools.

As an extension activity, have children use thermometers or other tools to plan and conduct an investigation to answer their questions.

Assessment

Lesson Quiz

See Assessment Guide, p. AG 88.

Record Your Data

Check children's work.

Record the weather. Glue picture cards into the chart.

Weather This Week

Monday	Tuesday	Wednesday	Thursday	Friday

Draw Conclusions

How is the weather alike from day to day?
How is the weather different from day to day?

Sample answer: The weather was cool every day. It was sunny on three days, but rainy on two days.

How did you make your prediction?

Sample answer: I looked at the weather for five days to help me predict the weather on the sixth day.

Ask More Questions

What other questions could you ask about the weather?

Sample answer: What is the temperature each day?

248

Picture Cards

Lesson 2 INQUIRY

Cut out the weather cards.

249

Teacher Notes

Differentiated Inquiry

Easy

Observe Weather

- Ask children to draw pictures that show three different kinds of weather.
- Have them write a caption to describe each one.
- Encourage children to show and discuss their weather pictures with a partner.

Average

Graph Weekly Weather

- Ask children to continue the Inquiry for another five days and graph the number of sunny, cloudy, and rainy days in a bar graph.
- Have children present the graphs to the class and explain their work.

Average

Observe Daily Rainfall

- Have pairs collect and measure the daily rainfall and snowfall (if any) each day for a week.
- Ask children to record their measurements in chart form. Then they can use the chart to write or draw a summary of any patterns they see in the data.

Challenging

Predict Weekend Weather

- Challenge children to look at the weather chart for this week and use it to predict the weather for Saturday and Sunday.
- Ask them to make a three-column chart for each weekend day. It should include the name of the day, a weather picture that shows the prediction, and a weather picture that shows the actual weather.
- On Monday, have children report on why they made the predictions they did and how well their predictions matched the actual weather.

People in Science

Objectives

- Describe what scientists do.
- Recognize that scientists come from all backgrounds.
- Identify the role of technology in the work of scientists.

Notebook Generate Ideas

Share the following information with children before you assign the feature. Ask questions to ascertain children's prior knowledge.

What is a meteorologist? A meteorologist is a person who studies weather.

Who is June Bacon-Bercey? June Bacon-Bercey is a meteorologist.

What did she do that was a first? She was the first female meteorologist on television.

Background

- June Bacon-Bercey earned a degree in meteorology. She then worked at a local television station in upstate New York, where she started a job as a weather reporter. She also would brief business leaders and government officials about major weather events.
- In the early 1970s, she became the first woman, and the first African American, to be awarded the "seal of approval" for excellence in television weathercasting from the American Meteorological Society.
- She established a scholarship fund using the money she won on a game show.
- She later worked closely with commercial airline pilots to help them land in stormy weather when she was a forecaster for the National Weather Service.
- June Bacon-Bercey enjoys teaching and has worked as a university lecturer and substitute science teacher.

TEKS 1.3C describe what scientists do

People in Scien

4 Things to Know About June Bacon-Bercey

1 June Bacon-Bercey i a meteorologist.

2 She was the first female meteorologis on television.

3 She won money, which she used to h other women becon meteorologists.

4 She enjoys teaching

Writing Connection

TEKS ELA 1.19

Write and Present a Weather Report Have children play the role of a meteorologist, and tell them to observe and report on the weather. Ask them to prepare a 15-second report that describes today's weather. The report should include the temperature and any words that describe the weather, such as *sunny, cloudy, windy, snowy,* and *rainy.* Have children present their reports to the class. If possible, tape-recor or make a video of the reports.

Word Whiz

▶ Learn weather words. Find the words in the word search below. Draw a circle around each word you find.

rnado | hurricane | lightning | thunder | storm | blizzard

l	i	g	h	t	n	i	n	g	q
w	m	r	n	o	t	b	y	v	h
b	d	l	z	r	x	s	p	c	u
l	t	h	u	n	d	e	r	b	r
i	j	g	s	a	y	z	q	m	r
z	q	f	g	d	g	f	d	s	i
z	w	s	t	o	r	m	h	j	c
a	r	d	k	y	y	p	l	k	a
r	t	s	h	p	q	w	r	t	n
d	y	p	f	j	s	d	c	b	e

Science, Technology, and Society

Remind children that June Bacon-Bercey began her career as a meteorologist in the 1970s. Explain that many of the tools meteorologists used then, such as thermometers, are in use today. Other tools, such as weather satellites, have changed a lot. Help children list some common weather tools. Then have them work in groups to research what each one does and how it has changed (or not changed) over the decades.

TEKS 1.3C

Develop Science Concepts

What do you call a person or scientist who studies weather? meteorologist

How was June Bacon-Bercey's experience as a meteorologist unique? She was the first female meteorologist on television.

What does a meteorologist say or do on television? A meteorologist tells people what the weather will be like in the next few days.

Develop Inquiry Skills

INFER Why is it important for people to know what the weather will be? It helps people to prepare, especially if the weather will be bad.

What skills and training does a meteorologist on television need? A meteorologist needs to know many areas of science. A meteorologist also needs to be organized and able to communicate ideas.

Notebook Summarize Ideas

Before children solve the Word Whiz, review the words in the word box. Explain that each word tells something about the weather, and review the meaning of each term.

Tell children that the words in the word search run from top to bottom or from left to right. No words run diagonally or backward. As an extension activity, challenge children to use the weather words in oral or written sentences.

Options for Inquiry

FLIPCHART P. 34

Children can conduct these optional investigations at any time before, during, or in response to the lesson in the Student Edition.

A **Keeping Warm**

How do animals stay warm in cold weather? Let's find out.

Materials
3 thermometers
ball of yarn
sock

Do This

1. Put 1 thermometer in a ball of yarn. Put 1 thermometer in the sock. Do not cover up the third thermometer with anything.
2. Place all 3 thermometers in a refrigerator for 20 minutes.
3. Take the thermometers out of the refrigerator. Record and compare each temperature.

Draw Conclusions

How are the yarn and the sock like animal fur? How does thick fur help animals in cold weather?

TEKS **1.2B** plan and conduct simple descriptive investigations . . . **1.2C** collect data and make observations using simple equipment . . . **1.2D** record and organize data using pictures, numbers, and words **1.4A** collect and compare information using tools, including . . . weather instruments such as classroom demonstration thermometers . . . **1.8C** identify characteristics of the seasons of the year . . .

B **Turn Over a New Leaf**

Identify what the different seasons are like. Make a plan. Record and organize your information into a chart. Draw and write to tell what happens in each season.

Spring	Summer	Fall	Winter

Science Notebook

Turn Over a New Leaf
My Planning Questions

Here is how one student began to p
her investigation

Questions	Answers
1. Which season is it now?	
2. What is the weather like in each season?	
3. How do the seasons affect plants, animals, and people?	

Directed Inquiry

A Keeping Warm

25 minutes
pairs

Prep and Planning Tips

Make sure that the thermometers register the same room temperature at the beginning of the investigation.

Check that the yarn balls are loose enough for children to insert a thermometer.

Use thick athletic or wool socks rather than dress socks.

If possible, have children put their thermometers beside each other in the refrigerator.

Expected Results

Children will collect and compare information using thermometers. They will observe that the thermometers in the sock and yarn register higher temperatures than the bare thermometer. They should conclude that the sock and yarn insulate, or protect, the thermometer from the cold.

Independent Inquiry

B Turn Over a New Leaf

20 minutes
individuals

Prep and Planning Tips

See the Planning for Inquiry page for more information. Before children begin to draw and write, have them fold their paper into fourths and label each section with a season. Encourage children to use previous knowledge of the four seasons in order to help them do the activity. If they have trouble, have them review the lesson pages.

Science Notebook

Children can use the Science Notebook as a model for planning and conducting their own investigations. Have them include the sample questions plus questions of their own. Additional questions may include *What is the order of the four seasons? How can I describe each season?*

TEKS **1.3B** make predictions based on observable patterns **1.8C** identify characteristics of the seasons of the year and day and night

Lesson 3

Essential Question

What Are Seasons?

Engage Your Brain!

Find the answer to the question in the lesson.

In which season do many trees have no leaves?

winter

Active Reading

Lesson Vocabulary

1. Preview the lesson.
2. Write the 2 vocabulary terms here.

season   weather pattern

Inquiry Flipchart p. 34—Keeping Warm/Turn Over a New Leaf

253

Go Digital

An interactive digital lesson is available in Online Resources. It is suitable for individuals, small groups, or may be projected or used on an interactive white board.

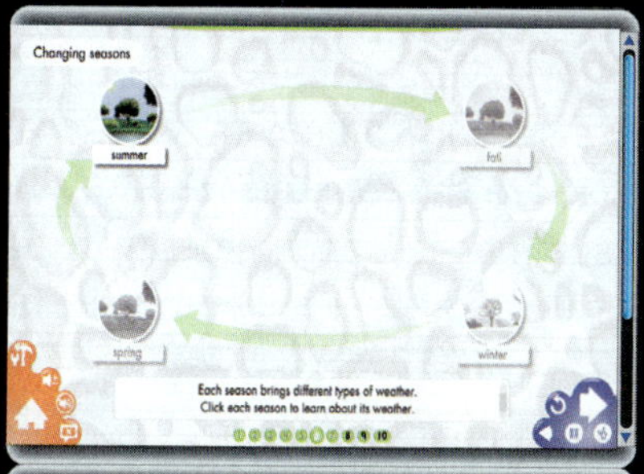

1 Engage/Explore

Objectives

- Plan and conduct simple investigations.
- Collect and compare information using thermometers.
- Record and organize data.
- Make predictions based on observable patterns.
- Identify characteristics of the seasons of the year.

Engage Your Brain!

Have children describe the picture and contrast the two types of trees. Ask them to review the four seasons and what the weather is like in each one. They should try to think about what trees look like in each season. Direct them to use all of that information to answer the question *In which season do many trees have no leaves?*

Remind children to record their final answer to the question when they find it on the eighth page of the lesson.

Active Reading Annotations

Remind children that active readers "make texts their own" by marking them or writing notes to help them understand what they are reading. Encourage children to use pencil to make annotations and to feel free to change their marks and notes as they read. The goal of annotation is to help children remember what they have read.

Vocabulary and Interactive Glossary

Remind children to find and list the yellow highlighted terms from the lesson. As they proceed through the lesson and learn about the terms, they can add drawings or words in the extra spaces provided in some entries in the Interactive Glossary.

2 Explain

Notebook Generate Ideas

Direct children to preview the heading, the captions, and the images on these pages and call on volunteers to discuss what they see. Ask them to use this information to figure out what these pages are about.

Active Reading Vocabulary

Explain that a vocabulary word may be highlighted in a color. Active readers pay attention to a highlighted word because its meaning is given in the same sentence or the next sentence.

Develop Science Vocabulary

season Write the names of the seasons on cards, and distribute them to four children. Have them read aloud their cards and arrange themselves in seasonal order, beginning with spring. Use the words *before* and *after* to ask: What season comes after spring? What season comes before winter?

weather pattern Draw a pattern of shapes on the board, such as square, square, circle, square, square, circle. Help children identify the pattern and discuss that a pattern is a change that repeats. Explain that the weather can also repeat. It is usually colder in winter than summer, for example. Challenge children to explain why that pattern is a weather pattern.

Develop Science Concepts

What are the four seasons? spring, summer, fall, winter **How often do the seasons repeat?** once a year

What do seasons have to do with weather patterns? Changes in the weather take place each season in a regular pattern.

Spring Into Spring

A **season** is a time of year. Spring, summer, fall, and winter are the four seasons. They form a repeating pattern.

The weather changes with each season. These changes form a weather pattern. A **weather pattern** is a change in the weather that repeats.

Active Reading

Find the sentence that tells the meaning of **season**. Draw a line under the sentence.

People plant flowers in spring.

254

Differentiation—Leveled Questions

Extra Support

What is a season? a time of year **What are the four seasons?** spring, summer, fall, and winter

Challenge

What are two changes in the weather from season to season? Sample answer: It is colder in fall and winter than spring and summer. It rains more in spring than in winter.

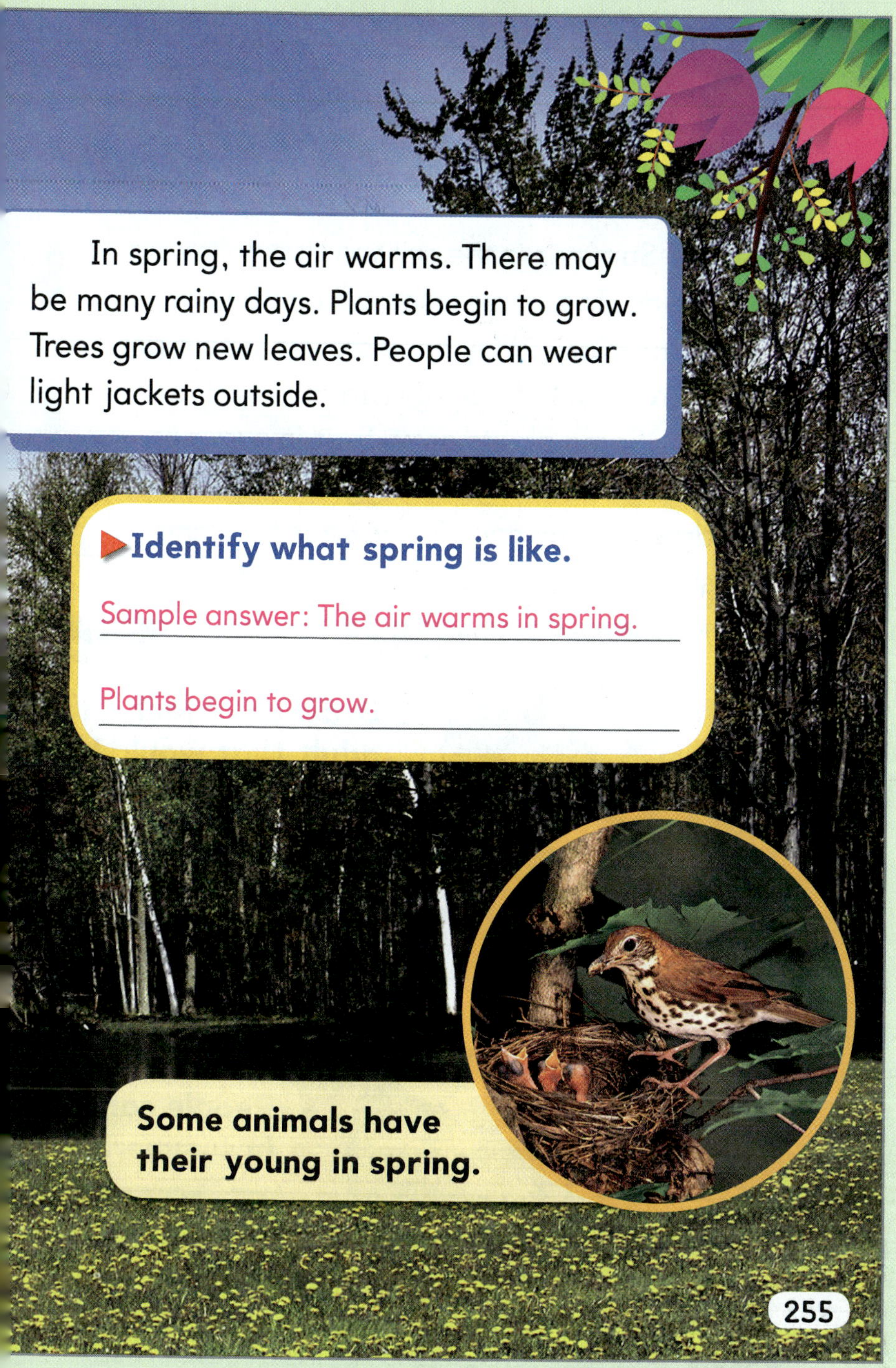

In spring, the air warms. There may be many rainy days. Plants begin to grow. Trees grow new leaves. People can wear light jackets outside.

▶Identify what spring is like.

Sample answer: The air warms in spring.

Plants begin to grow.

Some animals have their young in spring.

English Language Learners

ELPS 1E, 2C

Explore Word Meanings
Reinforce the meaning of *pattern*. Have children point to the word and read it aloud. Then have a group of three boys and three girls demonstrate an alternating girl/boy pattern. Lead the group in "reading" the pattern and discuss why it is a pattern. Have children make other patterns using classroom objects. For each one, ask children to use the word *pattern* in their explanations.

TEKS 1.3B, 1.8C

Interpret Visuals

Point out that captions are used to give information about the pictures. **What do the captions tell you about the pictures on these pages?** They give details about what some people and animals do in spring.

Have children point to the caption on the left page. **What can you learn from this caption?** You learn that people plant flowers in spring. **Have children point to the caption on the right page. What can you learn from this caption?** You learn that spring is a time for some animals to have young.

Call on volunteers to identify characteristics of spring. **Name some things that happen in spring.** Sample answers: The air warms and there may be many rainy days. Trees grow new leaves and some animals have their young. People wear light jackets and plant flowers. Have children use this information to help them answer the interactive.

Develop Inquiry Skills

COMPARE Remind children that when they compare, they tell how things are alike. **How are the seasons alike?** Sample answer: All of the seasons are a time of year.

Notebook Summarize Ideas

Direct children to use the words *season* and *weather pattern* as they summarize orally or in writing what they learned on these two pages.

2 Explain (continued)

Notebook Generate Ideas

Ask children to tell what they already know about summer weather. Call on volunteers to describe the weather and talk about summer activities they enjoy. Record these activity ideas on the board and add to this list after reading.

Develop Science Concepts

Use the information on these pages to help children identify characteristics of summer.

How does the weather change from spring to summer? Summer is usually hotter than spring and may have more storms.

How does summer weather affect what people wear and do? People dress to stay cool and to stay safe from the sun. They may enjoy outdoor activities such as canoeing or other water sports. When it is very hot, they may stay indoors to be cool.

Suppose you planted a vegetable garden in early spring. What might you expect to find in the middle of summer? Many fruits and vegetables would be ripe enough to eat.

Interpret Visuals

Focus attention on the boy and his dad in the canoe. **What is the boy wearing to help him stay safe from the sun?** a hat **How can the man stay safe from the sun?** Sample answer: by wearing a hat or sunglasses Have children draw their answers.

Sunny Summer

Summer is the season that follows spring. In summer, the air can be hot. Some places may have storms. There are more hours of daylight than in spring.

Some plants grow fruit in summer. Young animals grow bigger. People dress to stay cool. They wear hats and sunglasses to keep safe from the sun.

Children should draw a hat or sunglasses on the adult.

▶ **Draw an object on the adult that would keep him safe from the sun.**

People canoe in summer.

256

123 Math Connection

TEKS MATH 1.1C, 1.5

Solve Daylight Problems
Remind children that summer has more daylight hours than winter. Have children use a clock with moveable hands or other manipulatives to solve problems such as this one: *Suppose the sun comes up at 6 in the morning. It sets at 8 at night. How many hou of daylight are there?* (14 hours) *How many hours of darkness are there?* (10 hours)

▶ **Draw to show how most trees look in summer.**

Children should draw branches full of green leaves.

This hare's fur is brown in summer. The brown fur helps the hare hide.

257

Differentiation—Leveled Questions

Extra Support

What is summer? the season that follows spring

Challenge

Many people take vacations during summer. Why is summer a good time to take a vacation? Days are long, and the weather is usually hot and sunny. Summer is a good time to enjoy outdoor activities.

Interpret Visuals

Focus attention on the tree. Remind children that many trees also experience seasonal changes. If time allows, have children use books or online resources to look at summer trees. **How do many trees look in summer?** They have full, green leaves. Some have fruit.

Have children draw and color a tree in summer.

Misconception Alert

Children may think that seasonal weather patterns are the same everywhere in the United States. Show a U.S. map and explain that the seasonal patterns are generally true, but not identical, all over. Show places that do not quite fit the usual pattern, such as northern California or Maine. Maine gets warmer, but not very hot. Northern California may actually be warmer in other seasons than in summer.

Develop Inquiry Skills

INVESTIGATE Point out the photograph of the hare, and have children describe the color of its fur. **Where could this hare hide to stay safe? Explain.** It could hide in fields or places with tall grass that are the same color; it would blend in and be hard to find.

To help children better understand the concept of protective coloration, distribute small pieces of white, red, tan, black, and brown construction paper. Have them cut out small shapes and place them on the part of the photograph that shows the hare's environment. Ask children to determine which color best blends into this environment.

Notebook Summarize Ideas

Ask children to reread the title and then summarize orally or in writing three things they learned about summer.

2 Explain (continued)

Notebook Generate Ideas

Recite the following finger play as you act out the words with your hands: *Here are some colorful leaves, fluttering down. Here is a tree, tall and brown. Here is a frisky squirrel, with eyes so bright. She's hunting for nuts with all her might.* Ask children to identify which season is being described. Then tell them that they will learn about that season on these pages.

Active Reading Details

Explain that a detail sentence may give an example. Or, it may describe something. Active readers ask themselves, "What topic does this detail sentence tell about?" The answer will help readers keep the main idea in mind.

Develop Science Concepts

Use the information on these pages to help children identify characteristics of fall.

What season follows summer? fall **How is fall different from summer?** Days are shorter, and the weather is cooler.

Suppose you were a weather forecaster. What would you expect to tell people about the weather on a fall day? Sample answer: It will be cool and possibly cloudy.

How does fall weather affect what people wear? Cooler fall weather means that people wear warmer clothing than in summer. **How does fall weather affect animals?** Some animals leave to go to warmer places; other animals gather food and store it for later. **How does fall weather affect plants?** Leaves change color and drop off some trees.

Point out that these pages contain details about fall. Remind children to read the captions carefully to learn about those details.

Fall Into Fall

Fall is the season that follows summer. The air gets cooler. There are fewer hours of daylight than in summer.

Some leaves change color and drop off the trees. Some animals move to warmer places. People wear jackets to stay warm.

Children can underline the second, third, fourth, fifth, or sixth sentence. Children should draw an arrow from the detail to the first sentence.

Active Reading

A detail is a fact about a main idea. Draw one line under a detail. Draw an arrow to the main idea it tells about.

258

English Language Learners

ELPS 1E, 2C

Explore Word Meanings
Children may be confused by the heading that contains two meanings of the word *fall*. Point out the heading, and have children identify the word that appears twice. Explain both meanings of *fall*. Have children gesture or pantomime to demonstrate that *fall* means "to drop or go down." Review that *fall* also names a season. Have children share oral sentences using both meanings of the word.

S.T.E.M.
continued

Weather Tool Timeline

Use the timeline to answer the questions.

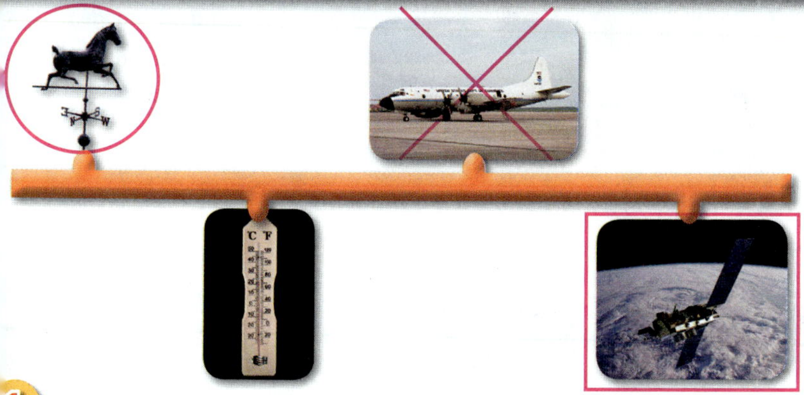

1 Which is the oldest weather tool? Circle it.

2 Which is the newest weather tool? Draw a box around it.

3 Which tool came after the thermometer? Draw an X over it.

Build On It!

Design and build your own rain gauge. Complete **Build It: Rain Gauge** on the Inquiry Flipchart.

Build On It!

In **Build It: Rain Gauge**, the design challenge associated with this lesson, children use the steps of the engineering design process to build a rain gauge. For more details, see the pages that follow.

Other opportunities to apply the design process appear throughout the *Inquiry Flipchart*.

Develop S.T.E.M. Concepts

When children have completed reading the feature, ask questions to help them reflect on how weather tools have changed throughout the years.

How do some weather tools allow us to do things that otherwise could not be done at all? Some new weather tools, such as weather satellites, can be placed in locations where people cannot go all the time.

How has weather technology changed the way people live? It has made it possible for people to observe and better predict and track weather. This helps people be prepared for weather, especially severe weather.

Develop Inquiry Skills

COMPARE/CONTRAST Ask children to carefully observe and compare and contrast the weather tools. **How are the tools alike?** They are all tools that people use to observe and record weather.

How are they different? Some are old; some are new. The old ones, such as the wind vane and the thermometer, are very simple. The new ones, such as the weather plane and weather satellite, are very complicated. They use computers and others kinds of technology to observe and record the weather.

ORDER **How do your comparisons of weather tools help you better understand the timeline?** Sample answer: The tools that are older are also simpler and have less advanced technology. The new ones have computers and other technology that was not invented a long time ago.

Notebook Summarize Ideas

Ask children to summarize what they learned about weather tools including how they are used and how they have changed over time.

S.T.E.M.

Engineering and Technology

FLIPCHART P. 35

20–25 minutes, plus 10 minutes each day for one day to 2 weeks

small groups

Objectives

- Record and organize data.
- Identify and explain a problem and propose a solution in his/her own words.
- Record weather information.

Prep and Planning Tips

- Ask children to help you collect clean, half-liter plastic bottles. Divide the class into as many groups as you have bottles. Cut the tops off the bottles in advance. Also have available a ruler, masking tape, and a permanent marking pen for each group.
- Allow 10 minutes each day for at least one day or as much as two weeks, depending on the available time, to record and measure. You can extend the activity if there is no precipitation for a two-week period.

Expected Results

Children will build a rain gauge. As an optional extension, they will use it to observe and measure precipitation that collects in it over a period of time.

1 Engage/Explore

Attention Grabber

Show a weather report, either as a video, online, or print version. Ask children to identify and explain the part that predicts or shows precipitation. Then ask small groups of volunteers to act as weather reporters by looking outside and telling the class the amount and kind of any precipitation they see.

Preview Activity

Before beginning the activity, have children review the directions on the Engineering and Technology Flipchart page.

Guide the Activity

Develop Inquiry Skills

OBSERVE Allow children time to observe the available materials. Encourage them to make sketches as they think about different design ideas.

MEASURE Explain that *measure* means "to find the size or amount of something." Remind children that tools, such as thermometers and rulers, are used to measure.

COMPARE Encourage children from different groups to compare their rain gauges to others and share ideas for improving them. Point out that the best ideas come from teams who share.

Strategies for Success

Before beginning the investigation, have children review the directions on the *Inquiry Flipchart*. As children draw their designs, remind them that the purpose of a rain gauge is to measure rain and other forms of water that fall from the sky.

Notebook Science Notebook

During the Activity Remind children to list all the materials they will need to build their design. Tell them to make their drawings clear enough to follow when they build the rain gauge.

2 Explain

Develop the Engineering Design Process

Use the following steps of the engineering design process to provide context and support for the analyses that children are doing in the flipchart activity.

1. FIND A PROBLEM **Use your own words to explain what you will design and build and what problem it will solve.** Sample answer: I want to design a rain gauge that will help me measure how much rain falls.
2. PLAN AND BUILD **How did your drawing help you build a rain gauge?** Sample answer: The drawing showed me the different materials and parts of the design.
3. TEST AND IMPROVE **How can you test your rain gauge?** Sample answer: I can put it outside and check to see how much rain falls each day for two weeks. Then I can see whether the rain gauge helps me measure rainfall.

3 Extend/Evaluate

Quick Check

How did you decide what your rain gauge would look like? Sample answer: I looked at other rain gauges.

How can you find out if your rain gauge works? Sample answer: I can use it to collect rainfall.

5. COMMUNICATE Have groups share their designs and explain how they followed their designs to build a rain gauge.

Notebook Science Notebook

After the Activity Check children's designs to see that they have drawn a rain gauge. If children use the rain gauge to measure precipitation, have them record the results in a chart in their notebooks.

! Michael DiSpezio's Tips & Tricks

Preparing Materials If you use plastic half-liter bottles for the rain gauges, you will need to prepare them. Carefully cut off the upper half of each container using sharp scissors, box cutters, or craft knives. As always, use caution and new blades when cutting. If you prefer not to cut the bottles, you can insert and secure a funnel in the container necks instead. Deli containers, peanut butter jars, and other plastic containers also work well. Emphasize to children how they are reusing "trash" for another purpose. If children mark the containers with permanent markers, remind them to recap the markers and take care not to make a mess with the ink.

Enduring Understandings

Revisit the Big Idea and Essential Questions

Big Idea **Weather changes from day to day and from season to season. You can use different tools to measure weather.**

To explore the Big Idea, post it on the board. Then, have children take turns telling how the content from each lesson supports it. Encourage children to use the vocabulary from the unit. Help children sort their ideas by breaking the Big Idea down into the following categories.

- Weather Changes from Day to Day
- Weather Changes from Season to Season
- Different Tools Measure Weather

Essential Questions

Post the Essential Questions, and use the following prompts to guide a discussion.

Lessons/Essential Questions	Prompts
L1 **What Is Weather?**	• Name three different kinds of weather.
L2 **What Can We Observe About Weather?**	• Tell what you can observe about today's weather.
L3 **What Are Seasons?**	• Describe the changes that happen from one season to the next.

Notebook **Science Notebook**

You may use the following strategies after children complete the unit or after each lesson.

- Have children review and edit the responses to the Essential Questions they drafted at the beginning of the unit. Suggest they cross out sentences or ideas that are unnecessary or inappropriate.
- Have children draft ideas for cards in their Science Notebooks to prepare for a memory game. Tell children to write on eight index cards. On four of the cards, have them write descriptions of weather, such as *cold and snowy, cold and rainy, warm and cloudy,* and *hot and sunny*. On the other four cards, have them draw clothing and accessories appropriate for each kind of weather. Then, explain the memory game's rules. Tell children to play with a partner. Ask them to turn all of one partner's cards facedown and look for weather and clothing matches. After all the matches have been found, have them play a second time with the other partner's cards.

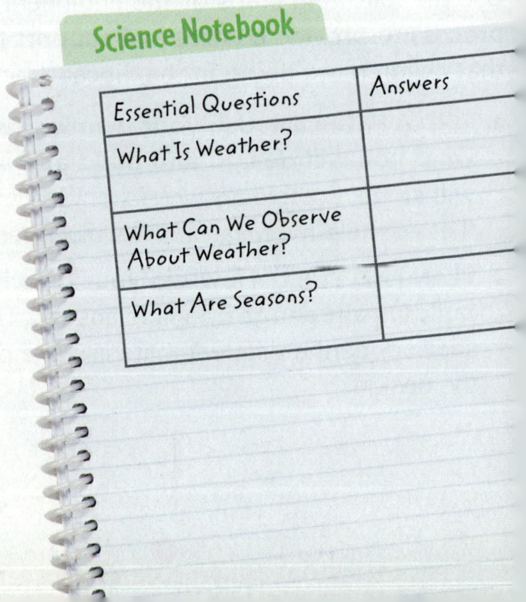

Unit 6 Review

Name ______________________

Vocabulary Review

Use the terms in the box to complete the sentences.

season
temperature
weather

TEKS 1.8A

1. In spring, you can record the weather as warm and rainy.

TEKS 1.3B

2. Winter is the season that comes after fall.

TEKS 1.8A

3. When you measure temperature, you tell how hot or cold something is.

Science Concepts

Fill in the letter of the choice that best answers the question.

TEKS 1.4A, 1.8A

4. What tool can you use to collect and record the temperature each day?
   - Ⓐ a rain gauge
   - Ⓑ a thermometer
   - Ⓒ a windsock

TEKS 1.3B, 1.8A

5. You see dark clouds in the sky. What kind of weather is **most likely** coming?
   - Ⓐ cold weather
   - Ⓑ rainy weather
   - Ⓒ sunny weather

Item Analysis

Items	TEKS	Depth of Knowledge	Cognitive Complexity
1	**1.8A**	1	Low
2	**1.3B**	1	Low
3	**1.8A**	1	Low
4	**1.4A, 1.8A**	1	Low
5	**1.3B, 1.8A**	2	Moderate

Unit Review

Answer Key

Vocabulary Review (5 points each)

1. weather
   Remind children that weather is a condition of the air over a short period of time. Air can be described in many ways. It may be cool or hot or cloudy.
2. season
   Have children name the seasons, and tell them that each season lasts about three months of the year. You may want to use a calendar to highlight the seasons.
3. temperature
   Draw children's attention to the phrase *how hot or cold something is* as an important clue to the answer. After children write the missing word, have them reread the sentence to make sure that the answer makes sense.

Science Concepts (7 points each)

4. B
   Have children tell how each tool is used. Make sure they understand that while all of the tools shown measure weather in some way, only a thermometer measures temperature.
5. B
   Point out that while dark clouds appear during cold weather, they almost always appear before rain so that is the best answer.

Assessment

Unit 6 Test and Performance Assessment

See Assessment Guide, pp. AG 92–AG 98, for Unit Test and Performance Task with Long Option rubric.

Unit Review *continued*

Answer Key

Science Concepts (7 points each)

6. B

Review how seasons affect animals. Help children recall that many young animals are born in the spring.

7. C

Review the characteristics of each season listed in the answer choices. Have children tell what type of weather might call for wearing heavy jackets.

8. C

Have children revisit each answer choice and ask themselves, "Could this be true for both fall and spring?" If the answer is *yes*, they will know it is not the correct answer.

9. C

Ask children to recall and describe what a rain gauge looks like. Then, have them tell what kind of weather dark clouds often accompany. Children can put these two clues together to figure out the answer.

UNIT 6

TEKS 1.8C

6. In which season was this young lamb born?

Ⓐ fall
Ⓑ spring
Ⓒ summer

TEKS 1.8C

7. The Han family is ice skating outside. They are wearing heavy jackets. Which season is it?

Ⓐ spring
Ⓑ summer
Ⓒ winter

TEKS 1.8C

8. How is fall **different** from spring?

Ⓐ Fall is a season.
Ⓑ People may wear jackets in spring.
Ⓒ Many trees lose their leaves in fall.

TEKS 1.8A

9. Pablo's rain gauge is full. There are dark clouds in the sky. He records what he observes. What does this tell you about the weather?

Ⓐ It is calm.
Ⓑ It is clear.
Ⓒ It is rainy.

Item Analysis *(continued)*

Items	TEKS	Depth of Knowledge	Cognitive Complexity
6	**1.8C**	1	Low
7	**1.8C**	2	Moderate
8	**1.0C**	2	Moderate
9	**1.8A**	2	Moderate

TEKS 1.8A

10. Look at this picture. What is the weather like?

Ⓐ calm and cold
Ⓑ cold and snowy
Ⓒ windy and warm

TEKS 1.2D, 1.8A, 1.8D

11. Pradeep shows that air is all around us by using a windsock. What can he observe and record?
Ⓐ the direction of the wind
Ⓑ the temperature of the air
Ⓒ the speed of the wind

TEKS 1.8C

12. Look at what the children are doing.

Which season is it?
Ⓐ fall
Ⓑ spring
Ⓒ summer

UNIT 6

Item Analysis *(continued)*

Items	TEKS	Depth of Knowledge	Cognitive Complexity
10	**1.8A**	2	Moderate
11	**1.2D, 1.8A, 1.8D**	2	Moderate
12	**1.8C**	2	Moderate

Unit Review *continued*

Answer Key

Science Concepts (7 points each)

10. B

Direct children's attention to details from the picture that indicate the weather is both cold and snowy, such as the snow and the children's clothing.

11. A

Have children refer back to the lesson pages as needed to identify what a windsock measures.

12. C

Point out that in some parts of the country and world, going to the beach can happen in more than one season. Explain that the purpose of the picture is to show what is typically the hottest season in the Northern Hemisphere—summer.

Short Option Performance Assessment

Task

Record the Weather
Have children fill in a weather chart with details about the weather for one day. Ask them to include weather vocabulary and other words used in the lessons. Also encourage them to include pictures.

Rubric

Preparation On a sheet of paper, make a chart for children to copy. Label the columns *Temperature, Rainfall,* and *Wind.*

Scoring Rubric—Performance Indicators

___ Includes accurate air temperatures.
___ Includes an accurate rainfall measure based on a rain gauge.
___ Identifies the presence/absence of wind.

Observations and Rubric Scores

3 2 1 0

Unit Review *continued*

Answer Key

Inquiry and the Big Idea (11 points each)

13.

a. snowy, cold, and icy

b. I would wear a winter coat, hat, scarf, and gloves.

c. I might make a snowman or go sledding.

Have children describe experiences they have had with snow and tell what they wore and what they did.

14.

a. The season is spring. I know this because the tree is just beginning to grow leaves and flowers.

b. summer

Point out the buds and growing leaves on the tree to children. Make sure they understand that this picture depicts a tree with leaves growing back after winter and not in the process of falling off.

UNIT 6

Inquiry and the Big Idea

Write the answers to these questions.

TEKS 1.8A

13. Look at the picture.

a. Record what the weather is like.

snowy, cold, and icy

b. What might you wear on a day like this?

I would wear a winter coat, hat, scarf, and gloves.

c. What might you do on a day like this?

I might make a snowman or go sledding.

TEKS 1.3B, 1.8C

14. Look at the tree.

a. Identify the season. Tell how you know which season it is.

The season is spring. I know this because the tree is just beginning to grow leaves and flowers.

b. Predict which season comes next.

summer

Item Analysis

Items	TEKS	Depth of Knowledge	Cognitive Complexity
13	**1.8A**	3	Moderate
14	**1.3B, 1.8C**	3	High

UNIT 7 Objects in the Sky

Big Idea and Essential Questions

This Unit was designed to focus on this Big Idea and these Essential Questions.

Big Idea

Many objects can be seen in the sky. The appearance of these objects can change.

Essential Questions

L1 **What Can We See In the Sky?**

L2 **How Does the Sky Seem to Change?**

L3 **How Does the Sun Seem to Move?**

Take It Home!
A School-Home Connection letter in English and Spanish is provided in Online Resources.

Professional Development

Houghton Mifflin Harcourt and **NSTA,** the **National Science Teachers Association,** have partnered to provide customized professional development resources for teachers using *ScienceFusion*.

The Professional Development Resources include:

- Do-it-yourself resources, where you can study at your own pace
- Live and archived online seminars
- Journal articles, many of which include lesson plans
- Fee-based eBooks, eBook chapters, online short courses, symposia, and conferences

Access to The NSTA Learning Center is provided in the *ScienceFusion* Online Resources.

NSTA National Science Teachers Association

The NSTA Learning Center

Unit Planning

Options for Instruction

Choose from **Interactive Worktext** and **Leveled Readers, Digital,** and **Inquiry** options to meet the Texas Essential Knowledge and Skills.

	LESSON 1	LESSON 2	LESSON 3
Essential Questions	**What Can We See In the Sky?**	**How Does the Sky Seem to Change?**	✔ **Guided Inquiry** **How Does the Sun Seem to Move?**
Texas Essential Knowledge and Skills	TEKS **1.8C**	TEKS **1.3B, 1.8B**	TEKS **1.2A, 1.2B, 1.2D, 1.4A, 1.4B, 1.8B**
Interactive Worktext	☐ **Student Edition** pp. 273–282 • Good Morning, Sunshine • Good Night, Sky • Eye on the Sky	☐ **Student Edition** pp. 285–294 • Hello, Shadow • Just a Phase • Cloudy Day, Starry Night	☐ **Student Edition** pp. 295–296 • Scaffolding for Inquiry
Leveled Readers	Parallel coverage of the lesson topics is provided in the **Extra Support, On-Level,** and **Enrichment** readers. See p. 271H for detailed reader information.		
Hands-On Inquiry	**Inquiry Flipchart** p. 36 **High in the Sky** ☐ Directed Inquiry **Star Fun** ☐ Independent Inquiry	**Inquiry Flipchart** p. 37 **Cloud Time** ☐ Directed Inquiry **Moon and Stars Calendar** ☐ Independent Inquiry	**Inquiry Flipchart** p. 38 **How Does the Sun Seem to Move?** ☐ Guided Inquiry
Digital Curriculum	☐ **Digital Lesson** Online Resources Interactive presentation of lesson content 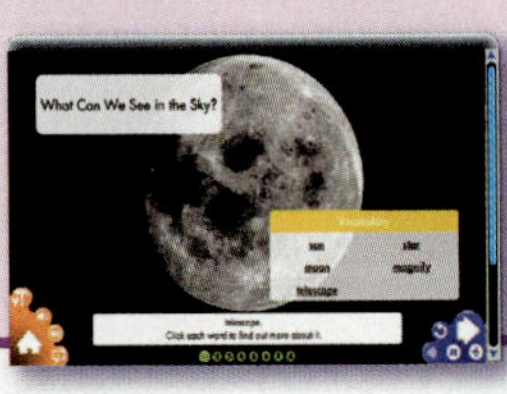	☐ **Digital Lesson** Online Resources Interactive presentation of lesson content 	☐ **Virtual Lab** Online Resources Interactive scaffolded inquiry 

OTHER UNIT FEATURES

People in Science, p. 283

S.T.E.M. Engineering and Technology, pp. 297–298B

Online Resources

Interactive Whiteboard Resources for Unit 7

Assessment

Formative Assessment
Sum It Up! and Brain Check
Student Edition, end of each lesson

Summative Assessment
Lesson Quizzes
Assessment Guide, pp. AG 99–AG 101

Unit 7 Review
Student Edition, pp. 299–302

Unit 7 Test
Assessment Guide, pp. AG 104–AG 108

Performance Assessment
SHORT OPTION: Teacher Edition, p. 301
LONG OPTION: Assessment Guide, pp. AG 109–AG 110

RTI Response to Intervention
RTI Strategies, p. 271I

Online Assessment
Test-taking and automatic scoring
Banks of items from which to build tests

Teacher Notes

Planning for Inquiry

Use the following preview of Inquiry Activities and Lessons to gather and manage the materials needed for each lesson.

Activity	Inquiry and Design Process Skills Focus	Materials	Prep Tips, Troubleshooting, and Expected Results
Lesson 1 DIRECTED INQUIRY **Flipchart** p.36 A **High in the Sky** **OBJECTIVES** Recognize the importance of safe practices. Plan and conduct simple investigations. Record and organize data. Identify characteristics of the day sky. 10 minutes each day for 5 days individuals TEKS **1.1B, 1.2B, 1.2D, 1.8C**	• Infer • Observe • Gather, Record, Display, or Interpret Data	• pencil • paper	**Prep Tips** If possible, have children make their observations first thing in the morning and soon after lunch. Allow 10 minutes each day for a week for children to observe and record their observations. Some children may find it easier to draw or dictate their observations. **Caution!** Remind children not to look directly at the sun. **Troubleshooting** Check the weather reports in advance, and conduct this investigation during a sunny week. If one day during the week is cloudy, skip that day and continue the following day. The days don't have to be continuous, although it will aid children's memories if they are. **Expected Results** Children will determine where the sun is in the morning and in the afternoon and conclude that the sun's position in the sky appears to change throughout the day. They should recognize that the sun seems to be higher in the sky around noon.
INDEPENDENT INQUIRY **Flipchart** p.36 B **Star Fun** **OBJECTIVES** Plan and conduct simple investigations. Record and organize data. Identify characteristics of the night sky. 15 minutes pairs TEKS **1.2B, 1.2D, 1.8C**	• Observe • Formulate or Use Models	• black construction paper • sharpened pencils • flashlights • shoebox (optional) • safety scissors (optional) • hole punch (optional)	**Prep Tips** You may wish to make holes in the paper for children or use a hole punch instead of having children punch holes with a pencil point. You may wish to have children set up their night sky models in shoeboxes. To do so, cut a square out of one end of the shoebox and a circle out of the other. Cover the square space with the black, pencil-pricked construction paper, and shine the flashlight into the circle space onto a blank wall, with the lights out. **Caution!** If children are using sharpened pencils, remind them to be careful. Also instruct them never to shine a flashlight in anyone's eyes. **Troubleshooting** You will need a darkened room for this activity. If turning out the lights and closing the blinds are not enough, you may wish to seek out a windowless room or closet in the school and have children test their models there. **Expected Results** Children make a model of a starry night sky using common classroom materials. They will recognize similarities and differences between the actual night sky and their models.

Take Notes ELPS 4G

As you read **TE pages 276–277,** give children practice taking notes.

Beginning	Intermediate	Advanced/Advanced High
Read aloud the first paragraph, and work with children to identify the key words and phrases. Model writing notes for the paragraph, and have children copy your notes.	Read aloud the first paragraph. Ask children to identify the most important information about the nighttime sky. Have them write key words and short phrases to record this information.	Have children take notes about these pages. Then, have pairs review their notes and determine if they recorded the key information.

Use Question Words ELPS 2C, 3B, 3F

After reading **TE pages 276–277,** have children practice using question words that are commonly used in the classroom.

Beginning	Intermediate	Advanced/Advanced High
Ask simple questions related to the nighttime sky: *Where would you see the moon? When can you see stars? What else do you see at night?*	Model asking simple questions: *What page are we reading? Where is the moon? How do you know when it is night?* Have children identify each question word.	Write *what, where,* and *when* on a chart. Have children use these words to ask partners questions about the nighttime sky. Have Advanced High ELLs ask questions with *why* and *how* as well.

Request Assistance ELPS 1D, 2D, 3F

After reading aloud **TE pages 286–287,** give children an opportunity to seek clarification of anything they did not understand.

Beginning	Intermediate	Advanced/Advanced High
Use gestures and visuals to help children understand the meaning of *shadow.* As you talk, have children give "thumbs up" to indicate they understand the information or "thumbs down" to show that they need clarification.	Model questions children can ask to clarify anything they do not understand: *Can you explain what a shadow is again? Can you show me what a shadow looks like? Can you repeat what you said about how shadows change?*	Review the information about how light from the sun makes shadows. Then, have children ask questions to seek clarification about what they heard.

Objects in the Sky

I Wonder Why

Ask children to consider why we see the moon at night, but not the sun. Use a diagram or materials such as a solar-system mobile to demonstrate where sunlight hits Earth and the moon at night. Encourage children to use the information you present to speculate on the answer to the "why" question.

Here's Why

Have children turn the page and read the response to the question. You may wish to share the following background with them.

More About...

The Moon

Like Earth, the moon is about 4.6 billion years old. It is the only natural object in the solar system other than Earth that humans have walked on. The moon moves in different ways. It spins around its own axis and also moves in a circular path around Earth. Where the moon is located in relation to Earth and to the sun determines how much of the moon people see from Earth. Sometimes we can see only a small sliver of the moon, and other times we can see a full moon.

Science Songs

See pp. TR40–TR45 for science songs you can use to reinforce content in this unit.

Professional Development Science Background

Use the keywords to access
- Professional Development from **The NSTA Learning Center**
- **SciLinks** for additional online content appropriate for children and teachers
- Teacher Science Background in the back of this Teacher Edition

Keywords

atmosphere
planetary cycles
solar system
stars

Here's Why The moon reflects light from the sun. This makes it look lit at nighttime.

In this unit, you will explore this Big Idea, the Essential Questions, and the Investigations on the Inquiry Flipchart.

Levels of Inquiry Key ■ DIRECTED ■ GUIDED ■ INDEPENDENT

Track Your Progress

Big Idea Many objects can be seen in the sky. The appearance of these objects can change.

Essential Questions

Science Notebook

Before you begin each lesson, be sure to write your thoughts about the Essential Question.

Go Digital

For a complete digital curriculum and resources that provide full coverage of the objectives for this unit, see the Online Resources for this program.

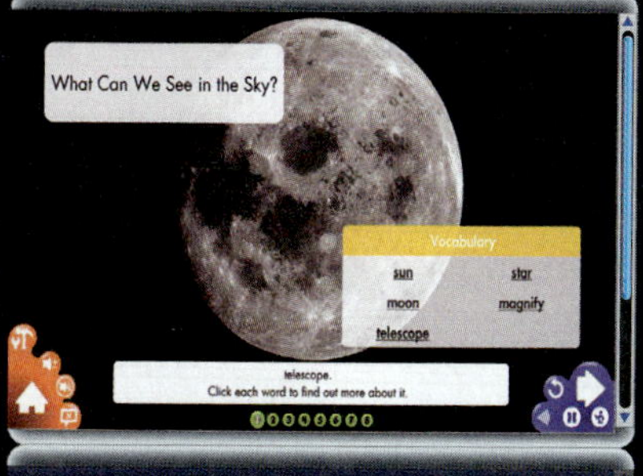

Big Idea and Essential Questions

Big Idea Many objects can be seen in the sky. The appearance of these objects can change.

Post the Unit Big Idea on the board. Have children read the Essential Questions, which are also the titles of the lessons in this unit.

- Discuss how the Essential Questions can help keep them focused on the Big Idea.
- Have children read the Big Idea statement. The statement describes the main science concept that they will be learning.
- Have children predict other ideas that will be taught in the lessons based on the titles, or have them give examples of pictures they expect to see.

Once they complete the unit, they should have a better understanding of the Big Idea.

Essential Questions You may use the following Science Notebook strategy for working with the Essential Questions before children begin the unit or before each lesson.

- Strategies for revisiting the Big Idea and Essential Questions are provided in Enduring Understandings on p. 299A.

Notebook Science Notebook

- Have children copy the Essential Questions into their Science Notebooks. Suggest they leave several writing lines between questions.
- Ask children to write responses to the Essential Questions. Urge them not to worry about whether their responses are correct. They should expect their ideas to change as they work in the unit. Comment that children will be able to review and revise their answers to the Essential Questions at the end of the unit.
- Tips and strategies for using Science Notebooks are provided throughout this unit, in the back of this Teacher Edition, and in the Online Resources.

Options for Inquiry

FLIPCHART P. 36

Children can conduct these optional investigations at any time before, during, or in response to the lesson in the Student Edition.

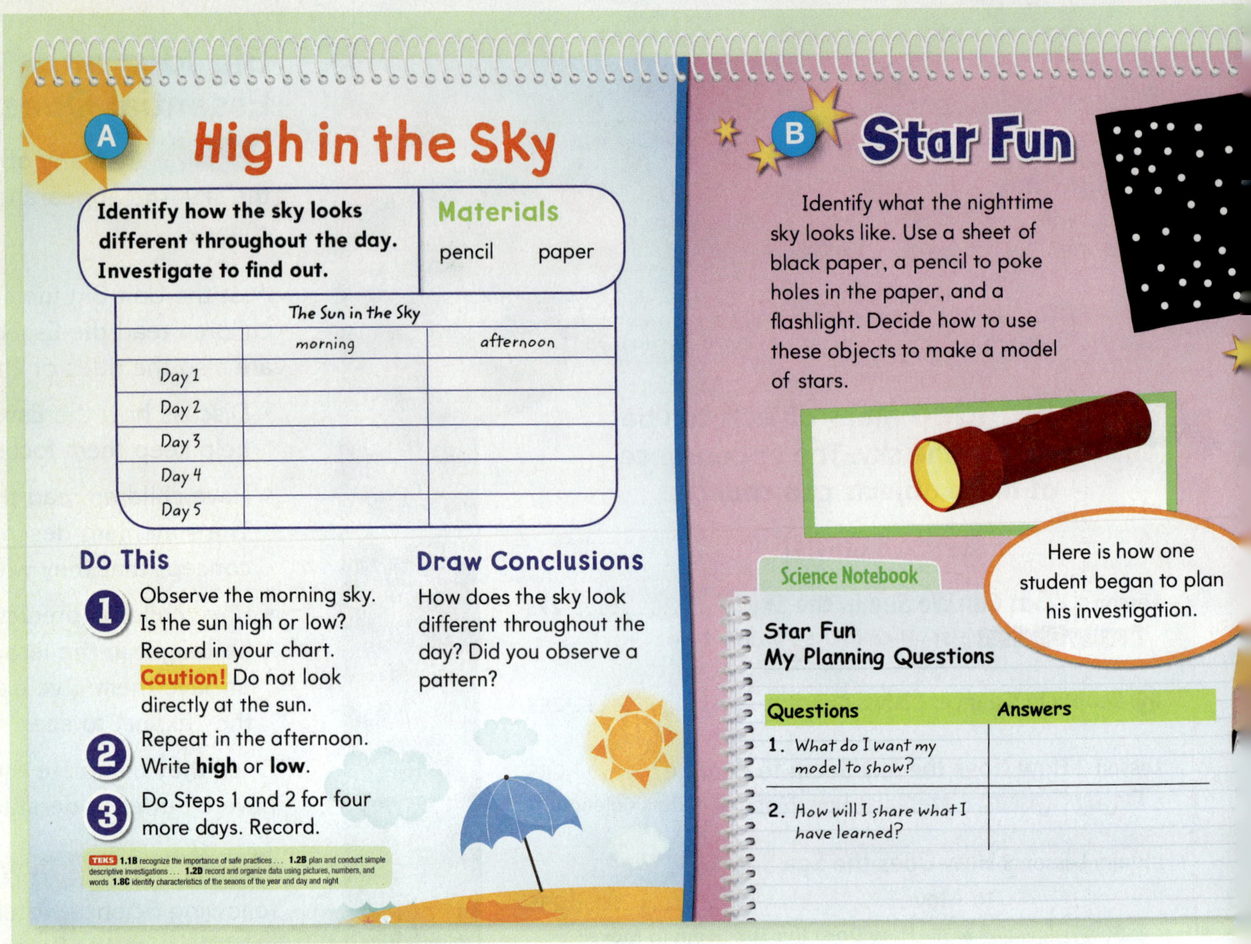

Directed Inquiry

A High in the Sky

10 minutes
individuals

Prep and Planning Tips

If possible, have children make their observations first thing in the morning and soon after lunch.

Allow 10 minutes each day for a week for children to observe and record their observations.

Some children may find it easier to draw or dictate their observations.

Caution! Be sure children recognize the importance of safe practices to keep themselves safe and healthy by reminding them not to look directly at the sun.

Expected Results

Children will determine where the sun is in the morning and in the afternoon and whether there is a difference in position between the two times. Guide them to conclude that the sun's position in the sky appears to change throughout the day.

Independent Inquiry

B Star Fun

15 minutes
pairs

Prep and Planning Tips

See the Planning for Inquiry page for more information. You may wish to make holes in the paper for children or use a hole punch instead of having children punch holes with the pencil point.

Caution! Be sure children recognize and demonstrate safe practices to keep themselves and others safe and healthy by reminding them to be careful when poking holes with a pencil point and never to shine a flashlight into anyone's eyes.

Science Notebook

Children can use the Science Notebook as a model for planning and conducting their own investigation. Encourage them to make a chart like the one shown and include the sample questions plus their own questions.

TEKS 1.8C identify characteristics of the seasons of the year and day and night

Lesson 1

Essential Question

What Can We See in the Sky?

Engage Your Brain!

Find the answer to the question in the lesson.

When can you see the moon?

at night and sometimes in the day

Active Reading

Lesson Vocabulary

1. Preview the lesson.
2. Write the 5 vocabulary terms here.

sun | magnify

star | telescope

moon

Inquiry Flipchart **p. 36—High in the Sky/Star Fun**

Go Digital

n interactive digital esson is available in Online esources. It is suitable for dividuals, small groups, or ay be projected or used n an interactive white oard.

1 Engage/Explore

Objectives

- Recognize the importance of safe practices to keep self and others safe and healthy.
- Plan and conduct simple investigations.
- Record and organize data.
- Identify characteristics of day and night.

Engage Your Brain!

Help children answer the question *When can you see the moon?* by asking them to think of their own experiences and describe what the moon looks like in the sky. Then focus their attention on the photograph and ask children whether they have ever seen the moon at any other time.

Remind them to record their final answer to the question when they find it on the second and fourth pages of the lesson.

Active Reading Annotations

Remind children that active readers "make texts their own" by marking them or writing notes to help them understand what they are reading. Encourage children to use pencil to make annotations and to feel free to change their marks and notes as they read. The goal of annotation is to help children remember what they have read.

Vocabulary and Interactive Glossary

Remind children to find and list the yellow highlighted terms from the lesson. As they proceed through the lesson and learn about the terms, they can add drawings or words in the extra spaces provided in some entries in the Interactive Glossary.

2 Explain

Notebook Generate Ideas

Read the heading on this page aloud to children. Then ask them to share what they know about objects that appear in the daytime sky. List their ideas on the board, and return to this list after reading this page and the next.

Active Reading Main Idea

Explain that the main, or most important, idea may be the first sentence in a paragraph. Or, it may be a different sentence. Active readers ask themselves, "What is this paragraph mostly about?" The answer will be the main idea.

Develop Science Concepts

Use the information on these pages to help children identify characteristics of the day.

Point out that the biggest difference between day and night is light. **Where does daylight come from?** It comes from the sun. **Why is the sky dark at night?** There is no sun providing light.

Read the first three sentences aloud. **Which sentence states the main idea? How do you know?** The second sentence states the main idea because it tells what the rest of the paragraph is about.

Point out that the rest of the page has details about things in the daytime sky. **What things might you see in the daytime sky?** the sun, clouds, and maybe the moon

Good Morning, Sunshine

Look up! You can see many things in the daytime sky. You can see the sun. The **sun** is the star closest to Earth. A **star** is an object in the sky. It gives off its own light. The sun gives light and heat to Earth. It warms Earth's land, air, and water.

You may also see clouds in the daytime sky. Sometimes, you can even see the moon.

Active Reading

The main idea is the most important idea about something. Draw two lines under the main idea.

274

Differentiation—Leveled Questions

Extra Support

How do you know that the sun is a star? I know the sun is a star because it is an object in the sky that gives off light.

Challenge

Why is it difficult to see the moon in the daytime when the sky is sunny? The sun is so brig that it makes it difficult to see the moon.

▶ **Look out your window. Identify what the daytime sky looks like. Draw what you see.**

Drawings will vary but should be reasonable representations of what children can see in the daytime sky.

275

Writing Connection

TEKS ELA 1.24C

Write a Sentence Share the poem "Star Light, Star Bright" with children:

"Star light, star bright,
The first star I see tonight,
I wish I may, I wish I might,
Have the wish I wish tonight."

Write this sentence starter on the board and help children read it: My wish is ______.

Have children draw a picture about a wish they might make and then copy and complete the sentence describing this wish.

TEKS 1.8C

Develop Science Vocabulary

sun Write the words *sun* and *sunny* on the board. Explain that *sun* is a naming word, or noun. Explain that *sunny* is a describing word, or adjective, that tells what it is like when the sun is shining. Have children use both words in a sentence.

star Explain that the word *star* comes from the Greek word *aster* and the Latin word *stella*. **What do you think the girl's name Stella might mean?** star

Misconception Alert

Children may think that the sun moves across the sky. Explain that the sun stays in one place while Earth rotates. Demonstrate by attaching a sticky note to mark the children's approximate location on a globe. Using the globe and a flashlight, rotate the globe and have children identify when they would see a daytime and a nighttime sky where they live.

Develop Inquiry Skills

INFER **Is the sun still in the sky on a stormy day? How do you know?** Yes; you know this because the sun is always in the daytime sky, although sometimes it is hidden behind clouds.

Notebook Summarize Ideas

Ask children to look back at the photographs and think about the main idea they learned about the daytime sky. Have them summarize this idea orally with partners by completing this sentence: "In the daytime, the sky ___."

2 Explain (continued)

Notebook Generate Ideas

Read the heading "Good Night, Sky" aloud to children. Remind them that this lesson is about things we see in the sky. Ask them what objects they might see in the nighttime sky. Record these responses on the board and review them after children have read these pages.

Active Reading Details

Explain that a detail sentence may give an example, or it may describe something. Active readers ask themselves, "What does this detail sentence tell about?" The answer will help readers keep the main idea in mind.

Develop Science Concepts

Use the information on these pages to help children identify characteristics of the night.

Think about what the moon is made of. Why can't the moon make its own light? A rock cannot make light.

What are two ways the moon and the sun are alike? Both are big, round spheres. Both are found in the sky.

Explain that there are many stars in the sky and that we can only see some of them. There are too many stars to easily count. Also tell children that the stars are not evenly spaced in the sky.

Good Night, Sky

moon

You can identify what the nighttime sky looks like. You may see the moon. The **moon** is a large sphere, or ball of rock. It does not give off its own light. You may also see clouds at night.

Active Reading

Draw one line under a detail. Draw an arrow to the main idea it tells about.

276

Differentiation—Leveled Questions

Extra Support

What do we call the large sphere of rock that we often see in the nighttime sky? the moon

Challenge

Could you sit outside at night and count all the stars in the sky? No there are too many star to count.

You may see stars in the nighttime sky. There are too many stars to count. They are not evenly spaced in the sky.

Do the Math!

Compare Solid Shapes

Many objects in the sky are spheres. A sphere is a round ball. The moon is a sphere. So is the sun. Color the spheres below. Children should color the first shape and the last shape.

277

English Language Learners

ELPS 1C, 2C, 2E

Reinforce Basic Vocabulary Write the word *moon* on the board. Have children repeat the word after you. Ask children to circle the word *moon* in their book. Then have children draw a picture of the nighttime sky and label the moon. Then ask children to identify other objects in their pictures, such as stars.

TEKS 1.8C

Develop Science Vocabulary

moon Write the word *moon* on the board and direct children's attention to the double *o*'s. Explain that an *o* reminds you of the full moon that you sometimes see in the nighttime sky. Have children use their fingers to make a round o shape and repeat the word *moon*.

Develop Inquiry Skills

USE MODELS Help children understand what it means when we say that stars are not evenly spaced. Display a U.S. flag and point to the stars. Explain that the stars make a regular pattern. Using pattern blocks, help children reproduce this pattern of alternating rows of six stars and five stars. Discuss what the flag might look like if the stars were not evenly spaced. Have children illustrate their ideas with a random arrangement of blocks.

Interpret Visuals

Focus children's attention on the photograph of the nighttime sky. Remind children that they can use information in this photograph to complete their answer to the Engage Your Brain! question.

Do the Math!

TEKS MATH 1.6E

Have children pronounce the word *sphere* as they circle the word. To help them observe the difference between a sphere and a circle, display a ball and a plate.

Notebook Summarize Ideas

Remind children that three objects—stars, the moon, and clouds are often found in the nighttime sky. Then have them identify which are spheres.

2 Explain (continued)

Notebook Generate Ideas

Remind children that large stars look tiny because they are very far away. Explain that scientists use tools called telescopes to look at faraway stars. If possible, display a toy telescope and demonstrate how to use it. Ask children what they know about telescopes, and record their ideas on the board. Add to this list after reading.

Develop Science Concepts

How do you use a telescope? You point the telescope at an object and look through the telescope to see a larger image of the object.

Why do scientists use telescopes when looking at objects in the sky? A telescope magnifies faraway things so we can see them better.

Suppose you wanted to view the nighttime sky through a telescope. Would you choose a clear night or a cloudy night to do your viewing? Why? a clear night because on a cloudy night, the stars and the moon might be behind the clouds

What are some other tools you know about that can make things look bigger? Sample answer: microscopes, magnifying glasses, cameras

Why It Matters

Eye on the Sky

Stars and other objects in the sky look small. We can magnify them to see them better. **Magnify** means to make something look bigger. A **telescope** is a tool that helps us magnify things in the sky.

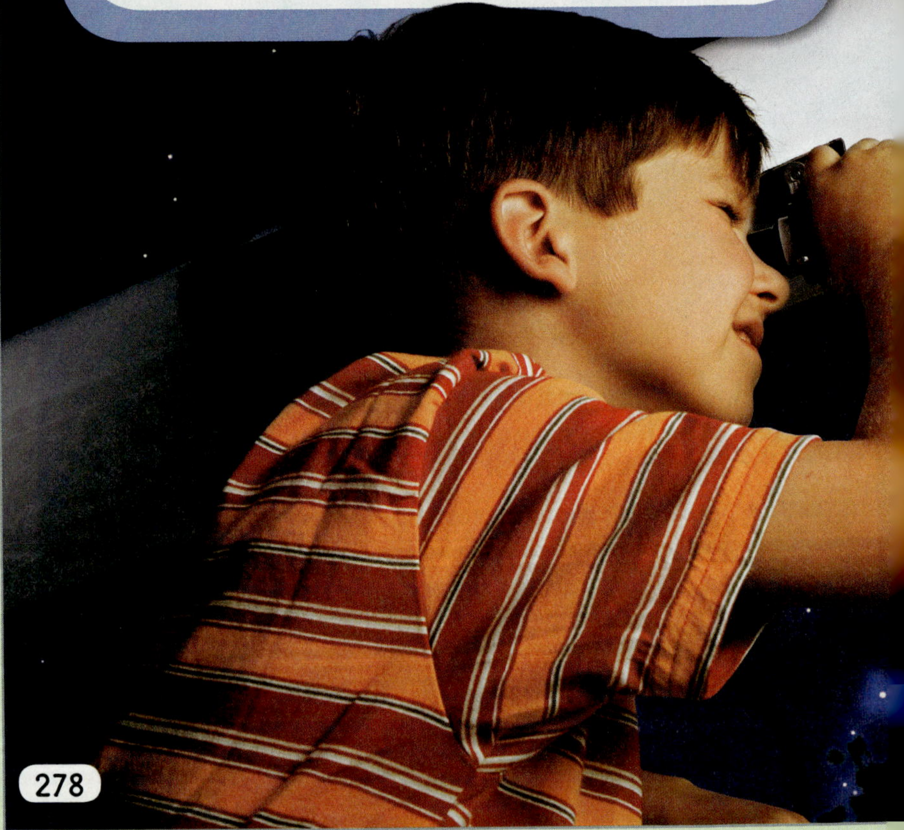

278

telescope

▶ Which picture shows the moon through a telescope? Mark an X on it.

Both pictures show the moon.

279

Writing Connection

TEKS ELA 1.19A

Write a Journal Entry Have children write short journal entries telling what else they would like to discover by viewing the moon with a telescope. Tell them to use the photographs on this page as well as what they already know about the moon.

TEKS 1.8C

Develop Science Vocabulary

magnify Demonstrate how a hand lens can magnify the print in a book. Have children describe which print is being *magnified.*

telescope Explain that the word *telescope* comes from two Greek words that mean "far-seeing." Give examples of near and distant objects such as a penny, the moon, an insect, and a mountain peak. Have children identify which things could be observed with a telescope.

Interpret Visuals

What is alike and different about the pictures on this page? Both show the moon; however, one shows what the moon looks like with your eyes and the other shows the view through a telescope. **How do you know which moon to mark?** You mark the one that shows more detail because a telescope magnifies things.

Develop Inquiry Skills

COMMUNICATE **Suppose I asked you to write a caption for each moon picture. What would you write?** Sample answer: the moon viewed with just your eyes; the moon viewed through a telescope

Notebook Summarize Ideas

Direct children to think about the details on these pages. Ask whether their ideas about telescopes and their use have changed from reading this section. Have them summarize these details orally or in writing.

3 Extend/Evaluate

Sum It Up!

1. **Solve It!** Read the riddle aloud with children and help them identify the three clues. If they need help figuring out the answer, have them reread the definitions of the yellow highlighted words on the "Why It Matters" pages.
2. **Circle It!** Before reading each statement aloud, remind children that circling the word *true* means they agree with the statement and circling the word *false* means they disagree with the statement. After children respond, have them rephrase the false statement to make it true.
3. **Draw It!** Before children draw, remind them that the picture in the left box should show the daytime sky and the picture in the right box should show the nighttime sky. Point out that the pictures can show what is alike and what is different about the sky at the two times.

Sum It Up!

1 Solve It!

Solve the riddle.

I am a tool. I make things look bigger. You can use me to observe things in the sky.
What am I?

telescope

2 Circle It!

Circle true or false.

Stars are evenly spaced in the sky.
true (false)

Stars give off their own light.
(true) false

3 Draw It!

Draw what you can see in the sky at both times.

daytime	nighttime

Drawings will vary but should reflect children's understanding of objects that can be seen in the daytime and nighttime sky.

280

ople in Science continued

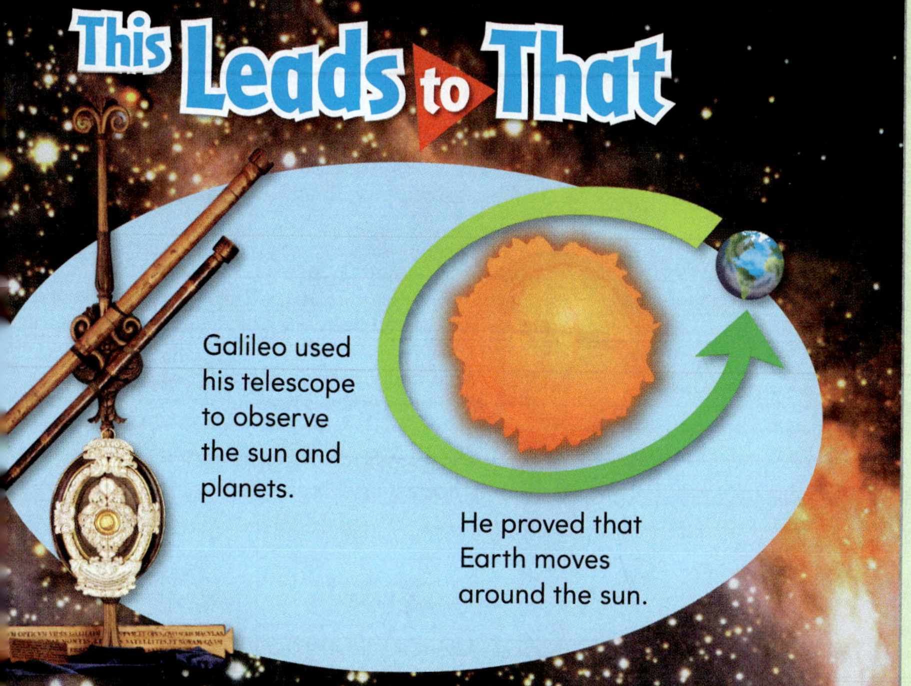

▶ **People used to think that the sun moved around Earth. Galileo proved this was wrong. Why is this important?**

Sample answer: It changed the way people thought about the sun and Earth.

Nature of Science

Share the following scenario: *You have just heard about the invention of a pair of eyeglasses that let people see in the dark. You want to improve this invention.* Tell children to think like scientists and list three questions they would ask themselves when trying to improve this invention. Sample answers: What can these glasses do? Who will use these glasses and how? How can I change these glasses so people can see farther or more clearly?

TEKS 1.3C

Develop Science Concepts

Describe what Galileo did. He used a telescope to observe the sun and planets. He proved that Earth moves around the sun.

How do you think the world would be different if Galileo had not made his discoveries? Sample answer: People might still think the sun moves around Earth. We would not know as much about the sun, moon, and planets.

Galileo made his telescope after hearing about someone else's magnifier made in another country. Why do you think scientists like Galileo build on the work of others? It lets them make new discoveries that improve our understanding of how things work or what things are.

How do you build on the work of your classmates? Sample answer: I listen to what they have to say; I compare their ideas with my ideas. I use some of their ideas to help me come up with my own ideas.

Develop Inquiry Skills

OBSERVE **What senses did Galileo use to make his discoveries?** He used his improved telescope to observe things in the sky using his sense of sight. Remind children that they, too, use their senses and tools like magnifiers to make observations that can change their thinking. **What is one way your observations changed the way you thought about something in the sky? Why was this important?** Answers will vary; children should give examples of how their thinking was changed by observation.

Notebook Summarize Ideas

Ask children what they learned about Galileo Galilei and his invention and discoveries, and how they changed people's understanding of the sun and planets. Have them summarize these ideas orally or in writing.

Options for Inquiry

FLIPCHART P. 37

Children can conduct these optional investigations at any time before, during, or in response to the lesson in the Student Edition.

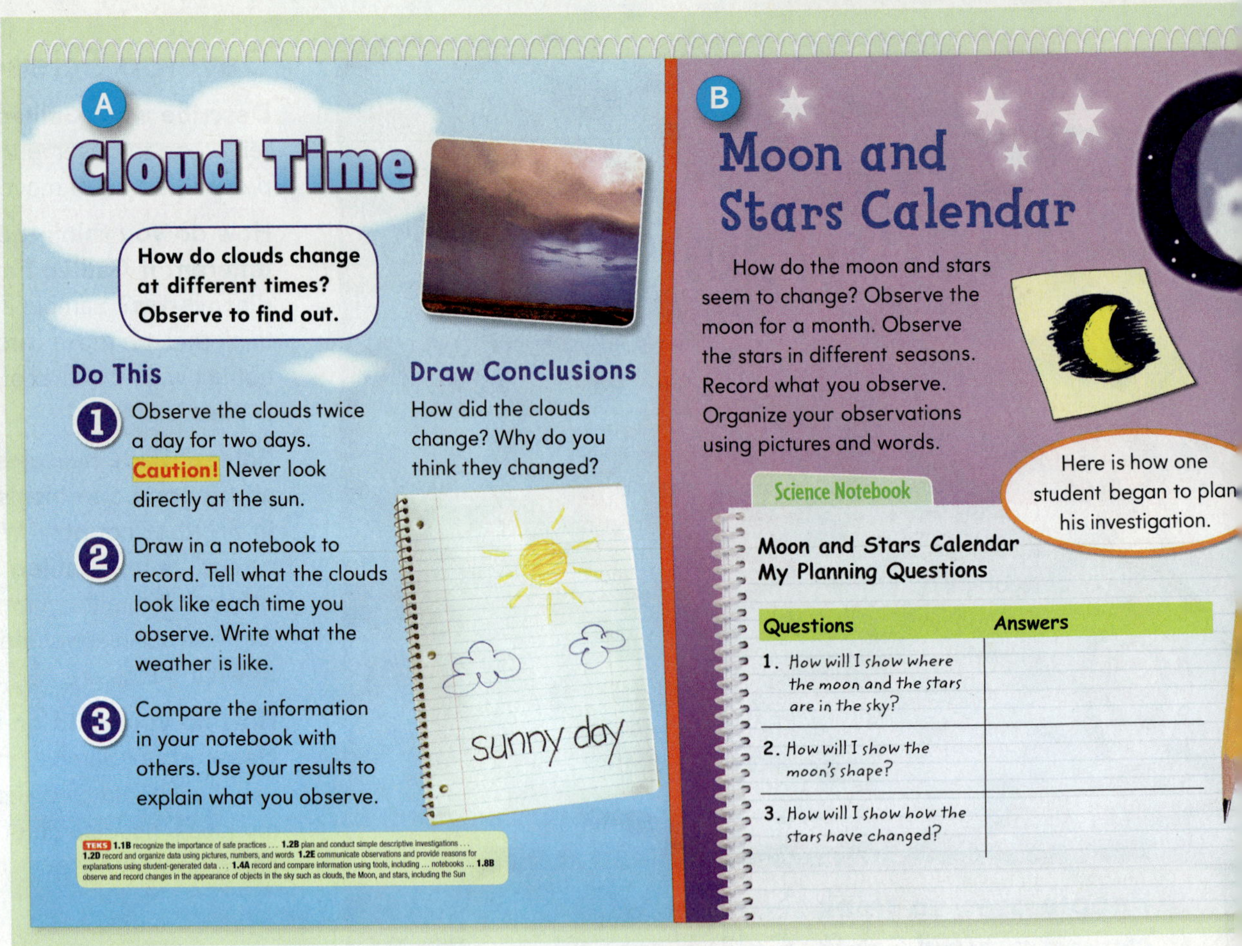

A Cloud Time

How do clouds change at different times? Observe to find out.

Do This

1. Observe the clouds twice a day for two days. **Caution!** Never look directly at the sun.
2. Draw in a notebook to record. Tell what the clouds look like each time you observe. Write what the weather is like.
3. Compare the information in your notebook with others. Use your results to explain what you observe.

Draw Conclusions

How did the clouds change? Why do you think they changed?

sunny day

TEKS **1.1B** recognize the importance of safe practices . . . **1.2B** plan and conduct simple descriptive investigations . . . **1.2D** record and organize data using pictures, numbers, and words **1.2E** communicate observations and provide reasons for explanations using student-generated data . . . **1.4A** record and compare information using tools, including . . . notebooks . . . **1.8B** observe and record changes in the appearance of objects in the sky such as clouds, the Moon, and stars, including the Sun

B Moon and Stars Calendar

How do the moon and stars seem to change? Observe the moon for a month. Observe the stars in different seasons. Record what you observe. Organize your observations using pictures and words.

Here is how one student began to plan his investigation.

Science Notebook

Moon and Stars Calendar
My Planning Questions

Questions	Answers
1. How will I show where the moon and the stars are in the sky?	
2. How will I show the moon's shape?	
3. How will I show how the stars have changed?	

Directed Inquiry

A Cloud Time

15–20 minutes for two days
individuals

Prep and Planning Tips

To help children organize their observations, you may wish to have them label two notebook pages Day 1 and Day 2, and then divide each page in half so that observations from the first viewing are recorded on the top of the page and observations from the second viewing go on the bottom of the page.

Caution! Remind children to recognize the importance of safe practices to keep themselves safe and healthy, by not looking directly at the sun while completing this activity. Remind them to focus on the clouds, and also take note of the weather conditions.

Expected Results

Children should observe that clouds change shape and color from day to day, and that certain types of clouds are more likely to correlate with certain types of weather (for example, white clouds appear on sunny days and gray clouds appear on rainy days).

Independent Inquiry

B Moon and Stars Calendar

5 minutes each day for a month
5 minutes one night during each season
individuals

Prep and Planning Tips

See the Planning for Inquiry page for more information. Remind children to have adult supervision when making their observations. Be sure children record the appearance of the moon each night for a month as well as taking one night during each season to record the appearance of the stars.

Science Notebook

Children can use the Science Notebook on the flipchart as a model for planning and conducting their own investigation. Encourage them to make a chart like the one shown and include the sample questions plus their own questions. Have children brainstorm safe and accessible places where they might be able to make their observations.

EKS 1.3B make predictions based on observable patterns 1.8B observe and record changes the appearance of objects in the sky such as clouds, the Moon, and stars, including the Sun

Lesson 2

Essential Question

How Does the Sky Seem to Change?

Engage Your Brain!

Find the answer to the question in the lesson.

Why does the sun seem to move across the sky?

Earth turns.

Active Reading

Lesson Vocabulary

1. Preview the lesson.
2. Write the 2 vocabulary terms here.

shadow phases

nquiry Flipchart p. 37—Cloud Time/Moon and Stars Calendar

Go Digital

n interactive digital esson is available in Online esources. It is suitable for ndividuals, small groups, or nay be projected or used n an interactive white oard.

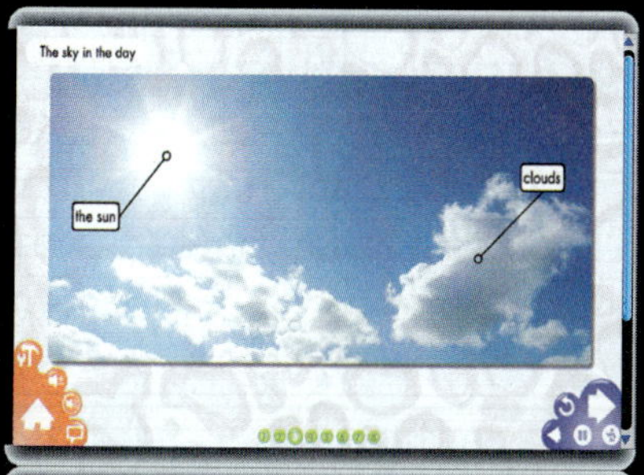

1 Engage/Explore

Objectives

- Recognize the importance of safe practices.
- Plan and conduct simple investigations.
- Record and organize data.
- Communicate observations and provide reasons for explanations from investigations.
- Make predictions based on observable patterns.
- Collect and compare information using notebooks.
- Observe and record changes in the appearance of objects in the sky.

Engage Your Brain!

Call on volunteers to describe the sun's position in the photograph. Then ask children to tell whether the sun stays in that position throughout the day and explain how they know. Have them use that discussion to help answer the question.

Remind children to record their final answer to the question when they find it on the second page of the lesson.

Active Reading Annotations

Remind children that active readers "make texts their own" by marking them or writing notes to help them understand what they are reading. Encourage children to use pencil to make annotations and to feel free to change their marks and notes as they read. The goal of annotation is to help children remember what they have read.

Vocabulary and Interactive Glossary

Remind children to find and list the yellow highlighted terms from the lesson. As they proceed through the lesson and learn about the terms, they can add drawings or words in the extra spaces provided in some of the entries in the Interactive Glossary.

2 Explain

Notebook Generate Ideas

Read aloud the heading with children. Then dim the lights, and use a flashlight and your hand to cast a shadow. Ask children what they think causes shadows outside during the day. Record their ideas, and review them after studying these two pages.

Active Reading Main Idea

Explain that the main, or most important, idea may be the first sentence in a paragraph. Or it may be a different sentence. Active readers ask themselves, What is this paragraph mostly about? The answer will be the main idea.

Read the first paragraph. **Which sentence states the main idea? How do you know?** The first sentence states the main idea because the paragraph is about the sun appearing to move.

Develop Science Concepts

The sun seems to move across the sky. Does it? Explain. No, the sun does not really move. Earth turns and makes the sun appear to move.

How does the sun appear in the sky in the morning and late afternoon? It appears low. **How does it appear at noon?** It appears high. **This is a pattern that repeats. Why?** It repeats every day because Earth turns each day.

For the interactive, remind children to not look directly at the sun. Guide them to make and record observations about how the appearance of the sun seems to change in the sky throughout the day.

Hello, Shadow

The sun seems to move across the sky. But the sun is not moving. It is really Earth that is moving. Each day, Earth turns all the way around.

In the morning and late afternoon the sun seems low in the sky. It seems high at noon. This is a pattern that repeats each day as Earth turns.

Active Reading
The main idea is the most important idea about something. Draw two lines under the main idea.

286

English Language Learners

ELPS 1E, 1F, 2I

Reinforce Basic Vocabulary
Write the words *sun*, *sky*, *light*, and *shadow* on the board and help children read them aloud. Have them draw and label a picture for each word. Then ask children to take turns reading the words to each other.

TEKS 1.3B, 1.8B

Light from the sun makes shadows. A **shadow** is a dark place made where an object blocks light. Shadows change as Earth moves. The sun's light shines on objects from different directions as the day goes on. Shadows change in size during the day. They change position, too.

▶ **Observe and record how the sun seems to change during the day.**

The sun seems low in the morning and late afternoon sky. It seems high at noon.

287

Differentiation—Leveled Questions

Extra Support

What is a shadow and how is it made? A shadow is a dark place that is made when an object blocks light.

Challenge

Can your shadow ever appear longer than you are tall? Explain. Yes, in the early morning and late afternoon, your shadow could be longer because the sun appears to be low in the sky.

Develop Science Vocabulary

shadow Use a lamp and your hand to show how an object blocks light to make a shadow. Help children use the demonstration to reinforce their understanding of the meaning of *shadow* as a place where light is blocked.

Interpret Visuals

Focus children's attention on the three pictures at the bottom of the pages. **What do these pictures show?** a girl's shadow in the morning, at noon, and in the afternoon

Remind children that something must block light for a shadow to form. **Where is the sun in the morning? How do you know?** The sun is on the left side of the girl. I know because the shadow is on the right side of the girl. **Ask similar questions about the other images.**

When is the girl's shadow the shortest? Why? It is shortest at noon because the sun is directly overhead, so less of the girl blocks the light.

Develop Inquiry Skills

MAKE A MODEL Provide children with a flashlight and a block. Have them hold the flashlight to the left, right, and directly above the block and note the position and length of the shadows. Ask them to summarize the results.

Notebook Summarize Ideas

Have children look again at the photographs on these two pages. Ask them to summarize orally or in writing why the sun appears to move and how it makes shadows that can change in size and position.

2 Explain (continued)

Notebook Generate Ideas

Write this riddle on the board and help children read it: *What is round, but not always around in the sky?* Before children guess, suggest that they preview these pages to help figure out the answer.

Active Reading Details

Explain that a detail sentence may give an example, or it may describe something. Active readers ask themselves, What topic does this detail sentence tell about? The answer will help readers keep the main idea in mind.

Develop Science Concepts

What might you see in the nighttime sky? some stars and the moon

What is the moon? a huge ball of rock

Think about the light from the moon. How is it different from the sun? The sun makes its own light; the moon reflects light from the sun.

Interpret Visuals

Direct attention to the diagram of the moon phases. Ask children to describe what they see.

What does this diagram show? Guide children to understand that it shows the phases, or moon shapes, that they can see in the sky as the moon moves.

What is the purpose of the captions in this diagram? The captions tell the name of each phase of the moon.

Just a Phase

Now it is night. You may see stars. You may see the moon. The moon is a huge ball of rock. It does not give off its own light. The moon reflects light from the sun.

Active Reading

A detail is a fact about a main idea. Draw one line under a detail. Draw an arrow to the main idea it tells about.

new moon

first quarter moon

Differentiation—Leveled Questions

Extra Support

What are the moon's phases? They are the moon's shapes that people can see from Earth.

Challenge

During which phase of the moon would you most likely se[e] nighttime shadows? Why? duri[ng] a full moon, because the moon i[s] brightest and reflecting the mos[t] light from the sun

The moon moves across the sky. Its shape seems to change. The **phases**, or shapes you see, change as the moon moves. The changes follow a repeating pattern. It lasts about a month.

▶ **Observe the full moon below. Predict what the moon's phase will be in about a month. Record it.**

a full moon

full moon

third quarter moon

English Language Learners

ELPS 1E, 1F, 2E

Reinforce Basic Vocabulary
Have children make their own picture dictionary of the four moon phases. The dictionary should include four pages, or cards. Each page should include a picture of one moon phase and a caption that labels the phase. Ask children to read their labels to a partner.

Develop Science Vocabulary

phases Write *phases* on the board and have children pronounce it with you, paying particular attention to the initial /f/. Point out the images at the bottom of these pages, and review that they show the phases of the moon. Have volunteers read the name of each phase.

Develop Science Concepts

Why does the moon appear to change shape during the month? The moon appears to change shape because it moves across the sky. **Why do we say that the phases of the moon follow a repeating pattern?** A pattern is anything that repeats, and the phases of the moon repeat about every month. **Suppose that there is a new moon today. About how long will it be until there is a new moon again?** about a month

Misconception Alert

Children may think that the unlit part of the moon in a certain phase disappears. It does not. That piece of the moon is just dark and difficult to see from Earth. In the pictures on these pages, on a very dark night, or with binoculars or a telescope, it is easy to see that the whole moon is still there.

Develop Inquiry Skills

MAKE A MODEL Have pairs model how the moon reflects sunlight by using a flashlight to represent sunlight and a white ball to represent the moon. **Why does the moon shine?** It reflects light from the sun.

Notebook Summarize Ideas

Reread the riddle and ask children to explain why the moon is round, but not always around (visible). Then have them summarize orally or in writing the details they learned about the moon and its phases.

2 Explain (continued)

Notebook Generate Ideas

Lead children in singing the first verse of "Twinkle, Twinkle, Little Star." Then ask them what they think stars are. Record those ideas on the board, and return to them to correct any ongoing misconceptions after children learn about stars.

Develop Science Concepts

When and where can you see stars? You can see stars in the nighttime sky.

How are nighttime stars like the sun? How are they different? Both give off their own light; both are kinds of stars. You can see the sun only in the day; you can see other stars only at night.

How are clouds like the moon? You can see clouds in the daytime and nighttime sky.

Why is it difficult to see stars on a cloudy night? The clouds block our view of the stars.

Misconception Alert

Children may think that stars go away during the day. Guide them to understand that stars are always there, but we just cannot see them in the daytime because the sun is so bright.

Cloudy Day, Starry Night

You can see stars in the nighttime sky. Stars give off light. You see different stars in each season.

You can see clouds in both the daytime and nighttime sky. Clouds change shape from day to day.

You may see these stars in winter.

You may see these stars in summer.

290

Writing Connection

TEKS ELA 1.18

Write a Poem Teach children the traditional wishing rhyme "Star Light, Star Bright." Then have them write a two-line poem that mimics the rhyming pattern of the first two sentences and tells one fact they have learned in this lesson. Have children use sensor details in their poems.

These kinds of clouds may bring rain.

These kinds of clouds can be seen on a sunny day.

▶ **Observe the clouds in the pictures. Record how they changed.**

In the left picture, the clouds are thin and white.

In the right picture, they are thick and gray.

291

Differentiation—Leveled Questions

Extra Support

What are two other things that you can see in the sky besides the sun and the moon? stars and clouds **Which of these things can you only see in the nighttime sky?** stars

Challenge

Why can't we see stars other than the sun in the daytime sky? The sun's light is so bright that it keeps us from seeing the light of other stars in the daytime sky. We can see the stars only when the sun has set and the sky is dark.

TEKS 1.3B, 1.8B

Interpret Visuals

Focus children's attention on the photographs of the clouds. **How do these clouds differ?** They are different sizes, shapes, and colors.

Have children describe the clouds in each picture and then record how the clouds changed.

Explain that clouds appear very dark when less light passes through them. **What might keep light from passing through a cloud?** Sample answer: Many raindrops in the cloud might keep light from passing through it.

You can observe how clouds change. What causes clouds to change shape from day to day? Sample answer: The weather can change the shapes of the clouds.

Develop Inquiry Skills

PREDICT **Suppose you saw dark gray clouds on your way to school. What would you predict the weather might be on your way home? Explain.** Sample answer: Dark clouds often bring rain, so I predict that the weather would be wet and rainy.

Notebook Summarize Ideas

Have children use these sentence starters to summarize orally or in writing what they learned about stars and clouds.

Stars can be seen _____. They are _____.

Clouds can be seen _____. They _____.

3 Extend/Evaluate

Sum It Up!

1. **Solve It!** Have children follow along as you read aloud the riddle. Ask them to picture in their minds, or draw pictures of, what is being described.
2. **Draw It!** Have children read the directions. Remind them that as the position of the sun seems to change, shadows change, too. Guide children to understand that in order to draw where the boy's shadow is in the morning, they will need to think about the sun's position in the sky and where the boy is standing. If children need help, encourage them to refer to the three shadow images in the lesson.
3. **Mark It!** Remind children that the moon appears to change shape in a repeating pattern. Call on a volunteer to read aloud the directions, and then ask children to restate them in their own words. If necessary, explain that "cross out" means the same as "mark with an X." Point out that a full moon and a new moon are moon phases, and children can refer back to the "Just a Phase" spread for help. After children have marked the full and new moon, encourage them to recall the names of the other two phases they learned.

Sum It Up!

1 Solve It!

Write the word to solve the riddle.

I am fluffy or thin.
I am white or gray.
I come out on some days and then go away.
I am a ___cloud___.

2 Draw It!

Draw the boy's shadow in the morning.

Children should draw a morning shadow.

3 Mark It!

Cross out the picture of the full moon. Put a box around the picture of the new moon.

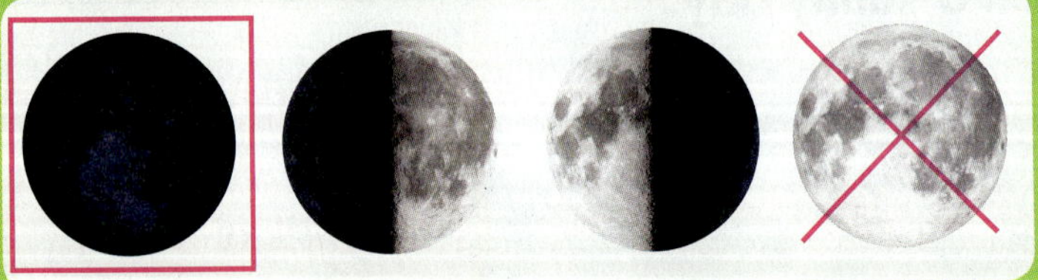

292

TEKS 1.3B, 1.8B

Brain Check

Lesson 2

Name ____________________

Word Play

Label each picture with a word from the box. Match the word to its meaning.

sun	phases	shadow

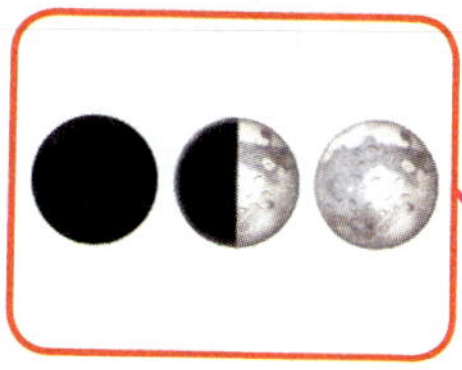

phases

shadow

sun

dark place made where an object blocks light

shapes you see of the moon

brightest object in the daytime sky

293

Answer Strategies

Word Play

- Call on children to read aloud the words in the word box. Point out that a picture and a definition for each word can be found below the word box.
- Review the directions. Explain that children will first label each picture with a word from the word box. Then they will draw lines to match each word with its meaning.
- If children have difficulty, refer them back to the pages in the lesson where the words are defined or discussed.
- Once children have matched the words with their pictures and meanings, have them further demonstrate understanding by using each one in a sentence.

Assessment

Lesson Quiz

See Assessment Guide, p. AG 100.

3 Extend/Evaluate (continued)

Answer Strategies

Apply Concepts

- Before children begin this activity, remind them that when things are put into categories, they are sorted into groups by how they are alike.
- Review the directions and emphasize that, unlike most activities children have done before, the words can be reused in more than one category.
- Point out the chart headings at the top of each column. Allow time for children to scan them.
- Complete the first column with children. Ask them to identify all of the objects that can be seen in the daytime sky. Once they identify clouds, sun, and moon, have them write these words in the column.
- Have children complete the rest of the columns either on their own or with a partner. Encourage them to find illustrations and/or sentences in the text that helped them decide which objects belonged in each category.

Take It Home!

Children and their family members will need to find a convenient time when they can observe how the clouds, the moon, and the stars seem to change. They can draw pictures to record what they see each time and label each picture with the date. Drawings can be shared with classmates.

Apply Concepts

Write the words that tell more about each column. Each word may be used more than once.

sun clouds stars moon

Daytime Sky	Nighttime Sky	Gives Off Its Own Light	Moves or Seems to Move
clouds	clouds	sun	sun
sun	stars	stars	moon
moon	moon		clouds
			stars

Take It Home!

Family Members: Observe objects in the sky, such as the clouds, the moon, and the stars. Ask your child to describe how each of these objects seems to change.

294

Make Connections

Easy

Physical Education Connection

TEKS PE 1.1A, 1.5A, 1.7A

Play a Game of Shadow Tag

- Take children to the playground on a sunny day to play a game of shadow tag, in which the players do not tag a person, but step on his or her shadow instead.

Caution! Remind children to only touch each other's shadows and not to have any physical contact with each other.

- After demonstrating the game, identify who is "it," and have children play several rounds.
- Conclude by asking questions such as: **Does it hurt to have someone step on your shadow? How far away can you be to step on one?**

Easy

Art Connection

TEKS ART 1.2A

Night Sky Scratchboard Pictures

- Distribute a 5" x 8" index card to each child.
- Have children cover the card with a thick layer of light-colored crayon and then paint over the surface with black poster paint mixed with a few drops of dishwashing detergent.
- When the paint is dry, have children use a bent paper clip to scratch a night sky scene through the paint. They should include the moon, clouds, and stars in the sky.

Average

Social Studies/ Art Connection

TEKS SS 1.17B; ART 1.2C

Explore and Make Shadow Puppets

- Provide information about shadow puppets that are popular in many Southeast Asian countries. Encourage children to do their own research to learn more.
- Discuss with children how shadow puppets are held in front of a light source so the shadow is cast on a piece of cloth. Have children work on their own to make the puppets and then collaborate to put on a show.

Challenging

Math Connection

TEKS MATH 1.3A

Interpret a Lunar Calendar

Provide children with a 12-month lunar calendar, which can be found at many online sites. Discuss the symbols used. Then display a list of questions such as the following, and have children use the calendar to answer them: **How many full moons are there this year? Do some months have more than one full moon? How many days are there from a new moon to a full moon? How many days from one full moon to the next?**

Guided Inquiry

FLIPCHART P. 38

20–25 minutes
pairs

Children should follow the directions on the Flipchart. The accompanying pages in the Student Edition provide scaffolding for guided inquiry.

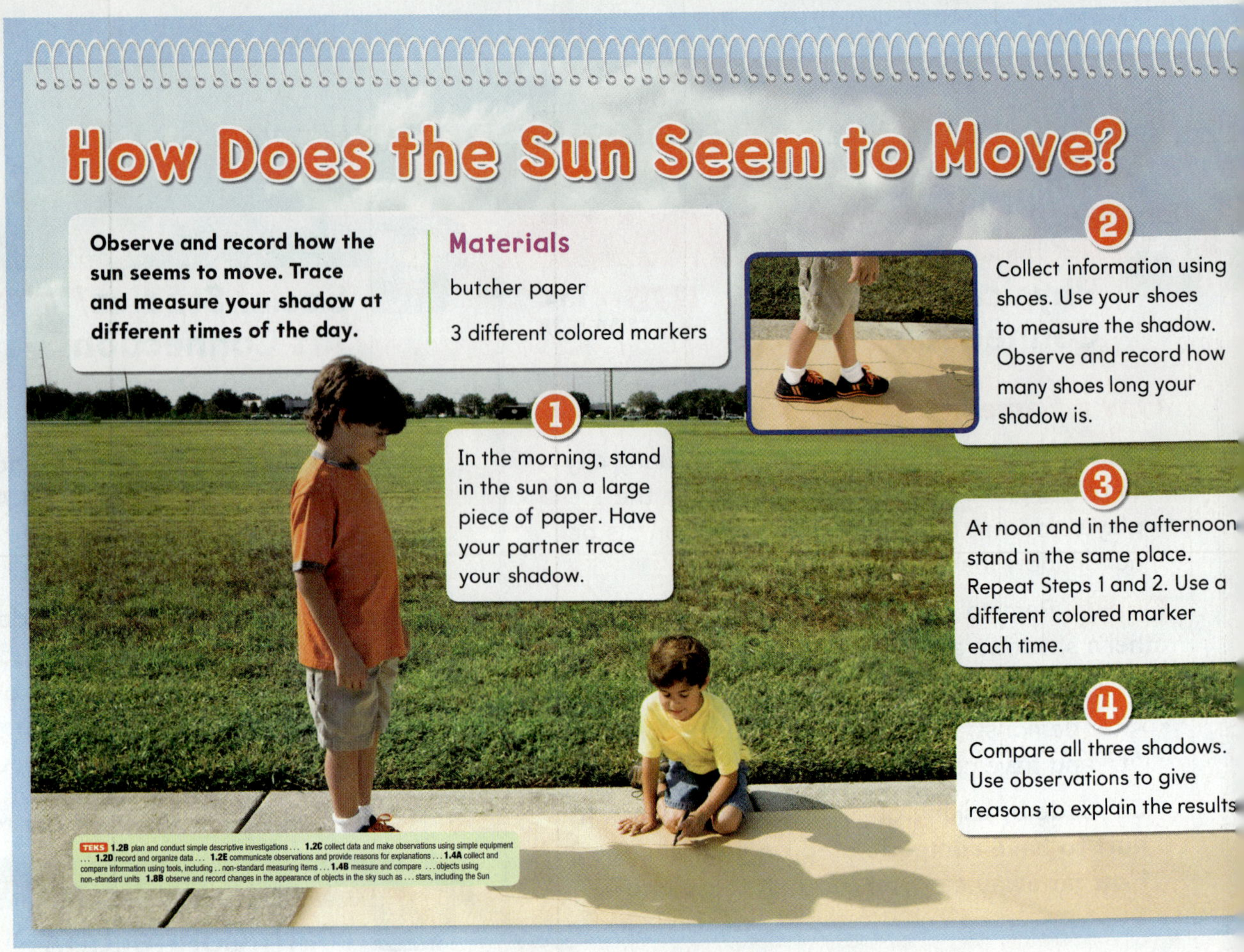

Inquiry Skills Focus Measure

Objectives

- Plan and conduct investigations. Record and organize data.
- Collect and compare information and make observations using non-standard measurement tools and measuring items.
- Communicate observations and provide reasons for explanations using student-generated data.
- Measure and compare objects using non-standard units.
- Observe and record changes in the appearance of objects.

Prep and Planning Tips

See the Planning for Inquiry page for more information.

- Children can also record shadows with chalk on a hard surface.
- Be sure children return to the same measuring spot each time.

Caution! Remind children never to look directly at the sun.

Expected Results

Children will observe that shadows are longer in the morning and afternoon than at noon. They will also find that shadows move during the day as the sun seems to move across the sky.

1 Engage/Explore

Attention Grabber

Share this riddle with children: "I pass before the sun, but make no shadow. What am I?" Once children identify the wind as the answer, ask them if they can think of other things that can pass in front of a light but make no shadow. Guide children to understand that only something "invisible" like the wind or transparent like glass will not cast a shadow if it comes in front of the sun.

Preview Activity

Before beginning the investigation, have children review the directions on the Inquiry Flipchart and the accompanying Student Edition response pages. Then have them complete the response pages as they follow the directions on the Flipchart.

Inquiry Flipchart p. 38

Lesson 3
INQUIRY

TEKS **1.2A** ask questions about organisms, objects, and events observed in the natural world **1.2B** plan and conduct simple descriptive investigations . . . **1.2D** record and organize data using pictures, numbers, and words **1.4A** collect and compare information using tools, including . . . non-standard measuring items . . . **1.4B** measure and compare organisms and objects using non-standard units **1.8B** observe and record changes in the appearance of objects in the sky such as clouds, the Moon, and stars, including the Sun

ame ______________________

Essential Question

How Does the Sun Seem to Move?

et a Purpose

ll what you want to find out.

vant to find out how my shadow changes as the sun seems to

ove during the day.

ink About the Procedure

When will you look at your shadow?

ill look at my shadow in the morning, at noon, and in

afternoon.

How will you know how your shadow changes?

ll trace my shadow and measure it.

295

Go Digital

irtual lab experience is ailable with the Online sources for this program.

1 Engage/Explore (continued)

Guide the Investigation

Develop Inquiry Skills

MEASURE Explain that *measure* means to determine the size or amount of something. Point out that people use different units to measure an object's size, weight, or temperature. Encourage children to discuss experiences that they have had being measured, or times they have measured things at home or in the classroom.

Suppose you wanted to measure the distance from your desk to the classroom door. What property would you be measuring? length

What are some ways you could measure length? Sample answer: You could use a ruler or a tape measure.

How could you measure the distance without using a ruler, yardstick, or tape measure? Sample answer: You could walk from your desk to the door and count your steps.

Point out that another option is to use shoes to measure the distance. Demonstrate how to do a toe-heel walk across the room from your desk to the door, and have children count the number of shoes with you. **How many shoes long is this distance?** Answers will vary. **What unit did we use to measure this distance?** a shoe length

How could we be sure that this measurement is correct? Sample answer: You could remeasure the distance and compare the number of shoe lengths to make sure that they are the same.

2 Explain

Develop Inquiry Skills

RECORD YOUR DATA Discuss with children how they will use the chart to record the length of their shadows at three different times in one day. Discuss the column headings, and have them identify when they will make their observations and in which column they will record each piece of information.

DRAW CONCLUSIONS Review with children that complete answers about shadows include information about changes in both length and position.

To help children understand why the shadows changed, ask them why the change occurred when they were careful to stand in exactly the same place each time. What moved if they did not? Encourage children to use what they know about the sun's apparent movement across the sky when explaining their answers.

3 Extend/Evaluate

ASK MORE QUESTIONS Discuss children's responses to the items. Some children may raise questions about other objects in the sky and whether they move or not. They may also wonder what would happen if they stood in a different place or what shadows would be like on a different day. As an extension activity, ask children to measure shadows in different times and places and compare the results.

Assessment

Lesson Quiz

See Assessment Guide, p. AG 101.

Record Your Data

Write the number of shoes in the chart. Compare them.

Check children's work.

My Shadow's Length

Morning	Noon	Afternoon
______ shoes long	______ shoes long	______ shoes long

Draw Conclusions

How did your shadow change from morning to noon?

It got shorter and changed position.

How did it change from noon to afternoon?

It got longer and changed position again.

Why do you think your shadow changed?

It changed because Earth turned and the sun appeared to be at different places in the sky during the day.

Ask More Questions

What other questions could you ask about how objects seem to move in the sky?

Sample answer: Do the stars move? Does the moon move?

296

Differentiated Inquiry

Easy

Explore a Change in a Nonstandard Measurement Unit

- Provide children with a nonstandard unit that is smaller than a shoe, such as an eraser.
- Have them use the eraser to remeasure their three shadows and record these measurements in another chart.
- Have children compare these measurements with the original ones they made. Guide them to conclude that while the length of the shadow stays the same, the number of units needed to measure it changes. As the unit of measurement gets smaller, it takes more of that unit to measure the same length.

Average

Explore Changes in Units of Measurement

- Direct children to complete the Easy activity using units of measurement that are both smaller and larger than their shoe.
- Have children draw conclusions about how changing the unit of measurement alters their results.

Average

Identify the Sun's Path in the Sky

- Have children place a stick upright through the center of a large piece of butcher paper in a sunny outdoor spot.
- Direct them to draw the stick's shadow at hour intervals and label each time.
- Children should use the drawings to explain the sun's apparent movement across the sky.

Caution! Warn children never to look directly at the sun.

Challenging

Explore Shadow Lengths

- Provide a rectangular block, a flashlight, and drawing paper.
- Have children investigate and draw conclusions about what happens to a shadow when the light source is at different heights and positions from the ground.

S.T.E.M.

Engineering and Technology

Objectives

- Identify and explain a problem and propose a solution in his/her own words.
- Compare the features of two flashlights.
- Demonstrate how to improve on the design of a product.

Notebook Generate Ideas

Share the background information before you assign the feature. Ask questions to ascertain children's prior knowledge.

What are some kinds of lights that help you see things at night? Sample answers: streetlights, headlights, lights in your home

When have you used a flashlight? How is it helpful? Sample answer: I have used a flashlight in my backyard at night. It is helpful because it is a light you can carry around with you.

Background

- People have been making "lamps" for at least 70,000 years. The earliest ones burned plant materials mixed with animal fat. The plant/fat mixture might be set in a rock or shell before being set on fire.
- Over time, people found new and better containers for the lamps. They also found different materials to burn and ways to control the fire or flame.
- Still, changes in lighting technology were small for hundreds of years. People basically just found new materials to burn, such as olive oil, sesame oil, kerosene, and coal gas.
- The invention of the incandescent light bulb changed lighting forever. Because the light bulb used electricity rather than fire, it was safe and easy to use. We use similar light bulbs today.

TEKS 1.3A identify and explain a problem such as finding a home for a classroom pet and propose a solution in his/her own words

S.T.E.M.

Engineering and Technolog

See the Light

Compare Flashlights

Lights help you see what you are doing. They help you get around at night. The lights in a building make it bright.

Flashlights can light up dark places. Flashlights work in different ways.

- uses a switch
- needs batteries
- lights up right away

- uses a hand crank
- does not need batteri
- takes time to light up

College & Career Readiness

CCRS I.E.1, I.E.2, III.C.1, I

Tool Designers This feature provides an opportunity to develop children's awareness of STEM careers related to engineering. Suggest children go online to find out more about engineers that design and make tools, such as flashlights.

Have children draw pictures of the different tools engineers m make that use light. Children should share the drawings wit the class and talk about the sk engineers would need to make these tools.

S.T.E.M. continued

ight Ideas

u have a problem. You need better
hting to read. How can you improve
lamp in your room? Draw your
sign. Tell how it works.

Check children's drawings.

heck children's work.

ild On It!

Design lights for a ballpark. Complete **Design It: Lights for a Park** on the Inquiry Flipchart.

Build On It!

In **Design It: Lights for a Park**, the design challenge associated with this lesson, children use the steps of the engineering design process to design a lighting plan for a ballpark. For more details, see the pages that follow.

Other opportunities to apply the design process appear throughout the *Inquiry Flipchart*.

TEKS 1.3A

Develop S.T.E.M. Concepts

When children have completed reading the feature, ask questions to help them reflect on the importance of improving upon different kinds of technology.

What problem do lights solve? They give light so people can see in dark places and at night.

What could make one light or lamp better than another? Sample answers: Some lamps or light bulbs may last longer, be nicer-looking, use less electricity, have a way to control them better, or have features that make them more useful for certain tasks.

Focus children's attention to the problem on this page. Read the scenario together. **Identify and explain the problem. What solution did you come up with?** Sample answer: I want to improve the lighting in my room. I thought about the white lamp by my bed. I added a switch so I could dim it, and I colored butterflies on the lampshade to make it prettier.

Develop Inquiry Skills

COMPARE/CONTRAST Ask children to carefully observe and compare and contrast the two flashlights on the previous page. **How are the flashlights alike?** They are both lights that you can carry with you. **How are they different?** One is powered by a battery and turns on right away; the other is powered by a hand crank and takes time to turn on.

Notebook Summarize Ideas

Ask children to summarize what they learned about how lighting technology helps them meet their needs. Have them tell about different kinds of lighting, the difference between the two flashlights, and how their new design for an existing light has made it better.

S.T.E.M.

Engineering and Technology

FLIPCHART P. 39

30 minutes

pairs

Objectives

- Record and organize data.
- Identify and explain a problem and propose a solution in his/her own words.

Prep and Planning Tips

- Provide or have children draw a simple map of a Little League ballpark that also includes a food stand and a parking lot.
- You may wish to draw a map of a ballpark on the board and have children use it as a model.

Expected Results

Children will design a lighting plan for a ballpark, taking into consideration the layout of the park and the intended purpose of the lights.

1 Engage/Explore

Attention Grabber

Provide pairs or small groups with hand mirrors. Have children look toward the light and observe their pupils in the mirror. Then turn out the lights, and make the classroom as dim as possible. Allow a few minutes so children's eyes adjust. Then have them look at their pupils again. Explain that their pupils get bigger in dim light so they can take in more light and help them see better when it is dark.

Preview Activity

Before beginning the activity, have children review the directions on the Engineering and Technology Flipchart page.

Guide the Activity

Develop Inquiry Skills

OBSERVE Allow children time to observe the picture of the ballpark on the flipchart and discuss where they would need lights if it were dark.

USE MODELS Have children draw a map of the ballpark and use it to discuss what people do in each area: the *playing field*, the *snack bar*, and the *parking lot*.

Strategies for Success

Before beginning the activity, have children review the directions on the *Inquiry Flipchart*. Write the following words on the board, and have children use them to label their ballpark maps: *playing field, snack bar,* and *parking lot*. Discuss the purpose of each of the areas.

Science Notebook

During the Activity Remind children to list all the areas of the ballpark that need light. Tell them to think about what people do in each place and why they would need lights at night. Partners should check each other's work to see that the designs are in agreement and that all areas are labeled.

2 Explain

Develop the Engineering Design Process

Use the following steps of the engineering design process to provide context and support for the analyses that children are doing in the flipchart activity.

1. **FIND A PROBLEM** **Identify and explain the problem. What solution can you design to solve the problem?** Sample answer: A ballpark needs lights at night so people can see. I will design a plan for placing lights at a ballpark so people can use the park at night.
2. **PLAN AND BUILD** **How will you make your plan?** Sample answer: I will draw a map of a ballpark with labels for the different parts, and then I will draw lights on the map to show where they should go.

3 Extend/Evaluate

Quick Check

How did you decide what your lighting plan would be? Sample answer: I thought about what people do in each area of the ballpark and where they would need lights. Then I drew lights in those areas.

What problems did you have when you made your design? How did you solve them? Accept all reasonable answers.

4. **REDESIGN** Help children research real ballparks online to see other ideas for lighting. They can use those ideas to redesign their lighting plans.
5. **COMMUNICATE** Have pairs share their designs and explain why they placed the lights where they did.

Science Notebook

After the Activity Check children's designs to see that they have labeled the areas of their maps, drawn lights in the appropriate areas, and written an explanation for why they placed the lights where they did.

Michael DiSpezio's Tips & Tricks

Evaluate and Extend Prior Knowledge To insure a common base of understanding among children, begin by surveying their familiarity with ballparks. Based upon the responses, you may need to offer an assortment of introductory references and resources. Select visually engaging and knowledge-appropriate materials. Try to profile ballparks that children may have visited or seen on television. Consider displaying online maps or high-altitude photographs that illustrate both local parks and major-league stadiums. Demonstrate how drawings and diagrams are used to represent structures in and around the park. If applicable, extend the engineering process by providing art materials children can use to construct models of their designs.

Enduring Understandings

Revisit the Big Idea and Essential Questions

Big Idea **Many objects can be seen in the sky. The appearance of these objects can change.**

To explore the Big Idea, post key terms from the unit on the board, and challenge children to find and explain different ways word pairs are connected. For example, a child might explain that the *moon* and the *sun* are both objects in the sky. Another child might explain that a *telescope* is a tool that is used to *magnify* objects in the nighttime sky. Prompt children with the following pairings.

- sun, star
- moon, phases
- telescope, star
- sun, shadow
- magnify, moon

Essential Questions

Post the Essential Questions, and use the following prompts to guide a discussion.

Lessons/Essential Questions	Prompts
L1 **What Can We See in the Sky?**	• Name three different objects you can see in the sky. Tell whether you see each one in the nighttime sky, the daytime sky, or both.
L2 **How Does the Sky Seem to Change?**	• Describe what seems to happen to the moon's shape over time.
L3 **How Does the Sun Seem to Move?**	• Demonstrate with your hand how the sun seems to move.

Science Notebook

You may use the following strategies after children complete the unit or after each lesson.

- Have children review and edit the responses to the Essential Questions they drafted at the beginning of the unit. Suggest they cross out sentences or ideas that are unnecessary or inappropriate.
- Ask children to draw sketches of four phases of the moon in their Science Notebooks. Tell them to draw the phases in order, starting with a full moon. Then, have them draw each phase on an index card. Ask children to scramble up the cards and exchange them with a partner. Have partners put each other's cards in order. Then, check their results against the sketches in their Science Notebooks.

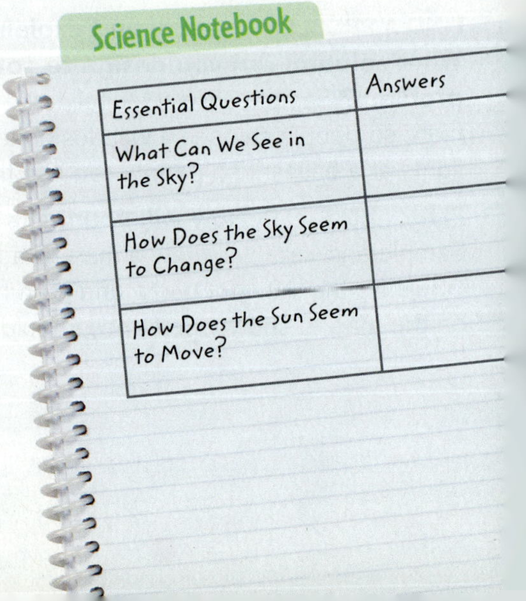

Unit 7 Review

Name ______________

Vocabulary Review

Use the terms in the box to complete the sentences.

phases
shadow
star

TEKS 1.8C

1. An object in the sky that gives off its own light is a star.

TEKS 1.8B

2. A dark place made where an object blocks light is a shadow.

TEKS 1.8B

3. The shapes of the moon you see as it moves are its phases.

Science Concepts

Fill in the letter of the choice that best answers the question.

TEKS 1.8C

4. You can see stars at night. How many stars are in the sky?
   - Ⓐ about 20
   - Ⓑ not enough to be counted
   - Ⓒ more than anyone can easily count

TEKS 1.8C

5. What objects can we see in the nighttime sky? Identify them.
   - Ⓐ the sun and clouds
   - Ⓑ the moon and stars
   - Ⓒ the sun and the moon

Item Analysis

Items	TEKS	Depth of Knowledge	Cognitive Complexity
1	**1.8C**	1	Low
2	**1.8B**	1	Low
3	**1.8B**	1	Low
4	**1.8C**	1	Low
5	**1.8C**	2	Moderate

Unit Review

Answer Key

Vocabulary Review (5 points each)

1. **star**
   Remind children that stars are made of hot gases and give off light and heat.
2. **shadow**
   Review how a shadow is made. Have children tell how shadows form when something blocks light.
3. **phases**
   Make sure that children understand that the moon does not actually change shape. Reiterate that the phases of the moon relate to how much of the sun's light is reflected off the moon's surface toward Earth and how much of the moon's surface is in darkness.

Science Concepts (7 points each)

4. **C**
   Point out that people who live in areas with a lot of light at night might not agree that C is the correct answer. Explain that it refers to what the stars look like in the sky on a dark, clear night.
5. **B**
   Go through the objects that appear in the answer choices and ask children if each object can appear in the daytime sky, nighttime sky, or both. Use those answers to guide children to the correct answer.

Assessment

Unit 7 Test and Performance Assessment

See Assessment Guide, pp. AG 104–AG 110, for Unit Test and Performance Task with Long Option rubric.

Unit Review *continued*

Answer Key

Science Concepts (7 points each)

6. B

Point out that if any part of an answer choice can appear in the night sky then the answer choice must be incorrect.

7. C

Direct children's attention back to the lesson pages on moon phases. Ask them to describe what each phase looks like.

8. C

Point out that the sun does warm the Earth, as in answer choice A, but that fact is related to the light and heat the sun gives off, not Earth's rotation. Remind children that the moon's phases are a result of its orbit around the sun, not Earth's rotation.

9. A

Refer children back to the photograph of stars in the nighttime sky, and ask them to describe what they see. Help them recognize that they do not look evenly spaced or patterned.

UNIT 7

TEKS 1.8B

6. Sophie observes how objects seem to change during the day. She records this in her notebook. Which objects did she observe?
   - Ⓐ the moon and the stars
   - Ⓑ the sun and the clouds
   - Ⓒ the stars and the sun

TEKS 1.8B

7. Observe the picture of the moon. Which moon phase does it show?

   - Ⓐ full moon
   - Ⓑ new moon
   - Ⓒ first quarter moon

TEKS 1.8B

8. Which happens because Earth turns?
   - Ⓐ The sun warms Earth.
   - Ⓑ The moon has phases.
   - Ⓒ The sun seems to move across the sky.

TEKS 1.8C

9. How do stars look in the nighttime sky?
   - Ⓐ They are scattered unevenly.
   - Ⓑ They are set in a pattern of rings.
   - Ⓒ They are set evenly across the sky.

Item Analysis *(continued)*

Items	TEKS	Depth of Knowledge	Cognitive Complexity
6	**1.8B**	1	Low
7	**1.8B**	2	Low
8	**1.8B**	2	Moderate
9	**1.8C**	2	Low

UNIT 7

TEKS 1.8B, 1.8C

10. Light from the sun makes shadows during the day. Which picture shows the flag's shadow at the end of the day?

Ⓐ The picture with the long shadow.
Ⓑ The picture with the short shadow.
Ⓒ Both pictures show the flag's shadow at the end of the day.

TEKS 1.8B, 1.8C

11. Yoon sees different stars on a winter night than he sees on a summer night. Why?
Ⓐ You can see stars only in the winter sky.
Ⓑ Clouds may block the stars in summer.
Ⓒ You can see different stars in different seasons.

TEKS 1.8C

12. Which object can you see in both the daytime and the nighttime sky?
Ⓐ 
Ⓑ 
Ⓒ 

Item Analysis *(continued)*

Items	TEKS	Depth of Knowledge	Cognitive Complexity
10	**1.8B, 1.8C**	3	Moderate
11	**1.8B, 1.8C**	2	Moderate
12	**1.8C**	2	Moderate

Unit Review *continued*

Answer Key

Science Concepts (7 points each)

10. A

Remind children that shadows formed by the sun move in correspondence with the apparent movement of the sun in the sky. Help them recall that shadows are longest at dawn and dusk.

11. C

Direct children's attention to the words *winter* and *summer* and ask them to tell what they name.

12. B

Have children identify each object pictured in the answer choices—sun, moon, and group of stars.

Short Option Performance Assessment

Task

In the Sky
Have children make a booklet titled "In the Sky." In it, children should include pictures of objects that can be seen in the daytime sky and objects that can be seen in the nighttime sky. Have children use their booklets to describe the differences in the daytime and nighttime sky to a partner.

Rubric

Preparation Provide children with crayons and blank booklets made from two sheets of folded drawing paper.

Scoring Rubric—Performance Indicators

___ Draws a picture of objects found in the daytime sky, such as the sun, clouds, and moon.

___ Draws a picture of objects found in the nighttime sky, such as the moon, clouds, and stars.

___ Describes how the daytime sky is different from the nighttime sky.

Observations and Rubric Scores

3 2 1 0

Unit Review *continued*

Answer Key

Inquiry and the Big Idea (11 points each)

13.

a. a telescope

b. It magnifies the stars, or makes them look bigger.

Ask children to tell the difference between looking at the stars with the naked eye and looking with a telescope. As needed, children can look back at Lesson 1 to review information about telescopes.

14.

a. Both can be seen in the nighttime sky.

b. Sample answer: Stars give off their own light. The moon does not. The moon can sometimes be seen during the day. The stars cannot.

Point out that the sun is a star, but the moon is not. Reinforce that stars are made of burning gases, but moons are made of rock.

UNIT 7

Inquiry and the Big Idea

Write the answers to these questions.

TEKS 1.2C, 1.8C

13. You want to get a closer look at the stars in the sky.

a. What tool can help you see the stars better?

a telescope

b. How does this tool help you?

It magnifies the stars, or makes them look bigger.

TEKS 1.8C

14. Compare and contrast the stars and the moon.

a. What is one way they are the same?

Both can be seen in the nighttime sky.

b. Name a way they are different.

Sample answer: Stars give off their own light. The moon does not. The moon can sometimes be seen during the day. The stars cannot.

302 **Unit 7** Unit Review

Item Analysis

Items	TEKS	Depth of Knowledge	Cognitive Complexity
13	**1.2C, 1.8C**	3	Moderate
14	**1.8C**	3	High

UNIT 8 Living Things and Their Environments

Big Idea and Essential Questions

This Unit was designed to focus on this Big Idea and these Essential Questions.

Take It Home! A School-Home Connection letter in English and Spanish is provided in Online Resources.

Big Idea

Living and nonliving things are found in environments. A living thing lives in an environment that meets its needs.

Essential Questions

L1 **What Are Living and Nonliving Things?**

L2 **Where Do Plants and Animals Live?**

L3 **What Is a Terrarium?**

Professional Development

Houghton Mifflin Harcourt and **NSTA,** the **National Science Teachers Association,** have partnered to provide customized professional development resources for teachers using *ScienceFusion*.

The Professional Development Resources include:

- Do-it-yourself resources, where you can study at your own pace
- Live and archived online seminars
- Journal articles, many of which include lesson plans
- Fee-based eBooks, eBook chapters, online short courses, symposia, and conferences

Access to The NSTA Learning Center is provided in the *ScienceFusion* Online Resources.

NSTA National Science Teachers Association

The NSTA Learning Center

Unit Planning

Options for Instruction

Choose from **Interactive Worktext** and **Leveled Readers**, **Digital**, and **Inquiry** options to meet the Texas Essential Knowledge and Skills.

	LESSON 1	LESSON 2	LESSON 3
Essential Questions	What Are Living and Nonliving Things?	Where Do Plants and Animals Live?	✔ Guided Inquiry What Is a Terrarium?
Texas Essential Knowledge and Skills	TEKS 1.9A	TEKS 1.9B, 1.9C	TEKS 1.2A, 1.2B, 1.2D, 1.4A, 1.9B
Interactive Worktext	☐ Student Edition pp. 305–314 • Living It Up! • What's Nonliving? • All Together	☐ Student Edition pp. 315–328 • All Around You • Salty Water • In a Rain Forest • Dry As a Bone • It's Cold Out Here! • On the Prairie • The Food Chain • Caring For Pets	☐ Student Edition pp. 331–332 • Scaffolding for Inquiry
Leveled Readers	Parallel coverage of the lesson topics is provided in the Extra Support, On-Level, and Enrichment readers. See p. 303H for detailed reader information.		
Hands-On Inquiry	Inquiry Flipchart p. 40 **It's Alive!** ☐ Directed Inquiry **Neighborhood Search** ☐ Independent Inquiry	Inquiry Flipchart p. 41 **Build an Aquarium** ☐ Directed Inquiry **Working Together** ☐ Independent Inquiry	Inquiry Flipchart p. 42 **What Is a Terrarium?** ☐ Guided Inquiry
Digital Curriculum	☐ Digital Lesson Online Resources Interactive presentation of lesson content 	☐ Digital Lesson Online Resources Interactive presentation of lesson content 	☐ Virtual Lab Online Resources Interactive scaffolded inquiry 

OTHER UNIT FEATURES

Careers in Science, p. 329

S.T.E.M. Engineering and Technology, pp. 333–334B

Online Resources

Interactive Whiteboard Resources for Unit 8

Assessment

Formative Assessment
Sum It Up! and Brain Check
Student Edition, end of each lesson

Summative Assessment
Lesson Quizzes
Assessment Guide, pp. AG 111–AG 113

Unit 8 Review
Student Edition, pp. 335–338

Unit 8 Test
Assessment Guide, pp. AG 116–AG 120

Performance Assessment
SHORT OPTION: Teacher Edition, p. 337
LONG OPTION: Assessment Guide, pp. AG 121–AG 122

RTI Response to Intervention
RTI Strategies, p. 303I

Online Assessment
Test-taking and automatic scoring
Banks of items from which to build tests

Teacher Notes

Planning for Inquiry

Use the following preview of Inquiry Activities and Lessons to gather and manage the materials needed for each lesson.

Activity	Inquiry and Design Process Skills Focus	Materials	Prep Tips, Troubleshooting, and Expected Results
Lesson 1 DIRECTED INQUIRY Flipchart p.40 A **It's Alive!** **OBJECTIVES** Recognize and demonstrate safe practices. Plan and conduct simple investigations. Record and organize data. Sort and classify living and nonliving things. 20–25 minutes pairs TEKS **1.1A, 1.1B, 1.2B, 1.2D, 1.9A**	• Observe • Compare	• magazines • safety scissors • glue	**Prep Tips** Gather magazines ahead of time that have photographs of both living and nonliving things. You may wish to choose wildlife, gardening, or travel magazines for children so that they will find pictures of living things as well as advertisements with pictures of nonliving things. Try to gather enough magazines so that each pair of children can have at least one magazine to look through. **Troubleshooting** If children do not find enough photographs to gather at least three living and three nonliving things, have them trade magazines with another group. If children are confused about whether something in a photo is living or nonliving, ask questions such as *Does it reproduce? Does it need food or water?* **Expected Results** Children should be able to distinguish between living and nonliving things. They should be able to sort and classify the pictures into a chart and explain the differences between the two groups.
INDEPENDENT INQUIRY Flipchart p.40 B **Neighborhood Search** **OBJECTIVES** Recognize the importance of safe practices. Plan and conduct simple investigations. Record and organize data. Collect and compare information using notebooks. Sort and classify living and nonliving things. 35 minutes individuals TEKS **1.1B, 1.2A, 1.2B, 1.2D, 1.4A, 1.9A**	• Observe • Compare • Classify • Plan and Conduct a Simple Investigation • Draw Conclusions	• Science Notebook • clipboards (optional)	**Prep Tips** If children are unable to complete this assignment in their neighborhoods, lead the class on a search around the school yard. You may wish to distribute clipboards so that children have a hard surface to write on. **Troubleshooting** As children brainstorm places to look for living and nonliving things in their neighborhoods, make sure the places they choose are safe and appropriate. **Caution!** Remind children that a parent or a trusted adult must accompany them when doing this activity at home. **Expected Results** In their searches, children should be able to find and determine living things, such as birds, trees, and grass, and nonliving things, such as cars and buildings. They should be able to classify things as either living or nonliving.

Additional teaching support for all inquiry activities is available in **Online Resources.**

Science Notebook Strategies

- Lists of Kit-Supplied Materials
- Meeting Individual Needs
- Investigate More—Extensions and Variations
- and More!

Activity	Inquiry and Design Process Skills Focus	Materials	Prep Tips, Troubleshooting, and Expected Results
Lesson 2 DIRECTED INQUIRY Flipchart p.41 A **Build an Aquarium** **OBJECTIVES** Record and organize data. Collect and compare information using tools, including materials to support the observations of habitats of organisms. Analyze and record examples of interdependence found in various situations. 30–35 minutes small groups TEKS **1.2D, 1.4A, 1.9B**	• Observe • Compare • Infer • Draw Conclusions	• large tank full of water • collecting net • fish • water plants • fish food	**Prep Tips** If you do not have enough tanks of water or fish to use, do the activity as a whole class. Pet stores may have tanks available to buy when you purchase the fish. Demonstrate for children how they should use the collecting net to gently lift and transport the fish and the plants to the aquarium. **Caution!** Warn children not to drink aquarium water, and have them wash their hands after handling the materials. **Troubleshooting** If you do not think children have the motor skills to pick up the fish, have them watch you as you move the fish into the aquarium. **Expected Results** Children should observe that the fish use plants as shelter and depend on humans for food. They should be able to compare how the plants and the fish move and meet their needs.
INDEPENDENT INQUIRY Flipchart p.41 B **Working Together** **OBJECTIVES** Recognize the importance of safe practices. Record and organize data. Gather evidence of interdependence among living organisms. 25–30 minutes individuals TEKS **1.1B, 1.2D, 1.9C**	• Observe • Gather, Record, Display, or Interpret Data • Plan and Conduct a Simple Investigation	• Science Notebook • clipboards (optional)	**Prep Tips** Find a place where animals might go, such as a bird feeder, pond, or stream near the school. Explain that if children stay still and quiet, they will have a better chance of seeing animals moving around or doing something. **Caution!** Warn children to observe animals from a safe distance. **Troubleshooting** If children are not finding enough living things to observe, you may wish to use online videos or assign the investigation for homework. **Expected Results** Children should be able to identify several animals that interact with plants or other animals. They should be able to gather evidence of how the animal depends on other living things in its environment for food and shelter.

Planning for Inquiry (continued)

Activity	Inquiry and Design Process Skills Focus	Materials	Prep Tips, Troubleshooting, and Expected Results
Lesson 3 INQUIRY GUIDED INQUIRY **Flipchart** p.42 **Student Edition** pp. 331–332 **What Is a Terrarium?** **OBJECTIVES** • Recognize and demonstrate safe practices. • Plan and conduct simple investigations. • Record and organize data. • Collect and compare information using tools, including materials to support observations of habitats of organisms. • Analyze and record examples of interdependence found in various situations. 25 minutes to set up; 10 minutes per day for 1 week to observe small groups TEKS **1.1A, 1.1B, 1.2B, 1.2D, 1.4A, 1.9B**	• Make a Model • Observe • Gather, Record, Display, or Interpret Data	• 2-L clear plastic bottle with cap, cut in half • potting soil • small plant • 10 pill bugs • gloves • damp leaf cuttings • rotten vegetables • water • tape • spray bottle (optional)	**Prep Tips** Prepare the bottles ahead of time by cutting them in half around the middle, 6 inches up from the bottom. Then, fill each bottle with 3 inches of soil and add the pill bugs, plant, leaf cuttings, and rotten vegetables. Finally, tape the bottles closed. You may wish to build just one terrarium for the entire class instead, having small groups take turns observing it in shifts each day. Large plastic mayonnaise jars or other large, clear plastic containers with covers provide good substitutes. If you choose to have children build their own terrariums from bottles you have cut, supervise them closely. Put newspapers down to capture loose soil. **Caution!** Tell children to wear gloves, be gentle with pill bugs, use all materials appropriately, and wash their hands after they are finished building. If children are bringing in their own plastic bottles, remind them to have an adult cut the bottles in half for them. **Troubleshooting** If you are ordering the pill bugs, be sure to plan ahead and have them shipped to arrive in time for your use. Have an appropriate means of disposal planned for the pill bugs once the activity is completed. Be sure to read any care and disposal information that comes with living materials used. Mist the soil in the terrarium with a spray bottle if it gets too dry. The pill bugs will need moisture to survive. If pill bugs are not available, consider using earthworms obtained from a local source. **Expected Results** Children will observe that the pill bugs are able to meet all of their needs within their environment. Children will be able to analyze and record examples of interdependence by observing how the pill bugs use the rotten vegetables for food and the leaf cuttings for shelter.

Go Digital! Virtual Lab

What Is a Terrarium?

Key Inquiry Skills: observe, infer

Children observe plants and animals in a model terrarium to infer the food supply of chameleons.

Additional teaching support for all inquiry activities is available in Online Resources.

Activity	Inquiry and Design Process Skills Focus	Materials	Prep Tips, Troubleshooting, and Expected Results
S.T.E.M. **Engineering and Technology** Flipchart p.43 **Design It: Butterfly Garden** OBJECTIVES • Record and organize data. • Identify and explain a problem and propose a solution in his/her own words. 30 minutes pairs or small groups TEKS **1.2D, 1.3A**	 **1 Find a Problem** **2 Plan and Build** **3 Test and Improve** **4 Redesign** **5 Communicate**	• pictures of butterflies • Science Notebook	**Prep Tips** Provide books or online resources that have photographs of butterflies. Discuss butterfly needs, such as flowers for the nectar butterflies use for food; shade to keep cool; puddles for drinking water; sunny places to get warm; and bushes and trees for shelter from wind, rain, and predators. **Expected Results** Children will design a garden where butterflies can meet their needs.

Differentiated Instruction

Leveled Readers

The Leveled Readers provide parallel coverage of the unit topics and Texas Essential Knowledge and Skills. Each Reader is available in English and Spanish. Both versions are available online and on touchscreen mobile devices.

ON-LEVEL This Reader reinforces unit concepts and vocabulary and focuses on the Texas Essential Knowledge and Skills. It includes student response activities.

EXTRA SUPPORT This Reader shares title, illustrations, vocabulary, and concepts with the On-Level Reader. However, the text is linguistically accommodated to provide simplified sentence structures and comprehension aids for students who need a little extra support with content-area reading and vocabulary development. It also includes student response activities.

ENRICHMENT This high-interest nonfiction Reader enriches and extends unit concepts. It reinforces some of the unit vocabulary, but also includes stretch vocabulary. It also includes student response activities.

TEACHER GUIDE
The accompanying Teacher Guide provides teaching strategies and support for using all the Readers, as well as English and Spanish worksheets that focus on vocabulary development. A correlation to the Texas Essential Knowledge and Skills is included.

DIGITAL VERSIONS

All of these Leveled Readers are available online. They are also available in an innovative and engaging format for touchscreen mobile devices. For information about accessing these versions, see page T9.

RTI Response to Intervention

Response to Intervention is a process for identifying and supporting students who are not making expected progress toward essential learning goals.

The following *ScienceFusion* components have the flexibility to be used to provide Core Classroom Instruction (Tier 1), strategic intervention (Tier 2), and intensive intervention (Tier 3).

Component	Location	Strategies and Benefits
Student Edition, Active Reading prompts, Sum It Up, Brain Check	Active Reading throughout each lesson, Sum It Up and Brain Check at the end of each lesson	Student responses can be used as screening tools to assess whether intervention is needed.
Assessment Guide, Lesson Quizzes and TEKS DOK Skill Builder	pp. AG 111–AG 115	Student responses can be used as screening tools to assess whether intervention is needed.
Inquiry Flipcharts	Inquiry Flipchart p. 42	Directed Inquiry for students who learn best through directed or teacher-led hands-on activities.
Teacher Edition, Unit Review Answer Strategies	TE pp. 335–338	Suggestions for intervention, guidance, and remediation for each review question.
Leveled Readers	TE p. 303H	Content support for students not meeting the learning needs during core classroom instruction.
Leveled Readers, Teacher Guides and Vocabulary Worksheets	TE p. 303H	Direct instruction with small groups of students needing additional content at various readability levels.
Extra Support for Vocabulary and Concepts (online worksheets)	Online Resources	Support for individualized instruction with practice in essential content.
Online Student Edition with Audio	Online Resources	Provides learners with multiple-modality access to science concepts and information.
Interactive Digital Lessons and Virtual Labs	Online Resources	Provides individualized learning experiences. Lessons make content accessible through simulations, animations, videos, audio, and integrated assessment.
Interactive Whiteboard Resources	Online Resources	Reinforces key unit concepts through interactive vocabulary games and visuals and graphic organizers.
Leveled Readers, online and tablet versions	Online and Tablet Resources	Highlighted words and sentences synced with audio provide support for emerging or struggling readers.

Differentiated Instruction

English Language Learners

Choose from these instructional strategies to meet the needs of English language learners.

Vocabulary Cards are provided in Online Resources.

Unit Vocabulary

Lesson 1	Lesson 2
living things	environment
reproduce	shelter
nonliving things	food chain
environment	

Preteach Vocabulary ELPS 2B

As you preteach vocabulary, model pronunciation and have children repeat. For Unit 8 vocabulary, draw attention to the long *o* sound in *reproduce* and the short *o* sound in *nonliving* and *environment.*

Language Acquisition Strategies

Express Ideas ELPS 1C, 3F, 3G

Use *Careers in Science* on **TE page 329** to give children a variety of ways to express ideas about what forest rangers do.

Beginning	Intermediate	Advanced/Advanced High
Write *forest ranger* in the center of a word web. Elicit words that describe what forest rangers do or what children think it would be like to be a forest ranger. Model expanding the responses into complete sentences.	Have children use these sentence frames to share their ideas: *A forest ranger is someone who* ___. *I would want to* ___. *I think it would be fun to be a forest ranger because* ___.	Have partners take turns completing this sentence frame: *I think a forest ranger is* ___ *because* ___. Then, have them tell what they would like and dislike about being a forest ranger.

Summarize Information ELPS 1C, 3F, 4G

Have children summarize the information about living things on **TE pages 306–307.**

Beginning	Intermediate	Advanced/Advanced High
Have children draw a picture to summarize what they learned. Have them work with a partner to label the drawings.	Have children use sentence frames to summarize the information: *Living things are ___. Living things need ___. Living things can ___. They make ___.*	Have partners take turns telling something they learned about living things. Then, have children review the material to make sure they told all the key information.

Prereading Support ELPS 4D, 4F

Before children read **TE pages 308–309,** use prereading strategies to support comprehension.

Beginning	Intermediate	Advanced/Advanced High
Explain that *nonliving* refers to anything that is not alive. Display each page, point to details in the picture, and use simplified language to describe each nonliving thing.	Remind children that *nonliving* refers to anything that is not alive. Have children find key words and visual details that relate to nonliving things.	Have children preview the text by reading the heading and looking at the picture. Ask them to predict what they will learn on these pages.

Coordinating Conjunctions ELPS 3C, 3F

Use **TE page 318** to help children speak with a variety of connecting words: *and, or, but,* and *so.*

Beginning	Intermediate	Advanced/Advanced High
Point out the word *and* in two places. Then, help children use *and* in a simple sentence: ___ *and* ___ *live in a rain forest.*	Model using connecting words in simple sentences to tell about the rain forest. Then, have children use *and* and *or* in short sentences that tell about the rain forest.	Have children read aloud the list of connecting words. Have children choose three words and use them to describe the rain forest and tell how it helps animals meet their needs.

UNIT 8

Living Things and Their Environments

I Wonder Why

Have children look at the photographs and describe what they see. Then ask them to share what they know about deer and where deer live. Discuss any other information or clues from the photographs that help children answer the "why" question.

Here's Why

Have children turn the page and read the response to the question. You may wish to share the following background with them.

More About...

White-tailed Deer

White-tailed deer can be found throughout the United States and southern Canada. They are common because they adapt easily to many different habitats and can live in open grasslands as well as on the edges of forests. In summer, white-tailed deer can be found in meadows and fields, using forest trees for shade. In winter, they stay in forests where they can find shelter from harsh weather.

White-tailed deer eat many kinds of plants, including tree shoots, leaves, grass, acorns, fruit, and corn.

White-tailed deer get their name from the white underside of their tails. In the spring and summer, their coat is reddish-brown. In autumn and winter, it turns to grayish-brown.

Science Songs

See pp. TR40–TR45 for science songs you can use to reinforce content in this unit.

Professional Development **Science Background**

Use the keywords to access

- Professional Development from **The NSTA Learning Center**
- **SciLinks** for additional online content appropriate for children and teachers
- Teacher Science Background in the back of this Teacher Edition

Keywords

living and nonliving things
animals
ecosystems

Here's Why A deer can meet its needs in the forest. It can find food, water, and shelter there.

In this unit, you will explore this Big Idea, the Essential Questions, and the Investigations on the Inquiry Flipchart.

Levels of Inquiry Key ■ DIRECTED ■ GUIDED ■ INDEPENDENT

Track Your Progress

Big Idea Living and nonliving things are found in environments. A living thing lives in an environment that meets its needs.

Essential Questions

Science Notebook

Before you begin each lesson, be sure to write your thoughts about the Essential Question.

Go Digital

For a complete digital curriculum and resources that provide full coverage of the objectives for this unit, see the Online Resources for this program.

Big Idea and Essential Questions

Big Idea Living and nonliving things are found in environments. A living thing lives in an environment that meets its needs.

Post the Unit Big Idea on the board. Have children read the Essential Questions, which are also the titles of the lessons in this unit.

- Discuss how the Essential Questions can help keep them focused on the Big Idea.
- Have children read the Big Idea statement. The statement describes the main science concept they will be learning.
- Have children predict other ideas that will be taught in the lessons based on the titles, or have them give examples of pictures they expect to see.

Once they complete the unit, they should have a better understanding of the Big Idea.

Essential Questions You may use the following Science Notebook strategy for working with the Essential Questions before children begin the unit or before each lesson.

- Strategies for revisiting the Big Idea and Essential Questions are provided in Enduring Understandings on p. 335A.

Notebook Science Notebook

- Have children copy the Essential Questions into their Science Notebooks. Suggest they leave several writing lines between questions.
- Ask children to write responses to the Essential Questions. Urge them not to worry about whether their responses are correct. They should expect their ideas to change as they work. Comment that they will be able to review and revise their answers to the Essential Questions at the end of the unit.
- Tips and strategies for using Science Notebooks are provided throughout this unit, in the back of this Teacher Edition, and in the Online Resources.

Options for Inquiry

FLIPCHART P. 40

Children can conduct these optional investigations at any time before, during, or in response to the lesson in the Student Edition.

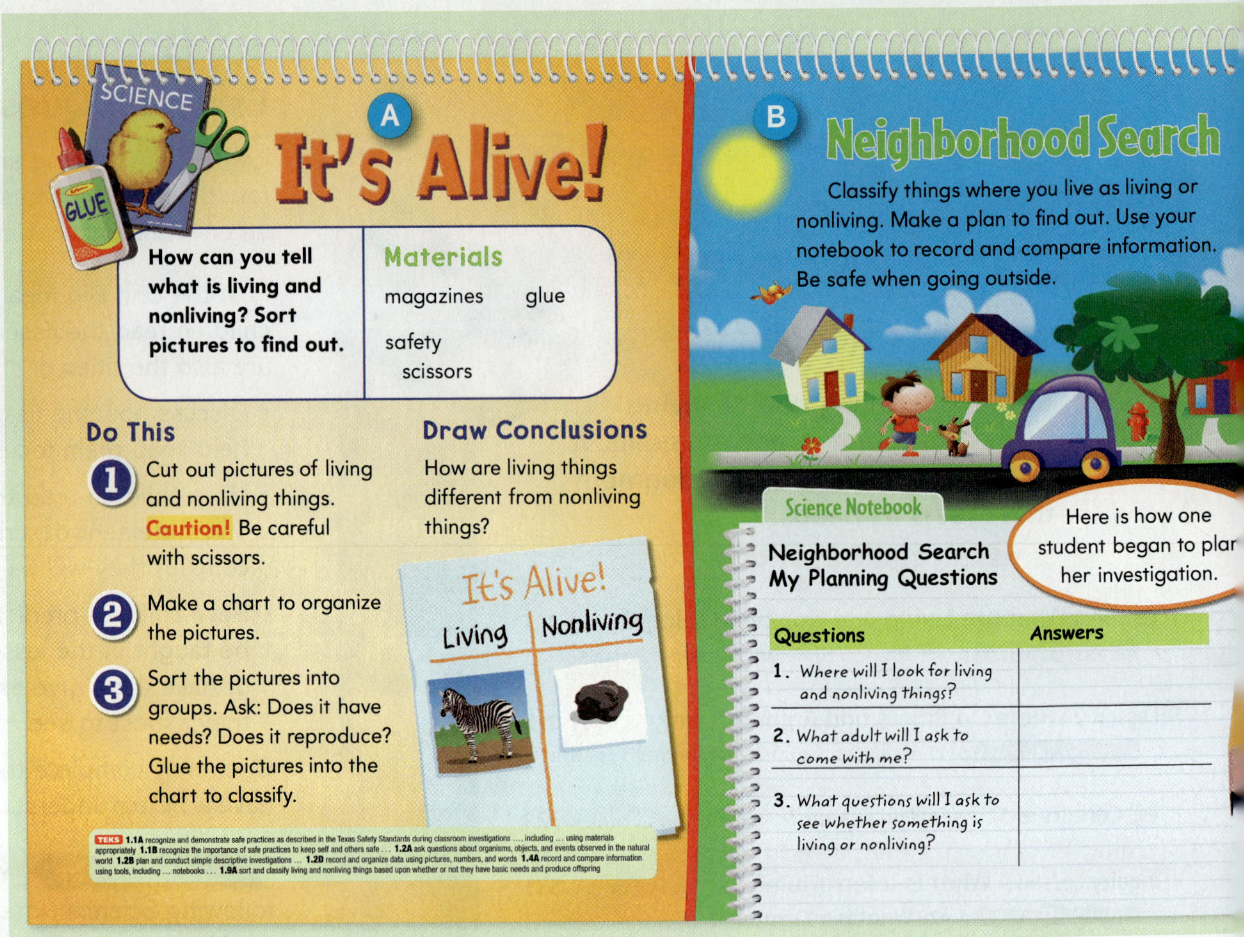

Directed Inquiry

A It's Alive!

20–25 minutes | pairs

Prep and Planning Tips

Review with children how to tell whether something is living or nonliving. You may wish to use living and nonliving classroom objects to demonstrate, and have children answer the questions *Does it have needs?* and *Does it reproduce?* for each one.

Provide child-friendly magazines with pictures of both living and nonliving things for each pair. Wildlife, gardening, or travel magazines, catalogues, and circulars should provide a good mix of living and nonliving things.

Caution! Be sure that children recognize and demonstrate how to use materials appropriately and handle scissors with care to keep themselves and others safe and healthy.

Expected Results

Children should be able to sort and classify living and nonliving things. They should understand that living things reproduce and have needs, and nonliving things do not.

Independent Inquiry

B Neighborhood Search

35 minutes | individuals

Prep and Planning Tips

See the Planning for Inquiry page for more information. If children are unable to complete this assignment in their neighborhoods, consider leading the class on a search around school. Caution! Remind children to have an adult accompany them.

Science Notebook

Children can use the Science Notebook as a model for planning and conducting their own investigation. Encourage them to make a chart like the one shown and include the sample questions plus their own questions. Additional questions may include *What time of day will I conduct the search? Does the weather affect what I might see?*

TEKS 1.9A sort and classify living and nonliving things based upon whether or not they have basic needs and produce offspring

Lesson 1

Essential Question

What Are Living and Nonliving Things?

Engage Your Brain!

Find the answer to the question in the lesson.

What do all living things need?

food, water, air, space to live

Active Reading

Lesson Vocabulary

1 Preview the lesson.

2 Write the 4 vocabulary terms here.

living	nonliving
reproduce	environment

Inquiry Flipchart p. 40—It's Alive!/Neighborhood Search

305

Go Digital

An interactive digital lesson is available in Online Resources. It is suitable for individuals, small groups, or may be projected or used on an interactive white board.

1 Engage/Explore

Objectives

- Recognize and demonstrate safe practices as described in the Texas Safety Standards.
- Ask questions about organisms and objects observed in the natural world.
- Plan and conduct simple investigations.
- Record and organize data.
- Record and compare information using notebooks.
- Sort and classify living and nonliving things.

Engage Your Brain!

Help children answer the question *What do all living things need?* Have them think about what they need to stay alive. Then focus children's attention on the picture and call on volunteers to describe what the child in the picture is doing. Point out that water is something that all living things need.

Remind children to record their final answer to the question when they find it on the next page of the lesson.

Active Reading Annotations

Remind children that active readers "make texts their own" by marking them or writing notes to help them understand what they are reading. Encourage children to use pencil to make annotations and to feel free to change their marks and notes as they read. The goal of annotation is to help children remember what they have read.

Vocabulary and Interactive Glossary

Remind children to find and list the yellow highlighted terms from the lesson. As they proceed through the lesson and learn about the terms, they can add drawings or words in the extra spaces provided in some entries in the Interactive Glossary.

2 Explain

Notebook Generate Ideas

Read aloud the heading on this page to children, and emphasize the word *living*. Have children preview the visuals to identify a farm. Explain that many living things are found on a farm. Ask children to name living things they might see there. Compile a list on the board and return to it after reading.

Develop Science Vocabulary

living things Write the words *live* and *living* on the board and point out the similarity. Explain that *living* forms from *live*. Tell children that when something lives, we call it a living thing. Have them identify other words they can form from *live*, such as *lives, lived, or alive*.

reproduce Write the word *reproduce* on the board. Circle the prefix *re-* and explain that this word part means "to do again." Underline the root *produce* and explain that it means "to make" or "to bring something into being." Show how the two word parts *re* + *produce* come together to mean "to make again."

Develop Science Concepts

Name two groups of living things. plants and animals

In which group do horses belong? Corn? Horses are animals; corn is a plant.

Draw children's attention to the second sentence on this page. **What information does this sentence provide?** It tells what living things need to live. **Point out that this information can be used to answer the Engage Your Brain! question.**

What questions could you ask to decide if something is a living thing? Does this thing grow, change, and reproduce? Does it need food, water, space, and air to live?

Living It Up!

Living things are people, animals, and plants. They need food, water, air, and space to live. They grow and change. Living things **reproduce**. They make new living things like themselves.

306

Differentiation—Leveled Questions

Extra Support

In what ways are plants, animals, and people alike? All are living things. They grow, change, and reproduce. They have needs in order to live.

Challenge

Is a farmer a plant or an animal? Farmers are people. People, or humans, are a kind of animal.

Writing Connection

TEKS ELA 1.6D, 1.24C

Label a Drawing Have children draw pictures showing living things in the classroom. Have them use a green crayon to label plants, a red crayon to label animals, and a blue crayon to label people.

TEKS 1.9A

Develop Science Concepts

Draw children's attention to the third sentence on the left page. **What happens when plants grow and change?** Their stems get longer. They get taller. They grow more leaves and longer roots. They might grow flowers.

What happens when animals grow and change? They get larger and taller. They change size and shape. They start to look more like their parents.

Interpret Visuals

To help children label the living things in this scene ask, **Which living things in this picture are plants?** the grass, the flowers, and the tree **Which living things are animals?** the cow, the dog, the sheep, the birds, and the groundhog

Develop Inquiry Skills

COMPARE **How are plants and animals alike?** They are both living things. They need food, water, air, and space to live. They grow, change, and reproduce.

Notebook Summarize Ideas

Pose these questions: **What are living things? What do they need to live?** Have children summarize the lesson concepts by answering these questions orally or in writing.

2 Explain (continued)

Notebook Generate Ideas

Read the heading aloud to children. Based on what children already know about living things found on a farm, have them brainstorm the meaning of *nonliving* as well as possible answers to the question. Record their ideas and return to them after reading to correct any inaccuracies.

Active Reading Vocabulary

Explain that a vocabulary word may be highlighted in a color. Active readers pay attention to highlighted words, because their meaning is given in the same sentence or the next sentence. Have children locate the highlighted vocabulary word on this page.

Develop Science Vocabulary

nonliving things Write the word *nonliving* on the board. Explain that the prefix *non-* means "not." Guide children to understand that *nonliving* means the opposite of *living,* or "not living."

Develop Science Concepts

What is different about living and nonliving things? Living things must have food, air, water, and space. They grow and change. Nonliving things do not need food, water, and air. They do not grow and change.

Have children recall examples of nonliving things mentioned in the text. (rock, air, water) **Look around the classroom. What nonliving things do you see?** Sample answer: desks, books, computers, bookcases, flag

Is fire a living thing? How do you know? No. It does not need food and water. It does not reproduce.

What's Nonliving?

Nonliving things do not need food, air, and water. They do not grow and change. What are some nonliving things? A rock is a nonliving thing. Air and water are nonliving things, too.

Active Reading

Find the sentences that tell the meaning of **nonliving things**. Draw a line under them.

▶ **List nonliving things you see.**

Sample answers: rake, shovel, gloves, tractor, and fence.

308

Differentiation—Leveled Questions

Extra Support

Which of these objects are nonliving: a dog, a paper clip, a cloud, a tulip, a baby, or a sandwich? The paper clip, the cloud, and the sandwich are nonliving things.

Challenge

Some people have kept "pet rocks" as pets. Why would a ro be an easy pet? Sample answe A rock is easy to care for becau it is a nonliving thing. It does no need food, water, or air. It will n grow or reproduce.

English Language Learners

ELPS 1E, 1F, 2E

Use Farm Words Children may be unfamiliar with the farm equipment shown in the illustration. Point to the tractor, say its name, and have children repeat the word after you. Repeat this procedure with other farm objects, including the rake, shovel, trowel, and gloves. Then point to each item and have children name it. Explain that these words may be helpful as children do the activity on the page.

TEKS 1.9A

Interpret Visuals

Call on volunteers to identify nonliving objects on the visuals of both pages. Remind children to use this information as they list several nonliving things they see.

Develop Inquiry Skills

EXPERIMENT Point out that wooden pencils are made from trees, which are living things. This source might make them wonder if the pencil is a living thing, too. Ask children how they could test whether a pencil is a living thing. Guide them to suggest that they could stick the pencil in soil, water it, and make sure that it has space and air. Then if the pencil grows, changes, and reproduces, they would know it is a living thing.

If possible, have children conduct this experiment and share their results. You may want to introduce children to the term *once-living,* which refers to things such as wood, dead plants, and so on, that were once alive but now are not.

Misconception Alert

Children may be confused about classifying or defining nonliving things, because a nonliving thing can have some characteristics of a living thing. Fire, for example, needs air and can seem to grow. Explain that a living thing meets all of the requirements of living things—it grows, changes, and reproduces, and needs air, water, space, and food. Something that meets only some, but not all, of those requirements is a nonliving thing.

Notebook Summarize Ideas

Remind children that nonliving things are the opposite of living things. Have them recall the definition of a *nonliving thing* and use it to explain how they can tell if something is nonliving. Have them summarize this information orally or in writing.

2 Explain (continued)

Notebook Generate Ideas

Have children follow along as you read the heading aloud. Ask children to share ideas about what clues the title provides about the information on this spread. Guide them to understand that it is about all the living and nonliving things together in a place called an *environment*.

Develop Science Vocabulary

environment Write the word *environment* on the board and have children pronounce it with you as they clap out the syllables. Explain that the origin of the word means "that which surrounds us." Then have children look around for living and nonliving things that surround them in their classroom environment.

Active Reading Main Idea

Explain that the main, or most important, idea may be the first sentence in a paragraph. Or, it may be a different sentence. Active readers ask themselves, What is this paragraph mostly about? The answer will be the main idea.

If children need help identifying the main idea, point out that this paragraph is about what makes up an environment. So they should look for a sentence that contains this information.

All Together

All the living and nonliving things in a place make up an **environment**. A farm is one environment. It has living and nonliving things.

Active Reading

The main idea is the most important idea about something. Draw two lines under the main idea.

310

English Language Learners

ELPS 1E, 1F, 2

Name More Environments Have children cut from magazines pictures of environments, such as forests, farms, parks, beaches, or cities. Then have them practice saying and identifying environments by presenting their pictures and completing th[e] sentence frame: *This picture shows a [beach] environment.*

Living things have basic needs and can reproduce. Nonliving things do not. Classify things in a farm environment by these properties.

Living	Nonliving
Sample answers: pigs, rooster, sheep, horse	Sample answers: barn, mud, weather vane

311

Writing Connection

TEKS ELA 1.19A

Write a Description Have children use what they have learned about an environment to write a three- to five-sentence description of an environment that is important to them. Remind them to include several living and nonliving things found in this environment. Have them share their descriptions in small groups.

TEKS 1.9A

Develop Science Concepts

Point out that some environments exist in nature, while people make others. **What natural environments are in your area?** Sample answers: a beach, a forest
What are some environments made by people? Sample answers: a city, a park

Is our school an environment? Yes, because a school has both living and nonliving things.

Interpret Visuals

Focus children's attention on the visual of the farm. **What is this environment?** a farm **What living things do you see in this environment?** rooster and chicks, sheep, horse, pigs **What nonliving things do you see?** fence, mud, hay, wind vane, barn, cloud

Direct children's attention to the chart on the right page. Remind children what it means to classify things. Point out the properties listed in the interactive that will help children classify. **What are you going to write in this chart?** living things and nonliving things I see on a farm **How will you fill it in?** I will write two living things in the left column. I will write two nonliving things in the right column.

Develop Inquiry Skills

COMPARE/CONTRAST Direct children's attention to the wind vane and identify it. **How are the wind vane and the rooster alike?** They both look like birds. **How are they different?** The wind vane is made of metal and is a nonliving thing; the rooster is a living thing.

Notebook Summarize Ideas

Direct children to think about the main idea on this spread. Have them complete this sentence to summarize it orally or in writing: *An environment is made up of all the ____ and _____ things found in a place.*

3 Extend/Evaluate

Sum It Up!

1. **Choose It!** Read the directions aloud to children, and ask them to tell in their own words what they are looking for. If they need help identifying and classifying living things and nonliving things, have them reread the definitions found on the second and fourth pages of this lesson.
2. **Draw It!** Have children think about parks they have visited. Then have them draw one living thing and one nonliving thing they might see in a park. After children complete their drawings, ask volunteers to explain how to tell the difference between living things and nonliving things.

Sum It Up!

1 Choose It!

Classify each thing. Circle the living things. Draw an X on the nonliving things.

2 Draw It!

Draw a living thing and a nonliving thing you might find in a park.

Children should draw one living thing and one nonliving thing they might see in a park.

312

Brain Check

Lesson 1

Name ______________________

Word Play

Classify parts of the picture as living or nonliving. Color the living things. Circle the nonliving things.

Children should color the trees and other plants as well as the cow, chickens, and other animals. Children should circle the barn, house, fence, water, soil, clouds, and other nonliving things.

313

Answer Strategies

Word Play

- Begin by helping children identify the things pictured on this page. Then talk about how to identify which things are living. **What are some living things?** People, animals, and plants are living things. Have them classify these things by coloring them.
- Then ask children how they can tell if something is nonliving. A nonliving thing does not need food, air, or water. It cannot grow or reproduce. Have children classify these things by circling them.
- To help children improve identification of living things and nonliving things, have pairs of children take turns reviewing the answers with each other.

Assessment

Lesson Quiz

See Assessment Guide, p. AG 111.

3 Extend/Evaluate (continued)

Answer Strategies

Apply Concepts

- If children have trouble completing the chart, remind them that the words *living* and *nonliving* are opposites (antonyms). Using the first line in the chart as an example, guide them to understand that entries on opposing lines in the chart are also opposites. Read each line in the chart aloud and pause to encourage discussion about its opposite meaning. Then have children record this information to complete each missing entry.
- Remind children that when they look around their classroom environment to name a living thing, they should keep the left column of their chart in mind. When they name a nonliving thing, they should make sure that it has the characteristics they described in the right-hand column of the chart.
- As a lesson follow-up, ask children to summarize what they learned in the lesson. Encourage them to share main ideas and use the terms *living thing, nonliving thing,* and *environment.*

Take It Home!

Suggest that children work with a family member to survey their home for living and nonliving things. Then have them make a two-column chart listing these items. Encourage children to bring their lists to class to share.

Apply Concepts

You can classify things as living or nonliving. Complete the chart to show how the groups are different.

Living Things	Nonliving Things
1 grow and change	do not grow and change
2 reproduce	do not reproduce
3 need air	do not need air
4 need water	do not need water
5 need food	do not need food

Look around your environment. Name one living thing and one nonliving thing.

Living Thing	Nonliving Thing
6 name of one living thing	7 name of one nonliving thing

Take It Home!

Family Members: Take a survey of your home with your child. Sort and classify the living things and the nonliving things you see.

314

Make Connections

Easy

Physical Education Connection

TEKS PE 1.1A

Play a Game

- Have children draw on an index card the picture of a living thing or a nonliving thing found in a farm environment. Place the cards in a bag and have each child select a card.
- In an open space, have them play a modified version of "Red Light, Green Light." To play, call out *Living things* or *Nonliving things,* and have children go or stop, based on the card they have. When all children cross the finish line, have them exchange cards and play again.

Average

Social Studies Connection

TEKS SS 1.5A

Identify Local Environments

- Have pairs of children use a local or state map to identify two or more environments, such as a park or a forest.
- If possible, have them mark and label the maps and present their results to the class.

Average

Math Connection

TEKS MATH 1.3D

Describe Objects in Terms of Number

Direct children's attention to an illustration with animals and have them use it to answer these questions:

How many animals in this picture have four legs? How many animals in this picture have two legs? Are there more four-legged animals or two-legged animals? How many more?

Challenging

Writing Connection

TEKS ELA 1.19A

Write Riddles

- Have children write riddles about living things and nonliving things. Explain that the first clue should identify if the thing is living or nonliving. The second clue should identify where you would find the living or nonliving thing. Other clues can give characteristics.
- To help children get started, share this example: *I am thinking of a living thing. It lives in a jungle. It is orange with black stripes. It has sharp teeth. What is my living thing?* (a tiger) Have children contribute their riddles to a class book.

Options for Inquiry

FLIPCHART P. 41

Children can conduct these optional investigations at any time before, during, or in response to the lesson in the Student Edition.

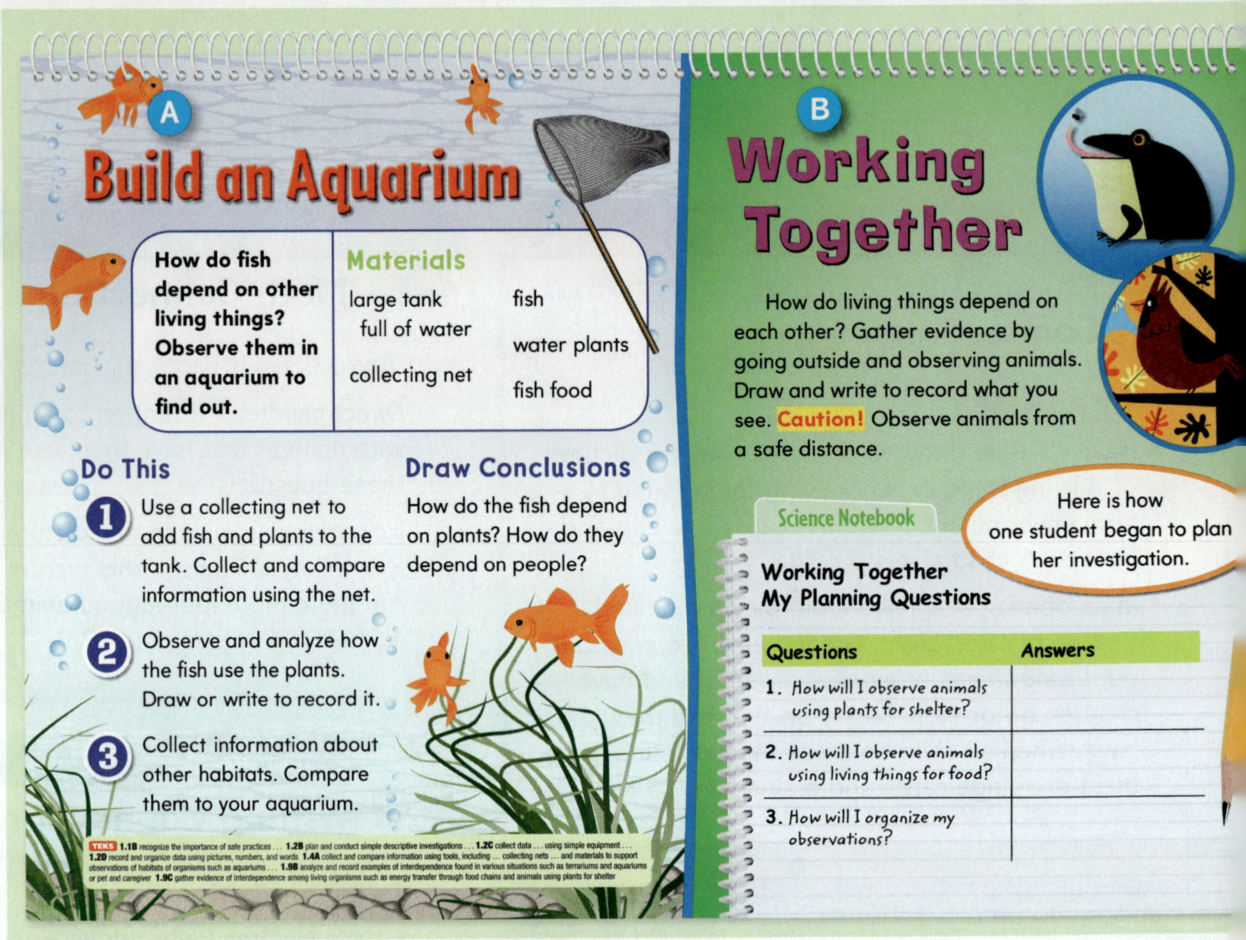

Directed Inquiry

A Build an Aquarium

30–35 minutes
small groups

Prep and Planning Tips

Demonstrate how to use a collecting net to gently transport fish and plants to the aquarium. If you don't think children have the motor skills or maturity to pick up a fish on their own, have them pick up plants only, and watch as you move the fish.

Explain that children can use the net to collect fish and plants, as well as compare them. For example, a fish will move in the net and a plant will not, even though they are both living.

Make sure children recognize the importance of safe practices to keep themselves safe and healthy. **Caution!** Warn children not to touch or drink aquarium water.

Expected Results

Children should observe that aquarium fish use plants as shelter and depend on humans for food. They should be able to compare the ways in which aquarium fish meet their needs to the ways in which other animals in different habitats meet their needs.

Independent Inquiry

B Working Together

25–30 minutes
individuals

Prep and Planning Tips

See the Planning for Inquiry page for more information. Have the class name some animals they may see. Remind children that they are gathering evidence, which means to find out about something. If children have difficulty finding animals to observe, you may wish to show online videos, such as live camera feeds from zoos.

Science Notebook

Children can use the Science Notebook page shown on the Flipchart as a model for planning and conducting their own investigation. Guide children in making a chart for the animals they observe. Children can write notes describing each animal they see and then ask if the animal used living things for food, used plants for shelter, or both.

Go Digital

n interactive digital lesson available in Online esources. It is suitable for dividuals, small groups, or ay be projected or used n an interactive white oard.

1 Engage/Explore

Objectives

- Recognize the importance of safe practices.
- Plan and conduct simple investigations.
- Record and organize data using pictures and words.
- Collect and compare information using tools, including collecting nets and materials to support observations of habitats of organisms such as aquariums and terrariums.
- Gather evidence and analyze and record examples of interdependence among living things or found in various situations.

Engage Your Brain!

Lead children in brainstorming answers to the question *How is this rain forest animal using the tree?* Have them tell what they observe about the place shown in the photograph and then expand with other facts they know about rainforests.

Remind children to record their final answer to the question when they find it on the fourth page of the lesson.

Active Reading Annotations

Remind children that active readers "make texts their own" by marking them or writing notes to help them understand what they are reading. Encourage children to use pencil to make annotations and to feel free to change their marks and notes as they read. The goal of annotation is to help children remember what they have read.

Vocabulary and Interactive Glossary

Remind children to find and list the yellow highlighted terms from the lesson. As they proceed through the lesson and learn about the terms, they can add drawings or words in the extra spaces in the Interactive Glossary.

2 Explain

Notebook Generate Ideas

Point out the highlighted vocabulary word *environment*. Have children review what they already know about environments and what they have learned about different places where plants and animals can live. Record that information on the board. Then ask children to preview the pictures in the lesson and tell what they think they will learn about environments.

Active Reading Vocabulary

Explain that a vocabulary word may be highlighted in a color. Active readers pay attention to each highlighted word, because its meaning is given in the same sentence or the next sentence.

Develop Science Vocabulary

environment Help children pronounce the word *environment*. Say each syllable slowly and clearly and have children repeat each one after you. You can also have children practice spelling the word by writing each syllable on separate index cards and then putting the pieces together.

shelter Explain that the word *shelter* comes from another word meaning "a roof or wall used as a shield." Ask children to explain how this meaning relates to *shelter*. Help them understand that a shelter shields, or protects, a living thing.

Develop Science Concepts

What is the difference between an environment and a shelter? An environment is all the living and nonliving things in a place. A shelter is a place where an animal can be safe.

All Around YOU

All the living and nonliving things around you make up your **environment**. A living thing lives in the environment that meets its needs.

Many animals need shelter. **Shelter** is a place where an animal can be safe.

Active Reading
Find the sentence that tells the meaning of **shelter**. Draw a line under the sentence.

Differentiation—Leveled Questions

Extra Support
Why is the log a shelter for the foxes? It is a place where the foxes can be safe.

Challenge
What kind of shelter do you liv[e] in? Explain. Sample answer: I liv[e] in a house. It is a shelter becaus[e] it keeps me safe from the weath[er].

TEKS 1.9B, 1.9C

Salty Water

An ocean environment is a large body of salt water. Its top layer is home to many living things. Here, plants and other living things get the sunlight they need. Animals can find food.

A jellyfish has body parts that help it catch its food.

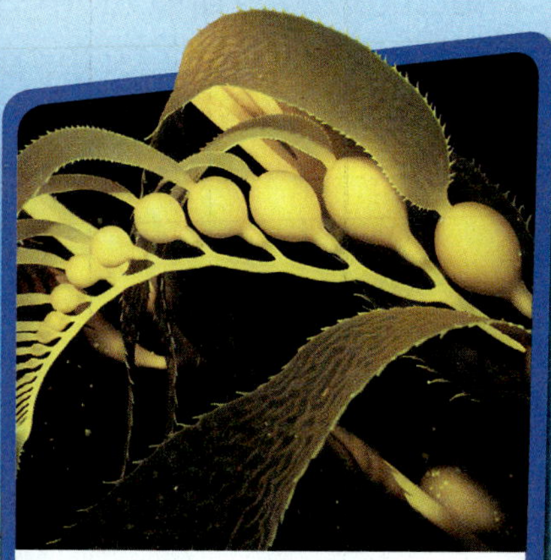

Kelp lives in the ocean. Many animals eat it.

▶ **Why do many plants live in the top layer of the ocean?**

Sample answer: to get the sunlight they need

317

Math Connection

TEKS MATH 1.2G

Solve a Problem Explain that ocean temperatures vary from place to place. Write these average ocean temperatures for March: Boston, Massachusetts: 37 °F; Miami, Florida: 75 °F; Los Angeles, California: 60 °F. Work with children to order these temperatures from lowest to highest and then from highest to lowest. Record each order with < and > symbols.

Develop Science Concepts

What are some characteristics of the ocean? It is a very large body of salt water. The top layer is home to many living things.

How is ocean water different from water in most lakes and ponds? Ocean water is salty, but water in lakes and ponds usually is not.

Interpret Visuals

Direct children's attention to the photographs of the environment where the foxes live and the ocean environment. **How are they alike and different?** Plants and animals live in both environments. Air surrounds the foxes, but water surrounds the ocean animals and plants.

Misconception Alert

Point to the picture of the kelp. Tell children that although kelp looks like a plant, it is actually algae, which is now considered a kind of protist. Explain that many of the living things on the top layer of the ocean that look like plants are actually protists. Kelp had been considered a plant until scientists reclassified it in the 2000s.

Develop Inquiry Skills

INFER **What might happen if you put an ocean fish in a freshwater pond? Explain.** It would probably not survive because it needs an environment with salt water.

Summarize Ideas

Notebook

Ask children to recall the meanings of *environment* and *shelter*. Have them use these terms to summarize orally or in writing what they learned about the relationship between living things and their environments.

2 Explain (continued)

Notebook Generate Ideas

Have children read the headings and preview the pictures on these pages. **What do you already know about rain forest and desert environments?** Rain forests get a lot of rain; deserts are dry. **What are some plants and animals that might live in each place?** Record children's ideas on the board. Add to these ideas as children read and discuss the pages.

Develop Science Concepts

Point out to children that a rain forest has layers like the layers of a cake.

In which layer would you likely find plants that need a lot of light? Explain. Plants that need a lot of light are found in the top layer, because thick plants block light from reaching the bottom layer.

Why are trees good places for some animals to live in the rain forest? Trees provide food and shelter from enemies and weather.

Tell children to check the text for information about rain forest animals before they draw their rain forest animal that lives in the trees.

Refer children to the next page on deserts to find the picture of the Gila monster. **What might happen if you released a Gila monster into a rain forest environment? Why?** It would probably die because it could not find the things it needs to survive.

Have children use the information on this page to answer the Engage Your Brain! question from the beginning of the lesson.

In a Rain Forest

A rain forest gets a lot of rain. The trees grow tall and block the sun. Many animals, such as birds and monkeys, use the tall trees for shelter. The shorter plants do not need much sunlight.

The rain forest provides everything this leopard needs to live.

▶ Draw a rain forest animal that uses trees or other plants for shelter.

Drawings could show a monkey, bird, or other animal that lives in rain forest trees or plants.

318

English Language Learners

ELPS 1E, 2C, 2

Understand and Use an Idiom Children may be unfamiliar with the idiom *dry as a bone*. Explain that this expression means "something that is very, very dry Have children use this idiom to describe examples of things tha are very, very dry.

Dry As a Bone

A desert environment ets little rain. Plants such s cactuses store water in heir thick stems. Other lants store water in their eaves. In hot deserts, many nimals hide during the day.

Joshua tree can e a shelter for mall animals.

Desert plants and animals can live with little water.

desert hare

Gila monster

▶ Draw a plant that stores water.

Drawings should show a cactus or other desert plant that stores water.

319

Writing Connection

TEKS ELA 1.19A

Write a Postcard Have children suppose they are visiting an ocean, a desert, or a rain forest. Have them write a postcard describing what they observe without naming the environment. Ask volunteers to read their postcards aloud, and have the class identify the place being described.

Develop Science Concepts

What is a cactus? A cactus is a plant that grows in dry places. It often has thick stems or leaves to store water. Some have spikes. Children might want to reference print or online resources to see examples of a cactus before they draw an example in the box.

Develop Inquiry Skills

INFER **Why might you have difficulty spotting animals during the day in a hot desert?** Animals often seek shelter from the hot sun during the day.

Since many deserts are dry, how can animals get water? Animals can get water from the foods they eat, such as plants that store water.

Misconception Alert

Children may think that all deserts are hot. Explain that some deserts are hot and some deserts are cold. The temperature depends on altitude, or how high the place is; distance from the equator; and whether cold or hot winds blow over it. Even a desert that is hot during the day can turn very cold at night. **How are all deserts alike?** They are dry. **How can deserts be different?** They can differ in temperature, altitude, location, and wind.

Notebook Summarize Ideas

Review with children what they learned about rain forests and deserts. Ask which place they would prefer to visit or live in and why. Have them use their ideas about the place they prefer to summarize what they learned.

2 Explain (continued)

Generate Ideas

Notebook

Direct children to follow along as you read the headings of these pages. Then have them preview the pictures. Ask children to identify details in the pictures that could help them answer this question: **How would you describe these two environments?** The environment on the left looks cold and snowy. The environment on the right looks sunny and dry; it has a lot of tall grass.

Develop Science Concepts

What do you think it would be like to live on the tundra? It would be cold and maybe windy. It would be hard to find food and a warm place to live.

Could a desert hare live in a tundra environment? Why or why not? No; a tundra environment would be too cold and snowy for a desert hare to survive.

Explain that there are two types of tundra. Alpine tundra is steep land found near the tops of mountains, and Arctic tundra is flat land found near the North Pole. **In which tundra would mountain goats live?** in an Alpine tundra **Where would you find polar bears?** in an Arctic tundra

Interpret Visuals

Draw attention to the caption next to the Arctic fox, and ask children to summarize the details in the caption.

How could this caption help you answer the question about an Arctic fox? It explains that white fur makes it hard to see an Arctic fox in winter.

You can put a white paper animal cutout in front of a piece of white paper to demonstrate the concept of camouflage.

It's Cold Out Here!

A tundra is a very cold environment. Plants grow close together near the ground. Animals have thick fur to stay warm.

An Arctic fox's white fur helps it hide in the snow.

Arctic flowers

▶ How does an Arctic fox's white fur help it in winter?

White fur makes it hard for other animals to see the fox.

320

Differentiation—Leveled Questions

Extra Support

Why do few plants grow in a tundra? A tundra is cold and snowy, so plants do not get the warmth they need to grow.

Challenge

The fur of an Arctic fox changes to brownish gray in summer. Why might this happen? Brownish gray fur would make it easier for the fox to blend in and hide when the snow melts in summer.

On the Prairie

A prairie environment is mostly dry. It has just a few kinds of trees and shrubs. Large animals eat the tall grasses. Smaller animals live in the grasses.

Active Reading

The main idea is the most important idea about something. Draw two lines under the main idea.

Some bison move to places with trees in the winter. The trees provide shelter from the cold.

coneflowers

prairie dogs

red-tailed hawk

321

Develop Science Concepts

Use a globe or map to show children the location of prairie land in the interior of North America.

What are the main features of a prairie? dry climate; tall grasses and wildflowers with a few trees or shrubs

What is the difference between the plants that grow on a tundra and the grasses that grow on a prairie? Tundra plants grow close to the ground. Prairie grass grows tall.

Active Reading Main Idea

Explain that the main, or most important, idea may be the first sentence in a paragraph. Or it may be a different sentence. Active readers ask themselves, **What is this paragraph mostly about?** The answer will be the main idea.

Develop Inquiry Skills

USE MODELS Help children understand how protective coloration helps animals survive. Have them cut out simple animal patterns from white and tan paper. Then have them place each animal against the photographs of the tundra and the prairie to see how the colors blend in or stand out.

Which color animal would have a better chance of survival on the prairie? Why? The tan animal; it would blend in better with the grasses and flowers.

Ask the same question about the tundra.

Notebook Summarize Ideas

Have children look at the visuals and captions to review important details about tundras and prairies. Have them summarize orally or in writing the main ideas they learned through those details.

English Language Learners

ELPS 1E, 2C, 2E

Recognize and Understand Prepositions Children may have trouble distinguishing the meanings of some prepositions. Read the heading of this page, "On the Prairie." Model the meaning of *on* by placing a book on a desk. Say: **The book is on the desk.** Have children repeat the sentence after you.

2 Explain (continued)

Notebook Generate Ideas

Draw or display a chain necklace or another kind of chain. Ask children to describe it and guide them to understand that a chain has links that connect from one to another. Read the highlighted term on this spread. Explain that the spread is about food chains, or ways that plants and animals link, or connect, by how one thing eats another.

Develop Science Vocabulary

food chain Write *food chain* on the board. Show how the term combines *food* + *chain*. Talk about the meaning of each separate word. Ask volunteers to put the meanings together to define *food chain* as the way plants and animals connect by how they use one another for food.

Develop Science Concepts

Remind children that plants and animals get what they need from their environments.

Why do all living things need the sun? They get light and heat from it.

How do plants use the sun? They use sunlight to make food.

How does the sun help animals? Some animals eat the plants that use the sun to make food. These animals get their energy from the plants.

What does a food chain show? how energy moves from plants to animals

The Food Chain

All living things need energy from the sun. Plants use sunlight to make food. Then animals eat the plants. They get the energy they need from the plants.

A **food chain** shows how energy moves from plants to animals.

The grass uses sunlight to make food.

▶ Trace the arrows to show the order of the food chain.

322

Writing Connection

TEKS ELA 1.14

Use Order Words to Write a Summary Remind children that words such as *first, next,* and *last* can help put events in order. Ask children to write a summary of the events in the food chain on these pages by using those words.

The cricket eats the grass.

The toad eats the cricket.

▶ How do living things depend on each other to get energy in this food chain?

The grass uses sunlight to make food.

A cricket eats the grass. Then the toad

eats the cricket.

323

Differentiation—Leveled Questions

Extra Support

Why do animals come after plants in a food chain? because animals eat plants

Challenge

Suppose an eagle eats the toad in the food chain shown here. How would you show that step? Draw an eagle. Then draw an arrow from the toad to the eagle.

TEKS 1.9B, 1.9C

Interpret Visuals

Guide children through the order of the food chain shown on these pages. **What happens first in this food chain?** Grass uses sunlight to make food. Have children write a 1 on the picture of the grass with sunlight.

What happens next? A cricket eats the grass. Have children number the cricket picture 2.

What eats the cricket? a toad **What number should you write on the toad picture?** 3 Ask children to number the toad.

Misconception Alert

Some children may think that a food chain involves actual pieces of chain between plants and animals. It does not. Reinforce the idea that a food chain is a picture or model that shows how energy is transferred from plants to animals in an environment. The picture makes it easier to understand which plants and animals an animal eats.

Develop Science Concepts

How do the living things in this food chain depend on one another? The grass needs the sun. The cricket needs the grass. The toad needs the cricket. Energy is passed from one living thing to the next which helps them grow.

Guide childen to use this information to help them answer the interactive on the right page.

Notebook Summarize Ideas

Have children review the photographs and captions so they can summarize orally or in writing what they learned about food chains. They should include the vocabulary term *food chain* in the summary.

2 Explain (continued)

Notebook Generate Ideas

Read the heading aloud to children. Have children who have pets describe what these pets are and what they need to live. Discuss what a new pet would need to grow and be healthy. Record children's ideas on the board.

Develop Science Concepts

Name some animals that are pets. Sample answers: dogs, cats, birds, guinea pigs, fish

What needs do pets have? food, air, water, shelter, space

Why does a pet need space? to exercise and play

Look at the pictures on these pages. Analyze and record how the pets depend on people. Sample answer: People are helping the pets meet their needs.

Misconception Alert

Children may have the misconception that certain types of animals are inherently pets, such as cats or dogs. Explain to children that pets are animals that have been chosen and trained, over time, to live with people. Some animals—such as small cats—have been kept as pets for hundreds or even thousands of years and are well-adapted to living alongside people. Other animals sometimes kept as pets, such as snakes or large cats, are more commonly found in the wild. To reinforce this concept, lead children in a brief discussion of what makes some animals more appropriate as pets, such as having a gentle temperament, being easily trained, and having needs that can be easily met by people (for example, not needing large amounts of space).

Why It Matters

Caring for Pets

Think about some pets you know. Where do they get their food and water? Who gives them shelter? They need people.

A pet needs space to exercise and play. You need to keep the pet and its shelter clean.

▶ Analyze how a person helps care for a pet. Record your answer.

A person helps a pet meet its needs.

324

Math Connection

TEKS MATH 1.8A, 1.8B, 1.8

Make a Graph and Solve Problems Take a survey of the kinds of pets children or their family members have. Write the type and number of each animal on the board. Then help children make a bar graph to show the survey results. Ask volunteers to summarize the information in the bar graph. Then ask children questions that involve adding an subtracting using information in the graph. For example: Fourtee people have dogs and 9 people have cats. How many dogs and cats are there in all?

People need to take care of pets and keep them clean.

People need to give pets food.

Do the Math!
Solve a Problem

This dog gets one cup of dog food in the morning and one cup of dog food at night.

How many cups of dog food does it get in one day?

  1 cup in morning
+ 1 cup at night

2 cups in one day

How many cups of dog food does it get in five days?

Ten cups

325

Writing Connection

TEKS ELA 1.17B

Describe What a Pet Does
Ask children to think about a pet that they have seen or that they have. Tell them to make a list of things about this pet such as how it looks, what it eats and drinks, how it moves, where it sleeps, and what it likes to do. Then work with children to write a topic sentence and three detail sentences about the pet. Suggest they illustrate their sentences. Children can share their drawings and sentences in small groups.

Do the Math!

TEKS MATH 1.3A, 1.3F

Solve a Problem

Ask children to explain what they are being asked to find out. Have children describe a way to solve the problem. Possible ways include drawing pictures and using counters. Then have them decide what computation will help them get the answer.

Have children solve the problem and describe their solutions. After they have found the solution, ask how they know that the solution makes sense. Have children discuss other ways they could solve the problem.

Interpret Visuals

Ask children to observe the photos. **How are the people taking care of animals?** They are feeding, brushing, and cleaning the animals.

Develop Inquiry Skills

COMPARE/CONTRAST **How are pets and animals in the wild alike?** Sample answer: They have the same needs.

How are pets and animals in the wild different? Sample answer: Pets depend on people to help them meet their needs. Animals in the wild must find their own way to meet their needs.

Notebook Summarize Ideas

Have children look at the list of their ideas about what they need to provide for a new pet so the pet will grow and be healthy. Ask what they learned from the lesson. Have them discuss their answers orally with partners.

3 Extend/Evaluate

Sum It Up!

1. **Draw It!** Help children make a list of the environments they learned about in this lesson. After they choose the environment they want to draw, they can look back at the lesson for clues to decide what living thing to draw. If necessary, review the needs that all living things have.
2. **Order It!** Tell children that the number 1 will stand for the first item in the food chain, 2 will be the second item, and 3 will be the last item. Children can try to find the right order by sketching the three parts of the food chain in this question on separate index cards. They can then order and reorder the cards until they find the one they think is correct.

Sum It Up!

1 Draw It!

Choose an environment. Draw a living thing meeting its needs there.

Children should draw any of the environments from the lesson and include at least one animal or plant meeting its needs for food, water, and shelter.

2 Order It!

Show how energy moves among living things. Put the parts of the food chain in order.

2

1

3

326

Brain Check

Lesson 2

Name ____________________

Word Play

Read the journal entry. Fill in the blanks using words from the box.

shelter	food chain	environment

Dear Journal,

Today I took a field trip to Mulberry Forest. It is an ___environment___ full of trees. Birds use the trees for ___shelter___.

The trees need sunlight to make food. The birds eat berries from the trees. The sun, the trees, and the birds are part of a ___food chain___. It was fun to learn about the forest.

Your Friend,
Swati

327

TEKS 1.9B, 1.9C

Answer Strategies

Word Play

- Ask children to scan the page to identify its general form and tell what they think they should do. Elicit that they will use the words in the word box to fill in the missing words in a journal entry.
- Point out that the words in the word box are highlighted terms from the lesson. Children can review those terms and their definitions by searching for the yellow highlights.
- Remind children that each term will be used only once, so they can cross it off in the word box after they use it.
- Encourage children to reread the journal entry from start to finish once they write all the terms in the blanks. If anything does not sound right, children should go back and check each answer.

Assessment

Lesson Quiz

See Assessment Guide, p. AG 112.

3 Extend/Evaluate (continued)

Answer Strategies

Apply Concepts

- Review the concepts of main idea and details: a main idea states a key thought, and details support the main idea.
- If children have trouble recalling details about a tundra, help them brainstorm a list of characteristics, and record their ideas on the board.
- If necessary, remind children that the word *nonliving* simply means "not living." All things that are not living are nonliving.
- As a lesson follow-up, ask children to summarize what they learned about environments. Encourage them to name new facts and ideas they learned about each environment while reading the lesson.

Take It Home!

Be sure children understand that in their environment living things depend on both living and nonliving things in order to survive. For the purposes of this activity, children can explore their home or immediate neighborhood. Remind children that they must have adult supervision if they decide to go out and look for examples. Encourage children to draw one example that they talked about with a family member and to bring the drawing to class to share with others.

Apply Concepts

Write two details that go with the main idea. Then answer the question.

Main Idea
A tundra is a cold environment.

Detail—Animals	Detail—Plants
Sample answer: Many animals grow thick fur to keep warm.	Sample answer: Plants grow close together near the ground.

What do all the living and nonliving things in a place make up? an environment

Take It Home! **Family Members: Talk about your environment with your child. Look for examples of animals using plants for food and for shelter.**

328

Make Connections

Easy

Health Connection TEKS HEALTH 1.1A

Draw a Food Chain

- Discuss that eating fruits and vegetables is part of a healthy diet. Point out that fruits and vegetables are plants and plant parts.
- Ask children to name the fruits and vegetables they have eaten that day. Then have them draw a food chain for each one. The food chain should include the sun, the plant (fruit or vegetable), and themselves.

Average

Art Connection TEKS ART 1.2C

Make a Collage

- Provide pairs of children with craft paper and art materials.
- Have children select an environment and make a collage to show how animals use plants for shelter as well as a food chain that can be found there.
- Provide sticky notes, and have children caption their mural before they display it.

Easy

Writing Connection TEKS ELA 1.19C

Write a Riddle

- Provide this riddle to children: "This is a dry place. Cactus plants and Gila monsters live here. What environment is it?"
- Discuss the clues with children, and have them use this format as a model to write their own riddles about an environment.
- Call on volunteers to share their riddles for the class to solve.

Challenging

Social Studies Connection TEKS SS 1.5B

Map Environments

- Provide children with research materials on environments in the United States, a U.S. outline map, and crayons.
- Have them research the locations of the Olympic Rainforest, the Mojave Desert, the prairies of the Great Plains, and the Atlantic and Pacific Oceans.
- Direct children to use four colors to show these environments on the map and to include a map key.

Careers in Science

Objectives

- Describe what scientists do.
- Explain how a forest ranger helps protect living things and their environments.

Notebook Generate Ideas

Display a picture of a healthy forest and ask children to identify the place they see. Then show a picture of an unhealthy forest—perhaps one that has suffered a fire or deforestation. Have children describe what they see, and compare and contrast the two places. Encourage children to talk about what they could do to make the unhealthy forest healthy again. Explain that the job of a forest ranger is to help make and keep forests healthy.

Background

- The first full-time professional forest rangers were hired in 1905. To apply for the job, a person had to be able to ride a horse and follow a map.
- Today, forest rangers manage many forest and grassland areas across the United States. They take care of 193 million acres, or about 300,000 square miles. That's an area just larger than the state of Texas.
- Forest rangers are the first line of defense against forest fires. They watch for signs of a fire and call in firefighters at the first sign of danger.
- Look at a map and find the Mississippi River. More than half of all forest rangers work east of the Mississippi River.
- Water coming from the national forests provides drinking water for over 60 million Americans.

TEKS 1.3C describe what scientists do

Careers in Scienc

Ask a Forest Ranger

What does a forest ranger do?

I take care of forests. I help keep plants and animals safe. I also teach about nature and how to care for it.

How does a forest ranger help keep plants safe?

I teach people how to keep forest fires from starting. I make sure no one cuts down trees.

How does a forest ranger help keep animals safe?

I make sure people do not feed them. I protect their homes by protecting the forest.

Now It's Your Tu

▶ What question would you ask forest ranger?

Sample answer: Whc kinds of living things be found in the fores that you help care fc

Writing Connection

TEKS ELA 1.24

Write to Inform Have pairs or small groups work together to make a poster that teaches people about protecting the forest. Children should research a tip to write on the poster and then illustrate it. After children present and explain their poster to the class, display them aroun the room.

Careers in Science continued

Protect the Forest

Draw or write the answer to each question.

1. Why are forest rangers important?

2. What would you like best about being a forest ranger? What would you like least?

3. Suppose you are a forest ranger. Draw one animal or plant you help protect in the forest.

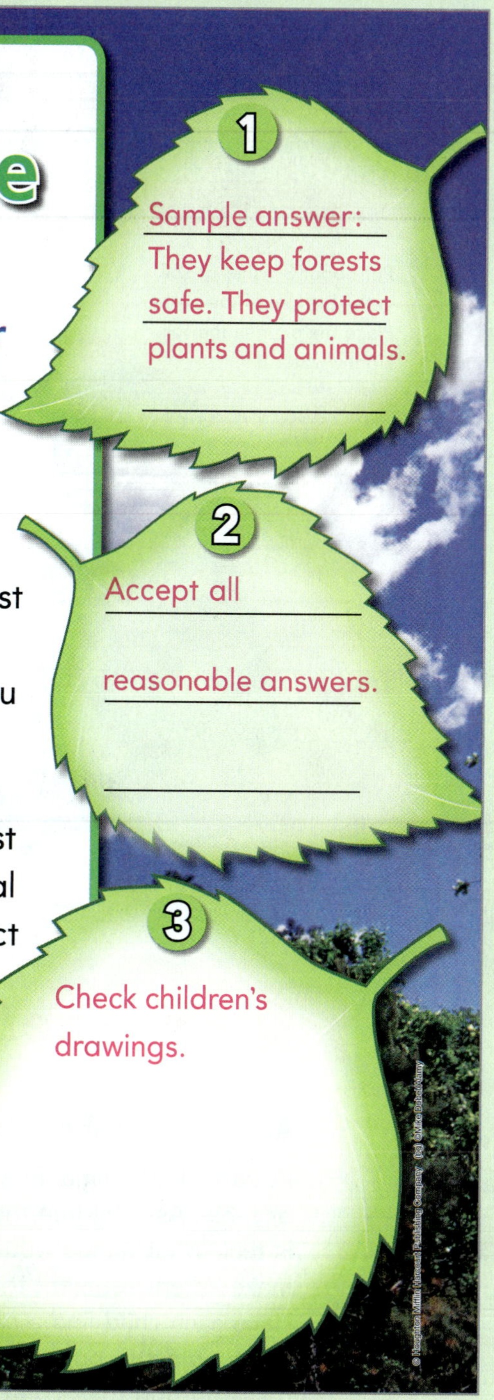

Nature of Science

Provide the following scenario: You are visiting a forest and want to learn more about plants or animals. That information is something scientists might want to know. Scientists can learn more about forests by asking questions and making observations to answer those questions. Have children write a question they want to study about plants or animals in the forest. Then ask them to describe three things they would observe to investigate that question.

TEKS 1.3C

Develop Science Concepts

What is a forest ranger? A forest ranger is a person who takes care of forests.

Describe what a forest ranger does. A forest ranger teaches people about nature and how to care for it. Forest rangers teach people how to prevent forest fires.

Suppose you were in a forest. How could you protect plants? Sample answer: I could be careful with campfires so I don't start a forest fire. **How could you protect animals?** Sample answer: I would not feed the animals.

Develop Inquiry Skills

INFER **What actions might forest rangers take if they see smoke? Why?** Sample answer: The smoke suggests that there is a forest fire. The rangers will warn people to leave the area. They will call for help from firefighters.

Why do you think a forest ranger warns people not to feed animals? Sample answer: Animals do not eat the same foods as humans. They might get sick if they eat human food.

Notebook Summarize Ideas

Have children look again at the photographs and review the questions on these pages. Have them use the answers to summarize what they learned about forest rangers.

Guided Inquiry

FLIPCHART P. 42

25 minutes plus 10 minutes per day for 1 week

small groups

Children should follow the directions on the Flipchart. The accompanying pages in the Student Edition provide scaffolding for guided inquiry.

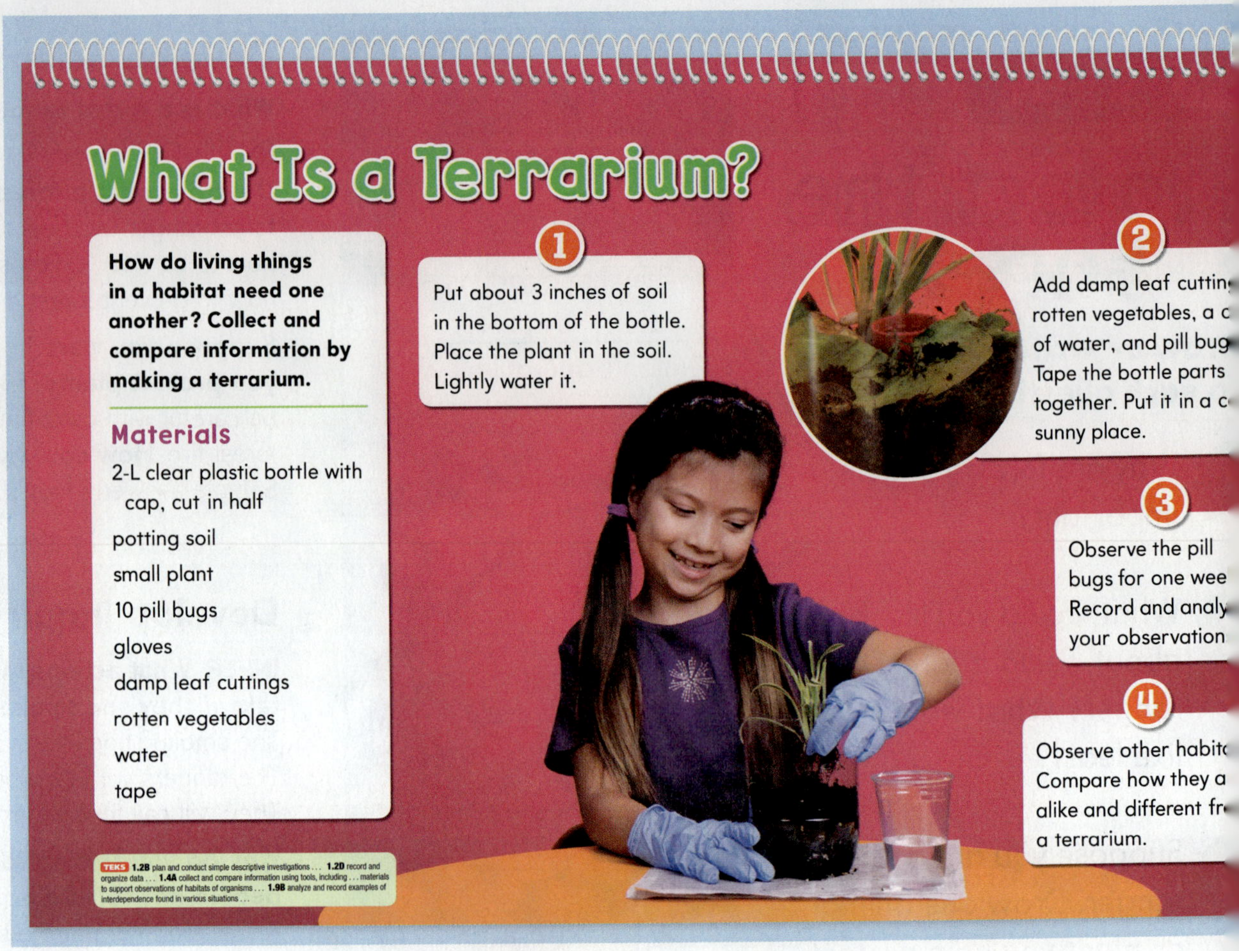

Inquiry Skills Focus Make a Model

Objectives

- Ask questions about organisms observed in the natural world.
- Plan and conduct investigations. Record and organize data.
- Collect and compare information using tools, including materials to support observations of habitats of organisms.
- Analyze and record examples of interdependence found in various situations.

Prep and Planning Tips

See the Planning for Inquiry page for more information.

- Cut the 2-L bottles in half, about six inches from the bottom. Large, wide-mouth jars or covered plastic bowls can substitute.
- When the soil gets dry, mist it with water to keep pill bugs alive.

Expected Results

Children will conclude that animals get what they need from their environment. They will record and analyze examples of interdependence, such as the pill bugs drinking water, eating rotten vegetables, and using the leaf cuttings for shelter.

1 Engage/Explore

Attention Grabber

Put a stuffed animal in a large box and place it on a desk or table. Ask children the following, "Suppose this animal is real. What things would we need to put in the box to make an environment that could keep the animal alive?" Have each child find a classroom object or draw a picture of an object to put in the box. Then have children take turns putting their contributions to the environment in the box as they explain their choices to the class.

Preview Activity

Before beginning the investigation, have children review the directions on the Inquiry Flipchart and the accompanying Student Edition response pages. Then have them complete the response pages as they follow the directions on the Flipchart.

S.T.E.M. continued

Map It!

This map shows a place designed for animals. People make sure the animals can meet their needs there. Use the map to find out how.

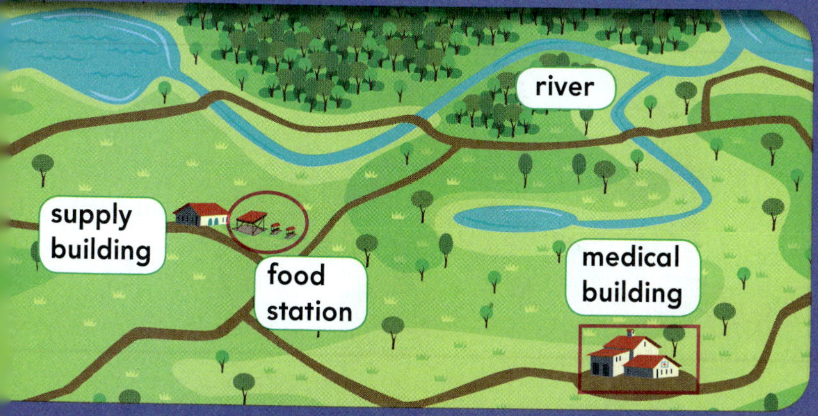

cle where animals can get food.
aw an X where animals can get water.
aw a box around where sick animals can get well.

Children can put an X over any part of the river.

ld On It!

Design a place for butterflies to live and grow. Complete **Design It: Butterfly Garden** on the Inquiry Flipchart.

Build On It!

In **Design It: Butterfly Garden**, the design challenge associated with this lesson, children use the steps of the engineering design process to design a garden, or sanctuary, for butterflies.

For more details, see the pages that follow.

Other opportunities to apply the design process appear throughout the *Inquiry Flipchart*.

TEKS 1.3A

Develop S.T.E.M. Concepts

When children have completed reading the feature, ask questions to help them reflect on ways sanctuaries help animals.

What problem does an animal sanctuary solve? It gives animals a safe place to live where they will be well cared for and protected.

Why do some animals need sanctuaries? Some animals need a place where they can get medical treatment and have a safe place to live.

How do sanctuaries meet animals' needs? They give the animals medical care, food, water, and shelter.

Develop Inquiry Skills

OBSERVE **Look at the map. Where can animals meet their needs for food, water, and medical care?** The animals get food at the food station, water from the rivers, and medical care at the medical building.

DRAW CONCLUSIONS **What makes this sanctuary a good place for animals?** Sample answer: It has places where animals can meet their needs for food, water, shelter, and medical care.

Notebook Summarize Ideas

Ask children to summarize what they learned about how technology can solve problems and help people help animals meet their needs. Have them tell what an animal sanctuary is and how it solves a problem.

1 Engage/Explore | 2 Explain | 3 Extend/Evaluate

S.T.E.M.

Engineering and Technology

FLIPCHART P. 43

30 minutes

pairs or small groups

Objectives

- Record and organize data.
- Identify and explain a problem and propose a solution in his/her own words.
- Use the steps of the engineering design process to design a butterfly sanctuary.
- Apply the scientific concepts of systems and system models and form and function.

Prep and Planning Tips

- Provide books or online resources that have photographs of butterflies.
- Discuss butterfly needs: flowers for the nectar that butterflies use for food; shade to keep cool; puddles for drinking water; sunny places to get warm; bushes and trees for shelter from wind, rain, and predators.

Expected Results

Children will design a garden where butterflies can meet their needs.

1 Engage/Explore

Attention Grabber

Ask volunteers to tell about butterflies they have seen. Then show children a photograph of a butterfly on a flower. Discuss why butterflies are often seen on or around flowers. Tell children that butterflies are attracted to certain kinds of plants. Suggest that children use those kinds of plants in their butterfly garden.

Preview Activity

Before beginning the activity, have children review the directions on the Engineering and Technology Flipchart page.

Guide the Activity

Develop Inquiry Skills

USE MODELS Have children use the map of the animal sanctuary as a model for their butterfly garden. Remind them to keep the specific purpose in mind. Have children label their designs and caption them with the purpose.

COMMUNICATE Ask children to present their completed designs to the class. Have them display their drawings and explain the different areas and why they were included.

Strategies for Success

Before the activity, have children review the directions on the *Inquiry Flipchart*. Show them photographs of butterflies in the natural environment in books or online. Suggest that they sketch each part of the garden in pencil before they color with crayons or markers. To be sure children provide for each butterfly need, have them list the needs and then check them off as they include them in the design.

Science Notebook

During the Activity Remind children to make their drawings clear enough to follow if someone were to build the garden. Partners should check each other's work to see that the designs are in agreement and that all parts are labeled.

2 Explain

Develop the Engineering Design Process

Use the following steps of the engineering design process to provide context and support for the analyses that children are doing in the flipchart activity.

1. FIND A PROBLEM **What will you design? Identify and explain the problem it will solve.** Sample answer: I want to design a butterfly garden that has everything a butterfly needs to live.
2. PLAN AND BUILD **How did you decide what to put in your garden? How did you decide where to put it?** Sample answer: I had to include places where the butterflies could meet all their needs. I decided to spread the places out so it wouldn't get too crowded in one area.

3 Extend/Evaluate

Quick Check

How did you decide what your sanctuary design would be? What problems did you have when you planned your design? How did you solve them? Accept all reasonable answers.

4. REDESIGN Help children research the needs of a particular butterfly and then use the information to refine their designs. Prompt children with questions such as: *What kinds of flowers does the butterfly like? Does it have other needs?*
5. COMMUNICATE Have groups share their designs with the class.

Science Notebook

After the Activity Check children's designs to see that they have drawn a butterfly garden Make sure that children have labeled the individual areas of the garden, captioned the design with its purpose, and written a sentence that tells how butterflies use it.

Michael DiSpezio's Tips & Tricks

Exchanging Ideas Prior to the activity, gather an assortment of print and online butterfly resources into a learning center. Allow time for children to learn about butterflies in general and a particular butterfly type they like. As children develop their garden ideas, organize them into teams. Encourage an idea exchange between team members. Have them discuss, assess, update, and record their designs. If applicable, extend the process by providing art materials that children can use to construct models of their proposed designs.

Enduring Understandings

Revisit the Big Idea and Essential Questions

Big Idea **Living and nonliving things are found in environments. A living thing lives in an environment that meets its needs.**

To explore the Big Idea, challenge children to work in groups of three or four to generate as many statements that support the Big Idea as possible. Then, have each group compare its list with the lists other groups make. Next, ask the class to work together to generate a master set of statements. Then, have them add their statements to their Science Notebooks. Prompt children with some sample environments to discuss.

- desert
- rain forest
- prairie
- tundra
- ocean

Essential Questions

Post the Essential Questions, and use the following prompts to guide a discussion.

Lessons/Essential Questions	Prompts
L1 **What Are Living and Nonliving Things?**	• Name two living things and two nonliving things.
L2 **Where Do Plants and Animals Live?**	• Name an environment and some of the plants and animals that live in it.
L3 **What Is a Terrarium?**	• Explain how you make a terrarium.

Science Notebook

You may use the following strategies after children complete the unit or after each lesson.

- Have children review and edit the responses to the Essential Questions they drafted at the beginning of the unit. Suggest they cross out sentences or ideas that are unnecessary or inappropriate.
- Help children draw a ten-by-ten grid on a page of their Science Notebook. Have them use the vocabulary words to make a word search. Instruct them to write the words from left to right in different parts of the grid. Then, have them fill in the empty boxes with random letters. Have children exchange their word searches with a partner.

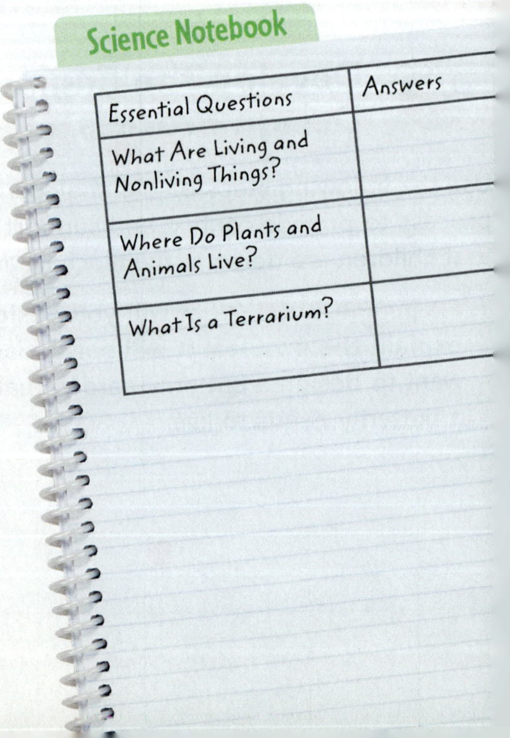

Unit 8 Review

Name ______________________

/ocabulary Review

Jse the terms in the box to complete he sentences.

environment
reproduce
shelter

EKS 1.9C

. An animal might use a plant for shelter.

EKS 1.9B

. All the living and nonliving things around you make up your environment.

EKS 1.9A

. When animals make new living things like themselves, they reproduce.

cience Concepts

ll in the letter of the choice that best nswers the question.

KS 1.9A

How are living things **different** from nonliving things?

Ⓐ They may be large or small.

Ⓑ They have needs and reproduce.

Ⓒ They can be found in many places.

TEKS 1.9B

5. A kangaroo rat needs little water to live. It lives underground to stay cool. Which **best** meets its needs?

Ⓐ a desert

Ⓑ an ocean

Ⓒ a tundra

Item Analysis

Items	TEKS	Depth of Knowledge	Cognitive Complexity
1	**1.9C**	1	Low
2	**1.9B**	1	Low
3	**1.9A**	1	Low
4	**1.9A**	3	Moderate
5	**1.9B**	2	Moderate

Unit Review

Answer Key

Vocabulary Review (5 points each)

1. shelter

   Discuss how animals have different ways to stay safe. Have children give examples of ways animals find shelter in their environment.

2. environment

   Ask children to name different kinds of environments.

3. reproduce

   Elicit from children that the words *make new living things like themselves* is the definition of the word that completes this sentence.

Science Concepts (7 points each)

4. B

   Point out the boldfaced word *different* in the question, and explain that children are looking for an answer choice that tells a way that living things are not like nonliving things.

5. A

   Have children describe each environment listed as an answer choice. Then, discuss why a desert is the best environment for a kangaroo rat. Ask volunteers to suggest other animals and plants that live in a desert environment.

Assessment

Unit 8 Test and Performance Assessment

See Assessment Guide, pp. AG 116–AG 122, for Unit Test and Performance Task with Long Option rubric.

Unit Review *continued*

Answer Key

Science Concepts (7 points each)

6. C

Review that *basic needs* are things that living things need to survive, or live. Ask volunteers to identify each picture in the answer choices. Ask, "Which of these pictures shows a living thing that has basic needs?"

7. A

Have children refer back to the section on a prairie environment. Have them describe what one is like and the animals that might live there.

8. B

Be sure children can see the subtle detail in the picture of the bird about to pull on the worm. Discuss how birds use worms.

9. B

Have children recall all the basic needs of animals. If necessary, refer children to the glossary definition of *shelter*.

UNIT 8

TEKS 1.9A

6. Which of these has basic needs?

Ⓐ 

Ⓑ 

Ⓒ 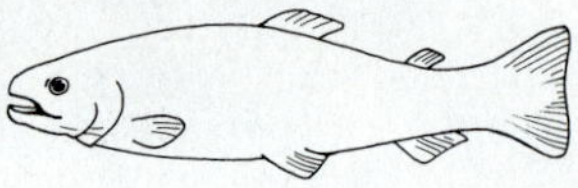

TEKS 1.9B

7. What kind of animal might live on the prairie?

Ⓐ an animal that eats grass
Ⓑ an animal that can live with little water
Ⓒ an animal that uses tall trees for shelter

TEKS 1.2B, 1.9A

8. Jamie is investigating the needs of animals. She observes the birds. Which need are these birds meeting?

Ⓐ air
Ⓑ food
Ⓒ water

TEKS 1.9C

9. How is this animal using the log?

Ⓐ for food
Ⓑ for shelter
Ⓒ for water

Item Analysis *(continued)*

Items	TEKS	Depth of Knowledge	Cognitive Complexity
6	**1.9A**	1	Low
7	**1.9B**	2	Moderate
8	**1.2B, 1.9A**	2	Moderate
9	**1.9C**	2	Moderate

TEKS 1.9B

10. Which is **true** about an animal you keep as a pet?

Ⓐ It does not have basic needs.

Ⓑ It needs people to help it meet its needs.

Ⓒ It does not need shelter or food.

TEKS 1.9C

11. How might one living thing depend on another living thing in an ocean environment?

Ⓐ A shark might use a fish for food.

Ⓑ A bird might use a tree for shelter.

Ⓒ A cow might use grass for food.

TEKS 1.2D, 1.9C

12. Felix draws this food chain in his science notebook.

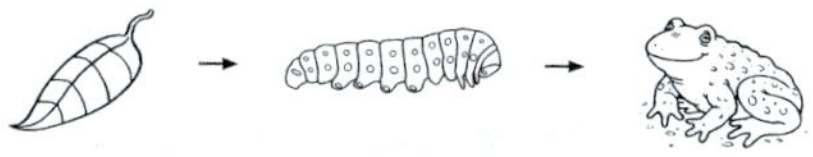

What does this food chain show?

Ⓐ The caterpillar uses the frog for food.

Ⓑ The frog uses the leaf for food.

Ⓒ The frog uses the caterpillar for food.

UNIT 8

Item Analysis *(continued)*

Items	TEKS	Depth of Knowledge	Cognitive Complexity
10	**1.9B**	2	Low
11	**1.9C**	2	Moderate
12	**1.2D, 1.9C**	2	Moderate

Unit Review *continued*

Answer Key

Science Concepts (7 points each)

10. B

Remind children that pets are living things and have the same basic needs as other animals.

11. A

Have children describe an ocean environment and name living things that can be found in one. If necessary, review the section on oceans.

12. C

Point out the arrows and their direction in the diagram. Have children explain what the arrows in a food chain show.

Short Option Performance Assessment

Task

Design and Build a Model Environment
Have children design and build a model environment for an animal. Have them describe the animal and its environment. Children should describe how the animal depends on other living things in order to surive, such as using plants for shelter or using plants and other animals for food.

Rubric

Preparation Provide the following materials: a shoebox, clay, cotton balls, scissors, glue, and other art materials.

Scoring Rubric—Performance Indicators

___ Chooses an animal.

___ Designs and builds a model of its environment.

___ Describes how the animal depends on other living things in order to help it survive.

Observations and Rubric Scores

3 2 1 0

Unit Review *continued*

Answer Key

Inquiry and the Big Idea (11 points each)

13.

a. the need for food

b. Sample answers: air, water, shelter, space

Tell children to remember that a deer is a living thing and that it needs the same things all living things need to survive.

14. The rotten vegetables provide food for the pill bugs. The pill bugs use the damp leaves for shelter.

Review with children all the basic needs of animals. Point out that the question is asking children to infer what has happened to the rotten vegetables that are gone. A good inference is that the pill bugs have eaten them.

UNIT 8

Inquiry and the Big Idea

Write the answers to these questions.

TEKS 1.9A, 1.9C

13. Look at this deer.

a. What need is this deer meeting?

the need for food

b. Name two other needs the deer has.

Sample answers: air, water, shelter, space

TEKS 1.9B, 1.9C

14. You can gather evidence of how living things depend on each other. You can make a terrarium. Put pill bugs in a jar with soil, damp leaves, and a few rotten vegetables. After a few days, you see that most of the vegetables are gone. You see pill bugs hiding under the damp leaves.

Analyze and record how the bugs need other things in the terrarium.

The rotten vegetables provide food for the pill bugs.

The pill bugs use the damp leaves for shelter.

338 **Unit 8** Unit Review

Item Analysis

Items	TEKS	Depth of Knowledge	Cognitive Complexity
13	**1.9A, 1.9C**	3	Moderate
14	**1.9B, 1.9C**	3	High

UNIT 9 Animals

Big Idea and Essential Questions

This Unit was designed to focus on this Big Idea and these Essential Questions.

Big Idea

Animals have adaptations that help them survive. Animals have different life cycles.

Essential Questions

L1 **How Do Animals Differ?**

L2 **How Can We Group Animals?**

L3 **What Are Some Animal Life Cycles?**

Take It Home! A School-Home Connection letter in English and Spanish is provided in Online Resources.

Professional Development

Houghton Mifflin Harcourt and **NSTA,** the **National Science Teachers Association,** have partnered to provide customized professional development resources for teachers using *ScienceFusion*.

The Professional Development Resources include:

- Do-it-yourself resources, where you can study at your own pace
- Live and archived online seminars
- Journal articles, many of which include lesson plans
- Fee-based eBooks, eBook chapters, online short courses, symposia, and conferences

Access to The NSTA Learning Center is provided in the *ScienceFusion* Online Resources.

Unit Planning

Options for Instruction

Choose from **Interactive Worktext** and **Leveled Readers**, **Digital**, and **Inquiry** options to meet the Texas Essential Knowledge and Skills.

	LESSON 1	LESSON 2	LESSON 3
Essential Questions	**How Do Animals Differ?**	✔ Guided Inquiry **How Can We Group Animals?**	**What Are Some Animal Life Cycles?**
Texas Essential Knowledge and Skills	TEKS 1.10A	TEKS 1.2A, 1.2B, 1.2D, 1.10A	TEKS 1.10C, 1.10D
Interactive Worktext	☐ **Student Edition** pp. 341–352 • Adaptable Animals • Move It! • Time to Eat • Hide Me!	☐ **Student Edition** pp. 353–356 • Scaffolding for Inquiry	☐ **Student Edition** pp. 359–370 • Animal Start-Ups • Hatch, Swim, Hop • Polar Parenting • The Mighty Monarch
Leveled Readers	Parallel coverage of the lesson topics is provided in the **Extra Support**, **On-Level**, and **Enrichment** readers. See p. 339H for detailed reader information.		
Hands-On Inquiry	**Inquiry Flipchart** p. 44 **Animals Adapt** ☐ Directed Inquiry **Picture Walk Safari** ☐ Independent Inquiry	**Inquiry Flipchart** p. 45 **How Can We Group Animals?** ☐ Guided Inquiry	**Inquiry Flipchart** p. 47 **Where's the Caterpillar?** ☐ Directed Inquiry **What's My Life Cycle?** ☐ Independent Inquiry
Digital Curriculum	☐ **Digital Lesson** Online Resources Interactive presentation of lesson content	☐ **Virtual Lab** Online Resources Interactive scaffolded inquiry	☐ **Digital Lesson** Online Resources Interactive presentation of lesson content

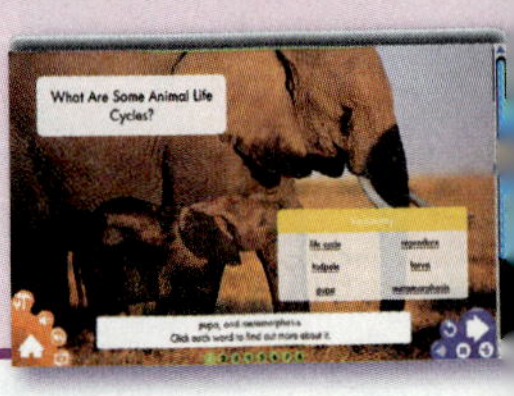

OTHER UNIT FEATURES

Careers in Science, p. 371

S.T.E.M. Engineering and Technology, pp. 357–358B

Online Resources

Interactive Whiteboard Resources for Unit 9

Assessment

Formative Assessment
Sum It Up! and Brain Check
Student Edition, end of each lesson

Summative Assessment
Lesson Quizzes
Assessment Guide, pp. AG 123–AG 125

Unit 9 Review
Student Edition, pp. 373–376

Unit 9 Test
Assessment Guide, pp. AG 128–AG 132

Performance Assessment
SHORT OPTION: Teacher Edition, p. 375
LONG OPTION: Assessment Guide, pp. AG 133–AG 134

Response to Intervention
RTI Strategies, p. 339I

Online Assessment
Test-taking and automatic scoring
Banks of items from which to build tests

Teacher Notes

Planning for Inquiry

Use the following preview of Inquiry Activities and Lessons to gather and manage the materials needed for each lesson.

Activity	Inquiry and Design Process Skills Focus	Materials	Prep Tips, Troubleshooting, and Expected Results
Lesson 1 DIRECTED INQUIRY Flipchart p.44 **A Animals Adapt** **OBJECTIVES** Plan and conduct simple investigations. Record and organize data. Communicate observations. Record information using notebooks. Investigate how the external characteristics of an animal are related to where it lives, how it moves, and what it eats. 25–30 minutes individuals TEKS **1.2B, 1.2D, 1.2E, 1.4A, 1.10A**	• Observe • Communicate • Draw Conclusions	• Science Notebook • index cards (optional)	**Prep Tips** Before the activity, talk about where children might find animals. Have children record their notes and drawings on index cards if they do not want to carry their Science Notebooks outdoors. If weather or other factors prevent outdoor observation, consider using classroom pets or online videos of animals in the wild. **Caution!** Remind children not to touch or get too close to any animals they find. **Troubleshooting** If children focus on only larger animals, they may not find many. Encourage them to look toward the sky and trees as well as looking for animals up close on the ground or on plants. **Expected Results** Children will observe that an animal's external features relate to where it lives, how it moves, and what it eats. Their drawings and notes should include information about body parts, such as teeth, legs, eyes, wings, beaks, fur, and feathers.
INDEPENDENT INQUIRY Flipchart p.44 **B Picture Walk Safari** **OBJECTIVES** Record and organize data. Collect, record, and compare information using computers. Investigate how the external characteristics of an animal are related to where it lives, how it moves, and what it eats. 30 minutes pairs TEKS **1.2D, 1.4A, 1.10A**	• Observe • Compare • Plan and Conduct a Simple Investigation	• computer	**Prep Tips** Prior to the activity, have sites already bookmarked for children to visit. Go over computer rules, such as going only to the sites designated by the teacher. Review how to use a computer ahead of time. Practice with children how to take notes from the sites they review. Have computers set up so that children know where to take notes while searching through the sites. **Expected Results** Children will learn how to collect, record, and compare information using a computer. They will investigate how external characteristics help animals survive.

Additional teaching support for all inquiry activities is available in **Online Resources.**

Notebook **Science Notebook Strategies**

- Lists of Kit-Supplied Materials
- Meeting Individual Needs
- Investigate More—Extensions and Variations
- and More!

Activity	Inquiry and Design Process Skills Focus	Materials	Prep Tips, Troubleshooting, and Expected Results
Lesson 2 INQUIRY GUIDED INQUIRY **Flipchart** p. 45 **Student Edition** pp. 353–356 **How Can We Group Animals?** **OBJECTIVES** • Recognize the importance of safe practices. • Plan and conduct simple investigations. • Record and organize data. • Communicate observations. • Investigate how the external characteristics of an animal are related to where it lives, how it moves, and what it eats. 20 minutes · individuals TEKS **1.1B, 1.2B, 1.2D, 1.2E, 1.10A**	• Classify • Observe • Compare • Gather, Record, Display, or Interpret Data	• picture cards from Student Edition p. 355 • safety scissors • 3 pieces of yarn, each about 3.5 feet long (per child) • index cards (to write labels for the animal groups) • tape (optional)	**Prep Tips** Have children cut out the animal picture cards on Student Edition p. 355. Guide children in forming their yarn-sorting circles so that each circle is large enough to hold up to eight picture cards. **Caution!** Remind them to be careful when using scissors. **Troubleshooting** To assure that the sorting circles keep their shape as children work, you may wish to tie the ends of the circles together and tape the circles down to a table or the floor. **Expected Results** Children will observe that some animals move in only one way, while others move in two or three ways. They may notice that the way an animal moves is related to the body parts it has.

Go Digital! Virtual Lab

How Can We Group Animals?

Key Inquiry Skills: observe, compare, order

Children observe the body coverings of different animals to separate them into groups.

Planning for Inquiry (continued)

Activity	Inquiry and Design Process Skills Focus	Materials	Prep Tips, Troubleshooting, and Expected Results
S.T.E.M. Engineering and Technology Flipchart p.46 **Design It: Guard the Lettuce!** **OBJECTIVES** • Record and organize data. • Identify and explain a problem and propose a solution in his/her own words. 25 minutes small groups TEKS **1.2D, 1.3A**	 **1 Find a Problem** **2 Plan and Build** **3 Test and Improve** **4 Redesign** **5 Communicate**	• toy stuffed rabbit • twine/wire • glue • netting • wood • Science Notebook	**Prep Tips** Display a life-size toy rabbit for children to examine. Tell them a rabbit can jump about 18 inches, and demonstrate with the toy. **Expected Results** Children will design a structure to surround a garden so that the structure's slats or openings are too small for a rabbit to squeeze through, high enough to block jumping, and far enough from the plants to avoid nibbling.

Additional teaching support for all inquiry activities is available in Online Resources.

Activity	Inquiry and Design Process Skills Focus	Materials	Prep Tips, Troubleshooting, and Expected Results
Lesson 3 DIRECTED INQUIRY Flipchart p.47 **A Where's the Caterpillar?** **OBJECTIVES** Plan and conduct simple investigations. Record and organize data. Observe and record life cycles of animals. 15 minutes for setup; 10 minutes per day for 2 weeks to observe small groups TEKS **1.2B, 1.2D, 1.10D**	• Observe • Gather, Record, Display, or Interpret Data • Draw Conclusions	• jars • caterpillars • leafy twigs • cheesecloth • rubber bands • soil, with grass attached	**Prep Tips** If ordering caterpillars, plan enough time for shipping. Follow care and handling instructions. Select a location for the containers where they will not be disturbed. Fill a jar with twigs, soil, and grass for each group. Cut the cheesecloth to cover the tops of the jars, and secure it with a rubber band. Children can use plastic spoons or other utensils to move the caterpillars into the jars so they do not have to touch them with their bare hands. If supplies are limited, you may wish to perform this investigation as a class. Allow 10 minutes per day for 2 weeks for children to observe and record their observations. **Caution!** Wear gloves. Remind children to wash their hands after the activity. **Troubleshooting** Remind children to be careful when replacing twigs in the jar. If necessary, instruct them to gently dislodge the caterpillar from the twigs before replacing them. **Expected Results** Children will be able to observe the caterpillars eating the leaves. Over time, they should notice that the caterpillars have grown. They will observe that a larva will become a pupa about two weeks after hatching.
INDEPENDENT INQUIRY Flipchart p.47 **B What's My Life Cycle?** **OBJECTIVES** Plan and conduct simple investigations. Record and organize data. Compare ways that young animals resemble their parents. Observe and record life cycles of animals. 30 minutes individuals TEKS **1.2B, 1.2D, 1.10C, 1.10D**	• Plan and Conduct a Simple Investigation	• nonfiction animal books • online sources • Science Notebook • index cards (optional)	**Prep Tips** In advance, compile kid-friendly books and online sources (such as zoo websites) that children can use to do their research. Before they begin their research, you may wish to go over the different kinds of animal life cycles. **Expected Results** To keep children on task as they do their investigations, check in after 10 minutes to make sure they have chosen an animal and moved on to researching its life cycle. **Expected Results** Children will choose one of the three animals mentioned on the flipchart and research its life cycle. They will be able to communicate the different stages of the animal's life cycle from birth to adulthood. They will compare ways that the young animal looks like its parents.

Differentiated Instruction

Leveled Readers

The Leveled Readers provide parallel coverage of the unit topics and Texas Essential Knowledge and Skills. Each Reader is available in English and Spanish. Both versions are available online and on touchscreen mobile devices.

ON-LEVEL This Reader reinforces unit concepts and vocabulary and focuses on the Texas Essential Knowledge and Skills. It includes student response activities.

EXTRA SUPPORT This Reader shares title, illustrations, vocabulary, and concepts with the On-Level Reader. However, the text is linguistically accommodated to provide simplified sentence structures and comprehension aids for students who need a little extra support with content-area reading and vocabulary development. It also includes student response activities.

ENRICHMENT This high-interest nonfiction Reader enriches and extends unit concepts. It reinforces some of the unit vocabulary, but also includes stretch vocabulary. It also includes student response activities.

TEACHER GUIDE

The accompanying Teacher Guide provides teaching strategies and support for using all the Readers, as well as English and Spanish worksheets that focus on vocabulary development. A correlation to the Texas Essential Knowledge and Skills is included.

DIGITAL VERSIONS

All of these Leveled Readers are available online. They are also available in an innovative and engaging format for touchscreen mobile devices. For information about accessing these versions, see page T9.

RTI Response to Intervention

Response to Intervention is a process for identifying and supporting students who are not making expected progress toward essential learning goals.

The following *ScienceFusion* components have the flexibility to be used to provide Core Classroom Instruction (Tier 1), strategic intervention (Tier 2), and intensive intervention (Tier 3).

Component	Location	Strategies and Benefits
Student Edition, Active Reading prompts, Sum It Up, Brain Check	Active Reading throughout each lesson, Sum It Up and Brain Check at the end of each lesson	Student responses can be used as screening tools to assess whether intervention is needed.
Assessment Guide, Lesson Quizzes and TEKS DOK Skill Builder	pp. AG 123–AG 127	Student responses can be used as screening tools to assess whether intervention is needed.
Inquiry Flipcharts	Inquiry Flipchart p. 45	Directed Inquiry for students who learn best through directed or teacher-led hands-on activities.
Teacher Edition, Unit Review Answer Strategies	TE pp. 373–376	Suggestions for intervention, guidance, and remediation for each review question.
Leveled Readers	TE p. 339H	Content support for students not meeting the learning needs during core classroom instruction.
Leveled Readers, Teacher Guides and Vocabulary Worksheets	TE p. 339H	Direct instruction with small groups of students needing additional content at various readability levels.
Extra Support for Vocabulary and Concepts (online worksheets)	Online Resources	Support for individualized instruction with practice in essential content.
Online Student Edition with Audio	Online Resources	Provides learners with multiple-modality access to science concepts and information.
Interactive Digital Lessons and Virtual Labs	Online Resources	Provides individualized learning experiences. Lessons make content accessible through simulations, animations, videos, audio, and integrated assessment.
Interactive Whiteboard Resources	Online Resources	Reinforces key unit concepts through interactive vocabulary games and visuals and graphic organizers.
Leveled Readers, online and tablet versions	Online and Tablet Resources	Highlighted words and sentences synced with audio provide support for emerging or struggling readers.

Differentiated Instruction

English Language Learners

Choose from these instructional strategies to meet the needs of English language learners.

Vocabulary Cards are provided in Online Resources.

Unit Vocabulary

Lesson 1	Lesson 3
adaptation	reproduce
	life cycle
	tadpole
	larva
	pupa

Preteach Vocabulary ELPS 3C

Pronounce each word and have children repeat. Use visuals and accessible language to define each vocabulary term. Then, have children define each term in their own words.

Language Acquisition Strategies

Sight Words ELPS 4C

Display a list of sight words from **TE page 342:** *have, and, are, is, or, that, to, where.* Have children practice reading and saying these words.

Beginning	Intermediate	Advanced/Advanced High
Point to each word and say it. Have children repeat after you. Do this several times. Then, point to each word and have children read it.	Have children make sight words flash cards. Have partners take turns displaying a card and reading it aloud.	Have children read aloud the list of words. Then, have children use the words in sentences. Ask them to read their sentences to a partner.

Retell Information **ELPS** 3B, 3H, 4F

Use the pictures on **TE pages 344–345** to have children practice retelling information.

Beginning	Intermediate	Advanced/Advanced High
Review the information in the pictures. Then, have children share one fact they learned about how an animal uses its body parts to move, using one of the pictures for support.	Read aloud the captions for the first two pictures. Have children explain how a monkey and a frog are alike.	Have children refer to the pictures as they retell what they learned about adaptations that allow animals to move.

Think, Pair, Share **ELPS** 1C, 2I, 3I

Have children collaborate with peers to share what they learned about adaptations that keep animals safe on **TE pages 348–349.**

Beginning	Intermediate	Advanced/Advanced High
Have children draw a picture to show one adaptation that allows an animal to hide. Ask partners to share and check each other's pictures. Then, have partners show their pictures to the class.	Have children identify adaptations that allow animals to hide. Then, have them work with a partner to complete these sentence frames: *An animal's ___ allows it to hide. An animal's __ also allows it to blend in.* Have partners share their sentences with the class.	Have children think about this question and then discuss it with a partner: *How do adaptations keep animals safe?* Have partners share their answer with the class.

Express Opinions **ELPS** 3C, 3G, 3H

Use *Careers in Science* on **TE page 371** to give children practice expressing their opinions.

Beginning	Intermediate	Advanced/Advanced High
Read aloud the information about what a zoo keeper does. Model sharing an opinion about this job. Then, have children do the same by sharing an opinion with a partner.	Have children use phrases or simple sentences to tell what they would like about being a zoo keeper.	Have children explain to a partner what they would like and dislike about being a zoo keeper.

UNIT 9

Animals

I Wonder How

Have children look at the photographs and describe what they see. Then ask them to share what they know about the different life cycles of animals, such as birds and dogs. Discuss any other information or clues from the photographs that help children answer the "how" question.

Here's How

Have children turn the page and read the response to the question. You may wish to share the following background with them.

More About...

Spoonbills

These long-legged pinkish wading birds are usually found in marshes, swamps, bayous, and lakes. Living mainly in southern Florida, parts of Texas, and southwest Louisiana, they eat small fish, amphibians, and some plants.

Spoonbills breed in their third year of life. Using twigs and other materials, the female builds a strong, deep nest. Florida spoonbills nest in red and black mangroves. Females usually lay about three eggs. Their young hatch after an incubation period of between 22 and 24 days.

Science Songs

See pp. TR40–TR45 for science songs you can use to reinforce content in this unit.

UNIT 9

Animals

Big Idea

Animals have adaptations that help them survive. Animals have different life cycles.

TEKS 1.2A, 1.2B, 1.2D, 1.3A, 1.3C, 1.10C, 1.10D

adult spoonbill

I Wonder How

Life cycles of animals can be different. How?

Turn the page to find out.

Professional Development Science Background

Use the keyword to access

- Professional Development from **The NSTA Learning Center**
- **SciLinks** for additional online content appropriate for children and teachers
- Teacher Science Background in the back of this Teacher Edition

Keyword

animals

SCILINKS. THE WORLD'S A CLICK AWAY

Here's How Some animals are born live. Some hatch from eggs. Some young look like their parents. Others do not.

In this unit, you will explore this Big Idea, the Essential Questions, and the Investigations on the Inquiry Flipchart.

Levels of Inquiry Key ■ DIRECTED ■ GUIDED ■ INDEPENDENT

Track Your Progress

Big Idea Animals have adaptations that help them survive. Animals have different life cycles.

Essential Questions

Now I Get the Big Idea!

Science Notebook

Before you begin each lesson, be sure to write your thoughts about the Essential Question.

Go Digital

or a complete digital urriculum and resources hat provide full coverage f the objectives for his unit, see the Online esources for this program.

Big Idea and Essential Questions

Big Idea Animals have adaptations that help them survive. Animals have different life cycles.

Post the Unit Big Idea on the board. Have children read the Essential Questions, which are also the titles of the lessons in this unit.

- Discuss how the Essential Questions can help keep them focused on the Big Idea.
- Have children read the Big Idea statement. The statement describes the main science concept that they will be learning.
- Have children predict other ideas that will be taught in the lessons based on the titles, or have them give examples of pictures they expect to see.

Once they complete the unit, they should have a better understanding of the Big Idea.

Essential Questions You may use the following Science Notebook strategy for working with the Essential Questions before children begin the unit or before each lesson.

- Strategies for revisiting the Big Idea and the Essential Questions are provided in Enduring Understandings on p. 373A.

Notebook Science Notebook

- Have children copy the Essential Questions into their Science Notebooks. Suggest they leave writing lines between questions.
- Ask children to write responses to the Essential Questions. Urge them not to worry about whether their responses are correct. They should expect their ideas to change as they work. Comment that children will be able to revise their answers to the Essential Questions at the end of the unit.
- Tips and strategies for using Science Notebooks are provided throughout this unit, in the back of this Teacher Edition, and in the Online Resources.

Options for Inquiry

FLIPCHART P. 44

Children can conduct these optional investigations at any time before, during, or in response to the lesson in the Student Edition.

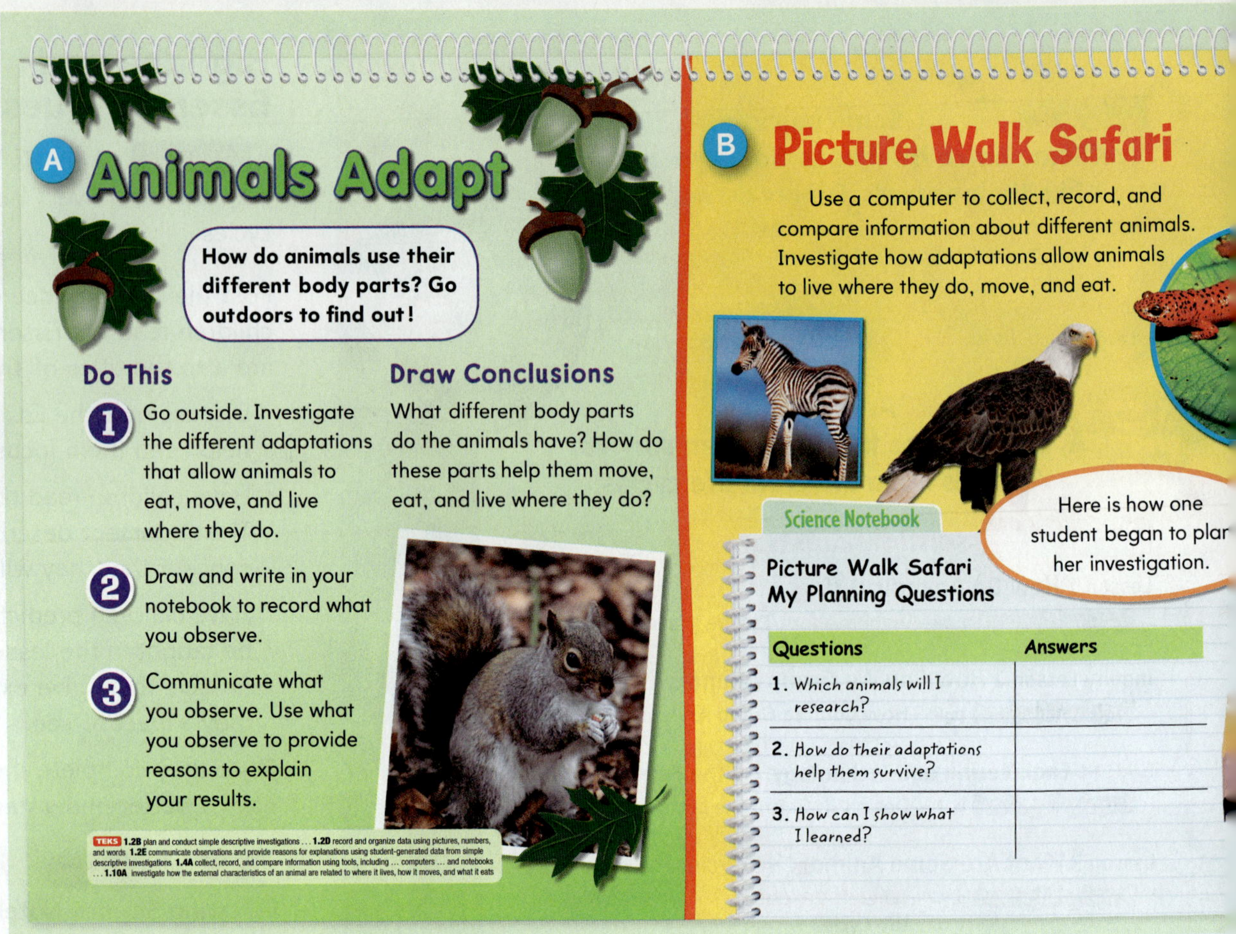

A Animals Adapt

How do animals use their different body parts? Go outdoors to find out!

Do This

1. Go outside. Investigate the different adaptations that allow animals to eat, move, and live where they do.
2. Draw and write in your notebook to record what you observe.
3. Communicate what you observe. Use what you observe to provide reasons to explain your results.

Draw Conclusions

What different body parts do the animals have? How do these parts help them move, eat, and live where they do?

TEKS **1.2B** plan and conduct simple descriptive investigations . . . **1.2D** record and organize data using pictures, numbers, and words **1.2E** communicate observations and provide reasons for explanations using student-generated data from simple descriptive investigations **1.4A** collect, record, and compare information using tools, including … computers … and notebooks . . . **1.10A** investigate how the external characteristics of an animal are related to where it lives, how it moves, and what it eats

B Picture Walk Safari

Use a computer to collect, record, and compare information about different animals. Investigate how adaptations allow animals to live where they do, move, and eat.

Science Notebook

Here is how one student began to plan her investigation.

Picture Walk Safari
My Planning Questions

Questions	Answers
1. Which animals will I research?	
2. How do their adaptations help them survive?	
3. How can I show what I learned?	

Directed Inquiry

A Animals Adapt

25–30 minutes
individuals

Prep and Planning Tips

To prepare, talk about places at school where children might be able to observe and investigate animals. Have them name the animals they think they will find.

Encourage children to investigate the larger environment, such as toward the sky and trees, in addition to looking for animals up close on the ground or on plants.

If children do not want to carry their notebooks, provide index cards for them to carry "into the field" to record notes and drawings.

Caution! Remind children to recognize the importance of safe practices to keep themselves safe and healthy by observing animals from a safe distance.

Expected Results

Children should observe that an animal's external characteristics (such as teeth, legs, eyes, wings, beak, fur, feathers) relate to where it lives, how it moves, and what it eats.

Independent Inquiry

B Picture Walk Safari

30 minutes
pairs

Prep and Planning Tips

See the Planning for Inquiry page for more information. Be sure to check with the school's Internet policies since children will be working on computers for this activity.

Science Notebook

Children can use the Science Notebook page shown on the Flipchart as a model for planning and conducting their own investigation. Encourage them to make a chart like the one shown and include the sample questions plus their own questions. Remind children that they are researching and investigating animals based on how their external characteristics allow them to eat, move, and live where they do.

EKS 1.10A investigate how the external characteristics of an animal are related to where it
es, how it moves, and what it eats

Lesson 1

ssential Question

How Do Animals Differ?

Engage Your Brain!

Find the answer to the question in the lesson.

This insect looks like a twig. How does this allow it to stay safe?

it hides it from other animals

Active Reading

esson Vocabulary

1 Preview the lesson.

2 Write the vocabulary term here.

daptation

quiry Flipchart p. 44—Animals Adapt/Picture Walk Safari

341

Go Digital

n interactive digital
esson is available in the
nline Resources. It is
uitable for individuals,
mall groups, or may be
rojected or used on an
teractive white board.

1 Engage/Explore

Objectives

- Plan and conduct simple investigations.
- Record and organize data using pictures and words.
- Communicate observations and provide reasons for explanations from investigations.
- Collect, record, and compare information using tools, including computers and notebooks.
- Investigate how the external characteristics of an animal are related to where it lives, how it moves, and what it eats.

Engage Your Brain!

Point out the picture and read the question. Have children brainstorm reasons why an insect might need to hide. Guide them by asking *What might happen to this insect if a bird saw it?* Record children's responses on the board.

Remind children to record their final answer to the question when they find it on the eighth page of the lesson.

Active Reading **Annotations**

Remind children that active readers "make texts their own" by marking them or writing notes to help them understand what they are reading. Encourage children to use pencil to make annotations and to feel free to change their marks and notes as they read. The goal of annotation is to help children remember what they have read.

Vocabulary and Interactive Glossary

Remind children to find and list the yellow highlighted terms from the lesson. As they proceed through the lesson and learn about the terms, they can add drawings or words in the extra spaces provided in some entries in the Interactive Glossary.

2 Explain

Notebook Generate Ideas

Have children look at the animals on these two pages. Ask them to name some of the animals' body parts, and use past experience to describe how the animals use these body parts.

Active Reading Vocabulary

Explain that a vocabulary word may be highlighted in a color. Active readers pay attention to highlighted words because their meaning is given in the same sentence or the next sentence.

Develop Science Vocabulary

adaptation Help children pronounce the word *adaptation*. Explain what it means and then allow time for children to practice saying, spelling, and writing it.

Develop Science Concepts

Ask children to investigate the different body parts that allow animals to live where they do. Have children look at the walrus. **In what kind of place does a walrus live?** It lives in a cold, icy place. **Suppose you are wearing a thick winter coat. How would it help you?** It would keep me warm. **A walrus has a thick layer of body fat called blubber. How does this allow the walrus to live in a cold place?** It keeps the walrus warm. Have children fill in the line in the interactive.

Develop Inquiry Skills

INFER **The walrus also has flippers. Why do you think the walrus needs flippers?** Flippers help it swim in the water.

Adaptable Animals

Animals have different body parts and behaviors. These are adaptations. An **adaptation** is a body part or behavior that helps a living thing survive. Adaptations allow animals to live where they do.

Active Reading

Find the sentence that tells the meaning of **adaptation.** Draw a line under the sentence.

Thick body fat lets the walrus live in a cold place.

342

English Language Learners

ELPS 1E, 2C, 2

Reinforce Content Words Point to the word *adaptation* in the paragraph, and have children circle the word. Say the word aloud, and have children repeat it after you. Explain that an adaptation is something that helps a living thing survive. It can be a body part, such as legs or wings or it can be a behavior. Work wit children to make a web of words that name body parts or behavio that help them, such as *legs*, *arr* and *teeth*. Read the list together and discuss why each one is an example of an adaptation.

Fish live in water. They use gills to take in air from the water.

▶ What allows a walrus to live in a cold place?

thick body fat

The elephant lives in a hot place. Big ears keep it cool.

343

Differentiation—Leveled Questions

Extra Support

Summarize why animals that live in different places have different body parts. They need body parts that will help them stay alive in the places where they live.

Challenge

What adaptations allow you to live where you do? Sample answer: I live on land and I use my legs to walk and my lungs to breathe.

Develop Science Concepts

Have children look at the external characteristics of the fish and the elephant.

Where do fish live? in water **What body parts do fish have that allow them to live in water?** gills, fins

Why are gills an important adaptation? Gills allow fish to take in oxygen from the water.

Where does the elephant live? in a hot land environment **How do elephants keep cool in a hot place?** Their large ears keep them cool.

Why do you think fish have gills, but walruses and elephants do not? Fish have gills because they need to live and breathe under the water. Walruses and elephants do not have gills because they live on land.

Develop Inquiry Skills

Remind children that when you compare and contrast things, you tell how they are alike and different.

COMPARE **What is alike about a walrus's fat, a fish's gills, and an elephant's ears?** They are all adaptations. They all help the animal survive in the place where it lives.

CONTRAST **How are a walrus's adaptations different from an elephant's adaptations? Why?** The walrus has thick body fat to live in a cold place. The elephant has big ears to keep it cool in a hot place. Their adaptations are different because they live in different places.

Notebook Summarize Ideas

Ask children to review what they know about the highlighted vocabulary word. Then have them summarize what an *adaptation* is, and give an example of how an adaptation allows an animal to live where it does.

2 Explain (continued)

Notebook Generate Ideas

Point out that animals move in many different ways depending on where they live. Guide children to brainstorm a list of verbs that describe different ways animals move (run, climb, fly, hop, jump, swim, slither). Invite volunteers to pantomime these words.

Develop Science Concepts

Ask children to investigate the different body parts that allow animals to move. **Look at the frog and the cheetah. How are these animals moving?** The frog is hopping and the cheetah is running.

What body parts are they using to move? They are both using their legs.

Now look at the monkey. Where is it sitting? in a tree

Why do monkeys need arms and legs to move? Monkeys live in trees. They need arms and legs to climb and swing in trees.

A monkey does not have fins. Why not? It lives on land, not in the water. It would not use fins to move.

Now look at the fish. What body parts do fish use to move? fins **Why do fish need fins, not wings or legs?** Fish live in water. They use fins to swim.

Monkeys and cheetahs move across the land, but where does a bird move? It flies through the air. **Which body part does a bird use to fly?** wings

A bird has wings, but a cheetah does not. Why? A bird needs wings to fly. A cheetah moves on land, so it does not need wings.

Move It!

Adaptations allow animals to move. Animals use different body parts to move in different ways. What body parts are these animals using to move?

Monkeys use arms and legs to climb and swing.

Frogs use strong back legs to jump.

Differentiation—Leveled Questions

Extra Support

Identify how legs and wings are the same. They both allow animals move.

Challenge

A mouse has short legs and a deer has long legs. How do you think this affects the way they move? Sample answer: The deer can move faster than the mouse.

Misconception Alert

Children may assume that all birds can fly. Explain that, although all birds have feathers and most have wings, not all can fly. Some birds, like ostriches, are fast runners. Other birds, like penguins, are good swimmers. However, ostriches and penguins do not fly.

Interpret Visuals

Have children point to and name the body part that each animal uses to move. Then ask questions to help them complete the interactive. **Which part of a bird's body does it use to fly? Circle it.** Children should circle the bird's wings. **Which part of the frog's body does it use to jump? Draw an X on it.** Children should draw an X on the frog's legs.

Develop Inquiry Skills

INFER **A cheetah has strong legs to run fast. Why might a cheetah need to run fast?** Sample answer: It needs to run fast so it can catch food or run from danger.

COMPARE/CONTRAST **How are legs, arms, wings, and fins alike?** They are all body parts that animals use to move.

How are a monkey, a frog, and a cheetah alike? They all live on land. They all use their legs to move.

How are a bird and a fish different from some of the other animals on these pages? The bird flies through the air. The fish lives and swims in water. Some of the other animals live and move on land.

Summarize Ideas

Notebook

Ask children to review the pictures and captions on this spread in order to identify the main idea that different body parts allow animals to move in different ways. Have them summarize this idea orally or in writing.

Writing Connection

TEKS ELA 1.6A, 1.20A

Write with Content Words Have children choose two animals that move in two different ways. Ask them to complete this sentence frame for each animal: *A ___ uses ___ to ___*. Children should complete the sentence by naming the animal, identifying the body part it uses to move, and then using an action word to describe that movement. For example: *A bird uses wings to fly.* Have children identify the nouns and verbs to a partner. They can then illustrate the sentence and share their work with their partner.

2 Explain (continued)

Notebook Generate Ideas

Read the heading aloud to children. Review from the last spread that animals have different body parts that allow them to move. Ask children to preview the heading and pictures on these pages. Ask: *Animals have different body parts that allow them to do something else. What is it?* Ask children to identify what the animals are using their body parts to do on these pages.

Active Reading Main Idea

Explain that the main, or most important, idea may be the first sentence in a paragraph. Or, it may be a different sentence. Active readers ask themselves, What is this paragraph mostly about? The answer will be the main idea.

Develop Science Concepts

Ask children to investigate to find out more about the body parts animals use to eat.

What do horses eat? grass, hay

Grass and hays are plants. What kind of teeth do horses have that let them eat plants? flat teeth

Why do horses have flat teeth instead of sharp teeth? They do not have sharp teeth because they do not eat meat. They do not need to tear up their food before they eat it. Flat teeth help them chew and grind down the plants they eat.

What do you notice about the lion's teeth? They are long and sharp.

What does a lion eat? meat

Why do animals like lions need sharp teeth? Sharp teeth let them tear and eat meat.

Time to Eat

Adaptations allow animals to eat. Animals that eat meat have sharp teeth. Animals that eat plants have flat teeth. Birds do not have teeth. You can tell what a bird eats by the shape of its beak.

Active Reading

The main idea is the most important idea about something. Draw two lines under the main idea.

A horse has flat teeth to eat plants.

A lion has sharp teeth to eat meat.

346

Differentiation—Leveled Questions

Extra Support

What body part do birds use to eat? beaks How is this different from the body part other animals use to eat? Many other animals use their teeth to eat.

Challenge

What do your teeth tell about the food you eat? Sample answers: Some of my teeth are flat and some are sharp. This means that I can eat plants and meat.

This bird has a short, rounded beak to eat seeds.

This bird has a long beak to eat insects.

Do the Math!

Solve a Word Problem

Solve the problem.

An adult horse has 20 teeth. An adult rabbit has 14 teeth.

How many more teeth does the horse have?

_20_ – _14_ = _6_ more teeth

Differentiation—Leveled Questions

Extra Support

Draw two shapes of bird beaks and then write a label that tells the kind of food the bird eats with each beak. Children should draw a short, rounded beak labeled "seeds" and a long beak labeled "insects."

Challenge

How does a short, rounded beak allow a bird to eat seeds? A short, rounded beak is stronger and better for cracking seeds than a long beak.

TEKS 1.10A

Develop Science Concepts

Look at each bird's beak. How are the beaks different? One beak is short and rounded and the other one is long. **What does each bird eat?** The bird with the short, round beak eats seeds. The bird with the long beak eats insects.

Why do birds have different kinds of beaks? They have different kinds of beaks because they eat different foods. **Why does the bird on the right need a long beak?** It uses its long beak to reach insects that are inside the tree.

Develop Inquiry Skills

INFER **Animals that eat plants have flat teeth. Besides horses, what other animals probably have flat teeth?** Sample answers: cows, pigs, goats **What makes you think so?** They are animals that eat plants and not meat.

Do the Math!

TEKS MATH 1.3F, 1.5D

Solve a Word Problem

Read aloud the word problem. Have children circle the two numbers. Explain that when a math problem includes the words *how many more,* this usually means it is a subtraction problem. Guide children to write the numbers they circled on the lines, solve the problem, and write their answer. Remind children that the greater number should come first in the number sentence.

Notebook Summarize Ideas

Direct children to think about the main idea of this spread. Ask them to summarize orally or in writing what they have learned about how animals use different body parts to eat different things, and name any details about this main idea that surprised them.

2 Explain (continued)

Notebook Generate Ideas

Ask: *When you play hide and seek, do you try to hide where people can see you, or where people cannot see you?* Have children talk about why people or animals might want to hide from other animals. Make a list or web of ideas on a chart or the board.

Develop Science Concepts

Ask children to investigate how and why animals hide themselves in the places where they live.

The animal on this page is called a leafy sea dragon. Where does this animal live? in the water **What do you see around it?** seaweed

What do you notice about how the leafy sea dragon looks and how the seaweed look? The leafy sea dragon has the same color and shape as the seaweed.

Why would it be hard for another animal to see the leafy sea dragon? It looks like floating seaweed in the water.

Why might the sea dragon want to hide itself? It does not want other animals to see it because it could be food for another animal.

How does the leafy sea dragon looking like seaweed keep it safe from other animals? If the leafy sea dragon is hard to see other animals have a hard time catching and eating it.

Misconception Alert

Children may assume that animals have the ability to change their external features instantly whenever they want to or need to. In fact, animals cannot change what body parts they have at will. Adaptations result from changes the animals are born with. Explain that adaptations often develop over long periods of time.

Why It Matters

Hide Me!

Adaptations allow animals to hunt. They can keep animals safe, too. Adaptations allow many animals to hide. Their colors and shapes let them blend in. You may not see the animals at all!

Color and shape allow this animal to hide.

348

English Language Learners

ELPS 1E, 2C,

Shades of Meaning
Children may have trouble understanding the scientific meaning of the phrase *blend in*. Explain that in everyday use, the word *blend* refers to mixing together ingredients. Explain that *blend in* also means to look like part of your surroundings. Point to the picture of the owl and sa *It is hard to see the owl because blends in with the tree.* Then hav children use *blend in* in their ow sentences to demonstrate their understanding of its meanings.

▶ Look at the pictures. Circle each animal hiding.

Brown feathers let the owl hide in the tree.

Rough skin lets the frog hide on the branch.

Stripes hide the tiger in tall grass.

349

Develop Science Concepts

To help children complete the interactive, have them circle the hidden animal as you discuss each picture.

Use your finger to trace the outline of the owl. Why is it hard to see the owl? It is the same color as the tree. **Which body part lets the owl blend in with the tree?** its brown feathers

Use your finger to trace the outline of the tree frog. Why is it hard to see the frog? It is the same color as the plants around it. **Which body part lets the frog blend in with its surroundings?** its green skin

What animal is hiding in the grass? a tiger

Use your finger to trace the tiger. Why is it hard to see the tiger? It blends in with the grass.

Which body part lets the tiger blend in with the grass? its stripes

Develop Inquiry Skills

INFER **All of the animals in these pictures blend in, but they all look very different. Why?** The animals look different because they live in different places. Each place has different colors and shapes, and the animals have different body parts that allow them to blend in with these colors and shapes.

Notebook Summarize Ideas

Have children look back at each picture to review details about how animals blend in with their surroundings. Ask children to explain orally to a partner or to write two sentences about how animals use their colors and shapes to blend in with their surroundings, and about how hiding helps them.

Math Connection

TEKS MATH 1.5D

Solve a Word Problem Share the following word problem with children: *Ana and Max are looking for hidden animals in a picture book. Ana spots 10 animals. Max spots 12 animals. How many animals did they find in all?*

Help children write an addition sentence to solve the problem: 10 + 12 = 22. Ask additional questions, such as *Who found more animals? How many more animals did Max find?*

3 Extend/Evaluate

Sum It Up!

1 **Circle It!** Before children complete the activity, ask them to describe the place shown in the picture. Ask them to recall the animal earlier in the lesson that lived in a cold place like this one. (walrus) Ask children which of the three animals has thick body fat like a walrus. Then read the directions with children and have them circle their answer.

2 **Match It!** Remind children that animals that eat plants have flat teeth and animals that eat meat have sharp teeth. Name each animal and ask children to identify what it eats.

3 **Write It!** Ask a volunteer to hop like a rabbit. Ask children which body part a rabbit uses to hop.

Sum It Up!

1 Circle It!

Circle the animal that could live here.

a seal (circled)

a lizard

a parrot

2 Match It!

Match the animal with the kind of teeth it has.

sharp teeth

flat teeth

3 Write It!

Write the name of the body part the rabbit uses to move.

legs

350

Brain Check

Lesson 1

Name ______________________

Word Play

Read each riddle. Then write the word that answers it.

teeth adaptation

That's me up there in the sky.
I have big wings.
They let me fly.
What do you call these wings
of mine?

adaptation

I have parts that allow me to eat.
They are very sharp.
They tear up meat.
What parts are these?

teeth

351

TEKS 1.10A

Answer Strategies

Word Play

- Read the directions with children and ask questions to check that they understand what to do. Review each word in the box at the top of the page by having volunteers read the words and explaining their meaning.
- Tell children to draw a line under the most important clues in each riddle. (sky, wings, fly; allow me to eat, sharp, tear up meat) Ask children to think about how each set of clues is related, and to choose the word that also relates to these clues.

Assessment

Lesson Quiz

See Assessment Guide, p. AG 123.

3 Extend/Evaluate (continued)

Answer Strategies

Apply Concepts

- Be sure children understand the meaning of the term *main idea*. Review that the main idea is the most important idea. Remind children that they can identify the *main idea* by asking *What is this mostly about?*
- Work together to complete the first row of the chart. Suggest that children look back at the lesson pages to review the adaptations that allow animals to live in different places. Then have children complete the chart in pairs or individually.
- If children have difficulty filling in the chart independently, do the activity orally and elicit responses by asking questions. For example, *What allows a walrus to live in a very cold place?*

Take It Home!

Some children may not have a pet or may be unfamiliar with local wildlife. As a group, talk about the animals that children could use for this activity. Write a few examples on the board. Invite volunteers to describe how each animal uses their body parts to eat, move, and live where they do.

Apply Concepts

Read each main idea. Add details that tell which body parts animals may use.

Adaptations

Main Idea	Details
Where Animals Live	Sample answer: thick fat Sample answer: gills
How Animals Move	Sample answer: wings Sample answer: fins
How Animals Eat	Sample answer: sharp teeth Sample answer: flat teeth

Take It Home!

Family Members: Work with your child to investigate how animals such as pets and local wildlife use their body parts to eat, move, and live where they do.

352

Make Connections

Easy

Physical Education Connection

TEKS PE 1.1B, 1.7A

Move It!

- Point out that children use a variety of body parts to move in different ways.
- Take children to the playground. Name an action for children to perform. Use words such as *jump, run, climb, swim,* and *swing*.
- Have children describe how they used different body parts for each action.

Average

Health Connection

TEKS HEALTH 1.1A, 1.4B

Make a Poster

- Remind children that they depend on their body parts to live, eat, and move, and it is important to keep their bodies healthy.
- Have children draw themselves on posterboard and label the body parts that allow them to live where they do, eat, and move. Ask children to share their drawings and tell what they do to keep their body healthy.

Average

Art Connection

TEKS ART 1.2A, 1.2C

Hidden Animal Picture

Have children draw a picture of an outdoor place or cut one out from a magazine and then draw an animal that is hiding in its surroundings. Remind children to use color and shape to hide their animal. Then have children share their picture and challenge partners to spot the hidden animal.

Challenging

Writing Connection

TEKS ELA 1.20A

Write a Riddle

- Review the riddles in the Brain Check activity. Point out how the writer used clue words to help children figure out the answer to each riddle.
- Ask children to write a riddle about an animal that uses an adaptation to live, eat, or move. Remind them to use descriptive nouns and verbs as clue words. Ask them to write the answer on the back of their paper.
- Collect the riddles and share them with the class.

Guided Inquiry

FLIPCHART P. 45

20 minutes
individuals

Children should follow the directions on the Flipchart. The accompanying pages in the Student Edition provide scaffolding for guided inquiry.

Inquiry Skills Focus Classify

Objectives

- Recognize the importance of safe practices.
- Ask questions about organisms observed in the natural world.
- Plan and conduct investigations. Record and organize data.
- Communicate observations.
- Investigate how the external characteristics of an animal are related to where it lives, how it moves, and what it eats.

Prep and Planning Tips

See the Planning for Inquiry page for more information.

- Yarn should be long enough to form large circles. You might want to precut the yarn or make the yarn circles in advance.

Caution! Be sure children recognize the importance of safe practices to keep themselves and others safe and healthy by reviewing scissors safety with children.

Expected Results

Children will observe the body parts that the animals use to move and then classify them by their movement.

1 Engage/Explore

Attention Grabber

Have children sit in a large circle to play animal charades. One child in the center of the circle moves like an animal while the other children use the movement clues to guess the identity. If they are unable to figure it out, the child in the center of the circle can give another clue, such as making the animal's sound. The child who guesses correctly takes a turn moving as a different animal.

Preview Activity

Before beginning the investigation, have children review the directions on the Inquiry Flipchart and the accompanying Student Edition response pages. Then have them complete the response pages as they follow the directions on the Flipchart.

Inquiry Flipchart p. 45

Lesson 2 INQUIRY

TEKS **1.2A** ask questions about organisms, objects, and events **1.2B** plan and conduct simple descriptive investigations such as ways objects move **1.2D** record and organize data using pictures, numbers, and words **1.10A** investigate how the external characteristics of an animal are related to where it lives, how it moves, and what it eats

ame ____________________

Essential Question

How Can We Group Animals?

et a Purpose

ll what you want to find out.

st, I want to find out the different ways animals move. Then,

ill find another way to classify the animals.

ink About the Procedure

How do you know which animals belong in the same group?

mals that move in the same way belong together.

How will you record the groups you make?

ll color the chart to show how each animal moves.

353

Go Digital

virtual lab experience is vailable with the Online esources for this program.

1 Engage/Explore (continued)

Guide the Investigation

Develop Inquiry Skills

CLASSIFY Explain that when children *classify,* they group things to show how they are alike. Point out that children use their observations to help them classify.

What do you want to find out about the animals? I want to find out how they move. **How will you use the information?** I will sort and classify animals into like groups by how they move.

Look at the picture cards to investigate the different body parts that animals use to move. What are some body parts that animals may use to move? Sample answers: legs, feet, wings, fins, tails

What are some ways animals move? swim, walk, fly

Look at the butterfly. How does it move? It flies. **What other animals on the picture cards fly?** Sample answers: duck, parrot, bat **A butterfly, parrot, duck, and bat all look very different. Why could they belong in the same group?** They all use their wings to fly.

Describe a duck's feet. A duck has webbed feet. **How do those feet allow it to move?** They help the duck paddle through water.

What other animals on the picture cards have the same kind of feet as ducks? penguins and alligators **What does this tell you about them?** They swim, too.

2 Explain

Develop Inquiry Skills

RECORD YOUR DATA Discuss with children how to move across and down the chart to record their data. Review the column and row headings as needed.

Explain that children will color each box that shows a way that an animal moves. Remind children that some animals move in more than one way.

DRAW CONCLUSIONS Be sure that children can justify their answers by using the information in the chart. Ask them to refer to the chart to explain their conclusions.

As children compare their observations, encourage them to summarize which animals can be grouped together. They should note that the butterfly, parrot, duck, and bat, for example, can be grouped together because they walk and fly.

3 Extend/Evaluate

ASK MORE QUESTIONS Discuss children's responses to the items. Children may raise questions about other ways to classify animals. Make a list of children's ideas about how else they could classify the animals, such as by size, number of legs, or by where they live. As an extension activity, ask children to sort the cards again and classify the animals in another way.

Assessment

Lesson Quiz

See Assessment Guide, p. AG 124.

Record Your Data

Color a box to show each way the animal moves.

How Does It Move?

	Walk	Swim	Fly
duck	■	■	■
butterfly	■		■
mouse	■		
fish		■	
bat	■		■
penguin	■	■	
parrot	■		■
alligator	■	■	
cow	■		

Draw Conclusions

How could you tell how an animal moves?

I look at its body parts to see how it moves.

Ask More Questions

What other questions can you ask about classifying animals?

Sample answer: Could I classify by the number of legs?

354

Picture Cards

Lesson 2 INQUIRY

Cut out each picture on the dashed lines.

duck

butterfly

mouse

fish

bat

penguin

parrot

alligator

cow

Teacher Notes

Differentiated Inquiry

Easy

Classify by Body Coverings

- Challenge children to classify the animals on the picture cards by body covering.
- Have children use the yarn circles and write new labels for the categories *fur/hair, feathers,* and *scales*. (If children cannot sort the butterfly into one of the groups, you may need to tell them that butterfly wings are covered with tiny scales.)
- After children sort the cards, have them make a new chart that summarizes the results.

Average

Research Animal Body Parts

- Ask children to select one of the animals shown on the picture cards and identify the main way it moves.
- Have children research how the animal's body parts allow the animal to move that way. For example, an alligator uses webbed feet and a tail to move through the water. Children can use what they know and do research using print or online resources.
- Ask children to present their information in a bulleted list, short paragraph, or labeled diagram.

Average

Identify Animals That Move in Many Ways

- Challenge children to list animals that can move in all three ways: walk, fly, and swim.
- Ask them to research additional animals to add to their lists.
- Children can present their results in a poster.

Challenging

Graph Animal Groups

- Have children make a picture graph that shows the number of animals in each group: walk, fly, and swim.
- Ask them to show their graph to the class and summarize the results.
- Ask children questions such as the following: *Which group has the most animals? Which has the fewest? How many animals are in each group?*

S.T.E.M.

Engineering and Technology

Objective

- Identify and explain a problem and propose a solution in his/her own words.

Notebook Generate Ideas

Display pictures of different farms, and ask children to describe what they see. Share the background information before you assign the feature. Ask questions to ascertain children's prior knowledge.

What is a farm? A farm is a place where people raise animals or grow crops to produce food or materials for clothing and other products.

What kinds of technology might you find on a farm? Sample answer: You may see tractors, trucks, and machines that help farmers care for animals or crops.

Background

- A farm can be large or small. It may have several kinds of animals and crops or specialize in certain animals, crops, or products. Specialized farms include dairy farms, egg farms, wheat farms, cotton farms, flower farms, cattle ranches, and apple orchards.
- A farm is made up of many parts that include people, animals, crops, buildings, tools, land, and weather. The parts work together to form a system.
- The farmer uses tools and technology to decide how to manage the farm, organize and maintain crops, harvest the product, and deliver it to the local community or to the world. If one part of the system breaks down—a machine does not work, a fence falls over, the weather is bad, or animals get sick—the farm system will not work properly.

TEKS 1.3A identify and explain a problem such as finding a home for a classroom pet and propose a solution in his/her own words

S.T.E.M.

Engineering and Technolog

On the Farm

Farm System

A farm is a kind of system. A system is a group of parts that work together. All parts must work for the whole system to run well. Some parts of a farm are the crops, animals, people, and tools.

Farmers use tools, such as fences, to protect their crops and animals.

College & Career Readiness

CCRS I.C.1, I.E.1, I.E.2, III.A. III.C.1, III.D

Agricultural Engineers This feature provides an opportunity to develop children's awareness of STEM careers related to farming, including agricultural engineers. Suggest children go online to find out more about agricultural engineers. Have children work together to write a resume for someone who wants to work as an agricultural engineer. Th resume should include a list of STEM skills an agricultural engineer needs.

S.T.E.M.
continued

'hat to Do?

ad the story. Then write how
ı would solve the problem.

ɔu have a small farm. Everything is working well. One
ay, wind knocks down part of a fence on your farm.

How could the broken fence affect the farm?
What would you do to fix the problem?

Sample answer: Farm animals might get out. Other
animals might get in. Those animals could eat crops or
harm the farm animals.
Sample answer: To fix the problem, I could nail wood to
he fence.

ld On It!

Design solutions to other problems on a farm.
Complete **Design It: Guard the Lettuce!** on the
Inquiry Flipchart.

Build On It!

In **Design It: Guard the Lettuce!**, the design challenge associated with this lesson, children use the steps of the engineering design process to design something that will keep rabbits from eating lettuce in a garden. For more details, see the pages that follow. Other opportunities to apply the design process appear throughout the *Inquiry Flipchart*.

Develop S.T.E.M. Concepts

When children have completed reading the feature, ask questions to help them reflect on the parts of a farm system.

Where have you seen fences? Sample answers: around playgrounds, yards, and buildings; along roads and train tracks.

Why were these fences developed? Sample answer: A playground fence stops children and toys, such as balls, from going into the street; it keeps animals and other people out of the playground so children can play safely.

Develop Inquiry Skills

INFER **Why might a farm need fences?** Fences keep farm animals from getting out and away from other farm animals and crops. They also keep wild animals from getting in and hurting farm animals or damaging crops.

DRAW CONCLUSIONS Ask children to describe the fence on their farm, telling what it looks like, what it is made of, and what its purpose is. Tell children to think about all these things as they decide how they would fix a broken fence. **What solutions do you have for fixing the fence?** Sample answer: A new piece of wood could be nailed to the fence.

COMMUNICATE Tell how your idea would solve the problem.

Notebook Summarize Ideas

Ask children to summarize what they learned about farm systems. Have them tell what can happen if one part of the system is missing or breaks down.

S.T.E.M.

Engineering and Technology

FLIPCHART p. 46

25 minutes

small groups

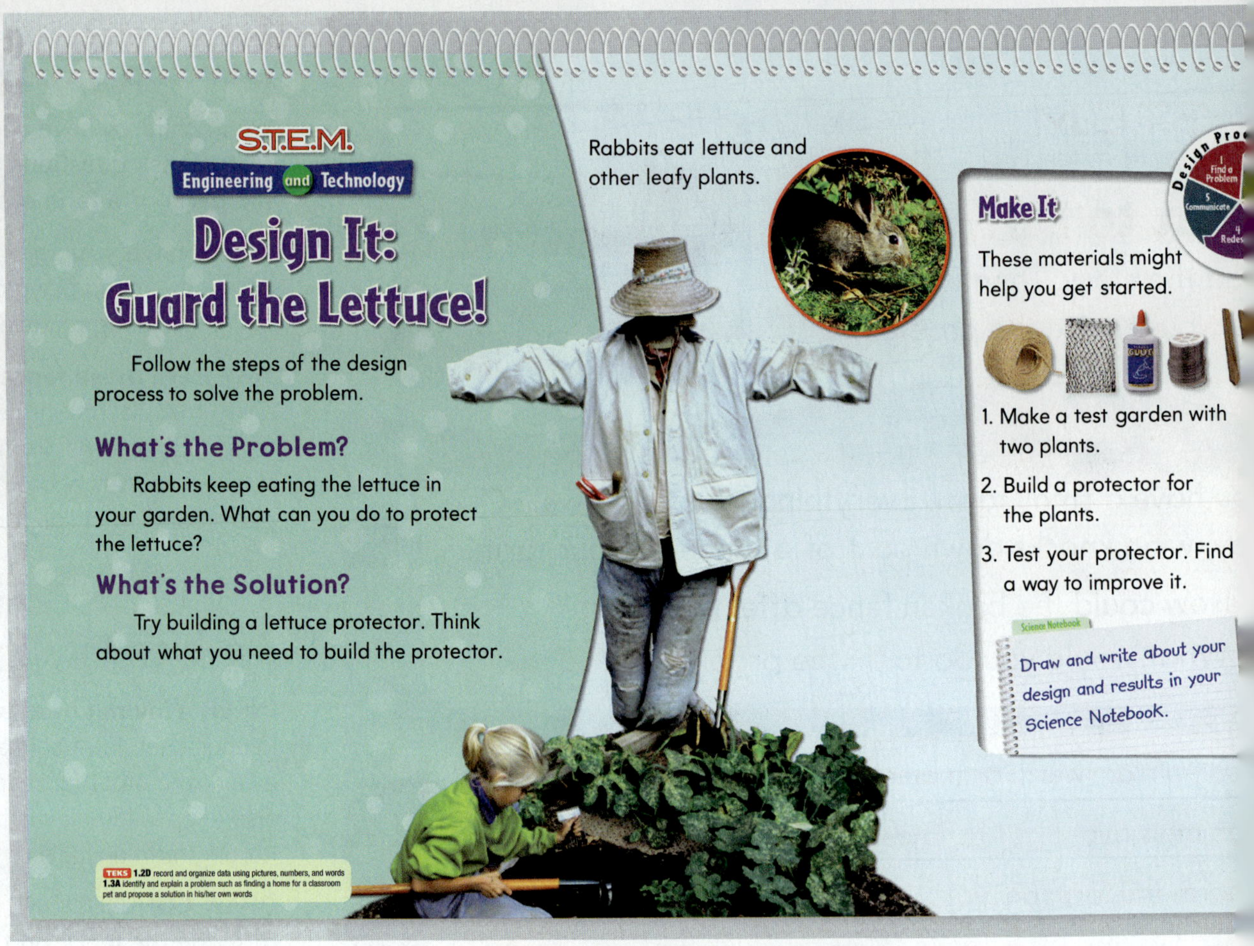

Objectives

- Record and organize data.
- Identify and explain a problem and propose a solution in his/her own words.

Prep and Planning Tips

- Display a life-size toy rabbit for children to examine. Tell them that a rabbit can jump about 18 inches, and demonstrate with the toy.
- You will likely need to cut the wire mesh or fencing with a wire cutter or very strong scissors. This step will be too difficult or dangerous for children to do themselves.

Expected Results

Children will design and build a structure to surround a garden so that the structure's slats or openings are too small for a rabbit to squeeze through, high enough to block jumping, and far enough from the plants to avoid nibbling.

1 Engage/Explore

Attention Grabber

Display a picture of a split-rail fence similar to one found around a pasture or a corral. If possible, choose a picture with an animal or a person in it to provide scale. Call out different animal names, and have children tell whether the fence would contain that animal. A split-rail fence, for example, could contain a horse or a cow but not a cat or a dog that is smaller and could squeeze under the rail of the fence.

Preview Activity

Before beginning the activity, have children review the directions on the Engineering and Technology Flipchart page.

Guide the Activity

Develop Inquiry Skills

OBSERVE Allow time for groups to observe the toy rabbit. Guide children to note its size. **What do you notice about the rabbit that will help you think of ideas for what to build?** Sample answer: I think about how big the rabbit is as I think of what to build.

ASK QUESTIONS Tell children to list their ideas. Have them ask questions about each idea to choose the best one, for example: *Is a rabbit small enough to go under the fence? Could a rabbit chew through a net fence?*

COMPARE Have children compare the size of the rabbit to items in the classroom. For example, can the rabbit fit through the legs of a chair or the opening in a desk?

Strategies for Success

Before beginning the investigation, have children review the directions on the *Inquiry Flipchart*. Suggest that they draw a rabbit in a corner of the design page to provide scale and perspective. Tell children to think about the rabbit's size as they draw. Remind them that the rabbit should not be able to squeeze through openings, jump over the structure, or reach the plants in any way.

Notebook Science Notebook

During the Activity Remind children to list the materials they will need for their design. If they plan to build a wooden fence, for example, they should list a hammer and nails among their materials. As children draw their designs, have them check that the design is to scale with the rabbit they drew and that all the parts are labeled.

2 Explain

Develop the Engineering Design Process

Use the following steps of the engineering design process to provide context and support for the analyses that children are doing in the flipchart activity.

1. FIND A PROBLEM **Use your own words to identify and explain the problem you want to solve.** I need to build something that will keep rabbits from eating my lettuce.

2. PLAN AND BUILD **What do you need to consider as you plan what to build?** I need to think about how small a rabbit is if I include any openings in my design.

3 Extend/Evaluate

Quick Check

What is the first thing you did to solve your problem? I brainstormed ideas with my group.

How did brainstorming help you plan what you would build? Sample answer: Thinking of different ideas helped my group choose one that we thought would work best.

4. REDESIGN **Explain that rabbits are burrowers; they can dig under the ground. How might the fact that rabbits can dig affect the design of your structure?** Sample answer: I would put part of my fence underground so that the rabbits couldn't dig under the fence.

5. COMMUNICATE Invite groups to share their designs. Provide groups with time to explain their designs and to answer questions from other groups.

Notebook Science Notebook

After the Activity Check children's designs to see that the structures they have drawn offer a viable solution to the problem. Make sure that the structure surrounds the garden and that any openings are too small for a rabbit to pass through. Also check that all parts of the design have been labeled.

! Michael DiSpezio's Tips & Tricks

Developing Background Talk about rabbits and how they survive in the wild. If available, display images of rabbits in their natural habitats. Talk about why it is important to know how high rabbits jump, how deep they burrow, and what frightens rabbits in order to solve this design problem. Have children make a list of all the things they would want to know in order to build the best solution. If appropriate, have children construct a scale model of their final design.

Options for Inquiry

FLIPCHART P. 47

Children can conduct these optional investigations at any time before, during, or in response to the lesson in the Student Edition.

A Where's the Caterpillar?

How does a caterpillar grow and change? Investigate to find out.

Materials

jar	rubber band
caterpillar	soil, with grass attached
leafy twigs	
cheesecloth	

Do This

1. Place a caterpillar in a jar with twigs, soil, and grass.
2. Cover the jar with cheesecloth. Secure it with a rubber band.
3. Keep the jar at room temperature.
4. Observe every day. Record how the caterpillar changes.

Draw Conclusions

What happened to the caterpillar?

TEKS **1.2B** plan and conduct simple descriptive investigations . . . **1.2D** record and organize data using pictures, numbers, and words **1.10C** compare ways that young animals resemble their parents **1.10D** observe and record life cycles of animals such as a chicken, frog, or fish

B What's My Life Cycle?

Observe and record the life cycle of a chicken, frog, or fish. Organize your information using pictures and words. Compare ways that young animals look like their parents.

Here is how one student began to plan his investigation.

Science Notebook

What's My Life Cycle?
My Planning Questions

Questions	Answers
1. *How will I find out about the animal's life cycle?*	
2. *How will I show the life cycle?*	

Directed Inquiry

A Where's the Caterpillar?

15 minutes
small groups

Prep and Planning Tips

Cut the cheesecloth to cover the top of the jar, and secure with the rubber band. Fill the jar with twigs, soil, and grass for each group. You may wish to have children use plastic spoons or other utensils to move the caterpillars into the jars.

Caution! Be sure children recognize and demonstrate the importance of safe practices to keep themselves and others safe and healthy by having them wear gloves, wash their hands after the activity, and to use all materials appropriately.

After placing the caterpillar in the jar, allow 10 minutes per day for 2 weeks for children to observe and record their observations.

Expected Results

Children will be able to observe the caterpillars eating the leaves. Over time, they should notice that the caterpillars have grown. If possible, measure a caterpillar every few days. A larva will become a pupa about two weeks after hatching.

Independent Inquiry

B What's My Life Cycle?

30 minutes
individuals

Prep and Planning Tips

See the Planning for Inquiry page for more information. Gather books and other resources that children can use to help them learn about each animal's life cycle.

Notebook

Science Notebook

Children can use the Science Notebook page as a model to plan and conduct their own investigation. Encourage them to make a chart like the one shown and include the two sample questions plus their own questions. Additional questions may include *What resources can I use? How will I tell about what I learned?* Ask volunteer to share their research with the class.

TEKS 1.10C compare ways that young animals resemble their parents 1.10D observe and
cord life cycles of animals such as a chicken, frog, or fish

Lesson 3

ssential Question

What Are Some Animal Life Cycles?

Engage Your Brain!

Find the answer to the riddle in this lesson.

When is a frog not like a frog?

When it is a ___tadpole___.

Active Reading

Lesson Vocabulary

1. Preview the lesson.
2. Write the 5 vocabulary terms here.

eproduce	larva
fe cycle	pupa
adpole	

quiry Flipchart p. 47—Where's the Caterpillar?/What's My Life Cycle?

Go Digital

n interactive digital sson is available in Online esources. It is suitable for dividuals, small groups, or ay be projected or used n an interactive white oard.

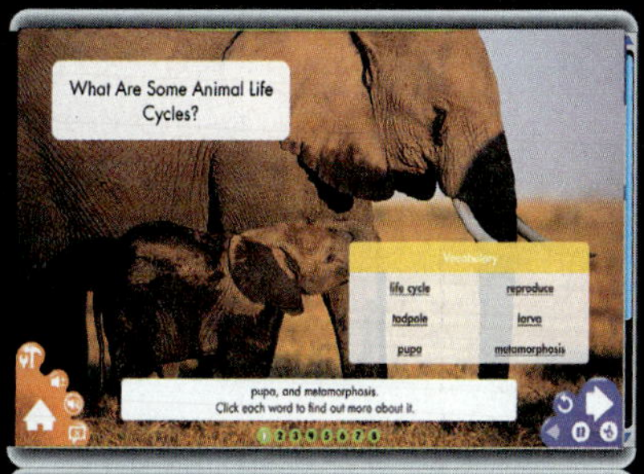

1 Engage/Explore

Objectives

- Plan and conduct simple investigations.
- Record and organize data.
- Compare ways that young animals resemble their parents.
- Observe and record life cycles of animals such as a chicken, frog, or fish.

Engage Your Brain!

Have children brainstorm answers to the riddle *When is a frog not like a frog?* Give them a hint by explaining that the answer to the riddle has to do with the changes a frog goes through during its life. Record children's responses on the board.

Remind children to record their final answer to the question when they find it on the fourth and fifth pages of the lesson.

Active Reading Annotations

Remind children that active readers "make texts their own" by marking them or writing notes to help them understand what they are reading. Encourage children to use a pencil to make annotations and to feel free to change their marks and notes as they read. The goal of annotation is to help children remember what they have read.

Vocabulary and Interactive Glossary

Remind children to find and list the yellow highlighted terms from the lesson. As they proceed through the lesson and learn about the terms, they can add drawings or words in the extra spaces provided in some entries in the Interactive Glossary.

2 Explain

Notebook Generate Ideas

Read the heading of the page aloud to children. Explain that all animals start life smaller than their parents, just as humans start life as babies. Have children brainstorm a list of young animals they have seen, such as their pets. Direct volunteers to describe how each young animal looked similar to, or different from, its parent.

Develop Science Vocabulary

reproduce Point to the pictures of the cat and the kitten. Explain that the adult cat reproduces to make the kitten. Write *reproduce* on the board. Point to the prefix *re-* and explain that it means "again." Then point to *produce* and explain that it means "make." Tell children that *reproduce* means "to make again."

Develop Science Concepts

Do you think the cat could reproduce and have a puppy? Could it have a fish? Why or why not? No; when animals reproduce, they make more animals of their own kind.

What kind of changes do you think a young animal goes through before it becomes an adult? It grows and changes. Some animals might grow more fur or get bigger. Some go through big changes in the way they look. The caterpillar changes a lot to turn into a butterfly.

Interpret Visuals

Direct children's attention to the kitten and the cat, then the caterpillar and butterfly.

Which pair has young that looks like its parent and which does not? The kitten looks like the cat. The caterpillar does not look like the butterfly.

Compare ways the kitten looks like the adult cat. They both have the same body shape, number of legs, and similar colors.

Animal Start-Ups

A dog can have puppies. A cat can have kittens. Adult animals can **reproduce**, or have young. Animals such as puppies and kittens look like their parents.

Other young animals look very different from their parents. They go through changes to become like their parents.

A young cat looks like its parents.

A young butterfly does not look like its parents.

▶ **Compare how a cat and a kitten are alike.**
They have similar colors and body shapes.

360

What's in the Egg?

Many animals begin life by ıatching from an egg. Animals hange as they grow. The hanges that happen to an ınimal during its life make up s **life cycle**.

▶ Observe the life cycles in the chart. Record the three stages of the life cycles.

egg, young, and adult

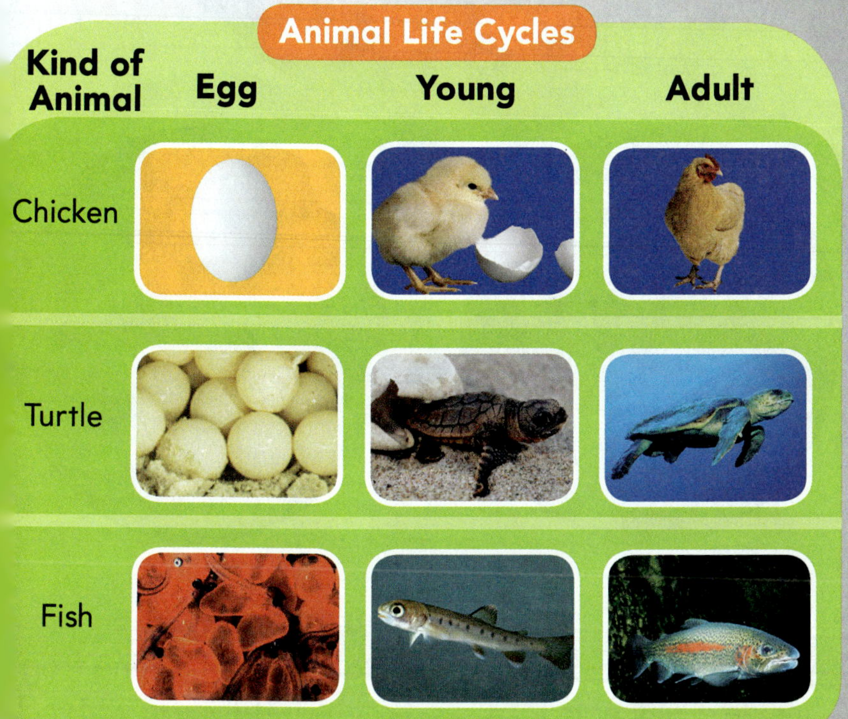

361

English Language Learners

ELPS 2C

Understand Words for Young Animals Help Spanish-speaking children understand that, in English, the words for young animals are often very different from the words for adult animals. For example, *kitten* is the name for a young cat. In Spanish, the word for kitten is *el gatito*, which is formed by adding the diminutive *-ito* to *gato*, the word for cat. *Gatito* literally means "little cat."

Develop Science Vocabulary

life cycle Explain to children that a *cycle* is a pattern that repeats over and over. During an animal's life cycle, an animal hatches or is born, grows into an adult, and has its own young. The pattern then begins again. Ask children to think about what might happen if animal life cycles did not repeat over and over.

Interpret Visuals

Help children read the title of the chart on this page. Then point to the first row.

What animal is shown in the first row of the chart? a chicken

Point to the picture of the young turtle that appears in the center of the chart.

What does this picture show? It shows a young turtle. The heading of the column is *Young* and the heading of the row is *Turtle*.

Observe the life cycles in the chart. What three stages does it show? egg, young, adult

Develop Inquiry Skills

COMPARE/CONTRAST **How are the animals in this chart alike?** They all begin life by hatching from an egg. They all grow and change as they become adults.

How are the animals in this chart different? They are different kinds of animals. Their eggs look different. The young turtle looks a lot like its parent. The young chicken and the young rainbow trout look somewhat different from their parents.

Notebook Summarize Ideas

Direct children to look at the photographs and the chart again and think about the main idea on these pages. Encourage them to summarize the main idea orally or in writing.

2 Explain (continued)

Notebook Generate Ideas

Read the heading aloud to children: "Hatch, Swim, Hop." Point out to children that when they swim, they must be in water. Then ask them where it would be easier to hop, in water or on land.

Ask children to name land animals and water animals. Tell children that they will learn about an animal that lives in water when it is young and on land when it is an adult.

Develop Science Vocabulary

tadpole Explain that *tad* comes from a word that means "toad" and that *pole* comes from a word that means "head" **Why do you think this is a good name for a young toad or frog?** Sample answer: A tadpole's head is very big compared to the rest of its body.

Develop Science Concepts

Have children preview and observe the life cycle of the frog using the numbered pictures.

Observe the life cycle of the frog. How is a young tadpole different from a growing tadpole? The young tadpole is smaller and does not have legs.

If you saw a growing tadpole in a pond, how could you tell it was not a fish? It has legs, and a fish does not have legs.

How is a frog different from a growing tadpole? The frog is bigger, lives on land, has no tail, and breathes with lungs.

Why do you think a tadpole loses its tail and gills when it becomes a frog? On land, a frog doesn't need a tail or gills.

1

Egg

A frog begins life inside a tiny egg.

2

Young Tadpole

A **tadpole**, or young frog hatches. It lives in water. I takes in oxygen with gills.

362

Differentiation—Leveled Questions

Extra Support
What is a tadpole? A tadpole is a young frog that lives in water.

Challenge
The tadpole uses its tail while i lives in water. Then it loses its tail when it becomes a frog. Wh do you think this happens? It n longer needs a tail to swim whe it is living on land.

Hatch, Swim, Hop

Did you know that a frog begins life inside a tiny egg? The young frog goes through many changes to become an adult. Observe the frog's life cycle below.

Active Reading

Find the sentence that tells the meaning of **tadpole**. Draw a line under the sentence.

3

4

Growing Tadpole

The tadpole gets bigger. It grows four legs. Later, it loses its tail.

Frog

The adult can live on land or in the water. It hops. It breathes with lungs.

363

Math Connection

TEKS MATH 1.5D, 1.5G

Solve a Problem The maximum leap recorded for a bullfrog is 214 centimeters. The maximum leap recorded for a Leopard frog is 163 centimeters. Use the data to have children complete addition and subtraction problems: **What is the difference between the length of the bullfrog's leap and the length of the Leopard frog's leap?** (214 – 163 = 51) **What is the sum of the length of the bullfrog's leap and the length of the Leopard frog's leap?** (214 + 163 = 377)

Misconception Alert

Children may be confused that a tadpole takes in oxygen from the water. Explain that all animals need oxygen, no matter where they live. Oxygen is in water and air. Some animals that live in water have developed certain body parts to take in oxygen from the water. These body parts are called gills.

Active Reading Vocabulary

Explain that a vocabulary word may be highlighted in a color. Active readers pay attention to highlighted words, because their meaning is given in the same sentence or the next sentence. Have children locate the highlighted vocabulary word on the left page.

Develop Inquiry Skills

SEQUENCE **How does a tadpole change as it grows?** First, it hatches from an egg and breathes with gills. Next, it gets bigger. Then it grows legs and loses its tail. Last, it becomes an adult and lives on land.

Notebook Summarize Ideas

To help children think about the life cycle of a frog, ask them to use time-order words, such as *first, next,* and so on, to summarize the changes a frog goes through.

2 Explain (continued)

Notebook Generate Ideas

With children, look at the pictures of the polar bears and read the heading aloud. Ask children how they think the way polar bears care for their young is similar to or different from the way humans care for their young. After children have read the pages, have them compare their answers with what they have read.

Develop Science Concepts

Have children preview and observe the life cycle of the polar bear using the numbered pictures.

How is the growing cub different from the newborn? The growing cub is bigger. It begins to explore outside the den.

How is the young polar bear different from the growing cub? The young polar bear is bigger. It begins to learn things it needs to know as an adult, such as how to swim and hunt.

Why do the cubs stay with their mother until they are almost grown? They cannot take care of themselves. They need to learn certain skills before they can live on their own.

Compare how the young polar bear is similar to the adult polar bear. The young polar bear and the adult polar bear both have the same body shape, color, and number of legs.

How is a polar bear's life cycle like a frog's life cycle? Both animals grow from young animals into adults.

How is a polar bear's life cycle different from a frog's life cycle? A polar bear is born live; a frog hatches from an egg. A polar bear lives on land its whole life; a frog lives on land only as an adult.

Polar Parenting

It is late October. A female polar bear gets a shelter ready for her cubs. She digs a den in the snow. The den will keep her young warm and safe. She gives birth in winter.

▶ **Compare how a young polar bear looks like its mother.**

It has fours legs and is the same color.

1

Newborn

A polar bear cub is born inside the den. It looks a lot like its parents.

2

Growing Cub

The cub begins to explore outside the den

364

English Language Learners

ELPS 1C, 1E, 2C, 2

Learn Words for Young Animals Point to the word *cub* and tell children that this is the word for a young bear. Make a list of other names for young animals, such as *puppy* for *dog*, *kitten* for *cat*, *chick* for *chicken*, *calf* for *cow*, *fawn* for *deer*, and *duckling* for *duck*. Help children read the list with you. Then ask them to draw or find pictures of the young animals ar say their names aloud.

3

4

Young Polar Bear

The young polar bear learns to swim and hunt.

Adult Polar Bear

The adult polar bear can live on its own. It can have its own young.

365

Interpret Visuals

Point out the numbers on the pictures, and ask children to use them as they describe the polar bear life cycle. Then ask children to use the pictures to compare the polar bears at different stages.

Develop Inquiry Skills

INFER Direct children to observe the weather where the polar bear lives. Help them recognize that it is cold and snowy. Then challenge children to figure out how the polar bear's body and behavior help it survive in that climate.

What is the weather like where polar bears live? Sample answer: I see a lot of snow so I think it is cold and snowy.

How do you think polar bears survive in this kind of climate? Sample answer: I see that they have thick fur to keep them warm. They build dens to keep their young warm and safe.

Notebook Summarize Ideas

Remind children to think about the life cycle of the polar bear. Ask them to use time-order words to summarize orally or in writing how the polar bear grows from a newborn into an adult.

2 Explain (continued)

Notebook Generate Ideas

Ask children to talk about when they have seen caterpillars and butterflies. Ask whether a caterpillar looks like a butterfly. Have children predict how a caterpillar changes during its lifetime and then read to find out whether their predictions are correct.

Develop Science Concepts

Have children preview and observe the life cycle of the butterfly using the numbered pictures.

Why do you think a female butterfly lays her eggs on a leaf? so the young will have something to eat when they hatch

What stage of the butterfly life cycle comes after the egg stage? the larval stage **Why do you think a larva must eat a lot?** It needs energy to grow quickly and go through a big change.

Describe a monarch butterfly pupa. The pupa has a hard covering. It hangs from a leaf or a branch. It does not move or eat. **What changes happen to the pupa?** The pupa grows wings, and changes shape and color.

How is an adult butterfly different from a larva? A butterfly larva is wormlike and crawls. An adult butterfly has a body with four wings and can fly.

How does the butterfly life cycle start over again? An adult female butterfly lays eggs.

Point out that all butterflies go through the same stages that a monarch butterfly does.

Misconception Alert

From looking at the picture, children may think that a butterfly lays only one egg. Tell them that a female butterfly actually may lay over 300 eggs during a 2-week period. Not all of the eggs will hatch, but the large number helps ensure that many survive .

The Mighty Monarch

A butterfly has a life cycle, too. An adult female butterfly lays a tiny egg. The egg is so small it is hard to see. This picture shows a close-up of an egg.

1 egg

Observe the life cycle of a butterfly. Record the four stages it goes through as it grows and changes.

egg, larva, pupa, and adult

366

Writing Connection

TEKS ELA 1.2

Write Fact Cards Have children write two fact cards based on the information about the animals in this lesson. Each card should include the name of the animal and two facts about it. Remind children that a fact is something that can be proved true. As a challenge, children could verify t facts by finding a second source of information either in an onlin or print encyclopedia or in nonfiction books about animals.

2 larva

A tiny **larva**, or caterpillar, hatches from the egg. A caterpillar is a young butterfly. The larva eats a lot. It grows quickly.

3 pupa

Then the larva stops eating and moving. The larva becomes a pupa. It makes a hard covering.

A **pupa** goes through many changes inside the covering. It grows wings.

4 adult

Finally, an adult butterfly comes out of the covering. It can have its own young.

Active Reading

Clue words can help you find the order of events. Draw a box around the clue words **then** and **finally**.

367

Differentiation—Leveled Questions

Extra Support

What are the stages of a butterfly's life cycle? egg, larva, pupa, adult

Challenge

What can you infer about the life cycles of other butterflies? Explain. Other butterflies go through many changes and have the same stages in their life cycles. Animals of the same kind usually have the same life cycle.

Develop Science Vocabulary

larva Tell children that *larva* is another word for caterpillar. Explain that the term comes from a word meaning "ghost" or "mask," perhaps because the larva is just a hint or ghost of the adult to come. Show children that the plural form of larva is *larvae.*

pupa Explain that the word *pupa* comes from a word meaning "doll" or "puppet." A pupa is less developed than an adult, just as a doll is small and unformed compared to a real person.

Active Reading Clue Words

Explain that some words are clues to ways ideas are connected. The clue words *then* and *finally* hint that information about order is coming. Active readers look for clue words to help them remember how ideas are connected.

Develop Inquiry Skills

OBSERVE AND COMPARE Mealworms (available at pet stores) are the larval form of beetles. Consider having children use a hand lens to carefully **observe** a mealworm and **compare** it to a caterpillar. With proper care, mealworms can be raised in the classroom so children can see their entire life cycle. Make sure that mealworms are disposed of responsibly.

Notebook Summarize Ideas

Have children think about the main idea of these pages. Ask whether the predictions they made about a butterfly's life cycle before they read the pages were correct. Have them summarize the main idea orally or in writing.

3 Extend/Evaluate

Sum It Up!

1. **Mark It!** Help children identify each animal as necessary. Then ask children to picture the young of each animal. If they need extra support, ask them what a tadpole looks like and whether it looks like an adult frog.
2. **Draw It!** Suggest that children look at the lesson to find a picture that looks like the one shown here.
3. **Solve It!** Tell children to underline the most important clue of the riddle: *Someday I will be an adult cat.*
4. **Think About It!** Remind children that a human baby looks like its parents and does not go through the many changes that a frog and butterfly do.

Sum It Up!

1 Mark It!

Draw an X on the animal that does not look like its young.

2 Draw It!

Draw a picture of this animal's mother.

3 Solve It!

Answer the riddle.

I am little now. I will change and grow. Someday I will be an adult cat.

What am I? kitten

4 Think About It!

Is a [baby] most like a [polar bear], a [tadpole], or a [caterpillar]? Why?

A baby is most like a polar bear. A baby and a polar bear are born looking like their parent

368

Brain Check

Lesson 3

Name ________________________

Word Play

Use these words to complete the puzzle.

tadpole pupa larva reproduce cycle

Across

1. The stage in a butterfly's life cycle after the egg
2. To make more living things of the same kind

Down

3. The stage in a butterfly's life between larva and adult
4. A young frog that lives in water
5. All the stages of an animal's life make up its life ________.

				4 t				5 c
1 l	a	r	v	a				y
				d				c
				p				l
2 r	e	3 p	r	o	d	u	c	e
		u		l				
		p		e				
		a						

TEKS 1.10C, 1.10D

Answer Strategies

Word Play

- If children have difficulty using the puzzle clues, guide them by rewording the clues as complete sentences. For example, instead of saying *The stage in a butterfly's life cycle after the egg*, say *What is the stage of a butterfly's life cycle that comes after the egg*? Encourage children to look at the lesson pages as needed.
- For additional reinforcement, ask children to use each puzzle answer in a sentence. If they have trouble, pair children and ask them to think of a sentence together.

Assessment

Lesson Quiz

See Assessment Guide, p. AG 125.

3 Extend/Evaluate (continued)

Answer Strategies

Apply Concepts

- If children have trouble using the chart, do the activity orally and elicit responses by putting the chart information in question form. For example, say *A butterfly hatches from an egg. How is this different from the way a polar bear is born?* Encourage children to look at the lesson pages as needed. Tell them to pay particular attention to the numbered steps in the lesson.
- As a lesson follow-up, ask children to summarize what they learned in the lesson. Encourage them to name new facts and ideas that they did not know before they read the lesson.

Take It Home!

Suggest that children use nonfiction books, reference materials, or reliable online resources to find out about the different life cycles of a chicken, frog, or fish. Have children cut out pictures from magazines or draw pictures of their own to organize, number, and caption the stages in the life cycle of one of the animals.

Apply Concepts

Compare the life cycle of a butterfly to the life cycle of a polar bear. Record how they are different. Sample answers provided.

Life Cycles

Butterfly	Polar Bear
A butterfly hatches from an egg.	A female polar bear gives birth to a cub.
A butterfly larva eats leaves.	A polar bear cub drinks milk from its mother's body.
A butterfly larva looks different from its parents.	A polar bear cub looks a lot like its parents.
A butterfly larva does not stay with its parents.	A polar bear cub stays with its mother for three years.

Take It Home!

Family Members: Discuss life cycles with your child. Observe and record the life cycle of a chicken, frog, or fish.

370

Make Connections

Easy

Art Connection

TEKS ART 1.2C

Make a Mobile

- Ask children to choose a butterfly or frog life cycle to complete this activity.
- Have children draw or cut out, number, and label pictures of each stage of the life cycle. Use a dowel or hanger for the top of the mobile. Children can then use string or yarn to hang the pictures from the top of the mobile.

Average

Health Connection

TEKS HEALTH 1.1A

Research Baby Health

Encourage children to use reliable online or print resources to identify three ways to promote good health in babies so that they become healthy toddlers, children, teens, and adults in the next stages of the human life cycle.

Average

Math Connection

TEKS MATH 1.5D, 1.5G

Calculate Weight

- Use the data below to have children calculate how much weight the polar bear gained from newborn to cub (16 pounds).
- As an added challenge, have them find the difference from cub to adult (282 pounds).

Newborn: 2 pounds

Cub: 18 pounds

Adult: 300 pounds

Challenging

Writing Connection

TEKS ELA 1.18A

Write an Animal Story

- Ask children to write a narrative story about an animal in this lesson that details how the animal changes as it grows and develops during its life cycle.
- Have them share their stories.

Careers in Science

Objectives

- Describe what scientists do.
- Recognize that scientists come from all backgrounds.

Notebook Generate Ideas

Preview the pictures with children. Ask questions to spark their interest in what a zoo keeper is and does.

What is the zoo keeper in the picture doing? feeding an animal

What would you like to ask a zoo keeper? Sample answer: How many times a day do you feed the animals?

You may wish to share some or all of the following background information with children before you assign the feature.

Background

- Much of a zoo keeper's job involves maintaining the cage or the area where an animal lives. This helps keep the animals safe and healthy.
- In large zoos, a zoo keeper might look after only one kind of animal. A zoo keeper cleans the cages, feeds the animals, and observes them for any changes in their behavior that might indicate that an animal is sick or injured.
- Most zoo keepers have gone to school to study and learn about animals.
- Some zoos have summer day camps and junior zoo keeper programs.

TEKS **1.3C** describe what scientists do

Careers in Scienc

Ask a Zoo Keeper

What does a zoo keeper do?

I feed the animals. I give them water. I make sure that the anim are healthy. I also keep their environments clean.

How do you know when an animal is sick?

Animals can not tell me when th do not feel well. So I observe th carefully. Sometimes an animal or moves very little. That could a sign that the animal is sick.

What else does a zoo keeper do?

I talk to people about the zoo animals. I have fun talking to children. They like animals so m

Now It's Your Turn!

▶ **Describe what a zoo keeper does.**

A zoo keeper takes care of animals.

Writing Connection

TEKS ELA **1.19C, 1.2**

Write to Describe Have each child write *zoo keeper* in the center of a sheet of paper or in their Science Notebooks. Then ask children to surround the word with four terms that describe some of the things a zoo keeper does. At the bottom of the page, have children write sentences that us three of the terms, leaving a bla where each term goes. Finally, have children switch notebooks and try to fill in each other's blanks, discussing the choices they made.

TEKS 1.3C

Now You Be a Zoo Keeper!

▶ A tiger cub was born at your zoo. Make a plan to take care of the cub.

My Zoo Keeper Plan

I will Sample answer: feed the cub and give it water.

I will Sample answer: observe it to make sure it stays healthy.

I will Sample answer: keep its environment clean.

Science, Technology, and Society

Explain to children that zoo keepers use many different tools. They may use tools to help them clean where the animals live, to check on the animal's health, or to research and share information about their animals. Have groups choose an animal that they might see at a zoo and write or dictate a paragraph describing how tools might help a zoo keeper take care of that animal. Guide them to include a topic sentence and details in their paragraph.

Develop Science Concepts

What is a zoo keeper? A zoo keeper is a person who takes care of animals in a zoo.

Describe what a zoo keeper does. Sample answers: A zoo keeper feeds the animals. He or she keeps the cages and the animals clean. The zoo keeper observes the animals' behavior to make sure they are healthy.

How can a zoo keeper tell when an animal is sick? The animal may not eat much. It may move very little.

How can a zoo keeper help the people who come to the zoo learn about the animals? Sample answer: The zoo keeper can tell people about the zoo animals and how they live in the wild.

Develop Inquiry Skills

OBSERVE **A zoo keeper is responsible for the health of the animals he or she takes care of. Why would observation be an important skill for a zoo keeper to use?** The zoo keeper would need to observe any changes in the way the animal behaves, such as how it moves and how much it eats. Changes in the animal's behavior might mean the animal is sick or injured.

When you learn about animals and plants, why is observing them important? Sample answer: You need to observe the plants and animals so you can learn how they are alike and different.

Notebook Summarize Ideas

Have children look again at the photographs and questions on these pages and review how they completed the right-hand page. Have children use the sentences they wrote to summarize what a zoo keeper does for animals.

Enduring Understandings

Revisit the Big Idea and Essential Questions

Big Idea **Animals have adaptations that help them survive. Animals have different life cycles.**

To explore the Big Idea, challenge children to work in groups of three or four to generate as many statements that support the Big Idea as possible. Then, have each group compare its list with the lists other groups make. Next, ask the class to work together to generate a master set of statements. Then, have them add their statements to their Science Notebooks. Prompt children with some sample adaptations to discuss.

- wings
- gills
- legs
- fins
- sharp teeth
- flat teeth

Essential Questions

Post the Essential Questions, and use the following prompts to guide a discussion.

Lessons/Essential Questions	Prompts
L1 **How Do Animals Differ?**	• Name two animals and tell how their adaptations help them survive.
L2 **How Can We Group Animals?**	• Explain one way to group three animals together.
L3 **What Are Some Animal Life Cycles?**	• Draw and label the stages in one animal's life cycle.

Notebook Science Notebook

You may use the following strategies after children complete the unit or after each lesson.

- Have children review and edit the responses to the Essential Questions they drafted at the beginning of the unit. Suggest they cross out sentences or ideas that are unnecessary or inappropriate.
- Have children draft ideas for cards in their Science Notebooks to prepare for a memory game. On six cards, children draw pictures of six animals. On another six cards, they write an adaptation that helps the animal survive. Review the game's rules. Children play first with one set of cards. Partners alternate turning up two face-down cards and looking for matches of an animal with its adaptation. After all the matches have been found, children can play again with the other partner's cards.

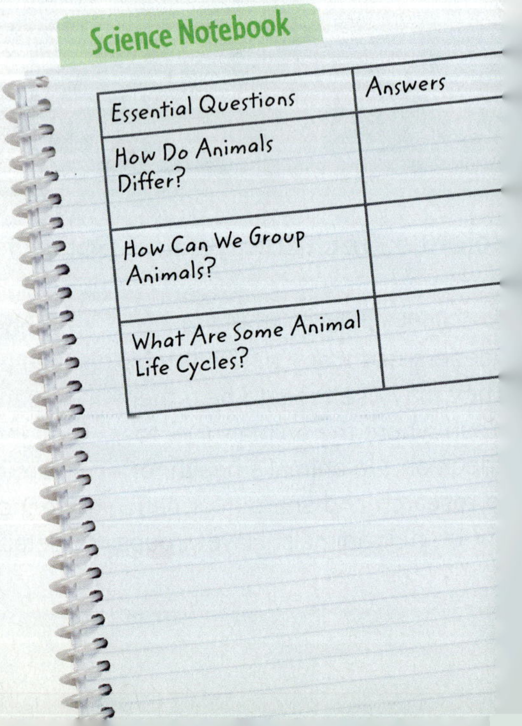

Unit 9 Review

Name ___________________________

ocabulary Review

se the terms in the box to complete
e sentences.

adaptation
larva
life cycle

S 1.10D

The changes that happen to an animal during its life make up its life cycle.

S 1.10A

Gills are an adaptation that let fish take in air from the water.

S 1.10D

A butterfly spends its larva stage as a caterpillar.

ience Concepts

in the letter of the choice that best
swers the question.

1.10D

How is a frog's life cycle the same as a turtle's life cycle?

Ⓐ Both animals hatch from an egg.

Ⓑ Both animals have shells.

Ⓒ Both animals look like their parents when they are born.

TEKS 1.10D

5. You see a butterfly flying. What part of its life cycle is the butterfly in?

Ⓐ adult

Ⓑ egg

Ⓒ larva

Item Analysis

Items	TEKS	Depth of Knowledge	Cognitive Complexity
1	**1.10D**	1	Low
2	**1.10A**	1	Low
3	**1.10D**	1	Low
4	**1.10D**	2	Moderate
5	**1.10D**	2	Moderate

Unit Review

Answer Key

Vocabulary Review (5 points each)

1. life cycle
   Have children reread the complete sentence to be sure that it makes sense.
2. adaptation
   Make sure children understand that gills are a body part that serve a function for fish. Have children tell what fish use gills for.
3. larva
   Elicit from children that the words *stage as a caterpillar* is the definition of the word that completes the sentence.

Science Concepts (7 points each)

4. A
   Point out the word *same* in the question so children understand that they are looking for a way that the life cycles of frogs and turtles are alike. Ask them to explain why answer choices B and C are incorrect.
5. A
   Children will need to figure out at which stage in the life cycle a butterfly can fly. They can refer back to the lesson pages that show and explain the stages of the butterfly life cycle for that information.

Assessment

Unit 9 Test and Performance Assessment

See Assessment Guide, pp. AG 128–AG 134, for Unit Test and Performance Task with Long Option rubric.

Unit Review *continued*

Answer Key

Science Concepts (7 points each)

6. A

Have children observe and describe the lion's pointed teeth. Ask, "What kind of food do animals with sharp, pointed teeth usually eat?"

7. B

Have children read the answer choices and tell what a rabbit uses each one for.

8. B

Have children look at the picture and ask them if it is easy or hard to see the zebra in the grass and tell why. Then, have them reread the question and answer it.

9. C

Discuss which animals—the butterfly, the frog, or the polar bear—hatch as eggs and which are born live. Then, talk about which of those animals would look like their parents as a result.

TEKS 1.10A

6. What can you tell by looking at the lion's teeth?

Ⓐ It eats meat.
Ⓑ It eats grass.
Ⓒ It eats seeds.

TEKS 1.10A

7. Which body part does a rabbit use to move?

Ⓐ flat teeth
Ⓑ strong legs
Ⓒ warm fur

TEKS 1.10A

8. How is the zebra using its stripes?

Ⓐ to run
Ⓑ to hide
Ⓒ to stay warm

TEKS 1.10C

9. Which animal looks like its parents when it is born?

Ⓐ a butterfly
Ⓑ a frog
Ⓒ a polar bear

Item Analysis *(continued)*

Items	TEKS	Depth of Knowledge	Cognitive Complexity
6	**1.10A**	2	Moderate
7	**1.10A**	1	Low
8	**1.10A**	2	Moderate
9	**1.10C**	1	Low

TEKS 1.10A

10. Why do seals need a thick layer of body fat?

Ⓐ to keep warm
Ⓑ to move
Ⓒ to hide

TEKS 1.10C

11. How are a young duck and a mother duck the same? Compare them.

Ⓐ They both have hair and use legs to walk.
Ⓑ They both have feathers and use wings to fly.
Ⓒ They both have scales and use fins to swim.

TEKS 1.10D

12. Which of these animals hatches from an egg?

Ⓐ 

Ⓑ 

Ⓒ 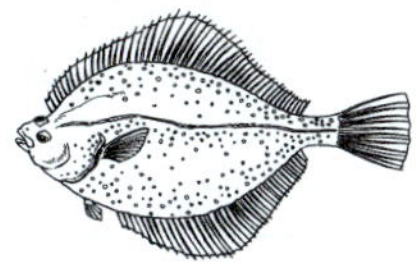

UNIT 9

Item Analysis *(continued)*

Items	TEKS	Depth of Knowledge	Cognitive Complexity
10	**1.10A**	2	Moderate
11	**1.10C**	2	Moderate
12	**1.10D**	2	Moderate

Unit Review *continued*

Answer Key

Science Concepts (7 points each)

10. A

Have children describe what they see in the picture and talk about the setting in which they see the seals. The ice sheet on which the seals sit should help children determine why seals need body fat.

11. B

Ask children to identify an example of an animal described in the incorrect answer choices A and C.

12. C

Be sure children can identify each animal pictured in the answer choices.

Short Option Performance Assessment

Task

Make a Life Cycle Diagram
After children choose an animal, such as a butterfly, chicken, frog, or fish, have them draw and label a diagram that shows the stages in its life cycle. Then, have children explain each stage of the life cycle to small groups or the class.

Rubric

Preparation Provide art materials children can use to draw and label diagrams, such as construction paper, colored pencils, and crayons.

Scoring Rubric—Performance Indicators

___ Chooses an animal that has distinct stages in its life cycle.

___ Draws and labels a diagram that shows the stages.

___ Explains each stage in the life cycle to others.

Observations and Rubric Scores

3 2 1 0

Unit Review *continued*

Answer Key

Inquiry and the Big Idea (11 points each)

13.

a. flat teeth

b. Sample answer: This animal is eating grass. Animals that eat plants have flat teeth.

Encourage children to look at the setting of the picture. Ask guiding questions such as, "Where is the animal?" or "What exactly is the animal eating?"

14.

a. Sample answer: They are alike because the young both look like their parents.

b. They are different because the bird hatches from an egg and the cat is born live.

Children might want to summarize the stages in the life cycle of both the cat and the bird in a list, chart, or diagram before comparing them.

UNIT 9

Inquiry and the Big Idea

Write the answers to these questions.

TEKS 1.10A

13. Look at the animal eating.

a. What kind of teeth do you think the animal has?

flat teeth

b. Why do you think so?

Sample answer: This animal is eating grass. Animals that eat plants have flat teeth.

TEKS 1.2D, 1.10C, 1.10D

14. Observe the animals. Think about their life cycles.

a. Record one way their life cycles are alike.

Sample answer: They are alike because the young both look like their parents.

b. Record one way their life cycles are different.

They are different because the bird hatches from an egg and the cat is born live.

Item Analysis

Items	TEKS	Depth of Knowledge	Cognitive Complexit
13	**1.10A**	3	High
14	**1.2D, 1.10C, 1.10D**	3	High

Additional teaching support for all inquiry activities is available in Online Resources.

Activity	Inquiry and Design Process Skills Focus	Materials	Prep Tips, Troubleshooting, and Expected Results
S.T.E.M. Engineering and Technology Flipchart p.51 **Design It: Greenhouse** **OBJECTIVES** • Record and organize data. • Identify and explain a problem and propose a solution in his/her own words. 45 minutes pairs or small groups TEKS **1.2D, 1.3A**	 1 Find a Problem 2 Plan and Build 3 Test and Improve 4 Redesign 5 Communicate	• liter soda bottle • clear, plastic mayonnaise jar • tiny potted plant • clear, plastic cups • tape • Science Notebook	**Prep Tips** Have available the following materials for each pair or small group: liter soda bottle, cut in half; clear, plastic mayonnaise jar; tiny potted plant; clear, plastic cups; tape. You may wish to have children grow their own plants beginning two weeks prior to this activity. **Expected Results** Children will design an indoor greenhouse for a small houseplant with clear, plastic bottles.

Differentiated Instruction

Leveled Readers

The Leveled Readers provide parallel coverage of the unit topics and Texas Essential Knowledge and Skills. Each Reader is available in English and Spanish. Both versions are available online and on touchscreen mobile devices.

ON-LEVEL This Reader reinforces unit concepts and vocabulary and focuses on the Texas Essential Knowledge and Skills. It includes student response activities.

EXTRA SUPPORT This Reader shares title, illustrations, vocabulary, and concepts with the On-Level Reader. However, the text is linguistically accommodated to provide simplified sentence structures and comprehension aids for students who need a little extra support with content-area reading and vocabulary development. It also includes student response activities.

ENRICHMENT This high-interest nonfiction Reader enriches and extends unit concepts. It reinforces some of the unit vocabulary, but also includes stretch vocabulary. It also includes student response activities.

TEACHER GUIDE

The accompanying Teacher Guide provides teaching strategies and support for using all the Readers, as well as English and Spanish worksheets that focus on vocabulary development. A correlation to the Texas Essential Knowledge and Skills is included.

DIGITAL VERSIONS

All of these Leveled Readers are available online. They are also available in an innovative and engaging format for touchscreen mobile devices. For information about accessing these versions, see page T9.

OTHER UNIT FEATURES

People in Science, p. 389

S.T.E.M. Engineering and Technology, pp. 403–404B

Online Resources

Interactive Whiteboard Resources for Unit 10

Assessment

Formative Assessment
Sum It Up! and Brain Check
Student Edition, end of each lesson

Summative Assessment
Lesson Quizzes
Assessment Guide, pp. AG 135–AG 137

Unit 10 Review
Student Edition, pp. 405–408

Unit 10 Test
Assessment Guide, pp. AG 140–AG 144

Performance Assessment
SHORT OPTION: Teacher Edition, p. 407
LONG OPTION: Assessment Guide, pp. AG 145–AG 146

Response to Intervention
RTI Strategies, p. 377I

Online Assessment
Test-taking and automatic scoring
Banks of items from which to build tests

Teacher Notes

Planning for Inquiry

Use the following preview of Inquiry Activities and Lessons to gather and manage the materials needed for each lesson.

Activity	Inquiry and Design Process Skills Focus	Materials	Prep Tips, Troubleshooting, and Expected Results
Lesson 1 DIRECTED INQUIRY **Flipchart** p.48 **A Are All Seeds Alike?** **OBJECTIVES** Plan and conduct simple investigations. Make observations using a hand lens. Record and organize data. Identify and compare the parts of plants. 25 minutes · small groups TEKS **1.2B, 1.2C, 1.2D, 1.10B**	• Observe • Compare	• seed packets for 3 different plants • zip-top bags • hand lenses	**Prep Tips** You may wish to organize the seeds into zip-top bags before the investigation. Consider making color copies of the seed packets and placing them in the zip-top bags with the seeds. Zinnia, marigold, and pansy seeds will provide a good basis for comparison, and they may be purchased at garden or home repair stores. Sunflower, pumpkin, and fennel seeds are available at many supermarkets. **Caution!** Remind children not to eat any seeds. Have them wash their hands after the investigation. **Troubleshooting** You may wish to focus children's investigation by encouraging them to observe such seed characteristics as color, shape, and size. As children observe the seeds in Step #2, have them compare the seeds to the pictures on the seed packets. If necessary, review how to use a hand lens. **Expected Results** Children will compare seeds and find that they come in different sizes, colors, and shapes.
INDEPENDENT INQUIRY **Flipchart** p.48 **B What Parts Do You See?** **OBJECTIVES** Plan and conduct simple investigations. Collect and compare data and make observations using a hand lens. Record and organize data. Identify and compare the parts of plants. 30 minutes · pairs TEKS **1.2B, 1.2C, 1.2D, 1.4A, 1.10B**	• Observe • Gather, Record, Display, or Interpret Data • Formulate or Use Models • Communicate	• plants • hand lenses • crayons • zip-top bags (optional)	**Prep Tips** Select flowering plants for observation. Consider placing plants in plastic zip-top bags, so children can observe their root structure. Plastic flats of small flowering plants, such as phlox and marigolds (available at many nurseries), may be easiest to move, since their soil will be compacted. Work with children to brainstorm ways they can show what they observe, such as by drawing or constructing a model. Make craft materials available to the class. **Troubleshooting** If necessary, lead the class in a quick review of plant parts. Review stems, roots, leaves, flowers, seeds, and fruits. Tell children that they may be able to observe only some of these parts. **Expected Results** Children will observe, identify, and compare plant parts, such as stems, roots, flowers, and leaves. They will choose a way to represent these parts. They will recognize that some plant parts, like fruit, do not appear on all plants.

Additional teaching support for all inquiry activities is available in **Online Resources.**

Science Notebook Strategies

- Lists of Kit-Supplied Materials
- Meeting Individual Needs
- Investigate More—Extensions and Variations
- and More!

Activity	Inquiry and Design Process Skills Focus	Materials	Prep Tips, Troubleshooting, and Expected Results
Lesson 2 DIRECTED INQUIRY **Flipchart** p.49 **A Rubbed Leaf Collection** **OBJECTIVES** Plan and conduct simple investigations. Record and organize data. Identify and compare the parts of plants. 40 minutes individuals **TEKS 1.2B, 1.2D, 1.10B**	• Observe • Compare • Formulate or Use Models	• leaves • drawing paper • crayons • masking tape (optional)	**Prep Tips** You may wish to collect leaves before children begin the investigation. Demonstrate how to place the leaves vein-side up. Thin copy paper works better than construction paper for this activity. To prevent the paper from moving, have children tape the corners to their desks with masking tape. **Caution!** If children collect their own leaves, make sure they do so with adult supervision and do not collect toxic leaves, such as poison ivy. Remind them not to touch their faces during the activity and to wash their hands after they complete their rubbings. **Troubleshooting** Make sure children choose leaves from three different trees and color over a wide enough swath of paper so the entire leaf appears in the rubbing. In Step #3, be sure children have the paper on top of the leaf, then rub the side of the crayon on the paper. **Expected Results** The rubbings will show the size, shape, and texture of each leaf as well as details of stems and veins. Children will recognize that while all leaves have stems and veins, their sizes, shapes, and textures differ depending on the type of tree.
INDEPENDENT INQUIRY **Flipchart** p.49 **B Fantastic Flowers** **OBJECTIVES** Plan and conduct simple investigations. Record and organize data. Identify and compare the parts of plants. 40 minutes individuals **TEKS 1.2B, 1.2D, 1.10B**	• Observe • Compare • Classify • Formulate or Use Models • Plan and Conduct a Simple Investigation	• real flowers, lifelike artificial flowers, or pictures of flowers • crayons or markers	**Prep Tips** Have children bring in flowers from home, or you can bring in flowers for the class. Real flowers are preferable. However, if children have allergies or real flowers are unavailable, lifelike artificial flowers or pictures of flowers will work, too. **Caution!** Be aware of possible allergies. If children are collecting flowers in their neighborhoods, remind them that a trusted adult should accompany them. **Troubleshooting** Discuss with children possible ways to present their flower observations. For example, children might draw the different flowers on a poster, making notes below each drawing about the parts, color, petal size, and other characteristics. **Expected Results** Children will observe that although flowers from different plants may have different colors, shapes, and petal sizes, they have certain parts in common.

Planning for Inquiry (continued)

Activity	Inquiry and Design Process Skills Focus	Materials	Prep Tips, Troubleshooting, and Expected Results
Lesson 3 INQUIRY GUIDED INQUIRY **Flipchart** p.50 **Student Edition** pp. 401–402 **How Can We Compare Leaves?** **OBJECTIVES** • Plan and conduct simple investigations. • Collect data and make observations using non-standard measurement tools. • Record and organize data. • Collect and compare information using non-standard measuring items. • Measure and compare organisms using non-standard units. • Identify and compare the parts of plants. 30 minutes pairs TEKS **1.2B, 1.2C, 1.2D, 1.4A, 1.4B, 1.10B**	• Measure • Compare • Observe • Communicate	• 3 leaves from 3 different trees • 10 large paper clips • 10 clothespins	**Prep Tips** Before the activity, demonstrate how to measure with nonstandard units. Show children how to line up the paper clips from end to end on top of each leaf. Call on a volunteer to count how many paper clips you used to measure. Note that measurements may not be exact so have children round to the nearest whole number. **Caution!** Be aware of possible allergies among children. Should you have any concerns about children handling leaves, have them use gloves. Wash hands after the activity. **Troubleshooting** Make sure children measure each leaf in the same way—starting at its stem and ending at its tip. **Expected Results** Children will see that the more paper clips and clothespins it takes to measure a leaf, the longer it is. They will observe that leaves are both the same *and* different and can be sorted by different characteristics.

Go Digital! Virtual Lab

How Are Plants of the Same Kind Different?

Key Inquiry Skills: observe, compare

Children compare young plants and their parents to see how the leaves and other structures vary from plant to plant.

RTI Response to Intervention

Response to Intervention is a process for identifying and supporting students who are not making expected progress toward essential learning goals.

The following *ScienceFusion* components have the flexibility to be used to provide Core Classroom Instruction (Tier 1), strategic intervention (Tier 2), and intensive intervention (Tier 3).

Component	Location	Strategies and Benefits
Student Edition, Active Reading prompts, Sum It Up, Brain Check	Active Reading throughout each lesson, Sum It Up and Brain Check at the end of each lesson	Student responses can be used as screening tools to assess whether intervention is needed.
Assessment Guide, Lesson Quizzes and TEKS DOK Skill Builder	pp. AG 135–AG 139	Student responses can be used as screening tools to assess whether intervention is needed.
Inquiry Flipcharts	Inquiry Flipchart p. 50	Directed Inquiry for students who learn best through directed or teacher-led hands-on activities.
Teacher Edition, Unit Review Answer Strategies	TE pp. 405–408	Suggestions for intervention, guidance, and remediation for each review question.
Leveled Readers	TE p. 377H	Content support for students not meeting the learning needs during core classroom instruction.
Leveled Readers, Teacher Guides and Vocabulary Worksheets	TE p. 377H	Direct instruction with small groups of students needing additional content at various readability levels.
Extra Support for Vocabulary and Concepts (online worksheets)	Online Resources	Support for individualized instruction with practice in essential content.
Online Student Edition with Audio	Online Resources	Provides learners with multiple-modality access to science concepts and information.
Interactive Digital Lessons and Virtual Labs	Online Resources	Provides individualized learning experiences. Lessons make content accessible through simulations, animations, videos, audio, and integrated assessment.
Interactive Whiteboard Resources	Online Resources	Reinforces key unit concepts through interactive vocabulary games and visuals and graphic organizers.
Leveled Readers, online and tablet versions	Online and Tablet Resources	Highlighted words and sentences synced with audio provide support for emerging or struggling readers.

Differentiated Instruction

English Language Learners

Choose from these instructional strategies to meet the needs of English language learners.

Vocabulary Cards are provided in Online Resources.

Unit Vocabulary

Lesson 1	Lesson 2
root	flower
stem	cone
leaf	
flower	
seed	
fruit	

Preteach Vocabulary ELPS 2B

As you preteach vocabulary, model pronunciation and have children repeat. For Unit 10 vocabulary, draw attention to the consonant blends in the words *stem, flower,* and *fruit.*

Language Acquisition Strategies

Use Content Area Vocabulary ELPS 2I, 3D, 3F

Have children use content words from TE pages 380–381 to share facts about plants. Display a bank of content words (*plant, soil, roots, water, needs, stem, grow*).

Beginning	Intermediate	Advanced/Advanced High
Model using several of the content words to state facts about plants. Then, have children share a fact with a partner.	Have children use content words to share one or two facts about plants.	Have children use content words to tell a partner what they learned about plants. Challenge children to use all the words in the word bank.

Reading Support ELPS 2E, 3E, 4F

Use **TE pages 382–383** to have children practice using teacher and peer support while reading.

Beginning	Intermediate	Advanced/Advanced High
Point out the pictures and labels. Explain that children should use these supports to learn about plant parts. Have children raise their hand if they need you to repeat or explain anything they hear.	Have children work in pairs. Provide questions they can ask to support their reading: *What should I pay attention to as I read? What is the main idea?*	Have partners skim the text before reading and identify words that are unfamiliar or difficult to pronounce. Discuss resources they could use to check these words.

Share Facts ELPS 3D, 3H, 4G

Display a bank of content words related to the information about plants and animals on **TE pages 392–393.** Have children use these words to talk about what they learned.

Beginning	Intermediate	Advanced/Advanced High
Use forced-answer questions to have children practice using content area words: *Are plants living or nonliving things? Do plants move or stay in one place? Do green plants make their own light or make their own food?*	Have children complete these sentence frames: *Plants and animals are both ___. Animals move, but plants ___. Green plants use light, ___, and ___ to make their own food.*	Have children compare and contrast plants and animals. Children should share facts in complete sentences.

Monitor Oral Language ELPS 1B, 2E, 3C

Have children make statements about plants using the information on **TE pages 394–395.** Guide them to use self-corrective techniques.

Beginning	Intermediate	Advanced/Advanced High
Say this sentence: *Shrubs are shorter than trees.* Model having difficulty saying *shrubs.* Use a dictionary to find the correct pronunciation and repeat the sentence.	If children make a mistake while speaking, model things they can say to correct their language: *I meant to say ___. Let me say that again. I should have said ___.*	As children make their statements, have them monitor their words and identify any words they mispronounced. Discuss resources they could use to check those words.

Answer Questions ELPS 3D, 3H, 4G

Have children answer questions about flowers and cones using the information on **TE pages 396–397.**

Beginning	Intermediate	Advanced/Advanced High
Have children respond to forced-choice questions such as: *Do flowers make seeds or leaves? Do some plants or all plants have flowers? Do cones hold a plant's flowers or seeds?*	Have children use words and phrases to respond: *What do flowers make? On what kinds of plants can flowers grow? What do cones hold?*	Have children respond in complete sentences: *Why are flowers important to a plant? Where can flowers grow? What would you find inside a cone?*

UNIT 10

Plants

I Wonder Why

Have children look at the photographs and describe what they see. Then ask them to share what they know about grapes, including how grapes taste and where they grow. If possible, bring in a bunch of grapes for children to observe. Discuss any other information or clues from the photographs that help children answer the "why" question.

Here's Why

Have children turn the page and read the response to the question. You may wish to share the following background with them.

More About...

Grapes

Grapes are a kind of fruit that grows on woody vines, in clusters of about 75 to 300 grapes. People eat grapes raw or use them to make products such as jam, juice, vinegar, and raisins. Grapes may be red, purple, dark blue, black, green, yellow, orange, or pink. "White" grapes are actually green.

People from as long ago as ancient Egypt grew grapes. Grapes are commonly grown in places with hot, sunny summers and cool winters, but some kinds of grapes can grow in places with freezing winters, such as Michigan. Grapes need the right amounts of sun and water and the right kind of soil.

Science Songs

See pp. TR40–TR45 for science songs you can use to reinforce content in this unit.

Professional Development Science Background

Use the keyword to access

- Professional Development from **The NSTA Learning Center**
- **SciLinks** for additional online content appropriate for children and teachers
- Teacher Science Background in the back of this Teacher Edition

Keyword

plants

Here's Why The leaves use the water, light, and air to make food.

In this unit, you will explore this Big Idea, the Essential Questions, and the Investigations on the Inquiry Flipchart.

Levels of Inquiry Key ■ DIRECTED ■ GUIDED ■ INDEPENDENT

Track Your Progress

Big Idea Plants have parts that help them grow and change. There are many kinds of plants.

Essential Questions

Now I Get the Big Idea!

Science Notebook

Before you begin each lesson, be sure to write your thoughts about the Essential Question.

Go Digital

or a complete digital urriculum and resources at provide full coverage the objectives for is unit, see the Online esources for this program.

Big Idea and Essential Questions

Big Idea Plants have parts that help them grow and change. There are many kinds of plants.

Post the Unit Big Idea on the board. Have children read the Essential Questions, which are also the titles of the lessons in this unit.

- Discuss how the Essential Questions can help keep them focused on the Big Idea.
- Have children read the Big Idea statement. The statement describes the main science concept that they will be learning.
- Have children predict other ideas that will be taught in the lessons based on the titles, or have them give examples of pictures they expect to see.

Once they complete the unit, they should have a better understanding of the Big Idea.

Essential Questions You may use the following Science Notebook strategy for working with the Essential Questions before children begin the unit or before each lesson.

- Strategies for revisiting the Big Idea and Essential Questions are provided in Enduring Understandings on p. 405A.

Notebook Science Notebook

- Have children copy the Essential Questions into their Science Notebooks. Suggest they leave writing lines between questions.
- Ask children to write responses to the Essential Questions. Urge them not to worry about whether their responses are correct. They should expect their ideas to change as they work in the unit. Comment that children will be able to review and revise their answers to the Essential Questions at the end of the unit.
- Tips and strategies for using Science Notebooks are provided throughout this unit, in the back of this Teacher Edition, and in the Online Resources.

Options for Inquiry

FLIPCHART P. 48

Children can conduct these optional investigations at any time before, during, or in response to the lesson in the Student Edition.

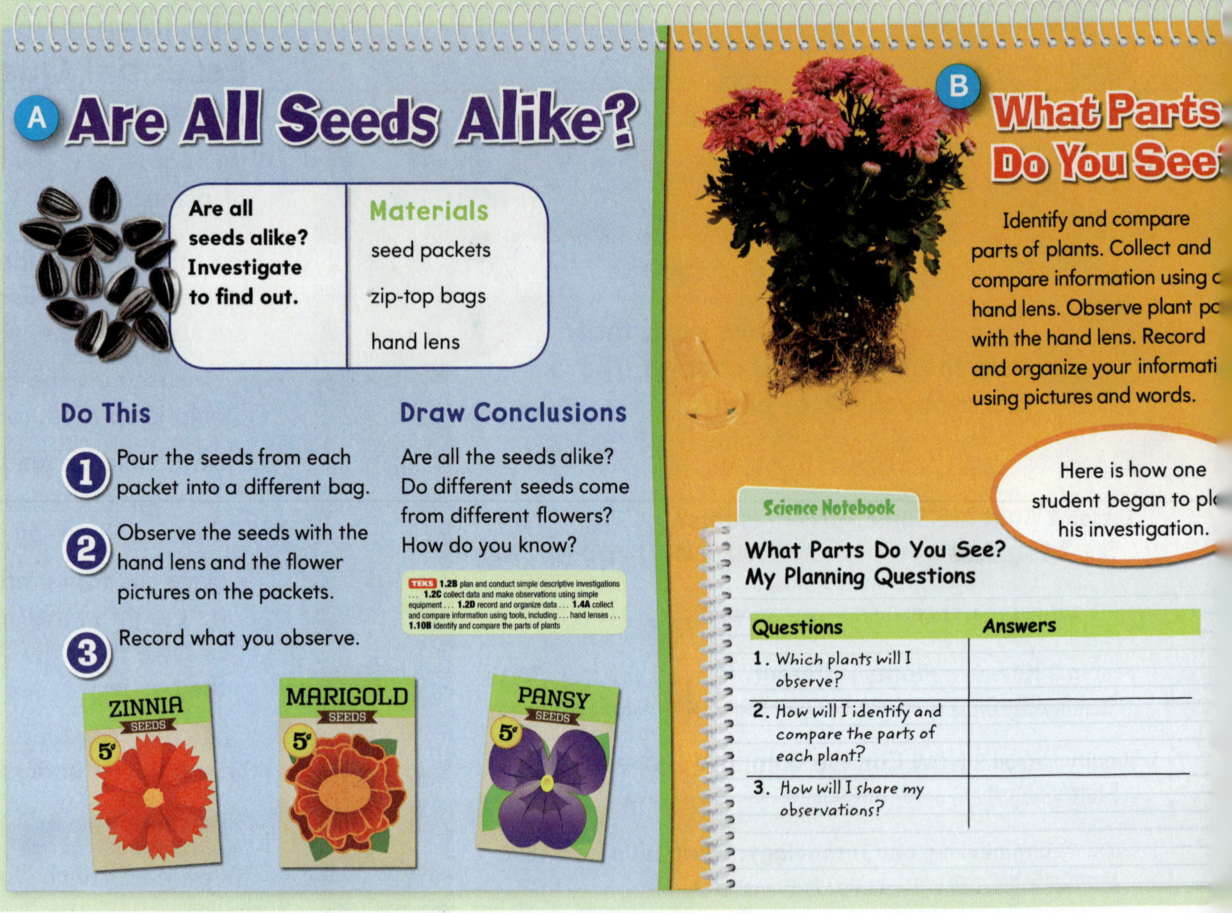

Directed Inquiry

A Are All Seeds Alike?

25 minutes
small groups

Prep and Planning Tips

You may wish to organize the seeds into zip-top bags before the investigation. Consider making color copies of the seed packets and placing them in the zip-top bags with the seeds.

Review how to use a hand lens to collect information and make observations. Remind children to record all of their observations.

Caution! Be sure children recognize and demonstrate safe practices to keep themselves safe and healthy by reminding them not to eat any seeds. Children should wash their hands at the end of this investigation and use all materials appropriately.

Expected Results

Children will find that seeds come in different sizes, colors, and shapes and that different seeds produce different types of plants.

Independent Inquiry

B What Parts Do You See?

30 minutes
pairs

Prep and Planning Tips

See the Planning for Inquiry page for more information. Select flowering plants for observation. Review how to use a hand lens to collect and compare information and make observations.

Caution! Have children wash their hands after the investigation.

Science Notebook

Children can use their Science Notebook as a model for planning and conducting their own investigation. Encourage them to make a chart like the one shown and to include the sample questions plus their own questions. Remind children to record and organize their information using pictures and words.

TEKS 1.10B identify and compare the parts of plants

Lesson 1

Essential Question

What Are Some Parts of Plants?

Engage Your Brain!

Find the answer to the question in the lesson.

What holds this tree in place?

its roots

Active Reading

Lesson Vocabulary

1. Preview the lesson.
2. Write the 6 vocabulary terms here.

root	flower
stem	seed
leaf	fruit

Inquiry Flipchart p. 48—Are All Seeds Alike?/What Parts Do You See?

379

Go Digital

n interactive digital esson is available in Online esources. It is suitable for dividuals, small groups, or ay be projected or used n an interactive white oard.

1 Engage/Explore

Objectives

- Plan and conduct simple investigations.
- Collect and compare information and make observations using a hand lens.
- Record and organize data.
- Identify and compare the parts of plants.

Engage Your Brain!

Help children brainstorm answers to the question, *What holds this tree in place?* Have them pantomime trees growing on a steep hillside. Have them think about what could help a tree stay in place instead of slipping down the hill.

Remind children to record their final answer when they find it on the next page of the lesson.

Active Reading Annotations

Remind children that active readers "make texts their own" by marking them or writing notes to help them understand what they are reading. Encourage children to use pencil to make annotations and to feel free to change their marks and notes as they read. The goal of annotation is to help children remember what they have read.

Vocabulary and Interactive Glossary

Remind children to find and list the yellow highlighted terms from the lesson. As they proceed through the lesson and learn about the terms, they can add drawings or words in the extra spaces provided in some entries in the Interactive Glossary.

2 Explain

Notebook Generate Ideas

Read the heading of this page aloud to children. Ask children to name parts that "make up" a plant. List the ideas on a chart and modify the list as you work through the lesson.

Develop Science Vocabulary

roots Write the word *roots* on the board and have children read it with you. As they do, have them bend one wrist and spread their fingers wide to imitate the root shape of many plants.

Active Reading Details

Explain that a detail sentence may give an example. Or, it may describe something. Active readers ask themselves, "What topic does this detail sentence tell about?" The answer will help readers keep the main idea in mind. Have children reread the second paragraph, looking for details that tell more about plant roots.

Develop Science Concepts

Identify the plant parts described on these two pages. roots and stems

Where do you find the roots of a plant? growing in the soil

What do the roots do? hold the plant in place; take in water and other things the plant needs from the soil

Why is it important to handle roots carefully when moving a plant? If roots are harmed, a plant cannot get the water and other things it needs to live.

Why do you think dandelions are difficult to pull out of a lawn? They have a long, thick root that makes them difficult to pull out.

A Plant's Makeup

A plant has parts that help it grow and change.

Taking Root

A plant has roots that grow into the soil. The **roots** hold the plant in place. They take in water from the soil. They take in other things from the soil that the plant needs.

Active Reading

A detail is a fact about a main idea. Draw one line under a detail. Draw an arrow to the main idea it tells about.

roots

380

English Language Learners

ELPS 1E, 2

Understand Multiple-Meaning Words Point to the word *Makeup* in the lesson title and have children repeat it after you. Explain that *makeup* combines *make* and *up*. Point out that *makeup* has different meanings. It can refer to cosmetics like lipstick. Scientists use *makeup* to describ the parts that create something, or make it up. Ask children whic meaning of *makeup* is used in these sentences: *The makeup of this soil is sand and clay. Jill put makeup before the play.*

Stems Stand Tall

The **stem** holds up the plant. It takes water from the roots to the other parts of the plant.

A flower has a thin, soft stem. A tree has a thick, woody stem.

▶ **Identify the roots and stems on these pages. Circle the roots. Put a box around the stems. Then compare how they are alike and different.**

Sample answers: Roots and stems are both parts of plants. Roots take in water from the soil. Stems take water to other parts of the plant.

381

Differentiation—Leveled Questions

Extra Support

Why do plants need roots and stems? Plants need roots to hold them in the ground and to take in water and other things from the soil. Plants need stems to hold them up and carry water from the roots to the other plant parts.

Challenge

Why might cutting the stems of flowers make a bouquet last longer? Cutting will keep the stems open so they can carry water up to the flowers to keep them fresh.

Develop Science Vocabulary

stem Write the word *stem* on the board and have children pronounce it with you. Have them underline the word *stems* in the heading on the right page. Ask children to tell how they think the other words in the title describe the word *stem*.

Develop Science Concepts

What do plant stems do? They hold up the plant. They carry water and other things a plant needs from the roots to other parts of the plant. **What can stems look or feel like?** They can be thin and soft or hard and woody. **Why do trees like the gum tree have thick, woody stems?** A thin, soft stem would not support the weight of a tree's heavy branches. A thick, woody stem can.

Interpret Visuals

Focus attention on the two pictures of the roots and the two pictures of the stems. Have children identify these plant parts and compare how they are alike and different.

Develop Inquiry Skills

EXPERIMENT To help children better understand the function of stems, snip the bottoms of white carnations and place them in colored water. Have children predict what will happen. Lead children to hypothesize that the flower petals may change color because the stem carries water up to other parts of the plant. Have children observe to determine if their predictions are correct.

Notebook Summarize Ideas

Have children recall details about roots and stems and summarize these details orally or in writing.

2 Explain (continued)

Generate Ideas

Notebook

Ask children to recall the two plant parts they have already learned about. Then have them read the headings on this spread to identify additional plant parts they will study.

Develop Science Vocabulary

leaf Write the words *leaf* and *leaves* on the board and have children read the words. Say that *leaves* is the plural form of *leaf.* Show how it forms by dropping *f* and adding *–ves.*

Active Reading **Vocabulary**

Explain that a vocabulary word may be highlighted in a color. Active readers pay attention to highlighted words because their meaning is given in the same sentence or the next sentence.

Develop Science Concepts

Identify the plant part you see on this page. leaf **What do leaves do?** They take in light and air. They use light, air, and water to make food for the plant.

Why might a plant have trouble staying alive if insects ate all its leaves? Without leaves, a plant cannot make the food it needs to stay alive.

Interpret Visuals

Focus children's attention on the banana leaf. **Why do you think this photograph shows children on either side of the leaf?** It helps show how large the banana leaf is.

What do the many different leaves on the left page show? They show that leaves come in many shapes and sizes.

Leaves at Work

A **leaf** is a plant part that makes food for the plant. It uses light, air, and water.

Active Reading

Find the sentence that tells the meaning of **leaf**. Draw a line under the sentence.

Leaves can be different shapes and sizes.

382

English Language Learners

ELPS 1C, 1E, 2

Make a Plant Part Glossary To help children recall the names of the plant parts they have learned, have them use labeled photographs, drawings, or real plant parts to make a picture glossary of these terms: *roots, stem, leaf, flower, fruit,* and *seed.* Once they have completed their glossaries, have them cover the labels and ask a partner to iden each plant part.

Flowers, Seeds, and Fruit

Many plants have flowers. A **flower** is a plant part that makes seeds. A new plant may grow from a **seed**. The new plant will look like the plant that made the seed.

Many flowers grow into fruits. A **fruit** holds seeds.

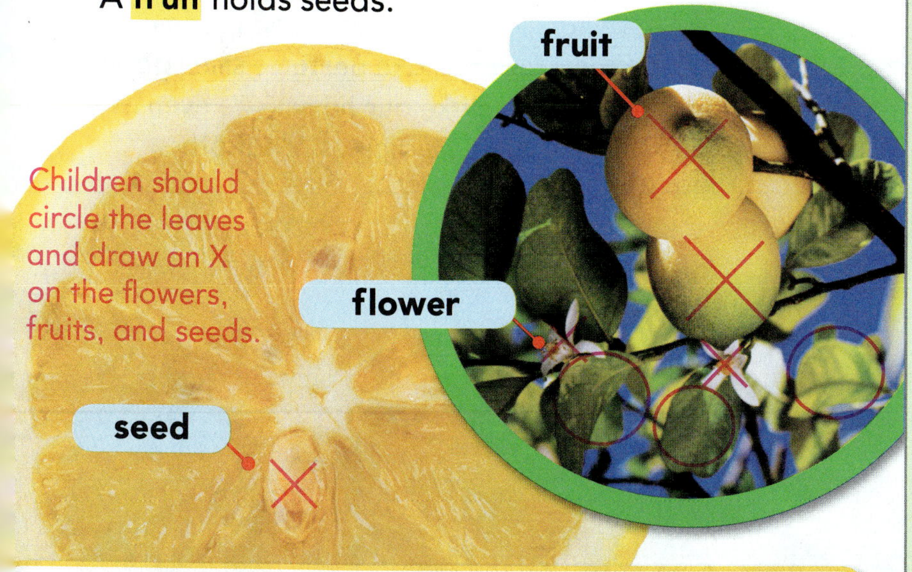

▶ **Identify parts of plants. Draw a circle around the leaves. Draw an X on the flowers, fruits, and seeds. Then compare how they are alike and different.**

Sample answer: All are parts of plants. Leaves make food. Flowers make seeds. Fruits hold the seeds. New plants may grow from seeds.

383

Writing Connection

TEKS ELA 1.19C

Write Help-Wanted Ads for Plant Parts Remind children that each plant part has an important "job" in making sure that the plant lives and gets what it needs. Have children choose a plant part and write a help-wanted ad that describes what this plant part does for the plant. For example, *Help wanted: A plant part that can take sunlight, air, and water and use them to make food for the plant.* Ask children to share their help-wanted ads and have classmates name the plant part that can do the job.

TEKS 1.10B

Develop Science Vocabulary

flower, seed, fruit Write *flower, seed,* and *fruit* on the board. Explain to children that flowers make seeds. New plants may grow from the seeds. Also discuss that many flowers grow into fruits. Fruits hold seeds.

Develop Science Concepts

Identify the plant parts you see on this page. flower, fruit, and seed **What is a flower?** the part of a plant that makes seeds **Why are seeds important to a plant?** Plants need seeds to make new plants. **What do some flowers grow into?** fruits **What does the fruit hold?** seeds

Have children compare how flowers, fruits, and seeds are alike and different. They can use this information to answer the interactive.

Misconception Alert

Children may think fruits are only berry or citrus varieties, such as grapes and oranges. Explain that plants we often call vegetables, such as pumpkins, tomatoes, and cucumbers, are actually classified as fruits because their fruits hold seeds.

Develop Inquiry Skills

PREDICT **What might happen if you cut open a ripe avocado fruit and planted the seed?** If the seed got what it needed, an avocado plant would grow from the seed. **How do you know?** The fruit holds a seed. Seeds grow into new plants.

Notebook Summarize Ideas

Direct children to think about the main ideas on these pages. Ask if their ideas have changed since they read this section. Have them summarize the main ideas orally.

2 Explain (continued)

Notebook Generate Ideas

Preview the images on this page and the next page and call on volunteers to describe what they see. Ask children what these images might have to do with "Plant Power" and the importance of plants in everyday life.

Develop Science Concepts

What are some ways people use plants? as food; to make things; as medicine As you go through the answers, have children number the different uses in their books.

How have plants been used to build or make things in our classroom? Sample answers: Woody stems are used to build walls, chairs, desks, and bookcases. Stems are used to make paper.

Explain that plant parts are also used to make fabrics, such as cotton and linen. Pair children and have them identify a fabric in the classroom made from plants. Sample answers: curtains, clothing, pillows, rugs

Develop Inquiry Skills

PREDICT **Think about our climate and things we can grow around here. What plants might you see if you visited a farmer's market in our community?** Answers will vary depending on where children live.

Why It Matters

Plant Power

We use plants for food. We also use plants to make things. Mint leaves are used in some toothpastes. Flowers make perfume smell good. Woody stems help make our homes. We even use plants to make some medicines. What other plant uses can you name?

384

Differentiation—Leveled Questions

Extra Support
Look around the room. What are two ways you see people using plant parts? Sample answer: wood in pencils, apples for snacks

Challenge
People use plant parts every d
What are some ways people ca
help protect this resource and
make it last? Sample answer:
reuse paper bags at the store, c
not waste food

Do the Math!
Solve a Problem

Look at the tomatoes. Use them to help you solve this problem.

A farmer has 24 tomatoes.
He picks 11 tomatoes.
How many are left?

24 - 11 = 13

385

Do the Math!

TEKS MATH 1.5D, 1.5G

Solve a Problem

Ask children what information they already know and what they need to find out in order to solve the problem. Have them decide whether they will add or subtract to get the answer. Remind them that they can use the picture of the tomato plants, counters, or other manipulatives to help solve the problem.

If children need guidance, suggest that they count the tomatoes on the plants and then cross out the number of tomatoes the farmer picked. Have them count the remaining tomatoes to see how many are left.

After children finish, have them look at their answer to decide if it makes sense. They should understand that the answer makes sense, for example, if it is less than the starting number.

Notebook Summarize Ideas

Direct children to think about the details and main ideas on these pages. Then have them identify the main idea these details support by completing this sentence orally or in writing: *Plants are important to people because* _________.

3 Extend/Evaluate

Sum It Up!

1. **Choose It!** Read the directions aloud and have volunteers name the pictures. If children have difficulty identifying which plant part takes in water, have them reread the definitions of the highlighted words in the lesson.
2. **Solve It!** Encourage children to read each riddle aloud with a partner and underline key words or phrases that will help them identify the plant part. To help children with spelling, they can look back through the lesson at the highlighted words. After children solve each riddle, review the answers and have them identify the most important clue that helped them figure it out.

Sum It Up!

1 Choose It!

Identify the plant part that takes in water. Circle it.

2 Solve It!

Solve each riddle.

I can be thick or thin.
I can be short or tall.
I help a plant get water and hold it up so it won't fall.

What am I?

stem

I can be different colors, shapes, and sizes.
I may fall to the ground.
I take in light and air to make food for a plant since it can't move around.

What am I?

leaf

386

Brain Check

Lesson 1

Name ______________________

Word Play

Identify the parts of the plant. Label it using words from the box.

flower	leaf	roots	stem

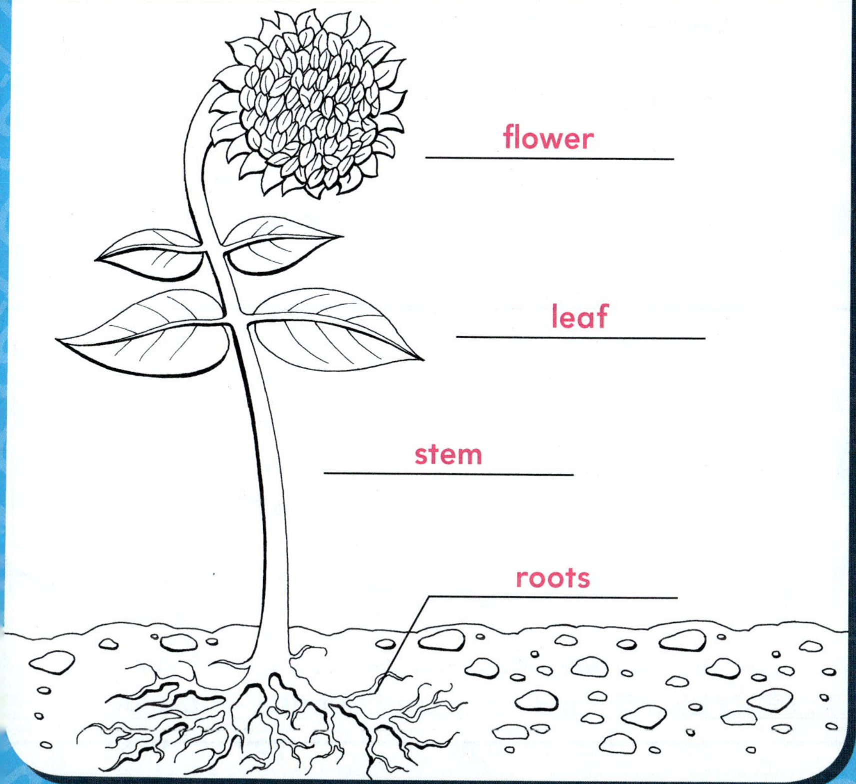

387

TEKS 1.10B

Answer Strategies

Word Play

- After reading the directions with children, review the words in the word box. Remind children that they will use each word only once to label the parts of the plant.
- Children can look back at the pictures showing roots, stems, leaves, and flowers for guidance or review. Remind them that while these plant parts will not be a perfect match for what they see in the pictures, they should be able to use them to help identify the correct label for each part.
- To help improve children's recall of plant parts and their functions, have pairs of children take turns using each plant part in a sentence. In their sentence, encourage them to identify how each plant part helps a plant get what it needs to survive.

Assessment

Lesson Quiz

See Assessment Guide, p. AG 135.

3 Extend/Evaluate (continued)

Answer Strategies

Apply Concepts

- Review how the chart is organized, with a *Problem* column on the left and a *Solution* column on the right where children should write one of the plant parts from the lesson. Point out that a problem and a solution go together across each row.
- If children have trouble completing the chart, remind them that the answer to each question is one of the six plant parts they have studied, and encourage them to look back at the lesson pages. Tell them to look for the names of each plant part and a description of what each part does to help the plant get what it needs to survive.
- As a lesson follow-up, ask children to summarize what they learned in the lesson. Ask them to name new facts and ideas they did not know about plant parts before reading this lesson.

Take It Home!

Suggest that children tell a family member what they have learned about plant parts. Together, they can identify and compare the parts of plants they have around their home and backyard. Encourage them to talk about plant parts that they use in their homes. Children may wish to classify these uses into groups by how they use the plant parts, such as food, and other uses. Have children report back to the class on the different plant uses they discovered.

Apply Concepts

Identify which plant parts a plant needs.

Problem	Solution
1 I need a plant part to hold seeds. What part do I need?	fruit
2 I need a plant part to take in water. What part do I need?	roots
3 I need a plant part to make fruit. What part do I need?	flower
4 I need a plant part to make food. What part do I need?	leaf
5 I need a plant part to hold me up. What part do I need?	stem
6 I need a plant part to make a plant just like me. What part do I need?	seed

Take It Home!

Family Members: Encourage your child to identify and compare the parts of a plant. Help your child name plants you eat and use everyday.

388

Make Connections

Easy

Writing Connection

TEKS ELA 1.19A

Write a Recipe for a Plant-Part Salad

- Display labeled pictures of the following salad ingredients: lettuce, spinach, carrots, onion, asparagus, and so on.
- Have children select items from the list and write a simple recipe for making a plant-part salad.
- Have them share their recipes in small groups and identify from which plant part each ingredient comes. Encourage them to take their recipes home to try with their families.

Easy

Social Studies Connection

TEKS SS 1.17A

Interview School Helpers About Plant Use

- Explain that many school helpers use plant parts in their work; for example, the school custodian may use a broom made from plant stems and the principal uses pencils made from woody plant stems.
- Have children interview school personnel to find out how they use plant parts.
- Have children share their findings in labeled drawings or in an oral report.

Average

Art Connection

TEKS ART 1.2C

Make a Seed Mosaic

- Provide construction paper, glue, and seeds such as birdseed, peas, beans, unpopped corn, and grass seed.
- Have children use them to make a seed mosaic of a plant and label its parts.

Challenging

Math Connection

TEKS MATH 1.8A, 1.8B

Make a Tally Chart and a Bar Graph

- Have pairs of children survey classmates to find out which fruit they like best.
- Have them collect the information in a tally chart and then present the results in a bar graph.

People in Science

Objectives

- Describe what scientists do.
- Recognize that scientists come from all backgrounds.
- Identify the role of technology in the work of scientists.
- Recognize that a scientist's work helps people.

Notebook Generate Ideas

Share the background information below with children before you assign the feature. Ask questions to ascertain children's prior knowledge.

Why do people need clean water? People need clean water to be healthy.

What would happen to people if the water they drank was dirty? Sample answer: They might get sick.

Background

- Dr. Norma Alcantar is a chemical engineer and a professor at the University of South Florida in Tampa. Some of the problems she works on involve Alzheimer's disease, chemotherapy, and finding ways to make drinking water clean.
- Many communities in Mexico have drinking water that contains harmful ingredients. Dr. Alcantar has begun using a process that involves the gooey substance mucilage, found in the prickly pear cactus. This substance allows the cactus to hold large amounts of water. When it is added to untreated water, it causes unwanted substances in the water to sink to the bottom.
- Dr. Alcantar wants to use the cacti as a filter so that more people can have access to clean water.

TEKS 1.3C describe what scientists do

People in Scienc

Get to Know ...
Dr. Norma Alcantar

Dr. Norma Alcantar studies materials. She makes them more useful. Dr. Alcantar wanted to find a way to make water clean.

She learned that some people in Mexico used prickly pear cactus plants to clean water. The plants have a gooey material. Dr. Alcantar studied it. She used the goo to make water clean

Fun Fact

She learned al using this kind cactus from he grandmother.

Writing Connection

TEKS ELA 1.1

Write to Explain Remind children that Dr. Alcantar learned about using the prickly pear cactus from her grandmother. Then have each child copy and complete the following sentence frames to share something they learned from a family member about how to meet one of their needs: *My ______ taught me to ______. T helps me to ______.* If children get stuck, ask them to think specifically about what family members such as grandparents have told them about what is a is not good to eat.

ple in Science continued

Clean It!

▶ **Answer the questions about Dr. Alcantar's work.**

1 Describe what Dr. Alcantar does.
She finds ways to make materials more useful.

2 Where did Dr. Alcantar get the idea for using the prickly pear cactus in her studies?
from her grandmother

3 Why is Dr. Alcantar's work important?
Sample answer: It gives people a way to get clean water. People need clean water to live.

4 What does Dr. Alcantar use from the cactus to make clean water?
goo

Nature of Science

Remind children that scientists form questions and then investigate to find answers. Have children imagine that the prickly pear cactus is able to meet the needs of people and animals in some way other than what Dr. Alcantar has studied.

Work with children to make a list of questions they could investigate to learn other uses for the prickly pear cactus. Possible questions could include *Can people or animals eat the prickly pear cactus? Can animals live inside the cactus or build homes from it?*

TEKS 1.3C

Develop Science Concepts

Describe what Dr. Alcantar does. She studies materials and finds ways to make them more useful to people.

How have people in Mexico used prickly pear cactus plants? to clean water

What material of the prickly pear cactus plant is Dr. Alcantar studying? the gooey material

Why is she studying this material? to find how to use the goo to make water clean

Do you think clean water could be helpful to animals in Mexico, too? Why or why not? Sample answer: Yes, I think animals in Mexico could use clean water, too. If they are drinking water that is dirty, they might get sick just as people can. People could give the clean water to their pets to keep them healthy.

Develop Inquiry Skills

DRAW CONCLUSIONS **Will Dr. Alcantar's work help people, plants, and animals in Mexico meet their needs? Why do you think this?** Sample answer: Yes, because people, plants, and animals need clean water to grow and be healthy. If the water is dirty and unhealthy, people might get sick, and plants and animals could die.

Notebook Summarize Ideas

Have each child summarize the information on these pages by telling a partner how Dr. Alcantar's work might help people and animals meet their needs.

Lesson 2

Options for Inquiry

FLIPCHART P.49

Children can conduct these optional investigations at any time before, during, or in response to the lesson in the Student Edition.

A Rubbed Leaf Collection

How can you show that leaves are different? Investigate to find out.

Materials
leaves
drawing paper
crayons

Do This

1. Collect several kinds of leaves.
2. Put a leaf on the table. Put the paper on top of the leaf.
3. Rub the side of a crayon over the paper and leaf.
4. Do the same thing with the other leaves. Compare your leaf rubbings.

Draw Conclusions

What do you observe? How are your leaves the same? How are they different? How many leaves have the same number of points?

TEKS 1.2B plan and conduct simple descriptive investigations ... 1.2D record and organize data using pictures, numbers, and words 1.10B identify and compare the parts of plants

B Fantastic Flowers

Are flowers from different plants different? Decide on a plan to find out. Compare how the flowers are the same and different. Draw and write to record what you observe.

Here is how one student began to plan his investigation.

Science Notebook

Fantastic Flowers
My Planning Questions

Questions	Answers
1. Where will I look for flowers?	
2. How will I compare the flowers I observe?	
3. How will I share my observations?	

Directed Inquiry

A Rubbed Leaf Collection

40 minutes
individuals

Prep and Planning Tips

You may wish to collect leaves before children begin the investigation. Demonstrate how to place the leaves vein-side up. Thin copy paper works better than construction paper.

Caution! Be sure children recognize and demonstrate safe practices to keep themselves and others safe and healthy. If children are collecting their own leaves, make sure they know to do so with adult supervision and do not collect toxic leaves such as poison ivy or poison oak. Remind children not to touch their faces during the activity, use all materials appropriately, and have them wash their hands after they complete their rubbings.

Expected Results

The leaf rubbings will show the size, shape, and texture of each leaf as well as details of the stems and veins. While all leaves have stems and veins, their sizes, shapes, and textures differ depending on the type of tree.

Independent Inquiry

B Fantastic Flowers

40 minutes
individuals

Prep and Planning Tips

See the Planning for Inquiry page for more information. If children are unable to collect flowers in their neighborhood, you may wish to provide flowers for them.

Caution! Remind children that a trusted adult should go with them and they should wash their hands after the investigation.

Science Notebook

Children can use their Science Notebook as a model for planning and conducting their own investigation. Encourage them to make a chart lik the one shown and include the sample questions plus questions of their own. Be sure children writ and draw to record what they observe in their Science Notebooks.

TEKS 1.10B identify and compare the parts of plants

Lesson 2

Essential Question

How Are Plants Different?

Engage Your Brain!

Find the answer to the question in the lesson.

How is this plant like some animals?

It eats insects and spiders

Active Reading

Lesson Vocabulary

1. Preview the lesson.
2. Write the 2 vocabulary terms here.

flower   cone

Inquiry Flipchart p. 49—Rubbed Leaf Collection/Fantastic Flowers

391

Go Digital

n interactive digital sson is available in Online sources. It is suitable for dividuals, small groups, or ay be projected or used an interactive white ard.

1 Engage/Explore

Objectives

- Plan and conduct simple investigations.
- Record and organize data.
- Identify and compare the parts of plants.

Engage Your Brain!

Lead children in brainstorming an answer to the question, *How is this plant like some animals?* Provide a hint by suggesting they think about how plants and animals usually get food. Then have them check the picture to determine if this plant is different from other plants in the way it gets food.

Remind children to record their final answer when they find it on the third page of the lesson.

Active Reading Annotations

Remind children that active readers "make texts their own" by marking them or writing notes to help them understand what they are reading. Encourage children to use pencil to make annotations and to feel free to change their marks and notes as they read. The goal of annotation is to help children remember what they have read.

Vocabulary and Interactive Glossary

Remind children to find and list the yellow highlighted terms from the lesson. As they proceed through the lesson and learn about the terms, they can add drawings or words in the extra spaces provided in some entries in the Interactive Glossary.

2 Explain

Notebook Generate Ideas

Read the heading on this page aloud to children. Have children recall whether a plant is living or nonliving and explain how they know. Ask children how they might tell a plant and an animal apart. Record their ideas on the board. Return to the list after reading this section and clarify any misconceptions.

Active Reading Compare

Explain to children that when they compare things, they are finding ways the things are alike. Active readers remember the way things are alike, because they keep in mind the things being compared.

Develop Science Concepts

Direct children's attention to the first sentence on this page. **What word in this sentence tells you that something is being compared? Explain.** Like—it tells how two things are the same. **How are plants and animals the same?** They are both living things.

Have children look at the second paragraph and explain that the sentences in this paragraph focus on differences between plants and animals.

What is different about how plants and animals get food? Plants make their own food. Animals eat plants or other animals for food. **What is another important difference between plants and animals?** Animals can move on their own, but plants cannot.

Is It a Plant?

Plants are living things, like animals. Plants are also different from animals.

Plants can not move like animals. They stay in one place. Green plants use light, water, and air to make their own food. Animals eat plants or other animals.

Active Reading

When you compare things, you find out ways they are alike. Draw triangles around two things that are being compared.

392

Differentiation—Leveled Questions

Extra Support

Which kind of living thing can make its own food? a plant **What does it need to do this?** light, water, and air

Challenge

How is a Venus flytrap like a spider? Both catch and eat insects for food. **How are they different?** A Venus flytrap cann move on its own, but a spider

TEKS 1.10B

Plants and Animals

▶ Complete the chart to tell how plants and animals are different.

	Plants	Animals
make their own food	Yes	No
eat plants or animals	No	Yes
move around on their own	No	Yes
grow and change	Yes	Yes

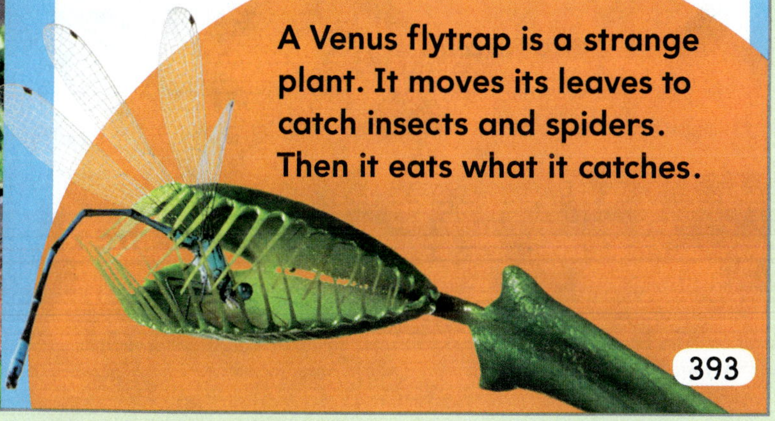

A Venus flytrap is a strange plant. It moves its leaves to catch insects and spiders. Then it eats what it catches.

393

Interpret Visuals

Direct children's attention to the chart on the right page.

What information does this chart compare? It compares the characteristics of plants and animals. **Point out the rows and the column heads for *Plants* and *Animals*. How will you fill in this chart?** I will read the characteristic in each row. Then I will write *Yes* in the column for *Plants* if the characteristic applies and *No* if it does not. I will do the same for *Animals*.

Point out the photo of the Venus flytrap at the bottom of the page and help children read the caption. **How can this information help you answer the Engage Your Brain! question?** Venus flytraps and some animals both catch and eat other animals. **Have children record their final answer to the Engage Your Brain! question.**

Develop Inquiry Skills

INFER **Suppose all plants suddenly disappeared. What would happen to animals and people? Explain.** Animals and people would die. I know this because most people and animals eat plants in order to live.

Notebook Summarize Ideas

Have children think about how plants and animals are the same and different. Have them use these similarities and differences to summarize the main ideas of these two pages orally or in writing.

:nglish Language Learners

ELPS 1A, 1C, 1E

:ecognize Plant and Animal :ognates Write *plant/planta* and *nimal/animale.* Point out the imilarity of the English words ɔ their Spanish cognates. Have hildren make word cards for these word pairs, with one word on each side of the card. Challenge children to make other word cards for related terms, including ones they find in the lesson, such as *flower* or *tree.*

2 Explain (continued)

Notebook Generate Ideas

Have a volunteer read the heading aloud. Clarify that *plenty* can mean "a lot." Then say that there are plenty of different kinds of plants in the world. Tell children to preview the photographs in the three sections on this spread, looking for differences in the types of plants shown. Ask them how these images help them figure out ways to tell plants apart. Record children's ideas on the board and return to them after they have read these pages.

Develop Science Concepts

What are the three groups of plants? trees, shrubs, and grasses Ask children to name some of the features of each group.

Have children use the lists of characteristics and photographs to compare and contrast the groups. Guide them with questions such as, **How do the sizes of trees and grasses compare? How are the stems of trees and shrubs alike? How are the leaves of shrubs and grasses different?**

Have children locate and observe the pictures of the oak tree and the boxwood shrub. **Suppose I showed you the leaves from these plants. How might observing the leaves help you identify and tell the plants apart?** The shapes and sizes of the leaves are different. I could identify the leaves and then use them to name the plant they came from.

Point out that some plants grow faster than others. **Based on the characteristics of trees and grasses, which one probably grows faster? Explain.** Sample answer: Grass probably grows faster because grasses are smaller and have a shorter life span than trees.

Plenty of Plants

How can you tell plants apart? You can compare their parts.They have different leaves. They have different shapes. They can be big or small.

Some plants have soft, thin stems. Some have thick, woody stems.

Trees
- tall
- woody trunk
- many branches
- different leaves
- long life

394

Math Connection

TEKS MATH 1.

Describe Objects in Terms of Number Display several leaves with different numbers of points. (Sassafras, sweet gum, and alder leaves work well.) Ask children to count the number of points each leaf has and record the information in a tally or other chart. Then have them report how many of the leaf types ha[v] one, three, or five points and h[o] many have two or four.

Shrubs

- shorter than trees
- smaller, woody stems
- smaller branches
- different leaves
- long life

boxwood shrub

Grasses

- small plants
- soft stems
- long, thin leaves
- shorter life

ornamental grasses

▶ **Compare parts of plants. Circle the names of the plants with woody stems. Draw a line under the name of the plant with soft stems.**

395

English Language Learners

ELPS 1E, 2C, 2E

Use the Names of Plant Parts Familiarize children with the names of plant parts. Display a plant or picture and point out the leaves and stem. Ask children to repeat *leaves* and *stem*. Then display a picture of a tree. Point out its branches and explain that branches grow out of a thick stem, also called a *trunk*. Have children repeat the words *branches, stem,* and *trunk*. Then point to plant parts on this spread and have children identify each.

TEKS 1.10B

Interpret Visuals

Direct children's attention to the shrubs section at the top of the right page. **What are some characteristics of shrubs?** Sample answer: They are shorter than trees and have woody stems.

Point out that a characteristic of shrubs is their woody stems. **How are trees and shrubs alike?** Both have stems that are hard and woody. Guide children to look at the information about grasses. **What kind of plant has soft stems?** grasses

Have children use these answers to follow the directions for answering the interactive.

Misconception Alert

Many children may think that trees and grasses are not plants because they have different characteristics and structures than the houseplants they know. Explain that plants throughout the world have a wide variety of characteristics, some quite surprising. Mention the Ghost Pipe, an entirely white plant, or remind them of the Venus flytrap—a plant that can eat insects!

Develop Inquiry Skills

CLASSIFY Give children three index cards and have them write one of these labels on each card: *trees, shrubs,* and *grasses.* Then display pictures of various trees, shrubs, and grasses found in your area. Have children hold up the card to identify each type of plant. Call on volunteers to tell how they know which group the plant belongs to based on its characteristics.

Notebook Summarize Ideas

Have children look again at the photographs and the accompanying lists in this section. Have them summarize orally or in writing the characteristics of trees, shrubs, and grasses.

2 Explain (continued)

Notebook Generate Ideas

Have children follow along as you read aloud the headings on these pages. Ask children to share what they know about flowers and cones and have them tell what purpose they think flowers and cones serve. Mention pinecones as a way to help children understand what a cone might be.

Develop Science Vocabulary

flower Write the words *flower* and *flour* on the board and have children read them with you. Explain that these two words are homophones. They sound the same but have different spellings and meanings. Ask children which word names a plant part and which word names something used in baking.

Develop Science Concepts

What kinds of plants can have flowers?
small plants, shrubs, and trees

To help children answer the interactive about which plant part makes seeds, focus their attention on the second sentence on the left page.

Why are flowers important to a plant?
Flowers make seeds.

Misconception Alert

Children may think that trees cannot have flowers. Explain that many trees, particularly fruit trees, have flowers. If possible, display a picture of a flowering fruit tree to correct this misconception. Ask children if they have heard of apple blossoms or orange blossoms and explain that *blossom* is another word for flower. Apple blossoms and orange blossoms are the flowers on apple trees and orange trees.

Plants with Flowers

Some plants have flowers. **Flowers** make a plant's seeds. Flowers can grow on small plants. They can also grow on shrubs and trees. Where have you seen flowers?

▶ **Identify the plant part that makes seeds.**

flower

396

Plants with Cones

Some plants have cones. **Cones hold a plant's seeds.** Cones grow on some trees. Where have you seen cones?

Active Reading

A detail is a fact about a main idea. Draw one line under a detail. Draw an arrow to the main idea it tells about.

397

Differentiation—Leveled Questions

xtra Support

ı which two places could you ɔok on a plant to find its seeds? could look at a plant's flowers or ɔnes to find the seeds.

Challenge

Why might you find many small pine trees growing from the ground below a very large pine tree? When pinecones fall to the ground, seeds in the cones may sprout and grow into small pine trees.

Develop Science Vocabulary

cone Display a model or pictures of, or draw, a solid geometric cone and a pinecone. Point out the similarity in shape. Discuss how a pinecone and a cone have a similar shape and name.

Active Reading Details

Explain that a detail sentence may give an example. Or, it may describe something. Active readers ask themselves, "What topic does this detail sentence tell about?" The answer will help readers keep the main idea in mind.

Help children identify the first sentence on this page as the main idea of the paragraph. Then have them read the other sentences and identify the details that support this main idea.

Develop Inquiry Skills

COMPARE **In what way are flowers and cones alike?** both contain seeds

Misconception Alert

Children may think all pinecones are alike in size. In fact, they vary widely. The largest pinecones in the United States are found on sugar pines. When open, these cones can reach 50 centimeters, or nearly 20 inches.

Notebook Summarize Ideas

Have children review the important details about plants and their seeds. Then have them identify the main idea these details support by completing this sentence orally or in writing: *Many plants have either* _____ *or* _____.

3 Extend/Evaluate

Sum It Up!

1. **Circle It!** Read the directions aloud. If children have difficulty recalling what a cone looks like, have them review the pictures on the previous page.
2. **Choose It!** Help children read aloud the list of characteristics. They can go back to the classification chart earlier in the lesson to review the *Animals* column of that chart. Although the directions have children circling animal characteristics, suggest that they also cross off phrases that do not match to keep track of the information as they go.
3. **Solve It!** Read the riddle aloud with children and focus their attention on the word *not* in the third line of the riddle. Make sure that children understand that the living thing described in the riddle cannot fly, walk, run, or swim.

Sum It Up!

1 Circle It!

Circle the plant that has cones.

2 Choose It!

Circle each group of words that tells about an animal.

- eats plants or animals
- makes its own food
- grows and changes
- moves around on its own

3 Solve It!

Solve the riddle.

Some living things fly.
Some walk, run, or swim.
I do not move on my own.
I stay in one place.
What am I? ___a plant___

Brain Check

Lesson 2

Name ____________________

Word Play

Color the letters to spell the vocabulary words. Write the words to complete the sentences.

c	t	o	t	r	e	e
f	l	o	w	e	r	o
t	a	g	l	d	e	i
e	j	c	o	n	e	b
i	r	s	w	g	h	l
k	e	m	e	o	a	d
r	s	h	r	u	b	Y

flower shrub
cone tree

1. A tall plant with a woody stem is a ___tree___.
2. A tree without a flower may have a ___cone___.
3. A ___flower___ makes seeds.
4. A plant that is smaller than a tree is a ___shrub___.

399

Answer Strategies

Word Play

- Begin this puzzle by helping children read the words in the word bank. Then have them locate each of these words in the puzzle. Point out that in this puzzle, the words are found only left to right (not up and down) and do not have overlapping letters.
- Once all the letters have been colored to spell the words, help children read the open sentences under the puzzle. Explain that one of the words in the puzzle will complete each sentence. After they write the word in the sentence, have them check that it makes sense by reading the sentence aloud.
- To help children improve recall of plant characteristics, pair children together and have them take turns using each vocabulary word in a sentence about plants. Point out that they can use the Sum It Up! page to help them review and study for tests.

Assessment

Lesson Quiz

See Assessment Guide, p. AG 136.

3 Extend/Evaluate (continued)

Answer Strategies

Apply Concepts

- Remind children that a Venn diagram organizes information with overlapping ovals. The overlap section in the middle shows ways that two things, plants and animals in this case, are alike. The left and right sections show how the two things are different.
- If children have trouble completing the Venn diagram, have them think of ways that plants and animals are alike and record these similarities in the center section. Then have them think of ways that plants and animals are different, and record this information in the outer sections.
- If children need help recalling how plant stems differ, encourage them to look back at the lists of characteristics for trees, shrubs, and grasses.
- Remind children that in assigning the size order of these plants, they should label the smallest plant with a *1* and the largest plant with a *3*.
- As a lesson follow-up, ask children to summarize what they learned in the lesson. Encourage them to tell how plants and animals are alike and different and how scientists use plant characteristics to put plants into different groups.

Take It Home!

As children and a family member go on a plant walk in their neighborhood, have them look for different kinds of plants to observe and compare how their parts and sizes are the same and different. Suggest that children draw their observations and bring them into class to share.

Apply Concepts

Complete the diagram to tell how plants and animals are alike and different.

Plants	Both	Animals
make own food, stay in one place	grow and change; are living things; need food, water, and air	eat plants and other animals, move around on their own

1 **Compare plant stems. How are they different?**

Plant stems can be soft and thin or they can be thick and woody.

2 **Write 1, 2, and 3 to put the plants in size order. Start with the smallest plant.**

3 tree   1 grass   2 shrub

Take It Home!

Family Members: Take a neighborhood walk with your child. Ask your child to compare plants and the different parts they have.

400

Make Connections

Easy

Art Connection TEKS ART 1.2C

Make a Dried Plant Collage

- Distribute construction paper, glue, and pieces of dried plants (grasses, flowers, stems, and leaves). Have children make a collage by gluing the parts on construction paper.
- Once the glue is dry, have children present their collages and identify and compare the plant parts they used. Encourage them to describe differences they observed in the size and shape of the leaves, flowers, and stems.

Average

Health Connection TEKS HEALTH 1.2E

Investigate Poisonous Plants

- Share the saying *Leaves of three, let it be!* and explain that it warns about poison ivy. The saying explains how to identify poison ivy from its shape and tells to stay away.
- Have partners use print or online plant guides to identify another poisonous plant and come up with a warning for the plant.
- Suggest that they share their work as a poster, a slogan, or a rhyme of their own.

Easy

Math Connection TEKS MATH 1.1C

Identify and Continue Leaf Patterns

- Provide pairs with an assortment of leaves.
- Have pairs of children use leaf characteristics to make a repeated pattern; for example, two wide leaves and one thin leaf.
- Have one partner describe the pattern and continue it. Repeat the activity so each child will have several turns to make and identify patterns.

Challenging

Social Studies Connection TEKS SS 1.6B

Classify Native Plants

- Provide simple illustrated nonfiction reference books or online tools about a local or state plant species.
- Have children identify five native plants and classify each one as grass, shrub, or tree.

Guided Inquiry

FLIPCHART P. 50

30 minutes
pairs

Children should follow the directions on the Flipchart. The accompanying pages in the Student Edition provide scaffolding for guided inquiry.

Inquiry Skills Focus Measure

Objectives

- Ask questions about organisms observed in the natural world.
- Plan and conduct investigations. Record and organize data.
- Collect and compare information and make observations using non-standard measuring items.
- Measure and compare organisms using non-standard units.
- Identify and compare the parts of plants.

Prep and Planning Tips

See the Planning for Inquiry page for more information.

- You might have children trace the leaves before measuring.
- Provide paper clips and clothespins that are all the same size.

Caution! Children should wash their hands after the activity.

Expected Results

Children will see that the more paper clips and clothespins it takes to measure a leaf, the longer it is. They will observe that all of their measurements are different because they used nonstandard measuring tools.

1 Engage/Explore

Attention Grabber

Ask each child to draw a large leaf without looking at what anyone else is drawing. Then ask the children, all a once, to hold up their drawings to the class. Talk about what makes the leaves "leaves." In other words, how are all the drawings the same, and what makes them recognizable as leaves? Guide children to see the variety in the drawings and point out that real leaves have man shapes and sizes, too. Show a collection of leaves to display that variety.

Preview Activity

Before beginning the investigation, have children review the directions on the Inquiry Flipchart and the accompanying Student Edition response pages. Then have them complete the response pages as they follow the directions on the Flipchart.

Inquiry Flipchart p. 50

Lesson 3 INQUIRY

TEKS **1.2A** ask questions about organisms, objects, and events observed in the natural world **1.2B** plan and conduct simple descriptive investigations such as ways objects move **1.2D** record and organize data using pictures, numbers, and words **1.4A** collect and compare information using tools, including . . . non-standard measuring items such as paper clips and clothespins . . . **1.4B** measure and compare organisms and objects using non-standard units **1.10B** identify and compare parts of plants

Name ___________________

Essential Question

How Can We Compare Leaves?

Set a Purpose

ell what you want to find out.

rst, I will compare the size of the leaves using paper clips.

ıen, I will compare the size of the leaves using clothespins.

hink About the Procedure

Why do you measure each leaf?

neasure each leaf to see how long it is.

How will you compare the leaves by size?

vill use the measurements to put the leaves in order from

ortest to longest.

401

Go Digital

virtual lab experience is ailable with the Online sources for this program.

1 Engage/Explore (continued)

Guide the Investigation

Develop Inquiry Skills

MEASURE Review that *measure* means to find the size or amount of something. People can measure in standard units, such as inches or centimeters for length. Standard units are the same everywhere. They can also use nonstandard units, such as paper clips and clothespins. Nonstandard units do not require a tool such as a ruler but are not the same for people all over.

What do you want to do in this activity? I want to find the lengths of the leaves so I can order them from shortest to longest.

What will you use to measure and compare the leaves? paper clips and clothespins

How will the paper clips and clothespins help you make observations and collect and compare information? I can use the paper clips and clothespins to help me make observations and collect information about how long each leaf is. I can use the information I learn to compare the lengths of each leaf.

Why should everyone in our class use paper clips? In other words, why can't you use paper clips and another child use erasers? We need to use the same object for measuring so we can compare our results.

How would this activity be different if you used a ruler instead of paper clips? Sample answer: I would measure the leaves in units of inches or centimeters instead of in paper clips and clothespins.

How will measuring the leaves help you order by length? Sample answer: After I count the number of paper clips and clothespins for the lengths, I can order those numbers.

2 Explain

Develop Inquiry Skills

RECORD YOUR DATA Discuss with children how to use the chart to record their data. Summarize that they will draw each leaf and write about how many paper clips and clothespins long it is.

Children might not understand why the answer allows for them to write "about" how many paper clips and clothespins long the leaves are. Explain that they might have to round their answers since the leaves will not always be exactly as long as a whole paper clip or clothespin. Talk about how to round up or down, depending on how close to the end of a paper clip or clothespin the leaf actually is.

DRAW CONCLUSIONS Be sure that children justify their answers by using the information in the chart. Remind children that they are to compare all of the measurements they took.

3 Extend/Evaluate

ASK MORE QUESTIONS Remind children that they can sort leaves in other ways besides length. As an extension, encourage them to sort in as many different ways as they can or make a two-column chart that summarizes the similarities and differences of two of the leaves in the activity.

Assessment

Lesson Quiz

See Assessment Guide, p. AG 137.

Record Your Data

Check children's work.

Record the length of each leaf. Circle the shortest leaf in each row. Draw an X on the longest leaf in each row.

Leaf Chart

Leaf 1	Leaf 2	Leaf 3
about ______ paper clips long	about ______ paper clips long	about ______ paper clips long
about ______ clothespins long	about ______ clothespins long	about ______ clothespins long

Draw Conclusions

Compare the measurements. Were they different? Why?

Yes, the measurements were different because the objects I used to measure with were different sizes.

Ask More Questions

What other questions could you ask about comparing leaves?

Sample answer: How could I compare leaf shapes?

402

Differentiated Inquiry

Easy

Describe Leaves

- If possible, take children on a nature walk to find leaves. Otherwise, ask them to bring in leaves from home.
- Provide rulers and hand lenses for children to use.
- Ask children to observe their leaves. Tell them to notice the color, shape, size, veins, and other characteristics. Then have them draw their leaves in detail on paper.
- Have children use a ruler to measure the length and width of the leaves. They should write the measurements on the drawing.
- Display the drawings around the classroom.

Average

Sorting Leaves

- Provide pairs with about six leaves or have them gather a group of leaves on their own.
- Ask children to observe the characteristics of their leaves, such as size, shape, and color.
- Have children sort the leaves according to one of those characteristics. Children should write the name of each category on a large poster and draw each leaf that belongs in that group under the name of the category.

Challenging

Estimate Area

- Provide pairs with leaves, about 100 beans (such as dried kidney beans), and paper.
- Ask children to trace a leaf on paper. Have them place ten beans inside the leaf tracing and estimate how many beans it will take to fill the entire area. They should record their estimates.
- Ask partners to fill the entire tracing with beans and then count to find the total. They should record the actual number and compare it to their estimate. Was the estimate high, low, or close? If it was off, why?
- Partners repeat the activity with other leaf tracings and see whether their estimation skills improve with practice.

Challenging

Measure and Graph Leaf Lengths

- Ask children to use a ruler to measure the lengths of ten leaves. (You can provide the leaves or ask children to collect them.) Remind them to measure the length of each leaf from tip to tip, and to round to the nearest inch.
- Have children make a bar graph to show the lengths of the leaves. Then ask them to summarize the information in the bar graph.

S.T.E.M.

Engineering and Technology

Objectives

- Identify and explain a problem and propose a solution in his/her own words.
- Explain how a greenhouse works.
- Compare two kinds of greenhouses.

Notebook

Generate Ideas

Share the background information before you assign the feature. Ask questions to ascertain children's prior knowledge.

What is a greenhouse? A greenhouse is a building with glass or clear plastic walls where plants are grown.

Why might people need a greenhouse? They might live in a colder place but want to grow fruits, vegetables, or flowers when it is too cold to grow them outside.

Background

- The glass or plastic walls of a greenhouse let in sunlight but keep the heat inside from escaping.
- Unlike an outdoor garden, the environment in a greenhouse is controlled. A greenhouse keeps out cold, rain, snow, wind, and insect pests. But people have to water the plants inside. They also have to make sure that the air stays at the right temperature and does not get too dry or too humid, or damp.
- An indoor greenhouse is attached to a house or another building. It might be as large as a wing of a house or as small as a box mounted on a house window. An indoor greenhouse uses the electricity, heat, and water from the building it is attached to.
- An outdoor greenhouse is separate from other buildings. It needs its own electrical, heating, and plumbing systems.

TEKS 1.3A identify and explain a problem such as finding a home for a classroom pet and propose a solution in his/her own words

S.T.E.M.

Engineering and Technolog

Warm It Up

Compare Greenhouses

Greenhouses are made of glass or plastic. Glass and plastic let in light. They also keep in heat. Light and heat help plants grow. Different plants can be grown at the same time.

indoor greenhouse

- needs only a small space
- for small plants only
- stays warm in winter

outdoor greenhouse

- needs a large space
- for small or large pla
- needs heating in wint

College & Career Readiness

CCRS I.E.1, I.E.2, III.C III.D.1, III.D

Botanists This feature provides an opportunity to develop children's awareness of STEM careers related to plants and flowers, including botanists. Suggest children go online to find out more about botanists, or scientists that study plants. Children should evaluate the online articles they read for reliability and currency. Have children draw a picture of a botanist. Then have children discuss as a class the different STEM skills a botanis needs.

S.T.E.M. continued

'hich Greenhouse?

ad the problem below.
en answer the questions.

u want to grow a large plant.
u have a lot of outdoor space.
e weather is not very cold.
nich greenhouse would you
oose? Why?

nple answer: I would choose an outdoor greenhouse
ause I want to grow a large plant. I have enough
door space for a greenhouse. It will work because the
ther is not too cold.

ld On It!

Design your own indoor greenhouse. Complete **Design It: Greenhouse** on the Inquiry Flipchart.

Build On It!

n **Design It: Greenhouse**, the design challenge associated with his lesson, children use the steps of the engineering design process o design a greenhouse for a small plant. For more details, see the pages that follow.

Other opportunities to apply the design process appear throughout the *Inquiry Flipchart.*

TEKS 1.3A

Develop S.T.E.M. Concepts

When children have completed reading the feature, ask questions to help them reflect on why people use greenhouses.

What problem does a greenhouse solve? It gives people a place where they can grow plants all year, without worrying about cold or other weather problems.

Why are greenhouses built with glass or clear plastic? These are good materials for their purpose; they let in sunlight and keep in heat.

Develop Inquiry Skills

COMPARE/CONTRAST Ask children to carefully observe and compare and contrast the two greenhouses on the previous page. **How are the greenhouses alike?** They are both made of glass; they are both places for plants to grow.

How are they different? The indoor one is a glass box attached to a window of a house. The outdoor one is a small glass house standing by itself in a yard.

DRAW CONCLUSIONS **What kind of greenhouse did you choose? How does its design make it better?** Sample answer: I have to look at what my needs are. The greenhouse that helps me meet my needs better is the better greenhouse for me. So I chose an outdoor greenhouse.

Notebook Summarize Ideas

Ask children to summarize what they learned about how technology can solve problems and help them meet their needs. Have them tell what a greenhouse is, how it solves a problem, and how to choose a greenhouse that would best meet their needs.

S.T.E.M.

Engineering and Technology

FLIPCHART p. 51

45 minutes

pairs or small groups

Objectives

- Record and organize data.
- Identify and explain a problem and propose a solution in his/her own words.
- Use the steps of the engineering design process to design and make a model of a greenhouse.
- Apply the scientific concepts of systems and system models and form and function.

Prep and Planning Tips

- Have available the following materials for each pair or small group: liter soda bottle, cut in half; clear, plastic mayonnaise jar; tiny potted plant; clear, plastic cups; tape.
- Ahead of time, cut clear, plastic liter bottles in half. You may wish to have children grow their own plants beginning two weeks prior to this activity.

Expected Results

Children will design an indoor greenhouse made out of clear plastic for a small houseplant.

1 Engage/Explore

Attention Grabber

Have children stand in a classroom with windows that are getting direct sunlight. Ask them to observe and describe the heat and light. Have them compare the same classroom at a different time of day when it is not getting direct sunlight.

Preview Activity

Before beginning the activity, have children review the directions on the Engineering and Technology Flipchart page.

Guide the Activity

Develop Inquiry Skills

OBSERVE Allow children time to observe the available materials. Encourage them to make sketches as they think about different design ideas.

USE MODELS Ask children to describe how each part of the model shows a part of a greenhouse. Have them compare and contrast the model with a real greenhouse.

COMPARE Encourage children from different groups to compare their greenhouses to others and share ideas that will make the greenhouses better. Point out that the best ideas come from teams who can share ideas and work together to solve a problem.

Strategies for Success

Before beginning the activity, have children review the directions on the *Inquiry Flipchart*. As children draw their designs, remind them that they should make it possible to open up the greenhouse to water the plant as necessary. The greenhouse will make a type of terrarium, with the existing moisture providing some water. But this water may not be sufficient, depending on the type of plant.

Notebook Science Notebook

During the Activity Remind children to list all the materials they will need to build their design. Remind them to make their drawings clear enough to follow when they build the model. Partners or group members should check each other's work.

2 Explain

Develop the Engineering Design Process

Use the following steps of the engineering design process to provide context and support for the analyses that children are doing in the flipchart activity.

1. FIND A PROBLEM **Use your own words to identify and explain the problem your design will solve.** Sample answer: I want to design an indoor greenhouse that will allow me to grow a plant without worrying about the weather.

2. PLAN AND BUILD **How did your drawing help you build your greenhouse?** Sample answer: The drawing showed me the different materials and parts of the design so I could just follow the drawing.

3 Extend/Evaluate

Quick Check

How did you decide what your greenhouse design would be? Sample answer: I thought about the needs of the plants. **What problems did you have when you built your design? How did you solve them?** Accept all reasonable answers.

4. REDESIGN Help children research the needs of the plants. Have them care for the plants according to these needs.

5. COMMUNICATE Have groups share their designs and explain how they followed their designs to build the greenhouse.

Notebook Science Notebook

After the Activity Check children's designs to see that they drew a greenhouse. Make sure that children have labeled the parts, captioned the design with its purpose, and written a sentence that tells how the design works.

! Michael DiSpezio's Tips & Tricks

Preparing Materials If using liter containers, prepare enough of them prior to class. Sharp, pointed scissors will cut the containers, but a carefully handled craft knife with a sharp blade might allow for easier cutting. Caution children about sharp or jagged edges. You might also substitute clear plastic produce containers if the plants are short in height. If tiny potted plants are not available, supply children with seeds that can be germinated in the greenhouses.

Enduring Understandings

Revisit the Big Idea and Essential Questions

Big Idea **Plants have parts that help them grow and change. There are many kinds of plants.**

To explore the Big Idea, post key terms from the unit on the board, and challenge children to find and explain different ways word pairs are connected. For example, a child might explain that *seed* and *cone* are related because a cone holds seeds. Prompt children with the following pairings.

- fruit, flower
- root, stem
- stem, leaf
- flower, seed
- seed, fruit
- flower, cone

Essential Questions

Post the Essential Questions, and use the following prompts to guide a discussion.

Lessons/Essential Questions	Prompts
L1 **What Are Some Parts of Plants?**	• Sketch a plant and name its parts.
L2 **How Are Plants Different?**	• Explain how two plants you know are different.
L3 **How Can We Compare Leaves?**	• Choose two different leaves shown in this unit. Tell how they are alike and different.

Science Notebook

You may use the following strategies after children complete the unit or after each lesson.

- Have children review and edit the responses to the Essential Questions they drafted at the beginning of the unit. Suggest they cross out sentences or ideas that are unnecessary or inappropriate.
- Ask children to draft sorting cards that show and label one picture of a plant part discussed in Lesson 1 in their Science Notebooks. Then, have them copy their sketches onto index cards. Have small groups combine their cards and sort them by what each plant part does.

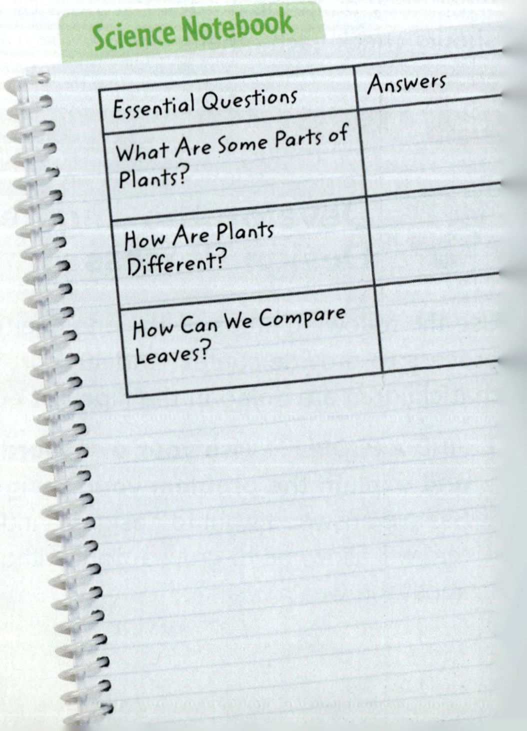

Unit 10 Review

Name ___________________

ocabulary Review

se the terms in the box to complete e sentences.

leaf
roots
seed

KS 1.10B

. A new plant may grow from a seed.

KS 1.10B

. A plant is held in place by its roots.

KS 1.10B

. The plant part that makes food is the leaf.

cience Concepts

l in the letter of the choice that best swers the question.

S 1.10B

Trey compares an apple and a pinecone. How are they alike?

Ⓐ They both are fruits.

Ⓑ They both hold seeds.

Ⓒ They both grow on the same kind of tree.

TEKS 1.2B, 1.10B

5. Umi is planning an investigation. She wants to plant something that will live a long time, but will not grow very tall. Which of these should she plant?

Ⓐ grass

Ⓑ shrub

Ⓒ tree

Unit Review **Unit 10** 405

Item Analysis

Items	TEKS	Depth of Knowledge	Cognitive Complexity
1	**1.10B**	1	Low
2	**1.10B**	1	Low
3	**1.10B**	1	Low
4	**1.10B**	2	Moderate
5	**1.2B, 1.10B**	3	Moderate

Unit Review

Answer Key

Vocabulary Review (5 points each)

1. seed

   Have children reread the complete sentence to be sure that it makes sense with their chosen word in place.

2. roots

   Remind children that roots act like straws taking in water and other things from the soil. Review that roots also help keep a plant in the soil, so it does not blow or wash away.

3. leaf

   Remind children that leaves are the plant part that take in sunlight. If necessary, have children review the plant parts in Lesson 1.

Science Concepts (7 points each)

4. B

   Explain that a pinecone is just a type of cone. Then, have children tell what they know about apples.

5. B

   Work with children to list the traits of each kind of plant named in the answer choices.

Assessment

Unit 10 Test and Performance Assessment

See Assessment Guide, pp. AG 140–AG 146, for Unit Test and Performance Task with Long Option rubric.

Unit Review *continued*

Answer Key

Science Concepts (7 points each)

6. A
Have children tell or draw what the picture would look like if Pavil had sorted the leaves by shape or number of points.

7. B
Remind children that the stem is the plant part that carries water and other things from the roots to the leaves.

8. C
Emphasize the word *all* in the question. Make sure children understand that if any kind of plant does not fit with what they read in the answer choice then that answer must be incorrect.

9. C
Review with children the different plant parts from Lesson 1.

UNIT 10

TEKS 1.10B

6. Pavil sorted leaves. This picture shows one group.

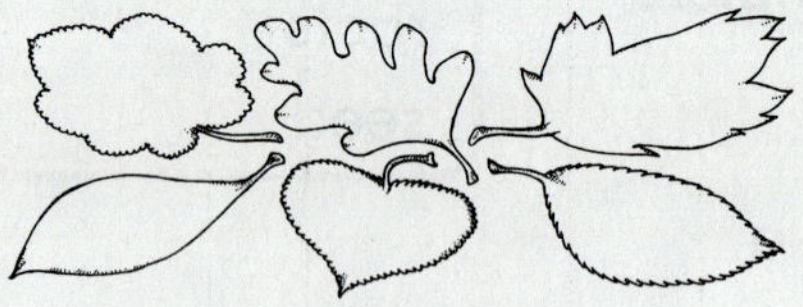

Which choice **best** describes how she sorted the leaves?

(A) by size
(B) by shape
(C) by number of points

TEKS 1.10B

7. Which of these plant parts can be identified as a stem?

(A) apple
(B) tree trunk
(C) pine needle

TEKS 1.10B

8. Which of these is a way that all plants are alike?

(A) They have flowers.
(B) They grow tall and have thick stems.
(C) They make their own food.

TEKS 1.10B

9. Which plant part does number 3 show?

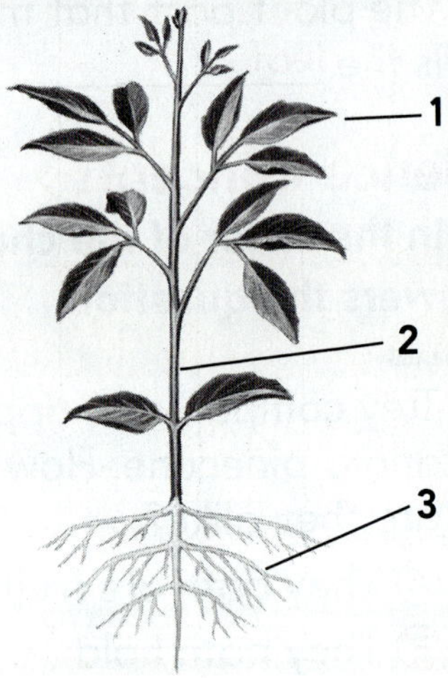

(A) leaf
(B) stem
(C) roots

406 **Unit 10** Unit Review

Item Analysis *(continued)*

Items	TEKS	Depth of Knowledge	Cognitive Complexity
6	**1.10B**	2	Moderate
7	**1.10B**	2	Moderate
8	**1.10B**	2	Moderate
9	**1.10B**	1	Low

TEKS 1.2D, 1.10B

10. Alex is comparing trees, shrubs, and grasses. He records his observations. Which sentence tells how all three are the same?

Ⓐ They grow and change.

Ⓑ They cannot make their own food.

Ⓒ They can move on their own.

TEKS 1.10B

11. Sara is identifying plant parts. What kind of stems do shrubs have?

Ⓐ green stems

Ⓑ soft stems

Ⓒ woody stems

TEKS 1.10B

12. Read these steps for how a plant gets and uses water.

1. The roots take in water from the soil.
2. ______?______
3. The leaves use water to make food.

Which step is missing?

Ⓐ The plant grows taller.

Ⓑ The flowers grow into fruit.

Ⓒ Water moves through the stem to all of the leaves.

UNIT 10

Item Analysis *(continued)*

Items	TEKS	Depth of Knowledge	Cognitive Complexity
10	**1.2D, 1.10B**	2	Moderate
11	**1.10B**	2	Moderate
12	**1.10B**	3	Moderate

Unit Review *continued*

Answer Key

Science Concepts (7 points each)

10. A

Remind children that trees, shrubs, and grasses are all plants.

11. C

Point out that the picture shows an example of shrubs, so it can help children see something about the stems. Ask, "Do these stems look soft?"

12. C

Ask children, "Which plant part helps water get from the roots in step 1 to the leaves in step 3?" Explain that this answer will help fill in missing step 2.

Short Option Performance Assessment

Task

All About a Plant

Assign children to small groups, and give each group a plant that has all its parts. Have children draw the plant and label each part. Then, ask them to tell at least one way this plant, or plants in general, can be used.

Rubric

Preparation Provide each group with drawing paper, crayons, and a plant, such as a carrot, a beet, or a bean seedling, that has all its parts. List the steps of the activity on the board so that children can refer to them as they work.

Scoring Rubric—Performance Indicators

___ Identifies the parts of a plant.

___ Accurately draws a plant and labels its parts.

___ Describes how plants can be used.

Observations and Rubric Scores

3 2 1 0

Unit Review *continued*

Answer Key

Inquiry and the Big Idea (11 points each)

13.

- **a.** makes seeds
- **b.** hold the seeds
- **c.** make new plants

  Have children look at a plant parts diagram and review the function of each plant part.

14.

- **a.** The stem of the tree is thick and woody. The stem of the grass is thin and soft.
- **b.** They both carry water to the leaves of the plant.

  Be sure children identify the picture on the left as the tree (they can label it) and the one on the right as the grass. The stem of the grass is less obvious than on the tree, so be sure children know which plant part they are looking at when they make their comparisons.

Inquiry and the Big Idea

Write the answers to these questions.

TEKS 1.10B

13. Explain what each of these plant parts does.

a. flowers

make seeds

b. fruits

hold the seeds

c. seeds

make new plants

TEKS 1.10B

14. Look at the pictures. Compare the stems of the tree and the grass.

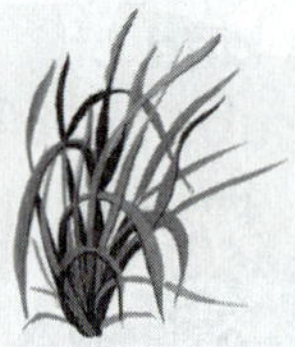

a. How are they different?

The stem of the tree is thick and woody. The stem of the grass is thin and soft.

b. How are they the same?

They both carry water to the leaves of the plant.

Item Analysis

Items	TEKS	Depth of Knowledge	Cognitive Complexit
13	**1.10B**	3	Moderate
14	**1.10B**	3	High

Resources, Professional Development, and Correlations

Teacher Notes

Professional Development

Enduring Understandings

Big Ideas, Essential Questions

It goes without saying that a primary goal for your students is to develop understandings of science concepts that endure well past the next test. The question is, what is the best way to achieve that goal?

Research and learning experts suggest that students learn most effectively through a constructivist approach in which they build concepts through active involvement in their own learning. While constructivism may lead to superior learning on a lesson-by-lesson basis, the approach does not address how to organize lessons into a program of instruction. Schema theory, from cognitive science, suggests that knowledge is organized into units and that information is stored in these units, much as files are stored in a digital or paper folder. Informed by our understanding of schema theory, we set about organizing *ScienceFusion*. We began by identifying the Big Ideas of science.

by Marjorie Frank

Big Ideas are generalizations—broad, powerful concepts that connect facts and events that may otherwise seem unrelated. Big Ideas are implicit understandings that help the world make sense. Big Ideas define the "folders," or units, of *ScienceFusion*. Each is a statement that articulates the overarching teaching and learning goals of a unit.

Essential Questions define the "files," or information, in a unit. Each Essential Question identifies the conceptual focus of a lesson that contributes to your students' growing understanding of the associated Big Idea. As such, Essential Questions give your students a sense of direction and purpose.

With *ScienceFusion,* our goal is to provide you with a tool that helps you help your students develop Enduring Understandings in science. Our strategy for achieving that goal has been to provide lesson plans with 5E-based learning experiences organized in a framework informed by schema theory.

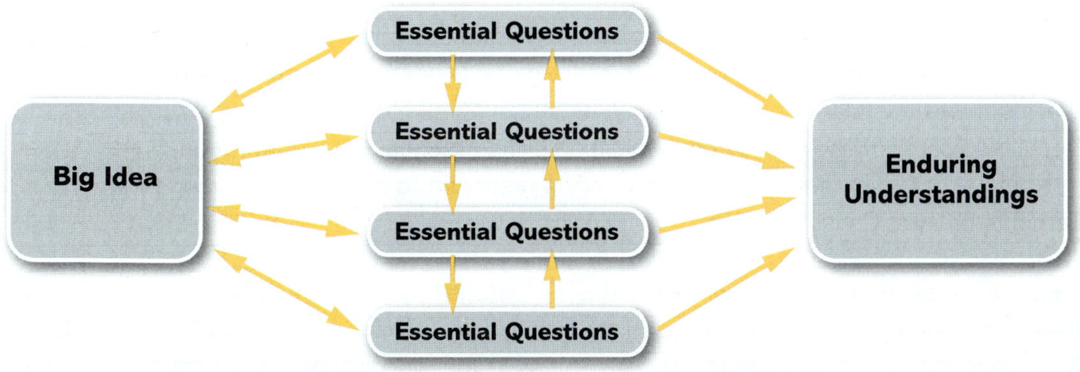

Professional Development

21st Century Skills/STEM

Skills Redefined

by
Michael A. DiSpezio

Our world has changed. Globalization and the digital revolution have redefined the skill set that is essential for student success in the classroom and beyond. Known collectively as 21st Century Skills, these areas of competence and aptitude go beyond the three Rs of reading, writing, and arithmetic. 21st Century Skills incorporate a battery of high-level thinking skills and technological capabilities.

21st Century SKILLS A Sample List

Learning and Innovation Skills

- Creativity and Innovation
- Critical Thinking and Problem Solving
- Communication and Collaboration

Information, Media, and Technology Skills

- Information Literacy
- Media Literacy
- ICT (Information, Communications, and Technology) Literacy

Life and Career Skills

- Flexibility and Adaptability
- Initiative and Self-Direction
- Productivity and Accountability
- Leadership and Responsibility

S.T.E.M.

Curriculum that integrates Science, Technology, Engineering, and Mathematics

21st Century Skills are best taught in the context of the core subject areas. Science makes an ideal subject for integrating these important skills because it involves many skills, including inquiry, collaboration, and problem solving. An even deeper level of incorporating these skills can be found with Science, Technology, Engineering, and Mathematics (STEM) lessons and activities. Hands-on STEM lessons that provide students with engineering design challenges are ideal for developing Learning and Innovation Skills. Students develop creativity and innovation as they engineer novel solutions to posed problems. They communicate and collaborate as they engage higher-level thinking skills to help shape their inquiry experience. Students assume ownership of the learning. From this emerges increased self-motivation and personal accountability.

With STEM lessons and activities, related disciplines are seamlessly integrated into a rich experience that becomes far more than the sum of its parts. Students explore real-world scenarios using their understanding of core science concepts, ability for higher level analysis, technological know-how, and communication skills essential for collaboration. From this experience, the learner constructs not only a response to the STEM challenge, but the elements of 21st Century Skills.

ScienceFusion provides deep science content and STEM lessons, activities, and Video-Based Projects that incorporate and develop 21st Century Skills. This provides an effective learning landscape that will prepare students for success in the workplace—and in life.

Differentiated Instruction

Skills Redefined

by Marjorie Frank

Your students learn in different ways, at different speeds, and through different means. Channeling the energy and richness of that diversity is part of the beauty of teaching. A classroom atmosphere that encourages academic risk-taking encourages learning. This is especially true in science, where learning involves making predictions (which could turn out to be inaccurate), offering explanations (which could turn out to be incomplete), and doing things (which could result in observable mistakes).

Like most people, students are more likely to take risks in a low-stress environment where they feel accepted and respected. Science, with its emphasis on exploring through hands-on activities and interactive reading, provides a natural vehicle for low-stress learning. Low stress, however, may mean different things to different people. For students with learning challenges, low stress may mean being encouraged to respond at the level they are able. Another factor in meeting the needs of diverse students is the instructional tools. Are they flexible? Inviting? *ScienceFusion* addresses the needs of diverse students at every step in the instructional process.

As You Plan

Select from these resources to meet individual needs.

- The planning pages at the beginning of each unit in the Teacher Edition identify resources and strategies geared to diverse learners.
- Online Resource: Digital lessons and virtual labs appeal to all students, especially struggling readers and visual learners. Extra Support for Vocabulary and Concepts are reproducible pages for use with struggling readers and students who need additional reinforcement.
- Student Edition with Audio for use with students who have vision impairments or learning difficulties.
- Leveled Readers reinforce, enrich, and extend concepts. A Teacher Guide for each Reader provides instructional strategies and includes reproducible worksheets for Vocabulary, Comprehension, and Oral Reading Fluency.

As You Teach

Take advantage of these point-of-use features.

- A mix of Directed Inquiries and Independent Inquiries suitable for different kinds of learners
- Interactive digital lessons
- Leveled questions for Extra Support, Challenge, and English Language Learners
- Make Connections: Easy, Average, and Challenging follow-up activities.

As You Reach Out to Families

Look for these school-home connections.

- Take It Home! at the end of every lesson in the Student Edition and Teacher's Edition
- Customizable School-Home Connection Letters for every lesson, available online.

The 5E Model and Levels of Inquiry

by
Michael A. DiSpezio

How do students best learn science? Extensive research and data show that the most effective learning emerges from situations in which one builds understanding based upon personal experiences. Learning is not transmitted from instructor to passive receiver; instead, understanding is constructed through the experience.

The 5E Model for Effective Science Lessons

In the 1960s, Robert Karplus and his colleagues developed a three-step instructional model that became known as the Learning Cycle. This model was expanded into what is today referred to as the 5E Model. To emulate the elements of how an actual scientist works, this model is broken down into five components for an effective lesson: Engage, Explore, Explain, Extend (or Elaborate), and Evaluate.

Engage—The engagement sets the scene for learning. It is a warm-up during which students are introduced to the learning experience. Prior knowledge is assessed and its analysis used to develop an effective plan to meet stated objectives. Typically, an essential question is then posed; the question leads the now motivated and engaged students into the exploration.

Explore—This is the stage where the students become actively involved in hands-on process. They communicate and collaborate to develop a strategy that addresses the posed problem. Emphasis is placed on inquiry and hands-on investigation. The hands-on experience may be highly prescribed or open-ended in nature.

Explain—Students answer the initial question by using their findings and information they may be reading about, discussing with classmates, or experiencing through digital media. Their experience and understanding of concepts, processes, and hands-on skills is strengthened at this point. New vocabulary may be introduced.

Extend (or Elaborate)—The explanation is now extended to other situations, questions, or problems. During this stage the learner more closely examines findings in terms of context and transferable application. In short, extension reveals the application and implication of the internalized explanation. Extension may involve connections to other curriculum areas.

Evaluate—Although evaluation is an ongoing process, this is the stage in which a final assessment is most often performed. The instructor evaluates lesson effectiveness by using a variety of formal and informal assessment tools to measure student performance.

The 5E lesson format is used in all the *ScienceFusion* Teacher Edition lessons.

Directed, Guided, and Independent Inquiry

It wasn't that long ago that science was taught mostly through demonstration and lecture. Today, however, most instructional strategies integrate an inquiry-based approach to learning science. This methodology is founded in higher-level thinking and facilitates the students' construction of understanding from experience. When offered opportunities to ask questions, design investigations, collect and analyze data, and communicate their findings, each student assumes the role of an active participant in shaping his or her own learning process.

The degree to which any activity engages the inquiry process is variable, from highly prescribed steps to a completely learner-generated design. Researchers have established three distinct levels of inquiry: directed (or structured) inquiry, guided inquiry, and independent (or open) inquiry. These levels are distinguished by the amount of guidance offered by the instructor.

Directed Inquiry In this level of inquiry, the instructor poses a question or suggests an investigation, and students follow a prescribed set of instructions. The outcome may be unknown to the students, but it is known to the instructor. Students follow the structured outline to uncover an outcome that supports the construction of lesson concepts.

Guided Inquiry As in Directed Inquiry, the instructor poses to the students a question to investigate. While students are conducting the investigation, the instruction focuses on developing one or more inquiry skills. Focus may also be provided for students to learn to use methods or tools of science. In *ScienceFusion*, the Teacher Edition provides scaffolding for developing inquiry skills, science methods, or tools. Student pages accompany these lessons and provide prompts for writing hypotheses, recording data, and drawing conclusions.

Independent Inquiry This is the most complex level of inquiry experience. A prompt is provided, but students must design their own investigation in response to the prompt. In some cases, students will write their own questions and then plan and perform scientific investigations that will answer those questions. This level of inquiry is often used for science fair projects. Independent Inquiry does not necessarily mean individual inquiry. Investigations can be conducted by individual students or by pairs or teams of students.

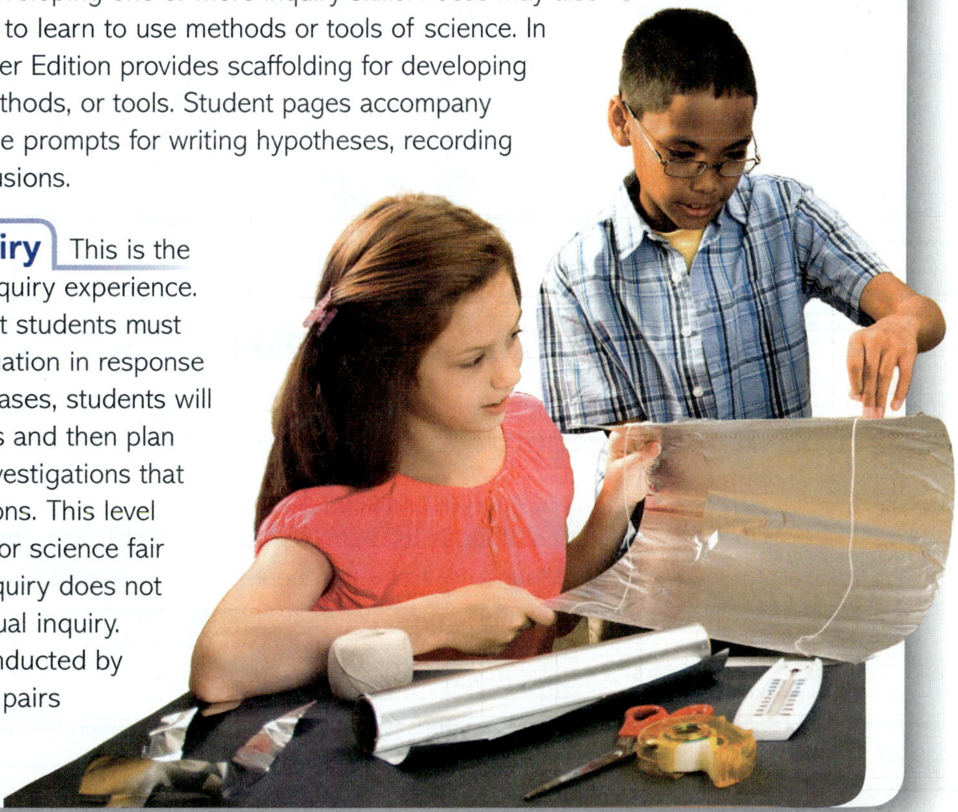

Response to Intervention

by Marjorie Frank

In a traditional model, assessment marks the end of an instructional cycle. Students work through a unit, take a test, and move on, regardless of their performance. However, current research suggests that assessment should be part of the instructional cycle, that it should be ongoing, and that it should be used to identify students needing intervention. This may sound like a tall order—who wants to give tests all the time?—but it may not be as difficult as it seems. In some ways, you are probably doing it already.

Assessment

Every student interaction has the potential to be an assessment. It all depends on how you perceive and use the interaction.

- Suppose you ask a question. You can just listen to your student's response, or you can assess it. Does the response indicate comprehension of the concept? If not, intervention may be needed.
- Suppose a student offers an explanation of a phenomenon depicted in a photo. You can assess the explanation. Does it show accurate factual knowledge? Does it reveal a misconception? If so, intervention may be needed.
- Suppose a student draws a diagram to illustrate a concept. You can assess the diagram. Is it accurate? If not, intervention may be needed.

As the examples indicate, assessing students' understandings can—and should—be an integral part of the instructional cycle and be used to make decisions about the next steps of instruction. For students making good progress, next steps might be exploring a related concept, a new lesson, or an additional challenge. For students who are not making adequate progress, intervention may be needed.

Assessment and intervention are tightly linked. Assessment leads to intervention—fresh approaches, different groupings, new materials—which, in turn, leads to assessment. Response to Intervention (RTI) gives shape and substance to this linkage.

RTI Response to Intervention

Response to Intervention is a process for identifying and supporting students who are not making expected progress toward essential learning goals.

RTI is a three-tiered approach based on an ongoing cycle of superior instruction, frequent monitoring of students' learning (assessments), and appropriate interventions. Students who are found not to be making expected progress in one Tier move to the next higher Tier, where they receive more intense instruction.

- **Tier I:** Students receive whole-class, core instruction.
- **Tier II:** Students work in small groups that supplement and reinforce core instruction.
- **Tier III:** Students receive individualized instruction.

How RTI and *Texas ScienceFusion* Work

Texas ScienceFusion provides many opportunities to assess students' understanding and many components appropriate for students in all Tiers.

TIER III Intensive Intervention

Individualized instruction, with options for auditory, visual, and second language learners. Special education is a possibility.

Online Student Edition

***Texas ScienceFusion* Components**

- Online Student Edition with audio
- Online and tablet versions of Leveled Readers with audio
- Online Extra Support for Vocabulary and Concepts

Appropriate for:
- Auditory learners

Appropriate for:
- Struggling readers
- Second-language learners

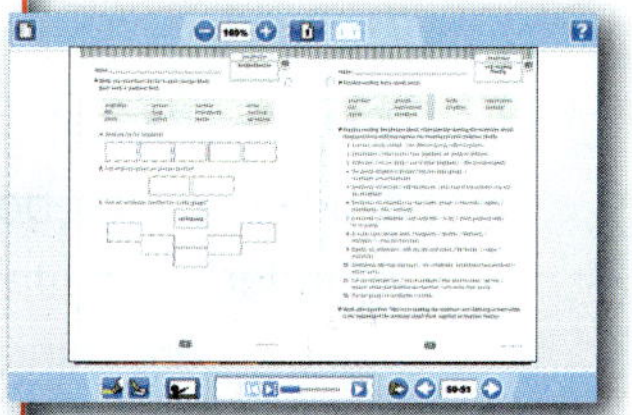

Extra Support

Students achieving at a lower level than their peers in Tier II

TIER II Strategic Intervention

Small Group Instruction in addition to core instruction

Leveled-Reader Teacher Guide

***Texas ScienceFusion* Components**

- Extra Support Leveled Readers
- Leveled Reader Teacher Guide
- Vocabulary Review Worksheets

Appropriate for:
- Struggling readers
- Visual learners
- Second-language learners
- Screening tools to assess students' responses to Tier II instruction

Extra Support Leveled Reader

Students achieving at a lower level than their peers in Tier I

TIER I Core Classroom Instruction

With the help of extensive point-of-use strategies that support superior teaching, students receive whole-class instruction and engage productively in small-group work as appropriate.

Teacher Edition

Student Edition

Assessment Guide

***Texas ScienceFusion* Components**

- Student Edition
- Teacher Edition
- Assessment Guide
- Online Digital Curriculum
- Interactive Whiteboard Resources

Appropriate for:
- Screening tools to access students' responses to Tier I instruction
- Tier I intervention for students unable to complete the activity independently

Digital Curriculum

Professional Development

Science Notebooks

The What, Why, Who, When, Where, and How!

Science Notebooks are powerful tools, and they play an important role in every teacher's in-box. They lead your students deep into the learning process, and they provide you with a window into that process as well as a means to communicate about it.

by Marjorie Frank

What Are Science Notebooks?

A notebook contains the writer's ideas, observations, and perceptions of events and endeavors. A Science Notebook contains ideas about and observations of scientific processes, data, conclusions, conjectures, and generalizations.

A Science Notebook can be in many formats—spiral-bound, tablet, loose pages in a binder, or digital. Like an ordinary notebook, it functions much like a storehouse, a place where things are collected and held. The "things" in a Science Notebook can be just about anything related to what students are doing and learning in science:

- observations and data
- drawings and diagrams of structures and processes
- graphs
- charts
- summaries of new concepts or a textbook lesson
- vocabulary words with definitions and drawings
- graphic organizers showing how ideas are connected
- responses to lessons or a specific learning experience
- reflections about their work and the meaning they derived from science experiences
- responses to questions
- new questions
- predictions and plans for an investigation
- observations and conclusions
- drawings or sketches from field trips
- original stories and poems about science topics
- science applications in daily life

A Science Notebook is especially important when students do inquiry-based or project-based learning. It offers students a single place to record their observations, consider possibilities, and organize their thoughts. As such, it is a learner's version of the logs professional scientists keep.

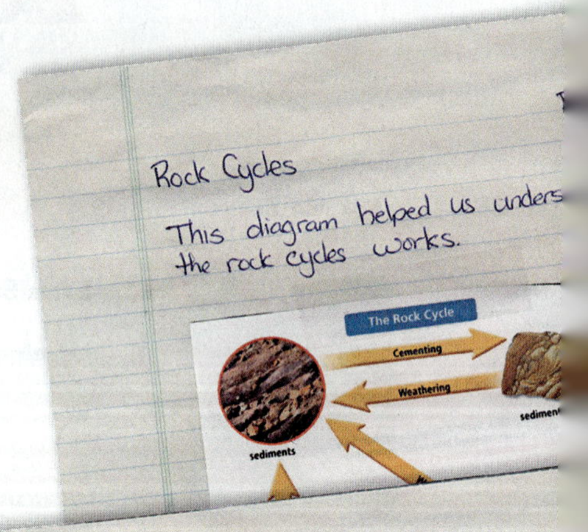

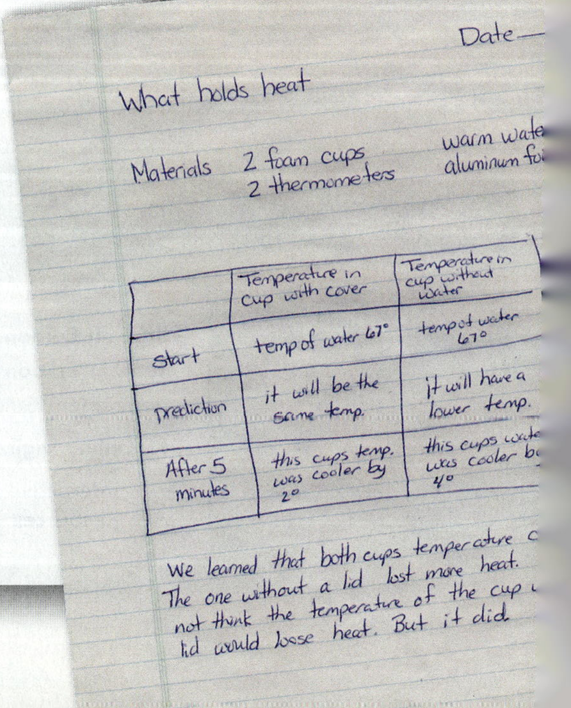

Why Bother with Science Notebooks?

No doubt, it takes time and effort to help students set up and maintain Science Notebooks, not to mention the time it takes you to review them and provide meaningful feedback. The payoff better be worth it, you're probably saying to yourself. And it is. Here's why.

Keeping a Science Notebook:

- leads each learner to engage with ideas (not just those who raise their hands in class)
- engages students in writing–an active, thinking, analytical process
- causes students to organize their thinking
- helps students develop 21st Century organizational skills
- enables students to express themselves creatively
- provides students with multiple opportunities and modes to process new information
- makes learning experiences more personal
- provides students with a record of their own progress and accomplishments
- doubles as a study guide for formal assessments
- creates a vehicle for students to improve their reading and writing skills

Who Should Keep a Science Notebook?

Every single student, regardless of age, aptitude, or language background.

Science Notebooks are well suited for differentiating instruction. By allowing students to draw about their investigations and use the glossary to label their drawings, you can include all students in the process. Students can also work in pairs to do shared writing.

Kindergarten and first grade learners may dictate brief captions to pictures that tell their science story. Or, they may benefit from working as a class to construct a science "big book."

When Should Students Work in Their Science Notebooks?

During every single science class.

On some days, students may only write a summary of a lesson, or write a response to an experience. On other days, they may attach a data sheet they completed during an investigation, or write a longer entry that includes diagrams, data, conclusions, and reflections.

Where Should Science Notebooks Be Stored?

In school. The Notebooks can be stored in a basket, in a bin, or behind a colored tab in a file cabinet. If students are working in groups or teams, each team may have its own basket or bin. Use color-coding for easy identification. Store the Notebooks near the science materials if there's space.

How Can I Get Started with Science Notebooks in My Class?

You'll want to have students set up their Science Notebooks as soon as possible after school begins, so they can be used throughout the year. If you are new to Notebooking, you might want to follow these steps or modify them to suit your needs.

1. After deciding on a Notebook format—spiral, pad, loose leaf in a binder, or digital—invite students to make a cover. Encourage students to decorate the cover so it can be easily distinguished and to include their names and other appropriate information, such as your name and the class period.
2. Use the first three or four pages to create a Table of Contents. Remind students to write "Table of Contents" at the top of each page.
3. Set up three columns on each Contents page and label the columns *Page, Activity,* and *Dates*.
4. Number the pages. While this may seem like a tedious task, it will pay off many times over during the year.
5. Although *ScienceFusion* has an interactive glossary at the back of the Student Edition, you may want students to use the last ten or twelve pages of their Science Notebooks for a glossary.

Now your students are all set!

For each activity or concept, students should start a new page. After they complete their work, they should return to the Table of Contents and fill in the information.

TIP
Keeping Place in the Notebooks

Students can lose valuable time trying to find their place in their Notebook. Here are some ways to get around the problem:

- **Have students use a binder clip to hold all the unused pages. During each lesson, they can remove newly used pages from the clip.**
- **Suggest that students tape a string to the spiral or spine of a binder and place the string between the used and unused pages.**
- **Encourage students to use a sticky-note to mark the last used page or first unused page.**

How Can I Give My Students Feedback on Their Notebooks?

Giving feedback is one of the most important strategies you can use to support students' learning. You'll want to review your students' Notebooks as often as possible. This is a case where more really is better. Students need to know their Notebooks are important. Regular feedback sends that message.

Many teachers provide critical feedback to coincide with points in the curriculum where mastery is key to moving on—for example, in the middle and at the end of a unit.

- Be sure you have a clear understanding of the lesson objective. This will help you decide how to comment on whether a student has met the objective. In *ScienceFusion*, a full answer to an Essential Question articulates the content of lesson objectives.
- Provide positive feedback directly in a Student's Notebook.
- Make suggestions for additional thought or work on sticky-notes, which can be removed when the work is completed.
- When possible, couch your suggestions as guiding questions such as, What conclusions can you draw from the evidence? Which of the variables will you need to control?

You may wish to have students conduct a self-evaluation of their Science Notebook. This page is available in the *ScienceFusion* Assessment Guide.

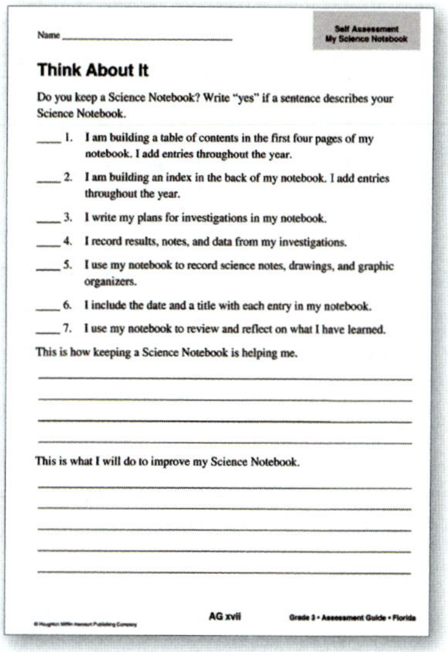
Name ______________________

Self Assessment
My Science Notebook

Think About It

Do you keep a Science Notebook? Write "yes" if a sentence describes your Science Notebook.

____ 1. I am building a table of contents in the first four pages of my notebook. I add entries throughout the year.

____ 2. I am building an index in the back of my notebook. I add entries throughout the year.

____ 3. I write my plans for investigations in my notebook.

____ 4. I record results, notes, and data from my investigations.

____ 5. I use my notebook to record science notes, drawings, and graphic organizers.

____ 6. I include the date and a title with each entry in my notebook.

____ 7. I use my notebook to review and reflect on what I have learned.

This is how keeping a Science Notebook is helping me.

This is what I will do to improve my Science Notebook.

AG xvii

Grade 3 • Assessment Guide • Florida

Science Notebooks and *ScienceFusion*

ScienceFusion Teacher Editions and the Inquiry Flipcharts include point-of-use suggestions and strategies for Science Notebook entries. Look for the Science Notebook features.

Strategies for using Science Notebooks with all the *ScienceFusion* Inquiry activities are provided in Online Inquiry Support in Online Resources.

The Teacher Edition also includes suggestions for summarizing ideas after each two-page spread. The Science Notebook is an ideal place for students to write their summaries.

As you and your students embrace Notebooking, you will surely find it to be an engaging, enriching, and very valuable endeavor.

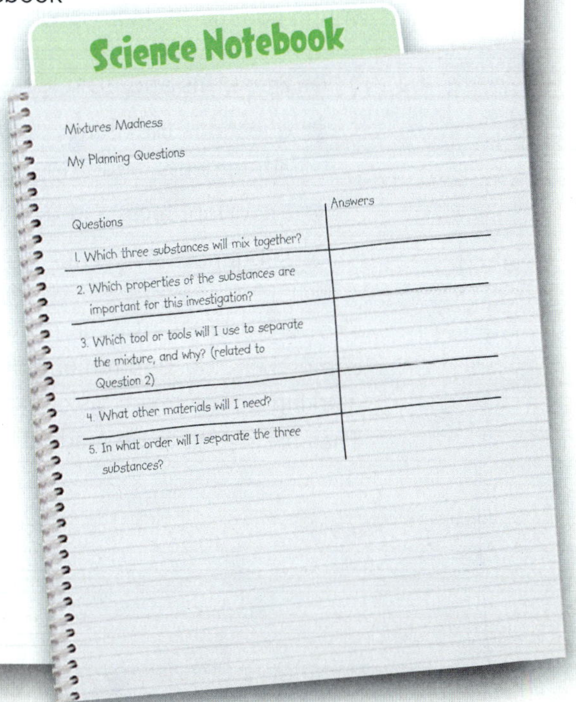

Active Reading

Reading is a complex process in which readers use their knowledge and experience to make meaning from text. Though rarely accompanied by obvious large-muscle movement, reading is very much an active endeavor.

by Marjorie Frank

Think back to your days as a college student when you pored over your textbooks to prepare for class or for an exam—or, more recently, concentrated on an article or book with information you wanted to remember.

- You probably paid close attention to the text.
- Perhaps you paused to ask yourself questions.
- You might have broken off temporarily to look up an important, but unfamiliar, word.
- You may have stopped to reread a challenging passage or to "catch up" if your mind wandered for a moment.

If you owned the reading material, you also may have used a pencil or marker to interact with the text right there on the page (or in a digital file).

In short, you were having a conversation with yourself about the text. You were engaged. You were thinking critically.

These are the characteristics of active readers. This is precisely the kind of reader you want your students to be, because research suggests that active reading enables readers to understand and remember more information.

Active Reading involves interacting with text cognitively, metacognitively, and quite literally. You can actually see active readers at work. They are not sitting quietly as they read; they're underlining, marking, boxing, bracketing, drawing arrows, numbering, and writing comments. Here is what they may be noting:

- key terms and main ideas
- questions they have, opinions, agreements, and disagreements
- important facts and details
- sequences of events
- words, such as *because, before,* and *but,* that signal connections between ideas
- problems/solutions
- definitions and examples

The very process of interacting actively with text helps keep readers focused, thinking, comprehending, and remembering. But interacting in this way means readers are marking up the text. This is exactly why *ScienceFusion* Student Editions are consumable. They are meant to be marked up.

Active Reading and *ScienceFusion*

ScienceFusion includes Active Reading prompts and strategies on most pages of the Student Editions. The prompts appear at the beginning of each lesson and on most two-page spreads.

The first page of each lesson includes an Active Reading prompt. These prompts give readers a heads-up about the text structure of the lesson—the way the ideas are organized. Reading experts suggest that knowledge of text structure improves comprehension since readers approach the text ready to think about ideas in the same way the writer has organized them. Cause and effect, sequence, compare/contrast, problem/solution, and main idea and details are ways to organize text.

Cause and Effect

Some ideas in this lesson are connected by a cause-and-effect relationship. Why something happens as a result of something else is an effect. Active readers look for effects by asking themselves, What happened? They look for causes by asking, Why did it happen?

Each prompt also includes a specific idea for readers to keep in mind, engaging self-monitoring or metacognitive strategies. This particular prompt gives readers specific questions to ask themselves so they remain focused on causes and effects. Other prompts urge readers to look for specific words that signal a text structure or to preview the text, turning headings into questions the text will answer.

Examples of Active Reading Prompts

- **Draw a star next to the names of animals that hatch from eggs and a check mark next to the names of animals that are born live.**
- **As you read these two pages, circle lesson vocabulary each time it is used.**
- **Find and underline four clues that a chemical change has occured.**
- **Put a *P* next to the sentences that describe a problem. Put an *S* next to the sentences that describe a solution.**

Students' Responses to Active Reading Prompts

Active Reading has benefits for you as well as for your students. You can use students' responses to Active Reading prompts and the other interactive prompts in *ScienceFusion* as ongoing assessments. A quick review of students' responses provides a great deal of information.

- Are students comprehending the text?
- How deeply do they understand the concepts developed?
- Did they get the main idea? the cause? the order in which things happen?

Answers to these questions are available in students' responses to Active Learning prompts throughout a lesson—long before you might see poor results on a test. These frequent and regular assessments are integral parts of an effective Response to Intervention program.

The Active Reading prompts in *ScienceFusion* help make everyone a winner.

Professional Development

Project-Based Learning

For a list of the *ScienceFusion* Video-Based Projects, see page T35.

by

Michael R. Heithaus

When asked why I decided to become a biologist, the answer is pretty simple. I was inspired by spending almost every day outdoors, exploring under every rock, getting muddy in creeks and streams, and fishing in farm ponds, rivers, and—when I was really lucky—the oceans. Combine that with the spectacular stories of amazing animals and adventures that I saw on TV and I was hooked. As I've progressed in my career as a biologist, that same excitement and curiosity that I had as a ten-year-old looking for a salamander is still driving me.

But today's kids live in a very different world. Cable and satellite TV, Twitter, MP3 players, cell phones, and video games all compete with the outdoors for kids' time and attention. Education budget cuts, legal issues, and the pressures of standardized testing have also limited the opportunities for students to explore outdoors with their teachers.

How do we overcome these challenges so as to inspire kids' curiosity, help them connect with the natural world, and get them to engage in science and math? This is a critical issue. Not only do we need to ensure our national competitiveness and the conservation of our natural resources by training the next generation of scientists, we also need to ensure that every kid grows up to understand how scientists work and why their work is important.

To overcome these challenges, there is no question that we need to grab students' attention and get them to actively engage in the learning process. Research shows that students who are active and engaged participants in their learning have greater gains in concept and skills development than students who are passive in the classroom.

Project-based learning is one way to engage students. And when the stimulus for the project is exciting video content, engaged and active learning is almost guaranteed. Nothing captures a student's attention faster than exciting video. I have noticed that when my university students have video to accompany a lesson, they learn and retain the material better. It's no different for younger students! Videos need to do more than just "talk at" students to have a real impact. Videos need to engage students and require participation.

Teachers and students who use *ScienceFusion* video-based projects have noticed the following:

- The videos use captivating imagery, dynamic scientists, and cool stories to inspire kids to be curious about the world around them.
- Students connect to the projects by having the videos present interesting problems for them to solve.
- The videos engage students with projects woven into the story of the video so students are doing the work of real scientists!

The start-to-finish nature of the video projects, where students do background research and develop their own hypotheses, should lead to students' personal investment in solving the challenges that are presented. By seeing real scientists who are excellent role models gather data that they have to graph and interpret, students will not only learn the science standards being addressed, they will see that they can apply the scientific method to their lives. One day, they too could be a scientist!

Based on my experiences teaching in the university classroom, leading field trips for middle school students, and taking the first project-based videos into the classroom, project-based learning has considerable benefits. The video-based projects generate enthusiasm and curiosity. They also help students develop a deeper understanding of science content as well as how to go about a scientific investigation. If we inspire students to ask questions and seek answers for themselves, we will go a long way toward closing achievement gaps in science and math and facilitate the development of the next generation of scientists and scientifically literate citizens.

Professional Development

Developing Visual Literacy

by
Donna M. Ogle

Science teachers can build the bridges between students' general literacy and their scientific literacy by focusing attention on the particular kinds of reading strategies students need to be successful. One such strategy is that of knowing how to read and interpret the various visual displays used in science.

Many young readers receive little instruction in reading charts, tables, diagrams, photographs, or illustrations in their language arts/reading classes. Science is where these skills can and must be developed. Science provides a meaningful context where students can learn to read visually presented forms of information and to create their own visual representations. Research studies have shown that students take longer to read science materials containing combinations of visual displays and narrative texts than they do to read narrative text alone. The process of reading the combination materials is slower and more difficult because the reader must relate the visual displays to the narrative text and build a meaning that is based on information from both.

We also know that students benefit when teachers take time to explain how each visual form is constructed and to guide students in the thinking needed to make sense of these forms. Even the seemingly simple act of interpreting a photograph needs to be taught to most students. Here are some ways to help students develop the ability to think more critically about what they view:

- Model for students how to look carefully at a photograph and list what they notice.
- Divide the photograph into quadrants and have students think more deeply about what the photographer has used as the focus of the image and what context is provided.
- Have students use language such as *zoom, close-up*, *foreground*, *background*, or *panorama views* to describe photographs.

The ability to interpret a photograph is clearly a part of the scientific skill of engaging in careful observation. This skill helps students when they are using print materials, observing nature, and making their own photographs of aspects of their experiments.

Attention to the other forms of visual displays frequently used in science is also important to students' learning of scientific concepts and processes. For example, students in grades 4 through 8 need to learn to interpret and then construct each of the types of graphs, from circle graphs and bar graphs to more complex line graphs.

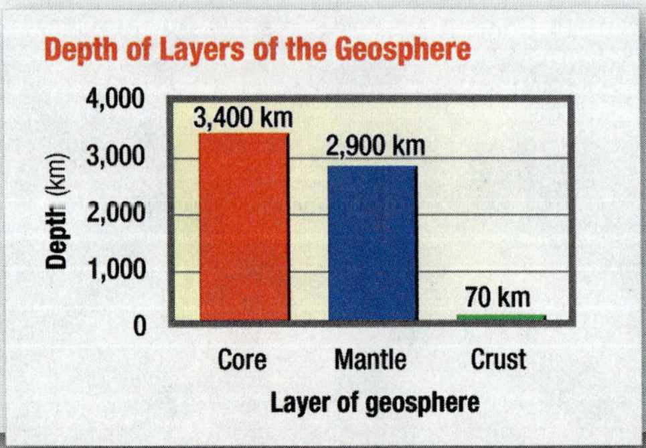

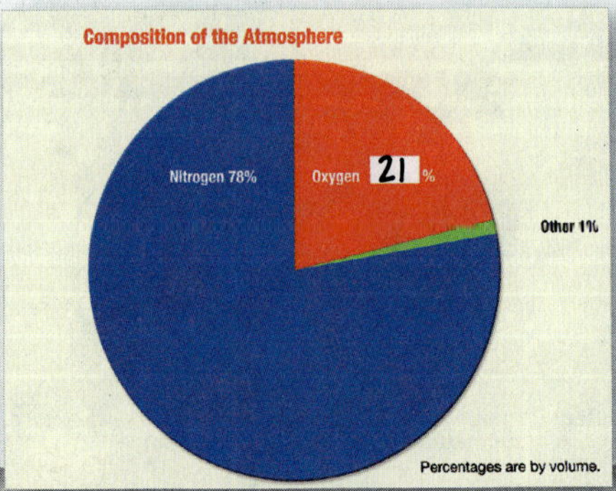

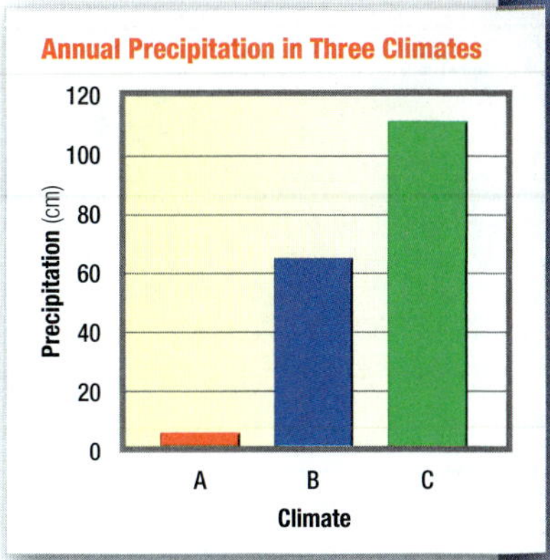

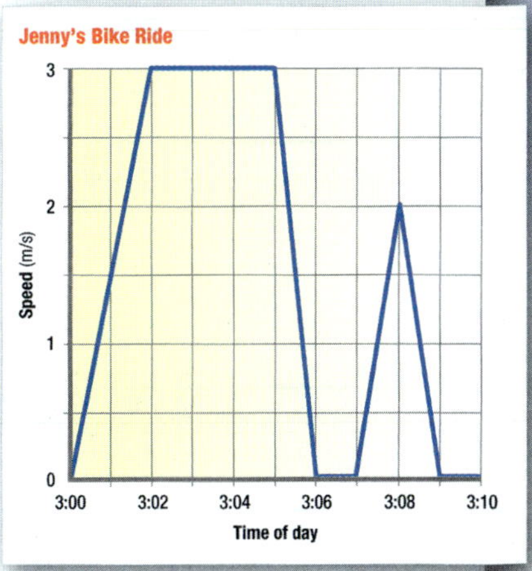

Students also need to be able to read diagrams and flow charts. Yet, in a recent study asking students to think aloud and point to how they visually scan tables and diagrams, we learned how inadequate many students were as readers of these visual forms. Because so much of the scientific information students will encounter is summarized in these visual formats, it is essential that students learn to interpret and construct visual displays.

A second aspect of interpreting visual displays is connecting the information in the visual formats with the narrative text information.
Some students misinterpret what they see in visuals when even a few words differ between the text and the illustration. For example, in this page from a Middle School Student Edition, the text says, "the arm of a human, the front leg of a cat, and the wing of a bat do not look alike . . . but they are similar in structure. "

The diagram labels (lower right) showing the bat's wing and the cat's leg use *front limb*, not *wing* or *leg*. For students who struggle with English, the differing terms may cause confusion unless teachers show students how to use clues from later in the paragraph, where limb and wing/arm are connected, and how to connect this information to the two drawings. In some cases, teachers have students draw lines showing where visual displays connect with the more extensive narrative text content. Developing students' awareness of how visual and narrative information support each other and yet provide different forms in which information can be shared is an important step in building scientific literacy.

Reading science requires students to use specific reading strategies. The more carefully science teachers across grade levels assess what students already know about reading scientific materials, the more easily they can focus instruction to build the scaffolds students need to gain independence and confidence in their reading and learning of science. Time spent explaining, modeling, and guiding students will yield the rewards of heightened student enjoyment, confidence, and engagement in the exciting world of scientific inquiry.

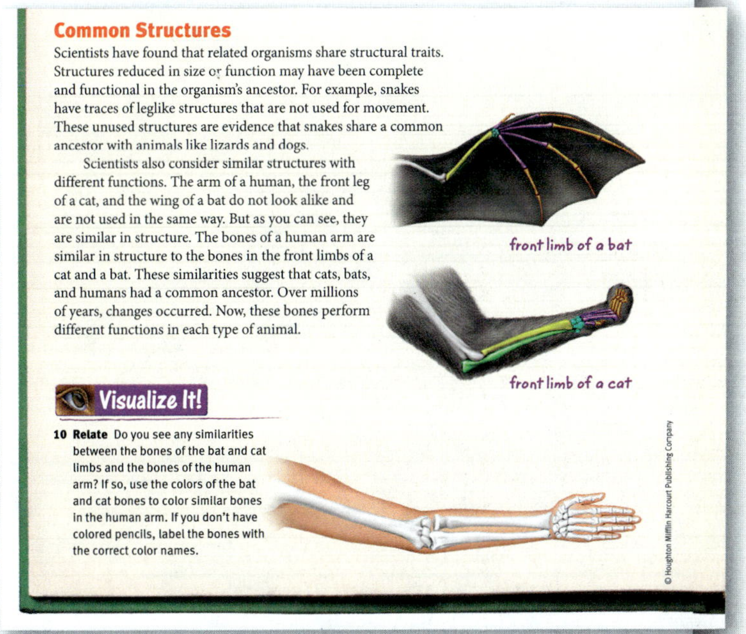

Common Structures

Scientists have found that related organisms share structural traits. Structures reduced in size or function may have been complete and functional in the organism's ancestor. For example, snakes have traces of leglike structures that are not used for movement. These unused structures are evidence that snakes share a common ancestor with animals like lizards and dogs.

Scientists also consider similar structures with different functions. The arm of a human, the front leg of a cat, and the wing of a bat do not look alike and are not used in the same way. But as you can see, they are similar in structure. The bones of a human arm are similar in structure to the bones in the front limbs of a cat and a bat. These similarities suggest that cats, bats, and humans had a common ancestor. Over millions of years, changes occurred. Now, these bones perform different functions in each type of animal.

front limb of a bat

front limb of a cat

Visualize It!

10 Relate Do you see any similarities between the bones of the bat and cat limbs and the bones of the human arm? If so, use the colors of the bat and cat bones to color similar bones in the human arm. If you don't have colored pencils, label the bones with the correct color names.

Teacher Notes

Teacher Science Background

These pages provide concise science background for the major topics and concepts in this program. The information is organized according to the following key words:

animals
atmosphere
changes in matter
climate
conservation
Earth's changing surface
ecosystems
energy
engineering and technology
engineering design process
exploring space
extinction
forces
fossils
gravity
human body
landforms
light
living and nonliving things
magnetism
measuring matter
meteorology
minerals
motion
natural resources
oceans
planetary cycles
plants
properties of matter
rocks
scientific method
scientific tools
seasons
soil
solar system
sound
stars
water cycle

SCILINKS. THE WORLD'S A CLICK AWAY

Additional background information is provided in Online Resources. The online content, appropriate for teachers and students, provides the following benefits:

- Free up-to-date web content to extend and expand student understanding
- Lessons, assessments, and deeper exploration of content for teachers
- Content that is constantly reviewed and vetted by experienced NSTA educators (National Science Teachers Association)
- Activities to bring science alive in the classroom

Animals

Adaptation

An adaptation is a characteristic of a plant or an animal that allows the organism to survive in a particular environment. Some adaptations have developed over many generations. Some, however, occur within a single generation. The key to adaptation is variation, or difference, within a species. In order for a species to survive, it must be able to adapt, or change, to better fit new circumstances that arise within an environment. Adaptations can take the form of changes both in an organism's body (physical adaptation) and in its behavior (behavioral adaptation). An example of the former is the long, pointed beak of the hummingbird, which is designed to fit inside tubular flowers. An example of the latter is the nest-building and courting-dance activity of the male bower bird that helps him attract a mate. These adaptations do not happen during one animal's lifetime, but over many generations. The shape of a bird's beak, the placement of a fish's eyes, and the shape of a mammal's teeth are just a few adaptations that help animals survive.

What Animals Need

Animals need food, water, air, and shelter. Different animals meet these needs in different ways. Physical adaptations for getting the necessary food include body parts (such as mouth parts, powerful hind legs, and acute vision) that allow animals to obtain food in the most energy-efficient way and to get the most nutrients from their food as they digest it. Adaptations for getting enough water vary as well. Animals such as camels do not sweat very much. That means their bodies don't lose water and they do not need to drink as often. They also get some water from food. Animals such as fish and tadpoles have gills that allow them to get the oxygen they need. Gills are different from lungs, which humans use, or from the respiratory system of insects.

How Animals Are Born and Grow

All animals produce offspring in one of two ways. Some animals hatch from eggs, while others develop inside the mother before she gives birth. Some animals look like their parents when they are born and others do not. Some need a lot of parental care; others need little. All need food, water, air, and shelter to survive. Either the parent helps the young meet these needs, or the young are equipped to meet them. In species where there is little or no parenting, the adults produce many offspring to compensate for those lost to predators. An animal's body covering also changes as the animal grows. Young animals that have to fend for themselves tend to develop mature body coverings faster than animals that receive parental care.

Butterfly Growth

In its life cycle, a butterfly goes through a complete *metamorphosis*. The young look nothing like their parents, and there are four distinct stages of the life cycle. First, an adult female lays eggs on a plant. The plant's leaves are food for the caterpillars, or larvae, when the eggs hatch. Most larvae have eyes on their heads, chewing or sucking mouth parts, and short antennae. Some larvae also have three pairs of true legs, which they retain during metamorphosis. A larva sheds its skin several times before changing into a pupa. In the pupa stage, body parts are reabsorbed and reorganized, and new parts grow. The adult emerges with crumpled wings and soft body parts. It takes just a few hours for these parts to harden, and then the adult is ready to reproduce and continue the life cycle

Protective Body Coverings

An animal's body covering protects the animal from harmful elements of its environment. The hard outer shell of an insect and the sharp quills of a porcupine act as shields around these organisms. Body coverings also protect animals from extreme temperatures. Thick hair traps an animal's body heat to insulate it in a cold environment. Thin, porous skin enables an animal to release body heat and keep cool in a warm environment.

Animal Classification

Living things can be grouped into domains and kingdoms. Two of the kingdoms are the plant kingdom and the animal kingdom. To organize the thousands of different species in the animal kingdom, zoologists group animals into categories according to their genectic makeup and their physical similarities and differences. Zoologists divide the animal kingdom into smaller and smaller groups called *subkingdoms*, *phylums*, and *subphylums*. This classification system is called a *taxonomy*. Animals can further be divided into smaller groups. The science of animal classification has been developing for more than 300 years. Because contemporary scientists can study the genetic makeup of animals, they can now group them in more ways. They have even found some new groups. Some animals may seem to belong to one group but actually belong to another. For example, a whale lives in water like a fish but it is a mammal. It has lungs instead of gills, and the female feeds milk to its young.

Animal Growth and Development

Different species of animals grow and develop in different ways. Most mammals grow inside their mother before they are born. The mother feeds them milk produced by her body after birth. All bird mothers lay eggs. Most bird parents incubate their eggs in nests. Other egg layers include amphibians, insects, and most reptiles and fish.

Atmosphere

The Sky

The appearance of the sky is an effect of layers of atmosphere surrounded by the vacuum of space. Earth's air, or atmosphere, is a mixture of several gases, including water vapor, nitrogen, and oxygen. The atmosphere protects Earth from the heat of the sun. Its water vapor is the source of clouds and weather.

Changes in Matter

Physical and Chemical Change

Cutting, bending, and wetting things with water are ways to cause physical changes in matter. When a physical change takes place, the substance itself does not change. Paper remains paper, no matter how it is changed physically. Matter can also be changed chemically, but chemical changes affect the basic nature of a substance. Chemical changes occur when a substance burns, oxidizes, or is dissolved in an acid. When a chemical change takes place, a new substance is formed, and the change is permanent.

Gases

Like solids and liquids, gases are a form of matter with properties that can be observed and described. Gases spread out to fill whatever empty space they occupy, from balloons and bubbles to rooms, or Earth's atmosphere. Water vapor, oxygen, and carbon dioxide are some gases that children are familiar with. They can see carbon dioxide bubbles in soda water and oxygen bubbles on the elodea plant in fish tanks. They can observe water evaporate and become invisible as water vapor. Many gases are odorless and colorless, but others can smell like rotten eggs or swampy muck. Children can experience how gases act when they squeeze an inflated balloon, open a bottle of soda, or stand in front of a fan.

Three Forms of Water

Water is the only matter naturally found in three forms—liquid, solid, and gas—within the normal temperature range on Earth. In liquid form, it is water. In solid form, it is ice. In gaseous form, it is water vapor. The molecules in water move about freely. Water evaporates because the molecules at the surface of the liquid break free and become water vapor. Most substances contract as they get colder. Water contracts until it reaches a temperature of 4 °C, or 39 °F. It expands when it becomes colder than that.

Climate

Climate

Recording and charting daily weather helps people understand the climate of an area. People make generalizations about climate based on recorded average weather conditions of an area over a long period of time. There are different kinds of climates, the three main types being polar, temperate, and tropical. In general, the greater a region's distance from the equator, the colder the climate will be.

Conservation

Natural Resources

Conservation is the protection, preservation, and careful management of Earth's natural resources. Natural resources are material resources, such as soil, forests, and water, that occur in a natural state. They also include energy sources, such as coal and oil. Natural resources are either renewable resources, such as trees, that can be replaced over time, or nonrenewable resources, such as oil, that cannot be replaced.

Earth's Changing Surface

Creep

Creep is a slow type of ground movement. During creep, soil gradually shifts downhill because of gravity. Unlike other types of ground movements such as landslides, creep is so slow that changes in landforms are hard to observe directly. The land may move only a few centimeters each year. But while creep cannot be seen occurring, over time it can move fences, utility poles, roads, and railroad tracks.

Types of Glaciers

There are two main kinds of glaciers. Valley glaciers are found in high mountain valleys. They flow slowly down mountainsides, eroding the mountain under them and forming U-shaped valleys. Only a few valley glaciers remain in North America, and even those are melting rapidly. Continental glaciers are ice sheets that cover large areas of Earth. They cover almost all of Greenland and Antarctica today. Thousands of years ago, when the global climate was colder, continental glaciers covered Europe, Canada, and the northern United States. The Great Lakes formed as retreating continental glaciers melted.

Erosion

Gravity is a force that pulls objects toward each other. It causes objects to fall toward Earth's surface and to roll down hills. Gravity can help erode mountains and hills by causing loose debris such as boulders and rocks to tumble down the slopes. Other agents, such as water, ice, wind, plants, and animals, also weather and erode rock, sand, and soil. In turn, rock, sand, and soil can further erode other rock. For example, a rolling boulder can cause erosion by breaking up rocks, causing material to fall, and destroying plants. Of all the agents of erosion, water is the most powerful. A large drop of water can splash sand grains 30 cm (1 ft) or more into the air.

Ecosystems

Ecosystems

Scientists define an ecosystem as any group of organisms interacting with one another and with their physical environment. Thus, an ecosystem can be as small as a drop of pond water or as large as the entire Earth. The Earth ecosystem is called the biosphere. Organisms within an ecosystem compete with each other for food, energy, and space. They also interact with the nonliving components of the ecosystem, for example, by taking minerals from the soil, consuming water and oxygen, and anchoring topsoil against erosion.

How Animals Help Plants

Animals help plants in two basic ways. First, they help plants grow better. Animals enrich the soil by leaving behind their wastes. They also enrich it by mixing humus, or dead organic matter, into the soil. This helps recycle nutrients plants need to grow. Small animals, such as earthworms and moles, also aerate the soil when they dig tunnels. Plant roots get air and water more easily in loose, aerated soil. Animals also help plants make new plants. Some plants need animals to scatter plant seeds and pollen. Many plants cannot make seeds unless they receive pollen from another plant, and they depend on animals such as insects, birds, and even some mammals to bring them the pollen they need. They produce sweet nectar to attract the animals to the part of the flower where the pollen is located.

Life in a Desert

A desert is any place that receives less than ten inches of rainfall in a year and that has a yearly evaporation rate of more than ten inches. Not all deserts are hot, nor are they all sandy. But they are all dry and support very little plant life. Between the Rocky Mountains and the Sierra Nevada in the United States, there are both hot and cold deserts. Idaho, Oregon, and northern Utah have cold desert conditions, while California, Arizona, Nevada, southern Utah, Texas, and New Mexico have hot desert conditions. Because a desert is so dry, anything that lives there has to have ways of surviving with very little water. Desert animals save water by staying where it is cool. Many choose to stay underground or in the shade during the day, feeding only at night. Some desert animals almost never drink water. They can survive on the water found in the food they eat.

Land Habitats

Animals that live on land are found in all of Earth's varied biomes. Each species is adapted to survive in and use the resources of its land habitat. Forest animals, for example, have adaptations that allow them to compete with trees for energy. They rely on the trees for food, shelter, and moisture. Only a little light reaches the forest floor, so plants that live there have to get their energy from the sun indirectly. Organisms like fungi use decaying trees and other decaying plant matter for food. Small animals, like insects, rodents, and reptiles, feed on fungi as well as some tree parts. Larger animals in a forest can eat the small animals. In addition, animals benefit from the shelter that the trees provide. Some plants and animals are so well adapted to forest conditions that, as their forest habitat is lost, they have difficulty surviving.

Water Environments and Habitats

The most important factors determining the kinds of plants and animals that live in water environments are the amount of salt in the water, the amount of dissolved oxygen in the water, and the amount of sunlight that reaches the water. **Freshwater environments** such as rivers, streams, lakes, and ponds contain little or no salt. Because the water of lakes and ponds is relatively still, it contains more plant growth than the water of faster flowing rivers and streams. Since ponds are shallow, sunlight usually reaches the bottom, promoting plant and algae growth. **Saltwater environments** include oceans, seas, and a few inland lakes. Many different saltwater ecosystems are found in the shallow waters of the coastal areas. Life in the open oceans is divided into zones based on the depth to which sunlight penetrates the water.

Energy

Energy

The scientific definition of *energy* is "the ability to cause changes in matter." Without energy, matter does not change. Without energy, no light, heat, sound, or motion could exist, and nothing would live or grow. Energy is neither made nor destroyed, but can be changed from one form to another and back. Energy is stored in natural resources such as coal, natural gas, and petroleum. Energy makes it possible to produce electricity, heat, and the power to run machines. Objects in motion, such as wind, flowing water, and a moving car, are examples of kinetic energy. Objects such as a hammer, a spring, and a rubber band—which are not moving but which could move—have potential energy. Batteries, food, coal, oil, and natural gas store chemical energy. Chemical energy is released when there is a chemical reaction.

Heat

Scientists define heat as "the movement of thermal energy." When this transfer of energy takes place, there usually is a decrease in temperature in the warmer body and an increase in temperature in the cooler body. However, a substance can absorb heat without increasing in temperature when it changes from one physical state to another. Examples of this occur when ice melts into a liquid and when water boils and changes from a liquid to water vapor. Heat is measured in degrees of temperature. When heat transfers to matter, the temperature of the matter goes up, and usually the matter expands.

Thermal Energy, Temperature, and Heat

Thermal energy is the total energy contained in an object or substance because of the motion of its particles. As energy from the sun strikes objects on Earth, the objects' particles absorb thermal energy. The particles move faster, and the thermal energy in the object increases. The average kinetic energy of the particles in a substance is measured as temperature. As a thermometer absorbs thermal energy, the liquid molecules within the thermometer move faster. The liquid expands, indicating an increase in temperature. Heat energy moves between objects with different temperatures: specifically, from warmer objects to cooler objects.

Engineering and Technology

Engineering

Engineering is the use of science knowledge to design products that solve problems and meet people's needs and wants. The products of engineering are *technology*. Technology can be as simple as a pencil or as complex as a car or computer. We're used to thinking of technology as only high-tech electronics. Actually, nearly everything that we see on a daily basis came from a factory that was designed by engineers—paper, aluminum cans, plastic cups, mirrors, roads, cars, fabric, ink pens, and on and on. Processes are also technology, for example, the steps for making steel, a cookie recipe, or a trouble-shooting script for computer hardware.

Engineering Design Process

The Engineering Process

Engineers often follow an iterative design process to develop a solution to a problem. The steps of the process vary and the divisions between steps are somewhat arbitrary. *ScienceFusion* uses a simplified five-step engineering design process:

1. Find a Problem—Identify a problem; describe an unmet need or want and who will use the solution.

2. Plan and Build—Decide the criteria the solution must meet to succeed; brainstorm designs; consider constraints, or limitations, such as budget, size, weight, and available materials; choose materials; draw detailed plans; and finally, construct a prototype.

3. Test and Improve—Test the prototype against the design criteria. If it is successful, make improvements to enhance its performance.

4. Redesign—Often, the first attempt at a solution fails to meet the design criteria. Engineers take what they learned from testing and start over with a new design.

5. Communicate—Document work throughout the process and communicate with team members. At the end of the process, engineers share the final design, explain the test results, and often write directions for how to use the product.

Exploring Space

Mars

People dream about space travel to other planets. Many scientists are now considering the possibility of humans traveling to Mars.

- The distance from Earth to Mars is approximately 80,000,000 km (49,700,000 mi). The trip would take a spacecraft many months to complete.
- Two rovers, *Spirit* and *Opportunity*, arrived on Mars in January 2004. Each rover carries a sophisticated set of instruments that allows it to search for evidence that liquid water may have been present on Mars in the past.
- Mars has an atmosphere that would not support life as we know it. NASA hopes to change that with ambitious plans to thicken the atmosphere of Mars and even melt its polar ice caps.

Trip to the Moon

- The *Saturn V* rocket had three stages. Each stage was mounted on top of the previous stage. The first stage produced more than 33 million N of thrust at liftoff.
- A command and service module (CSM) at the top of the *Saturn V* carried three astronauts into space and toward the moon. The CSM traveled the 384,000 km (about 239,000 mi) from Earth to the moon in four days.
- For comparison, it takes about four days to drive a car across the continental United States, a distance of about 3,000 miles.

Extinction

Habitats and Extinction

When a habitat changes, plants and animals may become *endangered*, meaning that fewer numbers of those plants or animals will survive each year. Over time, the plants or animals may die out, or become *extinct*. Extinction can occur when people cause habitats to change or when habitats change naturally.

Forces

Force

Force is what makes all objects move. Force can be either a push or a pull. Force can start or stop motion, speed up or slow down motion, or change the direction of motion. When a child slides down a slide, gravity pulls him toward Earth. When a child pushes a toy truck, the muscles contract and pull her bones to make her arm move and push. When a flag is blowing and waving, the wind is pushing it back and forth.

Fossils

Fossil Formation

Fossils rarely form. Whether plant or animal remains become fossils depends on what the organism is, where it lived, and whether the remains were protected from exposure. Organisms that are buried quickly and remain protected from air, water, bacteria, and scavengers are more likely to become fossils, because the remains will not be eaten and they will not decay too quickly. Hard materials, such as bones, teeth, wood, and shells, are more likely to become fossils than soft tissues. Marine organisms are more likely to become fossils than land-dwelling organisms. In a few cases, organisms such as woolly mammoths (prehistoric elephant-like animals) were preserved intact when they froze in the Arctic tundra.

Dinosaur Trace Fossils

When most people think of dinosaur fossils, they think of bones and large skeletons. Such "body fossils" are not the only kinds of fossil evidence, however. A trace fossil is indirect evidence of ancient life. It is not a body part but evidence of an organism's behavior. Examples of trace fossils left by dinosaurs include tracks, tooth marks, eggs, nests, gastroliths, and coprolites. A coprolite is fossilized animal droppings. Dinosaur coprolites reveal what dinosaurs consumed. Coprolites can contain either body fossils of plant material (indicating a herbivorous diet) or bones (indicating a carnivorous diet). Gastroliths, or "gizzard stones," can be difficult to distinguish from polished stones. Those most easily identified are found in the rib cages of dinosaur skeletons, which is where the dinosaur's stomach was.

Paleontology

Paleontology is the study of ancient life through analysis of plant and animal fossils.

- Paleontologists focus on the biology of ancient life. Their work involves investigating ancient life, trying to discover its connection to current life forms on Earth, and developing an understanding of the ancient forms' interrelationship with their environment.
- Paleontologists are also concerned with geology and have a major influence in determining the facts about the layers of rock that make up Earth. Using index fossils and other information about the rocks in which fossils occur, paleontologists aid petroleum geologists in their search for oil and gas.

Gravity

Gravity

Gravity is the attraction of one mass to another. It is the weakest force in nature, and yet it affects how bodies move throughout the solar system and in the larger universe. All bodies on Earth are influenced by gravity; how much depends on how much force Earth exerts on the object. The more mass the object has, the more gravity it has. The Earth's gravity pulls each particle with the same amount of force. So objects made up of more particles (matter) are subject to a greater gravitational force than are objects made up of less matter. To determine the amount of gravitational force pulling on you, you need only step on a scale. Your weight is a measure of the amount of gravitational force pulling you to Earth. If the matter that makes up an object is evenly distributed, the pull of gravity will also be evenly distributed, and the object will balance.

Gravity, Free Fall, and Air Resistance

The gravitational pull of Earth on an object in free fall causes the object to accelerate at 9.8 meters per second squared (9.8m/sec/sec). Acceleration because of gravity does not depend on an object's mass (mass being defined as a measure of the amount of matter contained in an object). However, free fall is rare on Earth because the upward force of air resistance opposes gravity's pull. Without air resistance, a feather would fall at the same rate as a brick.

Human Body

Bones

About 206 bones together form your skeleton. The head bones make up the skull, which sits on top of the spine. At the top of the spine sit the shoulder bones, which are linked to the arm bones. Twelve pairs of rib bones curve around the spine and connect at the front of the chest. At the bottom of the spine, pelvis bones connect to the leg bones. The places where bones meet are called **joints**. Knuckle and knee joints act like hinges and can bend naturally in only one way. Ball-and-socket joints in the shoulders and hips allow bones to move in a complete circle. There are more than 600 **muscles** in the human body. Some of these work under voluntary control, such as arm and thigh muscles. Others, such as those in the stomach, are involuntary.

How Bodies Grow

The human body grows, changing in both shape and size, from infancy to about the age of twenty. Growth is rapid during the first year of life. Weight will triple and height will increase by a half before a child turns one. When a baby is born, its head is 25% of its total body height. As the baby grows, the body's proportions will change. Arms, legs and torso grow so that the head becomes 12.5% of the body's size in an adult. During childhood, the growth rate is steady. It speeds up again between the ages of 10 and 16 when the child's body matures and becomes adult. This stage is called puberty. The adult body does not change much but may experience weight gain, shrinking, skin wrinkles, and loss of hair and muscle.

The Five Senses

The five senses are sight, hearing, smell, touch, and taste. Receptors for each sense are found on our faces in our eyes, ears, noses, mouths, and skin. Receptors for the sense of touch are also found in the skin on all parts of our bodies. Our senses send signals about their environment to the brain through the nervous system. The brain then processes the information from the senses. This enables us to learn about the world and to make decisions. The senses are survival tools because they send signals to the brain that help us detect danger and pain. Without the sense of touch to tell us that something is hot, we would be likely to seriously burn ourselves.

The Heart

The human heart is a muscle that pumps blood throughout the body. It is located just left of center in the chest. The heart has four chambers, or sections, called the *atria* and *ventricles*. Blood flows into the right atrium and is pumped through a valve to the right ventricle. From there it travels to the lungs, where it picks up oxygen and drops off carbon dioxide. Then blood travels back to the left atrium and is squeezed down into the left ventricle where it is pumped to the body. Blood carries nutrients and oxygen to the body.

The Lungs

The lungs are located in the center of the chest and surround the heart. Air travels down the *trachea*. The trachea divides into two main sections called *bronchi*. These lead to the lungs. Inside the lungs the bronchi branch out into thin bronchioles. At the tips of the *bronchioles* are structures called *alveoli* where the blood picks up oxygen and releases carbon dioxide.

Digestive System

Food is essential for life. It provides the energy and nutrients a body needs to grow, repair cells, and keep warm. Food must be changed into a form the body can use. The digestive system is basically a large tube that runs from the mouth to the anus. The process starts in the mouth where teeth and saliva break food down. It is then swallowed down the esophagus to the stomach. In the stomach the food is mixed with digestive fluids. The stomach muscles squeeze together to turn the food into a chunky liquid. This liquid enters the small intestine where the food breaks down into small molecules. The molecules pass into the blood, which carries the nutrients to all parts of the body. The food that is not digested in the small intestine enters the large intestine, where it is eliminated.

Landforms

What Are Landforms?

Landforms are natural features that make up Earth's surface. There are many kinds of landforms, including mountains, hills, valleys, plains, plateaus, beaches, and dunes. Some landforms, such as mountains and plateaus, form as a result of the upward movement of rock. Mountains can be found both on the ocean floor and on land. Other landforms are caused by erosion and by deposition of earth materials. Canyons are narrow, deep gorges that are cut into Earth by the action of running water, while valleys can be the result of erosion by streams and rivers and by glacial action. Landforms can also be caused by the movement of Earth's crust and by volcanic activity.

Light

Properties of Light

When light strikes a surface, the light may be reflected, refracted, or absorbed. What happens to light depends on the surface it hits. When light hits a smooth, shiny surface, it is reflected, or thrown back. Reflected light enables you to see yourself in a mirror. When light passes from one substance into another, it is refracted, or bent. That is why an object partially immersed in water appears to bend at the water line. Many surfaces absorb light. Some surfaces are opaque. They don't let light pass through, and you can't see through them. Surfaces that let some light through, such as wax paper, are translucent. Surfaces that let most light through are transparent. You can see through them.

Living and Nonliving Things

Living and Nonliving Things

Everything in the environment can be classified as living or nonliving. All living things eat, drink, digest, produce waste, breathe, reproduce, grow, and move. These characteristics are easier to observe in animals than in plants. Plants do not eat the way animals do. Rather, they make their own food and store it for use when they need it. Plants also do not move from place to place. Their movement and growth is in response to light, water, and gravity. Their movement may also be caused by external forces, such as wind. Nonliving things may sometimes have behaviors like those of living things. Fire, for example, may "grow" or "move." But unless something has all the characteristics of a living thing, it cannot be called living.

Magnetism

Magnets

A magnet is a solid, such as a piece of metal or a stone, that attracts objects that are made of iron or steel (which contains iron). Natural magnets, called *magnetite* or *lodestone*, are formed inside Earth. Centuries ago, sailors navigated by suspending a lodestone from a string to detect North. Today, magnets are found in computers and many appliances. They activate speakers in televisions, radios, stereos, and telephones. They are used as door latches and to separate items in recycling centers. To avoid damage, do not place magnets near computers or software. Do not drop, strike, or heat magnets, as demagnetization can result. Magnets attract only steel and iron and a few other metals, such as nickel and cobalt.

Magnetic Force

Magnets can be used to make some things move, even without touching them, because magnetic force reaches beyond the magnet. This area where the force extends is called the magnetic field. How far the force reaches, or the size of the magnetic field, depends on a magnet's strength. Most magnets used by children have small fields extending an inch or less. Earth has a magnetic field that extends more than 37,000 miles into space. Magnetic force happens in an iron object when groups of atoms, called domains, align. The domains cause an electromagnetic force that reaches beyond the object. The force is strongest within the magnet, and decreases as distance from the magnet increases. Scientists hypothesize that Earth's magnetic force comes from its core of hot iron surrounded by a fluid outer core.

Magnetic Poles

The poles of a magnet are named for the direction in which they point. Thus, a bar magnet suspended from a string tied around its center will swing until its north-seeking pole points north and the south-seeking pole points south. If a bar magnet is broken into two pieces, each piece will have its own north- and south-seeking poles. The poles of disk and circular magnets are not as easy to identify. For example, ring magnets can be magnetized so the inner edge is one pole, and the outer edge, the other pole; the two surfaces of a disk magnet may be the poles, and so on.

Measuring Matter

Mass and Weight

The mass and weight of an object are not the same. Mass and weight are different properties. Mass is the amount of matter an object has. Weight is the amount of pull that gravity has on an object. The mass of an object stays the same regardless of where it is. Its weight can change depending on the strength of the gravitational force that is pulling on it. An object would weigh more on Earth than on the moon because Earth has a stronger gravitational pull than the moon. Mass is measured with a balance. Weight is measured with a scale.

Meteorology

Clouds and Rain

Liquid water is constantly evaporating from Earth's surface. When water evaporates, it changes to a gas called *water vapor*. Water vapor condenses back to a liquid in the form of tiny droplets after 9 or 10 days. These tiny droplets make up clouds, or fog, or the dew we see on grass in the morning. If the tiny droplets form a cloud, and conditions allow, then the droplets grow until they are heavy enough to fall back to Earth as precipitation. Depending on the temperature conditions, precipitation can fall as either rain, snow, or ice, which might be either sleet or hail. About three-fourths of all Earth's precipitation falls over the ocean. The rest soaks into the ground or runs off into streams and rivers that flow into the ocean. Before long, the sun's heat causes the water to evaporate again, and the water cycle repeats.

Precipitation

Precipitation includes all forms of solid and liquid particles of water that form in clouds and then fall to Earth. Precipitation forms at temperatures that are above and below freezing. **Snow, ice pellets** or **sleet,** and **hail** are the main forms of precipitation that reach the ground in a frozen state. **Rain** (water drops with diameters of 0.5 mm or greater) and **drizzle** (water drops smaller than rain) are liquid forms of precipitation. When rain falls and freezes on impact on a cold surface, it is called *freezing rain*. **Dew** and **frost** do not actually fall from the atmosphere. A rain gauge is used to collect and measure rain and snow. Snow is melted before it is measured.

Wind

Moving air is called wind. The whole body of air surrounding Earth is constantly moving, in part because of Earth's spin, and because of an uneven distribution of heat in Earth's land and water. Since air is a gas, it expands and contracts according to its temperature and the temperature of whatever it moves across. Air over warm regions that has been heated by strong sunshine is less dense than air over cooler regions. The greater the difference in density between the two air masses, the faster the wind will move. This movement, plus the more complicated movements caused by Earth's spin, produces wind conditions that affect our weather. Wind can be both harmful and helpful. Strong unpredictable winds such as those found in hurricanes or tornadoes can be life-threatening if people do not take shelter. But predictable, steady winds can be helpful when people use them to power wind turbines that generate electricity.

Minerals

Minerals

There are more than 2,000 known minerals on Earth. For a material to be classified as a mineral, it must meet certain requirements. The material must be a solid, naturally occurring substance that has a definite chemical composition and internal arrangement of atoms, which is reflected in the mineral's outward appearance when the mineral has enough space to grow. The chemical makeup is responsible for the minerals' color, crystal shape, hardness, luster, streak, and other properties. People often think of minerals as gems, but not all minerals are gems. Many minerals are metal ores and salts. Likewise, not all gems are minerals. For example, pearls and amber are both produced through biological processes.

Iron and Steel

Iron is found in mineral compounds in Earth's crust. It is often used to make gates, railings, and fireplace tools. Iron is also used to make steel, an even harder and tougher metal alloy. Steel is made by treating molten (melted) iron with intense heat and mixing (alloying) it with carbon. Steel is used to make machines, cars, knives, and many tools.

Motion

Describing Motion

Many of the objects are in motion or have parts that are in motion. Even though these objects can be very different, the physical laws governing their motion are the same. When an object moves, its position changes as a function of time. The speed of an object is the rate at which the object covers distance. So, one way we can describe the motion of an object is to tell the speed at which it moves, or the distance it covers, in a specified period of time. The movement of an object can also be described in relation to its position. Position must be given in relation to some agreed-upon reference point. It is not enough to just specify the distance from the reference point; the direction must also be given. For example, you can tell the position of an object by describing its relationship to another object: For example, *the ball landed three feet to the right of the tree.*

Ways Things Move

As forces act upon them, different objects move in different ways. Marbles roll when pushed. Tops spin and eggs wobble. Rubber bands move back and forth very fast when pulled. Guitar strings vibrate. Some things, like falling rocks or diving hawks, move fast and make a straight path as they fall or dive. Others, like river barges or turtles, move slowly. We can observe and describe how different objects move, and categorize their movements by the paths they take, or their speed, or whether they move the same over and over again.

What Makes Things Move

A force is needed to make something move or stop moving. A force is always a push or a pull, whether gravity, friction, magnetism, or electricity. We use pushes and pulls to change the position and motion of objects. When you throw a ball, for example, your push sets the ball on a path. The ball may begin its path on a straight line, but that soon changes as the force of gravity pulls it down. The ball drops to Earth and the force of friction soon makes it roll to a stop. If you could escape from Earth's gravity and throw the same ball, the ball's straight path could be endless. With no forces acting upon it, the ball would never stop. Things in the universe tend to stay in motion unless forces act upon them.

Natural Resources

Energy Resources

Natural resources that provide people with energy are called *energy resources*. Sunlight is an energy resource that provides light and heat. The energy of sunlight can also be changed into electricity. Other energy resources include wind (moving air), tidal or current (moving water), and fuels such as wood, coal, gasoline, and oil.

Material Resources

Minerals, water, plants, animals, rocks, and soil are all *material resources*. Some of these things can be used to make different products. For example, sand is used to make glass, and wheat kernels are ground up to make flour. **Renewable Resources** are those that are regularly replaced or replenished by nature. Plants, animals, and water are renewable resources. Plants and animals reproduce to make more of their own kind. Thus when some plants are harvested, new plants can be grown to take their place. Water is replaced through the water cycle. Some natural resources are forever lost when used. Others take many years to be replaced by natural processes. **Nonrenewable resources** are those that can be used only once, or those that are not replaced by nature nearly as quickly as they are used. Oil, coal, and natural gas are considered nonrenewable resources because it takes millions of years for them to form. Minerals, including metals, are also considered nonrenewable resources. All natural resources must be used with care. Nonrenewable resources can be used up, making them unavailable to people in the future. Even renewable resources can be polluted or destroyed if not treated carefully.

Oceans

Ocean Plants and Animals

Algae are plant-like organisms that live in the oceans. They are not considered to be true plants because they have no transport system to carry water and nutrients. Algae include seaweeds and kelp. Some, such as kelp, can grow up to 30.5 m (100 ft) long. Others are single cells and can be seen only with a microscope. Ocean animals live where they can meet their needs. Most ocean plants and animals live in or near shallow water or near the surface of the open ocean.

Oceans

One large body of water covers almost three-fourths of Earth's surface. This body of water is separated into five regions—the Pacific, Atlantic, Indian, Southern, and Arctic Oceans. The largest ocean is the Pacific Ocean. It covers a third of Earth's surface and extends from the Arctic Ocean to Antarctica's Ross Sea. It contains about half of all the water on Earth. Oceans border all of Earth's large landmasses.

Sea Water

As water, wind, and chemical action eroded rocks, rivers carried the elements that make up salts into the ocean. On average, water in the world's ocean has a salinity of about 3.5 percent. However, sea water is not uniformly salty throughout the world. The Red Sea is the world's saltiest open sea, while Earth's freshest sea is the Gulf of Finland.

Planetary Cycles

Rotation and Revolution

Earth has two primary motions within the solar system. It rotates, or spins, on its axis once every 23 hours, 56 minutes, 4.1 seconds. A point at the equator spins at about 1,600 km per hour (about 1,000 mph); a point at 45° North rotates more slowly at approximately 1,073 km per hour (about 667 mph). In addition to its spinning motion, Earth is also revolving around the sun in an elliptical orbit. Traveling through space at about 106,000 km per hour (66,000 mph), it takes approximately 365 days for Earth to make one complete revolution around the sun, the length of one year. Every four years, the calendar includes an extra day to accommodate the additional time.

Plants

Types of Plants

Plants can be divided into two groups—flowering plants and nonflowering plants. Flowering plants have special parts that make seeds. Seeds are the first stage of growth for many plants. Roses and lilies are kinds of plants that have flowers. A conifer is one type of nonflowering plant. Conifers are plants that have cones instead of flowers. The seeds are made inside of cones, which hold and protect the seeds. After some time, the seeds will be ready to grow into new plants. When this happens, the cone will open and the seeds will fall out. Most conifers have needle-shaped leaves that stay green all year. Many conifers do not shed their leaves like other plants. Pines, spruce, firs, cypress, and yews are kinds of conifers.

What Plants Need

Plants need light, water, and air to produce food through a process called *photosynthesis*. This process takes place in the plant leaves and green stems. These parts contain chlorophyll, which enables the plant to use water, carbon dioxide from the air, and light energy from the sun to make sugars. Plants then use the sugars to grow and to form flowers, seeds, and fruit. Soil supplies nutrients, which are certain chemical elements that plants need to live. Plants grown hydroponically, or in a growing solution, get these nutrients from the solution. Plants that grow aeroponically, or in air, get the nutrients and moisture they need from air.

Plant Nutrients

All plants need certain chemical elements to live. Elements they need in large amounts, called macronutrients, include carbon, hydrogen, oxygen, sulfur, phosphorus, nitrogen, potassium, calcium, and magnesium. Nutrients needed in smaller amounts, called micronutrients, include copper, zinc, iron, nickel, and other minerals. Plants get oxygen and carbon through their leaves and absorb other elements through their roots. Most root absorption takes place from the soil; however, plants grown hydroponically, or in water, obtain the minerals they need from a mineral-rich growing solution. Plants grown aeroponically, or in air, have their roots sprayed with a mineral-rich solution.

Plant Parts

Plants have parts that are adapted to get what the plants needs. Most roots grow underground and absorb water and nutrients. Roots also anchor the plant. Some roots, called taproots, are thick. Other roots, called fibrous roots, are thin and spread out. Stems support a plant's leaves and flowers and improve the plant's ability to absorb water and nutrients. Some stems, such as tree trunks and limbs, are woody. Leaves make most of the food that the plant needs in a process called photosynthesis. The leaves contain chlorophyll, which enables them to use light energy to combine water and carbon dioxide to make the plant's food. Some plants reproduce from seeds. Seed plants are divided into two main groups. In flowering plants, the fruit protects the seeds. In conifers, such as pines and firs, seeds are made in cones.

Seeds

Seeds use their stored food to initiate sprouting. Seeds have three other requirements for continued growth—warmth, oxygen, and water. They absorb water from the soil through their coats. They get oxygen from air, which is trapped between soil particles. Warmth is usually provided by the sun.

Parts of a Seed

Seeds have many different sizes, shapes, and colors. The outside of a seed is the seed coat. This covering protects the seed. Some seeds, such as those of the coconut palm, have additional protection in the form of shells or husks. The fleshy part of the seed, called the cotyledon, is food for the embryo, which is the beginning of a new plant. The radicle is the first part of the plant to grow from the seed. It is the root of the plant embryo. The radicle holds the seedling in the soil and absorbs water that the seedling needs for growth. The shoot, which consists of both stems and leaves, emerges after the root.

Fruit

Most fruits contain seeds. Through fruits, plants are able to disperse their seeds with the help of various animals. Oranges, cherries, and tomatoes are all considered a kind of berry. Blackberries and strawberries are a different kind of berry. Both kinds ripen into a sweet, moist fruit, which is attractive to the animals that eat them. Then the seeds pass, unharmed, through the animal's digestive tract and are deposited on the soil in a new location. Fruits are an important part of the human diet because they provide the body with vitamins, such as vitamin C, and dietary fiber. Humans eat fruit in the forms of fresh fruit, jams, jellies, and pickles. Fruits can be packed in cans or jars or frozen to preserve them or transport them.

Properties of Matter

Density

The density of a material is a measure of how closely together its matter is packed. An object with a low density, such as a block of balsa wood, floats because its material is less dense than water. The opposite is true of a high density object, such as a golf ball. A golf ball sinks because it is denser than water. A large ship can float because its mass is spread out and a large part of its volume is air, so its average density is lower than that of water.

Matter

Matter refers to everything in the universe that occupies space and has mass. Matter is made up of microscopic particles called atoms. Matter generally exists in three states: solid, liquid, and gas. Although there is a fourth state called plasma, it is not common in our everyday world. Each kind of matter can be identified by its specific properties, or special qualities, such as smell, taste, size, shape, color, mass, and solubility. All matter shares two properties: taking up space and having mass. However, two objects cannot occupy the same place at the same time. All substances are made from more than 110 different elements, which, when combined differently, produce millions of materials with different properties.

Rocks

Rocks and How They Are Used

Rocks are naturally occurring solid objects made of one or more minerals. Rocks are found all over the surface of Earth, from the tops of mountains to the ocean floor. They vary in color, depending on the kinds of minerals in them, or in texture, depending on the size of the mineral grains. Earth's crust is made up of three different groups of rocks. Igneous rocks form when molten rock such as magma or lava cools. Granite and basalt are types of igneous rocks. Sedimentary rocks form when sediments are cemented together or when chemicals precipitate from ocean water. Sandstone, limestone, and shale are types of sedimentary rock. Metamorphic rocks form when any type of rock is subjected to enough heat and pressure to change it without melting. Slate and marble are types of metamorphic rock. People use rocks for building roads and structures, as well as for jewelry and other products, including materials such as chalk.

Weathering

Weathering is the process that changes the surface of rocks. There are two types of weathering, physical and chemical. During physical weathering, rocks are broken down into smaller rocks by force. One example of physical weathering is when water seeps into the cracks of large rocks. When this water freezes, it expands and breaks the rock into smaller pieces. Plant roots can also grow in the cracks of rocks and cause weathering. Physical weathering can also be caused by thermal expansion, which is the constant heating and cooling of rocks. Chemical weathering is when the makeup of a rock changes into a new substance when reacting to a chemical. Oxidation, hydrolysis, and acid rain are examples of chemical weathering.

Scientific Method

Scientific Method

The scientific method is based on evidence instead of belief. It permits the acquisition of new scientific knowledge that is based on physical evidence. The essential elements of the scientific method can be summarized in four steps—characterization of the subject of the investigation, which is accomplished by observation; the formulation of a hypothesis, which provides a causal explanation of the subject; the statement of a prediction that can be experimentally assessed; and the design of an experiment to test the hypothesis. The scientific process is iterative, which means that at any stage, scientists may repeat a part of the process. The results must also be verifiable, which means the results of an investigation must be able to be reproduced by others.

Scientific Tools

Temperature and Temperature Scales

Temperature is a measure of how hot or cold something is. It should not be confused with heat, a form of energy that flows. Temperature can be measured on three scales: Fahrenheit, Celsius, and Kelvin. On the Fahrenheit scale, the temperature of boiling water is 212 °F and of water freezing is 32 °F. There are 180° between them. On the Celsius scale, the temperature of boiling water is 100 °C and of water freezing is 0 °C. Each degree is one-hundredth of the difference between the two points on the scale. The Kelvin scale begins at the lowest theoretically possible temperature, which is called absolute zero, zero K, or zero Kelvins. This is the same as -273 °C.

History of the Microscope

Magnifiers are mentioned in writings dating from the first century A.D. The earliest simple microscope, called a flea glass, was a tube with a plate for the object at one end and a lens at the other. Late in the sixteenth century, two Dutch spectacle makers developed the forerunner of the compound microscope and telescope. In 1609, Galileo made an instrument with a focusing device. The father of microscopy, Anton van Leeuwenhoek, of Holland, taught himself to grind and polish tiny lenses with great curvature that yielded magnifications. This led to his building microscopes and his famous biological discoveries. He was the first to see and describe bacteria, yeast plants, and the teeming of life in a single drop of pond water.

Science Tools

Scales and balances are scientific tools used in homes as well as in scientific laboratories. A balance measures the mass of an object. The most basic tool for measuring mass is the pan balance. A pan balance uses a bar with a pan hanging from each end. At the center of the bar is a support, called a fulcrum, on which the bar can balance. The Egyptians used a balance of this kind as early as 2500 B.C. Scales measure weight and other forces.

Seasons

The Seasons

Earth's changing seasons are a result of Earth having a tilted axis that remains in a fixed position as the planet orbits the sun. As Earth orbits, its tilt affects how much sunlight reaches different parts of the planet. Opposite hemispheres experience opposite seasons. At the beginning of spring and fall, Earth's axis points neither toward nor away from the sun. On these days, called equinoxes, day and night are almost equal. From this point onward in spring in the Northern Hemisphere, days grow longer until the summer solstice (June 21 or June 22), which marks the longest day of the year. The converse happens in fall. The days grow shorter until the winter solstice (December 21 or December 22), which marks the shortest day of the year.

Soil

Soil and How It Is Used

Soil is a mixture of small particles, including bits of rock and decaying plant and animal matter. The particles are covered with a film of water and surrounded by air. The decaying material in soil, or humus, makes soil brown and fertile. The more humus, the darker brown a soil will appear and the richer it is for growing. Humus makes up the top layer of fertile soil. Beneath this is a layer of rocky soil that formed as solid rock eroded. Many plants and animals as well as helpful bacteria and fungi live in soil. Small animals, such as earthworms and centipedes, are large enough to be seen. Others, such as soil mites, require a hand lens to be seen. People use soil to grow plants and to build things. Adobe and clay bricks are examples of soil used as building materials. Animals also use soil to build things. Many birds and insects use mud to build nests.

Solar System

Earth's Rotation and Revolution

Earth revolves, or circles, around the sun. Earth also spins, or rotates, on its axis as it revolves around the sun. We cannot feel Earth spinning, but it makes one complete turn in one day. This is why we have day and night. When the part of Earth where we live is facing the sun, we have day. When the part of Earth where we live faces away from the sun, we have night.

The Moon

Although children may think the moon and sun are the same size, the sun is really about 400 times the size of the moon. What we call moonlight is actually sunlight reflecting off the moon's surface. The moon itself has no light. We see half of the illuminated side of the moon when looking at a first-quarter or third-quarter moon. The first-quarter phase of the moon is labeled as such because it is one-quarter of the way through the lunar cycle. The third-quarter moon is three-quarters of the way through the cycle.

Satellites

An artificial, or human-made, satellite is any object placed into orbit around Earth and used for scientific and technological purposes. Most satellites are used for communication, military purposes, or scientific research. Scientific research satellites are used to explore Earth's atmosphere and space near Earth, to make images of Earth's surface or ocean floor, to track weather patterns, and to image astronomical objects without the interference of Earth's atmosphere. *Sputnik 1*, launched by the Soviet Union on October 4, 1957, was the world's first artificial satellite. *Sputnik 1* was about the size of a basketball. Then on November 3, the Soviets launched a second satellite. It contained a small dog, named Laika. Three months later, the United States launched its first satellite, *Explorer 1*. Today, many satellites are orbiting Earth.

Sound

Loudness

The loudness of a sound refers to how strong the sound seems to people when they hear it. The intensity of a sound is determined by the amount of energy in the sound waves. Sound wave energy is less concentrated as it spreads outward in all directions from a source. As a result, the loudness of a sound decreases as the distance increases between the listener and the source of the sound. The word volume is also used to refer to the loudness of a sound.

Sound

All sounds make air vibrate. We describe these vibrations as sound waves. When sound waves strike our eardrums, they make the eardrums vibrate. The vibrations are passed on inside our ears, and signals are sent to our brain. When our brain gets the message, we "hear" the sound. Sounds travel through solids, liquids, and gases, but they travel fastest through solids.

Making Sound

All sounds—whether they are high or low, loud or soft—are made by a vibration. When an object vibrates, it causes the air around it to vibrate. The vibrations travel away from their point of origin in all directions. The vibrations can travel through gases, liquids, and solids. Humans produce sound in a section of the throat called the larynx. Two folds of membrane, called the vocal cords, cross the larynx. Between the vocal cords is an opening, or slit. When the vocal cords are relaxed, air rushes through the slit causing little or no vibration. When the vocal cords are tight, such as during speech, the rushing air causes the vocal cords to vibrate, which, in turn, causes sound. The tighter the vocal cords, the faster the vibration and the higher pitched the sound.

Stars

Stars

Stars are enormous bodies of gas in space. The sun is a star that provides light and heat to Earth. Although the daytime skies are as full of stars as the nighttime skies, distant stars are not visible in the daytime. This is because the amount of light the sun radiates to the part of Earth facing it outshines the light from other stars. At night, when Earth's rotation has turned us away from the sun's light, the more-distant stars are visible to us.

Constellations

There are billions of stars in the sky. Without using a telescope, a person can see about 2,000 stars on a clear night. Some of these stars form 88 official constellations, which include 14 people, 40 realistic animals, 2 centaurs, a flying horse, a dragon, and 30 inanimate objects. One constellation is called Ursa Minor. The seven brightest stars of this constellation comprise what is known as the Little Dipper. The star at the end of the handle of the Little Dipper is the North Star. It shows which direction is north. For hundreds of years, the North Star helped sailors navigate the ocean waters before compasses and other nautical tools were invented.

Water Cycle

The Water Cycle

Facts about the water cycle:

- People are part of the water cycle. A large percent of the human body is water. In fact, 75 percent of the brain is water!
- Earth contains the same amount of water today as it did when it first formed. Because water cycles continuously, the water you used to brush your teeth this morning could include water once used by dinosaurs.
- Water is one of the few substances that expands instead of shrinks when it freezes. This is why ice floats on liquid water.
- Only about 3 percent of Earth's water is fresh water (mostly ice); the rest is salt water.

Teacher Notes

Teacher Notes

Science Songs

ENGLISH LYRICS

Unit 1: How Scientists Work

My Senses (to the tune of I've Been Working on the Railroad)

I've been using all my senses,
All the live, long day.
I've been using all my senses,
Just to help me find my way.

I taste, touch, hear, see, and smell things.
Senses make me feel alive.
I taste, touch, hear, see, and smell things.
I like to use all five!

I use my eyes and ears
I use my eyes and ears
I use my eyes and ears and mouth and nose.

I use my eyes and ears
I use my eyes and ears
And my fingers and my toes!

Unit 2: Technology All Around Us

Technology Is All Around
(to the tune of Mary Had a Little Lamb)

Technology is all around.
All around,
all around.
Technology is all around.
It helps us to solve problems.

SPANISH LYRICS

Unidad 1: Cómo trabajan los científicos

Mis sentidos (al ritmo de I've Been Working on the Railroad)

Yo siempre uso mis sentidos,
los uso todos los días.
Yo siempre uso mis sentidos,
los sentidos son mi guía.

Oigo, toco, siento, veo, saboreo
y así me siento vivo.
Oigo, toco, siento, veo, saboreo
¡Uso todos mis sentidos!

Uso los ojos
uso los oídos
también la boca y la nariz.

Uso los ojos
uso los oídos
¡Y los dedos de los pies!

Unidad 2: La tecnología que nos rodea

La tecnología nos rodea
(al ritmo de Mary Had a Little Lamb)

La tecnología siempre está.
siempre está,
siempre está.
La tecnología siempre está.
para resolver problemas.

ENGLISH LYRICS

Unit 3: Matter

Matter Everywhere! (to the tune of Oh My Darling)

What is matter?
What is matter?
It is everything you see.
Toys and books and trees and flowers.
It is even you and me!

Classify it!
Classify it!
You can tell what matter's like.
Color, shape, and size and texture.
These are matter's properties.

SPANISH LYRICS

Unidad 3: La materia

¡Todo es materia! (al ritmo de Oh My Darling)

La materia
la materia
es todo lo que vemos.
Casas, libros, juguetes y flores.
¡También somos tú y yo!

Es muy fácil
es muy fácil
conocer sus cualidades.
Color, forma, tamaño y textura.
esas son sus propiedades.

ENGLISH LYRICS

Unit 4: Forces and Energy

In Motion! (to the tune of This Is the Way)

How do things get from here to there?
Here to there?
Here to there?

How do things get from here to there?
How do objects move?

Up and down and back and forth,
back and forth
back and forth.

Up and down and back and forth,
That's how objects move.

Round and round and fast and slow
fast and slow
fast and slow.

Round and round and fast and slow,
That's how objects move.

In a line or zig and zag,
zig and zag
zig and zag.

In a line or zig and zag,
That's how objects move.

SPANISH LYRICS

Unidad 4: Las fuerzas y la energía

¡En movimiento! (al ritmo de This Is the Way)

¿Cómo me muevo de aquí para allá?
¿De aquí para allá?
¿De aquí para allá?

¿Cómo me muevo de aquí para allá?
¿Cómo hace un objeto?

Arriba, abajo, atrás y adelante,
atrás y adelante
atrás y adelante.

Arriba, abajo, atrás y adelante,
se mueve un objeto.

Muy despacito y muy veloz
muy veloz,
muy veloz.

En circulitos, lento y veloz,
se mueve un objeto.

En línea recta o en zigzag,
en zigzag,
en zigzag.

En línea recta o en zigzag,
se mueve un objeto.

Unit 5: Earth's Resources

Reduce, Reuse, Recycle!
(to the tune of Pop Goes the Weasel)

You can help save resources.
Everyone is able.
Practice doing the three Rs,
Reduce, reuse, recycle!

Unidad 5: Los recursos de la Tierra

¡Reduce, reutilizar y reciclar!
(al ritmo de Pop Goes the Weasel)

Reduce, reutiliza y recicla también,
así ahorrarás recursos.
Erre, erre, erre,
¡erre sí se puede!

ENGLISH LYRICS

SPANISH LYRICS

Unit 6: Weather and Seasons

The Four Seasons (to the tune of I'm a Little Teapot)

I know all the seasons.
There are four.
Winter then spring, then summer and fall.
Earth orbits the sun,
It takes one year.
It makes the weather different here.

Unidad 6: El estado del tiempo y las estaciones del año

Las cuatro estaciones (al ritmo de I'm a Little Teapot)

Las cuatro estaciones
del año estas son.
Invierno, primavera, verano y otoño.
Pasa que la Tierra orbita al Sol,
cada año se repite la misma estación.
la vuelta se completa como una canción.

Unit 7: Objects in the Sky

Eye on the Sky (to the tune of Hot Cross Buns)

Daytime sky,
Daytime sky,
You see the sun,
It warms the Earth
And gives us light.

Nighttime sky,
Nighttime sky,
You see the moon,
And all the stars,
Way up high!

Unidad 7: Objetos en el cielo

Ojo con el cielo (al ritmo de Hot Cross Buns)

Cielo de día,
Cielo de día,
Sale el Sol, sale el Sol,
Da luz a la Tierra
y nos da calor.

Cielo de noche,
Cielo de noche,
Sale la Luna, sale la Luna,
junto a las estrellas
a las que acuna.

Unit 8: Living Things and Their Environments

Are You Living? (to the tune of Frere Jacques)

Are you living? Are you living?
Yes, you are! Yes, you are!
You can breathe and grow.
You can breathe and grow.
And move, you know.
And move, you know.

Unidad 8: Los seres vivos y sus medio ambientes

¿Estás vivo? (al ritmo de Frere Jacques)

¿Estás vivo? ¿Estás vivo?
¡Sí, lo estás! ¡Sí, lo estás!
Respiras y creces.
Respiras y creces.
Y te mueves.
Y te mueves.

ENGLISH LYRICS

Unit 9: Animals

Grow, Grow, Grow Little Butterfly

(to the tune of Row, Row, Row Your Boat)

Lay, lay, lay, some eggs,
That's how some life cycles go.
It's how it starts, and soon you know,
New butterflies will grow.

Hatch, hatch, little egg,
It's oh so very small.
A teeny, tiny larva,
It's hard to see at all.

Creep, creep, crawl and eat,
It munches on a leaf.
Crawling, munching, crawling, munching,
Eat and eat and eat.

Spin, spin, spin, and spin,
Spin a chrysalis,
It makes a very special shape,
Then soon it will escape.

Rest in the chrysalis,
It's changing right inside;
Soon you'll see, its time has come,
To be a butterfly.

Stretch, stretch, those wings,
Today's a special day.
The wings will soon be strong enough
For it to fly away.

Fly, fly, butterfly,
It flies from tree to tree.
It finds a spot to lay some eggs,
So they can grow like me.

SPANISH LYRICS

Unidad 9: Los animales

Crece, crece, crece mariposita

(al ritmo de Row, Row, Row Your Boat)

Pon, pon, pon huevitos
de vidas hermosas.
Así el ciclo comienza y ya,
saldrán las mariposas.

Rompe, rompe el cascarón,
pequeñita es.
La larvita diminuta,
que apenas sí se ve.

Come, come, se desliza,
mastica una hojita.
Come, come y se desliza,
en la hojita más rica.

Teje, teje y teje más,
la crisálida,
Teje una forma muy especial,
de donde escapará.

Descansa la crisálida,
le cambia cada cosa.
El tiempo pasa, pasa y pasa,
será una mariposa.

Estira, estira las alitas,
que el día está pasando.
Esas alitas te servirán,
para salir volando.

Vuela, vuela mariposa,
vuela de flor en flor.
Busca poner todos tus huevitos,
que crezcan como yo.

ENGLISH LYRICS

Unit 10: Plants

Amazing Plant Parts

(to the tune of John Jacob Jingleheimer Schmidt)

You can find plenty kinds of plants.
How can you tell them apart?
Different parts and shapes.
Different in many ways.
Stems, roots, and leaves, flowers, and seeds.
So many different plants!

SPANISH LYRICS

Unidad 10: Las plantas

Lo fantástico de las plantas

(al ritmo de John Jacob Jingleheimer Schmidt)

Hay muchas plantas que observar.
¿Cómo saber cuál es cuál?
Tienen formas sin igual,
que puedes diferenciar.
Tallo, raíz, hojas, flores y semillas.
¡Tan distintas maravillas!

Science Trade Books

Bibliography

Literature as Part of Science Instruction

This bibliography is a compilation of trade books listed for Grades 1–2. Many of the books are recommendations of The National Science Teachers Association (NSTA) and The Children's Book Council (CBC) as outstanding science trade books for children.

The panel has reviewed these books following rigorous selection criteria: they are of literary quality and contain substantial science content; the theories and facts are clearly distinguished; they are free of gender, ethnic, and socioeconomic bias; and they contain clear, accurate up-to-date information. Other selections are award-winning titles, or their authors have received awards.

As with all materials you share with your class, we suggest you review the books first to ensure their appropriateness. While titles are current at time of publication, they may go out of print without notice.

Grade 1

All the Water in the World by George Ella Lyon (Atheneum, 2011) gives a lyrical look at all the places that we can find water and how it interacts with its different environments. AWARD-WINNING AUTHOR

Animals: Mammals, Birds, Reptiles, Amphibians, Fish, and Other Animals by Shar Levine (Crabtree Publishing Company, 2010) illustrates the major animal groups and highlights the traits that set them apart from one another.

Baby Animals of the World by Carmen Bredeson (Enslow Elementary, 2011) depicts baby animals in a variety of habitats and shows the nature of their relationship with their animal parents and the world around them.

The Boy Who Harnessed the Wind by William Kamkwamba (Dial, 2012) tells the story of one young man who saves his village from a drought by building a machine that could harness the wind and turn it into energy, bringing electricity to everyone.

Bugs! Bugs! Bugs! by Jennifer Dussling (DK Publishing, 2011) studies a variety of bugs found around the world and how they have adapted to interact with their habitats and survive.

Carrots Grow Underground by Mari Schuh (Capstone Press, 2011) illustrates all of the processes that aid in the growth of a carrot while it's still under the ground.

Done in the Sun: Solar Projects for Children by Anne Hillerman (Sunstone Press, 2012) uses hands-on experiments to illustrate solar energy to children and teach them how they can use it in their daily lives.

The EARTH Book by Todd Parr (Little, Brown Books for Young Readers, 2010) introduces children to the idea of conservation and shows them how it benefits everyone on the planet to adopt Earth-friendly ways of using resources and space.

Evaporation by William B. Rice (Teacher Created Materials, 2010) explains the concept of evaporation and illustrates the process that water goes through in order to become a gas.

Even an Octopus Needs a Home by Irene Kelly (Holiday House, 2011) shows how different species of animals have the common need for a place of safety and security and depicts these places while highlighting their differences and similarities. AWARD-WINNING AUTHOR

Explore Water!: 25 Great Projects, Activities, Experiments by Anita Yasuda (Nomad Press, 2011) teaches children about the properties of water and uses hands-on experiments to show them what it can do and how we encounter it in our daily activities.

Explorers: Weather by Deborah Chancellor (Kingfisher, 2010) educates children about weather as a concept, its different patterns, and how it affects our everyday lives.

Friends: True Stories of Extraordinary Animal Friendships by Catherine Thimmesh (Houghton Mifflin Harcourt, 2011) depicts several unlikely friendships between different species of animals and shows how sometimes those differences are the things that make a relationship work. AWARD-WINNING AUTHOR

From Flower to Honey by Robin Nelson (Lerner Pub Group, 2012) illustrates in-depth the step-by-step process with which bees make honey from the pollen that they collect from flowers and shows how plants and animals need one another to thrive.

Wonder Why Stars Twinkle by Carole Stott (Kingfisher, 2011) takes an engaging and un look at facts about space, what stars are made of, and why we see them the way we do.

'm a Scientist: Kitchen (DK Publishing, 2010) explores the different technologies we use in our home kitchens and uses experiments s a way to make children comfortable with the nplements their parents use every day.

earning About Rocks by Mari Schuh Capstone Press, 2011) offers a look at the ifferent kinds of rocks used as the building ocks for both nature and the architecture ound us.

The Little Plant Doctor: A Story About George Washington Carver by Jean Marzollo (Holiday House, 2011) introduces the early life and work of George Washington Carver and encourages children to be curious about the world around them. AWARD-WINNING AUTHOR

Many Biomes, One Earth by Sneed B. Collard III (Charlesbridge Publishing, 2009) explores the different biomes and environments found on different parts of the planet, from icy tundras to tropical forests. AWARD-WINNING AUTHOR

Many Kinds of Matter by Jennifer Boothroyd (Lerner Classroom, 2011) depicts solids, liquids, and gases, how they are formed, and how they differ from one another.

Matter Comes in All Shapes by Amy Hansen (Teacher Created Resources, 2011) introduces children to the concept of different forms of matter and illustrates the characteristics that make them what they are.

Motion, Magnets, and More by Adrienne Mason (Kids Can Press, 2011) provides an introduction to the physical sciences and illustrates how the different forms of matter interact with one another.

National Geographic Readers: Planets by Elizabeth Carney (National Geographic Children's Books, 2012) depicts the planets in our solar system and explains what makes them different from each other and other solar bodies. AWARD-WINNING AUTHOR

Plant Adaptations by Julie K. Lundgren (Rourke Publishing Company, 2011) illustrates the ways in which plants adapt to different environments and explains the characteristics that make it possible for them to carry out that adaptation.

Roller Coaster by Marla Frazee (Live Oak Media, 2012) profiles roller coasters with the use of rhyming text.

Secrets of the Garden: Food Chains and the Food Web in Our Backyard by Kathleen Weidner Zoehfeld (Knopf Books for Young Readers, 2012) explores the ways in which plants and animals help each other through cohabitation and adaptation.

Snow Joe by Carol Green (Children's Press, 2011) shows the effect winter weather has on daily activities and the environment.

Super Simple Things to Do with Temperature by Kelly Doudna (Super Sandcastle, 2011) introduces children to the concept of temperature and how it affects the world around them through simple, hands-on science experiments.

Using Your Senses by Rebecca Rissman (Heinemann, 2011) explains the five senses to readers and shows how our senses help us in our daily lives.

What Floats? What Sinks? A Look at Density by Jennifer Boothroyd (Lerner Classroom, 2010) introduces the concept of density and shows the ways in which we can observe force being acted on an object in order to make it float or sink.

When Does Water Turn Into Ice? by Josephine Selwyn (Three Crows Media, 2012) teaches children about the freezing point of water and explains why and how water changes states with different temperatures.

Where in the Wild?: Camouflaged Creatures Concealed…and Revealed by David M. Schwartz, Yael Schy (Tricycle Press, 2011) takes a look at how body coverings help animals to survive through the use of camouflage in different environments. 2008 AMERICAN ASSOCIATION FOR THE ADVANCEMENT OF SCIENCE PRIZE FOR EXCELLENCE IN SCIENCE BOOKS; NTSA & CBC OUTSTANDING SCIENCE TRADE BOOK

Where the Sunrise Begins by Douglas Wood (Simon & Schuster, 2010) answers questions about how the sun seems to move around Earth by showing how the sun rises on different parts of the globe.

Why Do Moving Objects Slow Down? by Jennifer Boothroyd (Lerner Classroom, 2010) introduces the concept of friction and explores the ways it affects objects in motion.

The Wild, Wild Southwest! by Jeff Corwin (Puffin, 2012) uses a fictional park official and three budding naturalists to explore the wilds of New Mexico and explain its habitats for young readers.

Wow! Said the Owl by Tim Hopgood (Farrar, Straus, & Giroux, 2011) illustrates the differences between day and night in a fun fictional story about an owl who wants to see it all. AWARD-WINNING AUTHOR

Teacher Notes

Correlation to

ScienceSaurus

ScienceSaurus, ***A Student Handbook,*** is a "mini-encyclopedia" students can use to find out more about unit topics. It contains numerous resources including concise content summaries; an almanac; many tables, charts, and graphs; and a glossary. ***ScienceSaurus*** is available from Houghton Mifflin Harcourt.

ScienceFusion Grade 1	*ScienceSaurus* Topics	*ScienceSaurus* Pages
Unit 1 How Scientists Work		
Lesson 1 What Are Senses?	Doing Science, Science Is Observing	pp. 2–3
Lesson 2 How Can We Use Our Senses?	Doing Science, Science Is Observing	pp. 2–3
Lesson 3 What Are Inquiry Skills?	Doing Science, Science Is Observing Doing Science, Doing an Investigation	pp. 2–3 pp. 4–7
Lesson 4 How Do We Use Inquiry Skills?	Doing Science, Science Is Observing Doing Science, Doing an Investigation	pp. 4–7
Lesson 5 What Are Science Tools?	Doing Science, Using Science Tools	pp. 8–11
Lesson 6 How Do Scientists Work?	Doing Science, Doing an Investigation Doing Science, Using Science Tools	pp. 4–7 pp. 8–11
People in Science—Mary Anderson	Doing Science, Using the Design Process Earth Science, Weather and Seasons	pp. 12–15 pp. 64–68
Unit 2 Technology All Around Us		
Lesson 1 How Do Engineers Work?	Doing Science, Using the Design Process	pp. 12–15
Lesson 2 How Can We Solve a Problem?	Doing Science, Using the Design Process	pp. 12–15
Lesson 3 What Materials Make Up Objects?	Doing Science, Using the Design Process Earth Science, Natural Resources	pp. 12–15 pp. 80–87
Lesson 4 How Can Materials Be Sorted?	Doing Science, Using the Design Process	pp. 12–15
People in Science—Dr. Eugene Tsui	Doing Science, Using the Design Process Life Science, Living Things	pp. 12–15 pp. 18–45

ScienceFusion Grade 1	*ScienceSaurus* Topics	*ScienceSaurus* Pages
Unit 3 Matter		
Lesson 1 What Can We Observe About Objects?	Doing Science, Science Is Observing Physical Science, Matter	pp. 2–3 pp. 92–99
Careers in Science—Polymer Scientist	Doing Science, Doing an Investigation Doing Science, Using the Design Process Earth Science, Natural Resources	pp. 4–7 pp. 12–15 pp. 88–89
Lesson 2 How Can We Measure Temperature?	Doing Science, Using Science Tools Physical Science, Matter	p. 9 pp. 102–103
Lesson 3 How Does Heating and Cooling Change Matter?	Doing Science, Using Science Tools Physical Science, Matter Physical Science, Matter	p. 9 pp. 95–97 pp. 102–103
S.T.E.M. Engineering and Technology—Kitchen Technology	Doing Science, Using Science Tools Doing Science, Using the Design Process	pp. 8–11 pp. 12–15
Unit 4 Forces and Energy		
Lesson 1 How Do We Use Energy?	Physical Science, Energy	pp. 104–108
Lesson 2 How Do Magnets Move Objects?	Physical Science, Motion and Forces	pp. 118–119
Lesson 3 How Do Objects Move?	Physical Science, Motion and Forces	pp. 110–113
People in Science—Isaac Newton	Physical Science, Motion and Forces Physical Science, Motion and Forces	pp. 110–113 pp. 116–117
Lesson 4 How Can We Move a Ball?	Physical Science, Motion and Forces	pp. 110–117
Lesson 5 How Can We Change the Way Objects Move?	Physical Science, Motion and Forces	pp. 110–117
S.T.E.M. Engineering and Technology—Fly to the Sky	Physical Science, Motion and Forces	pp. 114–117

ScienceFusion Grade 1	*ScienceSaurus* Topics	*ScienceSaurus* Pages
Unit 5 Earth's Resources		
Lesson 1 What Can We Find on Earth?	Earth Science, Water and Land Earth Science, Natural Resources	pp. 54–55 pp. 80–89
People in Science—Dr. George Washington Carver	Doing Science, Doing an Investigation Earth Science, Water and Land Earth Science, Natural Resources Earth Science, Natural Resources	pp. 4–7 p. 63 p. 85 pp. 88–89
Lesson 2 What Is Soil?	Earth Science, Water and Land Earth Science, Natural Resources	p. 63 p. 85
Lesson 3 What Do We Find in Soil?	Earth Science, Water and Land Earth Science, Natural Resources	p. 63 p. 85
Lesson 4 How Do Soils Differ?	Earth Science, Water and Land Earth Science, Natural Resources	p. 63 p. 85
Lesson 5 Where Can We Find Water?	Earth Science, Water and Land	pp. 54–57
S.T.E.M. Engineering and Technology—Technology and the Environment	Doing Science, Using the Design Process Life Science, Animals Earth Science, Natural Resources	pp. 12–15 p. 36 pp. 86–89
Lesson 6 How Can We Save Resources?	Earth Science, Natural Resources	pp. 88–89
Unit 6 Weather and Seasons		
Lesson 1 What Is Weather?	Earth Science, Weather and Seasons	pp. 64–68
Lesson 2 What Can We Observe About Weather?	Earth Science, Weather and Seasons	pp. 64–68
People in Science—June Bacon-Bercey	Earth Science, Weather and Seasons	pp. 64–72
Lesson 3 What Are Seasons?	Earth Science, Weather and Seasons	pp. 69–72
S.T.E.M. Engineering and Technology—Weather Wisdom	Doing Science, Using Science Tools	pp. 8–11

ScienceFusion Grade 1	*ScienceSaurus* Topics	*ScienceSaurus* Pages
Unit 7 Objects in the Sky		
Lesson 1 What Can We See in the Sky?	Earth Science, Space	pp. 73–79
People in Science —Galileo Galilei	Doing Science, Using Science Tools Earth Science, Space	pp. 8–11 pp. 73–77
Lesson 2 How Does the Sky Seem to Change?	Earth Science, Space Earth Science, Space	pp. 73–75 pp. 78–79
Lesson 3 How Does the Sun Seem to Move?	Earth Science, Space	pp. 78–79
S.T.E.M. Engineering and Technology—See the Light	Doing Science, Using Science Tools Doing Science, Using the Design Process	pp. 8–11 pp. 13–15
Unit 8 Living Things and Their Environments		
Lesson 1 What Are Living and Nonliving Things?	Life Science, Living Things	pp. 18–19
Lesson 2 Where Do Plants and Animals Live?	Life Science, Living Things Life Science, Plants Life Science, Animals Life Science, Environments and Ecosystems	pp. 18–19 pp. 20–22 pp. 31–37 pp. 46–51
Careers in Science—Forest Ranger	Life Science, Plants Life Science, Animals Life Science, Environments and Ecosystems	pp. 20–28 pp. 29–45 pp. 46–51
Lesson 3 What Is a Terrarium?	Life Science, Plants Life Science, Animals Life Science, Environments and Ecosystems	pp. 20–28 pp. 29–45 pp. 46–51
S.T.E.M. Engineering and Technology—A Place for Animals	Doing Science, Using the Design Process Life Science, Plants Life Science, Environments and Ecosystems	pp. 12–15 pp. 29–37 pp. 46–45
Unit 9 Animals		
Lesson 1 How Do Animals Differ?	Life Science, Animals	pp. 29–37
Lesson 2 How Can We Group Animals?	Life Science, Animals Life Science, Animals	pp. 32–37 pp. 40–45
S.T.E.M. Engineering and Technology—On the Farm	Doing Science, Using the Design Process	pp. 12–15
Lesson 3 What Are Some Animal Life Cycles?	Life Science, Animals	pp. 40–45
Careers in Science—Zookeeper	Life Science, Animals	pp. 29–45

ScienceFusion Grade 1	*ScienceSaurus* Topics	*ScienceSaurus* Pages
Unit 10 Plants		
Lesson 1 What Are Some Parts of Plants?	Life Science, Plants	pp. 23–26
People in Science—Dr. Norma Alcantar	Life Science, Plants Earth Science, Water and Land Earth Science, Natural Resources	pp. 20–28 pp. 50–51 pp. 86–87
Lesson 2 How Are Plants Different?	Life Science, Plants	pp. 20–28
Lesson 3 How Can We Compare Leaves?	Life Science, Plants	p. 25
S.T.E.M. Engineering and Technology: Warm It Up	Doing Science, Using the Design Process Life Science, Plants	pp. 12–15 pp. 20–28
All Units		
These topics may be used with all units and lessons	Almanac, Units of Measure Almanac, Graphs and Time Lines Yellow Pages, Glossary of Science Terms	pp. 121–123 pp. 124–125 pp. 126–135
These topics may be used with all investigations	Doing Science, Science is Observing Doing Science, Doing an Investigation Doing Science, Using Science Tools Almanac, Units of Measure Almanac, Graphs and Time Lines	pp. 2–3 pp. 4–7 pp. 8–11 pp. 121–123 pp. 124–125
This topic may be used with all S.T.E.M. features and S.T.E.M. Investigations	Doing Science, Using the Design Process	pp. 12–15

Teacher Notes

English Language Proficiency Standards

A correlation to the Texas Essential Knowledge and Skills for Science is located in the front of this Teacher Edition. Correlations to the English Language Proficiency Standards are provided on these pages.

Grade 1 ELPS ENGLISH LANGUAGE PROFICIENCY STANDARDS	Teacher Edition Pages
Cross-Curricular Second Language Acquisition/Learning Strategies	
1) Cross-curricular second language acquisition/learning strategies. The ELL uses language learning strategies to develop an awareness of his or her own learning processes in all content areas. In order for the ELL to meet grade-level learning expectations across the foundation and enrichment curriculum, all instruction delivered in English must be linguistically accommodated (communicated, sequenced, and scaffolded) commensurate with the student's level of English language proficiency. The student is expected to:	
(A) use prior knowledge and experiences to understand meanings in English	1L, 39, 51K, 87K, 121M, 147, 233K, 271, 393
(B) monitor oral and written language production and employ self-corrective techniques or other resources	377K
(C) use strategic learning techniques such as concept mapping, drawing, memorizing, comparing, contrasting, and reviewing to acquire basic and grade-level vocabulary	1M, 37, 51J, 87K, 121M, 175L, 191, 194, 271J, 277, 303J, 303K, 339K, 364, 382, 393
(D) speak using learning strategies such as requesting assistance, employing non-verbal cues, and using synonyms and circumlocution (conveying ideas by defining or describing when exact English words are not known)	121M, 162, 271K
(E) internalize new basic and academic language by using and reusing it in meaningful ways in speaking and writing activities that build concept and language attainment	1M, 15, 19, 26, 29, 51J, 55, 58, 92, 94, 106, 110, 125, 131, 136, 140, 147, 160, 178, 191, 194, 219, 236, 239, 255, 258, 286, 289, 309, 310, 318, 321, 342, 348, 364, 380, 382, 393, 395
(F) use accessible language and learn new and essential language in the process	1M, 51K, 72, 87K, 106, 110, 121M, 125, 131, 136, 140, 160, 175M, 236, 239, 286, 289, 309, 310
(H) develop and expand repertoire of learning strategies such as reasoning inductively or deductively, looking for patterns in language, and analyzing sayings and expressions commensurate with grade-level learning expectations	149
(2) Cross-curricular second language acquisition/listening. The ELL listens to a variety of speakers including teachers, peers, and electronic media to gain an increasing level of comprehension of newly acquired language in all content areas. ELLs may be at the beginning, intermediate, advanced, or advanced high stage of English language acquisition in listening. In order for the ELL to meet grade-level learning expectations across the foundation and enrichment curriculum, all instruction delivered in English must be linguistically accommodated (communicated, sequenced, and scaffolded) commensurate with the student's level of English language proficiency. The student is expected to:	
(A) distinguish sounds and intonation patterns of English with increasing ease	131
(B) recognize elements of the English sound system in newly acquired vocabulary such as long and short vowels, silent letters, and consonant clusters	51J, 233J, 303J, 377J

Grade 1 ELPS ENGLISH LANGUAGE PROFICIENCY STANDARDS	Teacher Edition Pages
(C) learn new language structures, expressions, and basic and academic vocabulary heard during classroom instruction and interactions	1M, 15, 19, 29, 37, 55, 58, 68, 72, 74, 87K, 92, 94, 121L, 121M, 147, 149, 175M, 204, 209, 219, 224, 233K, 255, 258, 271K, 277, 318, 321, 342, 348, 361, 364, 380, 395
(D) monitor understanding of spoken language during classroom instruction and interactions and seek clarification as needed	51K, 271K
(E) use visual, contextual, and linguistic support to enhance and confirm understanding of increasingly complex and elaborated spoken language	1M, 5, 7, 19, 26, 29, 55, 58, 68, 72, 74, 92, 94, 106, 110, 121M, 125, 131, 136, 140, 149, 160, 162, 175L, 175M, 178, 204, 209, 219, 239, 277, 286, 289, 309, 310, 318, 321, 342, 348, 364, 377K, 382, 395
(G) understand the general meaning, main points, and important details of spoken language ranging from situations in which topics, language, and contexts are familiar to unfamiliar	87K
(I) demonstrate listening comprehension of increasingly complex spoken English by following directions, retelling or summarizing spoken messages, responding to questions and requests, collaborating with peers, and taking notes commensurate with content and grade-level needs	51K, 87K, 233J, 233K, 339K, 377J
(3) Cross-curricular second language acquisition/speaking. The ELL speaks in a variety of modes for a variety of purposes with an awareness of different language registers (formal/informal) using vocabulary with increasing fluency and accuracy in language arts and all content areas. ELLs may be at the beginning, intermediate, advanced, or advanced high stage of English language acquisition in speaking. In order for the ELL to meet grade-level learning expectations across the foundation and enrichment curriculum, all instruction delivered in English must be linguistically accommodated (communicated, sequenced, and scaffolded) commensurate with the student's level of English language proficiency. The student is expected to:	
(B) expand and internalize initial English vocabulary by learning and using high-frequency English words necessary for identifying and describing people, places, and objects, by retelling simple stories and basic information represented or supported by pictures, and by learning and using routine language needed for classroom communication	37, 74, 175M, 271K, 339K
(C) speak using a variety of grammatical structures, sentence lengths, sentence types, and connecting words with increasing accuracy and ease as more English is acquired	1L, 51K, 87J, 121L, 175L, 271J, 303K, 339J, 339K, 377K
(D) speak using grade-level content area vocabulary in context to internalize new English words and build academic language proficiency	1M, 51J, 121L, 121M, 233K, 377J, 377K
(E) share information in cooperative learning interactions	51K, 121M, 377K

English Language Proficiency Standards

A correlation to the Texas Essential Knowledge and Skills for Science is located in the front of this Teacher Edition. Correlations to the English Language Proficiency Standards are provided on these pages.

Grade 1 ELPS ENGLISH LANGUAGE PROFICIENCY STANDARDS	Teacher Edition Pages
Cross-Curricular Second Language Acquisition/Learning Strategies	
(F) ask and give information ranging from using a very limited bank of high-frequency, high-need, concrete vocabulary, including key words and expressions needed for basic communication in academic and social contexts, to using abstract and content-based vocabulary during extended speaking assignments	51K, 121L, 121M, 233K, 271K, 303J, 303K, 377J
(G) express opinions, ideas, and feelings ranging from communicating single words and short phrases to participating in extended discussions on a variety of social and grade-appropriate academic topics	121M, 303J, 339K
(H) narrate, describe, and explain with increasing specificity and detail as more English is acquired	1M, 51K, 121M, 175M, 339K, 377K
(I) adapt spoken language appropriately for formal and informal purposes	339K
(4) Cross-curricular second language acquisition/reading. The ELL reads a variety of texts for a variety of purposes with an increasing level of comprehension in all content areas. ELLs may be at the beginning, intermediate, advanced, or advanced high stage of English language acquisition in reading. In order for the ELL to meet grade-level learning expectations across the foundation and enrichment curriculum, all instruction delivered in English must be linguistically accommodated (communicated, sequenced, and scaffolded) commensurate with the student's level of English language proficiency. For kindergarten and first grade, certain of these student expectations apply to text read aloud for students not yet at the stage of decoding written text. The student is expected to:	
(A) learn relationships between sounds and letters of the English language and decode (sound out) words using a combination of skills such as recognizing sound-letter relationships and identifying cognates, affixes, roots and base words	220
(C) develop basic sight vocabulary, derive meaning of environmental print, and comprehend English vocabulary and language structures used routinely in written classroom materials	1M, 87K, 233J, 339J
(D) use prereading supports such as graphic organizers, illustrations, and pretaught topic-related vocabulary and other prereading activities to enhance comprehension of written text	303K
(E) read linguistically accommodated content area material with a decreasing need for linguistic accommodations as more English is learned	175L
(F) use visual and contextual support and support from peers and teachers to read grade-appropriate content area text, enhance and confirm understanding, and develop vocabulary, grasp of language structures, and background knowledge needed to comprehend increasingly challenging language	1L, 1M, 51K, 87K, 162, 175M, 233J, 233K, 271J, 303K, 339K, 377K
(G) demonstrate comprehension of increasingly complex English by participating in shared reading, retelling or summarizing material, responding to questions, and taking notes commensurate with content area and grade level needs	271K, 303K, 377K

Grade 1 ELPS ENGLISH LANGUAGE PROFICIENCY STANDARDS	Teacher Edition Pages
(I) demonstrate English comprehension and expand reading skills by employing basic reading skills such as demonstrating understanding of supporting ideas and details in text and graphic sources, summarizing text and distinguishing main ideas from details commensurate with content area needs	87K
(5) Cross-curricular second language acquisition/writing. The ELL writes in a variety of forms with increasing accuracy to effectively address a specific purpose and audience in all content areas. ELLs may be at the beginning, intermediate, advanced, or advanced high stage of English language acquisition in writing. In order for the ELL to meet grade-level learning expectations across foundation and enrichment curriculum, all instruction delivered in English must be linguistically accommodated (communicated, sequenced, and scaffolded) commensurate with the student's level of English language proficiency. For kindergarten and first grade, certain of these student expectations do not apply until the student has reached the stage of generating original written text using a standard writing system. The student is expected to:	
(B) write using newly acquired basic vocabulary and content-based grade-level vocabulary	1M, 51J, 220, 236
(F) write using a variety of grade-appropriate sentence lengths, patterns, and connecting words to combine phrases, clauses, and sentences in increasingly accurate ways as more English is acquired	1M
(G) narrate, describe, and explain with increasing specificity and detail to fulfill content area writing needs as more English is acquired	1L

TEKS for English Language Arts and Reading

A correlation to the Texas Essential Knowledge and Skills for Science is located in the front of this Teacher Edition. Correlations to the TEKS for English Language Arts and Reading are provided on these pages.

Grade 1 TEKS ENGLISH LANGUAGE ARTS AND READING	Teacher Edition Pages
1.4 Reading/Beginning Reading/Strategies. Students comprehend a variety of texts drawing on useful strategies as needed. Students are expected to:	
B ask relevant questions, seek clarification, and locate facts and details about stories and other texts; and	152B
1.6 Reading/Vocabulary Development. Students understand new vocabulary and use it when reading and writing. Students are expected to:	
A identify words that name actions (verbs) and words that name persons, places, or things (nouns);	111, 114A, 141, 144A, 345
D identify and sort words into conceptual categories (e.g., opposites, living things); and	78A, 165, 307
1.14 Reading/Comprehension of Informational Text/Expository Text. Students analyze, make inferences and draw conclusions about expository text and provide evidence from text to support their understanding. Students are expected to:	
B identify important facts or details in text, heard or read;	322
1.18 Writing/Literary Texts. Students write literary texts to express their ideas and feelings about real or imagined people, events, and ideas. Students are expected to:	
A write brief stories that include a beginning, middle, and end; and	208, 259, 370A
B write short poems that convey sensory details.	114A, 186A, 240, 282A, 290
1.19 Writing/Expository and Procedural Texts. Students write expository and procedural or work-related texts to communicate ideas and information to specific audiences for specific purposes. Students are expected to:	
A write brief compositions about topics of interest to the student;	64A, 81, 127, 129, 134, 168A, 246A, 279, 311, 314A, 319, 328A, 388A, 389
B write short letters that put ideas in a chronological or logical sequence and use appropriate conventions (e.g., date, salutation, closing); and	152A
C write brief comments on literary or informational texts.	16, 64A, 101, 181, 198A, 242, 251, 371, 383

Grade 1 TEKS ENGLISH LANGUAGE ARTS AND READING	Teacher Edition Pages
1.20 Oral and Written Conventions/Conventions. Students understand the function of and use the conventions of academic language when speaking and writing. Students continue to apply earlier standards with greater complexity. Students are expected to:	
A understand and use the following parts of speech in the context of reading, writing, and speaking: **(i)** verbs (past, present, and future); **(ii)** nouns (singular/plural, common/proper); **(iii)** adjectives (e.g., descriptive: green, tall); **(iv)** adverbs (e.g., time: before, next); **(v)** prepositions and prepositional phrases; **(vi)** pronouns (e.g., I, me); and **(vii)** time-order transition words;	57, 111, 141, 144A, 240, 345, 352A
1.23 Research/Research Plan. Students ask open-ended research questions and develop a plan for answering them. Students (with adult assistance) are expected to:	
A generate a list of topics of class-wide interest and formulate open-ended questions about one or two of the topics; and	64A, 283
1.24 Research/Gathering Sources. Students determine, locate, and explore the full range of relevant sources addressing a research question and systematically record the information they gather. Students (with adult assistance) are expected to:	
A gather evidence from available sources (natural and personal) as well as from interviews with local experts;	64A, 246A
C record basic information in simple visual formats (e.g., notes, charts, picture graphs, diagrams).	10A, 30, 40, 45, 57, 78A, 73, 100A, 129, 141, 144A, 153, 165, 187, 193, 214A, 221, 228A, 264A, 275, 307, 329, 366, 371
1.27 Listening and Speaking/Listening. Students use comprehension skills to listen attentively to others in formal and informal settings. Students continue to apply earlier standards with greater complexity. Students are expected to:	
A listen attentively to speakers and ask relevant questions to clarify information; and	64A
1.28 Listening and Speaking/Speaking. Students speak clearly and to the point, using the conventions of language. Students continue to apply earlier standards with greater complexity. Students are expected to share information and ideas about the topic under discussion, speaking clearly at an appropriate pace, using the conventions of language.	246A

TEKS for Math

A correlation to the Texas Essential Knowledge and Skills for Science is located in the front of this Teacher Edition. Correlations to the TEKS for Math are provided on these pages.

Grade 1 TEKS MATH	Teacher Edition Pages
1.1 Mathematical process standards. The student uses mathematical processes to acquire and demonstrate mathematical understanding. The student is expected to:	
A apply mathematics to problems arising in everyday life, society, and the workplace;	109, 207
C select tools, including real objects, manipulatives, paper and pencil, and technology as appropriate, and techniques, including mental math, estimation, and number sense as appropriate, to solve problems;	22A, 34A, 59, 94, 100A, 195, 256, 400A
E create and use representations to organize, record, and communicate mathematical ideas;	264A
F analyze mathematical relationships to connect and communicate mathematical ideas; and	210
1.2 Number and operations. The student applies mathematical process standards to represent and compare whole numbers, the relative position and magnitude of whole numbers, and relationships within the numeration system related to place value. The student is expected to:	
C use objects, pictures, and expanded and standard forms to represent numbers up to 120;	75
E use place value to compare whole numbers up to 120 using comparative language;	214A
F order whole numbers up to 120 using place value and open number lines; and	243, 246A, 317
1.3 Number and operations. The student applies mathematical process standards to develop and use strategies for whole number addition and subtraction computations in order to solve problems. The student is expected to:	
A use concrete and pictorial models to determine the sum of a multiple of 10 and a one-digit number in problems up to 99;	31, 69, 131, 139, 144A, 223, 225, 294A, 325
B use objects and pictorial models to solve word problems involving joining, separating, and comparing sets within 20 and unknowns as any one of the terms in the problem such as 2 + 4 = [ ]; 3 + [ ] = 7; and 5 = [ ] - 3;	186A
D apply basic fact strategies to add and subtract within 20, including making 10 and decomposing a number leading to a 10;	314A

Grade 1 TEKS MATH	Teacher Edition Pages
E explain strategies used to solve addition and subtraction problems up to 20 using spoken words, objects, pictorial models, and number sentences; and	186A
F generate and solve problem situations when given a number sentence involving addition or subtraction of numbers within 20.	325, 347
1.5 Algebraic reasoning. The student applies mathematical process standards to identify and apply number patterns within properties of numbers and operations in order to describe relationships. The student is expected to:	
B skip count by twos, fives, and tens to determine the total number of objects up to 120 in a set;	69, 131
D represent word problems involving addition and subtraction of whole numbers up to 20 using concrete and pictorial models and number sentences;	31, 69
1.6 Geometry and measurement. The student applies mathematical process standards to analyze attributes of two-dimensional shapes and three-dimensional solids to develop generalizations about their properties. The student is expected to:	
D identify two-dimensional shapes, including circles, triangles, rectangles, and squares, as special rectangles, rhombuses, and hexagons and describe their attributes using formal geometric language;	44A, 130, 131, 134A, 139, 161, 256, 345, 349, 363, 370A, 385
E identify three-dimensional solids, including spheres, cones, cylinders, rectangular prisms (including cubes), and triangular prisms, and describe their attributes using formal geometric language;	277
G apply properties of operations to add and subtract two or three numbers.	207, 363, 370A, 385
1.7 Geometry and measurement. The student applies mathematical process standards to select and use units to describe length and time. The student is expected to:	
C measure the same object/distance with units of two different lengths and describe how and why the measurements differ;	31
D describe a length to the nearest whole unit using a number and a unit ; and	31, 198A

TEKS for Math

A correlation to the Texas Essential Knowledge and Skills for Science is located in the front of this Teacher Edition. Correlations to the TEKS for Math are provided on these pages.

Grade 1 TEKS MATH	Teacher Edition Pages
1.8 Data analysis. The student applies mathematical process standards to organize data to make it useful for interpreting information and solving problems. The student is expected to:	
A collect, sort, and organize data in up to three categories using models/representations such as tally marks or T-charts;	93, 114A, 182, 388A, 394
B use data to create picture and bar-type graphs; and	93, 182, 388A
C draw conclusions and generate and answer questions using information from picture and bar-type graphs.	147

Teacher Notes

TEKS for Other Subject Areas

A correlation to the Texas Essential Knowledge and Skills for Science is located in the front of this Teacher Edition. Correlations to the TEKS for Other Subject Areas are provided on these pages.

Grade 1 TEKS SOCIAL STUDIES	Teacher Edition Pages
1.5 Geography. The student understands the purpose of maps and globes. The student is expected to:	
A create and use simple maps such as maps of the home, classroom, school, and community; and	22A, 214A, 314A
B locate the community, Texas, and the United States on maps and globes.	328A
1.6 Geography. The student understands various physical and human characteristics. The student is expected to:	
A identify and describe the physical characteristics of place such as landforms, bodies of water, natural resources, and weather;	64A, 246A
B identify examples of and uses for natural resources in the community, state, and nation; and	78A, 186A, 198A, 400A
1.16 Science, technology, and society. The student understands how technology affects daily life, past and present. The student is expected to:	
A describe how technology changes the ways families live;	114A, 144A, 228A
C describe how technology changes the way people work.	168A
1.17 Social studies skills. The student applies critical-thinking skills to organize and use information acquired from a variety of valid sources, including electronic technology. The student is expected to:	
A obtain information about a topic using a variety of valid oral sources such as conversations, interviews, and music;	228A, 388A
B obtain information about a topic using a variety of valid visual sources such as pictures, symbols, electronic media, maps, literature, and artifacts; and	282A, 294A
C sequence and categorize information.	134A
1.18 Social studies skills. The student communicates in oral, visual, and written forms. The student is expected to:	
A express ideas orally based on knowledge and experiences; and	134A
B create and interpret visual and written material.	134A, 144A

Grade 1 TEKS THEATRE	Teacher Edition Pages
1.1 Perception. The student develops concepts about self, human relationships, and the environment, using elements of drama and conventions of theatre. The student is expected to:	
D imitate and create animate and inanimate objects in dramatic play.	144A

Grade 1 TEKS MUSIC	Teacher Edition Pages
1.2 Creative expression/performance. The student performs a varied repertoire of music. The student is expected to:	
A sing or play a classroom instrument independently or in groups; and	22A, 214A, 228A, 282A
1.4 Creative expression/performance. The student creates and arranges music within specified guidelines. The student is expected to:	
A create short rhythmic patterns; and	34A
B create short melodic patterns.	34A

Grade 1 TEKS ART	Teacher Edition Pages
1.1 Perception. The student develops and organizes ideas from the environment. The student is expected to:	
A identify similarities, differences, and variations among subjects, using the senses; and	78A
B identify color, texture, form, line, and emphasis in nature and in the human-made environment.	186A
1.2 Creative expression/performance. The student expresses ideas through original artworks, using a variety of media with appropriate skill. The student is expected to:	
A invent images that combine a variety of colors, forms, and lines;	10A, 22A, 34A, 44A, 144A, 152A, 198A, 264A, 282A, 352A
C increase manipulative skills, using a variety of materials to produce drawings, paintings, prints, and constructions.	100A, 134A, 144A, 168A, 186A, 198A, 228A, 294A, 328A, 352A, 370A, 388A, 400A

TEKS for Other Subject Areas

A correlation to the Texas Essential Knowledge and Skills for Science is located in the front of this Teacher Edition. Correlations to the TEKS for Other Subject Areas are provided on these pages.

Grade 1 TEKS HEALTH	Teacher Edition Pages
1.1 Health behaviors. The student understands that personal health decisions and behaviors affect health throughout the life span. The student is expected to:	
A describe and practice activities that enhance individual health such as enough sleep, nutrition, and exercise; and	328A, 352A, 370A
1.2 Health behaviors. The student understands that safe, unsafe, and/or harmful behaviors result in positive and negative consequences throughout the life span. The student is expected to:	
E identify safety rules that help to prevent poisoning;	400A
1.3 Health behaviors. The student demonstrates basic critical-thinking, decision-making, goal setting, and problem-solving skills for making health-promoting decisions. The student is expected to:	
B describe how decisions can be reached and problems can be solved; and	64A
1.4 Health information. The student understands the basic structure and functions of the human body and how they relate to personal health throughout the life span. The student is expected to:	
A identify and demonstrate use of the five senses;	10A,
B identify major body structures and organs and describes their basic functions; and	168A, 352A
1.7 Influencing factors. The student understands the difference between sickness and health in people of all ages. The student is expected to:	
C explain common practices that control the way germs are spread.	44A
1.8 Influencing factors. The student understands factors that influence the health of an individual. The student is expected to:	
B describe ways in which a person's health may be affected by weather and pollution.	264A

Grade 1 TEKS PHYSICAL EDUCATION	Teacher Edition Pages
1.1 Movement. The student demonstrates competency in fundamental movement patterns and proficiency in a few specialized movement forms. The student is expected to:	
A demonstrate an awareness of personal and general space while moving at different directions and levels such as high, medium, and low;	114A, 294A, 314A
B demonstrate proper foot patterns in hopping, jumping, skipping, leaping, galloping, and sliding;	352A
1.3 Physical activity and health. The student exhibits a health-enhancing, physically-active lifestyle that improves health and provides opportunities for enjoyment and challenge. The student is expected to:	
A describe and select physical activities that provide opportunities for enjoyment and challenge;	10A, 44A
D lift and support his/her own weight in selected activities that develop muscular strength and endurance of the arms, shoulders, abdomen, back, and legs such as hanging, hopping, and jumping.	34A
1.5 Physical activity and health. The student knows and applies safety practices associated with physical activities. The student is expected to:	
A use equipment and space safely and properly;	294A
B describe the importance of protective equipment in preventing injury such as helmets, elbow/knee pads, wrist guards, proper shoes, and clothing;	78A
1.6 Social development. The student understands basic components such as strategies and rules of structured physical activities including, but not limited to, games, sports, dance, and gymnastics. The student is expected to:	
A demonstrate starting and stopping signals; and	114A
1.7 Social development. The student develops positive self-management and social skills needed to work independently and with others in physical activity settings. The student is expected to:	
A follow directions and apply safe movement practices;	10A, 100A, 152A, 294A, 352A

The Texas College and Career Readiness Standards

The Texas College and Career Readiness Standards (CCRS) specify the knowledge and skills necessary to succeed in entry-level community college and university courses. While ultimately intended for high school students, the CCRS for Science are incorporated into the K-12 Science TEKS–Texas Essential Knowledge and Skills. In the elementary grades, students initiate studies of science topics that eventually pave the way for in-depth studies and success with the CCRS in high school science.

In *Texas ScienceFusion*, many of the CCRS have also been incorporated into the instruction in this Teacher Edition. Specifically, the CCRS activities associated with the Science Technology Engineering and Mathematics (STEM) features provide opportunities to develop students' awareness of careers, training, and post-secondary education related to each topic. The STEM features also focus on problem-solving, collaboration, and deep content knowledge. Where possible, the features also strive to align with scientific applications of mathematics.

The following CCRS are addressed within the STEM features.

I. Nature of Science: Scientific Ways of Learning and Thinking

C. Collaborative and safe working practices

1. Collaborate on joint projects.

D. Current scientific technology

1. Demonstrate literacy in computer use.
2. Use computer models, applications, and simulations.

E. Effective communication of scientific information

1. Use several modes of expression to describe or characterize natural patterns and phenomena. These modes of expression include narrative, numerical, graphical, pictorial, symbolic, and kinesthetic.
2. Use essential vocabulary of the discipline being studied.

III. Foundation Skills: Scientific Applications of Communication

A. Scientific writing

1. Use correct applications of writing practices in scientific communication.

B. Scientific reading

1. Read technical and scientific articles to gain understanding of interpretations, apparatuses, techniques or procedures, and data.

3. Recognize scientific and technical vocabulary in the field of study and use this vocabulary to enhance clarity of communication.

C. Presentation of scientific/technical information

1. Prepare and present scientific/technical information in appropriate formats for various audiences.

D. Research skills/information literacy

1. Use search engines, databases, and other digital electronic tools effectively to locate information.
2. Evaluate quality, accuracy, completeness, reliability, and currency of information from any source.

Teacher Notes

Grade-Level Materials Lists

Quantities are indicated for one group of children.

Science Tools Activities, Guided Inquiry Lessons and S.T.E.M. Lessons

The following list provides materials needed for the Science Tools Activities and the Guided Inquiry and STEM Lessons—the core activities—in this grade level.

Consumable Materials

Material	Quantity per Group	Teacher Edition Page
bottle, soda	1	266A, 331A, 404A
celery	1 stalk	11A
cotton ball	5–10	216A
cup, foam	1	79A
cup, paper	1	216A
cup, plastic	quantity as needed	34B, 331A, 404A
fruit	1 piece	23A
gloves, disposable	1 pair	199A, 201A, 331A
glue	quantity as needed	247A
labels	3–5	353A
leaves, assorted	quantity as needed	23A, 331A, 401A
marker	quantity as needed	79A, 266A, 295A
nut	1	23A
paper	quantity as needed	34C, 65A, 116A, 298A, 334A, 358A, 404A
paper clip	quantity as needed	401A
paper, construction, assorted	quantity as needed	103A, 170A
paper, copy	quantity as needed	103A, 170A
pencil	quantity as needed	116A, 216A, 298A, 334A, 358A, 404A
pill bugs & food	quantity as needed	331A
plant	quantity as needed	331A, 404A

Consumable Materials (continued)

Material	Quantity per Group	Teacher Edition Page
plate, paper	quantity as needed	199A, 201A
sand	quantity as needed	199A, 201A, 216A
sand, coarse	1/2 cup	34B
sand, fine	1/2 cup	34B
soil, backyard	1/2 cup	34B
soil, clay	1/4 cup	201A
soil, loam	1/2 cup	34B
soil, loam	1/4 cup	199A
soil, potting	quantity as needed	199A, 201A, 216A, 331A
tape	quantity as needed	65A, 266A, 331A, 404A
toothpick	quantity as needed	199A
water	quantity as needed	216A, 331A, 404A
yarn	quantity as needed	155A, 353A

Nonconsumable Materials

Material	Quantity per Group	Teacher Edition Page
balance	1	23A, 34C
ball, rubber	1	155A
clock	1	34C
clothespins	6	34C
computer	quantity as needed	34B
cone, conifer	1	23A
container, plastic, 12 oz	2	34B
feather	1	23A
forceps	1	199A
goggles	1	199A, 201A
hand lens	1	11A, 23A, 199A, 201A
jar, plastic	1	404A
lid, metal	1	404A
net, insect	1	34B
nonstandard items to measure	1	295A
picture cards	1 set	247A, 353A
ramp	1	155A
rock specimen	1	23A
ruler	1	266A
scissors	1	65A, 79A, 247A, 353A
shell	1	23A
shelter (pill bugs)	1	331A
strainer	1	199A
tape measure	1	79A

Nonconsumable Materials (continued)

Material	Quantity per Group	Teacher Edition Page
textbook	1	65A
thermometer	quantity as needed	23A, 103A
vehicle, toy	1	79A

Directed and Independent Activities

The following list provides materials needed for the optional Directed and Independent activities in this grade level. The * indicates materials that also appear on the core activities materials list on the preceding pages.

Consumable Materials

Material	Quantity per Group	Teacher Edition Page
art supplies	quantity as needed	13A
bag, plastic	1	379A
battery, D-cell	2	273A
beads	quantity as needed	67A
bread, slice	1	123A
butterfly	quantity as needed	395A
cardboard	quantity as needed	67A
cheesecloth	1 piece	395A
chenille stick	quantity as needed	13A
clay, modeling	quantity as needed	13A
craft stick	quantity as needed	67A
crayons/markers	quantity as needed	35A, 89A, 105A, 203A, 235A. 253A, 273A, 315A, 341A, 391A
cup, paper*	1	157A, 189A
cup, plastic*	quantity as needed	35A, 105A, 145A, 177A, 189A, 203A
drink mix	1 spoonful	177A
egg, hard boiled	1	53A
fabric	1	53A, 67A
fiber fill, polyester	1 piece	53A
filter, coffee	1	189A

Consumable Materials (continued)

Material	Quantity per Group	Teacher Edition Page
fish/guppies & food	quantity as needed	315A
flower, marigold	2	379A
food coloring	5–10 drops	35A
gloves, disposable*	1 pair	189A
glue*	quantity as needed	305A
drink, grape	1/2 cup	189A
grass/sod	quantity as needed	217A, 395A
ice cube	quantity as needed	105A, 253A
ink or watercolor paint	quantity as needed	35A
label	quantity as needed	203A
leafy twig	1–2	395A
leaves*	3–6	391A
lettuce, romaine	2 leaves	203A
magazine	2–3	305A
moon calendar	quantity as needed	285A
oil, vegetable	1 cup	145A
paper clip*	quantity as needed	67A, 135A
paper*	quantity as needed	3A, 35A, 53A, 67A, 105A, 123A, 135A, 145A, 157A, 177A, 203A, 217A, 235A, 253A, 273A, 285A, 305A, 315A,341A, 391A, 395A

Consumable Materials (continued)

Material	Quantity per Group	Teacher Edition Page
paper, construction, assorted*	quantity as needed	105A, 235A, 273A
paper, crepe streamer (blue)	6–8 feet	235A
paper, crepe streamer (red)	6–8 feet	235A
paper, drawing	quantity as needed	341A
peanut, foam	quantity as needed	53A, 67A
pencil*	quantity as needed	3A, 35A, 53A, 67A, 89A, 105A, 123A, 135A, 145A, 157A, 177A, 189A, 203A, 217A, 235A, 253A, 273A, 285A,305A, 315A, 341A, 391A, 395A
plant, aquarium	1	315A
rock	quantity as needed	67A
rubber band	1	395A
salt	quantity as needed	203A
seed, impatiens	10	67A, 379A
seed, marigold	10	67A, 379A
seed, sunflower	3	67A, 379A
shampoo	1 cup	145A
shell	quantity as needed	67A
shoebox	1	3A
sock	1	253A
soil, clay*	quantity as needed	189A

Consumable Materials (continued)

Material	Quantity per Group	Teacher Edition Page
soil, potting*	quantity as needed	189A
soil, sandy	quantity as needed	189A
spoon	1	177A
tape*	quantity as needed	53A, 67A, 189A, 203A, 235A
toothpick*	quantity as needed	13A
tube, cardboard	1	53A
water*	quantity as needed	35A, 105A, 145A, 177A, 189A, 203A, 217A, 315A,
yarn*	quantity as needed	67A, 235A, 253A

Directed and Independent Activities (continued)

Nonconsumable Materials

Material	Quantity per Group	Teacher Edition Page
aquarium	1	315A
balance*	1	25A, 89A
ball, golf	1	157A
book	quantity as needed	13A
bowl, plastic	1	105A, 189A
classroom material (variety)	quantity as needed	3A, 25A, 67A, 89A, 135A, 145A, 157A, 217A
clock	1	105A
computer	quantity as needed	341A
cone, conifer*	1	67A
container, plastic, 12 oz	2	35A
dropper	1	105A
feather*	quantity as needed	67A
flashlight	1	273A
goggles	1	53A
hand lens*	1	35A, 379A
jar, plastic*	1	35A, 395A
magnet, bar	2	135A
magnet, donut	1	135A
marble	3	145A
measuring cup	1	35A, 189A
net, insect	1	315A

Nonconsumable Materials (continued)

Material	Quantity per Group	Teacher Edition Page
ruler*	1	13A, 67A, 89A
scissors*	1	13A, 67A, 89A, 235A, 305A
stopwatch	1	34A, 105A, 145A
tape measure*	1	13A, 25A, 157A
thermometer, indoor/outdoor	1	235A, 253A
toaster	1	123A

For information about Materials Kits, contact your Houghton Mifflin Harcourt sales representative.

Teacher Notes

Student Edition

Interactive Glossary

Interactive Glossary

This Interactive Glossary will help you learn how to spell a vocabulary term. The Glossary will give you the meaning of the term. It will also show you a picture to help you understand what the term means.

Where you see **Your Turn** write your own words or draw your own picture to help you remember what the term means.

A

adaptation A body part or behavior that helps a living thing survive. (p. 342)

Your Turn

attract To pull toward something. (p. 138)

C

clay Small bits of rock. It holds water so well that clay sticks together. (p. 193)

Interactive Glossary

condense To change from a gas to a liquid. (p. 111)

cone The part of a nonflowering plant that holds the plant's seeds. (p. 397)

Your Turn

conservation A way to protect resources and materials. (p. 220)

D

design process A plan with steps that help engineers find good solutions. (p. 55)

R2

Interactive Glossary

E

electricity A form of energy. People produce electricity by using energy from other sources. (p. 128)

energy Something that causes matter to move or change. Heat and light are kinds of energy. (p. 124)

engineer Someone who uses math and science to solve problems. (p. 54)

environment All the living and nonliving things in a place. (pp. 310, 316)

Your Turn

R3

Interactive Glossary

evaporate To change from a liquid to a gas. (p. 110)

F

flower The part of a plant that makes seeds. (pp. 383, 396)

food chain A path that shows how energy moves from plants to animals. (p. 322)

Your Turn

R4

Interactive Glossary

force Something that makes an object move or stop moving. (p. 158)

freeze To change from a liquid to a solid. (p. 106)

fruit The part of the plant that holds seeds. (p. 383)

Your Turn

R5

Interactive Glossary

H

heat Energy that makes things warmer. It moves from something warmer to something cooler. (p. 125)

human-made Materials made by people. (p. 72)

Your Turn

I

inquiry skills Skills that help you find out information. (p. 14)

investigation A test that scientists do. (p. 36)

L

lake A body of fresh water with land all around it. (p. 205)

larva Another name for a caterpillar. (p. 367)

Interactive Glossary

leaf The part of a plant that makes food for the plant. A leaf uses light, air, and water to make food. (p. 382)

Your Turn

Interactive Glossary

life cycle Changes that happen to an animal or a plant during its life. (p. 361)

light A kind of energy that lets us see. (p. 125)

living things Things that are living. People, animals, and plants are living things because they need food, water, air, and space to live. They grow, change, and reproduce. (p. 306)

M

magnet An object that can pull things made of iron or steel. A magnet can push or pull other magnets. (p. 136)

Your Turn

magnify To make something look bigger. A telescope magnifies the moon. (p. 278)

materials What objects are made of. (p. 70)

matter Anything that takes up space. (p. 90)

Interactive Glossary

melt To change from a solid to a liquid. (p. 108)

Your Turn

moon A large sphere, or ball, of rock. (p. 276)

Interactive Glossary

motion Movement. When something is in motion, it is moving. (p. 146)

N

natural Materials found in nature. (p. 72)

natural resource Anything from nature that people can use. (p. 178)

nonliving things Things that are not alive. Nonliving things do not need food, air, and water. They do not grow and change. (p. 308)

Your Turn

R10

Interactive Glossary

O

ocean A large body of salty water. (p. 206)

P

phases The shapes of the moon you see as it moves. (p. 289)

pole A place on a magnet where the pull is the strongest. (p. 137)

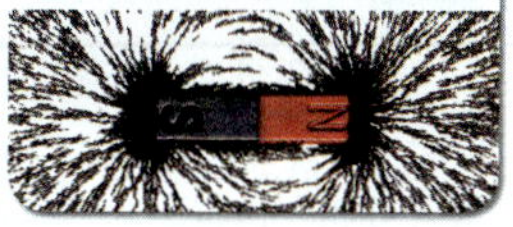

pollution Waste that harms land, water, and air. (p. 218)

product Something made by people or machines for people to use. (p. 179)

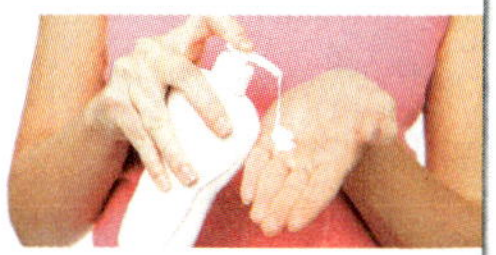

Your Turn

R11

Interactive Glossary

property One part of what something is like. Color, size, and shape are each a property. (pp. 92, 194)

pull To move an object closer to you. (p. 158)

pupa The part of a life cycle when a caterpillar changes into a butterfly. (p. 367)

push To move an object away from you. (p. 158)

Your Turn

R

recycle To use the materials in old things to make new things. (p. 222)

R12

Interactive Glossary

reduce To use less of a resource. (p. 222)

repel To push away from something. (p. 140)

Your Turn

reproduce To make new living things like oneself. (pp. 306, 360)

reuse To use a resource again. (p. 222)

river A large body of flowing water. (p. 204)

R13

Interactive Glossary

rock A hard, nonliving object from the ground. (p. 182)

roots The part of a plant that holds the plant in place. The roots take in water and nutrients. (p. 380)

Your Turn

S

sand Large bits of rock. It does not hold water well. (p. 193)

science tools Tools people use to find out about things. (p. 26)

Interactive Glossary

season A time of year that has a certain kind of weather. The four seasons are spring, summer, fall, and winter. (p. 254)

seed The part of a plant that new plants grow from. (p. 383)

senses The way you observe and learn. The five senses are sight, hearing, smell, taste, and touch. (p. 4)

shadow A dark place made where an object blocks light. (p. 287)

shelter A place where an animal can be safe. (p. 316)

Your Turn

Interactive Glossary

silt Medium bits of rock. It holds water fairly well. (p. 193)

soil It is made up of small pieces of rock and once-living things. It is the top layer of Earth. (pp. 183, 190)

sound A kind of energy you can hear. (p. 125)

speed The measure of how fast something moves. (p. 146)

star An object in the sky that gives off its own light. The sun is the closest star to Earth. (p. 274)

Your Turn

Interactive Glossary

stem The part of a plant that holds up the plant. (p. 381)

stream A small body of flowing water. (p. 204)

sun The star closest to Earth. (p. 274)

T

tadpole A young frog that comes out of an egg. It has gills to take in oxygen from the water. (p. 362)

Your Turn

telescope A tool that helps magnify things in the sky. (p. 278)

Interactive Glossary

temperature A measure of how hot or cold something is. (pp. 95, 238)

texture What an object feels like. (p. 92)

thermometer A tool used to measure temperature. (p. 27)

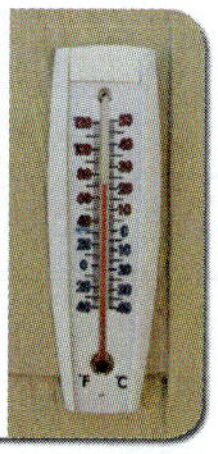

W

weather What the air outside is like. (p. 236)

Your Turn

Interactive Glossary

weather pattern A change in the weather that repeats. (p. 254)

weight The measure of how heavy an object feels. (p. 94)

wind Air that moves. (p. 236)

Your Turn

Interactive Glossary

windsock A tool used to show the direction of the wind. (p. 240)

Index

Note: Page numbers in plain type refer to the Student Edition; FC pages refer to the Inquiry Flipchart; page numbers in **boldface** indicate the Teacher Edition.

A

B

C

D

E

R

S

T

U

V

W

Z